THE
WORLD'S HISTORY

THIRD EDITION

VOLUME I: PREHISTORY TO 1500

THE WORLD'S HISTORY

THIRD EDITION

VOLUME I: PREHISTORY TO 1500

HOWARD SPODEK

PEARSON
Prentice
Hall

Upper Saddle River, N.J. 07458

Editorial Director: Charlyce Jones Owen
Executive Editor: Charles Cavaliere
Development Editor: Elaine Silverstein
Editorial Assistant: Shannon Corliss
Executive Marketing Manager: Heather Shelstad

Credits and acknowledgments borrowed from other sources and reproduced, with
permission, in this textbook appear on pages xiii–xiv.

Pearson Education LTD.
Pearson Education Australia PTY, Limited
Pearson Education Singapore, Pte. Ltd
Pearson Education North Asia Ltd
Pearson Education, Canada, Ltd
Pearson Educación de Mexico, S.A. de C.V.
Pearson Education–Japan
Pearson Education Malaysia, Pte. Ltd

This book was designed and produced by
Laurence King Publishing Ltd, London
www.laurenceking.co.uk
Every effort has been made to contact the copyright holders, but should there be
any errors or omissions, Laurence King Publishing Ltd would be pleased to insert
the appropriate acknowledgment in any subsequent printing of this publication.

Editor: Richard Mason
Picture Researcher: Emma Brown
Design: Newton Harris Design Partnership

Front cover: Ahmad Kashmiri, *The God Agni Creating Fire*, from the *Razmnama*, 1598.
Painting. The British Library, London.

10 9 8 7 6 5 4 3 2 1
ISBN 0-13-177316-X

BRIEF CONTENTS

CONTENTS

MAPS

AT A GLANCE

CHARTS

PICTURE CREDITS

I-6 British Library, London
I-11 Novosti (London)
3 (top) © Jonathan Blair/Corbis
3 (bottom) © Jonathan Blair/Corbis
4 © Paul A. Souders/Corbis
9 © Museum of Fine Arts, Houston, Texas, USA/Bridgeman Art Library
10 By permission of the Syndics of Cambridge University Library (DAR140.4)
14 Science Photo Library/John Reader
15 Natural History Museum, London
16 © Sygma Collection/Corbis
17 Natural History Museum, London
19 Natural History Museum, London
25 Royal Geographic Society/Bridgeman Art Library
27 Musée National de Préhistoire, Les Eyzies de Tayac, France
28 (top) Natural History Museum, London
28 (bottom) Jean Vertut, Issy-les-Molineaux
30 (top) Yan, Toulouse
31 J. Clottes, Ministère de la Culture et la Communication–Direction du Patrimonie, sous Direction de l'Archéologie
36 Howard Spodek
37 (top) Musée Guimet, Paris, France/Bridgeman Art Library
38 Photo courtesy of Science Museum of Minnesota
40–41 Bridgeman Art Library
42 © Dean Conger/Corbis
48 AKG Images/Erich Lessing
49 Hilprecht Collection, Friedrich-Schiller University, Jena
50 British Museum, London
53 (top) Hirmer Verlag, München
53 (bottom) University of Pennsylvania Museum
54 British Museum, London
55 British Museum, London
58 © Photo RMN
59 © Photo RMN
64 AKG Images
66 British Museum, London
68 British Museum, London
71 © Photo RMN
72 Egyptian Museum, Cairo
73 British Museum, London
74 AKG Images
78 Egyptian Museum, Cairo
82 (top) National Museum of India, New Delhi
82 (bottom) National Museum of Pakistan, Karachi
85 James Blair
90 Institute of Archaeology, Beijing
91 East Asian Library, Columbia University
93 Historical Museum, Beijing
95 Academia Sinica, Taipei
100 Museo Regional de Veracruz, Jalapa, Mexico
102 South American Pictures
103 British Museum, London

104 University of Pennsylvania Museum
110 South American Pictures
113 AKG Images
114 National Museum, Lagos, Nigeria
115 Private Collection
118 Museum of Anatolian Civilizations, Ankara, Turkey/Bridgeman Art Library
119 © Bettman/Corbis
120 Art Archive/Musée du Louvre, Paris
121 AKG Images
123 Stapleton Collection/Bridgeman Art Library
124 Art Archive/Dagli Orti
128 Photo Scala, Florence
131 British Museum, London
132 Robert Harding Picture Library
137 Giraudon/Bridgeman Art Library
141 National Archaeological Museum, Athens
144 (top) Staatliche Museen, Berlin
147 Alison Frantz, Princeton, N.J.
149 Acropolis Museum, Athens
151 British Museum, London
156 © Fotografica Foglia, Naples
158 Museo Capitolino, Rome
162 AKG Images
164 Museo Capitolino, Rome
169 (top) Photo Scala, Florence
169 (bottom) Art Archive
172 Photo Scala, Florence
174 Werner Forman Archive
176 Leonard von Matt
177 Alinari, Florence
179 Musei Vaticani, Rome
185 A.F. Kersting, London
186 Fototeca Unione, Rome
187 Alinari, Florence
193 Württembergisches Landesmuseum, Stuttgart
199 G.E. Kidder-Smith
204 Spectrum, London
206 Spectrum, London
215 Robert Harding Picture Library
219 British Library, London
221 British Museum, London
225 Werner Forman Archive
227 (top) Topham Picturepoint
227 (bottom) Idemitsu Museum of Arts, Tokyo
228 (top) Xinhua News Agency
228 (bottom) AKG Images/Jürgen Sorges
233 Werner Forman Archive
240 © Charles & Josette Lenars/CORBIS
245 Oriental & India Office, London
246 Oriental & India Office, London
249 Hulton Deutsch
250 (top) Boudot-Lamotte, Paris
250 (bottom) British Museum, London
251 (left) British Museum, London
252 British Museum, London
253 Robert Harding Picture Library
255 British Museum, London
258 Robert Harding Picture Library
259 Robert Harding Picture Library

264 AKG Images
265 Bridgeman Art Library
266 Mary Evans Picture Library
267 Alinari, Florence
269 AKG Images
270 AKG Images/Jean-Louis Nou
277 Hutchison Library/Nancy Durrell McKenna
280 © Lindsay Hebberd/Corbis
282 (left) Metropolitan Museum of Art, New York
282 (right) Boudot-Lamotte, Paris
283 Boudot-Lamotte, Paris
286 Archaeological Museum, Sarnath
288 Robert Harding Picture Library
289 Bridgeman Art Library
292 Anne and Bury Peerless
293 Nelson Atkins Museum of Art, Kansas City, Missouri. Purchase: Nelson Trust (34-10)
296 (top) British Library, London
296 (bottom) University of Pennsylvania Museum
306 © Domkapitel Aachen. Photo: Ann Münchow
311 Israel Museum, Jerusalem
313 Sonia Halliday Photographs
314 A.S.A.P. Tel Aviv
316 National Archaeological Museum, Damascus, Syria
318 AKG Images/Erich Lessing
319 Alinari, Florence
322 (right) Historiska Museet, Stockholm
331 AKG Images
334 Shimon Lev
338 (left) Musée des Antiquités, St.-Germain-en-Laye, France/Photo RMN
338 (right) © Photo RMN
340 © Angelo Hornak
344 Metropolitan Museum of Art, New York, 39.20
347 Bridgeman Art Library
348 Bibliothèque Nationale de France
353 Bibliothèque Nationale de France
356 Spectrum, London
358 Edinburgh University Library
362 Bibliothèque Nationale de France
371 Courtesy Institute Amattler d'Art Hispànic, Barcelona
374 Werner Forman Archive
375 A.F. Kersting
378 British Library, London
379 Spectrum, London
385 AKG Images
386 Stapleton Collection/Bridgeman Art Library
386 AKG Images
387 Courtesy Shri Swaminarayan Madir, Neasden, London
389 Bodleian Library, Oxford
390 Bridgeman Art Library/Bibliothèque Nationale de France

LITERARY CREDITS

SUPPLEMENTS

The World's History comes with an extensive package of supplementary print and multimedia materials for both instructors and students, many of which are available free to qualified adopters.

FOR THE INSTRUCTOR

- The *Instructor's Manual/Test-Item File* includes chapter outlines, overviews, key concepts, discussion questions, suggestions for useful audiovisual resources, and approximately 1500 test items (essay, multiple choice, true/false, and matching).

- The *Instructor Resource CDROM*, compatible with both Windows and Macintosh environments, provides instructors with such essential teaching tools as hundreds of digitized images and maps for classroom presentations, PowerPoint lectures, and other instructional material. The assets on the IRCDROM can be easily exported into online courses, such as WebCT and Blackboard.

- *Test Manager* is a computerized test management program for Windows and Macintosh environments. The program allows instructors to select items from the test-item file to create tests. It also allows online testing.

- The *Transparency Package* provides instructors with full color transparency acetates of all the maps, charts, and graphs in the text for use in the classroom.

- A *Correlation Guide to the Advanced Placement Exam* provides strategies and suggestions for using *The World's History* in AP World History courses.

FOR THE STUDENT

- *History Notes* (Volumes I and II) provides practice tests, essay questions, and map exercises to help reinforce key concepts.

- *Documents in World History* (Volumes I and II) is a collection of 200 primary source documents in global history. Questions accompanying the documents can be used for discussion or as writing assignments.

- Produced in collaboration with Dorling Kindersley, the world's most respected cartography publisher, *The Prentice Hall Atlas of World History* includes approximately 100 maps fundamental to the study of world history—from early hominids to the twenty-first century.

- *World History: An Atlas and Study Guide* is a four-color map workbook that includes over 100 maps with exercises, activities, and questions that help students learn both geography and history.

- *Reading Critically About History* is a brief guide to reading effectively that provides students with helpful strategies for reading a history textbook.

- *Understanding and Answering Essay Questions* suggests helpful analytical tools for understanding different types of essay questions, and provides precise guidelines for preparing well-crafted essay answers.

- Prentice Hall is pleased to provide adopters of *The World's History* with an opportunity to receive significant discounts when copies of the text are bundled with Penguin Classics titles in world history. Contact your local Prentice Hall representative for details.

MEDIA RESOURCES

- **Key** Prentice Hall's New Online Resource **OneKey** lets instructors and students in to the best teaching and learning resources—all in one place. This all-inclusive online resource is designed to help you minimize class preparation and maximize teaching time. Conveniently organized by chapter, OneKey for *The World's History, Third Edition* reinforces what students have learned in class and from the text. Among the student resources available for each chapter are: a complete, media-rich, interactive e-book version of *The World's History, Third Edition*; quizzes organized by the main subtopics of each chapter; over 200 primary-source documents; and interactive map quizzes.

  For instructors, OneKey includes images and maps from *The World's History, Third Edition*; instructional material; hundreds of primary-source documents; and PowerPoint presentations.

- *Prentice Hall OneSearch with Research Navigator: History 2005* This brief guide focuses on developing critical-thinking skills necessary for evaluating and using online sources. It provides a brief introduction to navigating the Internet with specific references to History web sites. It also provides an access code and instruction on using Research Navigator, a powerful research tool that provides access to three exclusive databases of reliable source material: ContentSelect Academic Journal Database, the New York Times Search by Subject Archive, and Link Library.

- The *Companion Website*™ (www.prenhall.com/spodek) works in tandem with the text and features objectives, study questions, web links to related Internet resources, document exercises, interactive maps, and map labelling exercises.

- *Prentice Hall World History Image Library* Bringing together hundreds of images—many of which have never before been digitized—this innovative new CDROM organizes images of fine art, culture, photographs, posters, cartoons, and manuscripts from around the world into thematic units, allowing instructors to efficiently export the material into customized PowerPoint lectures or other presentation platforms. In addition, interactive global maps showing change over time allow instructors to visually portray the large patterns of world history.

- *World History Documents CD-ROM* Bound into every new copy of this textbook is a free World History Documents CD-ROM. This is a powerful resource for research and additional reading that contains more than 200 primary source documents central to World History. Each document provides essay questions that are linked directly to a website where short-essay answers can be submitted online or printed out. A complete list of documents on the CD-ROM is found at the end of the text.

PREFACE

Why History?

The professional historian and the student of an introductory course often seem to pass each other on different tracks. For the professional, nothing is more fascinating than history. For the student, particularly one in a compulsory course, the whole enterprise often seems a bore. This introductory text is designed to help the student understand and share the fascination of the historian. It will also remind professors of their original attraction to history, before they began the specialization that has almost certainly marked their later careers. Furthermore, it encourages student and professor to explore together the history of the world and the significance of this study.

Professional historians love their field for many reasons. History offers perspective and guidance in forming a personal view of human development. It teaches the necessity of seeing many sides of issues. It explores the complexity and interrelationship of events and makes possible the search for patterns and meaning in human life.

Historians also love to debate. They love the challenge of demonstrating that their interpretations of the pattern and significance of events are the most accurate and the most satisfying in their fit between the available data and theory. Historians also love the detective work of the profession, whether it is researching through old archives, uncovering and using new sources of information, or reinterpreting long-ignored sources. In recent years historians have turned, for example, to oral history, old church records, files of photographs, cave paintings, individual census records, and reinterpretations of mythology.

Historical records are not simply lists of events, however. They are the means by which historians develop their interpretations of those events. Because interpretations differ, there is no single historical record, but various narrations of events each told from a different perspective. Therefore the study of history is intimately linked to the study of values, the values of the historical actors, the historians who have written about them, and of the students engaged in learning about them.

Professional historians consider history to be the king of disciplines. Synthesizing the concepts of fellow social scientists in economics, politics, anthropology, sociology, and geography, historians create a more integrated and comprehensive interpretation of the past. Joining with their colleagues in the humanities, historians delight in hearing and telling exciting stories that recall heroes and villains, the low born and the high, the wisdom and the folly of days gone by. This fusion of all the social sciences and humanities gives the study of history its range, depth, significance, and pleasure. Training in historical thinking provides an excellent introduction to understanding change and continuity in our own day as well as in the past.

Why World History?

Why specifically world history? Why should we teach and study world history, and what should be the content of such a course?

First, world history is a good place to begin for it is a new field for professor and student alike. Neither its content nor its pedagogy is yet fixed. Many of the existing textbooks on the market still have their origins in the study of western Europe, with segments added to cover the rest of the world. World history as the study of the inter-relationships of all regions of the world, seen from the many perspectives of the different peoples of the earth, is still virgin territory.

Second, for citizens of multicultural, multiethnic nations such as the United States, Canada, South Africa, and India, and for those of the many other countries such as the United Kingdom and Australia which are moving in that direction, a world history course offers the opportunity to gain an appreciation of the national and cultural origins of all their diverse citizens. In this way, the study of world history may help to strengthen the bonds of national citizenship.

Third, as the entire world becomes a single unit for interaction, it becomes an increasingly appropriate subject for historical study. The noted historian E.H. Carr explained that history "is an unending dialogue between the present and the past". The new reality of global interaction in communication, business, politics, religion, culture, and ecology has helped to generate the new academic subject of world history.

Organization and Approach

The text, like the year-long course, links *chronology*, *themes*, and *geography* in eight units, or parts of study. The parts move progressively along a time line from the emergence of early humans to the present day. Each part emphasizes a single theme—for example, urbanization or religion or trade—and students learn to use all eight themes to analyze historical events and to develop a grasp of the chronology of human development. Geographically, each part cover the entire globe, although specific topics place greater emphasis on specific regions.

REVISIONS TO THE THIRD EDITION

Readers of the first and second editions will find that this third edition builds on the strengths of the first two while adding new materials and new perspectives. Every aspect of the book's program has been exhaustively reviewed and revised. The pedagogical features were carefully examined. Revised and new, more useful elements were added including Review Questions, Key Topics, a running in-text glossary, up-to-date, annotated bibliographies, interactive maps, and Turning Point essays, which use visual sources to help the reader move from the themes of one part to the new themes of the next. The text has been reworked extensively to produce a narrative with improved coverage of gender issues, trade, technology and capitalism, the Islamic world and its influence, Africa and Latin America.

ORGANIZATIONAL CHANGES

Theme and Chronology

One of the most important organizational principles of this text from the beginning has been its emphasis on a thematic introduction to world history. Readers generally applauded this approach, but warned that sometimes it led us to neglect chronology. As in the first two editions, one theme is highlighted in each of the eight parts of the textbook, and the parts trace major chronological eras in the world's history, from the evolution of humans to the early 21st century. In this edition we have addressed much more effectively the problem of keeping chronology clear even as we continue to concentrate on themes. Readers should find this attention to consistent chronology—with much less of the moving back and forth in time periods that characterized earlier editions —also an important improvement.

Reorganization and New Materials

Readers familiar with the earlier editions will notice revisions and reorganization throughout the text, from beginning to end. The most striking difference appears in the final unit. It has been entirely reorganized, divided into two separate parts. The first of these looks at the world from the early twentieth century until about 1980, following much of the structure of the original and continuing to use the theme of "The Human Uses of Technology." A new unit has then been added that analyzes issues since about 1980 analyzed through the new theme of "Identity." Arguing that human action comes, in part, out of the sense of who we are, it examines new issues of religious, national, gender, and age identity. In each case it asks how new technologies, especially of communication, have affected these identities, and how these identities have affected technology. The final chapter will examine these new identity issues in several different regions of the world. Another major change is the addition of a new chapter, number 13, which examines European Visions 1000–1776. This chapter, along with Chapter 12 now forms a bridge between the pre-modern and modern worlds, and between volumes 1 and 2 in the paperback edition.

Historiography

A fundamental principal of the first two editions was the emphasis on the three questions: "What Do We Know?" "How Do We Know It?" and "What Difference Does It Make?" Teachers and students, both at the university level and, increasingly, in Advanced Placement courses appreciated the attention to these three historiographical issues, but they often found them cluttering the text. Discussions of the work and arguments of various historians appeared frequently, but inconsistently. In this edition each feature has been given a clearer place so that faculty and students can use them more effectively. In general, the main narrative conveys the "What Do We Know?" materials. Separate, color-coded, boxed features—usually two in every chapter—carry the "How Do We Know?" materials, demonstrating how historians sift through source materials and debate their interpretation. Questions accompany each of these "How Do We Know?" features to encourage students to appreci-ate the work of the historians in producing the records we have today. Additional color-coded boxed features in each chapter will introduce relevant primary sources for further analysis. Finally, each chapter ends with a discussion of "What Difference Does It Make?: Legacies to the Future." In another new feature, a set of questions end each chapter to guide students in their analyses of the material.

New Layout and Design

Readers will also see immediately a streamlined, cleaner design. A larger format provides for a more aesthetically-pleasing presentation, while the abundance of special feature boxes that filled the earlier editions have been reduced. More importantly, the basic material of many of the boxes has been incorporated into the narrative text. The text is now set in single-column, which allows for a more spacious layout. Each chapter now opens with a two-page spread that features an illustration embodying the core theme of each chapter.

CONTENT CHANGES

Within each part, materials have been updated, revised, and added. Examples of some of the more notable changes and additions include: a discussion of the fossils of early hominids discovered in Chad; additional materials on early urbanization in India and Africa; new evaluations for the decline of the Roman empire; consideration of the Gnostic gospels and their significance in understanding early Christianity; the assimilation of Islam into African empires in the

10th through the fifteenth centuries. Part Five, on world trade, 1000 to 1776 and Part Six, on migration and demography, 1200–1750, have been restructured into a single unit on the movement of goods, ideas, and people. The Scientific Revolution of the sixteenth, seventeenth, and eighteenth century gets more coverage. The Industrial Revolution has been placed into a wider context, more clearly setting the stage for the events that began to unfold in late eighteenth-century England. As noted, the twentieth century is now given expanded coverage, and divided into two chronological periods, each with its own theme. The region-by-region analysis presented in the closing chapters of the first two editions has been replaced by a more thematic consideration of global issues in the late twentieth century, more in keeping with the thematic approach of the rest of the text. Throughout the book increased prominence has been given to issues of gender.

In updating the book to cover most recent events, new materials have been added to reflect new developments, for example: the increasing importance of China in world trade; of religious/cultural militancy in India; of economic recovery in Southeast Asia and decline in parts of Latin America; of the global economy; of responses to the global AIDS epidemic, especially in Africa; of breakthroughs and cautions in cloning and applications of genome research; of the attacks on America of September 11, 2001, the American response; and global reactions to both the attacks and the American responses.

Chapter-by-Chapter Revisions

Chapter 1 incorporates the results of the most recent archaeological research, and new information on the discovery of a fossil skull in Chad that may extend hominid evolution 2.5 million years back in time

Chapter 2 includes improved coverage on the Sumerians and their contributions to the development of early civilizations.

Chapter 3 has been dramatically reorganized to treat various aspects of ancient Egyptian history to fit the thematic trajectory of the chapters. It contains new material on daily life and an extended analysis of gender roles in society. Much of the material previously included in this chapter has been moved to Chapter 5 on the rise of empires.

Chapter 4 has been revised to better connect themes within the Parts. In keeping with the overall desire to improve coverage of gender issues, more information is supplied on women in Chinese societies. The chapter now also contains more information on the Zhou.

Chapter 5 has been reorganized to include the Egyptian empire as among the early empires. The section on Alexander the Great has been brought up-to-date and expanded. In addition the coverage of gender has been improved.

Chapter 6 has been revised for improved readability and also includes a more detailed discussion of gender in the ancient world. It also includes fresh material on the decline of the Roman Empire.

Chapter 7 has been reorganized to present a clear discussion of China's earliest ideologists. It also has improved coverage of gender.

Chapter 8 contains a much clearer discussion of Indian culture, and includes additional thoughts on the comparison of different imperial systems.

Chapter 10 adds new materials on the controversial Gnostic gospels and their significance for the interpretation of Christianity.

Chapter 11 clarifies the chronology of the early caliphate and the wars of succession. It includes a reorganized and expanded section on Islam, which more clearly highlights gender issues in Islam and compares them with other religions.

Chapter 12 has been thoroughly revised. It is far more comprehensive on trade networks, and their significance, especially sea-borne networks.

Chapter 13 has been thoroughly revised to examine more fully the background to European overseas expansion. Medieval European history has been moved here and conceptually placed in a global context, including the decline of Mediterranean trade and the rise of Atlantic exploration. It also looks at the Medieval European revival of trade and its relationship to Renaissance ideas, and new worldviews in general.

Chapter 14 has been completely revised, with more attention to the nation-state and fuller discussion of "the great divergence," analyzing the economic restructuring of the world in which western Europe rose to prominence over China.

Chapter 15 has been restructured for greater clarity and clearer comparison of the various kinds of population movements, free, indentured, enslaved, settler, and conquest.

Chapter 16 adds more extensive coverage of the scientific revolution and clarifies issues of comparison among the several major political revolutions of the time.

Chapter 17 expands the discussion of the historical background to the industrial revolution, adds information on indentured labor, reorders the material for greater clarity and stronger indication of the connection among economic, political, and social relationships.

Chapter 18 has been restructured and updated for more careful consideration of the relationships between capitalism, the industrial revolution, imperialism, and responses to the imperial outreach.

Chapter 19 has been extensively revised and contains an enhanced discussion of the contests over the uses of technology. Greatly expanded coverage of World War I and the global depression, and their significance. The chronology has been restructured for greater clarity.

Chapter 20 includes extensive revisions to cover the ideologies of the combatants in World War II, the war and its consequences, including the early confrontations of the cold war.

Chapter 21 has been thoroughly revised to cover the cold war, the end of colonialism, the rise of newly independent nations, and the creation of a third world bloc.

Chapter 22 contains additional materials on Mao's planning, on Gandhi's work on behalf of industrial unions, and on problems and hazards of technology.

Chapter 23 is a new thematically-based chapter covering key identity issues of the late-twentieth and early twenty-first centuries, especially those created by the end of the cold war and the increasing network of economic globalization, but also considering the cultural identities that are emerging as a result of these changes.

Chapter 24 is a new chapter of brief case studies of contemporary themes in five geographical areas: the integration of the European Union, the dissolution of Yugoslavia, continuing warfare between Israelis and Palestinians, the Truth and Reconciliation Commission in South Africa, and the economic revival of contemporary China. Also coverage of global criminal networks.

PEDAGOGICAL ENHANCEMENTS

This edition retains many of the pedagogical features of the previous editions, including source boxes and timelines. We have introduced several new pedagogical features including a list of key topics at the beginning of each chapter, chapter review questions at the end of each chapter, one–two interactive maps per chapter, a running glossary of items highlighted in the text that appears in the margins as well as at the back of the book, and "Turning Points" essays at the end of each part use visual sources to highlight the key themes in each part. Each of these features is designed to make the text more accessible to students. Collectively, these materials provide a rich, comprehensive and challenging introduction to the study of world history and the methods and key interpretations of its historians.

- Substantially revised, the **Introduction** describes the key themes of the text and the methods historians use to practice their craft.
- The timelines have been completely redesigned to make the information easier to read and are now called **At a Glance**.
- New **Turning Points** essays illustrate visually the connections between one part and the next. In some cases, the **Turning Points** tell their own story as well, notably in the bridge into the twentieth century that uses the modern Olympic Games to illustrate and introduce many of the issues that are to follow.
- The **How Do We Know?** features have been separated from the text and placed in color-coded boxes. There are usually two in every chapter. Each **How Do We Know?** feature aims to help the student examine primary source materials, and each one ends with pertinent, thought-provoking questions.
- Each chapter ends with a discussion of legacies to the future, namely, **What Difference Does It Make?**
- This edition also continues the emphasis on the use of **Primary Sources**, for these are the kinds of materials from which the historical record is argued and fashioned. Each chapter usually has two primary sources, clearly highlighted in color-coded feature boxes.
- The **Bibliography** for each chapter has been thoroughly revised and up-dated to reflect current scholarship. In addition, each item in the bibliography is now annotated to direct students with their reading.
- Each chapter begins with a list of **Key Topics** that provide an overview of the chapter.
- Each chapter now ends with **Review Questions** to help students to re-examine the material. The questions are also useful for classroom debates and could serve as essay topics.
- The introduction to each of the eight **Parts** now includes more specific key references to the chapters that follow.
- **World History Documents CD-ROM.** Bound into every new copy of this textbook is a free World History Documents CD-ROM. This is a powerful resource for research and additional reading that contains more than 200 primary source documents central to World History. Each document provides essay questions that are linked directly to a website where short-essay answers can be submitted online or printed out. A complete list of documents on the CD-ROM is found at the end of the text.

Maps and Illustrations

To aid the student, extensive, clear and informative charts and maps represent information graphically and geographically. Several new maps have been added to provide better geographical context in the narrative. New to this edition one map in most chapter is now interactive. A wide range of illustrations, many in color, supplement the written word. For the third edition we have added more than 130 new illustrations.

One element that has not changed in this new edition is the mental image I keep before me of my own children—albeit at a younger age, since by now their knowledge in so many fields surpasses my own—and of my students. I write for them.

ACKNOWLEDGEMENTS FOR THE THIRD EDITION

Prentice Hall has taken an active role in the preparation of this edition. The wise interventions of Charlyce Jones-Owen, Editorial Director; the copy-editing of Marty Green and Elaine Silverstein, Developmental Editors; the content editing of Nancy Fitch, Professor of History at California State University, Fullerton; and the advice compiled from many external reviews by Charles Cavaliere, Executive Editor, have all resulted in many of the improvements evident in this edition. Laurence King Publishers in London continue to provide the excellent work in the production of the text and I am deeply indebted to them. Lee Ripley Greenfield, Director of College and Fine Arts, has assured that this transoceanic venture has proceeded reasonably smoothly, aided by Lesley Henderson, Senior Editor, Richard Mason, Senior Managing Editor, Nick Newton, Designer, and Emma Brown, Picture Researcher. Without them, there would be no third edition, and I am grateful for their patient and firm guidance and wise diplomacy. I have also benefited immensely from the kindness of many teachers and students who have used this book and took time to write to me with their advice and suggestions. I thank them and hope that they will see the benefits of their experience and wisdom in this edition.

Grateful acknowledgments are also extended to the following reviewers of the third edition: Wayne Ackerson, Salisbury University; Ewa Bacon, Lewis University, Illinois; Maurice Borrero, St. John's University; Stuart Borsch, Assumption College; Kenneth M. Chauvin, Appalachian State University; Jorge Cañizares-Esguerra, State University of New York, Buffalo; Nupur Chaudhuri, Texas Southern University; Mark Gunn, Meridian Community College; Phyllis Jestice, University of Southern Mississippi; Frank Karpiel, College of Charleston; David Kenley, Marshall University; Ane Lintvedt, McDonogh School; Angus Lockyer, Wake Forest University; John Langdon, University of Alberta; Louis McDermott, California Maritime Academy; Susan Maneck, Jackson State University; Michael Pavkovic, Hawaii Pacific University.

ABOUT THE AUTHOR

Howard Spodek received his B.A. degree from Columbia University (1963), majoring in history and specializing in Columbia's newly designed program in Asian Studies. He received his M.A. (1966) and Ph.D. (1972) from the University of Chicago, majoring in history and specializing in India. His first trip to India was on a Fulbright Fellowship, 1964–66, and he has spent a total of some seven years studying and teaching in India. He has also traveled widely throughout the United States, Latin America, Asia, Africa, and Europe. He has been a faculty member at Temple University since 1972, appointed Full Professor in 1984. He was awarded Temple's Great Teacher award in 1993.

Spodek's work in world history began in 1988 when he became Academic Director of a comprehensive, innovative program working with teachers in the School District of Philadelphia to improve their knowledge base in world history and facilitate a rewriting of the world history program in the schools. Immediately following this program, he became principal investigator of a program that brought college professors and high school teachers together to reconsider, revise, and, in many cases, initiate the teaching of world history in several of the colleges and universities in the Philadelphia metropolitan area. Those projects led directly to the writing of the first edition of the current text (1997).

Howard Spodek has published extensively on India, including *Urban-Rural Integration in Regional Development* (1976); *Urban Form and Meaning in South-East Asia* (editor, with Doris Srinivasan, 1993); and a wide array of articles, especially on urbanization—and on women's development issues—in India. He has written on his experiences with world history faculty at the college and high school levels in articles in The History Teacher (1992, 1995). In addition he wrote and produced the documentary film, *Ahmedabad* (1983). He has received funding for his research, writing, teaching, and film from Fulbright, the National Endowment for the Humanities, the National Science Foundation, the American Institute of Indian Studies, and the Smithsonian Institution.

INTRODUCTION: THE WORLD THROUGH HISTORIANS' EYES

THEMES AND TURNING POINTS

Most readers of this textbook have probably not taken many courses in history. Few are (thus far) planning to major in history, much less become professional historians. A lot therefore rides on this single text. It must present a general introduction to world history that interests, engages, and even fascinates the reader through its subject matter, its narrative, and its analysis. It must open the eyes, minds, and hearts of students who come to this course believing that history is only about the past, and mostly a matter of learning names, dates, and places. It must introduce them to the methods and "habits of mind" of the historian. It must demonstrate how knowledge of the contents and methods of world history—and of this book in particular—will broaden their horizons and also have practical usefulness.

"Usefulness" is not always associated with the study of history. Indeed, in everyday conversation, the phrase "that's history" means that an event is no longer significant. It may once have been important, but it is not now. From this point of view, "history" is a record of people and events that are dead and gone. For the historian, however, the opposite is true. The past has made us who we are, and continues to influence who we are becoming. In this sense, the past is not dead, just as people whom we have known personally and who have influenced our lives are not "dead," even though they may no longer be with us. This text will highlight ways in which the past continues to have profound effects on the present and future. It will help us understand who we have become.

History does not provide specific answers to today's problems, but it does provide examples and case studies that help us improve our thinking. Generals study past wars to understand how modern battles may be fought; economists study past periods of growth and recession to understand how we can encourage the former and avoid the latter. Understanding the ways in which families and relationships have functioned in the past helps us find ways to make our own families and relationships more satisfying today.

World history gives us the largest possible canvas on which to carry out these studies. We cannot, however, study everything that ever happened. We must choose what to include and what to exclude. We must choose strategies that maximize our ability to understand our lives today in the context of the whole range of human experience.

In this text we choose two fundamental organizing principles as our framework for the study and teaching of world history. First, we choose a series of eight chronological turning points, each of which changed the patterns of human life. Second, we explain the importance of each of these changes in terms of the new themes they introduced into human experience. These two elements—chronological turning points and interpretive themes—go together.

This text is organized around eight turning points and themes. Others might also have been chosen, but these turning points represent eight of the most important transformations in human life. The thematic analysis of these turning points encourages students to grapple with the origins and continuing presence of eight of the most significant themes in life: the biological and cultural qualities that make humans the special creatures that we are; the settlements we create and live in; the political power that we assemble and sometimes oppose; the religious systems through which many people find meaning in their individual lives and communities; the movement of trade and people that has linked the peoples of the world ever more closely, sometimes in cooperation, sometimes in competition, and sometimes in conflict; the political, industrial, and social revolutions, especially of the seventeenth through the twentieth centuries; the continuing technological developments that continue to re-shape our world; and the quest for personal and group identity, so prevalent in our own times.

Because real life does not fit neatly into exact chronological periods, there will be significant overlap among the turning points. Readers may argue that the themes are also not limited to single chronological periods. For example, political regimes, religious systems, and economic organizations appear at all times in history. This argu-ment is, of course, correct: "everything is related to everything else," and in reality each chronological period will include several themes. We have chosen, however, to highlight particular themes in particular historical periods so that students will under-stand these themes more thoroughly and learn to employ them as tools of analysis in forming their own understanding of our world.

CHRONOLOGICAL TURNING POINTS AND PART THEMES

PART ONE. TURNING POINT: The emergence of the first humans. Biological and early cultural evolution, 5 million B.C.E. to 10,000 B.C.E.
THEME: Historians and anthropologists search for and interpret artifacts and records to determine what is human about humans.

PART TWO. TURNING POINT: Creating settlements, first agricultural villages and, later, cities. 10,000 B.C.E. to 1000 C.E.
THEME: Settlements—villages, towns, and cities—are created to meet community needs.

PART THREE. TURNING POINT: The creation of early empires, 2000 B.C.E. to 1100 C.E., from Sargon of Assyria through Alexander the Great, Qin and Han China, Republican and Imperial Rome, and India of the Mauryas and Guptas.
THEME: Imperial political power is generated, increased, consolidated, and resisted.

PART FOUR. TURNING POINT: The creation and diffusion of global religions: Judaism, Christianity, Islam, Hinduism, and Buddhism. 2500 B.C.E. to 1500 C.E.
THEME: Spiritual feelings are mobilized into powerful religious systems, some of which attain global scope.

PART FIVE. Global movement of goods and people, and the linking of continents; 1000–1776.
THEME: The flows of goods and people are channeled into global networks.

PART SIX. TURNING POINT: Revolutions, both political and industrial, 1640–1914.
THEME: Vast, abrupt changes in political and economic systems create new social values and systems affecting individuals, families, and communities.

PART SEVEN. TURNING POINT: Technological change and its human control; 1914 to 1980.
THEME: New technological systems—both simple and complex—are instituted to improve or threaten human life.

PART EIGHT. TURNING POINT: The formation of new identities; global, national, regional, cultural, and personal, 1975 to the present.
THEME: Increasingly tight-knit webs of communication, trade, and power bring diverse individuals and groups into contact, forcing them to constantly reconsider their identities.

Global Scope

The scope of this text, and of each turning point and theme within it, is global. For example, the study of the industrial revolution in Europe includes its funding—in part—from the wealth that poured into Europe from its New World conquests of people, land, gold, and silver, and from African slave labor; its global extensions in the form of imperialism in Asia, Africa, Australia, and Latin America; and the interactions of colonizers and colonized in response to the new opportunities and challenges.

SOCIAL SCIENCE METHODS, COMPARATIVE HISTORY, AND THE STUDY OF VALUES

Comparative History and the Methods of the Social Sciences

The global, interactive, and comparative format of this text provides also an introduction to social science methodology. The methods of the social sciences are embedded in the structure of the book. Because each part is built on comparisons among different regions of the world, the reader will become accustomed to posing hypotheses based on general principles and to testing them against comparative data from around the world.

This method of moving back and forth between general theory and specific case study, testing the degree to which the general theory and the specific data fit each other, is at the heart of the social sciences. For example, in Part 2 we will explore the general characteristics of cities, and then examine how well the generalizations hold up through case studies of various cities around the world. In Part 3 we will seek general theories of the rise and fall of early empires based on comparisons of China, Rome, and India. In Part 4 we will search for commonalities among religious systems through a survey of five world religions. In Part 8 we begin with an analysis of new issues of political and cultural identity and then examine their significance in a series of six brief case studies in different regions of the world. These comparisons enable us more clearly to think about and to understand the workings of cities, empires, and religions not only of the past, but also of our own time and place.

Multiple Perspectives

The text highlights the importance of multiple perspectives in studying and interpreting history. The answers we get—the narrative histories we write—are based on the questions we ask. Each part suggests a variety of questions that can be asked about the historical event that is being studied and a variety of interpretations that can emerge in the process of answering them. Often there is more than one "correct" way of understanding change over time and its significance. Different questions will trigger very different research and very different answers. For example, in Part 5 we ask about the stages and processes by which Western commercial power began to surpass that of Asia. This question presupposes the fact that at earlier times Asian power had been superior and raises the additional questions why it declined and why European power advanced. In Part 7 we ask how the industrial revolution affected and changed relationships between men and women; this question will yield different research and a different narrative from questions about, for example, women's contributions to industrialization, which is a useful question, but a different one.

Through the systematic study of the past in this thematic, comparative framework, students will gain tools for understanding and making their own place in the world today. They will not only learn how the peoples of the world have gotten to where we are, but also consider the possibility of setting out in new directions for new goals.

Evaluating Values

This form of analysis will also introduce a study of values. In order to understand the choices made by people in the past, we must attempt to understand the values that informed their thinking and actions. These values may be similar to, or quite different from, our own. In order to understand the interpretations introduced by later historians, we must understand the historians' values as well. These, too, may be similar to, or different from, our own. Historians usually had personal perspectives from which they viewed the past, and these perspectives influenced their interpretations. Finally, in order for student-readers to form their own understanding of the past, and to make it more useful in their own lives, they must also see how their own values influence their evaluation of past events.

For most of the past century, social scientists spoke of creating "value free" disciplines. Today, most scholars believe that this is impossible. We cannot be "value free." On the contrary, we must attempt to understand the values that have inspired historical actors, previous historians, and ourselves. Coming to an understanding of the values of others – historical actors and historians who have studied them – will help readers to recognize and formulate their own values, a central part of a liberal arts education.

HISTORY AND IDENTITY

History is among the most passionate and bitterly contentious of disciplines because most people and groups locate a large part of their identity in their history. Americans may take pride in their nationality, for example, for having created a representative, constitutional democracy that has endured for over 200 years (see Part 7). Yet they may be saddened, shamed, or perhaps incensed by the existence of 250 years of slavery followed by inequalities in race relations continuing to the present (see Part 6). Christians may take pride in two thousand years of missions of compassion toward the poor and downtrodden, yet they may be saddened, shamed, or even incensed by an almost equally long record of religious warfare and of persecution of those whose beliefs differed from their own (see Part 4).

As various ethnic, religious, class, and gender groups represent themselves in public political life, they seek not only to understand the history that has made them what they are, but also to persuade others to understand that history in the same way, to create a new consciousness. Feminist historians, for example, find in their reading of history that patriarchy, a system of male-created and male-dominated institutions, has subordinated women. From available data and their interpretation of them, they attempt to weave a persuasive argument that will win over others to their position.

Some will not be persuaded. They may not even agree that women have been subordinated to men, but argue that both genders have shared in a great deal of suffering (and joy) throughout history (see Parts 1 and 7). The historical debates over the origins and evolution of gender relationships evoke strong emotions because people's self-image, the image of their group, and the perceptions others hold of them are all at stake. And the stakes can be high.

CONTROL OF HISTORICAL RECORDS

From earliest times, control over the historical records and their interpretation has been fundamental to control over people's thoughts. The first emperor of China, Qin

Shihuang (r. 221–207 B.C.E.), the man who built the concept of a united China that has lasted until today attempted to destroy all knowledge of the past:

> He then abolished the ways of ancient sage kings and put to the torch the writings of the Hundred Schools in an attempt to keep the people in ignorance. He demolished the walls of major cities and put to death men of fame and talent. (deBary, I: 229).

Lenin addressing troops in Sverdlov Square, Moscow, May 5, 1920. The leaders of the Russian Communist revolution crudely refashioned the historical record to suit the wishes of the winners. After Lenin's death in 1924, his second-in-command Leon Trotsky (pictured sitting on the podium in the left-hand picture) lost to Josef Stalin the bitter power struggle that ensued. Not only was Trotsky banished from the Soviet Union, but so was his appearance in the official archives (see doctored picture below).

So wrote Jia Yi (201–168? B.C.E.), poet and statesman of the succeeding Han dynasty. Shihuang wished that only his interpretation of China's past, and his place in it, be preserved. Later intellectuals condemned his actions—but the lost records were irretrievable (see Part 3).

In similar fashion, the first great historian of the Christian Church, Eusebius of Caesarea (c. 260–339) in his accounts of the early Christians in the Roman Empire, chose carefully to include elements that he considered of "profit" to his mission, and to exclude those that were not.

> It is not for us to describe their miserable vicissitudes [in persecution] ... just as it is not a part of our task to leave on record their faction-fights and their unnatural conduct towards each other, prior to the persecution. That is why we have decided to say no more about them than suffices for us to justify God's Judgment ... We shall rather set forth in our whole narrative only what may be of profit, first, to our own times, and then to later times. (MacMullen, p. 6).

Historical Revision

Interpretations of events may become highly contested and revised even after several centuries have passed. Colonial governments seeking to control subject peoples sometimes argued that the conquered people were so backward that they benefited from the conquest. Later historians, with more distance and more detachment, were often less kind to the colonizers. Some 1900 years ago the historian Tacitus was writing bitterly of the ancient Romans in their conquest of England: "Robbery, butchery, rapine, the liars call Empire; they create a desolation and call it peace" (*Agricola*, 30)

In our own era, the many nations that have won their freedom from colonialism echo similar resentments against their foreign rulers and set out to revise the historical record in keeping with their newly won political freedom. Jawaharlal Nehru, the first prime minister of independent India (1947–64), wrote in 1944 from the prison cell in which he had been imprisoned for his leadership of his country's independence movement:

> British accounts of India's history, more especially of what is called the British period, are bitterly resented. History is almost always written by the victors and conquerors and gives their viewpoint; or, at any rate, the victors' version is given prominence and holds the field. (Nehru, p. 289)

Philip Curtin, historian of Africa and of slavery, elaborates an equally critical view of European colonial accounts of Africa's history:

> African history was seriously neglected until the 1950s ... The colonial period in Africa left an intellectual legacy to be overcome, just as it had in other parts of the world. ... The colonial imprint on historical knowledge emerged in the nineteenth and early twentieth centuries as a false perspective, a Eurocentric view of world history created at a time of European domination ... Even where Europeans never ruled, European knowledge was often accepted as modern knowledge, including aspects of the Eurocentric historiography. (Curtin, p. 54)

Instead, Curtin continues, a proper historiography must:

> show the African past from an African point of view ... For Africans, to know about the past of their own societies is a form of self-knowledge crucial to a sense of identity in a diverse and rapidly changing world. A recovery of African history has been an important part of African development over recent decades. (p. 54)

Religious and ethnic groups, too, may seek to control historical records. In 1542, the Roman Catholic Church established an Index of Prohibited Books to ban writings it considered heretical. (The Spanish Inquisition, ironically, stored away many records that later scholars used to recreate its history and the history of those it persecuted.) More recently, despite all the evidence of the Holocaust, the murder of 6 million Jews by the Nazi government of Germany during World War II, a few people have claimed that the murders never took place. They deny the existence of such racial and religious hatred and of its consequences, and ignore deep-seated problems in the relationships between majority and minority populations.

The significance of the voyages of Columbus was once celebrated uncritically in the United States in tribute both to "the Admiral of the Ocean Sea" himself and to the courage and enterprise of the European explorers and early settlers who brought their civilizations to the Americas. In South America, however, where Native American Indians are more numerous and people of European ancestry often form a smaller proportion of the population, the celebrations have been far more ambivalent, muted, and meditative.

In 1992, on the 500th anniversary of Columbus' first voyage to the Americas, altogether new and more sobering elements entered the commemoration ceremonies, even in the United States. The negative consequences of Columbus' voyages, previously ignored, were now recalled and emphasized: the death of up to 90 percent of the Native American Indian population in the century after the arrival of Europeans; the Atlantic slave trade, initiated by trade in Indian slaves; and the exploitation of the natural resources of a continent until then little touched by humans. The ecological consequences, which are only now beginning to receive more attention, were not all negative, however. They included the fruitful exchange of natural products between the hemispheres. Horses, wheat, and sheep were introduced to the Americas; potatoes, tomatoes, and corn to Afro-Eurasia. Unfortunately, the spread of syphilis was one of

Indians giving Hernán Cortés a headband, from Diego Duran's *Historia de las Indias*, 1547. Bent on conquest and plunder, the bearded Spaniard Cortés arrived on the Atlantic coast of Mexico in 1519. His forces sacked the ancient city of Tenochtitlán, decimated the Aztec people and imprisoned their chief, Montezuma, before proclaiming the Aztec Empire "New Spain." By stark contrast, this bland Spanish watercolor shows local tribesmen respectfully paying homage to the invader as if he were a god; in ignoring the brutality exercised in the colonization of South America, the artist is, in effect, "rewriting" history. (*Biblioteca National, Madrid*)

the consequences of the exchange; scholars disagree on who transmitted this disease to whom (see Part 5).

Thugs sometimes gain control of national histories. George Orwell's satirical novel *Animal Farm* (published in 1945) presented an allegory in which pigs come to rule a farm. Among their many acts of domination, the pigs seize control of the historical records of the farm animals' failed experiment in equality and impose their own official interpretation, which justifies their own rule. The rewriting of history and suppression of alternative records by the Communist Party of the former Soviet Union between 1917 and 1989 reveals the bitter truth underlying Orwell's satire (see Part 8).

Although the American experience is much different, in the United States, too, records have been suppressed. Scholars are still trying to use the Freedom of Information Act to pry open sealed diplomatic archives. (Most official archives everywhere have twenty-, thirty-, or forty-year rules governing the waiting period before certain sensitive records are opened to the public. These rules, which are designed to protect living people and contemporary policies from excessive scrutiny, are the general rule everywhere.)

WHAT DO WE KNOW? HOW DO WE KNOW IT? WHAT DIFFERENCE DOES IT MAKE:

So, historical records are not simply lists of events. They are the means by which individuals and groups develop their interpretations of these events. All people develop their own interpretations of past events; historians do it professionally. Because interpretations differ, there is no single historical record, but various narrations of events, each told from a different perspective. Therefore the study of history is intimately linked to the study of values.

To construct their interpretations, historians examine the values—the motives, wishes, desires, visions—of people of the past. In interpreting those values, historians must confront and engage their own values, comparing and contrasting these values with those of people in the past. For example, they ask how various people viewed slavery, or child labor, or education, or art and music in societies of the past. In the back of their minds they compare and contrast those older values with values held by various people today and especially with their own personal values. They ask: How and why have values changed or remained the same through the passage of time? Why, and in what ways, do my values compare and contrast with values of the past? By learning to pose such questions, students will be better equipped to discover and create their own place in the continuing movement of human history. This text, therefore consistently addresses three fundamental questions:

> What Do We Know?
> How Do We Know It?
> What Difference Does It Make?

Even when historians agree on which events are most significant, they may differ in evaluating why the events are significant. One historian's interpretation of events may be diametrically opposed to another's. For example, virtually all historians agree that part of the significance of World War II lay in its new policies and technologies of destruction: nuclear weapons in battle and genocide behind the lines. In terms of interpretation, pessimists might stress the continuing menace of these legacies of terror, while optimists might argue that the very violence of the war and the Holocaust triggered a search for limits on nuclear arms and greater tolerance for minorities. With each success in nuclear arms limitation and in toleration, the optimists seem more persuasive; with each spread of nuclear weapons and each outbreak of genocide, the pessimists seem to win.

The study of history is thus an interpretation of significance as well as an investigation of facts. The significance of events is determined by their consequences. Sometimes we do not know what the consequences are; or the consequences may not have run their course; or we may differ in our assessments of the consequences. This play between past events and their current consequences is what historian E.H. Carr had in mind in his famous description of history as "an unending dialogue between the present and the past" (Carr, p. 30).

TOOLS

The study of history requires many tools, and this text includes most of the principal ones:

- Primary sources are accounts that were produced at the time an event occurred. Those who produced them were eyewitnesses with direct knowledge of what happened. The core of historical study is an encounter with primary materials, usually documents, but including other artifacts—for example, letters, diaries, newspaper accounts, photographs, and artwork. Every chapter in this text includes representative primary materials.
- Visual images, a strong feature of this book, complement the written text, offering non-verbal "texts" of the time. These are often central pieces of evidence. For example, in Chapter 9 we illustrate the influence of Hinduism and Buddhism in Southeast Asia through the temple architecture of the region.
- Maps place events in space and in geographical relationship to one another.
- Chronological timelines situate events in time and sequence.
- Brief charts supply summaries as well as contextual information on topics such as religion, science, and trade.

Review Questions

- Please review the eight themes and turning points selected here. From what you already know of world history, do these seem well-chosen? Would you select different or additional themes and turning points for your account? If so, which ones and why?
- Examine how one of the values in which you believe has come from historical experience, either your own experience or that of relatives and friends, or the experience of groups to which you belong.
- When you tell other people about yourself, what "records" from your past do you highlight? Which ones do you leave out of the story, or even conceal? Are there any that you would like to destroy? Can you destroy them? How does the audience you are speaking to affect your choice of "records"?

Suggested Readings

BASIC, COMPREHENSIVE, INTRODUCTORY MATERIALS

Carr, E.H. *What Is History?* (Harmondsworth, Middlesex: Penguin Books, 1964). A classic introduction to the study of history and historiography from the point of view of a master.

Tosh, John. *The Pursuit of History: Aims, Methods, and New Directions in the Study of Modern History*, 2nd ed. (London: Longman, 1991). Excellent, comprehensive introduction to the study of history, with discussions of many different kinds of historical study, their methods and purposes.

MORE SPECIALIZED MATERIALS

Bennett, Judith M. "Medieval Women, Modern Women: Across the Great Divide," in David Aers, ed., *Culture and History, 1350–1600: Essays on English Communities, Identities, and Writing* (New York: Harvester Wheatsheaf, 1992), 147–75. Discusses continuity, in contrast to change, in women's history.

Curtin, Philip D. "Recent Trends in African Historiography and Their Contribution to History in General," in Joseph Ki-Zerbo, ed., *General History of Africa, Vol. I: Methodology and African Pre-History* (Berkeley: University of California Press, 1981), 54–71. An excellent introduction to this fine series commissioned by the United Nations.

deBary, William Theodore, et al., comps. *Sources of Chinese Tradition*. 2nd ed. 2 vols. (New York: Columbia University Press, 1999, 2000). THE anthology of materials on the subject.

Lerner, Gerda. *The Creation of Patriarchy* (New York: Oxford University Press, 1986). A controversial study of patriarchy in ancient Mesopotamia by a distinguished historian of the United States. Lerner re-tooled to study this fundamental feminist question.

MacMullen, Ramsay. *Christianizing the Roman Empire (A.D. 100–400)* (New Haven: Yale University Press, 1984). Excellent analysis of the factors leading to Christianity's success in the Roman Empire. Gives major role to government support.

Nehru, Jawaharlal. *The Discovery of India* (Delhi: Oxford University Press, 1989). A history of his country, written in jail during the freedom struggle by the man who became India's first prime minister.

Orwell, George. *Animal Farm* (New York: Harcourt, Brace, 1946). A classic satire on government by thugs; aimed at the USSR.

Tacitus, Cornelius. *Tacitus' Agricola, Germany, and Dialogue on Orators*, trans. Herbert W. Benario (Norman: University of Oklahoma Press, 1991). One of ancient Rome's great historians who understood the cruelty underlying the power of empire.

THE
WORLD'S
HISTORY

THIRD EDITION

PART 1

Human Origins and Human Cultures

5 million B.C.E. –10,000 B.C.E.

BUILDING AN INTERPRETIVE FRAMEWORK: WHAT DO WE KNOW AND HOW DO WE KNOW IT?

Historians ask some very big questions. Of course, the stereotype of the historian as a person who searches in dusty archives for tiny, concrete bits of data is often correct. Detail and accuracy are important. Beneath this search for details, however, lie profound questions of fundamental importance. In this chapter we address some of the biggest questions of all: Where did humans come from? How did our collective life on earth begin? How are we similar to other living species, and how are we unique?

Many historians would consider such questions to relate to prehistory, for no written records exist to answer them. We choose, however, to include prehistory as part of our search, for we historians are eclectic in our methods; we begin with questions about the past and our relationship to it, and then choose whatever methods help us to find answers. In this chapter we find that until the mid-nineteenth century, stories, often religious narratives, provided the answers to our questions about human origins. Then a re-evaluation of religious and narrative traditions invited a search for additional answers with a scientific basis. About the same time, new techniques of archaeology developed to provide those answers.

What does it mean to be human? This profound question turns most historians and prehistorians to the study of human creativity. Humans are what humans do. We travel and migrate, often out of sheer curiosity as well as to find food and shelter. As we shall see, by about 15,000 B.C.E., humans had traveled, mostly over land, and established themselves on all the continents of the earth except Antarctica. We also create and invent tools. Our account begins with the simplest stone tools dating back millions of years and continues up to the invention of pottery and of sedentary farming some 10,000 years ago. Finally, we humans also express our feelings and ideas in art, music, dance, ritual, and literature. In this chapter we examine early evidence of this creativity in the forms of sculptures and cave paintings from 20,000 years ago.

For time periods more recent than 20,000 years ago, we usually adopt the notation "B.C.E." (Before the Common Era) and "C.E." (Common Era). These designations correspond exactly to the more familiar "B.C." (Before Christ) and "A.D." (Anno Domini, "in the year of our Lord"), but remove the specific reference to a single religion. For dates more than 20,000 years ago, "B.P." (Before the Present) is sometimes used.

A skeleton from Herculaneum, Italy, 2001. An archaeologist excavates the skeleton of an inhabitant from the Roman city of Herculaneum, which was buried by the eruption of Mount Vesuvius in 79 C.E.

THE DRY BONES SPEAK

5 million B.C.E.–10,000 B.C.E.

KEY TOPICS
- Human Origins in Myth and History
- Fossils and Fossil Hunters
- Humans Create Culture

HUMAN ORIGINS IN MYTH AND HISTORY

Where did we come from? How did humans come to inhabit the earth? These questions are difficult to answer because the earliest human beings left no written records or obvious oral traditions. For more than a century, we have sought the answer to these questions in the earth, in the records of the fossils that archaeologists and **paleo-anthropologists** (students of the earliest humans) have discovered and interpreted. But before the diggers came with their interpretations, human societies from many parts of the world developed stories based on popular beliefs to explain our origins. Passed from generation to generation as folk wisdom, these stories gave meaning to human existence. They not only tell *how* humans came to inhabit the earth, they also suggest *why*. Some of these stories, especially those that have been incorporated into religious texts such as the Bible, still inspire the imaginations and govern the behavior of hundreds of millions of people around the world.

paleoanthropologist A student of the earliest humans and the setting in which they lived.

Early Myths

As professional history developed, many historians considered that these stories were of limited value in the study of history and dismissed them as **myth**, an imaginative construction that cannot be verified with the kinds of records historians usually use. Nonetheless, myth and history are closely related, and many historians and anthropologists now accept myths as important commentaries that help us to understand how various societies have interpreted the origins of the human world. Myth and history share a common purpose—trying to explain how the world came to be as it is. Though there are limitations to mythical evidence, myths often contain important truths, and they can have powerful effects on people's values and behavior. Shared myths give cohesion to social relationships and bring them into a sense of shared community.

myth An interpretive story of the past that cannot be verified historically but has a deep moral message.

For thousands of years various creation stories have presented people with explanations of their place in the world and of their relationship to the gods, to the rest of creation, and to one another. The narratives have similarities, but also significant differences. Some portray humans as the exalted crown of creation, others as reconfigured parasites; some depict humans as partners with the gods, others as their servants; some suggest the equality of all humans, others stress a variety of caste, race, and gender hierarchies. To some degree, surely, people transmitted the stories as quaint tales told for enjoyment only, but they also provided guidance on how people should understand and live their lives.

One of the earliest known stories is the *Enuma Elish* epic of the people of Akkad in Mesopotamia. This account probably dates back to almost 2000 B.C.E. The goddess Tiamat and her consort Kingu revolt against the existing gods of Mesopotamia. These gods call on Marduk, a young, strong god, who defends the old order by defeating, killing, and dismembering the rebellious deities.

According to the *Enuma Elish*, the victorious gods created humans out of the blood of the defeated and slain leader of the rebels. The humans were to devote themselves

Opposite **A skeleton from Herculaneum, Italy, 2001.** An archaeologist excavates the skeleton of an inhabitant from Herculaneum.

to the service of the victors. In the context of the violent city-states of Mesopotamia at the time the epic was written down, this myth gave meaning and direction to human life and affirmed the authority of the powerful priestly class.

India, vast and diverse, has many different stories about the origin of humans. Two of the most widespread and powerful illustrate two principal dimensions of the thought and practice of Hindu religious traditions (see Chapter 9). The ancient epic *Rigveda*, which dates from about 1000 B.C.E., emphasizes the mystical, unknowable qualities of life and its origins:

> Who verily knows and who can here declare it, whence it was born and whence comes this creation?
>
> The Gods are later than this world's production. Who knows then whence it first came into being?
>
> He, the first origin of this creation, whether he formed it all or did not form it, whose eye controls this world in highest heaven, he verily knows it or perhaps he knows not.

In contrast to this reverent but puzzled view of creation, another of the most famous hymns of the *Rigveda*, the Purusha-sakta, describes the creation of the world by the gods' sacrifice and dismemberment of a giant man, Purusha:

> His mouth became the Brahmin; his arms were made into the Warrior, his thighs the People, and from his feet the Servants were born.
>
> The moon was born from his mind; from his eye the sun was born. Indra and Agni came from his mouth, and from his vital breath the Wind was born. (Ch. 10; v. 129)

AT A GLANCE : EARLY HUMANS AND THEIR ANCESTORS

DATE	PERIOD	HOMINID EVOLUTION	MATERIAL CULTURE
5 million	■ Pliocene	■ Fragments found in northern Kenya; possibly *Australopithecus*	
3.75 million	■ Pleistocene	■ *Australopithecus* genus, inc. Lucy (east and southern Africa) ■ *Homo habilis* (eastern and southern Africa) ■ *Homo erectus* (Africa) ■ *Homo erectus* thought to have moved from Africa into Eurasia	■ Tools ■ Stone artifacts ■ Use of fire
500,000		■ *Homo sapiens* (archaic form) ■ Remains of Peking Man (*Sinanthropus*) found at Zhoukoudian	
130,000– 80,000		■ *Homo sapiens* (Africa and western Asia)	■ Stone artifacts
100,000– 33,000		■ Neanderthals (Europe and western Asia)	
40,000	■ Aurignacian		■ Tools include long blades ■ First passage from Siberia to Alaska
30,000	■ Gravettian	■ Human remains of the Upper Paleolithic type, *Homo sapiens sapiens* (25,000) found in China	■ Venus figures (25,000–12,000)
20,000	■ Solutrean		■ Chauvet cave, France (18,000)
17,000	■ Magdalenian		■ Lascaux cave paintings (*c.* 15,000) ■ Altamira cave paintings (*c.* 13,550)

In this account, humans are part of nature, subject to the laws of the universe, but they are not born equal among themselves. Several groups are created with different qualities, in different **castes** or social, economic, and ritual positions inherited at birth. This myth of creation supported the hierarchical organization of India's historic caste system.

Perhaps the most widely known creation story is told in the Book of Genesis in the Hebrew Bible. Beginning from nothing, in five days God created heaven and earth; created light and separated it from darkness; created water and separated it from dry land; and created flora, birds, and fishes, and the sun, moon, and stars. God began the sixth day by creating larger land animals and reptiles, and then humans "in his own image."

The Book of Genesis assigns humans a unique and privileged place as the final crown and master of creation. Humans are specially created in God's own image, with dominion over all other living creatures. When the creation of humans and the charge to them are complete, God proclaims the whole process and product of creation as "good." Here humans hold an exalted position within, but also above, the rest of creation.

Until the late eighteenth century, these kinds of story were the only accounts we had of the origins of humans. No other explanations seemed necessary. In any case, no one expected to find actual physical evidence for the processes by which humans came to exist.

caste A hierarchical ordering of people into groups, fixed from birth, based on their inherited ritual status and determining whom they may marry and with whom they may eat.

Shiva Nataraja, Indian School, 13th century. Bronze. The cosmic dance of the Hindu Lord Shiva brings about a destruction that crushes evil underfoot and prepares the way for rebirth in the cycle of existence.

The Evolutionary Explanation

During the eighteenth century some philosophers and natural scientists in Europe, who were most familiar with the creation story told in the Bible, began to challenge its belief in the individual, special creation of each life form. They saw so many similarities among different species that they could not believe that each had been created separately, but they could not demonstrate the processes through which these similarities and differences had developed. They saw some creatures changing forms during their lifecycle, such as the metamorphosis of the caterpillar into the moth, or the tadpole into the frog, but they could not establish the processes by which one species metamorphosed into another. They also knew the processes of breeding by which farmers encouraged the development of particular strains in the farm animals and plants, but they lacked the conception of a timeframe of millions of years that would allow for the natural evolution of a new species from an existing one.

Challenging the authority of the biblical account required a new method of inquiry, a new system for organizing knowledge. By the mid-eighteenth century, a new intellectual environment had begun to emerge (see Chapter 15). Scientific method called for the direct observation of nature, the recording and analysis of observation, and the discussion and debate of findings throughout an international community of scholars. It rejected the authority of religious texts that asserted truths without presenting substantiating evidence.

Charles Darwin (1809–82) and Alfred Russel Wallace (1823–1913), separately, formulated the modern theory of

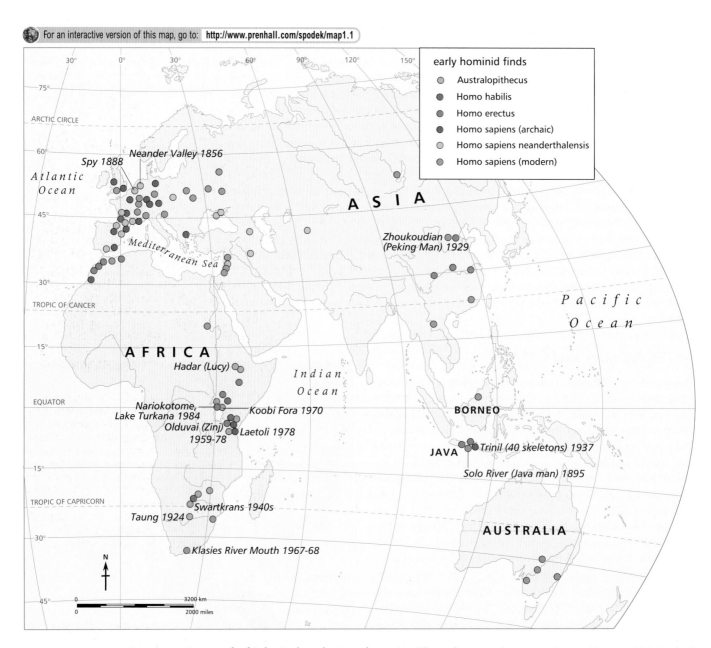

For an interactive version of this map, go to: http://www.prenhall.com/spodek/map1.1

early hominid finds
- Australopithecus
- Homo habilis
- Homo erectus
- Homo sapiens (archaic)
- Homo sapiens neanderthalensis
- Homo sapiens (modern)

Spy 1888
Neander Valley 1856
Atlantic Ocean
ASIA
Zhoukoudian (Peking Man) 1929
Mediterranean Sea
Pacific Ocean
AFRICA
Hadar (Lucy)
Indian Ocean
Nariokotome, Lake Turkana 1984
Koobi Fora 1970
BORNEO
Olduvai (Zinj) 1959-78
Laetoli 1978
Trinil (40 skeletons) 1937
JAVA
Solo River (Java man) 1895
Swartkrans 1940s
Taung 1924
AUSTRALIA
Klasies River Mouth 1967-68

3200 km
2000 miles

Human ancestors. Fossil remains of the earliest direct human ancestors, *Australopithecus* and *Homo habilis*, dating from 1 million to 5 million years ago, have been found only in tropical Africa. The unique soil and climatic conditions there have preserved the fossils. *Homo erectus* remains, from 1.5 million years ago, are the earliest to be found outside Africa. They, along with *Homo sapiens*, have been found throughout Eurasia.

the biological evolution of species. They also saw the mounting evidence of biological similarities among related species; they understood that these similar species were, in fact, related to one another, not separate creations, and they allowed a timeframe adequate for major transformations of species to take place. They then went on to demonstrate the method by which small differences within a species were transmitted from generation to generation, increasing the differentiation until new forms were produced.

Both Darwin and Wallace reached their conclusions as a result of extensive travel overseas. Darwin carried out his observations on a scientific voyage around the world in 1831–6 aboard the British warship *Beagle*, and especially during his stay in the Galapagos Islands off the equatorial west coast of South America. Wallace traveled for many years in the islands of southeast Asia. In 1855 he published a paper suggesting a common ancestor for primates and man. In 1858 Wallace and Darwin published a joint paper on the basic concepts of evolution.

In the isolated Galapagos Islands, Darwin had found various kinds of finches, all of which were similar to each other except in their beaks. He rejected the idea that each kind of finch had been separately created. Rather, he argued, there must have been an ancestor common to them all throughout the islands. Because each island offered slightly different food sources, different beaks were better suited to each separate island. The different ecological niches on each separate island to which the birds had immigrated had evoked slightly different evolutionary development. So from a single, common ancestor, new species evolved over time on the different islands.

Darwin compared natural selection to the selection process practiced by humans in breeding animals. Farmers know that specific traits among their animals can be exaggerated through breeding. Horses, for example, can be bred either for speed or for power by selecting those horses in which the desired trait appears. In nature the act of selection occurs spontaneously, if more slowly, as plants and animals that have traits more appropriate to an environment survive and reproduce while others do not.

In 1859 Darwin published his findings and conclusions in *On the Origin of Species by Means of Natural Selection*, a book that challenged humankind's conception of life on earth and of our place in the universe. Darwin explained that the pressure for each organism to compete, survive, and reproduce created a kind of natural selection. The population of each species increased until its ecological niche was filled to capacity. In the face of this population pressure, the species that were better adapted to the niche survived; the rest were crowded out and tended toward extinction. Small differences always appeared within a species: some members were taller, some shorter; some more brightly colored, others less radiant; some with more flexible hands and feet, others less manipulable. Those members with differences that aided survival in any given ecological setting tended to live on and to transmit their differences to their descendants. Others died out. Darwin called this process "natural selection" or "survival of the fittest."

The New Challenges. Darwin's argument challenged two prevailing stories of creation, especially the biblical views. First, the process of natural selection had no goal beyond survival and reproduction. Unlike many existing creation myths, especially biblical stories, evolutionary theory postulated no **teleology**, no ethical or moral goals and purposes of life. Second, the theory of natural selection described the evolution of ever more "fit" organisms, better adapted to their environment, evolving from existing ones. The special, separate creation of each species was not necessary.

For Darwin, the process of natural selection of more complex, better adapted forms also explained the evolution of humans from simpler, less well-adapted organisms. Perhaps this was "the Creator's" method. Darwin concluded *On the Origin of Species*:

Thus, from the war of nature, from famine and death, the most exalted object which we are capable of conceiving, namely, the production of the higher animals, directly follows. There is grandeur in this view of life, with its several powers, having been originally breathed by the Creator into a few forms or into one; and that, whilst this planet has gone cycling on according to the fixed law of gravity, from so simple a beginning endless forms most beautiful and most wonderful have been, and are being, evolved.

"That Troubles Our Monkey Again." **Cartoon of Charles Darwin from** *Fun,* **November 16, 1872.** As scientists and theologians struggled to come to terms with the implications of evolutionary theory, popular reaction was often hostile and derisive. In this cartoon from a contemporary British weekly, Darwin is caricatured as an ape checking the pulse of a woman—or, as the cartoonist ironically refers to her, a "female descendant of marine ascidian" (a tiny invertebrate).

teleology The philosophical study of final causes or purposes. Teleology refers especially to any system that interprets nature or the universe as having design or purpose. It has been used to provide evidence for the existence of God.

Note, however, that the words "by the Creator" did not appear in the first edition. Darwin added them later, perhaps in response to criticisms raised by more conventional Christian religious thinkers, who continued to find the biblical story a credible explanation for the origins of human beings.

Within a decade, Darwin's ideas had won over the scientific community. In 1871, Darwin published *The Descent of Man*, which extended his argument to the evolution of humans, concluding explicitly that "man is descended from some lowly organized form."

The search now began for evidence of the "missing link" between humans and apes, for some creature, alive or dead, that stood at an intermediate point in the evolutionary process. In this search archaeology flourished, and the adjunct field of paleo-anthropology, which explores the nature of early humans in their environment, developed. We shall now investigate the findings of these disciplines and the disputes they have engendered.

FOSSILS AND FOSSIL HUNTERS

The search for the "missing link" began in Europe, because that is where the major scientific researchers lived and worked, and that is where the discovery of Neanderthal skeletons in 1856 whetted their appetites for still more evidence. Later, the search led to Java, Indonesia, and Beijing, China. Still more recently, Africa has yielded the earliest specimens of the human species, *Homo sapiens sapiens*, fulfilling Darwin's prediction of an African origin of human evolution, based on the abundance of non-human primates—apes and chimpanzees—living on that continent.

As archaeologists discovered a variety of kinds of hominids—creatures that exhibited some characteristics of *Homo sapiens* but others of earlier primates—they concluded that there was no single missing link, but rather a variety of evolutionary paths that led to the emergence of humans. Our discussion will now follow the search for the missing link that ultimately led to this new understanding of the pattern of evolution. Readers who wish to know immediately the composite picture that has emerged from this research may now turn to the chart on pages 16–17.

The Puzzling Neanderthals

In August 1856, workers quarrying for limestone in a cave in the Neander Valley near Düsseldorf, Germany, found a thick skullcap with a sloping forehead and several skeletal bones of limbs. Some speculated that it was a deformed human. Others thought it was a soldier lost in a previous war. Other, similar, skeletal remains had been found, but without any clearer understanding of their meaning.

In 1863, Thomas Henry Huxley (1829–95), a leading advocate of Darwin's theory of evolution, argued that the skull was part of a primitive human being who stood between non-human primates and *Homo sapiens*, our own species. (The term *Homo sapiens* means "human, wise.") He claimed that it was the "missing link." In 1864, scholars gave the fossil a name that signified this intermediate position: *Homo neanderthalensis*.

One of the first questions archaeologists asked themselves was: What did *Homo neanderthalensis* look like? Reconstructing the appearance of Neanderthals was difficult, because soft tissue—hair, flesh, and cartilage—does not survive as fossils. Scientists had to use their imaginations.

The earliest efforts to picture Neanderthals showed them walking like apes, with a spine that had no curves, and hunchbacked, with their heads pushed forward on top

Diorama of "bovine" Neanderthals. Displayed for decades in the Field Museum of Natural History in Chicago, this reconstruction suggests that Neanderthals were unintelligent and clumsy. More recent interpretations portray a more intelligent, more graceful creature.

Alternate reconstructions from Neanderthal skull. Because soft tissues—hair, flesh, cartilage—don't survive as fossils, archaeologists must use their imaginations in adding these elements to the solid bone of excavated skeletons.

of their spines. Muscular but clumsy-looking, with heavy jaws and low, sloping foreheads, these pictures strongly suggested that *Homo neanderthalensis* was brutish and lacking in intelligence. For many years this interpretation, and others similar to it, carried great weight. Museum representations carried the message to the general public. Over the years, however, archaeologists have discovered more about Neanderthals' ability to make tools and survive in challenging environments. Impressed with these accomplishments, anthropologists now create reconstructions that show Neanderthals looking much less "primitive" and more like modern humans.

Moving beyond the individual skeleton in isolation, teams of experts from disciplines such as biology, geology, and climatology cooperate to reconstruct the natural setting of human and hominid development. As Neanderthal skeletons have been found from northern Europe to Africa, from Gibraltar to Iran, these natural settings vary greatly. Remains from caves near Gibraltar suggest that Neanderthals in that area lived in a nuclear family. Elsewhere, evidence shows that many Neanderthals lived in larger bands of up to twenty to thirty individuals.

One recent discovery suggests that at least some Neanderthals were cannibals. The evidence comes from a cave in southern France. A total of seventy-eight bones from at least two adults, two teenagers, and two children aged about seven show that the flesh from all parts of the bodies was carefully removed. Bones were smashed with rocks to get at the inside marrow and skulls were broken open. The Neanderthal bones and the bones of deer were tossed together into a heap and show similar marks from the same stone tools. On the other hand, there are many other examples of Neanderthals burying their dead carefully, suggesting that their cultural behavior differed from group to group.

While Neanderthals appeared to be *a* link between apes and humans, continuing excavations demonstrated that they were not *the* link. As researchers have continued to find additional examples of early hominids all over the world, it has become increasingly clear that there is no single link. There is no single chain leading directly from apes to humans. Rather, anthropologists now believe that many hominids contributed to a formation better described as a "bush" of various hominids with many branches. From the various interbreedings of these hominids, *Homo sapiens sapiens*, our species, evolved. All of the other intervening species died out and are no longer to be found

LANDMARKS IN EARLY LIFE

Years ago (millions)	Geological period	Life form
2500	Archaean	earliest living things
590	Cambrian	first fossils
505	Ordovician	first fish
438	Silurian	first land plants
408	Devonian	first amphibians
360	Carboniferous	first reptiles
286	Permian	reptiles expanded
248	Triassic	first mammals and dinosaurs
213	Jurassic	first birds
144	Cretaceous	heyday of dinosaurs
65	Cretaceous	mammals flourished; dinosaurs extinct
25	Tertiary	first hominoid (ancestor of apes and humans)
5	Tertiary	first hominid (human ancestor)
0.01	Quaternary	modern humans appeared

walking the earth. So it might appear that first there were apes and then, in a direct chain, there were humans. But the fossils of many different species in-between show that the evolutionary path was not so simple.

Homo erectus: A Worldwide Wanderer

Homo erectus The most widespread of all prehistoric hominids, and the most similar to humans. Evolved about 2 million years ago and became extinct 100,000 years ago.

The next of these prehistoric hominid species to be unearthed—the most widespread, and the closest to modern humans—was *Homo erectus* (the upright human). Examples of this species were discovered in widely dispersed locations throughout the eastern hemisphere and first named according to the locations in which they were found. Later, anthropologists recognized the similarities among them, named them collectively *Homo erectus*, and traced their migration patterns from their earliest home in Africa to new habitats across Asia.

In 1891, Eugène Dubois (1858–1940), a surgeon in the Dutch army in Java, Indonesia, was exploring for fossils. Employing the labor of convicts in Dutch prisons, along the bank of the Solo River, he discovered a cranium with a brain capacity of 900 cubic centimeters (compared to the modern human average of 1400 cc), a molar, and a femur. Dubois claimed to have discovered "pithecanthropus," ape-man. This find, widely referred to as Java Man, was the first early hominid discovered outside Europe. Dubois' Java Man forced scholars to consider the theories of the evolution of humans more seriously and to understand the process in a global context.

In 1929, in the vast Zhoukoudian cave 30 miles from Beijing, Chinese archaeologists discovered a 500,000-year-old skullcap. In the next few years, in this fossil-rich cave, they discovered fourteen more fossil skulls and the remains of some forty individuals, whom they dated from 600,000 to 200,000 years ago. The cave seems to have been the home of a band of hunters, who lived in a forested, grassy, riverine area and who ate plants as well as animals, such as bison and deer. Remaining bones and ash indicate their ability to use fire for light and cooking. With a brain capacity ranging from 775 to 1300 cubic centimeters and a height up to 5 feet 6 inches, anatomically Peking (Beijing) Man was almost identical to Java Man. About a decade later, further excavations in Java turned up the nearly complete skull of one hominid and the skeletons of some forty others who had lived some 100,000 to 900,000 years ago. Anthropologists soon recognized similarities between Java Man and Beijing Man and classified them collectively under the name *Homo erectus*. The forty skeletons from Java represent one-third of all the *Homo erectus* skeletons uncovered to this day in the entire world. Those in the Zhoukoudian cave represent another third. The most complete skeleton that we have of *Homo erectus* was discovered, however, in Africa, in 1984, on the shores of Lake Turkana, Kenya, by Richard Leakey. These fossils were later grouped as *Homo erectus*. The key problem was that the names were proliferating with no understanding of the relationships, and each discoverer considered his find to be a separate species.

The Search Shifts to Africa

In 1924, a medical student in South Africa called the attention of his professor, Raymond Dart, to some fossils in a quarry near Taung. Dart investigated and proclaimed the Taung skull to be *Australopithecus africanus*, "southern apelike creature of Africa," a 2-million-year-old ancestor of humans. Another medical doctor, Robert Broom, discovered additional hominid fossils including some of *Homo erectus*, similar to those discovered in Java and China. Between 1945 and 1955, Dart and his colleagues began to discover bone tools among the hominid fossils as well as evidence of the first controlled use of fire, about 1 million years ago. Their research extended beyond the archaeology of individual hominid skeletons to paleoanthropology, the study of the entire environment in which these hominids had lived. Their ecological analyses included, for example, the fossils of hundreds of animals discovered nearby the hominids.

Archaeologist Louis Leakey (1903–72) began his excavations in East Africa in the 1930s, although his most important discoveries were achieved with his wife Mary (1913–96) after 1959 in the Olduvai Gorge, where the Great Rift Valley cuts through northern Tanzania.

The Great Rift Valley runs from the Jordan River valley and the Dead Sea southward through the Red Sea, Ethiopia, Kenya, Tanzania, and Mozambique. The Rift is a fossil-hunter's delight. From at least 7 million years ago until perhaps 100,000 years ago, it was a fertile, populated region; it is geologically still shifting and, therefore, has covered and uncovered its deposits over time. Rivers that run through the Rift Valley further the process of uncovering the fossils, and it is volcanic, generating lava and ash that preserve the fossils caught within it and provide the material for relatively accurate dating.

Louis and Mary Leakey examining the palate of the Zinj skull, 1959. This husband-and-wife team revolutionized our understanding of anthropology. Their excavations in the Olduvai Gorge in East Africa led to the generally accepted belief that hominids originally evolved in Africa.

At Olduvai in 1959, the Leakeys discovered a hominid they called *Zinjanthropus boisei*, soon nicknamed Zinj. At first they hoped that Zinj might be an early specimen of *Homo*, but its skull was too small, its teeth were too large, its arms were too long, and its face was too much like an ape's. Zinj, who was 1,750,000 years old, was another *Australopithecus*, a hominid closer to apes than to modern humans. The *Australopithecus* clan was thus extended to include a new cousin, *Australopithecus boisei*. The australopithecine family tree—or "bush"—by now showed a number of branches, although the relationship among them and to us is not always clear. The chart on page 16 represents these branches and relationships.

Homo habilis. The Leakeys' continued excavations at Olduvai turned up skull fragments of creatures with brain capacities of 650 cubic centimeters, between the 400–500 cc of australopithecines and the 1400 cc of modern humans. The Leakeys named this new type of hominid *Homo habilis*, "handy person," because of the stone tools they made and used in scavenging, hunting, and butchering food. Dating suggested that *Homo habilis* lived at about the same time as Zinj, demonstrating that *Homo* and *Australopithecus* had lived side by side about 2 million years ago.

The Leakeys' discoveries at Olduvai furthered the search for the ancestors of modern humans in several directions: they pushed back the date of the earliest known representative of the genus *Homo* to 1.5–2 million years ago; they indicated the extent of the tool-using capacity of these early *Homo* representatives; and they reconstructed the ecology of the region 2.5–1.5 million years ago, placing *Homo habilis* within it as hunter and scavenger. Together with earlier discoveries, the findings enabled the Leakeys to identify Africa as the home of the earliest hominids and the earliest representatives of the genus *Homo*.

In the 1970s, Louis and Mary's son, Richard Leakey (1944–), discovered additional bones of the species *Homo habilis* at Koobi Fora on the east side of Lake Turkana in Kenya. The finds confirmed the size of its brain at about 650 cc; its opposable thumb, which allowed it to grip objects powerfully and manipulate them precisely, and thus to make tools; and its upright, bipedal (two-legged) walk, evident from the form of its thigh and leg bones.

Australopithecus afarensis. In 1974, at Hadar, Ethiopia, near the Awash River, Donald Johanson (1943–) discovered "Lucy," the first known representative of *Australopithecus afarensis*, named for the local Afar people. (Lucy herself was named for the popular Beatles song "Lucy in the Sky with Diamonds," which was playing on a tape recorder just as the Johanson team was realizing the importance of their find.) This discovery pushed back the date of the earliest known hominid to about 3.2 million years ago.

Lucy's overall height was between 3 feet 6 inches and 4 feet, and Johanson and his team estimated her weight as 60 pounds. The archaeologists were able to uncover about 40 percent of her total skeleton, making Lucy the earliest and most complete hominid skeleton known at the time. She had humanlike hands, but there is no evidence that she made or used tools, and her sturdy, curved arms are still consistent with tree-climbing. Later excavations at Hadar revealed numerous additional skeletons of *Australopithecus afarensis*, including the first complete skull, discovered by Johanson in 1992.

The cranial capacity of Lucy and her fellow *Australopithecus afarensis* was only 400 cubic centimeters, too small for her to be a *Homo*. Her pelvis was too small to allow the birth of offspring with a larger skull, but the form of that pelvis and the fit of her knee joints characterized Lucy as a two-legged hominid. Lucy had walked upright. She was a kind of bipedal ape, and, in her bipedalism, an ancestor of modern humans.

Further evidence of the bipedalism of these apelike creatures came from Laetoli, Tanzania. There, in 1978, Mary Leakey discovered the footprints of two *Australopithecus afarensis* walking side by side. In volcanic ash, she found seventy footprints walking a distance of 80 feet. The ash provided material for dating the prints; they were 3.5 million years old. The tracks suggest that *Australopithecus afarensis* had a slower, more rolling gait than modern man, although the prints reveal well-defined feet. Mary Leakey saw in them a slight sideward turn, a hesitation in direction, which she interpreted as the first evidence of human doubt.

In 1994, seventeen fossils of a new genus, *Ardipithecus ramidus*, "ground ape," were discovered in Aramis, Ethiopia, in the bed of the Awash River not far from the Lucy find. An international team of archaeologists analyzed them. Ten of the fossils were teeth, two were cranial fragments, and the remainder were bones from the left arm. Later, the team recovered about 80 percent of an *Ardipithecus ramidus* skeleton. It dated to 4.4 million years, pushing back the date of the earliest ape-like hominid by a half million years.

Then, in 2001, a team working in Chad, Africa, under the French paleoanthropologist Michel Brunet discovered a 6- to 7-million-year-old skull, nicknamed "Toumai," which means "hope of life" in the Goran language (see p. 19). Toumai is at least 2.5 million years older than any previously discovered hominid skull, and, remarkably, it is nearly complete. On the cusp between ape and human, its human characteristics include a relatively thick and continuous brow ridge, a relatively flat nose and face, and canine teeth which are shorter and more thickly enameled than those of chimpanzees. On the other hand, its cranial capacity is about the size of a chimp's, about one-fourth of a modern human's. It is not clear if Toumai was bipedal, but its spine entered its cranium in a pathway consistent with bipedalism. "Toumai" fits the dominant theories of

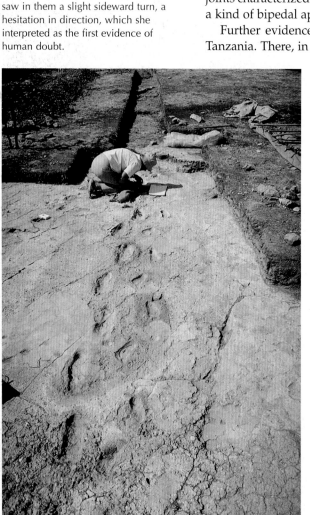

Hominid footprints, Laetoli, Northern Tanzania. These footprints in ash at Laetoli confirmed that hominids were walking upright 3.5 million years ago. The tracks suggest that *Australopithecus afarensis* had a slower, more rolling gait than modern man, although the prints reveal well-defined feet. Mary Leakey (pictured), who discovered the prints, saw in them a slight sideward turn, a hesitation in direction, which she interpreted as the first evidence of human doubt.

"Lucy" skeleton, *Australopithecus afarensis*, found at Hadar, Ethiopia. "Lucy" is thought to have lived about 3.2 million years ago and was at the time of her discovery in 1974 the earliest known hominid ancestor of modern man. She had humanlike hands and could walk upright; however, there is no evidence that she made or used tools, and her sturdy, curved arms are still consistent with tree-climbing. Until the discovery of Ardipithecus in 1994, Lucy was the most complete hominid skeleton from the period before 2 million years ago. (*Natural History Museum, London*)

evolution as to the time at which and the pattern by which the hominid line of evolution separated from the chimpanzee line, taking on its own distinct characteristics. It challenges most current beliefs, however, in suggesting that hominids evolved not only in the difficult, harsh, arid climate of the Rift Valley, where all the earlier hominids had been uncovered, but also in the more accommodating lush forests that covered western Chad 6 million years ago.

As paleoanthropologists assembled this record of the earliest human ancestors, they also found more recent skeletons that more closely resemble our own. The earliest known anatomically modern *Homo sapiens* fossil also appeared in Africa. It was discovered in 1967–8 in caves at the Klasies River Mouth on the coast of South Africa. These fossil remains of the oldest known example of the species *Homo sapiens* date to 75,000 to 115,000 years ago. They include lower and upper jaws, skull fragments, teeth, and bones of limbs. With them fossil-hunters found thousands of stone quartzite tools, an abundance of bones from numerous land mammals, and the remains of hundreds of thousands of shellfish, suggesting a diet rich in meat and seafood. The Klasies River Mouth discovery raised most provocatively the question of where the first *Homo sapiens* emerged and how they spread.

The Debate over African Origins

Almost all paleoanthropologists and archaeologists now believe that *Homo erectus* appeared first in Africa and spread from there to Asia and, perhaps, to Europe between 1 and 2 million years ago. But then the scholars split into two camps: the "multiregionalists" and the "out-of-Africa" camp.

The multiregionalists argue that *Homo erectus* evolved into *Homo sapiens* in each region of migration. Their thesis is often called the "candelabra" theory, since it sees the evolutionary branches beginning far back in history in many different locations.

The out-of-Africa group argues that *Homo erectus* evolved into *Homo sapiens* only once—in Africa. Then, about 100,000 years ago, the new humans emigrated to the rest of the world from Africa. This idea is often designated the "Noah's Ark" theory, since it proposes a much more recent common ancestry in Africa (see diagram, p. 18).

Both groups of scholars agree that the varieties of racial development—differences in physical characteristics such as skin color, characteristics of hair, bone structure, and minor genetic modification—are responses to different ecological niches. They differ, however, on the time and place of the development. If the evolution from *Homo erectus* to *Homo sapiens* began in several different locations up to 2 million years ago, then

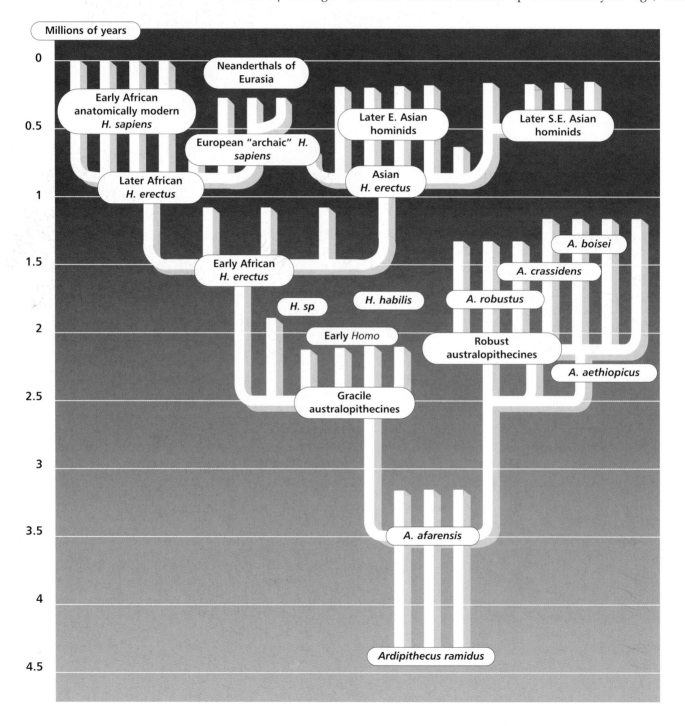

Skull reconstructions of some of the ancestors of modern man in chronological order. The generalized dates attached to each species imply that one followed the other, but actually some earlier species lived on for some time alongside more recent ones. By about 35,000 B.C.E., however, all except *Homo sapiens* were extinct.

Homo sapiens sapiens
present day

Homo sapiens (Neanderthal)
50,000 B.P.

Homo erectus
1.4 million B.P.

Homo habilis
1.8 million B.P.

Australopithecus boisei
1.9 million B.P.

Opposite **The human "bush."** Popular thought usually imagines a straight-line development from apes to humans, but anthropologists speak of a human "bush," a variety of interacting and inter-breeding species that finally produced *Homo sapiens*. Most anthropological models see *Ardipithecus ramidus* and *Australopithecus afarensis* as the first steps in the branching-apart of humans from apes about 5 million years ago. One line of further evolution led toward modern *Homo sapiens*. All the other hominid forms, those in our own line and those in other lines, subsequently became extinct.

Australopithecus africanus
2.7 million B.P.

racial differentiation is very old. Even so, the groups did not remain entirely separate from one another, and over time substantial interbreeding took place among the different regional groups despite their geographic distances. No race remained "pure." If, according to the alternative theory, all modern *Homo sapiens* share a common origin until just 100,000 years ago, and began to differentiate by race only after emigrating from Africa to new locations, then these differences are much more recent and even more superficial.

At present, the supporters of the "out-of-Africa" theory are in the majority. They point out that it is more common for just one branch of any particular species to evolve into another and ultimately to displace all the other branches than for all of the different branches to evolve simultaneously. They minimize the biological significance of race based on skin color as a relatively recent, and only "skin-deep," difference among the peoples of the earth. The advocates of both the multiregional and the out-of-Africa schools of thought agree that at deeper levels, such as blood types and the ability to interbreed, race has no significance.

Reading the Genetic Record

In the search for the time and place of the origins of *Homo sapiens*, a different kind of discovery, based on genetics rather than fossils, on laboratory research rather than field excavations, emerged about thirty years ago. Scientists began to study the DNA record of human and animal genes. DNA is each cell's chemical code of instructions

The candelabra, or multiregional, model. This suggests that *Homo erectus* emigrated from Africa throughout Europe and Asia and developed into *Homo sapiens* separately in all three regions. Some interbreeding did take place.

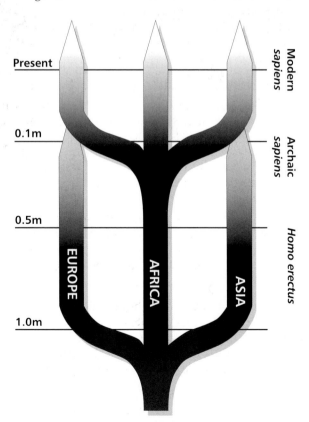

The Noah's Ark model. This suggests that *Homo erectus* did emigrate from Africa, but then died out everywhere else. The evolution to *Homo sapiens* took place only among those that remained in Africa—who later emigrated to Europe and Asia.

for building proteins, and the DNA research reveals the degrees of similarity and difference among the creatures studied.

Differences and similarities in the proteins and DNA of animals (including humans) living today suggest the date up to which they might have shared common ancestors before separating into different streams of evolution. In 1970, for example, biochemists first analyzed the protein albumin and the DNA of apes and humans and found that, genetically, modern humans are 97 percent the same as chimpanzees and 96 percent the same as gorillas. These data suggest that chimpanzees, gorillas, and humans shared common ancestors until 5–7 million years ago when evolutionary separation occurred. This genetic dating matches and reinforces the fossil record.

Extending the method further, researchers have used mitochondrial DNA (genetic material found outside the cell nucleus) to hypothesize that *Homo sapiens* emerged solely from Africa around 100,000 years ago. This confirmation of the "out-of-Africa" theory, however, remains controversial—and debate continues to rage. The journal *Nature* frequently carries these debates.

The Theory of Scientific Revolution

We have given a lengthy introduction to various explanations for the emergence of the first humans. Many historians would choose to move more quickly toward the present, although, of course, in covering 6 million years in one chapter we *are* moving swiftly! Some historians would be more comfortable covering "historic" times and places—that is, times and places with written records—but we have chosen to elaborate this account not only for its intrinsic interest but also because it helps to demonstrate most clearly our concern with "how we know" as well as with "what we know," since we believe that historians and paleoanthropologists share in the traditions of social science.

Paleoanthropologists maintain a lively debate about each of their findings and interpretations. They present their views and situate them within the ongoing debates in their field. This admirable procedure should inform all historical research and presentation, showing the historical record as an ongoing search and argument. Existing data may be re-evaluated; new data may be added; interpretations may be revised; new questions may arise. The historical record is never complete.

Amendments to the historical record, however, are usually minor additions to, or revisions of, a pattern already well known. Thomas Kuhn, in his pathbreaking study of the history of science, *The Structure of Scientific Revolutions*, wrote that

> normal science [like history] … is a highly cumulative enterprise, eminently successful in its aim, the steady extension of the scope and precision of scientific knowledge. Normal science does not aim at novelties of fact or theory and, when successful, finds none. (Kuhn, p. 52)

The history of the evolution of hominids usually follows this pattern of "normal science." Thus the discoveries of 4.5 million-year-old *Ardipithecus ramidus* in 1994 and of 6–7-million-year-old Toumai in 2001 did not surprise paleoanthropologists. The new fossils fit neatly into the expected

"Toumai," the oldest pre-human fossil, Chad, Africa, 2001. This skull was discovered by an international team of paleoanthropologists in Chad. It is from the earliest member of the pre-human family so far discovered, dating back 6–7 million years. "Toumai" is the name in Chad given to children born near the dry season.

paradigm A model of reality representing one viewpoint.

timeframe for the process of evolution from apes to hominids (although the geographical location of Toumai in Chad was unexpected). This was normal science filling in an existing model, or **paradigm**, with new detail.

Sometimes, however, new discoveries challenge existing paradigms. At first the new discoveries are discounted as exceptions to the rule. But when the exceptions increase, scientists seek new explanatory paradigms. Darwin's breakthrough followed this second pattern of scientific revolution. His discoveries on the voyage of the *Beagle* and his subsequent analyses of his findings challenged the existing concepts of creation that were based on biblical narratives. Darwin provided a radically different scientific explanation of the mechanisms of evolution that displaced the biblical paradigm. Both Darwin's scientific analysis and the Book of Genesis in the Bible, however, postulate the creation of an entire cosmos and world, replete with flora and fauna, before humans achieve their place in the universe and begin to name the other species.

Major revisions of the historical record often follow this trajectory. A general pattern of explanation is followed, until new research raises new questions and new theoretical paradigms provide more fitting explanations for all the available data and information. Throughout this text we shall continue to see changes in historical explanation over time. A "paradigm shift" may occur not only as a result of the discovery of new data, or of new interpretations better fitting the available data, but also as a response to new questions being raised that may not have been asked before. The historical record, like the scientific record on evolution, is always subject to re-evaluation.

HUMANS CREATE CULTURE

Biological Evolution and Cultural Creativity

Until now we have been examining biological evolution, "natural selection." Those organisms best able to survive did survive. By the time of *Homo habilis*, however, the *Homo* biological genus began creating simple tools through which it could shape nature to meet its needs. *Homo habilis* were already sculpting stone tools of increasing sophistication. They apparently hunted, scavenged, and gathered in groups and shared their booty. Throughout the intervening 2 million years up to our own day, *Homo* has continued to increase its sophistication in creating tools, art, rituals, settlements, concepts, and language, and in domesticating plants and animals—the basic elements of what anthropologists call culture. By the time that *Homo sapiens* had evolved, cultural creativity had superseded biology as the principal method by which humans coped with nature. Humans were no longer content to exist in nature. They sought to control it.

The cultural evolution seems to have been encouraged by biological evolution. As the *Homo* brain continued to develop and get bigger, it became impossible for the genus *Homo* to give birth through a relatively narrow birth canal to a child with a fully formed brain in a fully formed cranium. The brain capacity of human young must continue to develop for some time after birth. The brain of a newborn human weighs about 14 ounces, doubles to 35 ounces in about one year, and reaches its adult size of 45 ounces only by the age of six or seven. Within the genus *Homo*, therefore, parents must devote significant time to nurturing and teaching their young children. In addition, in female *Homo sapiens* the oestrus cycle, the alternating period of fertility and infertility, occurs each month rather than seasonally, allowing them to bear children more frequently than other primates. Increased childbearing further increases the time and energy devoted to nurturing the young. Because of the increased attention to nurturing, cultural life could flourish—and it did.

Since the earliest known appearance of *Homo sapiens* in the archaeological record about 120,000 years ago our species *Homo sapiens* has not changed anatomically. The skeletons unearthed at the Klasies River Mouth are no different from our own.

About 100,000 years ago, however, a new creativity appeared in the cultural and social life of *Homo sapiens*, perhaps the result of a modification in the internal structure of the brain. The people who lived before this development are called "archaic" *Homo sapiens*; those with the new cultural capabilities are considered a new subspecies, *Homo sapiens sapiens* (wise, wise human). They are us. Unlike their predecessors, *Homo sapiens sapiens* developed forms of symbolic expression, apparently spiritual and cultural in nature, including burial rituals and artwork that is sometimes stunningly beautiful and creative.

The remainder of this chapter presents seven creative behaviors that mark the arrival of *Homo sapiens sapiens*. First, we persisted. We are the lone survivor from among all the hominids of the last 6 million years. Second, we continued to spread to all parts of the globe in waves of migration that had begun even earlier. Third, we built small, temporary settlements to serve as base camps for hunting and gathering. Fourth, we continued to craft more sophisticated tools. Fifth, by about 25,000 B.C.E., on cave walls and in stone, we began to paint and sculpt magnificent

Two Aurignacian implements, France, Mesolithic era (c. 30,000 B.P.). Stone Age cultures first appeared in western Europe in 33,000 B.P. and underwent constant changes in technology—implying a gradual evolution in human behavior. By the Aurignacian era, flint-end scrapers (right) were employed in processing skins, woodworking, and carving artifacts like this bone spearpoint (left). (*Natural History Museum, London*)

KEY STAGES IN HUMAN DEVELOPMENT

4.5 m B.P.	First appearance of bipedalism. (*first clear appearance; Toumai of Chad, 6 m. B.C.E. was apparently bipedal*)
2 m B.P.	Change in structure of forelimbs— bipedalism is perfected. Gradual expansion and reorganization of the brain. Hunting, scavenging, and gathering cultures stimulate production of stone tools.
500,000 B.P.	Rapid brain growth.
200,000 B.P.	First forms of *Homo sapiens*. Early speech development. Fire now in use.
40,000 B.P.	Interglacial period. Existence of modern humans, with fully developed brain and speech. Tools constructed from component parts.
***c.* 25,000 B.P.**	Cave art and portable art in Europe. Human migration begins from Asia into America.
10,000 B.C.E.	Invention of bow and arrows. Domestication of reindeer and dog (N. Eurasia). Settled food production.
8000–4000 B.C.E.	Increase of human population by 1500 percent. Domestication of sheep and goats (Near East). Earliest pottery (Japan). Farming spreads to W. Europe. Rice cultivation starts in Asia.
3000 B.C.E.	Writing, metals.

HOW DO WE KNOW?

Dating Archaeological Finds

*Continuous improvements in dating techniques have changed our understanding of the relationships among the early Homo sapiens, and even among the earlier hominids, and their relationships to their environment. The most common technique, since its discovery in 1949, is **radiocarbon dating**, sometimes called the carbon 14 (C14) method. Living organisms breathe in air, and so they contain the same percentage of atoms of radioactive carbon as the earth's atmosphere. When an organism dies, its radiocarbon atoms disintegrate at a steady, known rate. By measuring the amount of radiocarbon remaining in a fossil skeleton, scientists can calculate backward to the date of death. Because the total amount of radiocarbon in any organism is small, little is left after 40,000 years, and the method does not work at all beyond 70,000 years into the past.*

For a broader spectrum of dates, scientists use a technique called

__thermoluminescence__, developed in 1987. This technique was applied to burned flints discovered in the caves where early humans had lived. Radioactivity occurring in nature releases electrons in flint and clay, but they can finally escape only when the substance is heated. When the flints were first burned by the people of the caves, the electrons freed up to that time were released. Reheating the flints in the laboratory today releases the electrons stored up since the first burning. Scientists calculate the date of the first burning by measuring the light of those electrons. This technique works not only for burnt flint of 50,000–300,000 years of age, but also for burnt clay, enabling scientists to date pottery from the last 10,000 years.

For much earlier dates, like those of the earliest hominid fossils that go back as much as 6 million years, scientists measure the decay of the radioactive element potassium 40 into argon 40, a process that takes place in volcanic rocks and soils. Potassium-argon dating, in use

since the 1950s, was invaluable in estimating the age of the soil in which stone tools and hominid remains were found in the Olduvai Gorge. This dating method was the clue to determining the deep antiquity of these fossils, and in shifting the search for the earliest hominids to Africa.

- *Biochemists and physicists have their contribution to make in understanding—and dating—the evolution of the earliest humans. What have been the contributions of other academic specialists encountered in this book?*
- *What are the similarities between radiocarbon, thermoluminescence, and potassium-argon dating? Why is each limited to a particular time period?*
- *Which of these methods directly dates fossil remains? Which dates the soil in which fossils are found? What might be the problems with dating fossils by the soil in which they are found?*

radiocarbon dating A method of dating artifacts by measuring their radioactive carbon. Useful for objects 40,000–70,000 years old.

thermoluminescence A method of dating burnt flint by measuring electrons in it from 50,000–300,000 years ago, or of burnt pottery from the last 10,000 years.

works of art and symbolism. Sixth, we elaborated more sophisticated use of language. Seventh, by 10,000–15,000 B.C.E., we began to domesticate plants and animals, introducing the art and science of agriculture.

How Did We Survive?

From about 120,000 years ago, when we first appear in the archaeological record, until about 35,000 years ago, anatomically modern *Homo sapiens sapiens* seem to have coexisted alongside archaic *Homo sapiens* in several sites. The best studied of these places are caves in the area of Mount Carmel near Haifa, Israel. These caves have revealed skeletons and tools of both Neanderthals and modern humans. The fossils from the Tabun, Amud, and Kebara caves seem to be Neanderthals; those from Skhul and Qafzeh appear more modern.

The oldest Neanderthal, from Tabun, dated to 120,000–100,000 years ago; the two *Homo sapiens sapiens* at Qafzeh and Skhul were almost equally old, at 92,000 years ago; the two Neanderthal specimens at Kebara and Amud are 60,000–50,000 years old. One can only conclude, therefore, that Neanderthals and modern humans coexisted in the area of modern Israel for tens of thousands of years. Moreover, they shared similar types of tools. Neanderthals seem to have used slightly simpler, smaller Mousterian stone tools (named for the village of Le Moustier in southwestern France where they have been most clearly documented). Their modern human neighbors used the thinner, longer, more precisely crafted Aurignacian tools (named for another hunter-gatherer site in southern France). The differences were marked but not huge.

How, then, did modern *Homo sapiens sapiens* eventually displace all other hominids?

Three principal interpretations, in various combinations, have been suggested. The first is that modern humans defeated all the other hominids through aggression, warfare, and murder. This theory suggests a violent streak in the earliest humans. The second theory suggests that processes of mating and reproduction among the species bred the new human. In other words, our immediate ancestors made love not war, and we contain a Neanderthal heritage. Finally, it has been proposed that modern humans successfully filled up the ecological niche available, outcompeting archaic *Homo sapiens* for the available resources. According to this third theory, modern humans did not directly confront the archaic forms but displaced them—in a sense, we ate them out of house and home.

Global Migration

Homo sapiens sapiens appeared in Africa no later than 120,000 years ago, evolving from *Homo erectus*. Within 30,000 years the species began to appear throughout Europe and Asia. Anthropologists suspect that early human migrations were not just aimless wanderings, but were purposeful and specific. From earliest prehistory, people weighed their choices and opportunities and then chose appropriate actions. Global migration was the ultimate outcome.

Early humans in the Ice Age. By 20,000 years ago, when ice covered much of Europe and much of Canada, virtually the whole world (except Polynesia) had been colonized. Early humans were able to spread north because water frozen into ice sheets reduced sea levels so much that land bridges appeared, linking most major areas. The cold was intense, and the migrants' survival depended on their ability to stitch together animal hides into primitive clothing, control fire, and hunt large mammals.

The colonization of the Pacific. The land bridges of the last Ice Age enabled early humans to spread south from China to Java and Borneo. There some knowledge of navigation was required to cross the Banda Sea to New Guinea and Australia. The most spectacular voyages were undertaken by the Polynesians, who journeyed hundreds and thousands of miles by canoe into the uncharted Pacific waters.

Changes in climate may have been one of the main reasons for migration. The Sahara, now a desert, provides one example. Until about 90,000 years ago, when the earth was in a warm, wet stage, the Sahara region was fertile and attractive to human settlement. People and animals from southern Africa migrated there. But then began an "ice age," one of the periods of global cooling that have affected the earth's climate over millions of years. Much of the earth's water froze. The Sahara dried up, turning the land to desert, and people and animals emigrated. Some may have turned back to southern Africa; some may have journeyed toward the North African coast; still others may have followed the Nile valley corridor into western Asia. So began one wave in a global process of migration.

To reach the most distant areas, such as Australia, the islands of the Pacific, and the Americas, took tens of thousands of years. These migrations required changes in

Charles Alexandre Lesueur, *Navigation in Van Diemen's Land*, pl. 14 from "Voyage of Discovery to Australian Lands," 1807. Engraving. When Europeans began settling Van Diemen's Land, now called Tasmania, in Australia, they found people who had arrived there some 40,000 years before, having crossed over from southeastern China. *(Royal Geographical Society, London)*

climate as well as in the skills of *Homo sapiens sapiens*. The successive ice ages of 90,000–10,000 years ago froze much of the water of the seas, reducing sea levels, extending the coasts of the continents, and creating land bridges that linked modern China with Japan, southeast Asia with the Philippines and Indonesia, and Siberia with Alaska. As long as the ice ages continued and the waters of seas and oceans were in frozen retreat, people could migrate across land passages.

There were exceptions. The Pacific islands known as Polynesia were not connected by land bridges to anywhere. As a result, they were peopled much later in history than most other regions. Only in 1000 B.C.E. did New Guineans, performing extraordinary feats of navigation in simple canoes, colonize Polynesia.

Increased Population and New Settlements

Gradually, as human population expanded, so, too, did the number of human groups and the closeness or "density" of their relationships to one another. Such increasing density and population pressure became a staple of human history. Frequently, the result was conflict among groups for the best lands and resources. Some groups chose to stand and fight for their territory, others reached accommodation with newcomers, and yet others emigrated, either by choice or by force, following losses in battle. These patterns, too, have repeated themselves for tens of thousands of years, and today there are some 20 million refugees in the world.

How large were these groups? They had to include enough members to provide security in defense and cooperation in work, yet be small enough to be able to subsist on the natural resources available and to resolve the interpersonal frictions that threatened the cohesion of the group and the safety of its members.

Calculated from the experience of modern hunter-gatherers, such as the Khoisan of the African Kalahari Desert, and theoretical mathematical models of group process, a five-family group of twenty-five persons seems the ideal balance. Mating and marriage rules might well have required, as they often do today, choosing a mate from outside the immediate band. For such an **exogamous** or external marriage pattern to function, a tribe would theoretically require at least nineteen bands of twenty-five members each, a total of 475 people, a figure reasonably close to the actual 500 found in modern hunter-gatherer societies.

How much territory did such bands require to support themselves? Anthropologists have calculated that an individual using the technology of Upper Paleolithic

exogamy The practice by which a person is compelled to choose a marital partner from outside his or her own group or clan, the opposite of endogamy, the choice of partner from within the group. Often the outside group from which the partner is to be chosen is specified.

times (150,000–12,000 years ago) would have required 77 square miles of relatively unproductive land or 7–8 square miles of fertile land to meet survival needs. At such densities, the area of the United States (excluding Alaska and Hawaii) might have supported a maximum of 600,000 people; the entire world, 10 million at most, although actual populations were less. As populations grew, bands began to stake out their own territories, and to mark out boundaries. They began to work out formal relationships with the occupants of neighboring areas.

Groups began to establish small settlements. The Neanderthals had occupied upland sites, but the later Cro-Magnon *Homo sapiens sapiens* (named for the region in France where this subspecies was originally discovered) moved down into the more valuable valleys and riverbeds. About half of their sites are within 1100 yards of a river, and all of them are near fords or shallows. These sites not only allow for easy crossing, but they are also at the points of animal crossings and therefore good for hunting. Tools took on regional patterns both in processes of manufacture and in styles of aesthetic appearance. These local patterns differentiated each group from its neighbors. Each group may have begun to develop a language, or a dialect, of its own.

HOW DO WE KNOW?

Man the Hunter or Woman the Gatherer?

In 1971 anthropologist Sally Slocum, writing under the pseudonym of Sally Linton, published one of the first feminist critiques of the current understanding of hominid evolution. She was responding to a set of papers published in 1968 entitled Man the Hunter. One of the papers asserted: "The biology, psychology, and customs that separate us from the apes—all these we owe to the hunters of time past." This argument, Slocum replied, put too much emphasis on aggressive behavior, the tools and organized planning required for hunting, the importance of fresh meat in the hominid diet, and male activities generally.

In "Woman the Gatherer: Male Bias in Anthropology," Slocum pointed out that gathering contributed more to group nutrition than hunting, as studies of modern hunter-gatherers showed. She also pointed out that tools usually linked to hunting might have been used for gathering instead, and she urged anthropologists to look afresh at the whole idea of tools:

Bones, sticks, and hand-axes could be used for digging up tubers or roots, or to pulverize tough vegetable matter for easier eating. If, however, instead of thinking in terms of tools and weapons, we think in terms of cultural inventions, a new aspect is presented. I suggest that two of the earliest and most important cultural inventions were containers to hold the products of gathering, and some sort of sling or net to carry babies.

Further, Slocum argued, the skills of raising and nurturing young children, usually women's tasks, evoked more innovation and perhaps more development of the brain than did hunting:

I suggest that longer periods of infant dependency, more difficult births, and longer gestation periods also demanded more skills in social organization and communication—creating selective pressure for increased brain size without looking to hunting as an explanation. The need to organize for feeding after weaning, learning to handle the more complex social–emotional bonds that were developing, the new skills and cultural inventions surrounding more extensive gathering—all would demand larger brains. Too much attention has been given to the skills required by hunting, and too little to the skills required for gathering and the raising of dependent young.

Slocum concluded that anthropologists needed to confront their own assumptions about male dominance. As she put it, "The basis of any discipline is not the answers it gets, but the questions it asks."

- Sally Slocum suggests that our historical searches are determined by the questions we ask. Are there questions about the paleoanthropological record that you want to ask that have not been addressed thus far? Can you suggest methods to find answers to these questions?
- Sally Slocum wrote of "Male Bias in Anthropology." Do you think that the different experiences of men and women influence the questions that they ask in historical time as well as in prehistory? Give examples. Keep this list at hand as you read this book to determine whether you seem to be correct.
- How do the resources available for answering questions—such as stone tools as compared with fibers and cloths, or tools for hunting compared with tools for child-raising— determine the agendas for scholarly research?

Changes in the Toolkit

Even as the pace of exploration, migration, and trade increased, the clearest changes in human development appeared in our stone toolkits. The steady improvements in tool technology give this period its archaeological names. The entire period is called the Old Stone Age or Paleolithic. Tools show a slow progression from the Lower Paleolithic, ending about 150,000 years ago, to the Upper Paleolithic, which continued to about 10,000 B.C.E. (The Mesolithic and Neolithic—Middle and New Stone Ages, 8000–6000 B.C.E. and 6000–3000 B.C.E., respectively—will be explored in Chapter 2.)

From about 2.5 million years ago until about 150,000 years ago, the dominant technology of *Homo erectus* had been Acheulian hand-held axes and cleavers made of stone (named for St. Acheul in northern France, but actually developed first in Africa and only later throughout Europe and Asia).

About 250,000 years ago some sites reveal a more sophisticated technique, the Levallois (named for a suburb in Paris where the first examples were discovered). This Levallois technique produced more precise tools, including side scrapers and backed knives, fashioned by more consistent patterns of preparing flakes from the stone, and a more standardized final shape and size. This technique marked the emergence of archaic *Homo sapiens*.

The technology of *Homo sapiens sapiens* developed much more rapidly. By about 40,000 years ago, Aurignacian tools were being produced in or near a cave near the present-day village of Aurignac in the Pyrenees. This technology included narrow blades of stone as well as tools crafted from bone, ivory, and antler. Gravettian styles followed, about 30,000 to about 20,000 B.P. Then came Solutrean styles, 20,000–17,000 years ago, which included the production of the first known needles. Magdalenian tools, about 17,000–12,000 years ago, included barbed harpoons carved from antlers. Finally Azilian, 12,000–8000 B.C.E., completed the Paleolithic sequence. Each location and time period had its own aesthetic style, and each produced an increasing variety of tools.

THE EARLIEST TOOL KITS

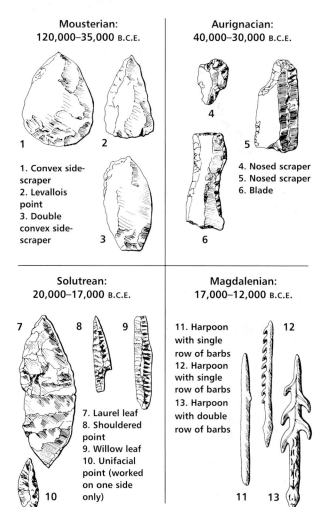

**Mousterian:
120,000–35,000 B.C.E.**

1. Convex side-scraper
2. Levallois point
3. Double convex side-scraper

**Aurignacian:
40,000–30,000 B.C.E.**

4. Nosed scraper
5. Nosed scraper
6. Blade

**Solutrean:
20,000–17,000 B.C.E.**

7. Laurel leaf
8. Shouldered point
9. Willow leaf
10. Unifacial point (worked on one side only)

**Magdalenian:
17,000–12,000 B.C.E.**

11. Harpoon with single row of barbs
12. Harpoon with single row of barbs
13. Harpoon with double row of barbs

Many of the earliest human tools were crafted from stone and show increasing sophistication. The "tool kits" shown here are named for the four different locations in which they were found. At first, humans simply chipped away at stone until edges and points were exposed. Later they began to carve the stone to meet more specific needs. The development took 100,000 years.

Bone flute, found in the Dordogne, France, c. 35,000 B.P.
Simple wind instruments like this 4½ inch-long flute were made from the hollowed-out bones of birds, reindeer, and bears. They date back to as long ago as 35,000 B.P. (*Musée National de Préhistoire, Les Eyzies de Tayac, France*)

Tools and artifacts, western Europe, 30,000–18,000 B.P.
(a) Bone used to make needle blanks;
(b) Bone needle;
(c & d) Harpoon head and barbed point carved from antler;
(e & f) Two heads carved in mammoth ivory.
(*Natural History Museum, London*)

Spearthrower, Montastruc, France, 12,000 B.C.E. More than 14,000 years ago, beauty played an integral part in purely functional objects. Spearthrowers allowed hunters to propel their missiles with a surer aim and added leverage, as is symbolized by the streamlined and powerful figure of this leaping horse. Did the shape of the bone suggest the animal, or did the artist search for a bone to match his (or her) preconceived idea?

Tool patterns began to differ increasingly from one region to another, suggesting the formation of new communities among small hunter-gatherer bands, and a greater sense of separation and distinction between groups.

Not all tools were directly related to food production, nor even to work. As early as 35,000 B.P., flutes made from the bones of birds, reindeer, and bears suggest that creating and performing instrumental music had already become part of the human repertoire. Aesthetics and play already had their roles.

The tools we have found represent only a small fraction of the daily objects that early humans probably made and used. Tools made of stone have endured, those made of wood have not. Those made from natural fibers have, of course, disintegrated, which means we know little about clothing or basketry or food preparation. In most hunter-gatherer societies, making clothing and preparing food are usually women's work. So a whole area of technological development, most likely in the hands of women, was long overlooked through the focus on stone tools.

Language and Communication

Language is an intangible innovation, invisible in the archaeological record. It must be inferred from more solid evidence: global migration, fixed settlement sites, new tools and new materials, regional differences in production, trade across long distances, social hierarchies often marked by personal adornment and ritual burials, and the creation of art and instrumental music. Many of these activities would have been difficult, if not impossible, without some kind of language.

Exactly when a system of spoken language emerged is much debated, especially because we can only infer the answer from circumstantial evidence. The craniums of archaic *Homo sapiens* were as large as, or even larger than, our own, and they seem to have indentations indicating the presence of areas in the brain that influence speech capacity. Archaic *Homo sapiens* probably possessed a larynx that had descended sufficiently low in the throat to produce the sounds of modern human language.

The dispute arises here. Some anthropologists believe that with this biological equipment, humans began to develop modern language and speech slowly through cultural evolution. Others, notably linguist Noam Chomsky, believe that a change took place within the organization of the brain that gave humans a new capacity for language. Chomsky draws his conclusion from analyzing similarities in the "deep structure" of languages around the world. These universal similarities suggest that the rules of syntax of human language are embedded in the brain. Chomsky argues that just as humans are born to walk so they are born to talk. Just as bipedalism is not a learned cultural capacity, but has evolved biologically, so talking is not culturally learned but has biologically evolved. The use of individual languages is, of course, culturally specific.

Modern language provided the ability to communicate with others on an individual basis. It also allowed for increasingly elaborate social structures and greater complexity in human relationships. It facilitated deliberation over ethical principles of conduct for guiding and regulating those relationships. Moreover, it allowed for increasingly sophisticated internal thought and reflection. We could become more introspective as well as more communicative with others. The sophisticated psychological and social relationships that make us human became possible only with the development of language.

Cave Art and Portable Art

Cave paintings and portable art suggest both individual creativity and group process. They may represent the sharing of information, hope, and feelings, and serve as a means of transmitting them to subsequent generations. Finds of artwork from before 35,000 B.P., such as beads, pendants, and incised animal bones, are rare and disputed. Cave paintings and statuettes came later, and they appeared in numerous sites around the world. At Kundusi, Tanzania, Mary Leakey discovered stylized ocher paintings of human beings dating back perhaps 25,000 years. On the southern coast of Australia, in the Koonalda Cave, a flint mine at least 20,000 years old, a crisscross of abstract finger patterns was engraved into the soft limestone. In eastern Australia at about the same time, people were stenciling images of a hand and a pipe and stem onto the walls of Kenniff Cave. And at Kakadu, in northern Australia, a series of rock paintings begin about 20,000 B.P. Local peoples continued to paint new ones almost to the present.

Clay bison, from Tuc d'Audoubert, Ariège, France, after 15,000 B.C.E. Most cave art owes its survival to the very particular atmospheric conditions formed in the limestone caves in which they were sealed thousands of years ago. Only a very small number of sculptures have survived. The one reproduced here—in high relief—shows a female being pursued by a male bison.

In Europe, the artwork begins with some figurines and some wall painting as early as 30,000 B.P. and climaxes about 17,000–12,000 B.C.E. More than 200 decorated caves and more than 10,000 decorated objects (portable art) have been discovered in Europe, 85 percent of them in southern France and northern Spain. Many of the tools from the Magdalenian period (17,000–12,000 B.C.E.), as noted above, were fashioned to be beautiful as well as practical. Many of the figurines include delicately carved features, such as the face and hair on the figurine from about 22,000 B.P. discovered at Brassempouy, France, and only about 1½ inches high (see p. 28e). Many others pay scant attention to face and personal features, but accentuate and exaggerate sexual organs and buttocks, such as the 25,000-year-old figurine discovered at Dolní Vestonice, Moravia. The portable art represents a desire to create and enjoy beautiful objects. The exaggerated forms of the female, "Venus" objects that appear throughout Europe and in northwestern Asia suggest also a desire for human fertility.

The first of the cave art was rediscovered only in 1868, at Altamira, Spain. Although the painting was 14,000 years old, it was not recognized as prehistoric until 1902. By now, 200 caves decorated with artworks have been discovered in Europe, most of them in the river valleys of southwest France and the adjacent Pyrenees and the Cantabrian Mountains of northern Spain. The most recent discoveries, stunning in the variety of animal life depicted and the artistry employed, have been the Cosquer Cave in 1991 and the Chauvet Cave in 1994.

The painters used natural pigments, like ocher, that produced reds, browns, and yellows, and manganese oxides that made black and violet. Blues and greens have not been found. Human figures are rare in the European caves. The usual representations are of large animals, such as bison, deer, wild oxen, and horses. Occasionally there are mammoths, lions, and even fish. Fantasy figures, such as unicorns, also appear. At caves such as Le Tuc d'Audoubert, France, sculptures of clay bison have been found. In many caves, the outlines of human hands have been stenciled onto cave walls by projecting pigment around

"Venus" figurine, found at Dolní Vestonice, Moravia, c. 23,000 B.P. Several hundred early female figures have been recovered, but no male figures. This seems to support the thesis that these statuettes were created, not so much as representations of ideal feminine beauty, but as fertility charms— notice how the breasts, buttocks, and thighs are emphasized to the exclusion of any individualizing facial traits.

the hands. No one knows how the pigments were applied, but the most common guess is that they were chewed and then either spat directly or blown through a pipe onto the walls.

Some of the cave art was abstract, some representational, some painted, some in relief. This rich artistic tradition did not continue past the Magdalenian period, about 12,000 B.C.E. Many of the techniques of the cave paintings, such as perspective and the feeling of movement, did not reappear in Western art until the Renaissance, about 1400 C.E.

Ever since the cave art was rediscovered, people have wondered about its function and meaning. The first interpretation to gain widespread acceptance argued that the paintings represented a kind of magic designed to bring good fortune to the hunters of the animals represented on the cave walls. The seemingly abstract geometrical patterns, some said, represented hunting equipment, such as traps, snares, and weapons. The mural paintings of animals may represent a hope for their fertility so that the hunters might find abundant prey. Another interpretation suggested that the caves were meeting grounds to which neighboring bands of people returned each year to arrange marriages and to cement political and social alliances. The different styles of paintings in each cave represent the artistic production of many different groups.

The art is often located not at the mouth of the cave, where it would have been on daily view of the campsites, but deep in the inner recesses. Why were so many images—about one-third of the total—painted so deep inside the caves? Some scholars of prehistoric art have suggested that they were not just decorative, but were links

Chauvet Cave, Rhône-Alpes region, France, 18,000 B.C.E. On Christmas Day 1994, a team of archaeologists led by Jean-Marie Chauvet discovered a cave 1640 feet deep in the Ardèche River Canyon. The cave's 300-plus Paleolithic wall paintings of horses, buffalo, and lions are the earliest examples anywhere in the world.

shaman In the religious beliefs of some Asian and American tribal societies, a person capable of entering into trances and believed to be endowed with supernatural powers, with the ability to cure the sick, find lost or stolen property, predict the future, and protect the community from evil spirits. A shaman may act as judge or ruler, and as a priest a shaman directs communal sacrifices and escorts the souls of the dead to the next world.

to ancient spirits, which were remembered and invoked in the dark depths of the cave through shamanistic rituals. Among the San people of the Kalahari desert, **shamans** are thought to communicate with spirits through trances induced through the use of drugs, breathing exercises, singing, dancing, and rhythmic clapping. They enter into trance states of increasing intensity in which they "see" first geometric patterns, then images from nature, and finally creatures not found in nature at all. Sometimes they see these various images as projections on the wall. Supporters of this theory believe that the Upper Paleolithic cave paintings represent such shamanistic hallucinations or visions from trance states.

The cave art and the portable art of 25,000–10,000 B.P. begin the known record of human aesthetic creation. For the first time we have examples of what humans regarded as beautiful and therefore worth creating and preserving. From this time onward, the desire to create and appreciate beauty is part of the human story. The cave creations also give us insight into their creators' search for meaning and purpose in life. Our art gives outward expression to our understanding of, and our deepest feelings about, our place in the world. In our art we express our fears and our hopes for ourselves, our loved ones, our communities, our world. Through our art we attempt to connect with larger forces in the world and to communicate with one another. By studying the form and meaning of ancient art, historians attempt to understand the external aesthetics and the inner world of the people who produced it.

Agriculture: From Hunter-gatherer to Farmer

Some hunter-gatherers began to stay for longer periods at their temporary campsites. They noted the patterns of growth of the wild grains they gathered and the migration habits of the animals they hunted. They began to experiment in planting the seeds of the largest, most nutritious cereals in the Middle East and Europe, maize in the Americas, and rootcrops in southeast Asia. In addition to pursuing animals as prey, people may have tried to restrict their movements to particular locations. Or hunters may have built their own campsites at points frequented by the animals, adjusting human movements to those of the animals. They learned to domesticate dogs, and domesticated dogs may have accompanied the first Americans on their travels across Beringia. In the Middle East, the sheep was the first species to be domesticated, perhaps 10,000 years ago.

By 15,000–10,000 B.C.E., humans had the biological and cultural capacity to farm and raise animals. But first they had to want to do so. Otherwise why give up hunting and gathering? Why settle down? Perhaps the transformation took place at sites with especially valuable and accessible natural resources, such as the fishing sites of the Jomon people of Japan, or the quarries of obsidian stone, used for making sharp cutting tools, around Çatal Hüyük in modern Turkey. A permanent source of food to eat or materials to trade might have outweighed the desire to shift with the seasons and travel with the herds.

Perhaps rising population pressures left humans no alternative. The press of neighbors may have restricted scope for travel. On limited land, hunter-gatherers found that planting their own crops and domesticating their own animals could provide them with more food than hunting and gathering. Despite the risks of weather and of plant and animal diseases that left agricultural settlements vulnerable, some groups began to settle. Ten thousand years ago, almost all humans lived by hunting and gathering. Two thousand years ago, most were farmers or herders. This transformation created not only the first agricultural villages, but cities as well. Cities grew up as the central administrative, economic, and religious centers of their regions. A new era was beginning. It is the subject of the next chapter and Part 2.

THE STORY OF PREHISTORY
WHAT DIFFERENCE DOES IT MAKE?

The materials of this chapter, which are largely based on the research of paleoanthropologists, make us more aware of different ways of knowing and their different kinds of usefulness. They lead us to be open-minded, yet skeptical, for example, of the uses of creation stories as a way of explaining the significance of human life, and to note that different myths and stories encourage different behaviors. Myths that are widely accepted within a society are not merely quaint stories, they are powerful explanatory messages that speak deeply to people's understanding of the world.

Similarly, they lead us to be open-minded, yet skeptical, of the powers of science to explain the world, noting, for example, that the process of evolution was not immediately evident until scientists began asking the right questions; the role of women in cultural evolution was not considered until feminist researchers began asking questions that had not been asked before; Africa as a location for the earliest hominids and humans was ignored until racial prejudices were put aside. Scientific enquiry is an enormously powerful tool in unlocking the mysteries of the world, but it addresses only those questions that we ask it to.

We have also learned to distinguish between "ordinary" science, which builds on what is already known and accepted, and revolutionary science, which puzzles over new information and anomalies, elements that do not fit into already existing patterns, until it may create "paradigm shifts," new ways of understanding the world.

We have seen that from the very earliest times human behavior has been characterized by migration, the creation of tools, the formation of ever-larger groups, which nevertheless apparently create distinctions between members and "others," communication through language, self-expression through art, and oscillation between accepting nature as it is and trying to control it as a means of advancing our own agendas. These are the principal legacies of the earliest hominids and humans to us, and the record of our successes in finding methods of understanding our world more clearly through historiography and through paleoanthropology.

Review Questions

- Most historians work with written documents, while paleoanthropologists work with different kinds of fossil materials. Nevertheless, many of their concerns in exploring the past are similar. Do you agree or disagree? Why?
- What are the images of humankind represented in the creation stories cited here from the *Enuma Elish*, the *Rigveda*, and the Book of Genesis? To what degree is the place of humankind in the world similar in each of the stories? To what degree is it different?
- In what sense did the work of Charles Darwin make the work of paleoanthropology possible?
- Would you like to participate in an archaeological dig in Africa seeking to discover further examples of early hominids? What elements of the work appeal to you? What elements do not?
- What is the difference between "normal science" and "revolutionary science"? What examples of revolutionary science appear in this chapter?
- To what degree is the creation of art a major step forward in cultural creativity? How do discoveries of art help us understand the lives of early *Homo sapiens sapiens*?

Suggested Readings

PRINCIPAL SOURCES

Bahn, Paul G., ed. *Archaeology* (Cambridge: Cambridge University Press, 1996).

Barber, Elizabeth Wayland. *Women's Work: The First 20,000 Years: Women, Cloth, and Society in Early Times* (New York: W.W. Norton & Co., 1994). Fascinating account of the earliest known production of cloth, and women's role in producing it.

Constable, George and the Editors of Time-Life Books. *The Neanderthals* (New York: Time-Life Books, 1973).

Darwin, Charles. *Darwin*, ed. Philip Appleman (New York: W.W. Norton & Co., 2nd ed., 1979). Excellent anthology of works by and about Darwin.

Fagan, Brian M. *People of the Earth* (Upper Saddle River, NJ: Prentice Hall: 10th ed., 2000). Outstanding textbook introduction to prehistoric human life around the globe.

Johanson, Donald, Lenora Johanson, and Blake Edgar. *Ancestors: In Search of Human Origins* (New York: Villard Books, 1994). One of the greatest paleoanthropologists tells of his work and its significance.

Leakey, Richard and Roger Lewin. *Origins Reconsidered* (New York: Doubleday, 1992). A great paleoanthropologist, continuing and expanding the accomplishments of his even more famous parents, presents his account of the fossil record of evolution.

Lewin, Roger. *The Origin of Modern Humans* (New York: Scientific American Library, 1993). Remarkably lucid presentation of the story of evolution and early humans.

Past Worlds: The (London) Times Atlas of Archaeology (London: Times Books Ltd., 1988). Text, maps, pictures are all superb on all aspects of archaeological understanding and accomplishment.

Scientific American, Special Edition, "New Look at Human Evolution," August 25, 2003.

ADDITIONAL SOURCES

Brown, Judith. "Note on the Division of Labor by Sex," *American Anthropologist* LXXII (1970), 1075–6. Argues that historically women's work has been compatible with child-care responsibilities.

Chauvet, Jean-Marie, Eliette Brunel Deschamps, and Christian Hillaire. *Dawn of Art: The Chauvet Cave, the Oldest Known Paintings in the World* (New York: Abrams, 1996). Gorgeous presentation of this recently discovered cave art.

Clottes, Jean and Jean Courtin. *The Cave Beneath the Sea: Paleolithic Images at Cosquer* (New York: Abrams, 1996). Another prehistoric artistic treasure in a magnificent presentation.

Conkey, Margaret W. *Art and Design in the Old Stone Age* (San Francisco, CA: Freeman, 1982). Analysis and presentation of early portable art.

Darwin, Charles. *The Origin of Species by Means of Natural Selection or the Preservation of Favored Races in the Struggle for Life*, reprinted from the Sixth Edition, ed. Edmund B. Wilson (New York: Macmillan Company, 1927). The classic, revolutionary work.

Darwin, Charles. *The Works of Charles Darwin*, ed. Paul H. Barrett and R.B. Freeman, Vol. XV *On the Origin of Species* 1859 (New York: New York University Press, 1988). The first edition, without mention of "the creator."

Defleur, Alban, Tim White *et al.* "Neanderthal Cannibalism at Moula-Guercy, Ardèche, France," *Science* (October 1, 1999), 286:128–131. Recent scientific finds concerning the Neanderthal diet.

Fagan, Brian M. *The Journey from Eden* (London: Thames and Hudson, 1990). A very readable, comprehensive account of biological and cultural evolution by an anthropologist with superb writing skills.

Fedigan, Linda. "The Changing Role of Women in Models of Human Evolution," *Annual Review of Anthropology* XV (1986), 22–66. Comprehensive introduction to feminist perspectives on evolution.

Gamble, Clive. *Timewalkers: The Prehistory of Global Colonization* (Cambridge, MA: Harvard University Press, 1994). Gamble ponders the migrations of humans from earliest times to all corners of the earth.

Gould, Stephen Jay. *Ever Since Darwin: Reflections in Natural History* (New York: W.W. Norton & Co., 1977). Lucid account of the Darwinian position and later amendments to it.

Gould, Stephen Jay. *The Structure of Evolutionary Theory* (Cambridge, MA: Harvard University Press, 2002). A comprehensive summary of all that we know of evolution today, by a master scholar-writer, published just months before his death.

Holm, Jean, with John Bowker, eds. *Myth and History* (London: Pinter Publishers, 1994). Analysis of the functions of myth and of history in human understanding.

Lewis-Williams, David. *The Mind in the Cave: Consciousness and the Origins of Art* (London: Thames and Hudson, 2002). Argues that in prehistoric caves "image-making," religion, and social discriminations were a "package deal," as humans realized a new capability for higher-order thought.

Linton, Sally (pseud. for Sally Slocum). "Woman the Gatherer: Male Bias in Anthropology," in Sue-Ellen Jacobs, ed. *Women in Perspective: A*

Guide for Cross-Cultural Studies (Urbana: University of Illinois Press, 1971). Asking new questions from a feminist perspective, Linton demonstrates a much-enhanced role of women in early cultural evolution.

McNeill, William H. *Mythistory and Other Essays* (Chicago, IL: University of Chicago Press, 1986). A master historian discusses the difference between myth and the professional study of history, and how the two perspectives intersect in the public mind.

Mellars, Paul and Chris Stringer, eds. *The Human Revolution: Behavioural and Biological Perspectives on the Origins of Modern Humans* (Princeton, NJ: Princeton University Press, 1989). Papers of a 1987 multidisciplinary conference at Cambridge on human origins and early behavior patterns.

Morell, Virginia. *Ancestral Passions: The Leakey Family and the Quest for Humankind's Beginnings* (New York: Simon & Schuster, 1995). The internal dynamics of the Leakey family, as down-to-earth as their excavations.

Nature. Interdisciplinary scientific journal related to biological concerns. Volume 418 (2002) contained numerous articles on the discovery of Toumai, and reprinted several classic articles on earlier archaeological discoveries, from Dart's in 1925 to the present.

The New English Bible (New York: Oxford University Press, 1976). For clarity and simple, basic annotation, my favorite edition.

Pfeiffer, John. *The Creative Explosion* (Ithaca, NY: Cornell University Press, 1982). Argues for a dramatic leap in human intellectual and artistic capacities about 35,000 years ago in Europe. Very well written. Now more controversial than ever.

Scott, Joan W. "Gender: A Useful Category of Historical Analysis," *American Historical Review* XCI (1986), 1053–76. A classic article in helping to bring feminist perspectives into mainstream historical research.

White, Tim D., Berhane Asfaw, and Gen Suwa. "Ardipithecus ramidus, A Root Species for Australopithecus," in F. Facchini ed. *The First Humans and Their Cultural Manifestations* (Forli, Italy: A.B.A.C.O., 1996), 15–23. Early reports on the archaeological find.

Wood, Bernard. "The Oldest Hominid Yet," *Nature* Vol. 371 (Sept. 22, 1994), 280–81. Another early report on *Ardipithecus ramidus*, including evaluation of its significance.

The Agricultural Village

The evolution of maize from the rather stunted cob of wild corn from the valley of Mexico about 5000 B.C.E. through to the more productive and nutritious plant of about 1 B.C.E. reveals the key reason for the creation of agricultural villages. (See Richard MacNeish, "The Origins of New World Civilization," *Scientific American*, November 1964.) Settled agriculture could greatly increase both the quantity and quality of the food supply. As human populations grew, the produce brought by hunting and gathering became insufficient to feed their numbers. People had to travel ever greater distances, and this became dangerous because it brought them into direct conflict with their neighbors—who were also hard pushed to find adequate food and were also expanding. Settled agriculture was the solution. Increased population made it necessary; the end of the most recent ice age made it possible. Careful attention to plant and animal patterns on the part of hunter-gatherers had already set the stage.

As they settled down, humans began to domesticate not only food crops but also animals, which served for food, for power and energy in carrying goods and pulling plows, and for products such as milk, wool, fur, and leather. Village dwellers produced tools that were increasingly

Model reconstruction of Ban Po.

narrow wooden poles

straw thatch

clay

reeds

millet stalks

central fire pit

brushwood

daubed or plastered interior partition

bare earth or plaster floor

sophisticated in terms of both usefulness and aesthetic beauty. Some of these tools were made of organic materials, such as bone and fiber, but many were made of stone. Village dwellers became skilled at grinding and polishing the stone tools, and this era is called the Neolithic or New Stone Age.

Settled agriculture began in the fertile crescent—that is, Mesopotamia, the valley between the Tigris and Euphrates Rivers—and the Nile valley, both about 12,000 years ago. One of the best preserved early villages was discovered, however, in China in 1953, at Ban Po, near Xian. The residents cultivated millet and domesticated pigs and dogs. They practiced slash-and-burn agriculture, and pollen samples show distinct alternating periods of cultivation and fallow. The most ancient layers of the excavation, which date to about 6000 B.C.E., give a very clear idea of the

Jomon vase, Kanto province, Japan. Earthenware. (*Musée Guimet, Paris*)

physical form of an early agricultural village.

Immediately adjacent to the excavation, archaeologists have reconstructed a model of the entire prehistoric village. It represents Ban Po's three housing styles: square, round, and an oblong, split level, part underground and part above. Ban Po villagers stored their grain in some 200 underground pits, which were dug throughout the village. A moat surrounds the entire residential settlement.

North of the village was a pottery production center with six kilns, and next to them was a public cemetery where some 250 graves have been excavated. The bodies of children were placed in urns and buried in the main residential area. Archaeologists found seventy-six such burial urns, and no one knows why adults and children were buried separately.

In the center of the settlement was a large square building. What was its function? Presumably it had political and social significance for the entire

Obsidian blades, Çatal Hüyük, c. 3000 B.C.E.

village. Was it a ruler's palace? A priest's shrine? The official posting on the excavation identifies this central structure as "a place for the Ban Po inhabitants to discuss public affairs." This assertion about the politics of the village is consistent with the general belief of archaeologists that villages were more or less egalitarian places. This viewpoint is especially consistent with the Marxist philosophy that relatively egalitarian villages preceded more hierarchical cities, an ideology held by the communist government of China. In fact, however, we cannot be sure of the function of this central structure nor of the political structure of the village as a whole.

Although agriculture was the basis of most early villages, there were exceptions. In southern Japan, the Jomon people created villages that supported themselves by fishing and hunting deer and wild boar with bows and arrows, and by gathering and storing acorns, nuts, and seeds. Some of the Jomon lived in caves, but others built villages with individual pit-houses and central, communal buildings. They may have also cultivated rootcrops and cereals, but they were not primarily agricultural. They created stone tools but are most famous for their distinctive pottery, some of the world's earliest and most beautiful pottery which dates to as early as 10,500 B.C.E. It was made by forming clay into cords and wrapping the cords by hand into pots. At first the cords were simply allowed to dry without firing in kilns. For sedentary peoples, pottery is a useful means of storage. Often, however, as with the Jomon people, it is also valued as an artistic medium of self-expression.

Jomon culture spread throughout Japan, from the southern island of Kyushu, reaching Hokkaido by 6500 B.C.E. The Jomon people began to build wooden houses with elaborate hearths and to practice settled agriculture. In all, 30,000 Jomon sites are known, dating from about 10,500 B.C.E. to about 300 B.C.E., most of them on the central island of Honshu.

Another non-agricultural development in villages occurred in eastern Anatolia (modern Turkey), around the shores of Lake Van. The presence of volcanic obsidian stone gave villagers a substance they could craft into blades of extraordinary sharpness, and they used these blades themselves and also traded them to villages hundreds of miles away on the eastern shores of the Mediterranean and the Persian Gulf. For most of these Anatolian villages, the trade in obsidian was complementary to agriculture. But one site, Çatal Hüyük, grew into a 32-acre town, based on the manufacture and trade of obsidian tools. The manufacture and trade in obsidian tools enriched Çatal Hüyük and improved the productivity of villagers who traded their agricultural produce for the valued tools. In the context of the villages surrounding it, Çatal Hüyük stands out as a village that became a new kind of settlement, combining agriculture with industry and trade. It was a transitional form in the development of early cities.

Farming in China. Evidence of the earliest established agriculture in east Asia is found in the arid but fertile regions of north central China, along the central reaches of the Huang He (Yellow River). Villages such as Ban Po grew up on the floodplain, rich in alluvial and loess deposits, where drought-resistant plants such as millet could be cultivated.

QUESTIONS

1. Why was the development of agriculture essential to the growth of the city?
2. What is the difference between a village and a city?
3. In what ways did settling down and abandoning nomadism change people's lives?

PART 2

Settling Down

10,000 B.C.E. –1000 C.E.

THE FIRST CITIES AND WHY THEY MATTER: DIGS, TEXTS, AND INTERPRETATIONS

The establishment of urban settlements introduced a new era in many parts of the world. The physical construction of the new cities, with their impressive buildings and crowds of inhabitants, most clearly marks the transformation, but many equally significant, though less tangible, developments also contributed to a revolution in human settlement patterns. Cities were nodes in the regional networks of exchange of goods and culture, and they encouraged the production of sophisticated arts, the specialization of labor, and the elaboration of a social hierarchy. Most significantly, cities signaled the emergence of a state organization for guiding and administering the city and its surrounding area. The new state, hand-in-glove with the new city, provided leadership, organization, and official control of armed power. It governed the people of the city, sometimes with their consent, often without it. The state enforced and helped to create the conditions of inequality that emerged among the people of the new cities. In all these characteristics, the ancient city reminds us of our own.

Unlike modern cities, however, almost all early cities were relatively small. The largest contained perhaps 100,000 people in 8 square miles; most had only a few thousand inhabitants. Until the industrial revolution in the late nineteenth century, a few thousand people concentrated in 100 acres might have constituted a city, for cities held only a tiny percentage of the total population of any region.

Most of the world's population were farmers or hunter-gatherers when the first cities developed. The multiplication of cities and urban residents that we see today took place only after the industrial revolution created new urban factories, transportation hubs, and mass labor forces. Moreover, many of the early cities, although small, were centers of independent city-states; most cities today are single points in much larger national and even international networks. Finally, the earliest cities emerged in each of seven regions around the world. Mostly, they took root along great river banks in Africa and Asia, reflecting the importance of water, irrigation, and agriculture to their development. The world's earliest cities emerged between the Tigris and

Northeastern façade of Ziggurat, Ur, present-day Iraq, c. 2100 B.C.E. Sacred buildings and temples dominated the center of Ur and this three-story-high ziggurat was the most famous of them. Each major Mesopotamian city had a ziggurat dedicated to its deity. Ur's was dedicated to Nanna, the moon God (see p. 51).

Euphrates Rivers in what is now modern Iraq. They developed along the Nile River in Egypt and in the Indus valley of modern Pakistan. In China the earliest cities flourished in the flood plain of the Yellow River. Finally, early cities appeared in West Africa near the great bed of the Niger River. The Americas provide some exceptions with the growth of great civilizations in the valleys and jungles of Mexico and on the heights of the Andes mountains.

Many of these early cities were dedicated to gods and were built on the foundations of existing shrine centers. As the cities grew, the shrines grew with them, providing a more profound meaning to the lives of their inhabitants by linking their mundane existence to transcendent and powerful supernatural forces.

FROM VILLAGE COMMUNITY TO CITY-STATE

FOOD FIRST: THE AGRICULTURAL VILLAGE
10,000 B.C.E.–750 B.C.E.

KEY TOPICS
- The Agricultural Village
- The First Cities
- Sumer: The Birth of the City
- The Growth of the City-State

Until about 12,000 years ago humans hunted and gathered their food, following the migrations of animals and the seasonal cycles of the crops. They established temporary base camps for their activities, and caves served them for homes and meeting-places, but they had not established permanent settlements. They had begun to domesticate some animals, especially the dog and the sheep, but they had not yet begun the systematic practice of agriculture. Then, about 10,000 B.C.E., people began to settle down, constructing the first agricultural villages.

Why did they do it? Is food production through agriculture easier than hunting and gathering? Surprisingly, the answer seems to be "no." Research suggests that, with the technology available at that time, adult farmers had to work an equivalent of 1000–1300 hours a year for their food, while hunter-gatherers needed only 800–1000 hours. Moreover, agricultural work was more difficult.

Why did they change? An appealing, although unproved, answer is that increasing population pressure, perhaps accompanied by worsening climatic conditions, forced people to take on the more productive methods of agriculture. Scientists estimate that even in a lush tropical environment, 0.4 square miles of land could support only nine persons through hunting and gathering; under organized, sedentary agricultural techniques, the same area could support 200–400 people. In the less fertile, sub-tropical and temperate climates into which the expanding populations were moving at the end of the last ice age, after about 13,000 B.C.E., hunting and gathering were even less productive. To survive, sedentary agriculture became a necessity.

The memory of this transition survives in myth. For example, the myth of Shen Nung, whom the ancient Chinese honored as the inventor of agriculture and its wooden tools (and of poetry), captures the transformation:

> The people of old ate the meat of animals and birds. But in the time of Shen Nung, there were so many people that there were no longer enough animals and birds to supply their needs. So it was that Shen Nung taught the people how to cultivate the earth. (Bairoch, p. 6)

In addition to increasing agricultural productivity, villages facilitated an increase in creativity of all kinds. It may have taken longer to raise food than to hunt and gather it, but the sedentary farmers did not stop work when they had secured their food supply. In their villages they went on to produce textiles, pottery, metallurgy, architecture, tools, and objects of great beauty, especially in sculpture and painting. Did the

Opposite **Sumerian ruins, Uruk, present-day Iraq, c. 2100 B.C.E.** A man and child stand amid what is left of the ancient city of Uruk.

AT A GLANCE : VILLAGE COMMUNITIES AND CITY-STATES

DATE	POLITICAL	RELIGION AND CULTURE	SOCIAL DEVELOPMENT
4500 B.C.E.	■ Ubaid people in Mesopotamia		
3500 B.C.E.	■ Sumerians (3300–2350) ■ Ziggurats built	■ Cuneiform writing ■ Sumerian pantheon	■ Urbanization in Mesopotamia
3000 B.C.E.	■ Hereditary kings emerge		■ Invention of the wheel ■ Bronze casting ■ Sumerian city-states (2800–1850)
2500 B.C.E.	■ Ur, First Dynasty (2500–2350) ■ Akkadian kingdoms (2350–2150); Sargon of Akkad (2334–2279) ■ 3rd Dynasty of Ur (c. 2112–2004)	■ Akkadian language used in Sumer ■ *Epic of Gilgamesh* (c. 2113–1991)	■ Sumerian Laws
2000 B.C.E.	■ Semitic rulers gain control of Mesopotamia ■ 1st dynasty of Babylon (c. 1894–1595) ■ Hammurabi (1792–1750) ■ Hittites in Asia Minor		■ Mycenaean traders in Aegean 1800–1000 B.C.E. ■ Hammurabi's Code of Law
1500 B.C.E.	■ Hittite Empire (c. 1460–1200)	■ "Golden age" of Ugarit	
1000 B.C.E.	■ Assyrian Empire (900–612)	■ Hebrew Scriptures recorded	
750 B.C.E.	■ Sargon II (d. 705) ■ Sennacherib (c. 705–681) ■ Ashurbanipal (d. 627) ■ Fall of Nineveh (imperial capital) (612) ■ Nebuchadnezzar (605–562)	■ *Gilgamesh* (complete version) ■ Homer (*fl.* 8th century) ■ Hesiod (*fl.* 700)	
600 B.C.E.	■ Neo–Babylonian Empire	■ Library at Nineveh	
500 B.C.E.	■ Persian Empire in control of Mesopotamia		

agriculturists work comparatively harder than the hunter-gatherers simply to survive under greater population pressure, or because they craved the added rewards of their extra labor, or both? We can never know for sure, but the agricultural village opened new possibilities for economic, social, political, and artistic creativity—while closing others. It changed forever humanity's concepts of life's necessities and potentials.

THE AGRICULTURAL VILLAGE

The first agricultural villages that archaeologists have discovered date to about 10,000 B.C.E. They are located in the "fertile crescent," which curves from the Persian Gulf and the Zagros Mountains in the east and south, on the border of today's Iraq and Iran, northwest into Anatolia, present-day Turkey, and then turns south and west through present-day Syria, Lebanon, and Israel on the Mediterranean Sea. In this region, wild grasses—the ancestors of modern wheat and barley—provided the basic grains, first for gathering, and later for cultivation. By 8000 B.C.E. the Natufians, named for their valley in northern Israel, and the peoples immediately to the south, in the Jordan River valley near Jericho, were growing fully domesticated cereals. Peas and lentils and other pulses and legumes followed. The peoples of the fertile crescent hunted gazelles and goats. Later, they domesticated the goat and the sheep. In Turkey they added pigs; around the Mediterranean, there were cattle.

In other parts of the world, agriculture and animal domestication focused on other varieties. In the western hemisphere, these included maize, especially in Mesoamerica, and rootcrops such as manioc and sweet potatoes in South America. Amerindians domesticated the llama, the guinea pig, and the turkey. Domesticated dogs probably accompanied their migrant masters across the Bering Straits about 15,000 years ago. Perhaps the process of domestication was then repeated with the dogs found in the Americas.

In southeast Asia and in tropical Africa, wild roots and tubers, including yams, were the staple crops. In the Vindhya Mountain areas of central India, rice was among the first crops to be cultivated, about 5000 B.C.E. Anthropologists are uncertain when rice was first cultivated, rather than just being harvested from the wild, in southeast and east Asia, but a date similar to India's seems likely. From earliest times, as today, China's agriculture seems to have favored rice in the south and millet in the north. Some crops, including cotton and gourds, were brought under cultivation in many locations around the globe.

Our knowledge of early agriculture continues to grow as the archaeological record is expanded and revised. European sedentary agriculture, for example, that was once thought to have been borrowed from the Near East, may have been a local response to changing climate conditions.

The era in which villages took form is usually called **Neolithic**, or New Stone Age, named for its tools rather than its crops. Farming called for a different toolkit from hunting and gathering. For cutting, grinding, chopping, scraping, piercing, and digging, village artisans fashioned new tools from stone. Archaeological digs from Neolithic villages abound with blades, knives, sickles, adzes, arrows, daggers, spears, fish hooks and harpoons, mortars and pestles, and rudimentary plows and hoes.

As villages expanded their economic base these stone tools often became valued as items of trade. Obsidian—a kind of volcanic glass with very sharp edges—was traded from Anatolia and is found in hundreds of digs from central Turkey to Syria and the Jordan valley. Among other items of trade, recognized by their appearance in digs a long distance away from their point of origin, are seashells, jade, turquoise, and ceramics.

Although ceramics occasionally appear among nomadic populations, the weight and fragility of clay make pottery essentially a creation of the more established Neolithic village. As a vessel for storage, pottery further reflected the sedentary character of the new village life. The fine designs and colors decorating its pottery became the most distinctive identifying mark of the Neolithic village, and archaeologists often designate eras, locations, and groups of people by descriptions of their pottery—the "grayware," the "red glazed," or the "cord-marked," for example.

Simple pottery is easy to make and accessible to anyone, but specialized craftspeople developed ceramics into a medium of artistic creativity. Fine ceramic jewelry, statuary, and figurines attained great beauty and were frequently used in religious rituals.

Historical change, however, does not proceed in a uniform, straight line. Historians must be alert not only to general patterns, but also to exceptions. Some villages did form on an economic base of hunting-and-gathering. In southern Japan, for example, a non-agricultural village society appeared among the Jomon people along with some of the earliest and most beautiful of

Neolithic "New Stone Age"—the last division of the Stone Age, immediately preceding the development of metallurgy and corresponding to the ninth–fifth millennia B.C.E. It was characterized by the increasing domestication of animals and cultivation of crops, established agricultural communities, and the appearance of such crafts as pottery and weaving.

The Fertile Crescent. The Tigris and Euphrates rivers gave life to the first known agricultural villages, about 10,000 years ago, and the first known cities in human history, about 5000 years ago. Fertile land extended to the Mediterranean and some contact apparently continued on to the Nile Valley. Its borders were defined to the south by arid regions receiving less than 10 inches of rainfall per year, and to the north by mountains and semi-arid plateaux.

The origins of agriculture and domestic animals. The development of agriculture and the domestication of animals took place independently in different parts of the world, but the Near East, Mesoamerica, southeast Asia, and China were among the first and most significant regions.

pottery. Jomon pottery, which is marked by distinctive cord lines, dates back to 10,500 B.C.E. and spread from the southern island of Kyushu, northward through Honshu, reaching Hokkaido by 6500 B.C.E. The Jomon villagers supported themselves from fishing, hunting deer and wild boar, and gathering and storing nuts. They created stone tools and lived in caves and in pit-houses in settled villages with central, communal buildings. Yet the Japanese did not develop agricultural cultivation for another several thousand years.

THE FIRST CITIES

The first cities were constructed on the economic base of sedentary village agricultural communities. In excavating these earliest cities around the globe, archaeologists ask which city forms were invented indigenously, by their own inhabitants, and which were borrowed from earlier examples or, perhaps, imposed from outside on local rural populations. Technically, the question is one of **innovation** versus **diffusion**. Thus far, most experts agree that innovative primary urbanization, not borrowed or imposed from outside, took place in seven places: five river valleys in the eastern hemisphere—Mesopotamia, the Nile, the Indus, the Huang He, and the Niger—and, in the western

innovation The explanation that similar cultural traits, techniques, or objects found among different groups of people were invented independently rather than spread from one group to another.

diffusion The spread of ideas, objects, or traits from one culture to another.

hemisphere, in Mexico and in the Andes Mountains. The birth of primary urbanization took place in these seven locations at very different times, with Mesopotamia the oldest at about 3300 B.C.E. and the Niger the most recent at about 400 C.E.

Cities transform human life. The physical form of the early cities tells the story vividly. Even today we can trace on the surface of the earth the 5500-year-old designs of the first cities and the irrigation systems that supported them. Remnants of walls and fragments of monuments of these first cities still rise from their sites. From under the surface archaeologists salvage artifacts: bricks; pottery; tools of wood, bone, stone, and metal; jewelry; and skeletons of citizens and slaves. The technology of the early cities included new means of transportation; we find the remains of wheeled vehicles and of sailboats. The earliest city dwellers advanced their skills in metallurgy, and products of their craftsmanship in copper, tin, and their alloys abound in the archaeological excavations. In recognition of these technological breakthroughs we often call the era of the first cities the Bronze Age.

But cities are more than bricks and mortar, metal and artifacts. They require institutions for their larger scale of organization and administration. As society and economy became more complex, new class hierarchies emerged. Professional administrators, skilled artisans, long-distance traders, local merchants, and priests and kings enriched the diversity and sophistication of the growing cities. External relations with other cities required skilled negotiations, and a diplomatic corps emerged. Armies mobilized for defense and attack. In short, with the growth of the city the early state was also born, with its specialized organization, centralized rule, and powerful armies.

THE EARLIEST URBAN SETTLEMENTS

3500 B.C.E.	Rise of Sumer, southern Mesopotamia.
3100	Emergence of Egyptian state; new capital at Memphis.
2500	Development of Mohenjo-Daro, urban civilization on the Indus plain.
2500	City-states in northern Mesopotamia and the Levant, dominated by palace complexes.
1800	Urban growth after Shang dynasty established in northeast China.
1200	Formative period in Mesoamerica, marked by first shrine centers, especially the Olmec.
c. **400** B.C.E.	City-states in Mesoamerica and South America.
400 C.E.	Urbanization of Jenne-jeno, Nigeria, sub-Saharan Africa.

The spread of civilizations. The first civilizations developed where unique local climatic and soil conditions, favorable to settled agriculture, occurred, mostly in major river basins. With the development of an agricultural surplus came the growth of urban centers, trade, and population. Related civilizations tended to develop in regions adjacent to these heartlands, or along trade routes between them.

core areas of earliest civilizations
extent of trading/cultural influence
core areas of subsequent civilizations

For an interactive version of this map, go to: **http://www.prenhall.com/spodek/map2.3**

To keep track of business transactions and administrative orders, the proclamations of rulers and the rituals of priests, the legends of gods and the histories of the city, new methods of record keeping were developed. At first these were tokens, pictures, seals, personalized markings, and, in the Andes, *quipu*, knots made in special lengths of string. By about 3300 B.C.E., in Sumer, which is geographically equivalent to today's southern Iraq, the world's first system of writing had evolved. This was one of the most revolutionary inventions in human history. The prestigious occupation of scribe was born, and schoolteachers soon followed.

From earliest times, city dwellers and analysts understood and commented on the significance of the first urban revolution. Today, we have more reason than ever to value and to evaluate its 5000-year-old heritage, for in modern times we are living through two new urban revolutions. By 1800 the industrial revolution opened a new era of urban development that re-invented the cities of western Europe and North America (see Chapter 17). In the twentieth century peasants streamed by the millions and tens of millions from rural villages to mammoth cities, creating massive, unprecedented urban environments around the globe (see Part 5). So we search humanity's earliest experiences with cities not only to understand our ancestors but also to understand ourselves.

SUMER: THE BIRTH OF THE CITY

A people called the Sumerians pioneered the world's first urban revolution in Mesopotamia, literally "between the rivers"—that is, the region between the Tigris and Euphrates Rivers, approximately modern Iraq. They migrated into southern Mesopotamia about 4000 B.C.E., perhaps from around the Caspian Sea, but no one knows for sure. They faced uncertain odds. While the area between the Tigris and Euphrates Rivers became known as the fertile crescent for its high agricultural productivity, high temperatures and unpredictable floods constantly challenged the Sumerians. To succeed in building cities in the region, peoples had to construct irrigation ditches and intricate canals.

The Sumerians were not the first to inhabit this land. Archaeological excavations of pottery show the earlier presence in Mesopotamia of the Ubaids, a Semitic-speaking people, beginning about 4500 B.C.E. The Ubaidians drained marshes and developed an early irrigation system. Although the language the Sumerians spoke was not Semitic, their use of Semitic word forms and names also suggests that Semitic-speaking people may have preceded them in the area.

Gradually, the Sumerians began to dominate the region, supplanting the Semitic-speaking populations. They dug better canals for irrigation, improved roads, and expanded urban developments. For a millennium, from 3300 B.C.E. until 2350 B.C.E., the Sumerians lived in warring city-states—Kish, Uruk, Ur, Nippur, Lagash, Umma, and dozens of smaller ones. Each of these city-states included a central city with a temple and the agricultural region surrounding it. The city controlled and protected the fields of grain, orchards, and land for livestock, which, in turn, provided enough food to support the cities' growing populations.

Stone tower and wall, Jericho, c. 8000 B.C.E. Before Sumer, a Neolithic community based at Jericho in the Jordan valley, Palestine, was the first to develop cereals of a fully domesticated type. In 8000 B.C.E these farmers, keen to secure their settlement in the arid environment, constructed a stone perimeter wall 10 feet thick that was strengthened at one point by a circular stone tower over 30 feet high. This wall is one of the earliest such defenses known.

Map of Nippur, 1500 B.C.E. This plan of Nippur, the ancient cultural center of Sumer, is the oldest known city map. Inscribed in a well-preserved clay tablet, 8¼ by 7 inches in size, the map is drawn accurately to scale and shows several of the city's key temples and buildings, its central park, its rivers and canals, and especially its walls and gates. The script is mostly Sumerian with a few words of Akkadian, the language of the Semitic people who eventually conquered the Sumerians. (*Hilprecht Collection, Friederich-Schiller University, Jena*)

With the city-states constantly at war with each other, their leaders began to think in terms of conquering others to create large empires. In *c.* 2350 B.C.E., Sargon, king of the city of Akkad, conquered the Sumerian cities one by one, allowing the Semitic-speaking Akkadians to overshadow the Sumerians. Calling himself the "king of Sumer and Akkad," Sargon was the first to unite the city-states under a single, powerful ruler. After some 200 years under Akkadian rule, the Mesopotamian city-states regained their independence under the third dynasty of Ur (2112–2004 B.C.E.), but they resumed their inter-urban warfare, which weakened them. Eventually, Hammurabi (1792–1750 B.C.E.), king of "Old Babylonia," launched a series of aggressive military campaigns. He extended his control over much of Mesopotamia, including Sumer and Akkad, and Sumerian influence waned. The cities they had built died out, having fought each other to exhaustion. A series of foreign powers—Hittites, Assyrians, Babylonians again, Achaeminid Persians, and Greeks under Alexander the Great—variously conquered and controlled Mesopotamia. The Sumerian cultural legacy lived on, however, assimilated into their conquerors' literature, philosophy, religion, law, and patterns of urbanization.

THE GROWTH OF THE CITY-STATE

What were the characteristics of the urban revolution in Mesopotamia? How did its cities differ from the earlier villages? The most obvious feature was that the scale of the city-state—its physical size, population, and territorial control—was much greater than that of the village.

The Neolithic village housed a few dozen or a few hundred residents on a few acres. The largest Neolithic site in the Near East, Çatal Hüyük in Anatolia, grew by 5500 B.C.E.

Standard of Ur, from Iraq. Sumerian, Early Dynastic II. *c.* 2800–2400 B.C.E. In Sumer the city-state was created as strong kings came to rule over walled cities and the surrounding countryside. This banqueting scene, found in a tomb in the royal cemetery at Ur, shows the court drinking to the health of the king. The boxlike "standard" is thought to have rested on top of a long pole during festive processions. (*British Museum, London*)

to occupy slightly more than 30 acres. It became a town. By comparison, the first cities of Mesopotamia were ten times larger, accommodating about 5000 people.

Over time, the larger cities reached populations of 35,000–40,000 and covered more than 1000 acres or 1½ square miles. The major cities were walled. The ramparts of Uruk (modern Warka, biblical Erech), the city of the king-god-hero Gilgamesh, stretched to a circumference of 6 miles, engirdling a population of 50,000 by 2700 B.C.E. By 2500 B.C.E. the region of Sumer held 500,000 people, four-fifths of them in its cities and villages! Urbanism in Sumer became a way of life.

To support these growing urban populations, the range of control of the Sumerian cities over the surrounding countryside, and its agricultural and raw material resources, continued to expand. For example, the total sway of Lagash, one of the major cities, probably extended over 1200 square miles. The king, priests, and private citizens controlled the fields of this area.

Networks of irrigation canals supported agriculture in this arid region and expanded Sumerian control over the land and its productivity. Irrigation permitted settlement to extend southward to central Mesopotamia, where cities would later emerge about 3300 B.C.E. The construction and maintenance of the canals required larger gangs of workers than the work teams that were based on family and clan alone. Loyalties that had been limited to blood relatives now extended beyond kinship to civic identity. In organizing these public works projects, a sense of citizenship, based on a shared space rather than on blood kinship, was born. It was enshrined in legal principles that made geographical residence the basis of citizenship. These new loyalties and laws marked the beginning of city life.

Organizing the canal systems required more powerful leaders than villages had known. At first, this leadership appears to have been exercised by councils of aristocratic elders, who worked closely with religious leaders. In times of crisis, especially during warfare with other cities, the council appointed a temporary single leader, but after about 2800 B.C.E., these men began to assume the position of hereditary kings and to rule in conjunction with temple priests. Political power and organization were both centralized and sanctified. Thus was the state born and consolidated.

Religion: The Priesthood and the City

Considerable power rested with the priests of the many deities of Sumer, because residents believed that their survival in the harsh environment of ancient Mesopotamia depended partly on the will of the gods. In contrast to modern patterns, in which the countryside is often considered more religious than the secular city, the authority of the ancient temple community gave the religious establishment enormous prestige and power in the city, and urban ritual practice was more fully elaborated than was its rural counterpart.

To consolidate their temporal and supernatural influences, the city priests built great temples, called **ziggurats**. Found throughout the region, ziggurats were a form of stepped temple built on a square or rectangular platform of small, locally produced, sun-baked bricks. The baked bricks were covered by glazed bricks, which may have had religious significance. A small sanctuary rested atop the structure, which could reach as many as ten stories high. The ziggurat lacked any internal chambers, and worshipers probably reached the sanctuary via external ramps. The walls themselves were more than 7 feet thick to support the weight of the massive edifice. (Ziggurats are probably the model for the Bible's Tower of Babel, which was depicted as a challenge to the power of the God Jehovah.) The ziggurats dominated the fields that the priests controlled and farmed, rented out, or turned over to their servants and favorites. As their power increased, the priests built the ziggurats taller and more massive. From within these vast temple complexes, they controlled huge retinues, including artisans and administrators, and retained gangs of field workers to farm the temple's estates. Temples employed and fed multitudes. The chief temple in the city of Lagash in Mesopotamia, for example, provided daily food and drink (ale) to some 1200 people by about 3000 B.C.E. The leading temples became virtual cities within cities.

Rituals, especially those of the priests and kings, suggest further the significance of religious thought in the minds of Sumerians. On New Year's day the king of Ur in Sumer proceeded to the top of the city's major ziggurat, where he was symbolically married to the goddess of fertility, Inanna. The entire population witnessed this affirmation of his divinity.

Royal burials also asserted the divinity and authority of the king. Royal tombs were elegant. Their arches, vaults, and domes suggesting new levels of architectural skill, were built of brick and stone, and many of the funeral objects interred with the dead were of gold and silver. As in the other ancient civilizations we shall encounter in later chapters, some of the royal dead were accompanied by attendants who might have been sacrificed for the purpose and were buried nearby. They, too, were adorned with jewelry of gold and silver. The British archaeologist Sir Leonard Woolley described the death pit adjacent to the royal burial place in Ur, which he excavated in the 1920s:

> Six men servants carrying knives or axes lay near the entrance lined up against the wall; in front of them stood a great copper basin, and by it were the bodies of four women harpists, one with her hands still on the strings of her instrument. Over the rest of the pit's area there lay in ordered rows the bodies of sixty-four ladies of the court. All of them wore some sort of ceremonial dress … Clearly these people were not wretched slaves killed as oxen might be killed, but persons held in honor, wearing their robes of office, and coming, one hopes, voluntarily to a rite which would in their belief be but a passing from one world to another, from the service of a god on earth to that of the same god in another place. (pp. 70–2)

ziggurat A temple tower of ancient Mesopotamia, constructed of square or rectangular terraces of diminishing size, usually with a shrine on top built of blue enamel bricks, the color of the sky.

In contrast to these elaborate royal burials, most common people were buried in small brick vaults in basement chambers of their own houses, and some were interred in cemeteries outside the city walls.

Occupational Specialization and Class Structure

The priests and the political-military rulers were only the most powerful of the new classes of specialists that emerged in the complex, large cities. Managers, surveyors, artisans, astronomers, brewers, warriors, traders, and scribes—all in addition to the farmers working their own fields and those of the temples and landowners—gave the cities a far more sophisticated hierarchical class structure than villages possessed.

Arts and Invention. Creativity flourished. Artisans crafted works of art in terra cotta, copper, clay, and colors surpassing village standards in their beauty and technical skill. Cylinder seals (small cylinders of stone engraved with designs for stamping clay tablets and sealing jars) became a common form of practical art in Sumer and spread as far as Anatolia and Greece. Astronomers established an accurate calendar based on lunar months that enabled them to predict the onset of seasons and to prepare properly for each year's planting and harvesting. Musicians created, designed, and played the lyre and composed and chanted songs, often dedicated to gods. Designers and architects, supervising armies of workers, built the canals of the countryside and the monuments of the cities.

Sumerians apparently invented the first wheels, the potter's wheel for ceramics and wagon wheels for transportation. They dramatically improved the plow, learning how to harness it to oxen. Metallurgists, smelting their new alloy of copper and tin, ushered in the Bronze Age. From the new metal they fashioned tips for the plow and an array of new tools: hoes, axes, chisels, knives, and saws. They turned their attention to

Mesopotamian trade. The Sumerian trading network, revealed by the wide range of valuable and exotic materials used by Mesopotamian craftsmen, was both extensive and sophisticated, drawing on resources often well over 2000 miles distant. Egyptian tomb paintings show Semitic merchants with donkey caravans, while some of the earliest writing is found on Sumerian clay tablets recording commercial transactions.

Engraved cylinder seal (left) and impression (right). Seals were first used as signatures before the invention of writing. The cylinders produce continuous patterns that are repetitive, but the figures themselves are remarkably naturalistic.

Lady Pu-abi's headdress (below). The splendor of this gold ornament, discovered in the 1920s in the royal burial place of Ur, reflects the wealth of this Mesopotamian urban society, the skill of its craftsmen, the hierarchy of its people, and the anticipation of some form of future life. (*University of Pennsylvania Museum*)

weapons and produced lance points and arrowheads, swords, daggers, and harpoons. They made bronze vessels and containers, as well as smaller items such as nails, pins, rings, and mirrors.

Trade and Markets: Wheeled Cart and Sailboat. Trade was central to urban life. Sumerian traders carried merchandise by land, river, and sea, in the world's first wheeled carts and sailboats, as well as by donkey caravan. Rich in agricultural commodities and artisan production but poor in raw materials, Sumerians traded with the inhabitants of hilly areas to the north for wood, stone, and metal. They sailed into the Persian Gulf to find copper and tin and then continued along the Arabian Sea coast as far east as the Indus valley for ivory and ceramics. They traveled east overland through the passes of the Zagros Mountains to bring back carnelian beads from Elam. Shells from the Mediterranean coast that have been found in Sumer indicate trade westward, probably overland, as well.

In the city marketplace, merchants sold locally produced foodstuffs, including vegetables, onions, lentils and beans, more than fifty varieties of fish taken from the Tigris and Euphrates Rivers, milk, cheese, butter, yogurt, dates, meat—mostly mutton—and ale. In vats in their homes, women, especially, brewed up to 40 percent of the barley and wheat harvest into ale for home use and for sale. For taste, effect, and storage purposes the Sumerians preferred ale to grain. (Hops had not yet been introduced to enable the processing of ale into beer.)

Thus, from king and priest through professionals, artisans, craftsmen, farmers, and laborers, specialization and division of labor and a hierarchical class structure marked the city's social and economic life as far more complex than that of the smaller, simpler village.

Monumental Architecture and Adornment

For the Sumerians, the size and elegance of their cities and monuments were a source of great pride. The earliest introduction to Gilgamesh, hero of the greatest surviving Sumerian epic, proclaims his excellence as city builder: "In Uruk he built walls, a great rampart, and the temple of blessed Eanna for the god of the firmament Anu, and for Ishtar the goddess of love. Look at it still today: the outer wall where the cornice runs, it shines with the brilliance of copper; and the inner wall, it has no equal."

Artwork adorned the city, especially the temple precincts. Sculptures, murals, mosaics, and especially stone **bas reliefs** (see p. 56) provided not only beauty and elegance, but represented pictorially key scenes in the history of the cities and their rulers. The magnificence of this monumental architecture and art defined the city's image, impressing residents and giving warning to enemies.

Writing

The Sumerians invented writing, thereby altering human history. Indeed historians so value writing as a means of communication and of recording events that they often call all the events prior to the invention of writing prehistory. For these historians, only when events are recorded in writing can they be called history since without writing we cannot know directly what people thought and said.

He-Goat and Flowering Tree. Offering stand for fertility god. Sumerian, from Ur, c. 2500 B.C.E. This offering stand was created with a magical as well as a functional purpose in mind, being intended to work as a fertility charm too. The goat, an ancient symbol of male sexuality, is shown rearing up against a flowering tree, emblem of nature's fecundity. (*British Museum, London*)

Pictographic c. 3000 B.C.E.									
Early cuneiform representation c. 2400 B.C.E.									
Late Assyrian c. 650 B.C.E.									
Sumerian phonetic equivalent and meaning	k / eat	mŭsen / bird	sag / head	gu⁴ / ox	še / barley	ud / day	sŭ / hand	ku⁶ / fish	a / water	b / cow

The earliest Sumerian scribes first used writing, beginning about 3300 B.C.E., for business purposes, to note the contents of commercial packages, the names of their owners, and to catalog this information into lists. They employed styluses made of bone or of hollow reed stems to incise **pictograms** (see p. 56), picture representations of the objects of their writing, onto clay tablets. By 3000 B.C.E. they were representing the key features of the pictures in wedge-shaped signs that we call **cuneiform** (see p. 56). Some cuneiform signs represented whole words, but others represented individual phonetic sounds based on words.

As the cuneiform became more sophisticated, so too did the subject matter, and by c. 2400 B.C.E. Sumerian writing began to transmit stories, proclaim political and military victories, sing the poetry of lovers, praise the glories of gods, and lament the fall of cities. Written literature took form and flourished. Archaeologists have excavated tens of thousands of Sumerian clay tablets, containing literature as well as business notations, and transferred them to research institutions around the world.

Many later peoples in the region—Elamites, Babylonians, Assyrians, and Akkadians—adopted cuneiform to write their own languages. The conquests of Alexander the Great in the fourth century B.C.E., however, helped to introduce alphabetic writing—of the Aramaic language—and cuneiform died out. The last known cuneiform text was written in 75 C.E.

Although some of the earliest town dwellers in other parts of the world—the settlers of the Niger valley of West Africa, the Olmec and Teotihuacanos of Mesoamerica, and the Chavin and Inca of the Andes Mountains of South America—achieved urban form and size without the use of any form of writing, most of the earliest cities did invent some system of recording. As in Sumer, these systems moved "from token to tablet"—that is, from a simple recording of business transactions and registration of ownership through designated tokens, often marked with individual notations, through picture writing, to **ideograms** (see p. 56), and finally to phonetic, alphabetical writing.

As we shall see in Chapters 3 to 5, not all civilizations followed this sequence. In China, for example, the first writing seems to have been symbols inscribed on oracle bones. They seem to have been an attempt to divine the future. Chinese as a written language has only recently been transliterated into a phonetic alphabet; its basic script is still ideographic. The Chavin and Inca developed a form of

Writing was invented in west Asia in the fourth millennium B.C.E. and developed from the need to keep a record of business transactions. From the wedge-shaped marks formed by a hollow-shaped reed, or stylus, cuneiform script evolved gradually. In this pictographic script, stylized drawings are used to represent words; each pictograph stands for a syllable, and abstract concepts are conveyed by using concrete notions that are close in meaning (e.g. "open mouth" for "eat").

Clay tablet with cuneiform, Jemdet Nasr, Iraq, 3000 B.C.E. This example of writing from Mesopotamia is among the earliest known anywhere in the world.

HOW DO WE KNOW?

Decoding Sumerian Writing

The Sumerians wrote no historical interpretive accounts of their accomplishments, but at least five kinds of written materials help us to reconstruct their past. King lists give us not only the names and dates of many of the principal kings of the major cities but also some chronology of their continuing warfare. Royal correspondence with officials illuminates relations with neighbors. Epics transmit Sumerian values and their sense of the heroic, and lamentations recount the continuing devastation wrought by their inter-city religious warfare. Finally, legal codes suggest the principles and hierarchies of their everyday life.

Despite Sumerian accomplishments, historians lost access to the Sumerians and their literature for at least 2000 years. The locations of even the grandest of the historic sites passed from memory. Biblical scholars, however, kept alive an interest in the region, searching for locations mentioned in Scripture, and British officials arriving with the British East India Company's outpost in Baghdad revived this interest. They began to investigate the ruins of Babylon and its

artifacts, and they dispatched artifacts, including written tablets, back to London. Still, no one knew what the wedge-shaped symbols meant.

Then, in the 1830s and 1840s, at Behistun, near Kermanshah, Persia, a British army officer began to copy a huge inscription that had been incised into a 300 foot high cliff to announce the military victories of the Persian king Darius I about 500 B.C.E. The officer, H. C. Rawlinson, had a scaffolding constructed so that he could reach the ancient writing, sometimes while hanging suspended from a rope 300 feet high above the surface of the earth. Rawlinson and other scholars found that the inscription actually included three scripts that represented different, but related languages: Old Persian, Babylonian, and Elamite. Old Persian and the Elamite were written in cuneiform scripts; the Babylonian in alphabetic script. The stone had probably been prepared to publicize Darius's triumphs in three of the major languages of his empire. The three inscriptions were translations of one another, enabling linguists who could already read the alphabetic script to crack the cuneiform—although it took several

generations before scholars completed this task.

Later archaeological digs in Mesopotamia uncovered tens of thousands of tablets and fragments, One especially rich cache was the royal library of the Assyrian king Ashurbanipal (r. 668–627 B.C.E.) at Nineveh. Through texts and digs, scholars resurrected the Sumerian economy, belief systems, and culture. Most of the texts deal with practical, everyday business transactions and administration. One contains the first known recipe for the ale that Sumerians enjoyed so much. Others recorded the world's first written literature.

- Why do you think the ancient language and literature of Sumer, like those of Egypt, were lost for 2000 years?
- How might the written records, once deciphered, complement the archaeological record known from excavations?
- How do the five kinds of records discovered in Sumerian writing differ from "historical interpretive accounts"? How do they contribute to an understanding of history even though they themselves may not be "historical interpretive accounts"?

---

bas relief In sculpture, relief is a term for any work in which the forms stand out from the background. In bas (or low) relief, the design projects only slightly from the background and the outlines are not undercut.

pictogram (alternative: pictograph) A pictorial symbol or sign representing an object or concept.

cuneiform A writing system in use in the ancient Near East from around the end of the fourth millennium to the first century B.C.E. The earliest examples are in Sumerian. The name derives from the wedge-shaped marks (Latin: *cuneus*, a wedge) made by pressing the slanted edge of a stylus into soft clay.

ideogram (alternative: ideograph) A character or figure in a writing system in which the idea of a thing is represented rather than its name. Languages such as Chinese use ideograms.

recording transactions and chronology through knots made in strings called *quipu*, but they did not develop an independent system of writing. Nor did the people of the Niger valley.

Writing facilitated communication, commerce, administration, religious ritual, and, later, the recording and transmission of literature. It enabled society to enlarge to a scale never seen before and it encouraged a self-consciousness and historical analysis previously unknown. It created a "knowledge industry," transmitted through systems of formal education and headed by scribes. By 2500 B.C.E., Sumerians had apparently established a number of schools where students could master the skill of writing. In a sense, this textbook had its origins in Sumer some 5000 years ago.

Achievements in Literature and Law

Much of what we know about the ancient Sumerian imagination and world vision comes from its literary works. *The Epic of Gilgamesh*, the most famous of the remaining literature, weaves together a series of tales about the hero Gilgamesh. Its most complete version comes from various shorter stories found in the library at Nineveh from about 750 B.C.E., but earlier fragments in the Sumerian excavations corroborate the antiquity of the core legends going back to the time when Gilgamesh ruled Uruk, about 2600 B.C.E.

SOURCE

The Epic of Gilgamesh

Like all epics, Gilgamesh *recounts the deeds of a larger-than-life hero. The Sumerian epic introduces the first hero in written literature:*

I will proclaim to the world the deeds of Gilgamesh. This was the man to whom all things were known; this was the king who knew the countries of the world. He was wise, he saw mysteries and knew secret things. ... When the gods created Gilgamesh they gave him a perfect body. Shamash the glorious sun endowed him with beauty, Adad the god of the storm endowed him with courage, the great gods made his beauty perfect, surpassing all others, terrifying like a great wild bull. Two-thirds they made him god and one-third man.

Aruru, the goddess of Uruk, who had also created Gilgamesh, created Enkidu, a forest dweller, who became Gilgamesh's friend and played a central role in the epic. Gilgamesh *highlights the suggestive myth of Enkidu's seduction by an urban harlot who lures him from the wilderness to the pleasures of the city as well as to his wrestling match with Gilgamesh. The implication is that sexuality is experienced very differently in the city—more intensely and in more sophisticated fashion—than in the countryside. So, too, is friendship:*

the harlot and the trapper sat facing one another and waited for the game to come ... on the third day the herds came; they came down to drink and Enkidu was with them ... The trapper spoke to her: "There he is. Now, woman, make your breasts bare, have no shame, do not delay but welcome his love. Let him see you naked, let him possess your body. When he comes near uncover yourself and lie with him; teach him, the savage man, your woman's art, for when he murmurs love to you the wild beasts that shared his life in the hills will reject him." She was not afraid to take him, she made herself naked and welcomed his eagerness; as he lay on her murmuring love she taught him the woman's art.

For six days and seven nights they lay together, for Enkidu had forgotten his home in the hills; but when he was satisfied he went back to the wild beasts. Then, when the gazelle saw him, they fled. Enkidu would have followed, but his body was bound as though with a cord, his knees gave way when he started to run, his swiftness was gone. And now the wild creatures had all fled away; Enkidu was grown weak, for wisdom was in him, and the thoughts of a man were in his heart. So he returned and sat down at the woman's feet, and listened intently to what she said. "You are wise, Enkidu, and now you have become like a god. Why do you want to run wild with the beasts in the hills? Come with me. I will take you to the strong-walled Uruk, to the blessed temple of Ishtar and of Anu, of love and of heaven: there Gilgamesh lives, who is very strong, and like a wild bull he lords it over men." When she had spoken Enkidu was pleased; he longed for a comrade, for one who would understand his heart. "Come, woman, and take me to that holy temple, to the house of Anu and of Ishtar, and to the place where Gilgamesh lords it over the people. I will challenge him boldly."

With Enkidu's first encounter with Gilgamesh in the city, the epic also recounts the first example of male bonding, forged through a test of physical strength. When Gilgamesh and Enkidu first meet, they engage in a mighty wrestling match:

They broke the doorposts and the walls shook, they snorted like bulls locked together. They shattered the doorposts and the walls shook. Gilgamesh bent his knee with his foot planted on the ground and with a turn Enkidu was thrown. Then immediately his fury died ... So Enkidu and Gilgamesh embraced and their friendship was sealed.

The epic also unveils the hero's driving ambition for fame and glory, both for himself and for his city, as Gilgamesh courageously chooses to enter the strongholds of Humbaba, guardian of the forest, and, with Enkidu, to fight him.

I will go to the country where the cedar is cut. I will set up my name where the names of famous men are written; and where no man's name is written I will raise a monument to the gods ... I, Gilgamesh, go to see that creature of whom such things are spoken, the rumour of whose name fills the world. I will conquer him in his cedar wood and show the strength of the sons of Uruk, all the world shall know of it.

The importance of metallurgy and metals, especially for weapons, is highlighted:

He went to the forge and said, "I will give orders to the armorers: they shall cast us our weapons while we watch them." So they gave orders to the armorers and the craftsmen sat down in conference. They went into the groves of the plain and cut willow and box-wood; they cast for them axes of nine score pounds, and great swords they cast with blades of six score pounds each one, with pommels and hilts of thirty pounds. They cast for Gilgamesh the axe "Might of Heroes" and the bow of Anshan; and Gilgamesh was armed and Enkidu; and the weight of the arms they carried was thirty score pounds.

The victory of Gilgamesh and Enkidu over Humbaba parallels the massive assault by urbanites on the natural resources of the world, turning the products of nature into objects of trade and commerce, and using them to build cities.

Now the mountains were moved and all the hills, for the guardian of the forest was killed. They attacked the cedars, the seven splendours of Humbaba were extinguished. So they pressed on into the forest ... and while Gilgamesh felled the first of the trees of the forest Enkidu cleared their roots as far as the banks of Euphrates.

Lower Mesopotamia has no stone, wood, or metal. To get these raw materials, Sumerians had to send parties over long distances to quarry, cut, and dig; to trade; and to conquer. The mixed responses of the gods to the murder of Humbaba suggest the deep ambivalence of the Sumerians to their own increasing power:

[Gilgamesh and Enkidu] set [the corpse of] Humbaba before the gods, before Enlil; they kissed the ground and dropped the shroud and set the head before him. When he saw the head of Humbaba, Enlil raged at them, "Why did you do this thing? From henceforth may the fire be on your faces, may it eat the bread that you eat, may it drink where you drink."

SUMER: KEY EVENTS AND PEOPLE

c. 3300 (B.C.E.)	Sumerians invent writing.
c. 3000 (B.C.E.)	Sumerians become dominant power in southern Mesopotamia.
c. 2800–2340	Sumerian city-states: early dynastic period sees spread of Mesopotamian culture to the north.
c. 2350	Sargon captures Sumer and establishes Semitic dynasty at Akkad, the new capital.
c. 2112–2004	Third dynasty of Ur.
c. 1900	Ammorites at Babylon.
1792–1750	Reign of Hammurabi; Babylon is the new capital of Mesopotamia.
c. 1600	Invasion by Hittites and Kassites, destroying Hammurabi's dynasty.

The Epic of Gilgamesh presents a world of many gods before whom humans are passive and frightened subjects. Gilgamesh, however, defers neither to human nor to god. Devastated by the death of his closest friend Enkidu, he sets off to the underworld in search of eternal life. Along the way he encounters the Sumerian prototype of Noah. This man, Utnapishtim, tells him of a flood that destroyed all human life except his family. A god who counseled him to build a boat had saved them. In the bleak underworld of the dead, Gilgamesh obtains a plant that will give eternal youth, but on his return voyage a snake rises from the water and snatches it from him. Gilgamesh recognizes a fundamental truth: Misery and sorrow are unavoidable parts of human life. Resigned to his losses, Gilgamesh returns to Uruk. Finally, he dies at a ripe old age, honored and mourned by his fellow citizens.

A second form of written document that marks the evolution to a more complex society is the legal code. Archaeologists discovered at Ur fragments of a legal code that dates to the twenty-first century B.C.E., and legal systems must have already existed even before this. Legal systems remained crucial for all Mesopotamian urban societies. The post-Sumerian code of the

The stele of vultures. This limestone tablet, or stele, depicts in bas relief Lagash's victory over Umma, in about 2450 B.C.E. Some 3600 of the enemy were slaughtered by King Eannatum of Lagash and his soldiers, who are seen here marching into battle. (*Louvre, Paris*)

The Code of Hammurabi

As states grew larger, formal, written law codes replaced the customs and traditions of the farming villages. Around 1750 B.C.E., the Babylonian ruler Hammurabi conquered Mesopotamia, uniting the warring city-states under his rule. To reinforce that unity he set forth a code of laws that covered many aspects of daily life and business.

The code provides a marvelous insight into the problems and nature of urban life at the time. It provides a detailed insight into property rights and urban crime, as well as the social and gender divisions in the society. Finally, it gives students and scholars some idea of how justice was perceived in Hammurabi's world. The code is a list of 282 laws; only some of them are represented here. In the original list, they are not particularly organized so we have reorganized them here.

Property

Property laws incorporated laws of consumer protection for house buyers, boat renters, contractors for services. In one case, a brutal punishment for faulty workmanship indicates that common people, too, were viewed as commodities. The sins of the fathers may be taken out on the children. Some of the specific laws included:

- If [the collapse of a building] has caused the death of a son of the owner of the house, they shall put the son of that builder to death.
- If any one steal the property of a temple or of the court, he shall be put to death, and also the one who receives the stolen thing from him shall be put to death.

Stele of Hammurabi, from Susa, Iran, c. 1760 B.C.E. Hammurabi, the great king of Babylon, is the first known ruler to have created a detailed legal code; other societies with unknown rulers developed much earlier codes. On this commemorative stone slab, he is shown receiving the Babylonian laws from the sun-god Shamash. The laws themselves are inscribed below on the stele. (Louvre, Paris)

Urban Crime

Many laws provided for punishment for robbery and for personal injuries. Many of the latter varied according to the social class of the person inflicting the injury as well as the person suffering the injury:

- If any one is committing a robbery and is caught, then he shall be but to death.
- If a gentleman has destroyed the eye of a member of the aristocracy, they shall destroy his eye.
- If he has broken another gentleman's bone, they shall break his bone.
- If he has destroyed the eye of a commoner or broken the bone of a commoner, he shall pay one mina of silver.
- If he has destroyed the eye of a gentleman's slave or broken the bone of a gentleman's slave, he shall pay one half his value.

Gender in Ancient Babylonia

Numerous laws governed marriage, bride price, dowry, adultery, and incest. Although women did own the dowries given them, their rights of ownership were limited. Marriage is presented in large part as a commercial transaction, in which the groom's family pays a bride-price to the bride's father, while the bride's father gives her a dowry. Childlessness is grounds for divorce but the husband must return his wife's dowry. Behavioral restraints in marriage are unequal: if the husband "has been going out and disparaging her greatly," the wife may leave, taking her dowry; if the wife is "a gadabout, thus neglecting her house (and) humiliating her husband," he may have her drowned.

- If a woman quarrels with her husband, and says: "You are not congenial to me," the reasons for her prejudice must be presented. If she is guiltless, and there is not fault on her part, but he leaves and neglects her, then no guilt attaches to this woman, she shall take her dowry and go back to her father's house.
- If she is not innocent, but leaves her husband, and ruins her house, neglecting her husband, this woman shall be cast into the water.

HOW DO WE KNOW?

Some Modern Critiques of Early Urbanization

Sumer's city-states had many accomplishments to their credit, but some historians have pointed out that their civilization came at the cost of increasing warfare, growing social inequality, and the oppression of women. These modern critiques reflect the importance of studying the past in order to understand the present more fully.

Politically, each of the major cities of Sumer was also a state, ruling over the contiguous agricultural areas and often in conflict with neighboring city-states. The artwork of the city-states often depicts royal armies, military expeditions, conquests, and a general appreciation, even an exaltation, of warfare. The fighting seems to have been frequent, and the main combatants were the largest of the city-states. Battles were fought hand-to-hand and also from donkey-drawn chariots.

The warfare was especially destructive because the kings and soldiers believed that they were upholding the honor of their gods. When cities are sacred, conflicts between them mean holy war, fights to the finish. The "Lamentation over the Destruction of Ur," which was addressed to Ningal, goddess of the Ekushnugal Temple, describes that city's utter destruction after the Elamites sacked it, exiled its ruler, and destroyed the temple c. 1950 B.C.E.:

> After your city had been destroyed, how now can you exist!
> After your house had been destroyed, how has your heart led you on!
> Your city has become a strange city; how now can you exist!
> Your house has become a house of tears, how has your heart led you on!
> Your city which has been made into ruins—you are no longer its mistress!
> Your righteous house which has been given over to the pickax—you no longer inhabit it,
> Your people have been led to slaughter—you are no longer their queen. (Kramer, The Sumerians, p. 142)

Lewis Mumford, one of the most respected modern commentators on the history of cities, regarded this early union of power, religion, and continuous warfare as a permanent curse of urban life. He wrote, "even when it is disguised by seemingly hardheaded economic demands, uniformly turns into a religious performance; nothing less than a wholesale ritual sacrifice."

The first Sumerian cities fostered division of labor into occupational categories. We have noted the roles of kings, priests, landowners, architects, scribes, long-distance traders, local merchants, artisans, cooks, farmers, soldiers, laborers—the whole panoply of occupational categories absent in villages but forming the backbone of a sophisticated urban economy and society. Priests and kings held great wealth and power and largely controlled the means of production, but it is not clear that they formed an exclusive category of "haves" versus "have nots." The spectrum seems to have been more varied, including a substantial group of middle classes. But there is, nevertheless, much evidence of the enormous power of the aristocracy.

At the bottom of the economic hierarchy were slaves. People entered slavery in four ways: some were captured in battle; some were sentenced to slavery as punishment for crimes; some sold themselves (or their family members) into slavery to cope with poverty and debt; and some were born into slavery. We have no record of the number or proportion of slaves in the general population of Sumer and its cities. The law codes' extensive regulations of slaves and slavery suggest, however, their widespread existence.

The socialist philosopher-historian Karl Marx argued that the rise of cities brought about "the division of the population into two great classes." Marx's formulation was too stark, ignoring the broad range of classes in the city, but he does force us to think about the class structure in our own cities, including the relationship between rich and poor, and its implications for the health of society.

Finally, the transformation of society from a rural, egalitarian, kin base to an urban, hierarchical, territorial, and class base may have provided the entering wedge for the subordination of women. Some women in Sumer had great power. Several seem to have held independent high administrative posts in major temples controlling large land holdings. The high status of Lady Pu-abi (c. 2500 B.C.E.) was revealed in her burial. She was adorned with gold and buried with several other bodies, presumably servants, suggesting a woman of high rank, perhaps a queen. Shagshag, wife of King Uruinimgina (also known as Urukagina), c. 2300 B.C.E., held great powers in the name of her husband.

Women in Sumer generally had certain basic rights, including the rights to hold property, engage in business, and serve as legal witness. Nevertheless, it is clear that women's legal rights were limited by their husbands. Even powerful women were often only pawns in the power struggles of men.

Feminist historian Gerda Lerner argues that before the evolution of city-states, with their warfare and hierarchical class structures, the status of women had been more equal. Kin groups had been the basic economic units of society, and women had had more power in these family groups than they did in the city-states that displaced them. Lerner claims that inequalities between men and women are not products of unchanging biological differences. Rather, the inequalities have been created by humans—and they can be altered by humans.

- What did Lewis Mumford learn about warfare from his study of ancient cities? How did this affect his view of modern warfare?
- What did Karl Marx learn about class relations from his study of ancient cities? How did this affect his view of class relationships in modern (nineteenth-century) cities?
- What did Gerda Lerner learn about gender relationships from her study of ancient cities?

Babylonian King Hammurabi, formulated *c.* 1750 B.C.E. (but rediscovered only in 1901–2), seems to have been built on the earlier concepts.

The modern critiques of Mumford, Marx, and Lerner remind us how seriously the past, and our preconceptions—or myths—about it, have influenced our thinking. They urge us to rethink the past in order to redirect our future from repeating some terrible mistake—for example, making warfare into a religious obligation, isolating city from countryside, establishing oppressive class distinctions, and institutionalizing patriarchal suppression of women.

Underlying these warnings, however, is yet another myth. The pre-urban agricultural village, it is widely believed, was more egalitarian, less warlike, and more integrated into nature. We do not know if this was so. Pre-urban villagers produced no written records, and their artifactual remains are thin, inconclusive, and subject to widely divergent interpretation. Scholars draw many of their conclusions concerning pre-urban life from observing isolated groups in today's world, such as the !Kung people of the African Kalahari desert of a generation ago. But here, too, both observations and interpretations differ.

THE FIRST CITIES
WHAT DIFFERENCE DO THEY MAKE?

We do know that early cities facilitated some of the accomplishments that people then and now considered vitally important: increases in human population (a questionable asset under today's conditions, but not then); economic growth; effective organization for common tasks; creative breakthroughs in technology, art, and, perhaps most significantly, in writing and literature; the inauguration of a rule of law; and the formation of a non-kin-based community with a sense of purpose and humanity.

They did not always succeed, however. The city-states could not work out a system of government and regulation that would enable them to live in peace. At the same time powerful and vulnerable, oscillating between psalms of victory and lamentations of defeat, they seemed to fall into one of two painful alternatives: inter-state warfare or conquest by imperial rulers. Their shortcomings cost them dearly. As long as each political entity was a law unto itself—as were the city-states of Sumer, pre-Han China, classical Greece, medieval Europe, and of India during much of its history—war was the likely result. This problem of warfare among competitive states persists to our own day, although the scale has escalated from the city-state to the independent nation-state.

The evolution of the large, complex city implies the evolution of a state capable of organizing and administering it. In aristocratic and monarchical Sumer, much depended on the disposition of the king. Even the legendary Gilgamesh ended his royal career devoted to, and honored by, his people, but his career had begun differently. The epic tells us that in Gilgamesh's youth, "the men of Uruk muttered in their houses" about his faults:

> his arrogance has no bounds by day or night. No son is left with his father, for
> Gilgamesh takes them all, even the children … his lust leaves no virgin to her lover,
> neither the warrior's daughter nor the wife of the noble.

They realized that it should have been different—"The king should be a shepherd to his people"—but they apparently had to submit. The only recourse they saw was muttering in their houses and praying to their gods.

This question of the proper organization of the state became the key question of urbanization. Two thousand years after Gilgamesh might have ruled—and two thousand years before our own day—in the city-states of ancient Greece, the philosopher Aristotle summed up the issue:

> When several villages are united in a single complete community, large enough to be nearly or quite self-sufficing, the state comes into existence, originating in the bare needs of life, and continuing in existence for the sake of a good life ... man is by nature a political animal [a creature of the polis or city-state] ... the association of living beings who have this sense makes a family and a state ... justice is the bond of men in states, for the administration of justice, which is the determination of what is just, is the principle of order in political society.

From the time of Sumer, the political questions, the questions of how to organize and administer the **polis** or city-state to achieve a good life, have been central to the process of urbanization. In Sumer the answers depended on the edicts of the king and the priests. In the next two chapters, we shall see how these questions and answers evolved in other primary cities and city-states around the world.

polis The city-state of ancient Greece. It comprised not only the town, which was usually walled with a citadel (acropolis) and a market place (**agora**), but also the surrounding countryside. Ideally, the *polis* comprised the citizens, who could reside in either town or country.

Review Questions

- Why did people create the earliest cities? Note that several of the reasons that are usually given are disputed. Which of the reasons seems to be most convincing to you? Why?
- Why did Sumer become the site of the first cities? Why did the Nile and Indus valleys become the next two sites?
- What is the connection between the creation of the first cities and the creation of the first states?
- What was the importance of writing to the creation of the first cities? Please consider all the uses of writing in your answer. Later we will encounter cities that had no writing. What do you think that they will lack in comparison to the cities of the fertile crescent that did have it?
- When ancient cities were defeated in warfare, lamentations were often composed over their loss. What was the nature of the losses that were lamented?
- In what ways are our modern cities like the ancient cities of Sumer? In what ways are they different?

Suggested Readings

PRINCIPAL SOURCES

Fagan, Brian M. *People of the Earth: An Introduction to World Prehistory* (Upper Saddle River, NJ: Prentice Hall, 2000). Excellent general textbook introduction to prehistory.

Gilgamesh, The Epic of, trans. and ed. N.K. Sandars (Harmondsworth, Middlesex: Penguin Books, 1972). Very readable edition of the classic epic.

Kramer, Samuel Noah. *History Begins at Sumer: Thirty-Nine "Firsts" in Recorded History* (New York: Doubleday and Co., Inc., 1959). One of the greatest scholars in the field presents Sumer's pioneering accomplishments.

Kramer, Samuel Noah. *The Sumerians: Their History, Culture, and Character* (Chicago, IL:

University of Chicago Press, 1963). A masterful, accessible summary by one of the greatest scholars in the field.

Lerner, Gerda. *The Creation of Patriarchy* (New York: Oxford University Press, 1986). Lerner brings a critical feminist perspective to studies of Sumer, although many scholars have criticized her scholarship here; her main field is American history.

Past Worlds: The Times Atlas of Archaeology (Maplewood, NJ: Hammond Inc., 1988). Excellent for its maps, pictures, time lines, brief discussions, and generally attractive presentation. Slightly dated.

Pritchard, James B., ed. *Ancient Near Eastern Texts Relating to the Old Testament* (Princeton, NJ:

Princeton University Press, 3rd ed. with supplement, 1969). Excellent compendium of primary source materials. Presentation is very scholarly and painstaking.

Roaf, Michael. *Cultural Atlas of Mesopotamia and the Ancient Near East* (New York: Facts on File, 1996). Another in the excellent Facts on File series, copiously supplied with maps and pictures as well as readable, scholarly, introductory text materials.

ADDITIONAL SOURCES

Aristotle. *Basic Works*, trans. and ed. Richard McKeon. (New York: Random House, 1941). Aristotle's *Politics*, in particular, presents very early, very thoughtful concepts of urban governance.

Bairoch, Paul. *Cities and Economic Development: From the Dawn of History to the Present*, trans. Christopher Braider (Chicago, IL: University of Chicago Press, 1988). Comprehensive presentation of the importance of cities in economic history. Europe is the main focus.

Cohen, Mark. *The Food Crisis in Prehistory* (New Haven, CT: Yale University Press, 1977). Asks why people began to settle into farming and continue it.

Hudson, M. and B. Levine, *Privatization in the Ancient Near East and the Classical World* (Cambridge, MA: Peabody Museum of Archaeology and Ethnology, 1996).

Marx, Karl. *Capital: A Critique of Political Economy*, trans. Ben Foulkes (New York: Vintage Books, 1977). Writing at the height of the industrial revolution in Western Europe, Marx explores the history of urbanization as part of his larger work.

Marx, Karl and Friedrich Engels. *The German Ideology* (New York: International Publishers, 1939). Includes a critical examination of the capitalist city.

Moore, Andrew M.T. "The Development of Neolithic Societies in the Near East," *Advances in World Archaeology*. Vol. 4., ed. Fred Wendorf and Angela E. Close (Orlando, FL: Academic Press, Inc., 1985). A fine, brief introduction.

Mumford, Lewis. *The City in History* (New York: Harcourt, Brace and World, Inc., 1961). The master examines the history of all cities, urging his readers to see the importance of social life and community as the key to the good city.

Oppenheim, A. Leo. *Ancient Mesopotamia. Portrait of a Dead Civilization* (Chicago, IL: University of Chicago Press, 1964). Scholarly articles covering a wide range of aspects of early Mesopotamian civilization, especially Babylonians and Assyrians.

Postgate, Nicholas. *The First Empires* (Oxford: Elsevier Phaidon, 1977). Comparative presentation of early city-states that preceded empires.

Redman, Charles L. *The Rise of Civilization: From Early Farmers to Urban Society in the Ancient Near East* (San Francisco, CA: W.H. Freeman and Co., 1978). Anthropologist's analysis of the basis of early cities, stresses ecological conditions and irrigation.

Sjoberg, Gideon. "The Origin and Evolution of Cities," *Scientific American*. (September 1965), 19–27. A sociologist, Sjoberg stresses the differences in political life and technological sophistication between pre- and post-industrial cities in this general introduction.

Wheatley, Paul. *The Pivot of the Four Quarters* (Chicago, IL: Aldine Publishing Company, 1971). For this enormously learned geographer, early cities were primarily concerned with their relationship with the gods and the cosmos, as reflected in their structure and leadership.

Woolley, C. Leonard. *Excavations at Ur* (London: Ernest Benn, Ltd., 1954). One of the greatest of the excavators describes his expeditions and their results. Well illustrated and very accessible.

◉ World History Documents CD-ROM

1.1 Lugal Sulgi: Role Model for Mesopotamian Royalty
1.2 The Nippur Murder Trial and the "Silent Wife"
1.4 *The Epic of Gilgamesh*

RIVER VALLEY CIVILIZATIONS

THE NILE AND THE INDUS 7000 B.C.E.–750 B.C.E.

KEY TOPICS
- Egypt: the Gift of the Nile
- The Indus Valley Civilization and its Mysteries

Two other urban civilizations flanked Mesopotamia: the Nile valley to the southwest and the Indus valley to the southeast. Scholarly opinion is divided as to whether these two cultures learned to build cities and states from the Mesopotamian example or invented them independently. Whatever the source of inspiration, the peoples of these three river valleys created separate and distinct patterns of urbanization and political life.

In Mesopotamia's Tigris–Euphrates valley, development of the physical city and the institutional state went hand-in-hand. In the Nile valley, the creation of the Egyptian state had greater significance than the growth of individual cities. In the Indus valley, we have extensive archaeological information on the cities, but we know next to nothing about the formation of the state. Until scholars learn to decipher the script and language of the Indus civilization, our knowledge of its institutional development will remain limited.

EGYPT: THE GIFT OF THE NILE

Egypt has often been called the "Gift of the Nile" because outside the valley of that great river the country is a desert. An immense, flowing ribbon of water, the Nile spans the length of the country from south to north, branching finally into an extraordinary delta as it approaches the Mediterranean. The river provides natural irrigation along its banks and invites further man-made irrigation to extend its waters to the east and west. Unlike the unpredictable floods of Mesopotamia, from prehistoric times until the mid-twentieth century C.E. a more-or-less predictable flood of water poured through the Nile valley every July, August, and September, not only providing natural irrigation, but also carrying nutrient-rich silt that fertilized the land. (As we shall see in Chapter 18, twentieth-century dam construction brought more control over the annual flood, and hydroelectric power, but also stopped the flow of silt.) Meanwhile, increased population filled in marshlands adjacent to the river bed.

The vital significance of the Nile appears in this 4000-year-old Egyptian poem:

> Food bringer, rich with provisions,
>   himself the author of all his good things,
> Awe-striking master, yet sweet the aromas rising about him
>   and, how he satisfies when he returns! –
> Transforming the dust to pastures for cattle,
>   bringing forth for each god his sacrifice.
> He dwells in the underworld, yet heaven and earth are his to command,
>   and the Two Lands he takes for his own,
> Filling the storerooms, heaping the grainsheds,
>   giving his gifts to the poor. (Foster, p. 113)

Opposite **Mohenjo-Daro, present-day Pakistan, c. 2600–1800 B.C.E.** When it flourished, Mohenjo-Daro held some 40,000 inhabitants in its carefully laid-out precincts and it continued to exercise an attraction for thousands of years. The round *stupa*, or burial mound, that now crowns the settlement was built as part of a Buddhist monastery some two thousand years after Mohenjo-Daro had ceased being a city.

AT A GLANCE : ANCIENT EGYPT

DATE	POLITICAL	RELIGION AND CULTURE	SOCIAL DEVELOPMENT
4000–3600 B.C.E.	■ Nagada I		
3500 B.C.E.		■ Hieroglyphics in use	■ Villages in Nile valley
3000 B.C.E.	■ Early Dynasty (c. 3000–2700)	■ Ruler of Egypt becoming godlike	■ First use of stone in building
2500 B.C.E.	■ Old Kingdom (c. 2700–2181)	■ Step pyramid at Saqqara ■ Pyramids at Giza, including Great Pyramid (of Khufu)	■ Irrigation programs along Nile
2000 B.C.E.	■ First Intermediate Period (c. 2200–2050) ■ Middle Kingdom (c. 2050–1750) ■ Second Intermediate Period (c. 1750–1550)	■ Golden age of art and craftwork (1991–1786)	■ Social order upset; few monuments built (2181–1991) ■ Country divided into principalities (1786–1567)

hieroglyphs The characters in a writing system based on the use of **pictograms** or **ideograms**. In ancient Egypt, hieroglyphics were largely used for monumental inscriptions. The symbols depict people, animals, and objects, which represent words, syllables, or sounds.

Figurine of bone and ivory, "Nagada I" period, c. 4000–3600 B.C.E. Egypt's rise to a mighty empire had modest roots: a string of loosely affiliated villages lining the Nile. This attractive figurine, whose eyes are inlaid with lapis lazuli, was unearthed from a tomb of this early, predynastic age. (*British Museum, London*)

The desert flanking the Nile valley protected Egypt from external invasion from the east and west; cataracts—precipitous, impassable waterfalls in the river—provided a buffer against Nubia to the south; and the Mediterranean provided a defensible northern border. As a result, for the first half of its 5000 years of recorded history, Egypt was usually ruled by indigenous dynasties. The rule of the kings began about 3100 B.C.E. and continued with few exceptions for nearly 2600 years, an unparalleled stretch of cultural and political continuity. These kings later were called pharaohs during the New Kingdom (see Chapter 5) after the palaces they constructed, and gradually, pharaoh became the generic name of all Egyptian kings.

Monumental structures—like the pyramids and Sphinx at Giza near modern Cairo in the north of Egypt, the temples at Karnak and Thebes in the south, and the pharaohs' tombs nearby in the Valley of the Kings—make clear the wealth, skills, and organizational capacity of ancient Egypt. Nevertheless, we know less about the physical form of Egypt's ancient cities than about those of Mesopotamia. The Nile has washed away many ancient structures and eroded their foundations. On the other hand, we know much more about the Egyptian state than almost any other. The written records of ancient Egypt, once they were deciphered, provided the institutional information.

Earliest Egypt: Before the Kings

In Egypt, as in Mesopotamia, agriculture provided the underlying sustenance for city life. By 12,000 B.C.E., residents of Nubia and Upper Egypt were using stones to grind local wild grasses into food, and by 8000 B.C.E. flour was being prepared from their seeds. (Upper or southern Egypt and Lower or northern Egypt derived their names from the flow of the Nile River. The river rises south of Egypt and flows north to the Mediterranean Sea.) By 6000 B.C.E. the first traces appear of the cultivation of wheat and barley, grasses and cereals, and of the domestication of sheep and goats. To the west, the Sahara was becoming drier and some of its inhabitants may have moved to the Nile valley bringing with them more advanced methods of cultivation.

By 3600 B.C.E. a string of villages lined the Nile River, at intervals of every 20 miles or so. The village economies were based on cereal agriculture. They were linked by trade along the river, although, since they mostly produced the same basic food-stuffs, trade was not central to their economy. The villages show little evidence of social stratification. These settlements characterized the "Nagada I" period (*c.* 3500 B.C.E.).

Gradually, population increased, as did the size of villages, and by 3300 B.C.E. the first walled towns appeared in the upper Nile, at Nagada and Hierakonpolis. Tombs for rulers and elites were built nearby, suggesting new levels of social stratification.

The Written Record

Writing began early in Egypt, almost simultaneously with ancient Mesopotamia, about 3500–3000 B.C.E. Egyptians may have learned the concept of writing from Mesopotamia, but in place of cuneiform, they developed their own script based on tiny pictographs called **hieroglyphs**, a word based on the Greek for "sacred carvings." Some scholars believe that hiero-glyphic writing in Egypt was completely independent of the Mesopotamian invention, and possibly preceded it.

Scribes, an important and highly regarded occupational group in ancient Egypt as in Mesopotamia, later invented two shorthand transcriptions of hieroglyphs, first, hieratic script, later, the even more abbreviated form of demotic script. They wrote on stone tablets, on limestone flakes, on pottery, and on papyrus—a kind of paper—made by laying crossways the inner piths of the stalk of papyrus plants and pressing them until they formed into sheets.

As in Mesopotamia, some of the earliest Egyptian writing is notation for business and administration. Over the millennia it grew into a rich literature, including chronological lists of kings, religious inscriptions, spells to protect the dead, biogra-phies and autobiographies, stories, wisdom texts of moral instruction, love poems, hymns to gods, prayers, and mathe-matical, astronomical, and medical texts. From this literature, scholars have reconstructed a substantial picture of the history of Egypt.

For the earliest 500 to 1000 years, until about 2400 B.C.E., the written records are thin. They do, however, provide a list of *nomes*, or administrative districts, suggesting the geographical organization of the Egyptian state as early as 2900 B.C.E. They also provide lists of the earliest kings of Egypt.

King lists written on stone about 2400 B.C.E., and on papyrus about 1200 B.C.E., combined with lists compiled by the Greek historian Manetho in the third century B.C.E., give the names of the entire sequence of Egypt's kings from about 3100 B.C.E, all

Land of the Nile. Stretching over 1000 miles along the Nile River, ancient Egyptian civilization depended on a strong government. The kingdom was divided into Lower and Upper Egypt, and further subdivided into *nomes* (tax districts).

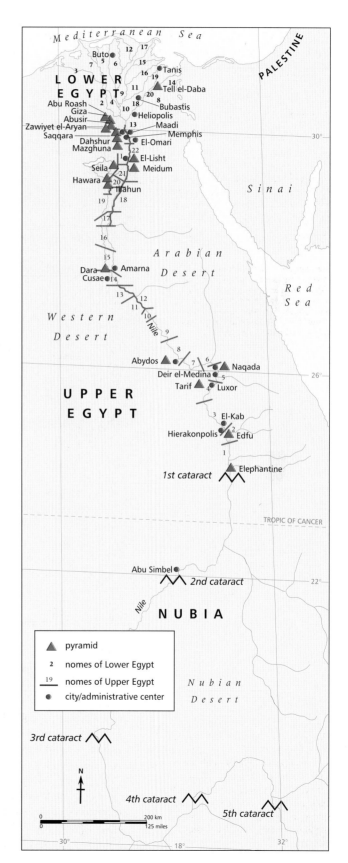

the way through the Persian conquest in 525 B.C.E. and the victory of Alexander the Great in 332 B.C.E. After that event we have many sources for constructing the basic chronology of Egypt's political history.

Unification and the Rule of the Kings

The king lists, records of the *nomes* (administrative units) of Upper Egypt, and inscriptions and designs on pottery suggest strongly that Egyptian national life and history began with the unification of the kingdom about the year 3100 B.C.E. This unity was forged from the diversity of peoples who came to inhabit Egypt. Semites from the desert to the east, Phoenicians from the sea coast, Blacks from Nubia and the heart of Africa, and Europeans from across the Mediterranean immigrated and amalgamated into a common national stock. They recognized each other and intermarried without apparent reference to race or ethnicity. Paintings of ancient Egyptians show them sometimes pale in color, sometimes black, very often red, perhaps reflecting their mixed ethnicity. Many historians believe that the colors may also be related to gender—women, mostly relegated to household chores, were usually depicted as pale; men, assumed to be outside of the household, were often painted much darker.

Who first unified the upper and lower Nile into the single kingdom of Egypt? Most king lists mention Menes, but some cite Narmer. Some scholars believe that these were two different names for the same person. The event took place about 3100 B.C.E., but tombs of kings excavated at Abydos predate it by about 200 years. Perhaps these were kings of local regions, or perhaps unification was actually accomplished under a "predynastic" king before Menes, or unification may have been a long process and "Menes" simply symbolizes the whole process.

As Egypt became unified, the kings grew steadily more powerful, finally gaining a position as gods, who lived on earth and were responsible for maintaining *ma'at*, justice and order, throughout the kingdom. They were responsible for keeping the forces of nature balanced and for inviting the annual flooding of the Nile River that made Egyptian agriculture possible. An increase in monumental tombs and funerary objects suggests an increasing hierarchy and an uneven distribution of wealth, two common characteristics of state building. A more or less unified artistic style in both pottery and architecture after that time mirrors the unification of Egyptian politics. This era, called the Early Dynastic period, lasted about 400 years, from *c.* 3100 to *c.* 2686 B.C.E. By this time Egypt exhibited the cultural complexity associated with early civilizations, including a national religious ideology and the centralized control of political administration and even of artistic productivity.

The **"Rosetta Stone," ancient Egyptian, 196 B.C.E.** The inscription is transcribed in three different forms: hieroglyphics, a later Egyptian shorthand called "demotic," and Greek. By comparing the three, scholars were able to decipher the ancient hieroglyphs. (*British Museum, London*)

The Gods, the Unification of Egypt, and the Afterlife

Egyptian religious mythology gives great prominence to the political unification of the country. The triumph of Isis, Osiris, and their son Horus—three of Egypt's most important gods—over disorder and evil represents in mythic terms the significance of the unification of Egypt. Osiris represented order (*ma'at*) and virtue; his brother, Seth, disorder and evil. Seth tricked Osiris into lying down inside a box that was to be his coffin, sealed it, and set it floating down the Nile. Isis, Osiris' wife and sister, found the box and brought Osiris back home. Seth, however, re-captured the body and cut it into fourteen separate pieces, which he scattered throughout Egypt and the eastern Mediterranean. Isis tracked down all the parts, brought them back to Egypt, re-attached them, and briefly restored life to them. From the restored body, she conceived a son, Horus. Horus defeated Seth in battle and gave Osiris new life, this time as king and principal god of the underworld. In some representations Horus and Seth are seen in reconciliation, binding Egypt into a single state. Seth represents southern areas around Nagada and Thebes; Horus, less specifically, represents the north.

Horus became the patron god of the Egyptian kings, the first Egyptian god to be worshiped nationally. In painting and sculpture he is often depicted in the form of a falcon, sometimes perched on the head or shoulder of the king, sometimes atop the double crown that symbolized the unity of Upper and Lower Egypt. The kings

HOW DO WE KNOW?

Written Texts and Archaeological Excavations

Few modern Egyptian scholars had been interested in recovering the ancient past of their country, apparently because its pharaonic, polytheistic culture did not connect with their own monotheistic Islamic and Christian cultures. In Europe, however, scholars and researchers were attempting to understand the early history of this civilization. The interest in this scholarship was so great that when Napoleon Bonaparte led a French military invasion of Egypt in 1798 he brought along with his armies a contingent of scientists, literary scholars, and artists.

In 1799 one of Napoleon's officers working at a fort on the western, Rosetta branch of the Nile delta, discovered a large, black, basalt stone slab. This "Rosetta Stone" (see p. 68) carried an inscription from the year 196 B.C.E. issued by the Greek ruler of Egypt and written in three languages: the most ancient Egyptian script, hieroglyphs, at the top; demotic Egyptian, a simplified script based on the hieroglyphs, in the middle; and Greek at the bottom. The French

dispatched copies of the inscription back to Europe, where scholars were working on deciphering the Egyptian hieroglyphs. Until this time, their efforts had not been successful because they mistakenly believed that all of the hieroglyphs were ideographs, a kind of picture writing in which each symbol stood for a word or a concept. Now, however, a young French scholar of linguistics, Jean-François Champollion (1790–1832), using the Rosetta Stone to compare the ancient Egyptian forms with the Greek, which he knew, recognized that hieroglyphic writing combined several forms—ideographic, syllabic, and alphabetic. Once he made this discovery, he was prepared to crack the script. In 1822, after fourteen years of research, which he had begun at eighteen, he published the results of his work.

Champollion himself made only one trip to Egypt, in 1828–9. With an Italian student, he produced the first systematic survey of the history and geography of Egypt as revealed in its monuments and inscriptions. He earned the informal title of "Father of Egyptology," and in 1831 a chair in Egyptian history and archaeology was created for him at the College de France.

Archaeological excavations, primarily in search of monumental objects, began in 1858, although tomb robbing and the theft of ancient artifacts had been continuous from earliest times. The annual expeditions of British Egyptologist W.M. Flinders Petrie, beginning in 1880, introduced more scientific archaeological studies of Egypt and of Nubia, immediately to the south. By about 1900 scholars had identified the basic outlines of Egypt's history from 3600 B.C.E. to their own time. Working with both text and artifacts they could produce a doubly-rich historical record.

- Why were modern Egyptian scholars no longer interested in the ancient past of their own country? Do you find this surprising? Why or why not?
- The earliest known alphabetic writing dates to about 1900 B.C.E. Its use in place of hieroglyphic writing has been described as revolutionary, "comparable to the invention of the printing press much later." Why?
- How do written accounts and monumental architecture complement each other in giving us a more complete understanding of ancient civilizations?

believed that if they lived proper, ordered lives they would be united with Osiris after they died.

This belief in the afterlife inspired the mummification of the dead—at least of those who could afford it—and the construction of Egypt's most spectacular monuments, the pyramids, as a final resting place for the dead kings until their soul and life force emerged for their journey through the afterworld. After passing through the ordeal of judgment in the next world, the souls might also revisit these elaborate tombs.

At first believed to be a preserve of the kings alone, later the afterworld was seen as a destination also for important officials and, still later, for a larger proportion of the population. The belief in a utopian afterlife seems to have made optimists out of most Egyptians. Even those who may not have shared in this belief were urged to enjoy life in this world to the full, as this 3100-year-old song suggests:

> All who come into being as flesh
> pass on, and have since God walked the earth;
> and young blood mounts to their places.
> The busy fluttering souls and bright transfigured spirits
> who people the world below
> and those who shine in the stars with Orion,
> They built their mansions, they built their tombs—
> And all men rest in the grave. . . .
> So, seize the day! Hold holiday!
> Be unwearied, unceasing, alive,
> you and your own true love;
> Let not your heart be troubled during your sojourn on earth,
> but seize the day as it passes! . . .
> Grieve not your heart, whatever comes;
> let sweet music play before you;
> Recall not the evil, loathsome to God,
> but have joy, joy, joy, and pleasure!
>
> (Foster, pp. 181–2)

GODS OF THE EGYPTIANS

Belief in one god (Aten, represented by the sun) was promoted during the reign of Akhenaten (r. 1353–1335), when the capital of Egypt was moved from Thebes to Amarna. At other times, the Egyptians worshiped a pantheon, whose main gods and goddesses are listed below:

Amon-Re	The universal god, depicted as ram-headed
Anubis	Jackal-headed god of funerals, son of Nephthus and Osiris. He supervised the weighing of souls at judgment
Hathor	The goddess of love, represented either as a woman with a cow's horns or as a cow with a solar disk
Horus	The falcon-headed god of light
Isis	Goddess of magic and fertility; sister and wife of Osiris; as mother of Horus, she was mother goddess of all Egypt
Nephthus	Sister of Isis, this funerary goddess befriended dead mortals at judgment
Osiris	Ruler of the underworld and chief judge of the dead, Osiris is normally depicted mummified or as a bearded man wearing the crown of Upper Egypt and with a flail and crook in his hands
Ptah	Magician and patron of the arts and crafts, Ptah later became judge of the dead. Normally represented as a mummy or holding an ankh (looped cross)
Seth	The god of evil and the murderer of Osiris
Thoth	The supreme scribe, depicted either with the head of an ibis or as a dog-headed baboon

Cities of the Dead

Burial sites, shrines, and sometimes towns were based on the need to provide final, collective, resting places for the bodies of the most prominent Egyptians. As early as 3100 B.C.E., kings and members of the court were buried at Abydos, a 300-mile boat trip upriver, south of Memphis. Their tombs, called *mastabas*, were made of sun-baked mud bricks, with flat roof and sloping sides, designed to last forever. Inside the structure were the food, weapons, tools, and furniture that the king might need in the afterlife. His body was mummified and buried in an underground chamber. Abydos later became the center for the worship of Osiris.

Another group of high officials was buried in the north, close to Memphis, near Saqqara, in mud-brick tombs. Their funerary goods included copper objects and stone vessels. Over the centuries a series of burial sites grew up nearby, stretching some 45 miles along the Nile. At the beginning of the second dynasty, 2770 B.C.E., the royal necropolis, the city of tombs, was sited at Saqqara itself.

Stele from the tomb of Djet (the "Serpent King"), Abydos, c. 3000 B.C.E. Horus, in the form of a falcon, is pictured above a serpent representing Djet, the "Serpent King," and the façade of a palace (*pharaoh* literally meant "great house" or "palace"). (*Louvre, Paris*)

Women of elite families were usually buried in simple pyramid tombs, but recently the more elaborate pyramid-tomb of Ankhesenpepi II was uncovered at Saqqara and explored. She was the wife of two Egyptian kings—first Pepi I (*c.* 2289–*c.* 2255), then his nephew Merenra (*c.* 2255–*c.* 2246)—and the mother of a third, Pepi II (*c.* 2246–*c.* 2152). Although her name means "she lives for Pepi," Ankhesenpepi II seems to have gained power also for herself . She is the first female known to have a magical, biographical, hieroglyphic text—a format found frequently in the tombs of kings—inscribed in her tomb to facilitate her access to the afterworld.

Adjacent to the burial sites were the towns of the workers who built the increasingly elaborate tombs for the kings and aristocrats. Several of these workers' towns have been excavated, most notably Deir el-Medina, in the south of Egypt, near the Valley of the Queens, opposite Thebes, although it dates to a later period. Mummification was also carried out in workshops in these towns.

The Growth of Cities

Unlike Mesopotamia, Egypt has almost no existing record of independent city-states. In Egypt, thousands of small, generally self-sufficient communities seem to have persisted under a national monarchy, but within a generally decentralized economy for the local production and consumption of food and basic commodities. The village economies were based on cereal agriculture, and they were linked by trade along the river, although, since they mostly produced the same basic foodstuffs, these villages traded only a little among themselves. They reveal little evidence of social stratification. These settlements characterized the "Nagada I" period (c. 3500 B.C.E.). Gradually, among the villages along the Nile, somewhat larger market towns must have grown up. Because administration, business, and transportation require some centralization, some of the villages began to house those functions. These selected villages, spaced strategically at larger intervals in the landscape, grew into larger settlements, and perhaps even into full-fledged cities.

In early dynastic Egypt, the siting of the administrative headquarters of the *nomes* would have given just such a boost to the towns in which they were located. Some settlements also hosted additional functions, including irrigation control and religious observance. The consolidation of villages into towns and towns into cities marks the beginning of "Nagada II" culture (c. 3300 B.C.E.) and the development of the site of Hierakonpolis along the Nile in Upper Egypt illustrates the process. Stretching for three miles along the banks of the Nile, Hierakonpolis ("Nekhen" in ancient Egyptian) did not have the form of a compact city, but it exercised many urban functions.

Archaeological excavations showed that the population of Hierakonpolis grew from a few hundred in 3800 B.C.E. to 10,500 by 3500 B.C.E. At least two cemeteries served the city, one for common people, another for the wealthier traders and more powerful administrators.

What precipitated the population growth, occupational specialization, and social hierarchy? One possibility is that local leaders introduced and implemented irrigation systems that saved agriculture and even enriched it during a period of severe drought. These changes enhanced the economy of the region and created subsequent growth and change. Indeed, Hierakonpolis seems to have been the capital from which King Menes, or Narmer, unified Egypt. The Narmer palette, a slate tablet illustrating this unification, was discovered here.

Political/administrative leaders continued to create irrigation systems along the Nile. These projects began in Old Kingdom Egypt, c. 2700–2200 B.C.E. They were expanded with the development of the Fayyum Lake region and the transfer of population to it during the Middle Kingdom, c. 2050–1750 B.C.E. New technology arose during the New Kingdom, c. 1550–1050 B.C.E., with the beginning of shaduf irrigation, which used buckets attached to a huge, turning wheel to dip into the river, bringing up water that then poured into man-made irrigation channels. The general predictability of the Nile's constant flow and annual flood meant that Egypt had fewer problems with its water supply than did Mesopotamia, but even here control of water resources influenced the formation of cities and the state.

Egypt's cities, like those of other early civilizations, had a religious base as well as an administrative one. Hierakonpolis, for example, housed a temple and prominent tombs as well as a ruler's palace. Perhaps the city flourished because its temple community and worship became especially attractive to surrounding villages. The combination of irrigation, administration, and worship built the city.

Earlier archaeological reports seemed to suggest that after unification under a single king Egyptian cities were not usually walled. The central government may have suppressed the kind of inter-city warfare that characterized Mesopotamia, rendering defensive walls unnecessary. Also, although invasions occurred from time

The Palette of King Narmer, c. 3200 B.C.E. This slate palette, used for ritual purposes, shows the power of King Narmer, who had just united Upper and Lower Egypt. In the top register, Narmer (left) inspects the bodies of dead enemies (right); at the bottom, the strength of the king is symbolized by the bull shown destroying the walls of a city. (*Egyptian Museum, Cairo*)

Wooden model of a sailing boat from Meir, Egypt, c. 2000 B.C.E. The presence of a mummy on board this Twelfth-dynasty model boat indicates that it was intended as a funerary artifact, used to symbolize the journey of the dead into the afterlife. We can glean important details about early Egyptian vessels— from the large central sail to the figures on deck, representing the pilot, the owner, and sailors working the halyards. (*British Museum, London*)

to time and required defensive precautions, the desert to the east and west of the Nile valley usually provided an adequate natural shield.

More recent excavations, however, question this view of open cities. The walls of some cities have been uncovered, and archaeologists are beginning to suspect that walls of other cities may have been removed and the materials used for other purposes. Excavations at El-Kab, across the Nile from Hierakonpolis, revealed a city enclosed in a wall, 1600 feet square, dating to 1788–1580 B.C.E. This wall, in turn, seems to have intersected a more primitive town, of circular or oval shape surrounded by a double wall.

Largest of all the Nile towns, presumably, were the political capitals, first in the north at Memphis, later in the south at Thebes, and occasionally at other locations. Most of the spectacular temples and monuments at Thebes today, for example, date only to the eighteenth and nineteenth dynasties, 1550–1196 B.C.E. This was a period of substantial population growth in Egypt, rising from 1.5 million to between 2.5 and 5 million people. Archaeologists cannot excavate below these monuments to reach older urban levels, and the residential buildings of that older city are probably below the current water table. They are irrecoverable.

Other types of cities completed the urban network. Trade cities, especially in the Nile delta, linked Egypt internally and to the outside world. As early as 3650 B.C.E., the city of Buto in the Nile delta near the Mediterranean served as the port of landing for shipping from the Levant (modern Syria, Lebanon, and Israel) and Mesopotamia. Further south but still in the delta, at El-Omari, many goods imported from the Mediterranean coast have also been found. In these ports, goods must have been off-loaded for transshipment in smaller boats or by donkey caravans to Maadi, near Memphis. Maadi was the trade link between the delta and Upper Egypt.

Monumental Architecture of the Old Kingdom: Pyramids and Fortresses

As in Mesopotamia, the increasing power of the Egyptian state inspired the construction of monumental architecture. In the third dynasty, 2649–2575 B.C.E., King Djoser's architect, Imhotep, elaborated the rather simple mastaba into a series of stepped stone slabs, one on top of the next, built to house the king's remains at death. This forerunner of the pyramids demonstrated an astonishing royal control over labor, finances, and architectural and building techniques. The administrative organization and economic productivity of government continued to increase, until, by the end of this dynasty, Egypt had extended its control of the Nile valley as far south as the first cataract, its classical southern frontier. At the same time, Egypt's artistic genius continued to develop the sculpture of its tombs and the sophistication of its script. The Old Kingdom had been established and Old Kingdom rulers spent fortunes constructing pyramid tombs to preserve their mummified bodies for the afterlife.

Within a half century, architects realized the beauty of filling in the steps of the multi-storied mastaba to create the simple, elegant, triangular form of the true pyramid. Kings of the fourth dynasty, 2575–2465 B.C.E., supervised the construction of the greatest pyramids in history. The 450-foot-high pyramids of Khufu (Cheops; r. 2551–2528 B.C.E.) and of Khefren (r. 2520–2494 B.C.E.), and the smaller pyramid of Menkaure (r. 2490–2472 B.C.E.), all arranged in a cluster with the Sphinx, proclaim creative vision, organizational power, and aspirations to immortality. The sculpture, reliefs, paintings, and inscriptions in the pyramids and in the many tombs of court officials and other powerful men of the time express the highest artistic achievements of the era. Tombs of queens and officials are situated in proximity to the kings' pyramids in accordance with their inhabitants' power and rank. (Tomb robbing was, however, so common that we have no idea how long any of them lay undisturbed in their tombs.) Following Menkaure, whose pyramid was already smaller than those of Khufu and Khefren, the building of such enormous monuments diminished, which may reflect a lessening of Egyptian power generally.

The Great Sphinx and the Pyramid of Khefren, Giza. The greatest of all the pyramids, the burial tombs of the kings, are at Giza, near modern Cairo, and date to around 2600–2500 B.C.E. The face of the sphinx—a mythological creature with a lion's body and a human head—is thought to be a likeness of King Khafre, who ruled Egypt some time after 2600 B.C.E.

Step pyramid of King Djoser, Saqqara, Egypt, c. 2700 B.C.E. This step pyramid, forerunner to the ancient architectural masterpieces at Giza, developed from the *mastaba*, a low rectangular benchlike structure that covered a grave. The purpose of this early pyramid, effectively a 200-foot-high ziggurat without a temple on top, was to mark and protect the underground tomb chamber 90 feet below.

Cutaway of Great Pyramid of Khufu, Giza. The rectangular plan and stepped form of Djoser's pyramid were gradually modified to become the colossal, smooth-faced monuments with which we are familiar. This pyramid is some 450 feet high on a square base occupying 13 acres and was built using forced labor.

Roof support

Outside covered in white limestone

Air shaft or the soul's exit

Unused burial chamber

King's chamber

Main shaft

Mortuary temple

Stepped construction can be clearly seen here

Causeway from the Nile

Original burial chamber

Escape shaft

At the height of the Old Kingdom, Egyptian trading, raiding, and mining initiatives began to extend southward into Nubia, above the first cataract of the Nile. These expeditions were protected and consolidated through the construction of the Buhen fortress at the second cataract, probably at about the time of the building of the great pyramids. That fortress, too, seems to have declined after about 2400 B.C.E., although trading and raiding expeditions continued. All of these architectural, spiritual, political, and military accomplishments date to the millennium we now call the pre-dynastic, early dynastic, and Old Kingdom.

The Disintegration of the Old Kingdom

Central authority weakened and provincial officials in each *nome*, called nomarchs, asserted their powers. They collected and kept the taxes for themselves, and their private armies ruled locally. Based on the size and records of cemeteries, the death rates seem to have increased at this time. Famine was prevalent. Apparently the Nile did not reach optimal flood heights for agriculture, and weak rulers could not create adequate irrigation works to compensate for the shortfall.

In 2181 B.C.E. the Old Kingdom fell. At first, several nomarchs held independent local power. Then two separate centers began to stand out in the contest for power: Herakleopolis in the north and Thebes in the south. This period of disunity, known as the First Intermediate Period, lasted for about a century.

SOURCE

The Egyptian Book of the Dead and the "Negative Confession"

Many ancient Egyptian texts concern the attempt to secure eternal happiness after death. A selection from these mortuary texts has been collected by modern scholars and titled The Book of the Dead. *A segment of these texts presents the "negative confession" of a deceased person in the court of judgment of the dead protesting his innocence of evil and crime:*

I have not committed evil against men.
I have not mistreated cattle.
I have not committed sin in the place of truth.
I have not tried to learn that which is not meant for mortals.
I have not blasphemed a god.
I have not done violence to a poor man.
I have not done that which the gods abominate.
I have not defamed a slave to his superiors.
I have not made anyone sick.
I have not made anyone weep.
I have not killed.
I have given no order to a killer.
I have not caused anyone suffering.
I have not cut down on the food or income in the temples.
I have not damaged the bread of the gods.
I have not taken the loaves of the blessed dead.
I have not had sexual relations with a boy.
I have not defiled myself.
I have neither increased or diminished the grain measure.
I have not diminished the measure of land.
I have not falsified the land records.
I have not added to the weight of the balance.
I have not weakened the plummet of the scales.

I have not taken milk from the mouths of children.
I have not driven cattle away from their pasturage.
I have not snared the birds of the gods.
I have not caught fish in their marshes.
I have not held up the water in its season.
I have not built a dam against running water.
I have not quenched a fire at its proper time.
I have not neglected the appointed times and their meat-offerings.
I have not driven away the cattle of the god's property.
I have not stopped a god on his procession.
I am pure: I am pure: I am pure: I am pure. …

Behold me—I have come to you without sin, without guilt, without evil, without a witness against me, without one against whom I have taken action. I live on truth, and I eat of truth. I have done that which men said and that with which gods are content. I have satisfied a god with that which he desires. I have given bread to the hungry, water to the thirsty, clothing to the naked, and a ferry-boat to him who was marooned. I have provided divine offerings for the gods and mortuary offerings for the dead. So rescue me, you; protect me, you.

(Pritchard, pp. 34–6)

SOURCE

The Autobiography of Si-nuhe and the Glorification of Court and Capital

Si-nuhe, a high-ranking official and royal attendant, fled from the Egyptian court when a new king came to the throne. Apparently he feared that his loyalty to the new ruler was suspect and his safety endangered. A skilled warrior and administrator, even in self-imposed exile he earned high positions in several Asian kingdoms. In Si-nuhe's old age, however, the king of Egypt and his family invited him back to the court so that he could spend his last years "at home" in comfort and be buried with appropriate rites.

This personal tale of reconciliation is almost certainly based on reality. Its glorification of Egypt over other countries, of the city over the countryside, and especially of the royal capital and the royal court represented the beliefs of the Egyptian elite. This account of the career and the moral personality of a court official, and of the excellence of the reigning king is an outstanding example of the autobiographies inscribed in ancient Egyptian tombs. Si-nuhe's story became one of the most popular classics of Egyptian literature, and manuscripts that include it began to appear about 1800 B.C.E. and continued to about 1000 B.C.E. One modern scholar refers to it as "the crown jewel of Middle Egyptian literature." (Lichtheim, I, 11)

Si-nuhe returned to the capital, then in the city of Lisht, near the Faiyum Lake.

So I went forth from the midst of the inner chambers, with the royal children giving me their hands. Thereafter we went to the Great Double Door. I was put into the house of a royal son, in which were splendid things. A cool room was in it, and images of the horizon. Costly things of the Treasury were in it. Clothing of royal linen, myrrh, and prime oil of the king and of the nobles whom he loves were in every room. Every butler was busy at his duties. Years were made to pass away from my body. I was plucked, and my hair was combed. A load of dirt was given to the desert, and my clothes to the Sand-Crossers. I was clad in fine linen and anointed with prime oil.

I slept on a bed. I gave up the sand to them who are in it, and wood oil to him who is anointed with it. I was given a house which had a garden, which had been in the possession of a courtier. Many craftsmen built it, and all its woodwork was newly restored. Meals were brought to me from the palace three or four times a day, apart from that which the royal children gave, without ceasing a moment.

There was constructed for me a pyramid-tomb of stone in the midst of the pyramid-tombs. The stone-masons who hew a pyramid-tomb took over its ground-area. The outline-draftsmen designed in it; the chief sculptors carved in it; and the overseers of works who are in the necropolis made it their concern. Its necessary materials were made from all the outfittings which are placed at a tomb-shaft. Mortuary priests were given to me. There was made for me a necropolis garden, with fields in it formerly extending as far as the town, like that which is done for a chief courtier. My statue was overlaid with gold, and its skirt was of fine gold. It was his majesty who had it made. There is no poor man for whom like has been done.

(Pritchard, pp. 18–22)

The Rise and Fall of the Middle Kingdom

Finally, about 2050 B.C.E., King Mentuhotpe of Thebes defeated his rivals in the north and reunited the kingdom, initiating the Middle Kingdom, *c.* 2050–1750 B.C.E. Trade revived, with two patterns achieving special prominence. One was the local caravan trade in spices, resins, and minerals between the Nile Delta and Palestine, across the northern Sinai desert. The other—the long distance trade carried by ship throughout the eastern Mediterranean—was commanded by royal families to bring in timber and resins, lapis lazuli, copper, and ivory for official construction and for adornment.

The fine arts and literature flourished. Among the finest literary gems of the Middle Kingdom was "The Autobiography of Si-nuhe," the narrative of a high-ranking court official who went into self-exile until, in his old age, he was recalled to the capital and awarded great honors. The story reveals not only the intrigues of the court and the royal family, but also the sharp contrast between the life of the elites of the capital and the harsh rigors of the surrounding desert.

Most important, the Middle Kingdom saw the state develop more organization and power than ever before. Egypt was administered efficiently and spread its power into Nubia and into the Middle East more aggressively than before. Egypt became an empire, ruling over more distant, foreign peoples. From this time onward, Egypt's fate would be intertwined with the fate of its empire. The Middle Kingdom ended in part because the Nubians drove out their Egyptian conquerors, but more importantly because of the invasions of the Hyksos, or "princes of the foreign lands," who spoke a Semitic language and probably came from the north and east of the Sinai desert. The New Kingdom (*c.* 1550–1050 B.C.E.) would rise again as an empire by once again asserting its authority over Nubia and over large regions of Palestine and adjoining segments of Syria. These issues of empire and its significance for Egypt are discussed in Chapter 5, "Dawn of the Empires." One fascinating event from the New Kingdom period—the construction and destruction of the city Akhetaten—belongs here, however, because it highlights the symbolic importance of capital cities.

Akhetaten, Capital City of King Akhenaten

Sandstone statue of Akhenaten, Amarna period. Akhenaten worshiped one God, the god of the setting sun, which was represented by a winged solar disk. (*Egyptian Museum, Cairo*)

Modern excavations at Amarna on the east bank of the Nile unearthed the ruins of an ancient Egyptian capital that owed its entire existence to the idiosyncratic vision of one ruler—King Amenhotep IV, better known as Akhenaten.

Within a few years of coming to the throne, King Amenhotep IV (r. 1353–35 B.C.E.) challenged the order of ancient Egypt by adopting a new monotheistic religion. Instead of worshiping a whole pantheon of gods, he offered his devotion to a single deity—Aten, god of the solar disk (or sun). Amenhotep appointed himself mediator between his people and the god. Symbolically, he abandoned his official dynastic name in favor of Akhenaten ("he who serves Aten"). The name of Amon, principal god of the old religion, was swiftly erased from inscriptions throughout Egypt, as were the words "all gods" in certain texts.

To bolster the new order and escape the power of the hostile priesthood, Akhenaten moved his capital 200 miles north from the established center of Thebes to an untouched site in the desert. The city that he built was named Akhetaten ("horizon of Aten"; present-day Amarna) and it was here that Akhenaten, the Great Royal Wife Queen Nefertiti, and their six daughters practiced the new religion.

The eccentricity of Akhetaten's ruler was reflected in the city's architecture, sculpture, and wall painting. Solid statements of eternity gave way to a freedom of expression that emphasized the here-and-now. Aten was worshiped in an open temple that ushered in the sun's rays rather than in the dark, austere sanctuary usually designated for worship. Residential buildings included spacious villas with large gardens and pools to house wealthy officials. In artistic expression, solemnity gave way to an unprecedented liveliness and invention. Artists showed the royal parents playing with their children or dandling them on their laps. Curious depictions of Akhenaten's drooping jaw and misshapen body capture his individuality, marking a departure from the highly stylized representations of previous pharaohs.

Akhenaten's isolated position, both geographically and intellectually, threatened the stability of Egypt's empire. When he died, Akhenaten's successors abandoned Akhetaten and later razed it to the ground. The capital returned to Thebes where the old religious and political order could resume. Subsequent pharaohs so hated Akhenaten's religion that they dismantled the city and used its building materials on other sites.

From this discussion of the varied cities of the Nile Valley with their abundance of archaeological and textual materials, we move eastward about 2500 miles to explore the earliest cities of the Indus valley with their very different structures and materials.

THE INDUS VALLEY CIVILIZATION AND ITS MYSTERIES

The civilizations of ancient Mesopotamia and Egypt never disappeared completely. Hebrew and Greek accounts and surviving artifacts, like the spectacular pyramids, kept them alive in popular imagination. Intermittent discoveries of tombs, and the thefts of their contents, added concrete evidence. Nevertheless, systematic excavating of sites and deciphering of texts did not occur in modern times until the mid-1800s.

The civilization of the Indus valley was lost almost entirely, so it is no surprise that its excavation did not begin until the 1920s and that its script is still not deciphered. The accidental discovery and systematic exploration of this long-lived and far-flung civilization is one of the great stories of mid- and late-twentieth-century archaeology.

The Roots of the Indus Valley Civilization

In 1856, the British colonial rulers of India were supervising construction of a railway between Lahore and Karachi, along the Indus River valley. As they progressed, construction workers discovered hundreds of thousands of old fire-baked bricks in the semi-desert area and used them to lay the road bed. Scattered among the old bricks, workers discovered steatite stone seals marked with artistic designs. These seals and bricks were the first clue that the area had once been home to an ancient and unknown civilization. Some were passed along to officers of the Archaeological Survey of India, and they took note of them, but formal systematic excavations began only in 1920 when John Marshall, Director General of the Archaeological Survey, commissioned his staff to survey a huge mound that rose above the desert floor where the seals had been found.

These excavations soon revealed a 4500-year-old city. They named the site Harappa, and archaeologists often used this name to designate the entire Indus valley civilization. Two years later, R. D. Banerji, an Indian officer of the Survey, recognized and began to excavate a twin site 200 miles to the southwest, later named Mohenjo-Daro, "Hill of the Dead." The two cities had many urban design and architectural features in common. Both were about 3 miles in circumference, large enough to hold populations of 40,000. With these two excavations, an urban civilization that had been lost for thousands of years was uncovered.

Before these excavations, scholars had believed that the civilization of India had begun in the Ganges valley with the arrival of Aryan immigrants from Persia or central

AT A GLANCE : THE INDUS VALLEY

DATE	POLITICAL	RELIGION AND CULTURE	SOCIAL DEVELOPMENT
7000 B.C.E.			■ Traces of settlements; trade with Mesopotamia
3000 B.C.E.			■ Cotton cultivated
2500 B.C.E.	■ Height of Harappan civilization in northern India (2500–2000)		■ Cities of Harappa and Mohenjo-Daro
2000 B.C.E.	■ Collapse of Harappan civilization (2000–1900)	■ Evidence of decline in standards of architecture	
1500 B.C.E.	■ Immigration of Aryans into India (c. 1250)		
1000 B.C.E.	■ Aryan immigrants reach west Ganges valley (c. 1000) and build first cities (c. 750)		■ Iron tools used to clear Ganges valley for agriculture (c. 1000)

Asia *c.* 1250 B.C.E. and the construction of their first cities *c.* 700 B.C.E. The discovery of the Harappan cities pushed the origin of Indian civilization back an additional 1500 years and located it in an entirely different ecological zone.

As archaeologists explored more widely in the Indus valley, they found that civilization there began earlier, lasted longer, and spread farther than anyone had suspected. Some of its roots seem to lie in a settlement called Mehrgarh, in the foothills of the Bolan Pass, that has yielded early settlement artifacts going back to 7000 B.C.E. and, with ever-increasing sophistication, coming forward to 2500–2000 B.C.E. At its height, it had major settlements as far west as the Makran Coast toward Iran, north and east into Punjab and even the upper Ganges River valley, and south and east to Dholavira in Kutch, and on to the banks of the Narmada River.

What was the relationship between this civilization and that of Mesopotamia? At first, many scholars assumed that the Indus valley people learned the art of city-building from the Sumerians and other peoples of Mesopotamia. But later scholars have argued that Harappa was not a derivative of Mesopotamia but had grown up independently. It is conceivable that the civilizations of both Mesopotamia and the Indus had a common ancestor in the settlements of the hills and mountains between them.

Written records, the key that re-opened the civilizations of ancient Mesopotamia and Egypt, are scarce in the Indus valley. The only written materials so far discovered are seal inscriptions that give only limited information. In addition, scholars have not succeeded in their attempts to decipher the script; they differ substantially in their interpretations. As a result, our understanding of Indus civilization is limited. Artifactual remains give a good representation of the physical cities and settlements, but not of their institutions. Moreover, while we can make educated guesses about the function and meaning of the remaining artifacts and physical structures from our own perspective, we do not have the words of the Harappans themselves to explain their own understanding of their civilization.

The Design and Construction of Well-planned Cities

Archaeological evidence to date reveals an urban civilization with its roots beginning as early as 7000 B.C.E. in simple settlements, such as Mehrgarh in the hills. Over the millennia, people moved down into the plains and river valley. At first, they may have moved into the forested river valley only in the colder months, herding their flocks of sheep and cattle, including the humped zebu, back to the hills for the summer. Over time they may have decided to farm the river-watered alluvial lands of the valley. They began to trade by boat along the Indus and even down the Indus into the Arabian Sea and, further, into the Persian Gulf and up the Tigris and Euphrates into Mesopotamia. Goods from the Indus valley have been found in Mesopotamia and vice versa.

Crafts and the Arts. Crafts of the Indus valley included pottery making, dyeing, metal working in bronze, and bead making. Bead materials included jade from the Himalayas, lapis lazuli from Afghanistan, turquoise from Persia, amethyst from Mewar in India, and steatite, which was found locally. All of these items suggest an active interregional trade. Small sculptures in stone, terra cotta, and bronze appear to represent priestly or governmental officials, dancing girls, and, perhaps, mother goddesses. Since there are no accompanying texts to explain exact identities, these can only be guesses. Dice and small sculptures of bullock carts were probably used as toys and games. The first known use of cotton as a fiber for weaving textiles occurred in the Indus valley, introducing one of India's and the world's most enduring and important crops and crafts.

For an interactive version of this map, go to: http://www.prenhall.com/spodek/map3.2

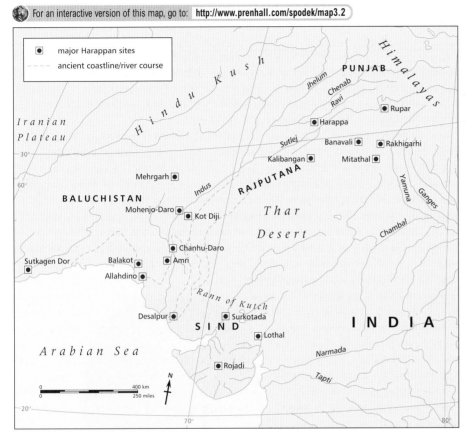

Legend:
- ● major Harappan sites
- ‒ ‒ ‒ ancient coastline/river course

Cities of the Indus. Confined to the north and west by mountains, and to the east by desert, the Indus valley had, by 2500 B.C.E., developed a sophisticated urban culture based on individual walled cities, sharing common patterns of urban design. In terms of geographical extent this civilization was the largest in the world in its time.

Planned Cities. With an area of 150 acres, and about 40,000 inhabitants, Mohenjo-Daro was a thriving Indus city. Excavations reveal a raised citadel area, containing ceremonial and administrative buildings, and a residential quarter centered on boulevards about 45 feet wide, with grid-patterned streets, an underground sewerage and drainage system, and a range of brick-built dwellings.

Carefully Planned Cities.

By about 2500 B.C.E., a thriving civilization encompassing 1000 known sites reached its apex and maintained it for about 500 years. Each of the two largest settlements, Harappa and Mohenjo-Daro, had a core area of about 3 miles in circumference, while Mohenjo-Daro also had a suburb—residential or industrial—about a mile away. Each city accommodated about 40,000 people.

Both cities share similar features of design. To the north is a citadel, or raised area; to the south is a lower town. In Mohenjo-Daro, the citadel is built on an architectural platform about 45 feet above the plain, and it measures 1400 by 450 feet. On the summit was a vast, communal bath 8 feet deep and 23 by 29 feet in area. Numerous cubicles—perhaps small, individual baths—flanked it. Adjacent to the large bath was a huge open space, identified as a granary, where food was stored safe from possible flood. Other spaces may have been used for public meetings. Fortified walls mark the southeast corner, and it appears that the entire citadel was walled.

The lower city was laid out in a gridiron, with the main streets about 45 feet wide. Here were the private houses, almost every one with its own well, bathing space, and toilet, consisting of a brick seat over a drainage area. Brick-lined drains flushed by water carried liquid and solid waste to sumps, where it would be collected and carted away, probably to fertilize the nearby fields.

The town plan was orderly and regular. Even the prefabricated, fire-baked bricks were uniform in size and shape. A uniform system of weights and measures was also employed throughout.

Excavation of the two largest cities has now reached severe limits. The city of Harappa was vandalized for thousands of years before, as well as during, the railroad construction, and few artifacts remain to be discovered. Mohenjo-Daro sits on a high water table, and any deeper excavation threatens to flood the site. It is impossible to dig down to the foundation level of the city.

Further exploration of Mohenjo-Daro's surface, however, continues to yield fascinating results. A recent survey revealed an outlying segment of Mohenjo-Daro about a mile away from the known city. Was it part of an industrial area or a residential suburb? It is impossible to determine. The discovery, however, identifies Mohenjo-Daro as a larger city than Harappa. Perhaps it was the capital city of the civilization. The regularity of plan and construction suggests a government with great organizational and bureaucratic capacity, but no truly monumental architecture clearly marks the presence of a palace or temple, and there is little sign of social stratification in the plan or buildings. Those burials that have been discovered are regular, with the heads pointing to the north, and with some grave goods, such as pots of food and water, small amounts of jewelry, simple mirrors, and some cosmetics. These were not the extravagant royal burials of Egypt or even of Mesopotamia.

In more recent years additional Indus valley cities have been discovered and excavated, giving a fuller idea of the immense geographical extent of this civilization. The new excavations generally confirm the

Limestone dancing figure from Harappa, c. 2300–1750 B.C.E. This dancing figure displays a grasp of three-dimensional movement and vitality rare in the arts until much later periods. Human sculptures in contemporary Mesopotamia and Egypt are by contrast symbols of pure power, either immutable ideals of divinity or semidivine kingship. Indeed, this Harappan accomplishment is so extraordinary that some scholars have cast doubt on its early date. (*National Museum of India, New Delhi*)

Limestone bust from Mohenjo-Daro, c. 2300–1750 B.C.E. This half-figure with horizontal slits for eyes, flat thick lips, and fringes of beard is thought to have represented a priest or shaman because of the way the robe is hung over its left shoulder. Despite its monumental appearance, the figure is only 7 inches high. (*National Museum of Pakistan, Karachi*)

urban design patterns of the earlier finds, but they add some new elements. The excavations at Dholavira, in Kutch, India, for example, begun in the late 1980s, revealed immense, ornamented gates at the principal entrances to the city and playing fields in the area between upper and lower cities. Dholavira was not located on a river, but in the elevated center of a small region that may have formed an island during the monsoon, when water levels around it were highest. Huge cisterns were cut into the rock of the upper city for collecting rain water in this extremely arid area. Dholavira also demonstrates a stark contrast between the relatively spacious quarters of the upper city and the more modest accommodations of the lower. Among the 20,000 artifacts uncovered, however, the extraordinary extremes of wealth and poverty of Egypt and Mesopotamia do not appear.

Questions of Interpretation. Interpretations of Indus valley artifacts stress the apparent classlessness of the society, its equality, efficiency, and public conveniences. Some interpreters view these qualities negatively, equating them with oppressively rigid governments and drab lives. While some scholars emphasize that the Harappans apparently survived and prospered for centuries, others argue that the cities changed little over long periods of time and lacked the dynamism of the cities in Mesopotamia and Egypt. With no contemporary literature to guide us, interpretation of what is found is in the eyes, and the value system, of the beholder.

We also do not know if this uniform, planned civilization had a single capital city, or several regional capitals, or no centralized political system at all. We see careful planning in the urban forms, but we do not know if the Indus valley civilization developed urban institutions for governance, trade, religion, or worship, much less the quality of any such institutions. While Egypt had a state but, perhaps, few cities, the Indus valley had cities but no clearly delineated state. Indeed, some scholars argue that the Indus valley did not create state structures at all. Was it like Egypt before unification or after unification? Was it like Mesopotamia, with numerous city-states all participating in a single general culture? All three suggestions have been made.

Until the Harappan language is deciphered, its civilization will remain mysterious: How was it organized? Why did it disperse? How did it move eastward? In what ways did it enrich its successor, the Aryan civilization of the Ganges River valley?

Legacies of the Harappan Civilization

Interchange between the resident Harappans and the invading Aryans produced new, hybrid cultural forms that we know primarily from the Aryan records. Ironically, these records are almost entirely literary and artistic. Reversing the Harappan pattern, the early Aryans have left a treasure of literature, but virtually no architectural or design artifacts.

Four legacies of Harappa stand out. First, the Aryan invaders were a nomadic group, who must have adopted at least some of the arts of settlement and civilization from the already settled residents. Second, as newcomers to the ecological zones of India, the Aryans must also have learned methods of farming and animal husbandry from the Harappans. Later, however, as they migrated eastward into the Ganges valley, they confronted

EARLY SCIENCE AND TECHNOLOGY (7000–1000 B.C.E.)	
7000–6000	Pottery made in Middle East
c. 5500	Copper, gold, and silver worked in Mesopotamia and Egypt
c. 4000–3500	In Asia and Africa, potter's wheel and kiln invented; mud bricks used; spindle developed for spinning; basket-making begins
c. 3500–3000	Plow and cart invented; bronze cast and cuneiform writing developed in Sumer
3100	Reed boats in Egypt and Assyria; appearance of hieroglyphs in Egypt
3000	Cotton cultivated in the Indus valley
c. 2500	Wooden boats used in Egypt; ink and papyrus writing material used
2050	First glass in Mesopotamia
1790	Mathematics and medicine practiced in Babylon
1740	War chariots introduced from Persia to Mesopotamia (and later Egypt)
1370	Alphabetic script used in western Syria
1000	Industrial use of iron in Egypt and Mesopotamia

HOW DO WE KNOW?

The Decline of Harappan Civilization

By about 2000 B.C.E. the architecture of the Indus civilization began to decline. New buildings and repairs to existing structures lacked attention to quality and detail. Residents began to leave the cities and towns along the Indus and to relocate northeastward into the Punjab to towns such as Kalibangan, and southeastward to towns such as Lothal in Gujarat. Meanwhile, newcomers—squatters—seem to have moved into the old cities.

Again, a variety of arguments suggest the reasons for the decline in the cities and the geographical redistribution of their populations. Perhaps the river changed course or became erratic; perhaps the soil became too saline; perhaps the forests were cut down and the topsoil eroded.

An older opinion—that the Indus civilization was destroyed by the invasion of Aryan peoples from somewhere northwest of India—is now less widely held. It rested on Harappan archaeological evidence and Aryan literature. Several sets of skeletal remains in Mohenjo-Daro indicate violent deaths, while Aryan religious texts suggest that the invaders burned and destroyed existing settlements. The Rigveda, one of the earliest and most important of these texts, tells of the destructive power of the god Indra:

> With all-outstripping chariot-wheel, O Indra, thou far-famed, hast overthrown the twice ten kings of men
> With sixty thousand nine and ninety followers …
> Thou goest on from fight to fight intrepidly, destroying castle after castle here with strength. (i, 53)
> … in kindled fire he burnt up all their weapons,
> And made him rich with kine and carts and horses. (ii, 15)

The Aryan god of fire, Agni, is still more fearsome:

> Through fear of you the dark people went away, not giving battle, leaving behind their possessions, when, O Vaisvanara, burning brightly for Puru, and destroying the cities, you did shine. (7.5.3)

Newer archaeological evidence, however, suggests that the decline, de-urbanization, and dispersal of the Indus civilization seem to have preceded the Aryan invasion. Further evidence suggests that the Aryans may not have swept into the region in a single all-conquering expedition, but in a series of smaller waves of immigration. The arrival of the Aryans may have only completed the Harappan decay.

- Why does the formation of new cities such as Kalibangan and Lothal suggest the decline of the Indus Valley civilization?
- Why did scholars once believe that Aryan invasions destroyed the Indus Valley civilization? Why do they now question that belief?
- What is the range of alternative explanations that have been offered? Why are scholars uncertain about the accuracy of these explanations?

a new ecology based on rice cultivation and the use of iron. Here Harappan skills were useless. Third, a three-headed figure frequently appearing in Harappan seals resembles later representations of the Aryan god Shiva. Perhaps an earlier Harappan god may have been adopted and adapted by the Aryans.

Finally, the Aryan caste system, which ranked people at birth according to family occupation, color, and ritual purity, and prescribed the people with whom they may enter into social intercourse and marry, may reflect the need of the Aryans to regulate relationships between themselves and the Harappans. To claim and maintain their own supremacy, the Aryans may have elaborated the social structures of an early caste system and relegated the native inhabitants to permanent low status within it.

The Aryan groups grew increasingly skilled and powerful as they moved east. The first known archaeological evidence of their urban structures dates to about 700 B.C.E. and is found in the Ganges valley. We will read more about it when we analyze the first Indian empire in Chapter 8.

THE CITIES OF THE NILE AND THE INDUS WHAT DIFFERENCE DO THEY MAKE?

To what extent do the river valley civilizations of the Indus and the Nile confirm or alter our views of the significance of cities? They do show us that cities come in very different forms and networks. In Mesopotamia they had appeared as warring city-states. Along the Nile they were part of a single state that was first unified by about

3000 B.C.E., and they continued to be unified through most of the next 2500 years. By 2000 B.C.E. they formed the core of an imperial state with foreign conquests. In the Indus valley we do not know if the cities were independent city-states or part of a unified state; it is apparent, however, from their design and cultural products that they were part of a single cultural unit. In all three areas, then, the city created the state and gave concrete form to its value system.

We also learn of the significance of archaeological and textual study in unearthing and recovering all these early civilizations. To greater or lesser degrees, all had been lost to history for thousands of years before being exhumed by scholars in the nineteenth and twentieth centuries. In the task of reconstruction, written records have been critical to understanding the social structures and value systems of these cities. In both Mesopotamia and the Nile valley, excavations and written records enable us to see clearly the presence of cosmo-magical religious elements, alliances between rulers and priests, extensive temple complexes and, in Egypt, burial complexes as well, and, in both civilizations, extensive specialization of labor and social stratification. But before we take these characteristics as the normal ancestry of city life, we pause at the Indus valley excavations, for here we see no record of such intense occupation with the otherworldly or the afterlife. We see no record of such extensive specialization of labor nor of such extreme stratification—although the more recent excavations at Dholavira exhibit significant differences between the richest and poorest residential areas. We also see little evidence of the levels of artistic accomplishments of Mesopotamia and Egypt. And, of course, without texts, we have no clear record of religious, philosophical, legal, or administrative systems in the Indus valley.

The citadel of Mohenjo-Daro, c. 2300 B.C.E. and later. The citadel at Mohenjo-Daro, a massive, mud-filled embankment that rises 43 feet above the lower city, was discovered by archaeologist Daya Ram Sahni while investigating the second-century C.E. Buddhist stupa (burial mound) that can be seen in the distance. The citadel's summit houses the remains of several impressive structures, of which the most prominent is the so-called Great Bath (foreground).

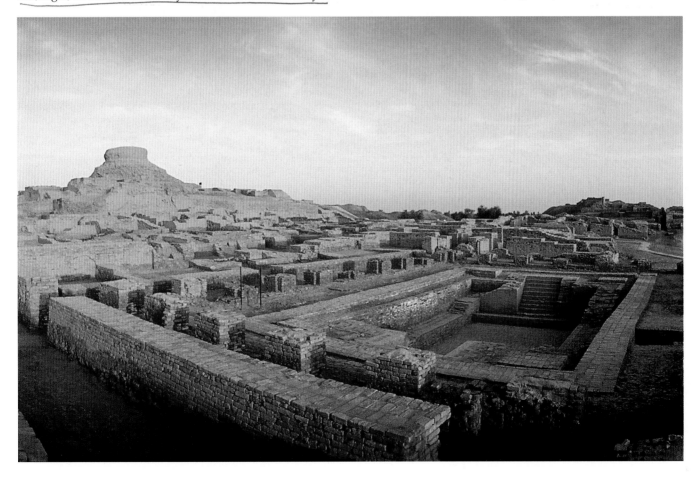

To further explore the global legacy of city and state formation, we now turn to four other regions of indigenous, early city and state formation in places far from those we have studied and far from each other: the Yellow River valley of China, Mesoamerica, South America, and the Niger River valley of West Africa. We are in for some surprises.

Review Questions

- Why is it difficult to determine which Egyptian settlements are cities? Why is Hierakonpolis sometimes called a city, although more often it is designated a very large settlement?
- In what ways did their belief in an afterlife influence the cities that the Egyptians built?
- What can we learn about cities from the autobiographical account by Si-Nuhe of his experience in exile and his return to the capital city of Lisht?
- What kinds of information are available in the written records of Egypt, and of Mesopotamia, that are unavailable for the Indus valley due to the scarcity of written materials and our inability to decipher them?
- In light of the discovery of the likely origins of the Indus valley civilization in the foothills to the west, and of its extensions as far north as Punjab and as far south as the Narmada river, is it appropriate to continue to call it "the Indus valley civilization?" Why or why not? If not, what other name might you give it?
- What is the evidence that scholars use to argue that the Indus valley civilization was more egalitarian, with less class differentiation, than the civilizations of the Nile valley and Mesopotamia?

Suggested Readings

PRINCIPAL SOURCES

Baines, John and Jaromir Malek. *Atlas of Ancient Egypt* (New York: Facts on File Publications, 1980). Another comprehensive and excellent introduction from these publishers, with well-chosen and copious maps, pictures, and charts.

Fagan, Brian. *People of the Earth: An Introduction to World Prehistory* (Upper Saddle River, NJ: Prentice Hall, 10th ed., 2000). The best available textbook introduction to prehistory.

Foster, John L., trans. and ed. *Ancient Egyptian Literature* (Austin, TX: University of Texas Press, 2001). A fine anthology of varied forms of literature, culled from the translator/editors of many previous collections, plus a few new pieces.

Hawass, Z. *Silent Images: Women in Pharaonic Egypt* (New York: Harry N. Abrams, 2000).

Kuhrt, Amélie, *The Ancient Near East, c. 3000–330 B.C.*, 2 vols (New York: Routledge, 1995).

Lesko, Barbara, "Women of Egypt and the Ancient Near East," in *Becoming Visible: Women in European History*, 2nd ed., ed. Renata Bridenthal, Claudia Koonz, and Susan Stuard (Boston, MA: Houghton Mifflin, 1998).

Lesko, Barbara S., ed. *Women's Earliest Records: From Ancient Egypt and Western Asia* (Atlanta, GA: Scholar's Press, 1989).

Manley, Bill. *The Penguin Historical Atlas of Ancient Egypt* (New York: Penguin Books, 1996). Through maps and pictures, an excellent review of Egyptian history from pre-dynastic times through Alexander's conquest. Special sections include coverage of foreign relations and warfare, urbanization, and women. Special emphasis on trade.

Nashat, Guity. " Women in the ancient Middle East," in *Restoring Women to History* (Bloomington, IN: Indiana University Press, 1999).

Past Worlds: The (London) Times Atlas of Archaeology (Maplewood, NJ: Hammond, Inc., 1988). The best available introduction to the archaeological exploration of the world, with attractive and useful maps, pictures, diagrams.

Possehl, Gregory L., ed. *Harappan Civilization: A Recent Perspective* (New Delhi: Oxford University Press and IBH Publishing, 2nd ed., 1993). An comprehensive update of the research.

Spodek, Howard and Doris Meth Srinivasan, eds. *Urban Form and Meaning in South Asia: The*

Shaping of Cities from Prehistoric to Precolonial Times (Washington: National Gallery of Art, 1993). The papers of an international conference by some of the leading archaeologists working in South Asian urbanization including Michael Janson, Jean-Francois Jarrige, Jim Shaffer, and others on the Indus valley civilization and its legacy.

ADDITIONAL SOURCES

Aldred, Cyril. *The Egyptians* (New York: Thames and Hudson, 1986). Useful general introduction, well illustrated.

Allchin, Bridget and Raymond. *The Birth of Indian Civilization: India and Pakistan before 500 B.C.* (Baltimore, MD: Penguin Books, 1968). Now dated, but clear and comprehensive introduction to what we know and how we know it by archaeologists who stress the archaeological record.

Fairservis, Walter. *The Roots of Ancient India* (Chicago, IL: University of Chicago Press, 2nd ed., 1975). An archaeologist's clear and accessible account of his own findings and those of his colleagues up to the date of publication.

Hassan, Fekri A. "The Predynastic of Egypt," *Journal of World Prehistory* II, No. 2 (June 1988), 135–85. Careful and comprehensive account of the research.

Kemp, Barry J. *Ancient Egypt: Anatomy of a Civilization* (London: Routledge, 1989). Stresses what we know about the social structures of ancient Egypt.

Lichtheim, Miriam. *Ancient Egyptian Literature: A Book of Readings* (Berkeley, CA: University of California Press, 3 vols., 1973). Wide-ranging, comprehensive account of 3000 years of literature.

Mumford, Lewis. *The City in History* (New York: Harcourt Brace, and World, 1961). Mumford looks only at cities of the western world, but he is thoughtful, opinionated, and persuasive on what makes a good city.

Noble Wilford, John. "Egypt Carvings Set Earlier Date for Alphabet," *New York Times* (November 14, 1999), A–1, 16. Records the discovery of the earliest alphabetic writing yet discovered.

Possehl, Gregory L., ed. *Ancient Cities of the Indus* (New Delhi: Vikas Publishing, 1979). Scholarly resume of what was known and debated among archaeologists up to the date of publication by an archaeologist practicing primarily in Gujarat.

Pritchard, James B., ed. *Ancient Near Eastern Texts Relating to the Old Testament* (Princeton, NJ: Princeton University Press, 3rd ed. 1969). The most comprehensive and accessible anthology of texts. Presented with full scholarly annotation.

Time-Life Books. *Time Frame 3000–1500: The Age of God-Kings* (Alexandria, VA: Time-Life Books, 1987). Beautifully illustrated, popular presentation of early civilizations including Mesopotamia, Nile valley, and Indus valley.

Wenke, Robert J. "The Evolution of Early Egyptian Civilization: Issues and Evidence," *Journal of World Prehistory* V, No. 1 (September 1991), 279–329. Historiographic study of what we know and how we know.

Wheatley, Paul. *Pivot of the Four Quarters* (Chicago, IL: Aldine Publishing Company, 1971). Very scholarly presentation of the argument that early cities were mostly cosmo-magical cities. Primary focus is China, but total range is global.

Wheeler, Mortimer. *Civilizations of the Indus Valley and Beyond* (London: Thames and Hudson, 1966). Head of the Archaeological Survey of India presents a clear view of its findings in layman's terms.

⊙ World History Documents CD-ROM

1.6 Daily Life in Egypt
1.7 A Humble Farmer Pleads His Own Case: The Workings of Ma'at
1.8 Some Commonsense Advice from the Scribe Any to His Son

A POLYCENTRIC WORLD

CITIES AND STATES IN EAST ASIA, THE AMERICAS, AND WEST AFRICA 1700 B.C.E.–1000 C.E.

KEY TOPICS
- China: The Xia, Shang, and Zhou Dynasties
- The Western Hemisphere: Mesoamerica and South America
- West Africa: The Niger River Valley

This chapter completes the survey of the seven areas of primary urbanization. It covers the four areas that developed primary urbanization somewhat more recently: the Yellow River valley of China; two regions of the western hemisphere—Mesoamerica and the South American Pacific coastal plain with the adjacent Andes Mountains that tower above it; and the Niger River valley of West Africa. The first cities in these regions date from as early as 1700 B.C.E. in China to as late as 400 C.E. in the Niger valley. They include cities that were not in major river valleys as well as some that were. They all show at least some evidence of state formation, long-distance trade, and religious practices. But they include settlements that did not have written languages and records, and therefore require us to base our understanding entirely on the archaeological record. In at least one of them—west Africa—the settlement pattern is so different from urbanization elsewhere that we are asked to stretch our definition of urbanization and challenge our value system in assessing the significance of it.

CHINA: THE XIA, SHANG, AND ZHOU DYNASTIES

The Earliest Villages

As early as the eighth millennium B.C.E., Neolithic pottery decorations marked the transition from hunting and gathering into the culture of farming and village life. This Yangshao culture, first excavated in 1921, was named for the location where it was discovered in China's western Henan province. Among other fascinating finds, in late 1999 archaeologists uncovered a set of tiny flutes carved some 9000 years ago from the wing bones of a large bird. Three thousand years older than the next known playable instruments, from Sumer, one of them is still playable.

The Yangshao lasted to *c.* 2700 B.C.E. Farmers of this era grew millet, wheat, and rice, and domesticated pigs, dogs, goats, and perhaps horses. They lived mostly in river valleys, and the villages were often surrounded with earthen walls for defense. Ban Po is the best excavated village of the Yangshao culture (see Turning Point, p. 36). From archaeological evidence, it appears that individual nuclear families occupied dwellings, but there was also a larger building found that may have housed clan meetings.

Slightly later and slightly to the northeast, a more sophisticated Neolithic culture, the Longshan, grew up. The people of the Longshan made their pottery on wheels, whereas the Yangshao had coiled or molded their pots by hand. The Longshan people domesticated sheep and cattle, which were not seen in Yangshao sites. Longshan graves were dug under their own homes, while the Yangshao had buried their dead in

Opposite **Warrior ear ornament (above), cleaned and reconstructed (tomb 1), and spider bead (below), cleaned and reconstructed (tomb 3), Moche Royal Tombs, Sipan, Peru, 1st–6th centuries C.E.** The spider that captures its prey in webs and later extracts its vital fluids, and the warrior—along with other human, animal, and ornamental grave goods—suggest a culture dominated by powerful warrior priests.

AT A GLANCE : CHINA

DATE	POLITICAL	RELIGION AND CULTURE	SOCIAL DEVELOPMENT
8000 B.C.E.		■ Neolithic decorated pottery	■ Simple Neolithic society established
5000 B.C.E.	■ Yangshao culture in China (5000–2700)	■ Marks on Yangshao pottery possibly writing	■ Penal code; defensive structures round villages
3500 B.C.E.	■ Longshan late Neolithic culture	■ Delicate Longshan ceramics	■ Farming, with domesticated animals
2000 B.C.E.	■ Xia dynasty (2205–1766) ■ Shang dynasty (1766–1122) ■ City of Zhengzhou (c. 1700) ■ Under Shang, bronze vases found in ceremonial burials	■ The "sage kings" in China known from legend; first known use of writing in this area	■ Agricultural progress ■ Cities (by 1700) under control of Shang kings
1100 B.C.E.	■ Zhou dynasty (1100–256)	■ Poetry extant from Zhou period	■ Under Zhou, iron, money, and written laws in use
500 B.C.E.	■ Warring States period (480–222) ■ Qin Dynasty (221–206)	■ Confucius (d. 479) ■ Great Wall of China begun (214) to keep out Xiongnu	■ Crossbow invented (c. 350)
100 B.C.E.		■ Sima Qian (d. 85)	

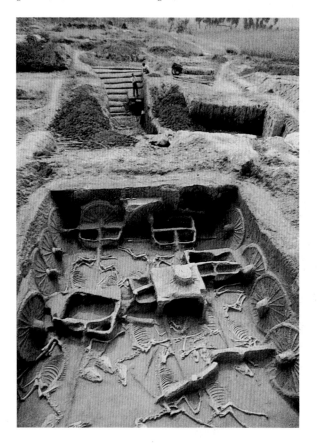

Burial pit, unearthed at Liulihe, Hebei province, Western Zhou period. Evidence for the centrality of ritual in ancient Chinese culture can be found in this tomb, which contains the remains of horses and chariots. These important instruments of rule would have been regarded as valuable offerings to the gods and were thus buried along with their owner.

graveyards far from their villages. Sometimes Longshan funeral urns were cemented into foundation walls, suggesting ancestor worship.

Several hundred miles to the east, somewhat further down the Yellow River in Shandong, and one or two centuries later, yet another branch of Longshan culture developed, with yet another distinct type of pottery, often distinctively reddish-brown and gray in color, quite different from the black pottery of the Longshan of Henan. Although the high points of Yangshao and the western and eastern Longshan cultures appeared at successively later times, they overlapped each other to a considerable extent.

The Henan Longshan culture seems to have been a harsh one. Excavations reveal the burials of victims of killing, some decapitated and showing signs of struggle, suggesting warfare between villages. The defensive walls of pounded earth that encircle some of the villages support this hypothesis, as does the presence of bronze knives.

The Beginnings of State Formation

Out of these struggles among villages, larger political units gradually emerged. Ancient Chinese historical texts tell of three early dynasties—the Xia, the Shang, and the Zhou—that ruled over large regions of China. In its time, each ruled over the most powerful single kingdom among the embattled states of northern China. All were based primarily around the Huang He (Yellow River) valley in north China. State formation may have begun under the Xia, c. 2205–1766 B.C.E., although records are too sparse to recreate its cities and institutions. The archaeological record on urbanization under the Shang, c. 1766–1122 B.C.E., is far more revealing and reliable. The Zhou, c. 1100–256 B.C.E., consolidated both city and state, and left extensive archaeological remains and written records.

None of the three dynasties succeeded in annexing all its enemies and building a single unified empire. That process would come later.

The traditional chronological dating suggests that the states succeeded one another, but recent evidence indicates that there may, in fact, have been considerable overlap. For centuries, they may have coexisted in neighboring regions, with first one, then another, having comparatively greater power and prestige.

By the time of the Shang, if not already in the Xia dynasty, people had founded cities in north China as centers of administration and ritual. State formation was well under way, and cities served as capitals and administrative centers. An urban network ruled the entire dynastic state. Capitals were frequently shifted, suggesting that new rulers wanted to make their mark through new construction, or that confrontations with neighboring, enemy states required strategic redeployments for improving offensive or defensive positions. Kings frequently entrusted the regional cities and their administrations to their blood relatives. It appears that rulers performed productive economic functions for their subjects, especially in water control. The ability to organize huge work gangs to construct irrigation channels and dikes for flood control confirmed their power and status. As a result, the lineages on top lived lives of considerable wealth while those on the lower levels had little, as sharp class differences emerged in the early dynastic states. The cemeteries of different classes were geographically segregated into different neighborhoods within the city and its suburbs, and were of different quality.

Like primary cities in other parts of the world, the Chinese cities were also religious centers, with the kings presiding over rituals as well as administration and warfare. Indeed, the warfare was necessary to supply the human and animal sacrifices that were central to the rituals.

Early Evidence of Writing. One of these early rituals has left us evidence of a crucial development in Chinese civilization—the invention of writing. Oracle bones—bones of birds, animals, and especially the shells of turtles—were inscribed with markings and writings for use in predicting the future. After they were marked, these bones were placed in a fire and tapped lightly with a rod until they began to crack. The cracks were then interpreted by specialists in predicting the future. A poem from the later Zhou dynasty noted the use of oracle bones in deciding the location of a new city:

The plain of Chou was very fertile,
Its celery and sowthistle sweet as rice-cakes.
"Here we will make a start; here take counsel,
Here notch our [turtle]."
It says, "Stop," it says, "Halt.
Build houses here."   (Chang, *Shang Civilization*, pp. 31–2)

Shang China. Centered where the Huang He (Yellow River) enters its floodplain from the mountains of northeast China, the Longshan farming communities of about 2500 B.C.E benefited from rich alluvial soils and extensive metal ore deposits. By 1800 B.C.E. a powerful, highly organized, urban, metal-working culture, the Shang, had developed.

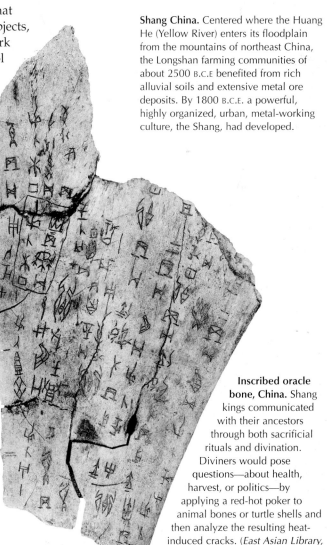

Inscribed oracle bone, China. Shang kings communicated with their ancestors through both sacrificial rituals and divination. Diviners would pose questions—about health, harvest, or politics—by applying a red-hot poker to animal bones or turtle shells and then analyze the resulting heat-induced cracks. (*East Asian Library, Columbia University*)

EARLY CHINESE CULTURE

5000 (B.C.E.)	Rice cultivation, basketry, weaving, use of wooden tools, primitive writing
3000	Domestication of sheep, cattle, water buffalo
2000	Human grave sacrifices
1900	Metal working, class system, domestication of horse
1200	Chariots in warfare

Some of the oracle bone inscriptions confirm the names and approximate dates of Xia and Shang rulers. Other bones suggest that their purpose was to communicate with the gods. The location of the bones and the content of their inscriptions encouraged archaeologists to search further in the north central Chinese plains, near the point where the Yellow River flows out of the mountains for evidence of China's early dynastic period.

Historical Evidence of the Xia Dynasty. Chinese legend long spoke of three ancient dynasties—the Xia, the Shang, and the Zhou. While many written records exist on the Zhou dynasty, historians were often skeptical of the existence of the earlier dynasties until relatively recently. At Erlitou, east of Luoyang, in western Henan, archaeologists found a culture in precisely the areas described by ancient texts as the

HOW DO WE KNOW?

Ancient China

Three kinds of sources provide most of our direct information about early Chinese cities and dynasties: written texts, oracle bones, and artifacts uncovered archaeologically. (Scholars also sometimes take records, such as poetry, from later eras and infer that they may represent earlier conditions as well, as we shall see in the next pages.)

Texts
We have no literary texts remaining from the Xia and Shang dynasties. Some scholars believe that the Zhou dynasty destroyed those that did exist. Much later texts ascribed to the Chinese teacher Confucius (551–479 B.C.E.) refer to the Xia and Shang dynasties, but give little detail. Later, Sima Qian (Ssu-ma Ch'ien; c. 145–85 B.C.E.), court historian of the Han dynasty, wrote the first of China's official historical annals. Sima, who had access to many texts that have not survived, devoted a chapter to the Shang royal house beginning with its legendary founder Xie, who located his capital to a town called Shang, now believed to have been in eastern Henan. Successive rulers moved this capital eight times. Xie's fourteenth successor, Tang, established the hereditary dynasty of Shang. Sima's sources of information were limited, however, and his chapter mostly outlined the genealogy of the rulers, recounted moralistic tales of their rule, and briefly noted their capital cities.

Oracle Bones
A new source of information came to light in the 1890s and early 1900s. Numerous oracle bones—some apparently hidden away for many years, others recently uncovered—appeared in antique markets in China. Over the decades more than 10,000 were discovered, mostly in the central plains of north China. These bones of birds and animals, and shells of turtles, were inscribed with symbolic notations, placed in a fire, and tapped with a rod until they began to crack. Specialists then "read" the marks to predict the future.

Some of the oracle-bone inscriptions confirmed Sima Qian's accounts of early Shang rulers. The location of the bones and the content of their inscriptions encouraged archaeologists to search further for additional oracle bones and other artifacts in the area around the ancient Shang capital of Anyang.

Archaeology
Archaeology was in fashion in China in the 1920s. Peking Man had been discovered at Zhoukoudian, and in the process a new generation of Chinese archaeologists had received on-the-job training. Meanwhile, the new "doubting antiquity" school of Chinese historiography began to question the dating and to challenge the authenticity of many ancient Chinese historical events. In response, the newly established National Research Institute of History and Philology dispatched the young archaeologist Dong Zobin to explore the Anyang region. Dong recommended excavating for oracle bones. These excavations, mostly under the direction of Li Ji, uncovered not only bones but also sites from the Shang dynasty. These led to the discovery of artifacts from earlier eras as well. Scholars understood these to be evidence of the existence of the Xia dynasty. Ancient texts, bronzes, oracle bones, and excavations reinforced one another in recounting parts of ancient China's urbanization and state formation. Civil war in China, beginning in 1927, and war with Japan, beginning in 1937 (see Chapter 20), interrupted excavations until 1950, but since then continuous archaeological research has yielded new understandings.

- What historical evidence enabled the Xia dynasty to emerge from the realm of legend to its current status as the accepted first dynasty of ancient China?
- Politics and fashion as well as scholarly motives influence the kind of research that archaeologists can and do undertake. Please discuss this assertion in terms of the excavation of the sites of early Chinese cities and dynasties.
- What kinds of skills do you think a "reader" of oracle bones must have had to be successful? What would have been considered success in this profession?

site of the legendary Xia dynasty. The pottery at Erlitou seemed intermediate in style and quality between the earlier Longshan and the later Shang. Although the link is not certain, many archaeologists took Erlitou to be representative of the Xia dynasty.

The Xia, like the later Shang and Zhou, seems to have been ruled by specific internal clans, each with its own king. As in many cultures, kingship and kinship were linked. As head of both his biological clan and his geographical realm, the king performed rituals, divinations, and sacrifices; waged war; constructed irrigation and flood control works; and administered his government. The king mediated between the world of the spirits and the world of humans. He was thought to be descended from the god of the spirits who controlled human health, wealth, agriculture, and warfare. The king's assertion of his right to perform sacrifice in any particular place was, in effect, his assertion of his right to rule over that place. Rights over ritual implied rights over land and people.

Another critical task of the ruler was taming the waters of the mighty, and hazardous, Yellow River. China's first settlements had avoided the immediate flood plain of the Yellow River, one of the most treacherous in the world. Its bed filled with the silt from the mountains, the Yellow River has jumped its course twenty-six times in recorded history, wreaking untold devastation. As early as the Longshan culture, people built great levees and canals for flood control, drainage, and irrigation. Chinese legend credits the first success in taming the Yellow River to one of the cultural heroes of ancient history, Yu the Great of the twenty-third century B.C.E., legendary founder of the Xia dynasty. The legend reflects the reality of a royal house's gaining power in part through its ability to organize great gangs of laborers to construct a system of water control.

The Xia dynasty went further with human organization. It assembled armies, built cities, carved jade, cast and worked bronze into both weapons and ritual vessels, created the pictograms that would evolve into Chinese script, and may have designed China's first calendar.

Shang dynasty bronze wine vessel, fourteenth to eleventh century B.C.E. The thousands of Shang bronze vessels that survive today continue to astonish us with their technical mastery and elegance. They testify to the elite's willingness to devote huge quantities of a precious resource to ritual purposes. During times of war, such bronzes were often melted down to produce weapons but once peace resumed, they were recast into ritual objects. (*Historical Museum, Beijing*)

Similarities Among the Three Dynasties. All three of these earliest dynasties, the Xia, Shang, and Zhou, built walled towns. Indeed, in written Chinese the same character, *cheng*, represents both city and city wall. At times these towns were loosely connected to one another, forming a network of rule and trade. At other times, when a single powerful king headed the dynasty, a single capital city predominated. Archaeologists see many similarities among the towns and the political structures of all three dynasties.

In the absence of earlier written records, scholars sometimes use literary evidence from later dynasties as evidence for patterns in the earlier dynasties. For example, in arguing for the supremacy of royal rule during the Shang Dynasty, they find supporting proof from "Pei shan," a poem of the Zhou dynasty:

Everywhere under Heaven
Is no land that is not the king's
To the borders of all those lands
None but is the king's slave. (trans. Arthur Waley)

There is some evidence that women could wield power in the earliest of Chinese dynasties, but it is otherwise difficult to say much about gender relations in ancient China. By the time of the Shang dynasty, however, all evidence points to China as a very patriarchal society wherein women had many fewer options than men.

City and State under the Shang and Zhou

By the time of the Shang dynasty, the ruler directly controlled a growing network of towns. The king ruled from his capital city. He apportioned regional cities to his designated representatives, who were usually blood relatives. These relatives received

SOURCE

The Cosmo-Magical City

In his classic and convincing Pivot of the Four Quarters, *Paul Wheatley argues that ancient Chinese cities, like most ancient cities, began as ritual centers. He calls these cities "cosmo-magical." Archaeological and textual records support this interpretation for China. Consider, for example, this Zhou poem illustrating the siting of a royal capital. The process begins with reading the oracle shell of a tortoise to determine its location and ends with sacrifices to mark the completion of construction:*

Of old Tan-fu the duke
At coming of day galloped his horses,
Going west along the river bank
Till he came to the foot of Mount Ch'i.
Where with the lady Chiang
He came to look for a home.

The plain of Chou was very fertile,
Its celery and sowthistle sweet as rice-cakes.
"Here we will make a start; here take counsel,
Here notch our tortoise."
It says, "Stop," it says, "Halt.
Build houses here."

So he halted, so he stopped,
And left and right
He drew the boundaries of big plots and little,
He opened up the ground, he counted the acres
From west to east;
Everywhere he took his task in hand.

Then he summoned his Master of Works,
Then he summoned his Master of Lands
And made them build houses
Dead straight was the plumb-line,
The planks were lashed to hold the earth;
They made the Hall of Ancestors, very venerable.

They tilted in the earth with a rattling,
They pounded it with a dull thud,
They beat the walls with a loud clang,
They pared and chiselled them with a faint *p'ing, p'ing;*
The hundred cubits all rose;
The drummers could not hold out.

They raised the outer gate;
The outer gate soared high.
They raised the inner gate;
The inner gate was very strong.
They raised the great earth-mound,
Whence excursions of war might start.

The rituals seem to have conferred worldly benefits. Potential enemies fled. The poem continues:

And in the time that followed they did not abate their sacrifices
Did not let fall their high renown;
The oak forests were laid low,
Roads were opened up.
The K'un tribes scampered away;
Oh, how they panted!

Oracle records recognize more than twenty titles of officials grouped into three categories: ministers, generals, and archivists, "but the most important categories of officials insofar as our available data are concerned are the diviners … and the inquirers. . .. Jao Tsung-yi enumerated the activities of as many as 117 diviners and inquirers in the oracle records. Ch'en Meng-chia counted 120." (Chang, p. 192)

Besides the diviners, a cadre of priests performed religious rituals, including human sacrifices.

Military force was needed to sustain these rituals, by providing the prisoners-of-war to be sacrificed when rituals demanded. Oracle records speak of Shang military campaigns of 3000, 5000, and even 13,000 troops. As many as 30,000 prisoners-of-war were claimed in one large battle, and 300 prisoners were sacrificed in a ritual of ancestor worship. Archaeological finds show that 600 humans were sacrificed at the completion of a single house; 164 for a single tomb.

title to land, shares in the harvests, and rights to build and control the regional capital cities. In exchange, they represented and served the king and his interests in the provinces.

Territorially, the Shang dynasty was always based in northern and central Henan and southwestern Shandong. At its most powerful it extended as far south as Wucheng, south of the Yangzi River; east to the Pacific, incorporating the Shandong Peninsula; north into Hebei and southern Manchuria; and west through Shanxi into the mountains of Shaanxi. At its greatest extent it may have controlled 40,000 square miles. On the fringes, Shang territories were interspersed with those of other rulers, and warfare between them was apparently frequent.

Early Royal Capitals. The capital shifted often, but always remained within the core area of Shang urbanization. One of the earliest capitals was located at Luoyang; later, and for many decades, it was at Zhengzhou; and, finally, *c.* 1384 B.C.E., at Anyang. Luoyang has been difficult to excavate because it lies directly under a modern city. Zhengzhou, however, has been excavated extensively. Founded *c.* 1700 B.C.E., its core covered about 1¼ square miles, enclosed by a wall 4½ miles long and, in places, still surviving to a height of 30 feet.

Inside the walled area lived the royal family, the nobility, and their retainers. Outside this palace/ritual center was a network of residential areas; workshops making bone, pottery, and bronze artifacts; and cemeteries. The class divisions written into this spatial pattern were reinforced by the geography of the suburbs: to the north were the dwellings and graves of the wealthy and powerful, marked by ritual bronze vessels and sacrificial victims; to the south were the dwellings of the commoners and their burial places in trash pits. Occupations tended to be inherited within specific family units (compare the caste system of India discussed in Chapters 8 and 9). Many *zu*, or lineage groups, corresponded to occupational groups.

Anyang: The Last Shang Capital. The final, most powerful, and most elaborate capital of the Shang dynasty was at Anyang. Shang texts report that the nineteenth king, Pan Gieng, moved his capital to Yin and that the dynasty remained there until its fall 273 years later. Archaeologists identify that site as Anyang. This capital was the center of a network of sites stretching about 200 miles from northwest to southeast. The core area around Anyang is difficult to excavate fruitfully. The city burned to the ground,

Headless skeletons of human sacrificial victims, tomb 1001, Anyang, China. The royal tombs discovered at Anyang testify to the wealth and power of the Shang rulers. Numerous servants and prisoners-of-war gave their lives willingly or unwillingly to accompany their masters to the grave. The heads of the decapitated figures shown here were located elsewhere in the tomb.

and farmers have been plowing the area, and robbers pillaging it, for 3000 years. Remains of royal graves and of buildings that appear to be royal palaces hint at the greatness of the ancient city, but they do not yield many secrets. Nonetheless scholars have found yields of bronze treasures in royal graves.

The Shang excelled in crafting bronze. They produced bronze axes, knives, spears, and arrowheads as well as bronze utensils, ritual vessels, and sculptures. They also used horse-drawn chariots, which may have been derived from Indo-Europeans who migrated into China. The ability to use bronze in their weapons gave Chinese kings and warriors a decided advantage over their enemies, but it appears that most bronze was crafted for ritual uses.

The Zhou Dynasty. The Shang dynasty fell to the Zhou around 1122 B.C.E., but it did not disappear, just as the Xia had not disappeared when it had fallen to the Shang. Instead, in defeat, these kingdoms continued to exist, albeit with diminished territories and powers. Until the Qin dynasty unified China in 221 B.C.E., the defeat of a dynasty did not mean that it completely disappeared. Rather, it became one of the many smaller kingdoms competing for power in continuous warfare in north China.

The Zhou survived for more than 600 years, making it one of the longest lasting Chinese dynasties. The Zhou made several important conceptual contributions to Chinese thinking about culture, politics, and military strategy. Moreover, with the advent of substantial written sources, we know much more about the Zhou than the earlier Chinese dynasties.

One of the most important written sources for Zhou political thought is the *Book of Documents*, which describes the Zhou conquest of the Shang. As is often the case, such a book is written from the perspective of the winners. In this case, the Zhou portray their victory as one of heroic soldiers over decadent soldiers led by a clueless king. Nonetheless, they wanted to portray their strong connections and good relations with previous kings so that they will appear legitimate.

They also develop a heretofore unique explanation of why they should be considered the legitimate rulers of the region: the idea of the "Mandate of Heaven." The *Book of History* assumed a close relationship between Heaven and the king, but the king only had the mandate to rule if he acted in the interests of the people. If a king was weak, the theory argued that others had the right to remove him, with the "Mandate of Heaven." This doctrine would shape Chinese thinking on leadership for centuries.

While they were in power, the Zhou made several important contributions to Chinese culture. One of the most important was the *Book of Songs*, which includes a collection of China's earliest poetry, some of which appears to have been from earlier societies and transmitted orally until it was recorded. The poetry focuses on the exploits of kings and aristocrats, but also provides powerful insights into family life and gender relations in early China.

One poem, for example, describes the anxiety of a woman who became too old to marry. It makes clear that men would pursue women in courtship and not the other way around and that the woman would leave her family to join her husband's. Others speak of a deep distrust of women in politics and argue that men alone should be in the public sphere and that women belonged at home. Challenging the notion of the Mandate of Heaven, at least one poem argues that women in politics, not Heaven, sowed disorder in dynasties. Still others deal with the give and take of seduction and love outside of marriage.

The Zhou also transformed warfare, turning away from the chariots that seemed so useful earlier. They both developed the cavalry in which soldiers fought successfully with bows and arrows on horseback, and introduced infantry troops of draft foot soldiers who could effectively fight the cavalry with crossbows.

The Zhou expanded significantly, creating a much larger state than that ruled by the Shang. Recognizing the difficulty of ruling such a large state, the Zhou created a decentralized administration that left much power in local hands. In the end, this contributed to much instability with the Zhou remaining in power at least nominally at the top, while Zhou rulers faced competition from subordinates throughout China. Because of the chaos, by 480 B.C.E. a period subsequent scholars have named "the Warring States period" emerged, which lasted until the Qin dynasty unified the country in 221 B.C.E. (We will continue with this discussion as China enters an imperial age, Chapter 5.)

THE WESTERN HEMISPHERE: MESOAMERICA AND SOUTH AMERICA

The first cities of the Americas share several characteristics with those of east Asia. They began as religious shrine centers, linked by shamans, individuals who had special powers to communicate with the spiritual world on behalf of the community. They developed into city-states with important functions in politics and trade as well as in religion, and some even incorporated whole empires under their sway. Specific individual cities, most notably Teotihuacán, had enormous cultural influence over other settlements that were spread across great distances.

AT A GLANCE : THE EARLY AMERICAS

DATE	POLITICAL	RELIGION AND CULTURE	SOCIAL DEVELOPMENT
6000 B.C.E.		■ Stone tools in Mexico (6700)	
5000 B.C.E.			■ Plants (including maize) cultivated in Mesoamerica
3000 B.C.E.			■ Villages established in Mesoamerica; gourds and beans grown
2500 B.C.E.	■ Maya culture originated (2000)	■ Pottery from Mesoamerica	
1500 B.C.E.	■ Olmecs, Gulf of Mexico (c. 1500 B.C.E.–400 B.C.E.) ■ Zapotecs, S. Mexico (1400 B.C.E–900 C.E.)	■ Olmec center of San Lorenzo; pottery, mirrors, ceramics	
1000 B.C.E.	■ Chavin, N. Peru (c. 900–200 B.C.E) ■ Tiwanaku, Bolivia (c. 800 B.C.E–1200 B.C.E.)		
200 B.C.E.	■ Moche, N. coast of Peru (200 B.C.E.–600 C.E.)	■ First Teotihuacán buildings, Valley of Mexico	
100 B.C.E.	■ Nazca, Peru (1–600 C.E.)		
500 C.E.	■ Maya culture (S. Mexico, Guatemala, Belize) at peak (325–900) ■ Huari, Peru (c. 650–800)	■ Teotihuacán population 100,000 ■ First fully developed towns in the Mississippi valley (c. 700) ■ Teotihuacán culture at peak (500–650)	
1000 C.E	■ Toltecs (c. 900–1170) ■ Chimu, N.W. Peruvian coast (c. 1000–1470)		
1200 C.E	■ Aztecs (c. 1100–1521) ■ Inca, Andean S. America (c. 1200–1535)	■ Aztec pictographs and hieroglyphs ■ Aztec gold, jade, and turquoise jewels, textiles, and sculptures	■ Aztec tribute empire over surrounding lands from capital of Cuzco

There were also great differences between the hemispheres. Geographically, the cities of the western hemisphere were built at water's edge, usually near lakes or small rivers, but not on major river systems. Technologically, the people of the Americas did not use metals in their tools. In fact, they hardly used metal at all except for ornaments, jewelry, and artwork. They used neither wheels nor draft animals in transportation, perhaps because the Americas had no large, domesticable animals to use for pulling carts until horses and cattle were introduced by the Spaniards. Llamas served as pack animals for small loads in the Andes in South America, but otherwise goods were carried by hand, dragged, or shipped by canoe. Construction and transportation were thus far more labor intensive than in most of Afro-Eurasia. Finally, except for the Maya, the native Americans did not create writing systems. Some, like the Zapotecs and Toltecs, used limited hieroglyphic symbols and calendar formats, but these did not develop into full, written languages. In Afro-Eurasia, only in the Niger River area did settlements grow into cities without developing writing systems.

In many respects, the cities of the western hemisphere still had one foot in the stone age. Urban society evolved much later in the Americas. Stone tools ground by hand first appeared in central Mexico about 6700 B.C.E.; the domestication of plants began about 5000 B.C.E.; villages were established about 3000 B.C.E.; pottery appeared about 2300 B.C.E.; and population suddenly increased in about 500 B.C.E. These processes were much slower than in the river-valley civilizations of Eurasia, perhaps because humans arrived in the New World relatively recently.

Origins: Migration and Agriculture

Humans arrived in the western hemisphere from across the Beringia land bridge (connecting Alaska and Siberia) about 15,000 years ago and then spread throughout both North and South America. By 5000 B.C.E., they were cultivating maize, at least in small quantities, as well as gathering wild crops and hunting animals. By around 3000 B.C.E. they also grew beans and gourds.

Archaeologists and botanists have documented the beginnings of domestication of maize in the valley of Tehuacan, 200 miles southeast of Mexico City. Beginning with wild corn cobs about 5000 B.C.E., farmers slowly bred larger and more nutritious varieties, producing an early form of modern corn about 2000 years ago. Later excavations in Peru showed that the cultivation of maize began there by 4000 B.C.E., perhaps introduced from Mesoamerica. In both regions, at about the same time, the other two staples of the American diet, beans and squashes, also appear. Further, in the Andes Mountains, potatoes and rootcrops were also grown. The valley of Mexico and the high Andes of Peru thus became incubators of much of the civilization of the Americas from an early date. Agricultural innovation, urbanization, and the foundation of empires originated in these regions and spread outward.

Mesoamerican Urbanization: The First Stages

By 2000 B.C.E., the agricultural foundations for an urban civilization were in place in Mesoamerica. Farmers throughout present-day Mexico and central America were cultivating maize, gourds, beans, and other food crops. In addition to farming dry fields, their methods included "slash-and-burn agriculture," which kept them moving from place to place in search of new land; "pot irrigation," dipping pots into wells and simply pouring the water onto the fields; canal irrigation; and, in low-lying swamplands, the creation of *chinampas*, raised fields or so-called "hanging gardens." *Chinampas* were created by piling up the mud and the natural vegetation of the swamps into grids of raised land crisscrossed by natural irrigation channels. When the

For an interactive version of this map, go to: http://www.prenhall.com/spodek/map4.2

Classic cultures of the Americas. Sophisticated urban cultures developed in two tropical regions of the Americas: humid southern Mexico and the more temperate valleys of the central Andes. Both regions witnessed a succession of distinctive cultural and political centers. The Maya civilization of the Yucatán emerged, by 250 C.E., as the outstanding power in Mesoamerica, while the Huari empire of the Andes prefigured that of the Inca. In South America, urban civilizations appeared both near sea level along the Pacific coast and in the Andes Mountains, at altitudes from 6,500 to 12,000 feet.

Spanish arrived in 1519, they estimated that the *chinampas* could feed an impressive four persons per acre; more recent archaeological estimates of their productivity suggest eight people.

Olmec Civilization along the Gulf Coast. On the basis of these agricultural systems, localized permanent settlements that centered on religious shrines and were led by local chiefs began to emerge. Trade and shared cultural and ceremonial practices gave a common character to specific geographical regions within Mesoamerica. Along the Gulf coast of Mexico, the earliest of these civilizations, the Olmec, took shape from about 1500 B.C.E.

The Olmec built raised platforms, settlements, and shrines above the low-lying woodlands. The first that we know of was built at San Lorenzo about 1150 B.C.E. Labor brigades constructed *chinampas*, and the population of the settlement may have reached 2500. Olmec artwork—representations of animals and mythological creatures in sculpture and bas relief—suggests a shared religious basis of the society. They also developed rudimentary hieroglyphics, but as of today, no one has been able to decipher them. About 900 B.C.E. the San Lorenzo site was destroyed, its artwork defaced. No one today knows why.

About one hundred years later, some 100 miles to the northeast and closer to the Gulf, Olmec peoples at La Venta built a small island in the middle of a swamp, and constructed on it an earth mound, half again as large as a football field and 100 feet high. Buildings atop the mound were probably used as temples. Monumental stone sculptures, including some of the giant stone heads typical of Olmec art, also mark the space. Some of them probably served also as altars. The stone building materials were transported here from at least 60 miles away, the jade from much further. La Venta flourished for four centuries until about 400 B.C.E. it, too, was destroyed and its monuments defaced. Again, no one today knows why.

Zapotec Civilization in the Oaxaca Valley. Olmec products—pottery, ritual objects, mirrors, and ceramics—appeared in the highlands around modern Oaxaca as early as 1150 B.C.E., along with natural products, such as obsidian and seashells from around the Gulf of Mexico. At first, therefore, scholars believed that the Zapotec culture of the Oaxaca valley was an offshoot of the Olmec. More recent finds in the village of San Jose Mogote, dating to 1400–1150 B.C.E., demonstrate, however, that the Zapotec settlements began as early as the Olmecs. The imported products reflected trading between the two groups.

Zapotec civilization peaked on the slopes of Monte Albán. By 400 B.C.E. ceremonial and public buildings dotted the summits of the hills. The settlement grew over the centuries, reaching its peak in the centuries after 200 C.E., when up to 50,000 people lived there. The settlement was not entirely concentrated into a single city, but extended over 15 square miles, with some 2000 terraces built into the hills, each with a house or two and its own water supply. Temples, pyramids, tombs, and an array of religious images suggest the importance of symbolism among the Zapotecs, too. Monte Albán peaked in population and creativity about 700 C.E. and then declined.

Colossal head from San Lorenzo, Veracruz, Mexico, before 400 B.C.E. Weighing around ten tons, this massive sculpted head is one of nine that were found at San Lorenzo. Made from basalt and carved with stone tools, the heads originally stood in rows on the site and are most probably portraits of Olmec rulers. All display the same full, resolute lips and broad, flat noses. Similar sculptures were also found at La Venta. (*Museo Regional de Veracruz, Jalapa, Mexico*)

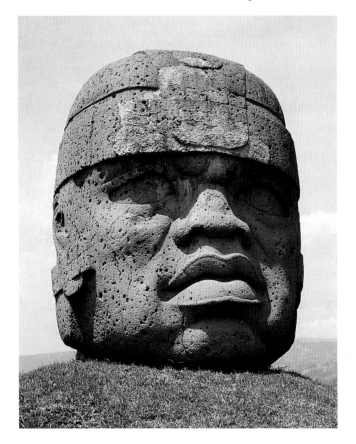

The Urban Explosion: Teotihuacán

Meanwhile, in the valley of Mexico, another civilization was coalescing, dominating the lands near it, and finally creating a substantial empire. At its core, about 40 miles to the northeast of present day Mexico City, stood Teotihuacán, one of the great cities of the ancient world. Teotihuacán represented a totally new kind of settlement in the Americas. It marked the beginning of a true urban revolution. At its peak, about 550 C.E., Teotihuacán accommodated about 100,000 inhabitants on some 8 square miles. Teotihuacán civilization had no system of writing so, again, our knowledge is limited to the excavation and interpretation of physical artifacts.

The first buildings of Teotihuacán appeared about 200 B.C.E. One hundred years later, there were still only about 600 inhabitants. By 150 C.E., however, the population had grown to 20,000 and the area to 5 square miles. Then the population multiplied as the city exploded with religious, trade, artisanal, and administrative functions and personnel.

The city sat astride the major communication line between the valley of Mexico and the passes eastward to the Gulf of Mexico. Life in the city was a gift of the low-lying lake system of the valley of Mexico, especially of nearby Lake Texcoco. The lakes provided irrigation waters for the fields of the Teotihuacán valley and salt, fish, and waterfowl. Basalt, limestone, and chert stone for building and clay for pottery were readily available in the valley, but other raw materials were imported, notably obsidian for tools and weapons from Pachuca and Otumba in the surrounding mountains. Marine shells and copal (a tree resin used as incense) were imported from the Gulf region, and feathers of the quetzal bird came from the Maya regions of the southeast. Trading outposts of Teotihuacán appeared 700 miles south in Maya areas, and Teotihuacán ceramics have been found as far south as Tikal (see the discussion of Maya civilization on pp. 103–106). More than 400 workshops in the city produced pottery, obsidian manufactures, ornaments fashioned from seashells, and art and jewelry from jade and onyx.

A huge pyramid, the Pyramid of the Sun, at its base as broad as the great pyramid of Khufu in Egypt, though only half as high, dominated the Teotihuacán cityscape. The pyramid sits above a natural cave that early inhabitants enlarged into a clover-leaf-shaped chamber. The combination of natural cave and pyramid suggests that local people may have believed that this cave was the "navel of the universe." As Mircea Eliade, the historian of religions, has demonstrated, the belief that all human life, or at least the lives of the local people, had emerged upward onto earth from a "navel," a single specific geographical point, was widely held in many civilizations of the ancient world. (The Garden of Eden story is a later variant of this belief.) Two additional massive shrines—the adjacent, smaller Pyramid of the Moon, and a central temple dedicated to the god Quetzalcoatl—enhance the religious dimensions of the city. Throughout its lifetime, and indeed even afterward until the Spanish conquest, Teotihuacán attracted multitudes of pilgrims from as far away as Guatemala.

The city was laid out on a monumental, geometric grid that centered on the 150-foot-wide Avenue of the Dead, the north–south axis of the city. More than seventy-five temples line this road, including the Pyramid of the Sun. The Pyramid of the Moon

Teotihuacán. Between 400 and 750 C.E., high in the valley of Mexico, Teotihuacán was the dominant power in Mesoamerica. Covering over 7.5 square miles, with a population of 100,000, the city was laid out on a regular grid plan connecting the elements of a massive ceremonial complex. The residents thrived on agriculture, craftwork, and trade in ceramics and locally quarried obsidian.

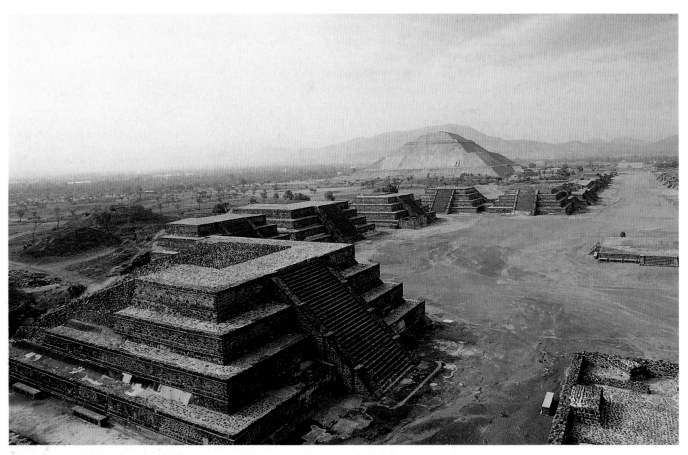

Teotihuacán, Mexico, with the Pyramid of the Moon (foreground) linked to the Pyramid of the Sun by the Avenue of the Dead. By 200 B.C.E. in the valley of Mexico, the combined effects of intensified trading, growing religious activity, and huge surpluses of food led to the founding of this major city, which for centuries enjoyed religious, political, and economic dominance in the region. Teotihuacán reached an enormous size (8 square miles) and population (100,000) before eventually being deliberately, and mysteriously, burned down in 650 C.E.

demarcated its northern terminal. The regularity of the city plan suggests a powerful government and, indeed, a large administrative headquarters, the Ciudadela, dominates the southeastern terminus of the Avenue. The placement of the central Temple of Quetzalcoatl within the Ciudadela implies a close relationship between religion and administration.

At its peak, 500–650 C.E., Teotihuacán exercised a powerful imperial force over its immediate surrounding area and exerted spiritual, religious, cultural, economic, and military influence for hundreds of miles, especially to the south, into Maya areas. In 650, however, the city was deliberately burned down. Teotihuacán began to decline in significance. By 750 its power was broken, and its population scattered to smaller towns and rural areas. Several reasons have been suggested: the region may have become increasingly arid, incapable of supporting so large a population; increasing density of population, augmented by government programs for moving rural populations into the city, might have led to conflict and revolt from within; neighboring city-states, pressured by the increasing militarization in Teotihuacán, may have attacked the city. These are, however, only educated guesses. In the absence of written records, no one knows for sure.

Cities interact with one another in networks of exchange, so advances or declines in one usually echo in the others. Teotihuacán and Monte Albán both declined simultaneously about 750 C.E., but smaller, nonurban centers kept the political, cultural, and religious legacies of Teotihuacán alive in the region. (Compare this with the experience of western Europe after the decline of Rome, discussed in Chapter 6.) Three subsequent civilizations—the Toltec, the Aztec, and the Maya—absorbed and perpetuated its influence.

Successor States in the Valley of Mexico

When the Toltecs arrived in the valley of Mexico from the north and came to dominate the region from a new capital at Tula, about 900 C.E., they apparently ruled on Teotihuacán foundations and built their chief ceremonial center in honor of Quetzalcoatl. Their rule, however, was shortlived. About 1170 C.E. still newer immigrants destroyed the Toltec temples and government.

After Tula fell, the Aztecs entered the valley. They established settlements on the southeastern shores of Lake Texcoco and built Tenochtitlán as their capital only 40 miles from the earlier site of Teotihuacán. As the Aztecs built their large, militaristic empire, the population of Tenochtitlán grew to 200,000. Militarism and the demand of their gods for human sacrifice led the Aztecs into a constant quest for captives to sacrifice and, therefore, into constant warfare with their neighbors. When the Spanish conquistadores arrived in 1519, the neighboring peoples helped them overthrow the Aztecs and their empire. The Spanish then razed Tenochtitlán to the ground and established their own capital, Mexico City, atop its ruins (see Chapter 12).

The Rise and Fall of the Maya

Teotihuacán's third legacy was to the Maya. The Maya lived where their descendants still dwell today—in the Yucatán peninsula of Mexico, in Guatemala, and in Belize. The Maya built on Olmec and Teotihuacáno foundations as well as on their own practices. Arriving in the Yucatán and central America, they began to construct ceremonial centers by 2000 B.C.E. Between 300 B.C.E. and 300 C.E., they expanded their centers to plazas surrounded by stone pyramids and crowned with temples and palaces. The classic phase, 300–600 C.E., followed with full-fledged cities and monumental architecture, temples, extensive sacrifices, and elaborate burials, and the Olmec and Teotihuacán cultural influences are evident. Maya culture flourished in the southern lowlands, and major construction took place at Palenque, Piedras Negras, Copán, Coba, and elsewhere.

The Great City of Tikal. Tikal, in today's Guatemala, is one of the largest, most elaborate, and most completely excavated of these cities. In its center, Tikal holds five temple pyramids, up to 200 feet high and built from 300 to 800 C.E. (One appeared so massive, powerful, and exotic that film-maker George Lucas used it as a setting for *Star Wars*.) As the first modern archaeologists hacked away the tropical rainforest and uncovered this temple core, they concluded that Tikal was a spiritual and religious center. Later they uncovered housing and water cisterns that accommodated up to 50,000 people outside the

A blood-letting rite, limestone lintel from Yaxchilán, Mexico (Maya), c. 725 C.E. The king, Lord Shield Jaguar, in his role of shaman, brandishes a flaming torch to illuminate the drama about to unfold. His principal wife, Lady Xoc, kneeling, pulls through her tongue thorn-lined rope that falls into a woven basket holding blood-soaked strips of paper cloth. These will be burned and thereby transmitted to the gods. Few works of art made by the Maya capture so completely the link between their political and religious ideas in an appropriately sacramental style. (Having deciphered the hieroglyphics of the Mayan calendar, scholars know that this event took place on October 28, 709 C.E.) (*British Museum, London*)

temple precincts. This find led them to change their assessment of Tikal. Instead of viewing it as a purely religious shrine, they began to see it as a large city of considerable regional political and economic significance as well. At the height of its powers, Tikal's authority covered almost 1000 square miles containing 360,000 people.

Most Maya states held only 30,000–50,000 subjects. The number of states ruled by kings grew from perhaps a dozen in the first century B.C.E. to as many as sixty at the height of the lowland civilization in the eighth century C.E.

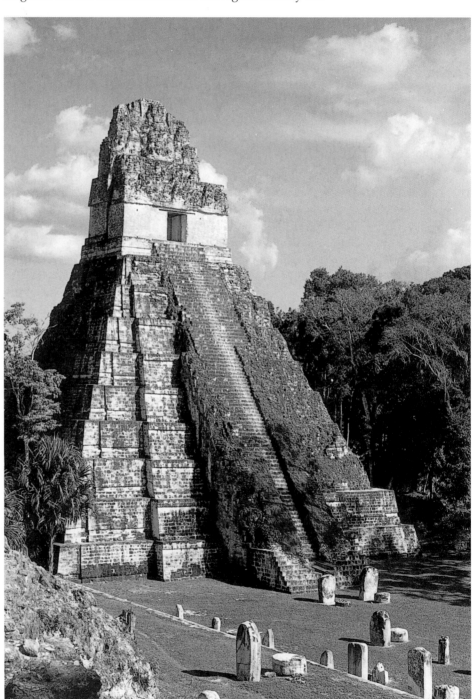

Temple I at Tikal, Guatemala (Mayan), before 800 c.e. At its height the city-state of Tikal covered almost 1000 square miles and was home to 360,000 inhabitants. Its symbols of authority were centralized in its monumental shrines. This unusually steep stepped pyramid—230 feet high—would have been the backdrop for self-inflicted blood-letting and the sacrifice of prisoners-of-war as offerings to the gods.

SOURCE

The Popol Vuh

The Popol Vuh *is the most complete existing collection of creation myths to survive the Spanish conquistadores. Originally written in Maya hieroglyphs, it was transcribed into Latin in the sixteenth century and then translated into Spanish by a Dominican priest in the eighteenth century. The selection cited here is reminiscent of the biblical story of the tree in the garden of Eden whose fruits were forbidden. But the tale in* Popol Vuh *has even more significant differences. The tree, a calabash, is forbidden because the skull of a god, named One Hunahpu, was placed on a fork in it. As a young woman reached out to take the fruit of the tree, the skull spat out saliva on her, making her pregnant and thus preserving the god's lineage among humans.*

And this is when a maiden heard of it, the daughter of a lord. Blood Gatherer is the name of her father, and Blood Woman is the name of the maiden.

And when he heard the account of the fruit of the tree, her father retold it. And she was amazed at the account:

"I'm not acquainted with that tree they talk about. 'Its fruit is truly sweet!' they say." "I hear," she said.

Next she went all alone and arrived where the tree stood. It stood at the Place of Ball Game Sacrifice:

"What? Well! What's the fruit of this tree? Shouldn't this tree bear something sweet? They shouldn't die, they shouldn't be wasted. Should I pick one?" said the maiden.

And then the bone spoke; it was here in the fork of the tree:

"Why do you want a mere bone, a round thing in the branches of a tree?" said the head of One Hunahpu when it spoke to the maiden. "You don't want it," she was told.

"I do want it," said the maiden.

"Very well. Stretch out your right hand here, so I can see it," said the bone.

"Yes," said the maiden. She stretched out her right hand, up there in front of the bone.

And then the bone spat out its saliva, which landed squarely in the hand of the maiden.

And then she looked in her hand, she inspected it right away, but the bone's saliva wasn't in her hand.

"It is just a sign I have given you, my saliva, my spittle. This, my head, has nothing on it—just the bone, nothing of meat. It's just the same with the head of a great lord: it's just the flesh that makes his face look good. And when he dies, people get frightened by his bones. After that, his son is like his saliva, his spittle, in his being, whether it be the son of a lord or the son of a craftsman, an orator. The father does not disappear, but goes on being fulfilled. Neither dimmed nor destroyed is the face of a lord, a warrior, craftsman, orator. Rather, he will leave his daughters and sons. So it is that I have done likewise through you. Now go up there on the face of the earth; you will not die. Keep the word. So be it," said the head of One and Seven Hunahpu—they were of one mind when they did it.

This was the word Hurricane, Newborn Thunderbolt, Raw Thunderbolt had given them. In the same way, by the time the maiden returned to her home, she had been given many instructions. Right away something was generated in her belly, from the saliva alone, and this was the generation of Hunahpu and Xbalanque.

And when the maiden got home and six months had passed, she was found out by her father. Blood Gatherer is the name of her father. (Tedlock, p. 106)

The Maya also created an elaborate calendar that recorded three related chronologies: dates and events in cosmic time periods of thousands of years; historic events in the lives of specific rulers and their states; and the yearly cycle of agricultural activity. Maya rituals were permeated by the sense of living at once in the world of here-and-now and in a spiritual realm connected with other worlds and gods. Their kings were shamans, bridges between the two worlds.

Maya Civilization in Decline. By 900 C.E., the great classical period of the Maya in the southern lowlands ended. No one knows why. The most frequent hypotheses include: excessive population pressure on natural resources, especially agriculture; climatic changes beyond the ability of the Maya to adjust; excessive warfare that wore out the people and destroyed their states. No one knows for sure.

No one knows, either, why at the time of the Maya decline in the lowlands, new Maya cities and states grew up in the northern highlands of the Yucatán peninsula, notably at Uxmal and Chichén Itzá. These cities, in turn, declined by 1200, and the last Maya capital, Mayapán, was constructed between 1263 and 1283. It adapted many of the cultural monuments of Chichén Itzá, but grew only to some 10,000 to 20,000

HOW DO WE KNOW?

Great-Jaguar-Paw: Mayan King of Tikal

By deciphering, translating, and interpreting the stelae at Tikal, Linda Schele and David Freidel recreate an heroic moment of military victory in the life of the king Great-Jaguar-Paw and in the history of his kingdom. Their interpretation is based primarily on the stela illustrated here and on comparison with later stelae representing the same event:

Jaguar paw ax blade

God dangling from the royal belt

Captive

Tikal location

Despite the fact that he was such an important king, we know relatively little about Great-Jaguar-Paw's life outside of the spectacular campaign he waged against Uaxactun. His reign must have been long, but the dates we have on him come only from his last three years. On one of these historical dates, October 21, A.D. 376, we see Great-Jaguar-Paw ending the seventeenth katun [a ritual cycle of twenty years] ... This fragmentary monument shows him only from the waist down, but he is dressed in the same regalia as his royal ancestors, with the god Chac-Xib-Chac dangling from his belt. His ankle cuffs display the sign of day on one leg and night on the other ... He holds an executioner's ax, its flint blade knapped into the image of a jaguar paw. In this guise of warrior and giver of sacrifices, he stands atop a captive he has taken in battle. The unfortunate victim, a bearded noble still wearing part of the regalia that marks his noble station, struggles under the victor's feet, his wrists bound together in front of his chest. He will die to sanctify the katun ending at Tikal.

Warfare was not new to the Maya. Raiding for captives from one kingdom to another had been going on for centuries, for allusions to decapitation are present in even the earliest architectural decorations celebrating kingship. The hunt for sacrificial gifts to give to the gods and the testing of personal prowess in battle was part of the accepted social order and captive sacrifice was something expected of nobles and kings in the performance of their ritual duties. Just as the gods were sustained by the bloodletting ceremonies of the kings, so they were nourished as

well by the blood of noble captives. Sacrificial victims like these had been buried as offerings in building terminations and dedications from late Preclassic times on, and possibly even earlier ...

The war waged by Great-Jaguar-Paw of Tikal against Uaxactun, however, was not the traditional hand-to-hand combat of proud nobles striving for personal glory and for captives to give to the gods. This was war on an entirely different scale, played by rules never before heard of and for stakes far higher than the reputations or lives of individuals. In this new warfare of death and conquest, the winner would gain the kingdom of the loser. Tikal won the prize on January 16, A.D. 378 ...

The subjugation of Uaxactun by Great-Jaguar-Paw and Smoking Fog [his commander-in-chief], which precipitated this new kind of war and rituals, survives in the inscriptional record almost entirely in the retrospective histories carved by later rulers at Tikal. The fact that these rulers kept commemorating this event shows both its historical importance and its propaganda value for the descendants of these conquerors.

(Schele and Freidel, pp. 144–8)

- What are all the symbols through which this stela represents the power and strength of Great-Jaguar-Paw?
- What does the war between Tikal and Uaxactun tell us about the increasing power of the state?
- What do you think Schele and Freidel mean by "the propaganda value" of commemorating the victory of Tikal over Uaxactun?

---

inhabitants. Mayapán seemed militaristic, beleaguered, and possessed of tough sensibilities as evidenced by wholesale human sacrifices. The city was later destroyed in civil wars in the mid-1400s.

By the time the Spanish conquistadores reached Mesoamerica in 1517, only a few small Maya towns remained. The period of Maya power and splendor had ended. The Toltecs, too, had fallen by then. The Aztecs had become the reigning power, and the Spaniards destroyed them.

Urbanization in South America

South America had few established trade links with Mesoamerica, but the two regions share many similarities. Both regions constructed religious shrine centers that seem to have dominated their general cultural foundations by about 1500 B.C.E. Both developed small city-states that defined local cultural variations from 300 to

HOW DO WE KNOW?

The Mysteries of Maya Writing

For centuries the connection between today's Maya—living an often impoverished existence—and the glories of their civilization in the third through the tenth centuries C.E. had been lost. Then, in 1839–41, a New York lawyer, John Lloyd Stephens, and a Scottish artist, Frederick Catherwood, discovered the remnants of the cities of Copán and Palenque in the rainforests of Mesoamerica, and the temples of Uxmal and Chichén Itzà in the Yucatán peninsula. Stephens and Catherwood wrote and painted what they saw and made rubbings of the designs they found on Maya stelae, stone marker tablets. Their research, published in 1841, opened the way for the modern academic study of the Maya at almost exactly the same time as H.C. Rawlinson and others were discovering the great archaeological sites of Mesopotamia and deciphering its language.

Stelae and other inscriptions demonstrated that the Maya had created a written language, but no one could read it. Even the Maya themselves, prevented by the Spanish from keeping their language alive (see Chapter 13), had forgotten the script. Scholars could read parts of the elaborate and sophisticated Maya calendar system, but they could not discern whether the events recorded were historical, mythical, or some combination of the two.

In the 1950s and 1960s, at Harvard University, Tatiana Proskouriakoff began to demonstrate that the Maya stelae recorded the reigns and victories of real kings who had ruled real states. Then the Russian scholar Yuri Knorozov demonstrated, against fierce opposition, that the Maya script included representations of phonetic sounds as well as of full words. By the 1970s a new generation of linguistic scholars began to decode the syntactical structure of the writing. They learned to distinguish the signs for nouns and those for verbs, and their place in the structure of the narrative. They were well on their way to discovering Maya history, and they were surprised by what they found.

The archaeologists Linda Schele and David Freidel finally mastered the hieroglyphs and scripts of the people of the city of Palenque. In contrast to previous beliefs that the Maya were peaceful and somewhat otherworldly in their concerns, as their massive temples seemed to indicate, Schele and Freidel found records of constant warfare among the local shaman kings and their profoundly religious local city-states. The Maya kingdoms fought in order to gain captives who would serve as slaves and human sacrifices to their demanding gods. The temples, it turned out, were the altars on which the sacrifices were performed. Schele and Freidel also discovered the exact lineage of the Palenque kings, and the picture of a tree used to symbolize the king, for the Maya represented their royal families as forests of trees and forests of kings.

- Why was it easier to decipher the cuneiform of Sumer and the hieroglyphs of Egypt than the symbols of Maya writing?
- Why had the Maya forgotten their own written language? Does the reason surprise you? Why or why not?
- On p. 106 you can see an example of Maya writing. As you look at it, what seem to you to be the difficulties in deciphering the Maya written language?

---

200 B.C.E. Both created proto-empires throughout significant regions about 500–600 C.E.; and generated large, urban empires—the Aztecs in the valley of Mexico, the Inca in the Andes—and developed trading relationships between their coastal regions and their mountainous inland cores. But the contrast between coast and inland mountains is far more striking in South America. The Pacific coast of Ecuador, Peru, and Chile is a desert in most places. The prevailing winds come not from the Pacific, but from the Amazon basin to the east. The Andes Mountains thus have little rainfall from the Pacific Ocean to trap on their western slopes, but they do intercept the precipitation from the Atlantic, making the eastern slopes fertile while leaving the west coast dry. The most spectacular urban civilizations of South America took root in the 10,000-foot-high plains and passes of the Andes rather than in the arid Pacific coast below. The contrast with the river-basin civilizations of Afro-Eurasia could not be more vivid.

Coastal Settlements and Networks

The Pacific coast is not, however, uninhabitable. It yields abundant quantities of fish, seaweed, and salt. Even today these ocean products are traded to the mountain cities in exchange for their food crops. In some areas the cultivation of cotton is also

CIVILIZATIONS FLOURISHING IN CENTRAL AMERICA BEFORE COLUMBUS

Olmec	*c.* 1500–400 B.C.E. Gulf of Mexico. First complex society in region, with centralized authority. Known for carvings of giant stone heads and jade animals.	**Teotihuacán**	*c.* 300 B.C.E.–750 C.E. Valley of Mexico. Major trading and cultural center. At its peak populated by 100,000 inhabitants in an area (8 square miles) larger than Rome. Contains huge Pyramid of the Sun, Mexico's largest pre-Columbian edifice.
Maya	*c.* 2000 B.C.E.–900 C.E. S. Mexico, Guatemala, Belize. Most enduring of the Middle American civilizations, the Mayans had by 325 C.E. become superb astronomers who built stepped pyramids, smelted metal tools, and developed hieroglyphs.	**Toltec**	*c.* 900–1170 C.E. Central Mexico. Toltecs ruled much of the country from Tula (northeast of Mexico City), where symbols of blood and war predominate, and the similar city of Chichén Itzá in Yucatán.
Zapotec	*c.* 1400 B.C.E.–900 C.E. S. Mexico. Built ceremonial center of Monte Albán and peaked as a civilization around 200 C.E.	**Aztec**	*c.* 1100–1521 C.E. Central Mexico. Sophisticated culture run by priestly aristocracy that built capital of Tenochtitlán. Known for their architecture, textiles, and a complex sacred calendar, the Aztecs were conquered by the Spanish in 1519–21.

possible, and coastal Peru rivals the Indus valley as the home of the first production of cotton textiles, about 4500 B.C.E. The quality of the textiles and the colorful designs dyed into the cotton show up most clearly in the burial cloths of semi-mummified bodies in the Paracas peninsula near Pisco, Peru.

In addition, although climatically a desert, the coast does have some small mountain-fed rivers running through it. People who could organize labor brigades to channel the rivers for irrigation also created ceremonial centers along the coast, beginning perhaps by 2000 B.C.E. The oldest of these shrine centers, and the one closest to the Pacific, is El Paraiso, near modern Lima, at the mouth of the Chillon River. Built in a typically U-shaped complex of buildings, El Paraiso appears to have been constructed by people from many separate villages and kin groups. Few lived at El Paraiso, but apparently the shrine served them all, and many used the location as a burial place.

The largest of the shrine centers is Sechin Alto, a 130-foot-high mound, 1000 by 800 feet, on which was built a U-shaped ceremonial complex surrounded by houses and platforms. The oldest building dates to 1300 B.C.E. It continued to expand until 400 B.C.E.

The Moche. In the Moche valley of coastal northern Peru, settlements of up to 2000 separate structures had grown up by 200 B.C.E. From about 200 B.C.E. to 600 C.E., in this and neighboring valleys, the Moche state established itself. The Moche created irrigation systems, spectacular monuments, and important tombs. In the late 1980s, at nearby Sipan, archaeologists discovered three royal tombs that demonstrate the social and political stratification of the society. Each tomb housed a lord, buried in shrouds and adorned with jewellery, some made of gold, and surrounded by servants and perhaps family members, and by animals—llamas, and at least one dog and one snake—that had been buried with him. Paintings and ceramic designs within the tombs show priests engaged in warfare and performing human sacrifices of prisoners-of-war. The Moche built provincial centers in nearby river valleys from which they apparently ruled, traded, and introduced irrigation systems.

The Chimu. By about 600 C.E. the Moche left the region, for reasons that are not entirely clear, and were succeeded by the Chimu kingdom that controlled twelve coastal river valleys. The Chimu built irrigation and water storage facilities, trade networks, and a powerful state that stretched some 1000 miles along the Peruvian coast. Their monumental capital, Chan Chan, built near the earlier Moche, was surrounded by a 35 foot high mud wall, and it covered nearly 4 square miles, with palaces, temples, administrative offices, and housing for the common people. Chan Chan contained ten royal compounds. Apparently each king in turn built his own center, ruled from it during his life, and was buried in it after his death.

In each area they dominated, the Chimu built subsidiary administrative centers that formed a network reaching as far south as modern Lima. The Chimu empire reigned until it was conquered by the Inca in 1470. Ironically, thanks to the Inca transportation and communication network, Chimu artwork influenced western South America even more after the Inca conquest than it had before.

Urbanization in the Andes Mountains

Despite these coastal settlements and networks, most scholars believe that the core areas of South American urbanization were in the Andes, the 20,000-foot-high mountain chain that parallels the Pacific coast for the entire length of South America. From earliest times to today, there has been considerable "vertical trade," linking coastal lowlands with high mountain areas in an exchange of the different products of their different ecologies. With the trade came networks of cultural, religious, and political communication, and some archaeologists have argued that the civilization of the Andes Mountains was developed from a prior foundation along the sea coast far below.

The Chavin. The first known civilization of the Andes, the Chavin, flourished for about a millennium, 1200–200 B.C.E. The civilization is named for its best known and largest ceremonial center at Chavin de Huantar, which flourished in central Peru from about 900 to about 200 B.C.E. Chavin temples include a pantheon of gods preserved in paintings and carvings, including jaguar-like humans with serpents for hair, eagles, caymans, and many mixed figures, part-human, part-animal, reminiscent of similar figures in China. Like El Paraiso and the coastal shrines, Chavin seems to have been built by the joint efforts of many nearby kin and village groups. At its height, it held only 2000 inhabitants, but its culture and its gods inspired common religious forms in the vicinity, and carried them throughout the high Andes.

The Tiwanaku, Huari, and Nazca. Some 600 miles to the south, south of Lake Titicaca, on today's border between Peru and Bolivia, at an elevation of 12,000 feet, lay the largest open, flat plain available for agriculture in the Andes. By 200 C.E., Tiwanaku (Tihuanaco) at the southern end of the lake, near the modern city of La Paz, became the capital of the region. Its rulers irrigated their high plains, *altiplano*, region to support perhaps 20,000 people and to create a ritual center of monumental structures and religious and spiritual practices that suffused the Andes and the coast. When Tiwanaku collapsed, for reasons now lost to history, successor states in the region, notably at Huari and Nazca, kept alive many of their administrative and religious practices.

CIVILIZATIONS OF SOUTH AMERICA	
Chavin	*c.* 1200–200 B.C.E. N. Peru. Farming society, comprising different regional groups, whose main town may have been a pilgrimage site.
Moche	200 B.C.E.–600 C.E. N. coast of Peru. Modeled ceramics of animals in a realistic style. Religious and political life focused on the Huaca de la Luna (artificial platform) and Huaca del Sol (stepped pyramid).
Nazca	?1–600 C.E. Peru. Known principally for its series of enormous figures drawn with lines of pebbles. Best seen from the air, the largest (a hummingbird) is 900 feet long.
Tiwanaku	*c.* 200 C.E.–1200 C.E. Bolivia. Named for the ancient city, near Lake Titicaca, that was occupied by a series of five different cultures, then abandoned.
Huari	*c.* 650–800 C.E. Peru. Empire whose style of architecture and artifacts, similar to Tiwanaku's, was dispersed throughout the region.
Chimu	*c.* 600–1470 C.E. Northwest Peruvian coast. Large urban civilization (capital: Chan Chan) responsible for fine gold work, record-keeping, and aqueducts. Conquered by the Aztecs.
Inca	*c.* 1476–1534 C.E. Andean South America. Last and largest pre-Columbian civilization (capital: Cuzco) that was destroyed by Spanish conquistadores in the 1530s.

Nazca lines, San Jose pampa, Peru desert, c. 500 c.e. Another of the successor states of Tiwanaku, the Nazca, created great patterns of lines drawn with pebbles on the desert surface. The designs, like this 900-foot-long hummingbird figure, are visible only from the air, and their function and meaning are as elusive as the culture that fashioned them.

The Inca. These five states—Chimu, Chavin, Tiwanaku, Huari, and Nazca—established foundations on which the Inca built their powerful but shortlived empire, which stretched for 2000 miles from north to south and as far as 200 miles inland, between 1476 and 1534. The Inca adapted many of the gods and religious symbols, artwork, ceramics, and textiles of these earlier states. They built a new capital, Cuzco, at 10,000 feet, and connected it to all the mountain and coastal regions of their empire by an astonishing 25,000-mile system of roads, with tunnels, causeways, suspension bridges, travel lodges, and storage places. The roads were sometimes broad and paved, but often narrow and unpaved, especially because the Inca had no wheeled vehicles. Enforced, *mit'a* labor was exacted from local populations for the construction.

In 1438, Cusi Yupanqui was crowned "Inca," or king-emperor, after he won a victory over a neighboring tribe, and forged his quarreling peoples into a conquering nation. Thereafter, the whole nation was called Inca. Cusi Yupanqui established an hereditary monarchy, and his descendants built a great empire from his early conquests. They employed the *mit'a* system, demanding unpaid labor for public construction for part of each year from all adults in the empire. The Inca did not develop writing, but they did create an abacus-like system of numerical recording through the use of knots tied on strings. These *quipu* held the administrative records of the empire.

In each conquered region, the Inca established administrative centers, from which tax collectors gathered two-thirds of the crops and the manufactured products, like beer and textiles, half of it for the state, half for the gods and their priests. They established state workshops to produce official and consumer goods, and they seem to have encouraged significant standardization of production, for Inca arts and crafts show little variation over time and place. Inca religion apparently encouraged different gods and worship for different people. The sun god was the chief deity, and the emperor was considered his descendant; the nobility worshiped the military god Viracocha; while the common people continued to worship their own indigenous spirits, along with the newer sun god. The organization and the study of empire, however, take us to Part 3.

Agricultural Towns in North America

Agricultural settlements took root in many locations in continental North America in the first few hundred years c.e. Several grew into small towns, reaching their maximum size about 1000–1400 C.E., and some scholars see the signs of early urbanization. Nevertheless, these towns are not included among the seven sites of primary urbanization because few of them reached a population size that might be considered urban; nor do they demonstrate clearly a non-agricultural base to their economies. They may also be derivative of earlier settlements to the south. For example, those in the southwestern United States, like the Hohokam, Mogollon, and Anasazi peoples, show evidence in their artwork and building patterns of influences from Mexico and even South America.

The first fully developed towns in the Mississippi valley appeared about 700 C.E. Their inhabitants built temple mounds and left evidence of elaborate, ritual funerals, suggesting a hierarchical social and political organization. The largest of the temple mound towns, Cahokia, occupied land along the Mississippi, across the river from and a few miles east of present-day Saint Louis. Cahokia held a population of 10,000 in the city and 38,000 in the region in the twelfth and thirteenth centuries. Such a large population probably included many craft specialists. Around the town were sited some 100 mounds, which served as burial tombs or as platforms for homes of the elite. The mounds resemble those of Mexican cities and suggest interchange between the two regions. Evidence indicates that a strong central authority controlled the town. Cahokia, like almost all the towns of North America, was in decline, or even deserted, before the arrival of European invaders, in the early 1500s, for reasons that are not entirely clear. Archaeologists continue active research in the towns of North America, their cultures, and their links to one another and to other regions.

WEST AFRICA: THE NIGER RIVER VALLEY

Until the late 1970s, all the cities in sub-Saharan Africa that were known to archaeologists had developed along patterns introduced from outside the region. Meroe and Kush on the upper Nile had adapted urban patterns from Egypt. Aksum in modern Ethiopia had followed examples of urbanization from both the Nile valley and the trading powers of the Indian Ocean. Port cities along the East African coast, such as Malindi, Kilwa, and Sofala, had been founded by traders from across the Indian Ocean. The walled stone enclosures, called **zimbabwes**, built in the region of modern Zimbabwe and Mozambique to house local royal rulers, had been initiated through contact with Swahili traders from the coast.

In west Africa, the first known cities, such as Timbuktu, Jenne, and Mopti along the Niger River, and Ife and Igbo Ukwu deeper south in the Yoruba lands near the tropical forests, had been built as centers of exchange. They were thought to be responses

zimbabwes Stone-walled enclosures or buildings built during the African Iron Age in the region of modern Zimbabwe and Mozambique. The structures were the courts of local rulers. They have been associated with foreign trade, integrated farming and animal husbandry, and gold production.

AT A GLANCE : THE EARLY AFRICAS

DATE	POLITICAL	RELIGION AND CULTURE	SOCIAL DEVELOPMENT
500 B.C.E.		■ Nok terra cotta sculptures ■ Bantu adopting settled agricultural lives	■ Iron smelting
250 B.C.E.	■ Jenne-jeno founded	■ Copper and semi-precious stone ornaments from Niger	
500 C.E.	■ Ancient Ghana		■ Cities in Niger valley (400) recorded by Arab visitors
1000 C.E.	■ Foundation of Benin (c. 1000)		
1200 C.E.	■ Ghana falls; Kingdom of Mali founded		

Trade across the Sahara. Ivory, gold, hardwoods, and slaves were the magnets which drew trading caravans south across the arid Saharan wastes, often following routes established before the desert had formed. These routes linked the classical cultures of the Mediterranean and southwest Asia with an array of rich trading states strung along the Sahel/Sudan axis.

to the arrival of Muslim traders from north Africa who crossed the Sahara southward after the seventh century C.E. Archaeologists believed that Africans, like Europeans, had learned of city building from outsiders. But this viewpoint has now been challenged.

West Africa before Urbanization

The most important developments of pre-urban west Africa were iron smelting, apparently initiated by contact with north Africa; the development of new artistic traditions, especially by the Nok peoples; and the spread of agricultural civilization by the Bantu people. Iron smelting entered the archaeological record in west Africa suddenly about 500 B.C.E. In most places the technology jumped from stone to iron directly, with only a few examples of copper-work in between. Most archaeologists interpret this technological jump to indicate that iron working was introduced from outside, probably from the Phoenician colonies along the north African coast, and they find evidence for this idea in the rock art of the Sahara desert. Along the routes crossing the desert, rock engravings and paintings dating from between 1200 B.C.E. and 400 B.C.E. depict two-wheeled chariots that suggest trans-Saharan traffic.

In northern Nigeria, the Nok peoples were producing terra cotta sculptures, especially of human heads, from about 500 B.C.E. Living in settlements along the Niger, near its confluence with the Benue in modern Nigeria, the Nok also built iron-smelting furnaces, dating to 500–450 B.C.E.

Meanwhile, also in the lower Niger, some Bantu peoples were giving up nomadic pastoralism for settled agriculture, although many remained nomadic for a long time. They began great, but gradual, migrations southward and eastward over thousands of miles, introducing their languages, their knowledge of iron production, and their experience with settled agriculture. In one thousand years, 500 B.C.E. to 500 C.E., the Bantu carried their languages, their new, settled way of life, and their metallurgical skills almost to the southern tip of Africa.

Jenne-jeno: A New Urban Pattern?

Neither the Nok nor the Bantu built cities. Other people of the Niger River, however, apparently did. In excavations that began in 1977 and continue today archaeologists Susan and Roderick McIntosh uncovered Jenne-jeno, "Ancient Jenne," the first known indigenous city in sub-Saharan Africa. The Jenne-jeno settlement began about 250 B.C.E. as a small group of round mud huts. Its herding and fishing inhabitants were already using iron implements, and the village grew to urban size by 400 C.E., reaching its peak of settlement by about 900 C.E.

The physical form of the city was different from that of the other six centers we have studied. A central inhabited area of some 80 acres was surrounded by a city wall 10 feet wide and 13 feet high with a perimeter of 1¼ miles. Near this central area were some forty smaller, but still substantial additional settlements. They extended to a radius of 2½ miles. By the year 1000, the settled area may have included 50,000 persons.

Excavations through numerous levels revealed that the people of Jenne-jeno ate fish from the river, rice from their fields, and beef from their herds. They probably drank the cows' milk as well. At least some wore jewelry and ornaments of imported copper and semi-precious stones. Dozens of burial urns, each up to 3 feet high, yielded human skeletons arranged in fetal position. The urns date from 300 to 1400 C.E., and their burial inside and adjacent to the houses suggests a reverence for ancestors. Statuettes in a kneeling position set into walls and under floors further suggest the probability of ancestor worship.

This part of the religious and cultural heritage of Jenne-jeno seems to have endured. Although not built primarily as a shrine center, Jenne-jeno included religious functions as an important part of its activities, as its modern counterpart does today. There are also similarities between the arrangement of the huts of Jenne-jeno 1000 years ago and the grouping of family huts there today. In ancient times as in modern, it appears that the husband–father lived in one large central hut while one of his wives occupied each of the surrounding huts.

Jenne-jeno must have engaged in trade, because even in 250 B.C.E. its inhabitants were using iron and stone that had to be brought from at least 30 miles away. Sandstone for their grinding stones had to have been imported from at least 60 miles away, while copper and salt came from hundreds of miles away. The McIntoshes have also discovered one gold

Two men with an ibex, Tanzoumaitak, Tassili Mountains, Sahara, 7000–6000 B.C.E. Rock painting. Rock art of the Sahara at first represented wild animals such as buffalo, rhinoceros, hippopotamuses, giraffes, and elephants. By 6000 B.C.E. it was representing domesticated animals such as ibex or goats, dogs, horses, and camels, suggesting a transition from hunting to pastoralism and settled agriculture.

The spread of Bantu. About 1500 B.C.E. an extraordinary cultural migration began to transform sub-Saharan Africa. From their homeland near the Niger delta, groups of Bantu-speaking farmers began to move east and south, spreading cattle domestication, crop cultivation, and iron-working. By about 500 C.E. southern Africa had been reached, the original hunter-gatherers having been marginalized to remote regions such as the Kalahari Desert.

Head from Jemaa, Nigeria, c. 400 B.C.E.
The Nok were a nonliterate farming people that occupied the Jos Plateau in northern Nigeria during the first millennium B.C.E. Their distinctive sculptures—of elephants, snakes, monkeys, people, and even a giant tick—are all boldly modeled and skillfully fired in terra cotta. This powerful lifesize head would probably have formed part of a full-length statue. (*National Museum, Lagos, Nigeria*)

earring, dating to about 750 C.E., in the region. The nearest site of gold mining was 500 miles away. Perhaps the people of Jenne-jeno traded the fish of the Niger and the rice of their fields for these imports. Some Jenne-jenoites may have become professional merchants.

Innovation in architectural concepts may also have come to Jenne from external contacts. By about 900 C.E. some rectangular houses began to appear among the circular ones, perhaps introduced through contact with northern peoples. Outside contacts increased with the introduction of camel transportation across the Sahara about 300 C.E. and with the Muslim Arab conquest of north Africa about 700 C.E. Especially after 1200 C.E., Muslim traders crossing the Sahara linked the savanna and forest lands of the south to the cities of the Mediterranean coast. Most scholars have argued that these external contacts and trade possibilities encouraged the growing importance of new cities like Timbuktu, Jenne, Niani, Gao, Kano, and, further south, Benin. The McIntoshes suggest an opposite perspective: these cities predate the northern connections, and, indeed, their prosperity and control of the trade routes and the gold further to the south encouraged the northerners to dispatch their camel caravans across the Sahara. This debate remains unresolved.

By 1100, the settlements peripheral to Jenne-jeno began to lose population. Some of their inhabitants apparently moved to the central settlement. In another century the rural population also began to decline. By 1400, Jenne-jeno and its satellites were no more. Why? Perhaps warfare and slave-trading upset local stability. It is also possible that land rights and family structures shifted, reducing residents' interest in the region. Finally, it is possible that migration to other places along the Niger River simply allowed Jenne to slowly decline. We just do not know.

State Formation?

Could the settlements of the Middle Niger at Jenne-jeno be an example of early urbanism without a strong centralized government? Without a state? It is possible. The population at Jenne-jeno lived in neighboring clusters that were functionally interdependent rather than in a single urban center with a prominent core marked by large scale, monumental architecture as was found in most of the other centers of primary urbanization. This kind of development might be viewed as "a precocious, indigenous, and highly individual form of urbanism" (R. McIntosh, p. 203). In this case, it is possible that Jenne-jeno rose on the basis of trade and expanded into geographically neighboring, interactive settlements, but without a hierarchical social structure or a strong, central authority. In contrast to primary urbanization in all the other regions of the world we have examined, Jenne-jeno may have experienced relative equality and cooperation among its citizens rather than competition, dominance, and coercion.

On the other hand, a comparative assessment might suggest that Jenne had developed only to about the stage of the Olmec settlements and had not yet created the kind of centralized authority that emerged clearly and powerfully among the later Maya. Had Jenne-jeno persisted longer and grown larger, perhaps centralization and stratification would have developed. Indeed the presence of a central settlement surrounded by smaller adjacent settlements suggests that some hierarchy was already emerging. Did Jenne-jeno represent an alternative kind of urbanization, or was it a settlement that was on its way to full-scale conventional urbanization? These are the kinds of questions of comparison that archaeologists—and historians—love to debate.

THE FIRST CITIES
WHAT DIFFERENCE DO THEY MAKE?

With the creation of cities, humanity entered into many new forms of living. The first of these cities, in the river valleys of Mesopotamia and the Nile almost 5500 years ago, introduced not only new scale and density in human settlement patterns but also new technology in the metallurgy of copper, tin, and bronze; monumental scale in architecture; and specialization and hierarchy in social, political, and economic life. These cities flourished also as nodes in networks for the exchange of goods and ideas. The invention of writing in these cities not only gave new life to cultural creativity, but also provided new means of record keeping for the bureaucrat, businessperson, and scholar. These new cities allowed and demanded complex and hierarchical government to keep them functioning. Although we sometimes see cities today as homes of secularism and heterogeneity, these early cities were also religious in the sense that they often existed to promote dedication to specific gods through their physical and ritual organization. Differences in climate and culture separate Egyptian from Mesopotamian urbanization, but they also shared many similarities. We know somewhat less about Egyptian urbanization because the Nile itself washed away many of its foundations, but more recent archaeology has uncovered Egyptian as well as Sumerian city walls and residential structures, suggesting that they also needed to protect their inhabitants from outsiders.

Sumer and Egypt provide what scholars sometimes refer to as a "master narrative," a conventional, widely accepted view of historical transformation, suggesting that the historical process at other times and places will follow similar patterns. Each of our subsequent case studies has reinforced some dimensions of the "master narrative" while challenging others.

- Indus valley urbanization suggested that a generally consistent civilization could extend over an immense geographical space, over thousands of years. A few of its distinctive, planned cities stood out as capitals, but even after they were evacuated, other cities of the far-flung network kept the civilization alive. Moreover, Indus agricultural practices were adopted and adapted by invaders who transplanted some of them from the Indus valley to the Ganges valley.
- Early Chinese urbanization, represented in the historical record through oracle bones and through the geometrical design of city plans, placed added emphasis on the religious dimension of cities, although the rulers did not neglect to mobilize large and powerful armed forces.
- In the Americas, cities like Teotihuacán and the later cities of the Maya demonstrated again the importance of monumental, religious architecture, although each additional excavation reveals the extent of both long-distance trade and of everyday, mundane activities as well. Urbanization in the Andes mountains indicates that not all early cities needed river beds. Urban rulers could construct fabulous networks for trade, communication, and troop movement at forbidding altitudes. From their capital cities they could launch empires. They could also administer cities, and even empires, without having invented writing.
- In the Niger River valley of west Africa, the single primary urban settlement that has been excavated challenges the "master narrative," suggesting that cities may develop through the interrelationship of adjacent smaller settlements without the need for hierarchy, centralization, government structure, and written language. The data presented thus far may be, however, subject to different interpretations. Perhaps the central mound in Jenne-jeno does, in fact, represent some hierarchical

Bronze kneeling figure, Jenne, Mali, c. 1100–1400. Archaeological activity over the last quarter century has revealed Jenne-jeno, "Old Jenne," as a commercial center on the Niger River from about 250 B.C.E. Its traditions seem to have persisted through the centuries and into "new" Jenne, the city which now stands adjacent to the older excavation. Statuettes such as this one, produced in Jenne, may have been used in worship of and for ancestors. (*Private collection*)

structure. Or perhaps it is a collection of contiguous villages rather than an urban center. The interpretation depends in part on how far the definition of a city and its functions may be—and ought to be—stretched. Continuing excavation and interpretation will help decide the degree to which the "master narrative" concerning early urbanization will hold up, and to what degree new, less rigid ideas of the role of urbanization in human history are yet be formulated.

Review Questions

- Archaeologists working with the earliest cities of Mesopotamia and Egypt asserted that a true city must have writing. In light of the findings in the Americas and in Jenne-jeno, do you agree with those archaeologists that the settlements in these regions are not cities; or do you think that they are cities and that a city's definition should be changed?
- How has the discovery and deciphering of ancient writing helped to form our understanding of urban life in ancient China and Mesoamerica?
- Anthropologist Jared Diamond says that Mesopotamia and Egypt had an advantage in technological and social development over other areas of the world because they were ecologically rich in animal and plant resources. As you compare the early urban developments in China, the Americas, and Jenne-jeno, would you agree or disagree with Diamond? Why?
- In at least six of the early seven urban locations, we find evidence of human sacrifice, or of killing some of the ruler's companions to accompany him (or her) to an afterlife. Why do you think these practices stopped?
- In which of the four urban centers represented in this chapter did the ruler seem to have the most power? What evidence can you cite to support your view?
- Are you convinced by the arguments of the McIntoshes that Jenne-jeno is an example of an unusual kind of city that challenges our understanding of early urbanization? Why or why not?

Suggested Readings

PRINCIPAL SOURCES

Blunden, Caroline and Mark Elvin. *Cultural Atlas of China* (New Haven, CT: Facts on File, 1983). One in the excellent series by this publisher, prepared by an historian and an archaeologist, with text, maps, pictures.

Coe, Michael, Dean Snow, and Elizabeth Benson. *Atlas of Ancient America* (New York: Facts on File, 1986). One in the excellent series by this publisher, prepared by experts, with text, maps, pictures.

Fagan, Brian. *People of the Earth: An Introduction to World Prehistory* (Upper Saddle River, NJ: Prentice Hall, 2000). Outstanding anthropological textbook on prehistory.

McIntosh, Roderick James. *The Peoples of the Middle Niger: the Island of Gold* (Oxford: Blackwell, 1998). Most recent book publication on Jenne-Jeno by one of the two principal archaeologists.

Murray, Jocelyn, ed. *Cultural Atlas of Africa* (New York: Facts on File, 1982). One in the excellent series by this publisher, prepared by an expert with text, maps, pictures, time lines.

Schele, Linda and David Freidel. *A Forest of Kings: The Untold Story of the Ancient Maya* (New York: William Morrow, 1990). Tells how the Mayan language was deciphered, by those who did it.

Times (London). *Past Worlds* (Maplewood, NJ: Hammond Inc., 1988). Excellent, comprehensive, scholarly introduction to archaeological prehistory, lavishly illustrated with maps and pictures.

ADDITIONAL SOURCES

Alva, Walter and Christopher Donnan. *The Royal Tombs of Sipan* (Los Angeles, CA: Fowler Museum of Cultural History, University of California, Los Angeles, 1993). Lavishly illustrated account of the excavation.

Chang, Kwang-chih. *The Archaeology of Ancient China* (New Haven, CT: Yale University Press,

3rd ed., 1977). THE expert's account, somewhat dated, but still the standard.

Chang, Kwang-chih. *Shang Civilization* (New Haven, CT: Yale University Press, 1980). Comprehensive account by an archaeologist who participated in some of the most significant excavations.

Connah, Graham. *African Civilizations* (Cambridge: Cambridge University Press, 1987). Excellent, comprehensive textbook on prehistoric Africa. Covers the entire continent.

Curtin, Philip, Steven Feierman, Leonard Thompson, and Jan Vansina. *African History from Earliest Times to Independence* (New York: Longman, 2nd ed., 1995). A standard textbook by four distinguished experts.

deBary, William Theodore, *et al.*, comp., *Sources of Chinese Tradition. Vol. 1.* (New York: Columbia University Press, 1998). The best available anthology of classic writings. Good section on oracle bones.

Demarest, Arthur and Geoffrey Conrad, eds. *Ideology and Pre-Columbian Civilizations* (Santa Fe, NM: School of American Research Press, 1992). Scholarly argument on the importance of ideas, both cosmo-magical and political, in the construction of pre-Columbian civilizations.

Eliade, Mircea. *The Sacred and the Profane* (New York: Harper and Row, 1959). The classic argument for the importance of sacred spaces in city development, by a pre-eminent historian of religion.

Keightly, David N., ed. *The Origins of Chinese Civilization* (Berkeley, CA: University of California Press, 1983). An excellent account.

MacNeish, Richard S. "The Origins of New World Civilization," *Scientific American* (November 1964). Reprinted in *Scientific American, Cities: Their Origin, Growth, and Human Impact* (San Francisco, CA: W.H. Freeman and Company, 1973), 63–71. Brief introduction, especially interesting on domestication of crops and animals.

McIntosh, Susan and Roderick McIntosh. "Finding West Africa's Oldest City," *National Geographic* CLXII No. 3 (September 1982), 396–418. Popular introduction based on early archaeological expeditions.

McIntosh, Susan Keech, ed. *Excavations at Jenné-Jeno, Hambarketolo, and Kaniana (Inland Niger Delta, Mali), the 1981 Season* (Berkeley, CA: University of California Press, 1995). Comprehensive, scholarly documentation on the excavations.

Millon, René. "Teotihuacan," *Scientific American* (June 1967). Reprinted in *Scientific American, Cities: Their Origin, Growth, and Human Impact*, 82–91. Basic introduction to the early professional excavations of Mesoamerica's largest prehistoric metropolis.

Moseley, Michael E. *The Maritime Foundations of Andean Civilization* (Menlo Park, CA: Cummings, 1975). Argues that the Andean cities were founded on the basis of the Pacific coastal developments.

Scientific American, ed. *Cities: Their Origin, Growth, and Human Impact* (San Francisco, CA: W.H. Freeman and Company, 1973). Anthology of articles on urbanization culled from *Scientific American* articles. Still useful.

Tedlock, D., trans. *Popol Vuh* (New York: Simon & Schuster, 1985). The definitive edition of the Mayan *Book of the Dawn of Life and the Glories of Gods and Kings*.

Time-Life Books. *Time Frame 3000–1500 BC: The Age of God-Kings* (Alexandria, VA: Time-Life Books, 1987). Popular but authentic, engaging, introduction to many areas of early urbanization: Mesopotamia, the Nile valley, the Indus valley, and the Yellow River valley.

Waley, Arthur, trans. *The Book of Songs* (New York: Grove Press, 1996). Marvelous translation of poetry from the age of Confucius.

◉ World History Documents CD-ROM

2.1 Might Makes Right: the "Shu ching" Sets Forth the Mandate of Heaven
2.2 The Spirit World
2.3 Ch'u Yuan and Sung Yu: Individual Voices in a Chaotic Era
2.4 Confucius: *Analects*
2.5 Mencius: the *Counterattack on Legalism*
2.6 Taoism

From City-State to Empire

Developing military force was the key to transforming a city-state into an empire. City-states already had their offensive and defensive powers: walls, moats, soldiers and troops, and, for those situated at the water's edge, ships and sailors. The literature from Mesopotamia, pre-imperial China, ancient Greece, and Mayan Mesoamerica abounds with evidence of fighting among city-states. From Gilgamesh onward, the rulers of city-states were builders of city walls and commanders of armed forces, famed as much for their military prowess as for their administration. They were engaged in incessant warfare.

Military force turned these city-states into empires. Almost 4000 years earlier, Sargon of Akkad (c. 2330–2280

Deer hunt relief, Hittite, 9th century B.C.E. Stone. (*Museum of Anatolian Civilizations, Ankara, Turkey*)

B.C.E.) had set the example. His victories over the quarreling city-states of Mesopotamia around 2250 B.C.E. created the first empire recorded in history.

Sargon's troops were apparently equipped with the usual weaponry of the day: wooden spears with sharp points made of stone or bone and a range of perhaps 150 feet, simple bows and arrows with a range of somewhat more than 300 feet, leather slings capable of hurling stones with deadly force up to 600 feet, and war chariots—rough wagons with solid wooden wheels, pulled by asses—bearing their spear hurlers and quivers filled with arrows. We do not have visual evidence of Sargon's armies, but we do for the Sumerians whom he defeated. The military standard from Ur depicts not only the foot soldiers, chariots, and weapons of the victors, but also the defeated enemy soldiers, some already dead, some awaiting their fate. Sargon's armies were probably not much different from Ur's in their equipment, but they were greater in numbers, organization, skill, and energy.

Sargon proceeded to conquer the cities of the middle and upper Euphrates and moved on into southern Anatolia. Then he turned eastward to dominate Susa in western Iran, the capital city of the Elamites. Sargon's empire lasted for only about a century, but from his time onward,

Macedonian troops in formation, after a painting by G.D. Rowlandson.

Mesopotamia was usually ruled by one empire or another, most frequently an invading force, like his own, but sometimes a revolutionary army arising from within. City-states did not return.

Egypt also established an empire early on, by moving southward, above the first cataract—one of a series of impassable rapids—on the Nile River, into Nubia, a land famed for its gold. As early as 2500 B.C.E., the Egyptians built a city at Buhen, just below the second cataract, in an area not much populated at the time, and held it for centuries as a basis for mining and trade, until it was taken by Nubians. During the twelfth dynasty (1991–1786 B.C.E.), however, Egypt returned to the area. The Egyptians secured passage for ships around the first cataract by constructing a canal and added a parallel land route over the desert sands. At Buhen Egyptian engineers directed the construction of one of the greatest fortresses known to

ancient history. Low, outer walls and towering inner walls were each protected by ditches and crenellated on top with loopholes for archers and spear- and stone-throwers. The fortress housed soldiers' barracks surrounded by their own walls, a market, government offices and residences, and, later, a temple dedicated to Horus. Buhen served as the chief outpost of Egyptian military activity, administration, and trade in Nubia. It was once again conquered by Nubians after Egypt itself was defeated by Hyksos invaders, probably from across the deserts of Sinai, about 1600 B.C.E.

At about that time, new instruments of war were being introduced into the fertile crescent by new immigrant groups, probably from the mountains to the northeast. The most significant was a new two-wheeled war chariot, light, fast, easily maneuverable, pulled by horses and commanded by archers in bronze

The Assyrian army and musicians, from the Palace of Ashurbanipal, Nineveh, 7th century B.C.E. **Limestone relief.** (*Louvre, Paris*)

Although chariots, horses, and asses were employed by early armies, the mainstay of most was the infantry: Greek hoplites, protected by their heavy bronze armor and massed in phalanxes several rows deep; Roman legions, less heavily armed, and grouped into smaller units for greater mobility; and Chinese foot soldiers, also by the thousands. Chinese historical records are abundant in their descriptions of armies and warfare, but archaeologists were nevertheless astonished to uncover in 1974 a ceramic army of 7000 life-sized soldiers and horses (see p. 206) arranged in military formation and armed with bronze weapons, spears, longbows, and crossbows (a Chinese invention). In 1976 a second excavation uncovered the cavalry, 1400 chariots and mounted soldiers in four military units. The next year a much smaller pit was discovered, holding what appeared to be a terra cotta officer corps. These thousands of figures were not mass produced. Each figure was modeled and painted separately, even down to its elaborate hairstyle that symbolized its specific military office. The figures apparently represented the elite of the imperial troops, and were fashioned to accompany the first emperor of China, Qin Shi Huangdi (r. 221–210 B.C.E.), to his own tomb and afterlife.

War took place on sea as well as land. In the eastern Mediterranean, in the fifth century B.C.E., the trireme (see p. 145) was the principal warship of both the Persians and the Greeks as they contested for power. With approximately 170 oarsmen arranged about equally in three tiers along each side, these ships could reach speeds of up to nine knots per hour. When such speeds were not necessary, the ships might hoist square-rigged sails and travel with the wind.

The trireme's hull was of light wooden construction, with the Greek ships usually somewhat lighter than

armor shooting bronze-tipped arrows. This chariot powered the armies of the Middle East for a thousand years. The first to use it successfully were the Mitanni, centered on northern Mesopotamia, about 1500 B.C.E. They were succeeded by the Hittites, based in their capital of Hattushash (Boğazköy) in eastern Anatolia from about 1650 to about 1200 B.C.E. The Hittites, in particular, also developed the use of iron and even steel for use in weapons—defensive armor and offensive spear-, arrow-, and sword-points—and in farm tools that increased agricultural productivity.

the Persians'. This enabled faster speeds, but it also left the ships vulnerable to the bronze-covered rams that they carried as an offensive weapon. At first, spearmen and archers accompanied the rowers. By the end of the fourth century B.C.E., the construction changed, as decks were introduced to accommodate the armed soldiers, and multiple rows of oarsmen replaced the tiers.

Psychological weapons had their place as well. One of the earliest and most common was the use of sound and instruments in urging on one's own troops—and providing communication among them—while frightening and confusing the enemy. There are ancient references to the use of trumpets and other instruments as accompaniments of warfare. The Bible includes instructions in their use as the Hebrews traversed the desert in their exodus from Egypt. As they finally reached their promised land, their leader Joshua's assault on the walled city of Jericho was accompanied by trumpeters blasting on rams' horns that, according to the Book of Judges, caused the city walls to collapse.

The legendary founding of the Persian Empire was recorded long afterwards by the tenth-century C.E. poet Firdowsi in Iran's national epic the *Shah-nameh* ("Book of Kings"). Beloved by its readers, the epic describes the victory by Rustum, one of the legendary founders of the Persian nation, over his arch-enemy Turani. The epic also captures the sounds of musical instruments used in battle.

The written record of warfare is filled with the images of death, destruction, and captivity, from virtually all imperial conquests. One of the closing scenes depicts corpses from the warfare of Mesopotamia, the earliest and most continuous site of imperial battles. The lamentations over the destruction of the third city

of Ur, Ur III, is one of the earliest ever recorded, between 2000 and 1500 B.C.E. It reminds us that empire building is deadly business:

O Father Nanna, that city into ruins was made; the people groan.

…

Its walls were breached; the people groan. In its lofty gates, where they were wont to promenade, dead bodies were lying about;

In its boulevards, where the feasts were celebrated, scattered they lay. In all its streets, where they were wont to promenade, dead bodies were lying about; In its places, where the festivities of the land took place, the people lay in heaps.

…

Its dead bodies, like fat placed in the sun, of themselves melted away.

(Pritchard, p. 459)

Battle of Til-Tuba between the Assyrian king Ashurbanipal and the king of Elam, from the palace of Ashurbanipal, 645 B.C.E. Stone relief. (*British Museum, London*)

QUESTIONS

1. How important are warfare and murder in the construction of empire?
2. How closely can you correlate the development of new weapons of warfare with the creation of new empires?
3. What kinds of skills and powers, beyond the military, are necessary in the construction of empires?

3

Empire and Imperialism

2000 B.C.E. –1100 C.E.

WHAT ARE EMPIRES AND WHY ARE THEY IMPORTANT?

The first empires grew up in the areas of the civilizations we studied in Part 2—that is, in Mesopotamia, the Nile valley, and the Yellow River valley. The Akkadian Empire of Sargon, which flourished *c.* 2350 B.C.E., is the first for which we have documentary evidence, and it was followed in the same part of Mesopotamia by the Babylonians and, later, by the Assyrians. In their successions we see a pattern that will become familiar: the building of a large, powerful military force in the hands of a strong ruler, followed by a decline, a challenge by an outsider, the overthrow of the old empire, and the rise of a new one.

Chapter 5 begins with Akkad as the earliest example of empire building. Egypt provides the second example, and then we turn to the Persian Empire. In Persia's struggle against the Greeks in the fifth century B.C.E., we see a fundamental clash between monarchy and democracy and between empire and city-state. A confederation of small, local city-states stopped the conquering force of the world's most powerful empire. Ultimately, however, in the subsequent dissolution of the Greek system into civil war and the succession of Alexander the Great, we see one of the great ironies of history. Those cities that had earlier prided themselves on their independence and their victory over the largest empire of the time lost their independence and became integrated into Alexander's empire.

Chapter 6 will consider in greater depth the empire of Rome, while Chapter 7 examines those of China and, briefly, its daughter civilization in Japan. Chapter 8 explores India and touches on southeast Asia. These three systems controlled vast areas, had an enormous impact on tens of millions of people, and have continued to make their influence felt to our own time. They represent turning points in the history of most of humankind.

Rome, China, and India were so successful that their ideologies of empire—their explanations of why they should rule—prevailed for centuries. Indeed, the Roman Empire endured for almost a thousand years, from about 500 B.C.E. to almost 500 C.E., and if we include the Eastern

Roman soldiers besieging a town, from *The History of the Nations*. Aquatint engraving by A. Nani. Rome's array of military devices— battering rams, equipment for scaling walls, catapults, and horses and chariots waiting at the ready—facilitated its policy of the "new wisdom," namely, to defeat the enemy through patient, deliberate preparation, and the demonstration of overwhelming force. (*Private Collection*)

Empire, based in Constantinople, Rome's duration is some 2000 years. Moreover, Rome inspired an imperial image that was expressed throughout later Europe in the so-called Holy Roman Empire. In the nineteenth and early twentieth centuries, many commentators compared the British Empire with Rome, and in the late twentieth and early twenty-first centuries, many drew a similar comparison with the United States. The Chinese Empire, founded in 221 B.C.E., lasted more or less continuously until 1911 C.E., and some would argue that it persists even today in new, communist garb. The first emperor to rule almost all of the Indian subcontinent, Ashok (Asoka) Maurya (r. 273–232 B.C.E.), is still commemorated today on every rupee currency note printed in India. Throughout these chapters, we also consider the trade routes that kept these three great empires in communication with each other.

DAWN OF THE EMPIRES

EMPIRE-BUILDING IN NORTH AFRICA, WEST ASIA, AND THE MEDITERRANEAN 2000 B.C.E.–300 B.C.E.

KEY TOPICS
- The Meaning of Empire
- The Earliest Empires
- The Persian Empire
- The Greek City-States
- The Empire of Alexander the Great

THE MEANING OF EMPIRE

New York proudly calls itself the Empire State; Chrysler advertises its Chrysler Imperial luxury automobile; until recently, Britain maintained the "imperial gallon" as a measure of volume. Yet today the word "imperialism" has a generally negative connotation. The demise within the past generation of many empires, most recently that of the Soviet Union, has met with general approval around the world. Why does the concept of empire evoke such conflicting attitudes? What is an empire?

Empires grow from the conquest of one people by another—in fact, a definition of empire is the extension of political rule by one people over other, different peoples. Empires have been as natural in human history as the desire of people to exert control over other peoples and their resources, and they have arisen as frequently as rulers have been able to build military organizations capable of attaining those goals.

The word "empire" stirs conflicting images and feelings in most of us. We think of the monumental structures of palaces and the ruling establishments of the emperor and the leadership cadre. In our imaginations we see majestic buildings adorned with the finest artworks. The emperor and the imperial administrators, we imagine, wear the finest clothes, eat the choicest foods, enjoy the most select luxuries, and support and command the most powerful technologies. Often they encourage great creativity in the arts and in learning. Sometimes, however, we see them using their power over others in acts of cruelty, arrogance, irresponsibility, and decadence.

We see, too, vast marketplaces and, perhaps, ports and dockyards processing goods from the far corners of the empire, since one purpose of empire building is to bring natural resources to the mother country. Leading into the capital city, connecting it with the remotest areas of empire, are lines of communication and transportation, sea lanes, and, most important of all, roads. Specific examples stand out. Notable are the grand canals linking the rich agricultural lands of south China to the capital in the north and dating back as early as the Sui dynasty, in the seventh century C.E. Similarly, the phrase "All roads lead to Rome," the capital of an equally powerful empire, may have been an exaggeration, but its central idea was correct. Empires bring exotic goods and diverse peoples together under a common ruler. People of different languages, religions, ethnic origins, and cultural and technological levels are brought under a single, centralized rule.

In order to organize and maintain communication and exchange among all parts of the empire, a system of administration must be established. The administrators and rulers must also regulate the fate of conquered peoples in accordance with the needs of the empire. Some are granted full citizenship, most of the remainder receive fewer rights and privileges, while those at the bottom, especially war captives, might be

Opposite **Apadana, principal audience hall, Persepolis, Iran, 521–486 B.C.E.** Persepolis was destroyed by Alexander the Great. Visible here are columns from the Apadana of Darius I.

enslaved. A few—those who proved particularly dangerous or costly to the imperial rulers—might be executed as a warning to potential rebels.

The administration must ensure either that different kinds of monies from various parts of the empire are consolidated into a single system of coinage or that means of exchanging them are readily available. It must communicate across the many languages of the empire, and it may adopt and impose a single administrative language so that the writ of empire is universally understood. It must establish a legal system with at least some degree of uniformity. Indeed, the administration must provide sufficient uniformity in language, currency, weights, measures, and legal systems to enable it to function as a single political structure. Perhaps the most significant administrative task of all is the collection of taxes from its subjects and tribute from the conquered. Such revenues represent the continuing financial profits to the rulers.

Twentieth-century scholars emphasize two forms of imperial rule: **hegemony** and **dominance**. For the imperial power, hegemony is to be preferred, for this is rule that subjects accept willingly if they can be persuaded that it is in their best interests. They may benefit from the stability and peace it imposes; from the technological improvements it introduces; from the more extensive networks it develops and opens to their trade and profit; from the cultural sophistication it exhibits and shares with them; or from the opportunities for new kinds of advancement that membership in the empire may offer. If imperial membership is perceived to have such benefits, the subject peoples may welcome it peacefully, even eagerly. They may accept the ideology of the imperial power and its explanation for the legitimacy and benefit of its foreign rule. In short, hegemony may be defined as foreign rule that governs with the substantial consent of the governed.

Should the imperial ideology not be acceptable, however, rulers will impose their government through dominance, the exercise of sheer power. In these circumstances, military force, and the threat to exercise it, are central to the empire's existence, so the state expends vast sums on recruiting, training, and equipping its armies. The troops mobilize across the vast spaces of empire, using the same roads that carry the imperial commerce.

Resistance to imperial rule is as normal as empires themselves. Rulers of empires usually dominate because they are able to mobilize more power than the peoples they control. Often, intentionally or unintentionally, the secrets of their power spread among the conquered, thereby enriching their lives. The subject populations learn from the technology introduced by their conquerors, whether it is the use of weapons, materials, military formations, agricultural methods, administrative organizations, or techniques of production. Empires that begin by using their superiority to rule, eventually produce change among the peoples they conquer. Subject peoples, who may originally have felt some gratitude toward their imperial benefactors, may later grow resentful, restive, and finally rebellious. Goths, for example, no longer wished to be subordinate to Romans, nor Mongols to Chinese, as we shall see in Chapters 6 and 7. Empires are not static. They rise and they fall. Ironically, the imperial masters are often forced to trade places with those they had subjugated.

The causes of the decline and fall of empires include:

- Failure of leadership—the inability of the empire to produce or select rulers capable of maintaining the imperial structures;
- Overextension of the administration—the inability of the imperial rulers to sustain the costs of a far-flung empire while coping simultaneously with critical domestic problems;
- Collapse of the economy—the overextension of empire to territories so remote or so difficult to subdue and govern that costs outrun benefits;

hegemony The predominance of one unit over the others in a group, for example one state in a confederation. It can also apply to the rule of an empire over its subject peoples, when the foreign government is exercised with their substantial consent.

dominance The imposition of alien government through force, as opposed to hegemony.

- Doubts over the ideology—the end of belief in the justice or benefit of empire, which may occur either when cynical colonizers abandon the colonial enterprise, or when frustrated colonized peoples revolt, or both;
- Military defeat—external enemies and the colonized people combine in revolt.

THE EARLIEST EMPIRES

Mesopotamia and the Fertile Crescent

Mesopotamia's earliest power centers were independent city-states that could not reach political accommodation among themselves. They fought constantly for land, irrigation rights, and prestige, as we can see from the scenes of warfare that fill the bas relief artwork from third-millennium Sumer. From this artwork and from cuneiform records, archaeologists have reconstructed two main antagonists, the cities of Lagash and Umma in Mesopotamia, which, with their allied forces, dominated the warfare of the time. Victory by either one, however, or by any of the city-states over any of the others, was frequently avenged in the next generation.

Sargon of Akkad. Geographically, the city-states of Mesopotamia were also vulnerable to immigrant groups crossing their territory and challenging their powers. About 2350 B.C.E., Sargon (r. *c.* 2334–2279 B.C.E.), leading an immigrant group of Semitic peoples from the Arabian peninsula, entered Sumer. The new arrivals settled in and around northern Sumer and called their land Akkad. Sargon led the Akkadians to victories over the leading cities of Sumer, over the Elamites to the east, over northern Mesopotamia, and over a swath of land connecting Mesopotamia to the Mediterranean. He founded the Akkadian capital at Agade, a city whose exact location is now unknown.

The Empire of Sargon. During the third millennium B.C.E. Sargon established his control over the city-states of southern Mesopotamia, creating the world's first empire. Building a capital at Agade, he founded the Akkadian dynasty, which for a century ruled the fertile crescent, from the Persian Gulf to the Mediterranean Sea.

Bronze head of an Akkadian ruler (Sargon I?), c. 2250 B.C.E. Exuding royal self-confidence, this near-lifesized bronze head probably depicts Sargon I, founder of the Akkadian dynasty. For over half a century, Sargon dominated one city-state after another until he had conquered most of Mesopotamia. After his death, his successors worshiped him as a god.

Historical records are skimpy, but those that do exist correspond to our assessment of the key characteristics of empire. First, the Akkadians conquered widely. Administrative tablets of the Akkad dynasty have been found as far away as Susa, several hundred miles to the east in Persia, suggesting a far-flung governmental administration. Second, after razing the walls of the major cities of Ur, Lagash, and Umma, Sargon displaced the traditional local civilian hierarchies with his own administrators, designated the "sons of Akkad." Third, the Akkadian language was used in administrative documents in Sumer. Fourth, measurements of length, area, dry and liquid quantities, and probably weight were standardized throughout the empire; indeed, people in the region used the Akkadian units of measure for more than a thousand years, far longer than the empire itself survived. Finally, Sargon imposed his own imagery and ideology of empire. Documents were dated from the founding of the Akkadian kingdom, legal oaths were taken in the name of the Akkadian king, and Sargon installed his own daughter as high-priestess of the moon-god Nanna at Ur.

Sargon's empire lasted for about a century and was followed by other outsiders, the Gutians, and then by a revival of internal Sumerian power under Ur-Nammu (r. *c.* 2112–*c.* 2095 B.C.E.). Culturally, Sumer was so advanced that it influenced even its conquerors, the Akkadians, the Gutians, and later arrivals. The Akkadian language, however, did supplant Sumerian by about 2000 B.C.E.

Waves of Invaders: The Babylonians and the Hittites. Throughout this time, waves of immigrants continuously entered the fertile crescent, perhaps attracted by empty land on its fringes, perhaps by the presence in its heartland of already settled peoples on whom they could prey. Historians have not always been able to determine the specific origins of the immigrants, but two groups have stood out most clearly, Semites and Indo-Europeans. Each is designated by the family of languages that it spoke and later wrote; a common language probably indicates a degree of internal ethnic relationship as well.

Among the Semitic groups were the Amorites, who invaded and conquered Sumer about 1900 B.C.E. and founded their own new dynasty slightly to the north at Babylon. At first they employed Sumerian cultural and administrative forms, but over time they created new systems of their own. Their sixth ruler, Hammurabi (r. 1792–1750 B.C.E.), is most famous for his law codes, but he was also a skilled military leader who defeated the Sumerian city-states that had remained independent. He created the Babylonian Empire, imposing an administrative network that stretched from the Persian Gulf to Syria and endured for 250 years, until its defeat about 1500 B.C.E. by the Hittites, a new group of invaders.

While the Semitic Amorites had apparently immigrated from the south, the Hittites arrived as part of a vast movement of Indo-European peoples that originated from the north, apparently from the mountain regions of the Caucasus. This group of peoples spoke "Indo-European" languages, from which developed many of the principal languages of the lands to which they migrated and settled, from Britain in the northwest to Persia and India in the southeast.

In the course of their migrations, the Indo-Europeans also invented the decisive weapon of the age, the two-wheeled war chariot. Drawn by a horse, which bore part of the weight of the chariot, this new war machine had light wheels with a hub and spokes and carried three warriors, at least one of whom could continuously shoot his wooden bow, reinforced with bone and sinew. Unlike the four-wheeled chariot, the new design of the Indo-Europeans had great maneuverability.

The Hittites shared in this invention. When they settled in Anatolia, they also helped usher in another innovation, iron-working technology that they developed in this iron-rich region. They established their capital in Hattushash, modern Boğazköy, Turkey, in the early second millennium B.C.E., extending their power over much of Anatolia and northern Syria. Much of what we know about them comes from some 25,000 cuneiform tablets that were discovered there. About 1590 B.C.E. they invaded and conquered Babylonia. About 1400 to 1200 B.C.E., during the New Kingdom of Egypt, the Hittites ruled as one of the most powerful nations of the Middle East. In c. 1274 B.C.E., in one of the greatest battles of the Middle East, they confronted the Egyptian armies at Qadesh, Syria. The two armies, each with about 20,000 men, and the Hittites with 2500 two-wheeled chariots, fought to a draw. Within a few years these two great powers had concluded treaties of peace and mutual defense, re-affirmed by royal marriages.

The Hittite Empire suddenly collapsed about 1193 B.C.E., perhaps under an onslaught from invaders, the Sea Peoples, who arrived via the Mediterranean. City-state and regional outposts of Hittites survived until about 710 B.C.E., when they were defeated and incorporated by the Assyrians.

The Assyrians. Assyrians, descendants of the Akkadians, were additional major participants in the continuous warfare in Mesopotamia. In the twentieth century B.C.E. they established an independent state and, through the trade of their private businessmen, achieved some prosperity. Then, subjugated by the Mitanni, they regained

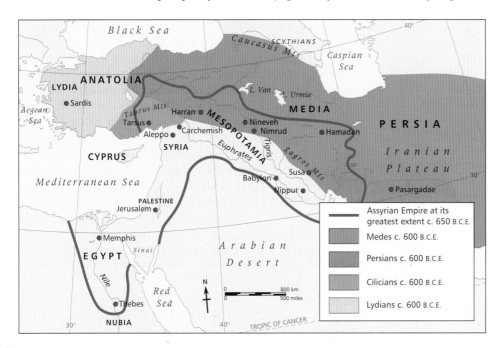

Assyria and its rivals. The shifting political map of southwest Asia was dominated between 850 and 650 B.C.E. by the powerful and martial Assyrians, who even occupied Egypt. Anatolia was fragmented into smaller states. To the north a powerful federation of Median tribes was a growing threat. In 614, in alliance with the Babylonians, they crushed Assyria.

their independence in the thirteenth century only to lose it again to the Arameans *c.* 1000 B.C.E.

Around 900 B.C.E. a Neo-Assyrian (New Assyrian) kingdom began a series of conquests, sweeping westward to the Mediterranean coast, northward to Syria and Palestine, and southeastward into Babylon. Infantry provided their main force, while archers riding in chariots led the attacks, and battering rams and siege towers assaulted fixed positions.

More than most ancient empires, the Assyrians controlled conquered peoples through policies of terror and forced migration. They tortured those they captured to instill fear. They also deported some nations into exile from their homelands, including ten of the tribes of Israel, which were subsequently "lost"—that is, they lost their sense of ethnic and religious identity and presumably ceased their opposition to the Assyrians, just as the conquerors had hoped. In other regions, the Assyrians imported their own people to settle among the defeated peoples and keep them under control.

King Esarhaddon (r. 680–669 B.C.E.) conquered Egypt in 671 B.C.E., making Assyria the greatest power of its day. His successors held the entire province, driving the Nubians from the southern regions and suppressing rebellions. Assyria finally withdrew from Egypt, defeated not primarily by the Egyptians but by internal dynastic struggles and by the combined forces of Babylonians, Arameans, the Medes of Iran, and Scythian invaders, who attacked Assyria's Mesopotamian heartland. The Assyrian capital, Nineveh, fell in 612 B.C.E.

Only the last of the Neo-Assyrian kings, Ashurbanipal (r. 668–627 B.C.E.), is known to have been literate, and he constructed a great library in his capital at Nineveh. Some 20,000 tablets are still preserved from that library, including the earliest complete version of *The Epic of Gilgamesh*.

The city-state organizational structure of Mesopotamia and its geographical openness had left the region very vulnerable. As the city-states fought destructively among themselves, they were repeatedly attacked by, and absorbed into, powerful empires. Some of these empires were based outside the region, others grew up, or transplanted themselves through immigration, within the region. The Mesopotamians had to expend their resources on military technology and organization as their local units of government faced increasing challenges from ever-greater external powers.

Middle and New Kingdom Egypt. By 2040 B.C.E. the unification of Egypt into a centralized, militaristic state was under way. Its hierarchic society focused on the priesthood and the dynastic succession of semi-god rulers, the pharaohs. The consolidation of power was reflected in the size and scale of royal building projects, including fortifications, new cities, temples, and grandiose tombs, and by conquests in Nubia.

Egypt and International Conquest

Egypt's background to empire was very different from Mesopotamia's. From early times Egypt was governed as a unified state. Geography had encouraged Egypt to become a single administrative unit, incorporating the entire Nile valley from the first cataract northward to the Mediterranean Sea. From 3000 B.C.E. to the present, Egypt has usually remained a single political unit, so we think of it as a kingdom with a single government ruling a single civilization rather than as an empire of one people ruling over others.

Egyptian forces did not always stay within their own borders, however. During the Middle Kingdom, c. 2000–1650 B.C.E., Egyptians conquered Nubia, the territory stretching southward some 900 miles from just above the first cataract in the Nile, at present-day Aswan in Egypt, to present-day Khartoum, capital of the Sudan. At first, this imperial conquest was only into lower Nubia, and Nubia's success in driving out the Egyptian conquerors was one of the factors that brought Egypt's Middle Kingdom to an end.

During the second intermediate period (1650–1550 B.C.E.), a time of disunity between periods of consolidation, immigrant Semitic groups, referred to in Egyptian texts as the Hyksos, ruled Lower Egypt. It is not clear if the Hyksos first came as traders or as nomadic immigrants, but as the Egyptian kingdom disintegrated they came to rule parts of it. Although later Egyptian rulers despised them, they are recognized as the legitimate sixteenth dynasty. A Semitic people, the Hyksos introduced bronze-making technology and horses and chariots to Egypt.

One of the establishing events of the New Kingdom, as Egypt became consolidated once again (c. 1550–c. 1070 B.C.E.), was the expulsion of the Hyksos. In pursuing the Hyksos into Palestine, where they apparently had allies, the Egyptians began an active, direct involvement in Middle Eastern affairs that led to their imperial presence in the region for several centuries. Thutmosis I (r. 1504–1492 B.C.E.) not only extended Egypt's control further into Nubia than ever before (see below), but also northeast as far as the Euphrates River, creating Egypt's greatest historical empire. The small states of Syria and Palestine managed to remain self-governing, but Egypt stationed army units and administrative officials in the region and collected taxes. Egypt seemed more interested in access to these taxes, to raw materials, and to trading opportunities than in imperial governance.

Relief from the temple of Beit el-Wali (detail), Lower Nubia, c. 2000–1850 B.C.E. The rich variety of produce here presented to Ramses II after his conquest of Lower Nubia—bags of gold, incense, tusks, ebony logs, ostrich eggs, bows, shields, fans, and wild animals—seems to mirror the ethnic diversity on display. Pale-, brown-, and black-skinned peoples coexisted in Egypt and Nubia. (*British Museum, London*)

Royal pyramids and adjacent iron slag heaps at Meroe, Sudan, *c.* 600 B.C.E. The rulers of Meroe and Egypt shared many artistic traditions, but often gave them a distinctive local interpretation, as can be seen in the forms of their pyramids and palaces.

The Art of Palace and Temple. The colonies of the New Kingdom enriched Egypt, helping to produce a period of great opulence and creativity. Because the pharaoh often traveled throughout the country, the Egyptians built a number of elegant palaces at various points along the Nile, from the delta all the way to the northern edge of Nubia. The state religion and the state administration were closely linked, so temple complexes and the towns that grew up around them were also constructed and reconstructed as important centers of power, faith, and governance. One of the greatest of these temples was constructed by Pharaoh Ramses II (r. *c.* 1279–1213 B.C.E.) at Abu Simbel, just north of the first cataract, and dedicated to the greatest gods of the New Kingdom and to Ramses II himself. The entire complex, including its grand sculptures, was saved from total destruction in the 1970s by being moved to a new location at the time of the building of the Aswan dam, which completely flooded the entire site. Art was abundant and highly stylized, with fixed proportions for various parts of the body, and fixed, usually stiff, poses.

In addition to Ramses II, at least two other pharaohs call for special note. One of the four female pharaohs, Hatshepsut (*c.* 1473–*c.* 1458 B.C.E.) was the widow of one pharaoh and served as regent to her stepson when he succeeded to the throne. For fifteen years, however, until the boy grew up and she died, Hatshepsut declared herself "king," since there was no official sanction for a female ruler. She encouraged artists to represent her as a man, wearing male clothing and with a male king's beard. She built a temple at Deir el-Bahri near Thebes, which was devoted to the worship of the traditional god Amon but which she also hoped would promote her as a deity after her death.

Also departing from Egyptian traditions, in the fifth year of his reign, Amenhotep IV (r. 1352–1336 B.C.E.) changed his name to Akhenaten, "he who serves Aten," the lord of the sun. He challenged the order of ancient Egypt by adopting a new monotheistic religion. Instead of worshiping a pantheon of gods, he worshiped only the sun, and designated himself as mediator between his people and the god. He had the name of

Amon, principal god of the existing religious practice, erased from inscriptions throughout Egypt, and similarly had the words "all gods" removed from certain texts.

To bolster the new order and escape the power of the hostile priesthood, Akhenaten moved his capital 200 miles north from the established center of Thebes to an untouched site in the desert. He named his new city Akhetaten, or "horizon of Aten," present-day Amarna. Here he and his queen Nefertiti and their six daughters practiced their new religion. Akhenaten's religious revolution never caught on. His geographic and intellectual isolation from his people threatened the stability of Egypt's empire. When he died, Akhenaten's successors abandoned Akhetaten and later razed it to the ground. They returned to Thebes where the old religious and political order resumed.

The End of Empire. Egypt's imperial control over remote and diverse peoples met resistance from local powers within the fertile crescent. The Hittites, the Babylonians, and, especially, the Mitanni mounted frequent revolts. (Egyptian pharaoh Ramses II

For an interactive version of this map, go to: http://www.prenhall.com/spodek/map5.4

core Egyptian (New Kingdom) state

extent of Egyptian conquests (Middle and New Kingdom)

core Hittite state

extent of Hittite conquests c. 1250 B.C.E.

core Mitanni state

extent of Mitanni conquests c. 1500 B.C.E.

Babylonian state

The empires of southwest Asia. Toward the end of the second millennium B.C.E. three empires fought for control of the fertile crescent. Egyptians, Mitanni of northern Mesopotamia, and Hittites of Anatolia came into direct conflict. Building on strong political control over their core regions, each dispatched powerful armies with the most up-to-date weapons to seize more territory from the others.

reported the great, but indecisive, battle against the Hittites at Qadesh, noted above, as a brilliant victory, neither the first nor last time that a government would falsely claim military honors that it had not won.) Egyptian control ended by about 1200 B.C.E., although its trading interests and political and economic influence in the region continued for centuries.

After suffering defeats in the Levant, Egypt was pushed back within its river domains, but by now these once again included Nubia. Early in the New Kingdom, Egypt had once again conquered the heartland of central Nubia, the core of the sophisticated, independent state and a source of gold, minerals, wood, and recruits for Egypt's army and police. It maintained its imperial power over this southern colony until c. 1050 B.C.E., when the colony broke free. The loss of empire, together with the loss of the gold, supplies, and slaves it had provided, helped to bring an end to the unified New Kingdom of the Egyptians and to usher in the third intermediate period of divided rule (c. 1069–747 B.C.E.).

Three centuries later Nubia marched northward to capture Egypt itself, reversing the relationship between colonizer and colonized. For half a century, 712–657 B.C.E., Nubia ruled over an empire of its own, which included all of Egypt. Thereafter Nubia remained strong, with its capital first at Napata and later at Meroe, while Egypt fell into decline.

In 671 B.C.E., while Nubians ruled southern Egypt, Assyrians conquered and occupied the north. Egypt's fall into the possession of others continued as the Persians conquered it in 525 B.C.E. Two centuries later, in 332 B.C.E., Alexander the Great captured Egypt from Persia, and in 30 B.C.E., Egypt passed to the next great Mediterranean empire, that of Rome. Some of these conquests are noted below.

THE PERSIAN EMPIRE

Medes and Persians began to appear in the region east of Mesopotamia about 1300 B.C.E., bringing with them the use of iron. Written cuneiform records of the mid-ninth century B.C.E. confirm the archaeological evidence of their arrival. At first the Medes were more numerous and powerful, but later the Persians came to predominate. Like the Hittites, both groups were Indo-Europeans—that is, in language and cultural heritage they were related to some of the same major groups who came to inhabit Europe and northern India.

Cyaxares of Media (r. 625–585 B.C.E.) established an army; conquered the Scythians, another immigrant group in the region; sealed an alliance with the Babylonians by marrying his granddaughter to the son of their ruler; and, together with them, captured Nineveh, the capital of Assyria. They destroyed Assyria as a major military force, and a new **balance of power** among the Egyptians, Medes, Babylonians, and Lydians emerged in western Asia.

balance of power In international relations, a policy that aims to secure peace by preventing any one state or alignment of states from becoming too dominant. Alliances are formed in order to build up a force equal or superior to that of the potential enemy.

Persian Expansion

Cyrus II, the Great, of Persia (r. 558–529 B.C.E.), however, broke the balance when he defeated the other three kingdoms of western Asia and incorporated them into his own empire. He conquered, first, the Medes in 550; then, in 546, the Lydians with their king, the fabulously wealthy Croesus; and finally, in 539, the Babylonians. Under Cyrus, the Achaemenids (named in honor of their legendary ancestor Achaemenes) dominated the entire region from Persia to the Mediterranean.

The story of Cyrus' greatest conquest, his capture of the city of Babylon, also has larger-than-life qualities. Cyrus' legend had grown so great that the Babylonians welcomed their new foreign king without even giving battle. Cyrus was also careful to observe the principal ritual of the Babylonian New Year festival, showing honor to the statue of Bel-Marduk, the king of the Babylonian gods. Herodotus' story of Cyrus' death is also of legendary proportions. In conquering the Massagetai nomads, Cyrus killed the son of the woman who ruled them, and the young man committed suicide. The mother swore revenge and ultimately killed Cyrus. This legend is, however, not consistent with the more illustrious story of Cyrus' death in battle. According to this, Cyrus was killed in battle in 529 B.C.E., defending his empire against attacks from the north by a nomadic group of Scythians led by their queen Tomyris.

His eldest son, Cambyses II (r. 529–522 B.C.E.), expanded Cyrus' conquests. Crossing the Sinai Desert, he captured Memphis, the capital of Egypt, and carried its pharaoh back to Susa in captivity, thus completing the conquest of all of the major powers that had influenced the Middle East. Egypt frequently revolted, and large garrisons were required to keep it under control, so the Achaemenids under Darius I (r. 522–486 B.C.E.) completed a canal across the desert, connecting the Nile River and the Red Sea. This early "Suez Canal," first envisioned by the Egyptians as a trade route, became a troop supply line for Persian control over Egypt.

Darius also extended the Persian Empire more deeply into the Indian subcontinent, as far as the Indus River. The Achaemenids now controlled some of the most valuable trade routes in Asia; the **satrapy**, or province, of "India" submitted one-third of the annual cash receipts of the Achaemenids, and Indian troops served in the Achaemenid armies. From this time, Indian- and Persian-based powers would regularly confront one another across the borders of what are today Afghanistan and Pakistan. Meanwhile, in the west, Darius expanded onto the fringes of Europe, capturing Thrace and Macedonia, and bringing the Persian Empire to its greatest extent.

Achaemenid Persia. The Medes and the Persians were united under Cyrus the Great in 550 B.C.E. to form the Achaemenid or Persian Empire. Cyrus and his successors, notably Darius and Xerxes, extended the empire to the Indus in the east and to Egypt and Libya in the west, and twice invaded Greece.

satrapy A province or colony in the Achaemenid or Persian Empire ruled by a satrap or governor. Darius I completed the division of the Empire into provinces, and established 20 satrapies with their annual tributes. The term satrapy can also refer to the period of rule of a satrap.

Attempts to move further were stymied. The Scythians to the north and west fought a kind of guerrilla warfare that the massed forces of the Persians could not overcome. To the south and west, the Greeks defeated Persian armies of invasion. As you will read later in this chapter, a confederation of small, democratic, Greek city-states managed to repulse the mighty Persian Empire. Herodotus' *The Persian Wars*, written in the late fifth century B.C.E. and presenting the story from a Greek perspective, is the first great book of secular history still preserved.

Imperial Policies

The Persian imperial form of rule and administration changed in the three generations from Cyrus II, its chief architect, through his son and successor Cambyses II, to Darius I, its most powerful emperor. The differences among the three emperors became especially clear in their policies for achieving a balance between the power of the central government and the desire of local, conquered peoples for some degree of autonomy. Under Cyrus and Darius, Persia respected local customs and institutions even as the empire expanded. Cambyses was more dictatorial, and met an early end.

Cyrus II. Cyrus (r. 558–529 B.C.E.) respected the dignity of his opponents. When he conquered the Medes, he allowed their king to escape with his life. He administered his newly acquired lands through the existing Median bureaucracy and army, allowing Median officials to keep their positions, though under Persian control. When Cyrus conquered Lydia, he spared Croesus and even enlisted his advice as a consultant. In conquered Ionian cities he retained local rulers who were willing to work under Persian direction. On defeating Babylon, his most powerful rival, Cyrus chose to rule in the name of the Babylonian god Marduk and to worship daily in his temple, thus keeping the support of the priests. He continued to employ local bureaucrats and to protect and secure the trade routes that brought wealth to the empire and secured the loyalty of the merchant classes.

Perhaps most strikingly, Cyrus allowed the peoples that Babylonia had captured and deported to return to their homes. For example, he permitted the Jewish community of exiles in Babylon to return home to Judaea and to rebuild their temple in

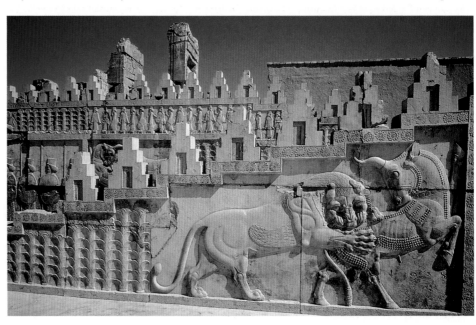

Lion killing a bull, bas relief, Persepolis, Iran, 550–330 B.C.E. The great palace complex of Persepolis, encompassing many smaller palaces within it, was designed as the central symbol of Darius' empire. Construction began in 518 B.C.E. and took some seventy years to complete. Scenes such as this bas relief of a lion killing a bull seem to emerge from Achaemenid mythology, which read the signs of the zodiac, Leo following Taurus, as representing the end of the old year and the coming of the new.

Homage rendered to Darius, bas relief, Persepolis, Iran, 550–330 B.C.E. On New Year's Day, ambassadors of each of Persia's twenty and more satrapies presented themselves to the emperor in his audience hall at Persepolis. Darius, bejeweled and arrayed in royal robes of purple and gold, received them.

Jerusalem. He also returned to them the gold and silver that had been taken from the temple. The 40,000 exiles who returned over 1000 miles to Judaea hailed Cyrus as their political savior and kept their renewed state loyal to the Persian Empire.

Cambyses II. Unlike his father, Cambyses II (r. 529–522 B.C.E.) seems to have lost sight of the need for restraint in both the expansion and the administration of his empire. His conquest of Egypt and his use of Egyptians in his own administration of that land followed Cyrus' model, but then he overextended his reach. His attempted campaign against the Phoenician city of Carthage in distant north Africa failed when Phoenician sailors in his own navy refused to fight. An army sent south from Egypt to Nubia, attempting to capture its fabled gold supplies, failed to reach its destination and retreated from the desert in tatters. Cambyses may not have been emotionally stable, and it was rumored that he kicked to death his pregnant wife/sister. When he died, as he was returning to Persia to put down an insurrection, it was further rumored that he had committed suicide. His seven-year rule had been costly to Persia.

Darius I. Darius (r. 522–486 B.C.E.), a general in the Persian army and prince of the Achaemenid dynasty, succeeded to the throne by murdering Bardiya (r. 522), who ruled briefly after Cambyses. Darius ruled for thirty-five years. He was more deliberate, more balanced, and more capable as an administrator than Cambyses, and he became much richer as emperor than either of his predecessors. Like Cyrus, he used local administrators to staff local governments. He sought to create smaller, more efficient units of government by increasing the number of administrative units, or satrapies, even faster than he expanded the empire. Some of the regional administrators, or satraps, were local elites; some were Persian. In each satrapy, loyalty to the empire was assured by the presence of Persian army units, which reported directly back to the king, and by a secretary, who monitored the actions of the satrap and also reported back to Persia.

Darius commissioned the design of the first written Persian script. He established the tradition that royal inscriptions were to be trilingual—in Old Persian, Babylonian, and Elamite. Among these inscriptions were those on the Behistun stone, a proclamation of Darius' ascent to power, that twenty-three centuries later became the key to unlocking cuneiform writing. In the midst of the multitude of languages used across the empire, these were to be the official written languages of administration. The most widely spoken public language was Aramaic, however, and this language of the common people throughout much of the eastern Mediterranean greatly influenced the development of formal Persian.

Legal codes varied among the satrapies to reflect local usage, and the Persian rulers frequently codified and recorded these laws. They rationalized tax codes. They evaluated, measured, and recorded the size and productivity of agricultural fields, and fixed the tax rate at about 20 percent. In each satrapy a Persian collector gathered the various taxes—on industry, mining, ports, water, commerce, and sales. The satraps remitted most of the revenues to Persia, but some were retained locally for administrative and development expenses.

Darius built, maintained, and guarded an imperial system of roads, the most famous of which was a 1700-mile royal road, stretching from his capital at Susa to Sardis across Anatolia (but not quite reaching the Mediterranean). Along these roads he established a series of inns for travelers and a royal courier service with stations at about every 15 miles. He completed the construction of the Nile–Red Sea canal, which the Egyptians themselves had abandoned.

To increase agricultural production, Darius renewed the irrigation systems of Mesopotamia, and encouraged the introduction of new crops from one part of the empire to another. He standardized the empire's gold coinage, and permitted only his own imperial mints to strike the official coinage, the gold daric, in his name. Agriculture and commerce flourished, and not only for the benefit of the wealthy. Craftsmen produced goods for everyday use—leather sandals, cheap cloth, iron implements and utensils, and pottery—in increasing quantities.

Substantial sums of the enormous wealth of the flourishing empire went to the construction of four capital cities. The most sumptuous and lavish of them, and the one most Persian in style, was built by Darius and named "Parsa," Persia. The Greeks later called it "Persepolis," the city of the Persians.

Symbols of Power

Although the records of ancient Persia speak of painting as one of its arts, little has been found. Our greatest knowledge of Persian art comes from imperial architecture and design, most especially at Persepolis. The outstanding architectural monument in this capital was a fortified citadel that held ceremonial and administrative buildings. Immediately below it was a large complex of residential palaces, probably the homes of the court.

Alexander and subsequent conquerors looted and burned the city, and the dominant remains today are forests of 60-foot high columns, which have survived to indicate the grandeur of the city at its height. The largest and highest of all the remaining structures in the palace is the audience hall of Darius. Its façade is covered by creatures—lions, bulls, and griffins—asserting the power of the emperor and intimidating visitors. These visitors—many of them representatives from Persia's subject lands come to pay their respects in a procession before the emperor—are immortalized in bas reliefs on the façades of the building and its stairways. The array of reliefs suggests the imperial power of Persia over its empire, and yet a place of honor seems to have been found for each of the delegates.

In accordance with the political theory that had evolved in imperial Persia, the emperor legally possessed all the property of the realm as well as the power of life and death over his subjects. Darius did not, however, choose to become a god. He was probably a follower of the religion of the teacher Zarathustra, or Zoroaster as the Greeks called him. Zoroastrian scriptures date him to about 600 B.C.E., although modern scholarship places him as much as 1000 years earlier. In a series of hymns, called *Gathas*, Zoroaster described a conflict between Ahuramazda, the god of goodness and light, and Ahriman, who embodied the forces of evil and darkness. Individuals had to choose between them and they would be rewarded or punished for their choice on a final day of judgment. The *Avesta*, a later, fuller book of Zoroastrian scripture, further elaborated on the concept of an afterlife and the resurrection of the dead. Although, like Cyrus, Darius did not impose his own religious beliefs on the peoples he conquered, Zoroastrianism, with its roots in Persia, did spread rapidly under his rule. Darius also tried to soften the imposition of imperial administration and tax collection by maintaining local traditions and by enlisting local elites to serve in his administration. Like Cyrus, Darius managed to balance imperial majesty with local autonomy. At the western end of his empire, however, his neighbors and rivals, the Greeks, fought back against his attempts to rule over them.

THE GREEK CITY-STATES

The Greek city-states had deep historic roots of their own. Long before the Persian Empire, civilizations had risen and fallen on the Greek peninsula, its neighboring islands, and the island of Crete in the eastern Mediterranean Sea. Archaeological excavations show that for some five hundred years in Greece and for a thousand in Crete, local, brilliant, urban civilizations had flourished.

Early City-states of the Aegean

The Minoans. Immigrants began to settle on Crete about 6000 B.C.E. By 3000 B.C.E., they had built villages, and by 2000 B.C.E. at Knossos they erected the first and largest of at least four major palace complexes on the island. The palaces combined three functions:

HOW DO WE KNOW?

Discovering Troy and Mycenae

Until the 1870s, scholars of classical Greece believed that the Greek city-states had begun their slow evolution about the ninth century B.C.E. after hundreds of years of political and military turmoil. Naturally, they knew of Homer's great epic poems of the Trojan War, the Iliad and the Odyssey, in which the king of Mycenae led the Greek city-states in war against Troy around 1400 B.C.E., but they understood these tales of earlier times to be myths without foundation in fact.

Then, in the 1870s, Heinrich Schliemann, a classicist and amateur archaeologist, discovered evidence of the existence of city kingdoms at both Troy and Mycenae dating to about 1600 to 1450 B.C.E. Schliemann popularized archaeology and began to standardize its methods. He sought to buy the site of Knossos located on the island of Crete, but he couldn't afford to pay what the Ottoman Empire wanted for it. When Crete became independent, another archaeologist, Arthur Evans, was able to buy it. Excavating it in 1900, Evans discovered a massive palace complex that confirmed the possible reality of the

mythical king Minos. Thus archaeologists discovered two ancient kingdoms, with trade links, confirming popular folk legends and locating some of the roots of Greek civilization a thousand years further back in time.

- Languages and civilizations have been lost to history. How does the past become lost?
- Nineteenth- and twentieth-century archaeologists recovered some lost languages and civilizations. Besides Troy and Mycenae, what other examples come to mind?

they were elaborately furnished royal residences, centers for religion and ritual, and headquarters for administering the Cretan economy. The craftspeople of Crete produced bronze tools, gems, and extraordinarily fine pottery in the form of eggshell-thin vessels, which they exported throughout the eastern Mediterranean. As an island kingdom located at the crossroads of multiple trade routes, Crete excelled in commerce. Pictographic writing existed from at least 2000 B.C.E., and syllabic writing was introduced *c.* 1700 B.C.E. Known as Linear A, this script has not yet been deciphered.

About 1450 B.C.E., some, now unknown, disaster led to the destruction of three of the major palaces. (For a time scholars believed that eruptions of the volcano Thera might have caused the destruction, but deep-sea excavations show that the eruption was too early, *c.* 1625 B.C.E., and too far distant to have caused such devastation.) Crete seems to have become more deeply enmeshed in the affairs of the Greek mainland at this time. A new script, known as Linear B, was created for transcribing Greek, suggesting that this had now become the language of Crete. In 1370 B.C.E. the palace at

AT A GLANCE : ANCIENT GREECE AND ITS NEIGHBORS

DATE	POLITICAL	RELIGION AND CULTURE	SOCIAL DEVELOPMENT
600 B.C.E.	■ Cyaxares of Media (r. 625–585) ■ Age of Greek tyrants (657–570)	■ Zoroaster (630–553)	■ City-states in Greece
550 B.C.E.	■ Cyrus II (r. 558–529); defeat of Medes, Lydia, Babylon ■ Peisistratus (d. 527) controlled Athens ■ Cambyses II (r. 529–522) conquered Egypt	■ Pasargadae and Susa developed	■ Nile–Red Sea canal
500 B.C.E.	■ Darius I (r. 522–486); Persian Empire extended to Indus River; war against Greek city-states ■ Ionian revolt (499) ■ Battle of Marathon (490) ■ Xerxes I (r. 486–465) ■ War between Athens and Sparta: 1st Peloponnesian War (461–451)	■ Pythagoras (d. *c.* 500) ■ Piraeus established as port of Athens ■ Persepolis built	■ Athens at the height of its power. Acropolis built (*c.* 460); architecture, city-state democracy, political philosophy flourish
450 B.C.E.	■ Pericles (d. 429) and Delian League ■ 2nd Peloponnesian War (431–404) and end of Athenian power	■ Persian script written down ■ "Golden Age" of Athens ■ Aeschylus (d. 456) ■ Herodotus (d. *c.* 420) ■ Sophocles (d. 406) ■ Euripides (d. 406) ■ Thucydides (d. *c.* 401)	■ Persian Empire: regional laws codified; roads built; centralized administration; irrigation systems extended
400 B.C.E.		■ Socrates (d. 399)	
350 B.C.E.	■ Philip II (r. 359–336) and Alexander the Great (r. 336–323) extend Macedonian Empire ■ Athens and Thebes defeated (338), ending Greek independence ■ Alexander conquers Asia Minor (334) and Egypt (332), and reaches Indus (326)	■ Aristophanes (d. *c.* 351) ■ Plato (d. 348) ■ Aristotle (d. 322) ■ Demosthenes (d. 322) ■ Alexandria (Egypt) founded (331) ■ Persepolis burned (331)	■ Spread of Hellenistic culture
300 B.C.E.	■ Ptolemies in Egypt ■ Seleucids in Asia		

Knossos was also destroyed, and Crete came under the sway of Mycenae, the leading city-state of mainland Greece. Finally the glories of Knossos were lost, preserved for thousands of years only in legend.

The Mycenaeans. Homer portrays the Mycenaeans as brave and heroic warriors as well as active sailors and traders. They carried on extensive trade and cultural exchange with Crete, including sharing the use of Linear B script. After 1450, when several of Crete's important towns were destroyed, Mycenae came to dominate the relationship.

Mycenae was home to several small kingdoms, each with its own palace or citadel and accompanying cemetery of beehive-shaped tombs. The greatest of the cities was Mycenae itself, capital of the legendary king Agamemnon. This administrative center of the entire region was surrounded by a colossal wall up to 25 feet thick. Its massive entrance gate was adorned with huge stone lions looking down on all who entered and left. The site is rich in the evidence of warfare: weapons, armor, paintings of warriors, and, at the seashore a few miles distant, ships of war. Some of the kings, at least, were quite wealthy: one was buried with 11 pounds of gold, and the funeral "mask of Agamemnon" was a work of consummate craftsmanship in gold. Scholars have been unable to discover the reason for the fall of Mycenaean civilization; perhaps it was invaded, perhaps it imploded in internal warfare. By the end of the twelfth century B.C.E., all the palaces and towns of Mycenae had been destroyed or abandoned.

Their fall ushered in the Greek "Dark Ages," a period of general upheaval throughout much of the eastern Mediterranean. The Greeks even lost their knowledge of how to write. Apparently, additional waves of nomadic immigrants entered Greece from the north. By about 850 B.C.E. the peoples of Greece began to emerge from an age of darkness and once again to settle, to build towns, to trade overseas, to receive new waves of immigrants that increased their population, and to restore their written culture.

Death mask ("Mask of Agamemnon"), 16th century B.C.E. Gold. When archaeologists in the late nineteenth century discovered this brilliant death mask, in this leading city-state of ancient Greece, they naturally claimed that it represented Mycenae's King Agamemnon himself, leader of the Greek forces in their war against Troy. Later judgments differed, because the date of the mask was too early. (*National Archaeological Museum, Athens*)

The Greek Polis: Image and Reality

By the time the Persian emperor Darius I began to conquer the Greek city-states of western Anatolia (present-day Turkey), the Greeks had developed a very different form of political organization from that of the Persian imperial structure. The Greek city-state, or polis, was an intentionally small, locally organized government based on a single central city with enough surrounding land to support its agricultural needs. Most of the city-states had populations of a few thousand, with only the very largest of them exceeding 40,000 people.

Geography and topography played a large part in limiting the size of the Greek city-state. In and around the Greek peninsula, mountains, rivers, and seas had kept the units of settlement rather small and isolated. (To the north, where farmland was more expansive, as it was in Macedonia, geographically larger states developed within such

SOURCE

Homer and the Value System of Early Greece

Historical folk tales survived from the era of Mycenae through the Dark Ages. From these tales, which had probably circulated orally since the twelfth century B.C.E., the poet Homer (c. eighth century B.C.E.) wove his two great epic poems, the Iliad and the Odyssey. The Iliad tells of the Trojan War, which, Homer writes, a coalition of Greek city-states launched against the Trojans in response to the seduction of Helen, the wife of the king of Sparta, by Paris, the son of the king of Troy. Just as the war begins in a personal vendetta, so, too, individual feuds during the war break out among the Greeks themselves, for personal more than for political reasons. The bitter personal quarrel between Agamemnon, brother of the king of Sparta and himself king of Mycenae, and Achilles, the mightiest of the Greek warriors, cripples the effectiveness of the Greek coalition and dominates the storyline of the Iliad. The Odyssey tells the still more personal post-war story of Odysseus' ten-year struggle to reach his home in Ithaca and of his ultimate reunion with his wife and son in that kingdom.

Although some literary critics believe that "Homer" was really more than one author, most today believe that just one person wrote, or dictated, the epics. The stories on which Homer bases his poetic accounts were probably well known among the Greeks of his time. Homer's lasting reputation and fame rest on his skill in crafting these stories into coherent narratives told in poetry of great power. Further, by focusing on personal stories within the national epics, Homer created images of human excellence (arete in ancient Greek) at levels of heroism that inspire readers to this day. He writes with equal power of excellence in war and in love.

Bravery in warfare is a cardinal virtue, and, in the Iliad, Homer portrays Hektor, the mightiest of the Trojans, praying that his son might inherit his own strength in battle, and even surpass it. The child's mother would apparently share this vision of her son as warrior:

> Zeus, and you other immortals, grant that this boy, who is my son,
> may be as I am, pre-eminent among the Trojans,
> great in strength, as am I, and rule strongly over Ilion;
> and some day let them say of him: "He is better by far than his father,"
> as he comes in from the fighting; and let him kill his enemy
> and bring home the blooded spoils, and delight the heart of his mother.   (*Iliad*, VI: 476–81)

Praising excellence in warfare and combat, Homer portrays Odysseus, Telemachus, and their followers in the Odyssey as fierce raptors swooping down upon their prey:

> After them the attackers wheeled, as terrible as falcons
> from eyries in the mountains veering over and diving down
> with talons wide unsheathed on flights of birds,
> who cower down the sky in chutes and bursts along the valley—

> but the pouncing falcons grip their prey, no frantic wing avails,
> and farmers love to watch those beaked hunters.
> So these now fell upon the suitors in that hall,
> turning, turning to strike and strike again,
> while torn men moaned at death, and blood ran smoking over the whole floor. (XXII: 310–19)

Homer sang equally vividly, and far more sweetly and poignantly, of excellence in love. As the Odyssey moves toward its conclusion, hero and heroine, Odysseus and Penelope, are reunited after a wartime separation of twenty years:

> Now from his breast into his eyes the ache
> of longing mounted, and he wept at last,
> his dear wife, clear and faithful, in his arms,
> longed for as the sunwarmed earth is longed for by a swimmer
> spent in rough water where his ship went down
> under Poseidon's blows, gale winds and tons of sea.
> Few men can keep alive through a big surf
> to crawl, clotted with brine, on kindly beaches
> in joy, in joy, knowing the abyss behind:

> and so she too rejoiced, her gaze upon her husband,
> her white arms round him pressed as though forever.
> … (XXIII: 234–44)

> So they came
> into that bed so steadfast, loved of old,
> opening glad arms to one another,
> Telemachus by now had hushed the dancing,
> hushed the women. In the darkened hall
> he and the cowherd and the swineherd slept.
> The royal pair mingled in love again
> and afterward lay reveling in stories:
> hers of the siege her beauty stood at home
> from arrogant suitors, crowding on her sight,
> and how they fed their courtship on his cattle,
> oxen and fat sheep, and drank up rivers
> of wine out of the vats.
>   Odysseus told
> of what hard blows he had dealt out to others
> and of what blows he had taken—all that story.
> she could not close her eyes till all was told.
>   (*Odyssey* XXIII: 298–313)

War and love, the bloody heroism of the battlefield and the warm intimacy of family life—Homer addressed both in imagery that has inspired readers, and listeners, to this day.

centralized city capitals.) When a region could no longer support an expanding population, it hived off colonies to new locations. Most of the Greek city-states in Anatolia seem to have originated as colonial settlements of older cities on the Greek mainland, part of an array of Greek city-states that spread throughout the Mediterranean coast, extending as far west as present-day Marseilles in France and Catalonia in Spain. Although separate and usually independent politically, the city-states were united culturally by the use of the Greek language, a myth-history centered on the *Iliad* and *Odyssey* of the poet Homer, and such festivals as the Olympic games, held every four years after 776 B.C.E.

The physical design of a Greek polis told much about its origins, functions, and ideals. Many cities were built on hillsides, at least partly for defense, but also partly because of the mountainous geography of Greece. As the city rose, with each level upward its functions and architecture became more exalted. At the bottom were the houses of the common people, built simply from local materials of stone and mud, with little concern for architectural merit. Private dwellings were relatively plain; the fine art and architecture went into public buildings.

Further up the hill was the **agora**, or civic and market center, with clusters of buildings for trade in goods, ideas, and political maneuvers. These public buildings were more elegant, designed for greater comfort and show. Nearby were gymnasia for exercise and competition. The *agora* and gymnasia demonstrated the value the Greeks placed on public life and physical prowess and discipline. Further off, built into the side of the hill, was an amphitheater where plays were regularly performed, often representing scenes from Greek mythological history and suggesting their significance in understanding the moral issues of the day. In the city of Athens, at the top of the hill, on the Acropolis ("city on high"), surrounded by a wall, were the chief temples of the city, especially the shrine to the goddess Athena who was considered the divine guardian of the city.

agora A central feature of ancient Greek town planning. Its chief function was as a town market, but it also became the main social and political meeting place. Together with the acropolis, it normally housed the most important buildings of the town. Later, the Roman forum fulfilled this function.

Athens and the Development of Democracy

Each polis developed its own form of government. Councils of nobles governed some cities, while others fell under the rule of a single powerful individual. We recount the fate of the city of Athens, in particular, for three reasons: It was a leader among the Greek city-states; it gave birth to the modern concept of political democracy; and it has left us the most historical records. Of all the major cities of Greece—for example, Sparta, Corinth, Thebes, and Syracuse—Athens seems to have moved farthest from rule by kings and oligarchies in the direction of rule by the people, democracy.

In 600 B.C.E., Solon (*c.* 630–*c.* 560 B.C.E.), who had risen to high office as a general and a poet, ended the monopoly over public office held by the Athenian hereditary aristocracy. He opened to all free men participation and voting in the decision-making public assembly, although only those meeting certain income levels could be elected to high public office. The Council of Four Hundred, which Solon also created, represented the interests of the wealthy and noble factions, while the assembly balanced them with the voices of more common men. Perhaps more importantly, Solon canceled all public and private debts, and abolished the practice of enslaving people to pay off their debts.

Solon's reforms crumbled when he left office, and decades of struggle between rich and poor and between men of different hereditary clans ensued until about 550 B.C.E., when Peisistratus seized control of the government as a "tyrant," the Greek term for a one-man autocratic ruler. Peisistratus (d. 527 B.C.E.) fostered economic growth through loans to small farmers; export promotion programs; road construction; and public works, including major building programs for the beautification of Athens and its

Two halves of a red-figure cup by the sculptor Douris, fifth century B.C.E. The figures depict four scenes from the education of a young man: learning to play the lyre and flute, and learning to read and write, all under the watchful eye of a pedagogue.

deme A rural district or village in ancient Greece, or its members or inhabitants. The demes were a constituent part of the polis but had their own corporations with police powers, and their own cults, officials, and property.

Acropolis. On Peisistratus' death, the city-state again fell into disarray and even civil war. In 510 B.C.E., at the invitation of a faction of Athenian noblemen, the king of Sparta, already Athens' greatest rival, invaded Athens, besieged the Acropolis, and deposed the descendants of Peisistratus.

Through all the warfare and strife, the ideals of Solon survived. A new ruler, Cleisthenes (c. 570–c. 508 B.C.E.), came to power as a tyrant and dramatically reorganized the city and its surrounding countryside. He did away with the aristocratic family centers of power by registering each Athenian as a citizen according to his geographical residence, or **deme**, in the city. Similarly, he reorganized the electoral districts of Attica, the region around Athens, into ten electoral units, creating new political identities and allegiances. The assembly resumed meeting about every ten days, and all male citizens were expected to participate; 6000 were necessary for a quorum. Above the assembly, and setting its agenda, was a Council of Five Hundred, even more open than Solon's Council of Four Hundred had been, since members were selected from each deme, or neighborhood, for one-year terms by lottery, and members were not allowed to serve for more than two terms. In organizing themselves by deme, Athenians based their political identity on geographical residence in the city, not on heredity and kinship, nor on class and wealth.

This new concept of civic identity allowed the city to welcome new residents and the ideas they brought with them, regardless of their place of origin. It allowed people of different ethnic origins, even of enemy ethnic stocks, to enter the city, although they were not eligible for full citizenship, which was restricted to free men born in the deme. The human interaction in the small Greek city-state nurtured the intellect of its citizens. Life in the polis meant constant participation in a kind of ongoing public seminar. As Socrates (c. 470–399 B.C.E.), the leading philosopher of fifth-century Athens, said: "I'm a lover of learning, and trees and open country won't teach me anything, whereas men in the town do."

When Darius I's Persian Empire challenged the Greek city-states, Athens took the lead in forming a coalition against it. The contrast between the combatants was stark: city-state versus empire; local administration versus imperial power; evolving, decentralized democracy versus established, centralized imperial control. Persia was a huge, centrally governed empire; each Greek city-state was individually independent, although many had joined into regional confederations and leagues for mutual assistance and trade. A single emperor who set policies for the entire empire headed Persia; an assembly of all its adult, free, male citizens, for the most part, governed each individual Greek city-state. These assemblies passed laws, judged criminal and civil cases, provided for administration and implementation of legislation, and arranged for military defense as the need arose. The Greek city-states were moving toward democracy; they understood their legal systems to be their own creation and responsibility, neither ordained by the gods nor imposed by a powerful external emperor.

Greek trireme. The Greeks developed triremes (with three banks of oars) as warships and had them specially strengthened so that they could ram other ships. The triremes were slower and less maneuverable than the Persian ships. To compensate, the Greeks put soldiers aboard and, at Salamis, relied mostly on hand-to-hand combat.

War with Persia

Some of the Greek city-states in Anatolia had earlier fallen under Darius' empire. Although they were permitted to retain their own form of local government as long as they paid their taxes to Persia, some of them revolted and called on the Greek cities of the peninsula for help. Athens tried, half-heartedly and unsuccessfully, to assist its overseas relatives with ships and soldiers. According to Herodotus, Darius was furious at this interference. He ordered one of his servants to remind him, every day at dinnertime, "Master, remember the Athenians." In 490, Darius I dispatched a naval expedition directly across the Aegean to punish Athens for its part in the revolt in Anatolia.

War with the Persians tested the Greeks' fundamental mode of political organization. How could the tiny Greek city-states hold off Darius' imperial armies and keep their incipient democracies alive? First, they had the enormous advantage of being close to home, with a good knowledge of local geography and conditions. Second, the largest among them, especially Athens and Sparta, chose to cooperate in defense against a common enemy.

hoplite A heavily armed foot soldier of ancient Greece, whose function was to fight in close formation, usually in ranks of eight men. Each soldier carried a heavy bronze shield, a short iron sword, and a long spear for thrusting.

When the Persian fleet of 600 ships landed 48,000 soldiers at Marathon in 490 B.C.E., a force of some 10,000 Greek **hoplite** soldiers, joined by about 1000 soldiers from Plataea and another 1000 slaves, confronted them. The hoplite forces were deployed in solid phalanxes, columns of soldiers arrayed in tight lines, the left arm and shield of one man pressed against the right shoulder of the other, in row on row. If a soldier in the front row fell, one from the next line took his place. (In these hoplite formations, each individual soldier is crucial to the welfare of all. Many analysts have seen in this egalitarian military formation the rationale for Athenian political democracy.)

The discipline of the Athenians defeated their enemy. At the Battle of Marathon in 490 B.C.E., Persia lost 6400 men, Athens 192. The Athenian general sent his fastest runner, Pheidippides, racing back to Athens to tell of the victory at Marathon to strengthen the resolve of the Athenians at home and to hasten their preparations for battle against the surviving Persian forces. Pheidippides delivered the message, and died of exhaustion on the spot. (The marathon race of today is named for his 26-mile run.)

Xerxes I (r. 486–465 B.C.E.), Darius's son, succeeded him and mounted a renewed attack on the Greek mainland by land and sea in 480 B.C.E. Courageous resistance by the Spartan general Leonidas and his troops at Thermopylae cost the lives of all the defenders, but won time for the Athenians to evacuate their city and regroup their forces. Xerxes continued to push onward to Athens, capturing, burning, and plundering the city and its Acropolis, but the Athenian warriors had withdrawn to the nearby port of Piraeus and the Bay of Salamis. At Salamis, a force of some 1000 Persian ships confronted a much smaller fleet of some 300 Greek triremes, named for the three levels in which its approximately 170 rowers were arranged. One of Xerxes' most trusted naval advisers, Artemisia, a widowed queen among the people of Halicarnassus, and a captain of one of the ships, counseled waiting and watching. Xerxes, however, followed the majority and sailed into battle. The Athenians maneuvered the Persians into a bottleneck in the Salamis Channel and destroyed 200 of their ships while losing only 40. Xerxes sailed for home, and Persia never again attacked Greece by sea.

The Persians did, however, continue to fight by land. In 479 B.C.E., in alliance with their subjects in Macedonia and some northern Greeks, they prepared an army of some 100,000 men on the edge of the plains opening southward to Athens and the Peloponnese. Sparta and Athens formed an alliance with some other city-states to field an opposing army of about 40,000. Despite initial confusion in the ranks, the allied Spartan and Athenian forces destroyed the Persian armies and their camp, annihilated the elite guard, and killed the leading Persian general. At about the same time, the Greek fleet defeated the surviving Persian fleet at Mycale, on the Ionian coast of Anatolia.

In the face of these losses, and with weaker leadership at home, Persia left Europe, never to return in such force. The small Greek city-states, led by arch-rivals Athens and Sparta, had shown an ability to combine in the face of a common enemy. They had demonstrated the virtues of small-scale, local units of society and the resilience of popular, democratic forms of government. Conversely, the Persians had exhibited one of the great flaws of empire: the tendency to overextend its powers.

Athens: from City-State to Mini-Empire

Ironically, the city-state of Athens, having led the Greeks in their struggle against the Persian Empire, subsequently began to construct an empire of its own. For purposes of the war, Athens had assembled its principal allies into the Delian League, with its council and treasury situated in Delos. At first, membership was voluntary, but soon Athens forbade withdrawal. When Naxos left the league in 470 B.C.E., the Athenians attacked the city, forced it to return, and terminated its independence. Other allies also revolted, usually because they could not meet Athens' demands for tribute and ships. As Athens continued to suppress these revolts, Thucydides reports, "the Athenians as rulers were no longer popular as they used to be."

By 461 B.C.E., many of the Greek city-states turned to Sparta to help them resist Athenian power. For ten years, from 461 to 451, Athens and its allies confronted Sparta and its allies in a series of intermittent battles sometimes called the First Peloponnesian War. During these wars Athens exploited its allies. In 454 B.C.E. the Athenians moved the treasury of the Delian League to Athens and appropriated its funds in order to create in the city a spectacular center of culture and grace. These self-serving actions antagonized its allies and precipitated further war with Sparta. Here we explore Athens, first in its brilliant century of splendor, and later in its wartime suffering and defeats.

Parthenon, Athens, 447–432 B.C.E. The Parthenon on the Athenian Acropolis was a temple dedicated to the goddess Athena, the city's patron-deity. It was built at the instigation of Pericles as a symbol of Athens' growing importance and represents, in architectural terms, the summit of classical Greek achievement.

The Golden Age of Athenian Culture

Under the military and civic leadership of Pericles (*c.* 495–429 B.C.E.), Athenians took immense pride in their city-state, its democratic philosophy and artistic creativity. During the war years, the Persians had destroyed and burned much of Athens. When victory was secure, the Athenians began the rebuilding of their city.

Athens rose from a plain, and with each level upward its functions and architecture became more exalted. At the bottom were the houses of commoners, built simply from local materials of stone and mud, with little concern for architectural merit. Further up the hill was the *agora*, or civic and market center, with clusters of buildings for trade in goods, ideas, and political decision-making. These public buildings were more elegant, designed for greater comfort and show. In the splendor of the *agora* Athenians demonstrated the value placed on public life and on physical prowess and discipline. Nearby were gymnasia for exercise and competition. An amphitheater where plays were regularly performed was carved out of the hillside. At the top of the hill, on the Acropolis ("city on high"), surrounded by a wall, were the chief temples of the city, especially the shrine of the goddess Athena, the divine guardian of the city. Architects and urban designers Ictinus and Callicrates planned the new Acropolis and built the Parthenon, while the sculptor Phidias carved the friezes on the Parthenon and created a 40-foot-high statue of Athena, the city's patron goddess, to reside within it.

As the architectural projects flourished, Pericles founded a colony in southern Italy and took a fleet into the Black Sea. More important, he encouraged naval battles against Sparta and Corinth, as well as Persia, to promote his radical egalitarian democracy at home. Rowers typically were poorer than hoplites, but benefited from regular salaries and the spoils of war and empire. Eventually, he realized his strategy was flawed, concluding that his imperial ambitions threatened the very Athenian democracy he cherished.

sophist An itinerant professor of higher education in ancient Greece, who gave instruction for a fee. The subjects taught, which included oratory, grammar, ethics, mathematics, and literature, had the practical aim of equipping pupils for successful careers.

Plan of Acropolis. The construction of the Acropolis (Greek for "high city") beginning in *c.* 460 B.C.E. under the leadership of Pericles, signified the beginning of a Golden Age for Athens. The plan above indicates some of its most celebrated buildings—the Parthenon (1), the Erectheum (2), the Propylaea (3), and the Temple of Athena Nike (4).

Historians. The city's historians began to reflect on its origins, accomplishments, and the challenges it had faced. Indeed, the modern profession of history as a systematic attempt to understand the influence of past experience on the present began in Athens. Two of the most outstanding historians of the fifth century B.C.E. have given us the history of the city and its relationships with its neighbors. Herodotus (d. *c.* 420 B.C.E.) wrote *The Persian Wars*, and in the narrative recaptured a general, if anecdotal, history of the whole eastern Mediterranean and eastward as far as Persia and India from a Greek perspective. Thucydides (d. *c.* 401 B.C.E.), far more systematically and carefully, recounted the subsequent *History of the Peloponnesian War*, the war between Athens and Sparta that lasted from 431 B.C.E. until 404 B.C.E.

Philosophers. Philosophers such as Socrates and his student Plato introduced questions, methods of analysis and of teaching, and examinations of the purpose of life, which continue to command attention for their range and depth. Plato's prize student, Aristotle, later wrote that man is a "political animal," a creature of the city-state, and many of the key works in Greek history, drama, and philosophy explored the working of the city-state itself and the relationship of the individual to it.

For the philosopher Socrates (*c.* 470–399 B.C.E.), the Athenian state was father and mother; he derived his sense of self and purpose from the education the state gave him and from his continual debates with fellow citizens both in public and private. Socrates argued for the supremacy of the city-state over the individual. The citizen had obligations to the state for all the benefits he received from it, but had no rights to claim against the power of the state.

Socrates took philosophy personally and seriously. He opposed and satirized the **sophist** philosophers of his day who earned their salaries by training future statesmen how to argue any side of any question without necessarily staking any personal commitment. Through his incessant questions, he taught *his* students to be thoughtful but critical about the truths of others and about their own truths, and, after having reached their own conclusions, to live their own truths fully even if it meant their death, as it did for Socrates himself.

Plato (*c.* 428–348 B.C.E.) was Socrates' leading pupil and the founder of the Academy, which endured for centuries as Athens' leading school of philosophy. His philosophical works dealt with many topics, including love, justice, courage, and the nature of the state. Plato conceived of ideal situations, whether realistic or not. The ideal state, according to Plato, would be administered by a philosopher-king, who by virtue of innate good character and intensive training would know and do what was best for all citizens in the state. Similarly, Plato saw love ascending from the emotional and sexual passion for an individual to the contemplation of universal ideals.

Aristotle (384–322 B.C.E.), Plato's greatest pupil, addressed an astonishing array of subjects—logic, physics, astronomy, metaphysics, religion, rhetoric, literary criticism, and natural science—but he, too, devoted some of his most important writing to ethics and politics. His analysis of the principal forms of constitutional government in his *Politics* remains a useful introduction to the field even today. Aristotle later tutored Alexander the Great of Macedon, although that world-conqueror seems to have thoroughly rejected his teacher's argument for small units of government like the city-state: As Aristotle argued:

> If the citizens of a state are to judge and to distribute offices according to merit, then they must know each other's characters; where they do not possess this knowledge, both the election to offices and the decision of lawsuits will go wrong. When the population is very large they are manifestly settled at haphazard, which clearly ought not to be. (*Politics* VII: 4; p. 326)

Dramatists. Drama developed and flourished in the theaters of Athens. The pursuit of justice, morality, and equity was a core theme. Athenian playwrights invented the

A marble, second-century-C.E. copy of the statue of Athena Parthenos, dedicated in 438 B.C.E. Phidias' 40-foot Athena, the divine guardian of the city, dominated the central chamber of the Parthenon on the Acropolis. This miniature Roman copy of the destroyed statue hardly suggests the glittering magnificence of the enormous gold-and-ivory original, a powerful symbol of the might of the goddess and her city, Athens. (*Acropolis Museum, Athens*)

SOURCE

Socrates on the Rights of the State over the Individual

Condemned to death on trumped-up charges of corrupting the political morals of youth and blaspheming against the gods of Athens, Socrates is offered the opportunity to escape and live out his life in another city-state. He refuses. He notes that the state has acted through formal legal process and has the right to execute him. He, in turn, has the obligation to accept the sentence.

Are you too wise to see that your country is worthier, more to be revered, more sacred, and held in higher honor both by the gods and by all men of understanding, than your father and your mother and all your other ancestors; and that you ought to reverence it, and to submit to it, and to approach it more humbly when it is angry with you than you would approach your father; and either to do whatever it tells you to do or to persuade it to excuse you; and to obey in silence if it orders you to endure flogging or imprisonment, or if it sends you to battle to be wounded or to die? That is just. You must not give way, nor retreat, nor desert your station. In war, and in the court of justice, and everywhere, you must do whatever your state and your country tell you to do, or you must persuade them that their commands are unjust. But it is impious to use violence against your father or your mother; and much more impious to use violence against your country. (Plato, *Crito* XII: 51: b)

dramatic forms of tragedy and comedy, and their most important plays all include themes related to the evolution of their city and its institutions.

The *Oresteia* trilogy by Aeschylus (525–456 B.C.E.) follows three generations of murders within the royal family of Atreus, as one act of revenge provokes the next, until finally, in a trial at Athens, Athena, patron goddess of the city, acquits Orestes, suggesting that divinely ordained vengeance will be replaced by human justice and the cycle of murder will be ended.

Oedipus Rex of Sophocles (*c.* 496–406 B.C.E.), perhaps the most famous single play of ancient Athens, centers on the family tragedy of Oedipus' murder of his own father, the king of Thebes, and his subsequent marriage to his own mother. (Oedipus, who had been abandoned as an infant and raised by shepherds, did not know that the man he killed was his father and that he had married his mother.) The play opens with the people of Thebes gathered round King Oedipus, before his tragedy is revealed, crying out for his help in arresting a plague that is afflicting the city. Oedipus' own moral corruption has brought the plague on the city, although that is revealed only later. Sophocles' *Antigone* confronts the conflict in loyalty to family versus loyalty to the city-state, as Antigone chooses to bury her brother, Polynices, despite the royal decree to leave his corpse unattended as an enemy of the state.

Euripides (480–406 B.C.E.) saw more clearly Athens' move toward imperialism, and criticized it in *The Trojan Women*. The hilarious, sexually explicit comedy, *Lysistrata*, by Aristophanes (*c.* 450–385 B.C.E.) portrays the women of Athens and Sparta agreeing to go on strike sexually until their men stop fighting the Peloponnesian Wars. As long as the men make war the women will not make love! The best of the Athenian dramatists addressed directly the political and social issues that confronted their city.

The Limits of City-State Democracy

Socrates' justification of the state demonstrates that even in the most democratic Greek city-state, government could exact respect and service from the citizen, but the citizen had few rights vis-à-vis the state. The citizen had the right, and indeed the obligation, to participate in the activities of the state and to serve the state, but not to have the state serve him.

For women, even the right of participation was absent. Women born of two Athenian parents were regarded as citizens, enjoyed some legal protection, and had responsibilities for performing certain religious rituals of great importance for the state. But, like slaves, they were excluded from attending the meetings of the assembly, holding annual public offices, serving as jurors, initiating legal cases on their own, or owning property in their own names. They had to have a man speak for them before judges and juries. Women's segregation from public life in ancient Greece perpetuated longstanding beliefs that there is a public sphere and a private sphere, and that women should be confined to the latter. Pericles captured this belief in his famous funeral oration, when he delivered this advice to the widows of fallen warriors: "Great will be your glory in not falling short of your natural character; and greatest will be hers who is least talked of among the men, whether for good or for bad."

Since many Greeks believed that true friendship was possible only among equals, many Greek men sought relationships, including sexual relationships, with other men outside their households, even when they held their marriages in high esteem. Greek vases, especially those used in male drinking parties, often carried paintings that glorified the phallus. Given this evidence, some feminist historians have concluded that this culture was misogynistic—hating women—and that the exaltation of masculinity could have been at the root of the constant warfare and militarism of ancient Greek society.

Plato (c. 428–348 B.C.E.) recognized the prejudices against women in his society. When he suggested in his visionary *Republic* that women should be treated equally with men in their access to the highest professional and civic responsibilities, and in the education needed to achieve them, he knew that his ideas were revolutionary for Athens in his time and that they would be greeted with derision. Plato himself believed that men were generally more talented than women, but he argued that both should be offered equal access to political opportunity. On the issue of gender equality, he seemed to remain consistent with his general philosophy: the state should encourage each citizen to reach his or her educational potential, and should direct the most talented into governmental affairs. Plato wrote:

> There is no occupation concerned with the management of social affairs which belongs either to women or to men, as such. Natural gifts are to be found here and there in both creatures alike; and every occupation is open to both, so far as their natures are concerned, though woman is for all purposes the weaker ... Now, for the purpose of producing a woman fit to be a Guardian, we shall not have one education for men and another for women ... If we are to set women to the same tasks as men, we must teach them the same things. They must have the same two branches of training for mind and body and also be taught the art of war, and they must receive the same treatment.

Aristotle confirmed Plato's apprehensions, but not his optimism nor his sense of potential equality. Aristotle wrote of women: "The temperance of a man and of a woman, or the courage and justice of a man and of a woman, are not, as Socrates maintained, the same; the courage of a man is shown in commanding, of a woman in obeying." He quotes with approval the general view that "Silence is a woman's glory."

Psykter (wine cooler) painted by Douris with cavorting satyrs, 500–490 B.C.E. Feminist historian Eva Keuls argues that, contrary to the cradle-of-civilization clichés, Athenian society was excessively warlike and women-hating. She finds much of her evidence on Greek vases of the type used in male drinking parties. (*British Museum, London*)

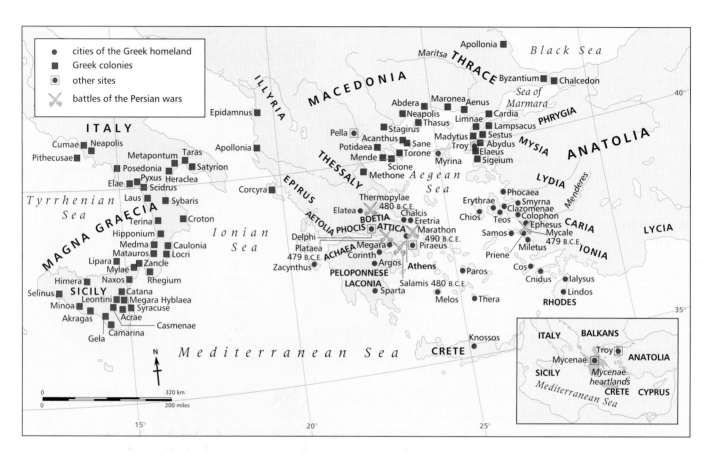

Classical Greece. The hilly terrain and sea-boundaries of Greece discouraged the growth of large settlements, and Greek philosophers also stressed the importance of local community. When population grew too great the citizens encouraged their younger cohort to establish new city-states of their own. The resulting spread of settlements established Greek influence all the way from Sicily to Anatolia.

In practice, Athens followed Aristotelian rather than Platonic views on the role of women in public life.

Even among males, only the sons of native-born Athenian mothers and fathers were eligible for citizenship. Slaves captured in war, and even allies, could not gain citizenship. When Classical Athens reached its maximum population, 250,000, only about one adult Athenian in six qualified for citizenship. These limits on Athenian democracy increased domestic social strains.

Ironically, the city-state of Athens, having led the Greek city-states in the struggle against the Persian Empire, subsequently set out to construct an empire of its own. Following major victories in the Persian wars, Athens assembled its principal allies into the Delian League, with its council and treasury situated in Delos. At first, membership was voluntary, but soon Athens forbade withdrawal. Some cities left the League, usually because they could not pay the tribute Athens demanded. They found it particularly difficult to supply triremes, because they frequently lacked the shipyards of their larger ally. In response, Athens might declare war against them. As a result, "the Athenians as rulers," in the words of Thucydides, "were no longer popular as they used to be."

By 461 B.C.E., many of the Greek city-states turned to Sparta to help them resist Athenian coercion. For ten years, from 461 to 451, Athens and its allies confronted Sparta and its allies in intermittent warfare. During these wars Athens exploited its allies. In 454 B.C.E. Pericles moved the treasury of the Delian League to Athens and appropriated its funds in order to create at Athens a spectacular center of power and authority, particularly by building the Parthenon and expanding the fleet. A democracy at home, Athens was fast becoming an imperial power holding sway over its neighbor.

The Peloponnesian War

Relationships between Athens and its neighbors also deteriorated. Pericles' imperialistic policies encroached on its own allies and on those of Sparta. Fearful that the Athenians would use their navy to destroy Spartan control over its own alliance system, the Peloponnesian League, Sparta became determined to destroy Athens' power. In 432 B.C.E. Sparta attacked Athens, and the Peloponnesian War began in earnest. The struggle was for power, not for higher ideals.

Thucydides, historian of the conflict, portrays Athens setting forth its claims increasingly bluntly in statements of **realpolitik** (power politics). He reports the arrogant Athenian ultimatum ordering the people of the island of Melos to submit to Athenian authority:

> Our opinion of the gods and our knowledge of men lead us to conclude that it is a general and necessary law of nature to rule whatever one can. (V:105; p. 404)

Much weaker than Athens, Melos nevertheless chose to resist. When the Athenians finally conquered the Melians in 415 B.C.E., they killed all the men of military age whom they captured and sold the women and children into slavery. Throughout Greece, admiration for Athens turned to loathing.

By 404 B.C.E. Sparta, supported by Persian funding, defeated Athens and captured the city. The Peloponnesian War between Athens and Sparta and their allies had dragged on for a full generation. Both sides were exhausted. Nevertheless, warfare

realpolitik A German term meaning practical politics, that is, a policy determined by expediency rather than by ethical or ideological considerations.

SOURCE

Pericles' Funeral Oration

As political and military leader of Athens, 460–429 B.C.E., Pericles delivered this eulogy at a mass-funeral of troops who had died in battle in the early years of the Peloponnesian War. As reported by Thucydides, it is one of the great proclamations of the civic, aesthetic, moral, and personal virtues of the Athenian city-state:

Our system of government does not copy the institutions of our neighbors. It is more the case of our being a model to others, than of our imitating anyone else. Our constitution is called a democracy because power is in the hands not of a minority but of the whole people. When it is a question of settling private disputes, everyone is equal before the law; when it is a question of putting one person before another in positions of public responsibility, what counts is not membership of a particular class, but the actual ability which the man possesses. No one, so long as he has it in him to be of service to the state, is kept in political obscurity because of poverty …

We [obey] those whom we put in positions of authority, and we obey the laws themselves, especially those which are for the protection of the oppressed, and those unwritten laws which it is an acknowledged shame to break …

When our work is over, we are in a position to enjoy all kinds of recreation for our spirits … all the good things from all over the world flow in to us, so that to us it seems just as natural to enjoy foreign goods as our own local products …

Our love of what is beautiful does not lead to extravagance; our love of the things of the mind does not make us soft. We regard wealth as something to be properly used, rather than as something to boast about. As for poverty, no one need be ashamed to admit it: the real shame is in not taking practical measures to escape from it. Here each individual is interested not only in his own affairs but in the affairs of the state as well: even those who are mostly occupied with their own business are extremely well informed on general politics—this is a peculiarity of ours: we do not say that a man who takes no interest in politics is a man who minds his own business; we say that he has no business here at all. We Athenians, in our own persons, take our decisions on policy or submit them to proper discussions: for we do not think that there is an incompatibility between words and deeds; the worst thing is to rush into action before the consequences have been properly debated …

I declare that our city is an education to Greece, and I declare that in my opinion each single one of our citizens, in all the manifold aspects of life, is able to show himself the rightful lord and owner of his own person, and do this, moreover, with exceptional grace and exceptional versatility. (Book II:37–41; pp. 145–8) soon resumed among the Greeks, with Thebes and Corinth now entering the lists as major contenders. Each major city-state sought advantage over the others, and the stronger continued to force the weaker into subordinate alliances as intermittent warfare sputtered on.

THE EMPIRE OF ALEXANDER THE GREAT

To the north of the major Greek city-states lay the rougher, less urbanized Macedonia, a borderland between Greece and the Slavic regions to the north and east. The principal language and culture of Macedonia were Greek, but other languages and cultures were also present. Here in 359 B.C.E., in the Macedonian capital of Pella, Philip II (r. 359–336 B.C.E.) persuaded the Macedonian army to declare him king, in succession to his brother, who had died in warfare.

The Conquests of Philip

The Empire of Alexander. In 338 the Greek city-states were defeated by Philip of Macedon. His son, Alexander, extended the imprint of Greek culture far beyond its Mediterranean homeland. In a series of whirlwind campaigns between 334 and 323 B.C.E., Alexander gained control of Syria and Egypt and then destroyed the might of Persia. He took his armies east to the Indus and north to central Asia, but died age 33 in Babylon.

After consolidating his power in Macedonia, Philip declared two goals. The first of these was to unify and bring peace to Greece; the second was to liberate the Greek city-states in Asia Minor from Persian control. Skillful as a diplomat and careful to introduce economic improvements in the lands he conquered, Philip nevertheless realized that his army was the real key to achieving his goals. He built up its phalanxes, armed the soldiers with spears up to 15 feet long, and augmented the foot soldiers with powerful and swift cavalry. Philip led the troops himself, suffering numerous, serious wounds in battle.

Between 354 and 339 Philip conquered the Balkans from the Danube to the Aegean coast and from the Adriatic to the Black Sea. To pacify and administer the area, he established new towns, which were populated by both Macedonians and local peoples. Similarly, he employed many local people in his administration. Within Greece proper, his accomplishments were more mixed. He won some allies, such as Thessaly; defeated the armies of several city-states; and mediated the end of a war between two coalitions of Greek city-states. He was honored with election as president of the Pythian Games at Delphi in 346, but Athens and Thebes bitterly opposed his overtures for greater power in Greece.

The orator Demosthenes (384–322 B.C.E.) delivered three "Philippics," public addresses calling Athens to battle against the Macedonian king and predicting the end of Athenian democracy if Philip defeated the city-state. In the face of this opposition, Philip met in battle with Athens and its allies, defeating them at Chaeronea in 338 B.C.E. Philip now sought to create a self-governing league of Greek city-states, to accomplish his first goal, and to forge an alliance between Macedonia and the league to fight Persia, his second goal. But he was assassinated in 336. His twenty-year-old son, Alexander, continued his father's mission.

The Reign of Alexander the Great

No stranger to warfare, Alexander had fought by his father's side just two years beforehand as he defeated Athens at the Battle of Chaeronea. Applauded by the army, Alexander succeeded to the throne without opposition and continued his father's career of conquest. Over the next twelve years, his disciplined army traversed some 22,000 miles, conquering lands that stretched from Egypt in the west to the Indus River in the east. Alexander's empire became the largest known up to his time, and in 324 B.C.E. he declared himself a god.

Like his father Philip and like the Persian emperors Cyrus II and Darius I, Alexander (r. 336–323 B.C.E.) followed a policy of benevolent despotism much of the time. But, also like them, he implemented this policy only after his power had been amply demonstrated. Unfortunate Thebes provided an early site for this demonstration. Soon after assuming the throne, Alexander had marched north to the Danube River to suppress revolts in Thrace. Mistakenly informed that Alexander had been killed in battle, Thebes revolted against his local forces. Alexander quickly marched his troops back to Thebes, captured and sacked the rebel city, killed 6000 of its inhabitants, and sold into slavery 20,000 of those who survived.

In 334 Alexander was ready to cross into Asia, where his first major victory came at Granicus. From there he continued southward, forcing the Persians out of the Greek cities that lined the Ionian coast. To make sure that the Persians would not return, Alexander marched eastward through Anatolia with 35,000 Greek troops, routing the 300,000-man army of the Persian emperor Darius III at Issus in 333 B.C.E. and forcing Darius himself into flight.

Alexander continued southward down the coast of the eastern Mediterranean. At Tyre, which held out in siege against him for seven months, he again demonstrated power and brutality, killing 7000 men and selling 30,000, mostly women and children, into slavery. Elsewhere, however, Alexander showed the velvet glove, respecting local religions, ruling through local hierarchies, and maintaining local tax rates. To drive Persia from the Mediterranean basin and to establish his own control, Alexander continued south and then west, conquering Egypt. He was welcomed as Egypt's liberator from Persian rule and treated as a god by the Egyptian priests of the god Amon, whose shrine he visited. At the western end of the Nile delta, Alexander laid the foundation of what would be for several centuries the most attractive and cultured city of the Mediterranean coast, Alexandria.

The "Alexander Mosaic," first century B.C.E. mosaic copy from Pompeii of a painting by Philoxenos, c. 300 B.C.E. This mosaic portrays the Battle of Issus (333 B.C.E.) in terms of a personal duel between Alexander the Great and Darius III, Emperor of Persia. Darius (right) is shown about to turn and flee in his chariot as the youthful Alexander (left), wild-haired and helmetless, charges toward him. (*Museo Archeologico Nazionale, Naples*)

His appetite whetted, again a common experience with empire builders once they begin their careers, Alexander moved onward to conquests previously unplanned. He set out to conquer the Persian Empire and make it his own. He marched northeastward across the fertile crescent and through Mesopotamia. At Gaugamela in 331 B.C.E. he again faced the Persian emperor, Darius III, and again routed him. The historical capital cities of Babylon, Susa, Persepolis, and Pasargadae lay open to Alexander. He destroyed Persepolis, Darius' own capital, almost totally. Then, having captured the heartland of the Persian Empire, he set off to conquer the eastern half as well, finally reaching and capturing the Indus River valley in the east, and Sogdiana, across the Oxus River, in the northeast.

Although Alexander wanted to continue into India as far as the Ganges, his troops mutinied. They would go no farther. As he was returning from his new frontiers, Alexander contracted a fever. Weakened both by the hardships of war and by heavy drinking, he died in Babylon in 323 B.C.E., only thirty-three years old. Several accounts report that he was poisoned; some said the instigator was his own former teacher Aristotle. On his deathbed he reputedly declared, "Let the job go to the strongest." In the battle for succession among his generals, Alexander's wife, Roxane, and their thirteen-year-old son were murdered.

The empire Alexander created did not survive two generations. In the east, local rulers regained power in India and Afghanistan. In the west, the Greeks returned to their internal warfare, finally breaking up once more into individual city-states, kingdoms, and leagues. Macedonia remained a separate kingdom and meddled in Greek affairs.

Two major kingdoms emerged from the wreckage of Alexander's empire: Egypt under the dynasty of Ptolemy, which ruled through a Greek and Macedonian elite until the Roman conquest; and the empire established by Seleucus I Nicator (d. 281 B.C.E.), who was governor of Babylon when the empire split apart, and who added to his own domain Iran, Afghanistan, and Anatolia. But the Seleucid Empire, too, fragmented. Parthians reclaimed Persia in the east, and Anatolia divided into numerous local governments. By 200 B.C.E. the Seleucid Empire was limited primarily to the area around Syria.

HOW DO WE KNOW?

Evaluating Alexander the Great

Alexander remains a controversial figure. He was reputed to have murdered hundreds of thousands to achieve his power, yet his admirers see in him a creative genius who aimed at forging a unified Greco-Persian culture that extended into central Asia. By some he was called Alexander the Great; by others Iskander the Accursed. Subsequent historians and other scholars are unsure whether he was an innocent multiculturalist or an imperial monster. There seems to be no question that he believed in his own divinity, but much about this young man remains unknown.

By the end of his life, however, there were few who sorrowed over Alexander's death. Historian Peter Green, who has written an historiographical sketch of Alexander's reputation through the ages, found that the conqueror's image has changed dramatically over time.

The earliest remaining accounts of Alexander's life date from the first century B.C.E., at least 200 years after his death, while the most reliable and fullest of the earliest biographies still extant, that written by Arrian Flavius Arrianus, dates to the second century C.E. For the most part, all historians work from these same basic records, but their assessments reflect the issues and conditions of their own day.

Arrian, who lived at the height of the Roman empire, and approved of it, praises Alexander for his conquests. Alexander was the prototype of Rome's own Caesars. Closer to our own times, in the late eighteenth and nineteenth centuries, during the democratic era of the American and French revolutions, and of the Greek War for Independence (see Chapter 15), historical opinion turned against Alexander. George Grote's History of Greece (1888) represented both Philip and Alexander as "brutalized adventurers simply out for power, wealth, and territorial expansion, both of them inflamed by the pure lust for conquest" (Green, p. 482).

On the other hand, Johann Gustav Droysen, an ardent advocate of a reunified, powerful Germany (see Chapter 17), saw Alexander as a model. Droysen's scholarly biography, Alexander der Grosse (1833), praised Alexander for introducing Greek culture into large parts of Asia.

As the British Empire expanded in the nineteenth and early twentieth centuries, many British scholars also adopted a favorable view of Alexander. William Tarn's two-volume biography saw his conquests as instrumental in spreading a social philosophy of the Brotherhood of Man, bringing together Greeks and Persians, the conquerors with the conquered. Even in our post-imperial day, Cambridge University scholar N.G.L.

Hammond agrees, citing the essay by the biographer Plutarch (c. 46–126 C.E.):

> He harnessed all resources to one and the same end, mixing as it were in a loving-cup the lives, manners, marriages and customs of men. He ordered them all to regard the inhabited earth as their fatherland and his armed forces as their stronghold and defense.

Nonetheless, Green remains critical, arguing that his own assessment is closest to that at the time of Alexander's death:

> his all-absorbing obsession through a short but crowded life, was war and conquest. It is idle to palliate this central truth, to pretend that he dreamed ... of wading through rivers of blood and violence to achieve the Brotherhood of Man by raping an entire continent. He spent his whole life, with legendary success, in the pursuit of personal glory, Achillean kleos; and until very recent times this was regarded as a wholly laudable aim. The empire he built collapsed the moment he was gone; he came as a conqueror and the work he wrought was destruction. (p. 488)

- What seems to be the basis for Green's interpretation of Alexander's career?
- Would you consider Alexander a hero or a villain?
- In light of America's increasing use of power overseas, how do you think scholarly interpretations of Alexander might change?

The Legacy of Alexander: The Hellenistic Ecumene

What were the legacies of the empire Alexander built? He made the language and culture of Greece dominant among the ruling intellectual and commercial elites from the Mediterranean, east to India, Afghanistan, and the borders of Russia, and south as far as Egypt. A common dialect of Greek, known as Koine, spread as the language of educated people throughout the ancient western world.

Waves of Greek administrators, businessmen, and soldiers followed Alexander's conquests and helped to transmit Greek culture. At the same time, local customs, especially the imperial ceremonial forms of Persia, endured and transformed the simplicity of the earlier Hellenic culture into the more complex, elaborate, and cosmopolitan Hellenistic culture that flourished from the time of Alexander until the death of the last Macedonian queen of Egypt, Cleopatra, in 30 B.C.E. One striking example of the mixture of Hellenistic and local cultures—this time from India—can be seen in some

Dying Gaul, Roman copy in marble of a bronze original of c. 230–220 B.C.E. When Attalas I of Pergamum defeated an enemy force of Gauls, a series of statues showing dead or dying invaders was cast. This poignant example illustrates the many artistic developments in sculpture that epitomize Hellenistic Greece: a special emphasis on the portrayal of suffering and pain, dramatically conveyed through facial expression; a widening subject-matter (not merely male and female nudes); a twisting pose for the body; and a design that allows the composition to be viewed from all sides. (*Museo Capitolino, Rome*)

ecumene A Greek word referring to the inhabited world and designating a distinct cultural-historical community.

of the first representations of the Buddha in sculpture from the area of India/Pakistan after it was conquered by Alexander. These sculptures represent the Buddha wearing a toga (see p. 251).

To facilitate travel and commerce, as well as conquest and administration, Alexander built roads, canals, and whole new cities, including at least sixteen Alexandrias across the length and breadth of his conquests, using the gold and silver captured from Persia to finance many of these constructions. The most famous and illustrious Alexandria was the metropolis in Egypt, which became the leading city of its day. Egyptian Alexandria housed palaces, administrative centers, theaters, stadia, the greatest library of Greek knowledge, containing 700,000 manuscripts, and the final resting place of Alexander himself.

At the eastern end of the empire, on the Oxus River in today's Uzbekistan, the Greeks constructed, on Persian foundations, Ai Khanoum, a small, well-defended city centered on a palace. Ai Khanoum was rediscovered and excavated only in the 1960s, and archaeologists believe it may prove to be Alexandria Oxiana, a lost city from the age of Alexander the Great.

Between Alexandria in Egypt and Ai Khanoum in central Asia were dozens of cities and small towns, which served as seeds of Greek culture throughout the empire. The Alexandrian Empire and its successors built a Hellenistic **ecumene**—that is, a unified urban culture, encompassing vast lands and diverse peoples. Some of its cities, which had long, independent Greek heritages, retained strong elements of their pre-Alexandrian culture and even their autonomy. These were the cities of the Greek heartland, such as Athens, Sparta, Thebes, Corinth, and Delphi. Others were cities of empire, built later by Alexander and his successors either from the ground up or on existing but relatively minor urban bases. These cities served as new regional capitals, to administer the new empire, to extend its economy, and to broadcast its culture.

Alexander and his successors also administered their empire through the already existing indigenous urban framework, but added to it the principal institutions and monuments of Hellenistic culture: temples to Greek gods frequently located on a walled acropolis; theaters; an *agora*; civic buildings such as a council chamber and town hall; gymnasia; and stadia. Examples of this style of urban Hellenization in newly conquered lands included Susa, Damascus, Tyre, Kandahar, and Merv. Residents of these varied cities might feel themselves to be both citizens of the locality and participants in a semi-universal ecumene, although the balance of these feelings might vary from city to city and from time to time. A sharp division intensified between the cities with their high culture, now very much Hellenized throughout the empire, and the rural areas, which continued their traditional patterns of life without much change.

The empire encouraged the flow of trade and culture in many directions. Greek ships have been found as far west as the British Isles as well as in the Indian Ocean in the east. European, African, and Asian trade routes intersected at Taxila, Ai Khanoum, Begram, and Merv. The Persians had begun to create an Asian–African–European ecumene; Alexander carried the process further and deeper. Rome, already beginning to rise by the time of Alexander, would later extend a similar imperial mission throughout much of Europe to the west and north, although Rome would not control the east, as we shall see in Chapter 6.

EMPIRE-BUILDING
WHAT DIFFERENCE DOES IT MAKE?

Mesopotamians, Egyptians, Persians, Greeks, and Macedonians launched their imperial ambitions from very different backgrounds. Mesopotamians and Greeks began as city-states, while Egyptians and Persians started as consolidated nations. Out of the fractious chaos of the Greek city-states Macedon built its small state to imperial dimensions under a father and son who ruled as ambitious and skillful kings. Although our coverage was necessarily sketchy, we have seen that each empire erected a central capital; administered a government based in that center that could control the provinces; provided a uniform language, coinage, and legal system across the empire; constructed a road and communication network; articulated an ideology of empire that won the loyalty of many of its citizens and subjects; and created art and architecture to impress on friend and foe alike the power of the empire. Each assembled military forces to apply coercion where necessary.

A time finally came for each empire to rein in its ambitions and limit further expansion. Sometimes it reached the limit of its capacity to conquer and administer profitably; sometimes it was defeated in warfare; often it encountered a combination of both these humbling experiences.

The imperial armies of Alexander the Great refused to proceed to newer, more distant conquests beyond the Indus River. So he turned back toward home. Ironically, Alexander's school tutor had been the philosopher Aristotle, who had written: "To the size of states there is a limit." Aristotle's ideal political unit was the Greek city-state because it promoted the maximum personal participation in democratic government through intense social and political interaction among the citizens.

In choosing to build an empire, Alexander was neither the first nor the last student to disregard his teacher's advice. (Alexander wanted the Greek city-states to be self-governing, but he did not want other areas to have such powers.) Nor was Aristotle the first or last to weigh the relative merits of small, local democratic government units against those of large, centralized bureaucracies. Similar debates still go on in our own day. Debates over the usefulness, limits, and legitimacy of empire were also central to the political thought of ancient Rome, China, and India, the three huge empires that are the focus of Chapters 6, 7, and 8.

Review Questions

- Define "empire" and discuss the chief characteristics generally shared by empires.
- Choose an empire from this chapter. Indicate the degree to which it shares the characteristics noted above.
- Give examples of a culture becoming an empire by conquering an existing empire. Give examples of people creating an empire of their own.
- Apart from the use of sheer military force, what policies do successful empires adopt in order to establish and maintain their power over the peoples they conquer?
- What seem to be the causes of the decline and fall of empires?
- Thucydides wrote, "Our opinion of the gods and our knowledge of men lead us to conclude that it is a general and necessary law of nature to rule whatever one can." Do you agree? Why or why not? Use this chapter's materials to support your view.

Suggested Readings

PRINCIPAL SOURCES

Baines, John and Jaromir Malek. *Atlas of Ancient Egypt* (New York: Facts on File Publications, 1980). Two noted experts continue the excellent books in this series with fine text, maps, pictures, time lines, and breadth of coverage.

Green, Peter. *Alexander of Macedon* (Berkeley, CA: University of California Press, 1991). An excellent, thoughtful, up-to-date biography with good historiographical coverage as well.

Green, Peter. *The Greco-Persian Wars* (Berkeley, CA: University of California Press, 1996). A revision of an older classic on the wars.

Hanson, Victor Davis. *The Wars of the Ancient Greeks* (London: Cassell & Co, 1999). A readable volume that incorporates recent scholarship on Greek warfare.

Kagan, Donald. *The Peloponnesian War* (New York: Viking, 2003). Distills the great scholarship, and increases the readability, of his earlier four-volume work. Based largely on Thucydides, but includes considerable additional scholarship and new perspectives.

Levi, Peter. *Atlas of the Greek World* (New York: Facts on File Publications, 1982). The series continues its excellent, broad coverage with outstanding text, maps, pictures, time lines.

Past Worlds: The (London) Times Atlas of Archaeology (Maplewood, NJ: Hammond, Inc., 1988). Beautifully produced, superbly researched atlas with fine text and excellent pictures as well.

Postgate, J.N. *Early Mesopotamia* (London: Routledge, 1992). Scholarly analysis and clear presentation.

Thucydides. *History of the Peloponnesian War*, trans. Rex Warner (Harmondsworth: Penguin Books, 1972). The definitive primary source, cynically philosophical about political motives, the product of bitter and cynical events.

Wycherley, R.E. *How the Greeks Built Cities* (Garden City, NY: Anchor Books, 1969). Excellent introduction to the urban plans of the Greek cities, with good attention to the significance of the buildings and designs, and to the variety of city-states.

ADDITIONAL SOURCES

Aristotle. *Basic Works*, ed. and trans. Richard McKeon (New York: Random House, 1941). Direct introduction to the work of the philosopher, whose works continued authoritative for at least two thousand years.

Bernal, Martin. *Black Athena: The Afroasiatic Roots of Classical Civilization* (New Brunswick, NJ: Rutgers University Press, 1987). Bernal demonstrates the influence of Egyptian culture on ancient Greece. Because of the title the book became involved in racial debates, but the text does not concentrate on race.

Hamilton, J.R. *Alexander the Great* (London: Hutchison University Library, 1973). A standard biography.

Hammond, Mason. *The City in the Ancient World* (Cambridge, MA: Harvard University Press, 1972). A kind of history of the ancient western world through an analysis of its cities.

Hammond, N.G.L. *The Genius of Alexander the Great* (Chapel Hill, NC: The University of North Carolina Press, 1997). A standard biography.

Herodotus. *The Persian Wars*, trans. George Rawlinson (New York: Modern Library, 1942). Some consider this the first secular book of history. Mixes myth with history in recreating the great clash of civilizations between the Greeks and the Persians.

Homer. *Iliad*, trans. Richmond Lattimore (Chicago, IL: University of Chicago Press, 1951). The story that inspired the ancient Greeks in warfare, and gave us insight into their world.

Homer. *Odyssey*, trans. Robert Fitzgerald (New York: Doubleday & Co., 1961). The great story of the odyssey of Odysseus through one trial after another from the Trojan war back to his home in Greece.

Hornblower, Simon. *The Greek World 479–323 BC* (London: Methuen, 1983). A standard historical survey.

Keuls, Eva C. *The Reign of the Phallus: Sexual Politics in Ancient Athens* (New York: Harper and Row, 1985). Opinionated, belligerent, engaging feminist critique of ancient Athens; evidence based on painting on drinking vessels.

Mumford, Lewis. *The City in History* (New York: Harcourt, Brace and World, 1961). Classic history with a strong argument for small, manageable cities with strong sense of community.

O'Brien, John Maxwell. *Alexander the Great: The Invisible Enemy* (London: Routledge, 1992). Critical biography.

Plato. *The Collected Dialogues of Plato,* ed. Edith Hamilton and Huntington Cairns (New York: Bollingen Foundation [distributed by Pantheon Books], 1961). The complete works of the classic philosopher of ideal types.

Plutarch. *The Lives of the Noble Grecians and Romans,* trans. John Dryden, revised by Arthur Hugh Clough (New York: Modern Library, n.d.). Writing from the height of the Roman Empire, this Greek historian preserves many materials that have otherwise been lost as he assesses the accomplishments of many of the Greek and Roman greats.

Robinson, Eric W., ed. *Ancient Greek Democracy: Readings and Sources* (Malden, MA: Blackwell, 2004). Very useful selection of primary documents on the functioning and limits of ancient Greek democracy.

Saggs, H.W.F. *The Might that Was Assyria* (London: Sidgwick & Jackson, 1984). Fine general survey.

Sophocles. *Oedipus Rex and Oedipus at Colonus,* trans. Robert Fitzgerald in *The Oedipus Cycle* (San Diego: Harcourt Brace Jovanovich, 1969). Two of the most famous plays from ancient Greece.

Tacitus. *The Annals of Imperial Rome,* trans. Michael Grant (Baltimore, MD: Penguin Books, 1959). Primary source by this government official and historian of Rome, often very critical of the growth of empire.

Tarn, W.W. *Alexander the Great.* 2 Vols. (Cambridge: Cambridge University Press, 1948). Laudatory biography.

⊚ World History Documents CD-ROM

1.3 The Reign of Sargon
1.5 The Code of Hammurabi
1.10 Assyrian War Tactics
4.1 Homer: The *Iliad*
4.2 Empires and Military Glory: Herodotus Relates the Story of Thermopylae
4.3 Thucydides
4.4 From Confederacy to Empire: Thucydides
4.5 The City-State of Sparta
4.6 The First Philippic: A Great Orator Warns of Macedonian Imperialism
4.7 The Figure of Alexander
4.8a Against Communism
4.8b Virtue and Moderation: The Doctrine of the Mean

ROME AND THE BARBARIANS

THE RISE AND FALL OF EMPIRE
750 B.C.E.–500 C.E.

KEY TOPICS
- From Hill Town to Empire
- The Barbarians and the Fall of the Roman Empire

All roads, by land and sea, led to Rome, the capital of one of the longest lasting and most influential of empires. Situated on the Tiber River, not far from the sea, Rome served as the center of communication and trade for the entire Italian peninsula. To the surrounding sea the Romans gave the name "Mediterranean," the middle of the earth, for it is itself surrounded by the three continents that they knew: southern Europe, northern Africa, and western Asia. Later, as Roman armies conquered and ruled an empire that encompassed all these lands and many territories still more distant, they began to call the Mediterranean *Mare Nostrum* ("Our Sea").

At its greatest extent in the second century C.E., the Roman Empire ruled between 70 and 100 million people of vastly diverse ethnic, racial, religious, and cultural roots. Geographically, it sprawled over 2700 miles east to west and 2500 miles north to south, extending from Scotland to the Persian Gulf. At its most powerful, between 27 B.C.E. and 180 C.E., Rome enforced the **Pax Romana**, the Roman peace, a reign of stability and relative tranquility throughout all these vast regions.

From the first, this empire evoked both praise and condemnation. The Latin poet Virgil (70–19 B.C.E.) led one of the greatest choruses of praise, describing Rome as a gift of the gods, and praising its citizens for successfully carrying out their mandate: "Remember Romans/ To rule the people under law, to establish/ The way of peace." Virgil praised the sheer size of the empire, its roads, its cities, its trade, and its monuments. Most of all, however, he cited the peace and prosperity established through Rome's rule of law, the Pax Romana, enforced by Rome's armies.

The historian Tacitus (*c.* 56–*c.* 120 C.E.) mocked this praise of peace and prosperity: "Robbery, butchery, and rapine they call 'Empire.' They create a desert and call it 'Peace.'" Writing a century after Virgil, and viewing the empire through the eyes of a defeated Celtic chieftain, Tacitus characterized the Pax Romana as a policy of brute military conquest and destruction. This chapter will explore the conditions underlying both of these contradictory points of view.

Pax Romana The "Roman Peace," that is, the state of comparative concord prevailing within the boundaries of the Roman Empire from the reign of Augustus (27 B.C.E.–14 C.E.) to that of Marcus Aurelius (161–180 C.E.), enforced by Roman rule and military control.

FROM HILL TOWN TO EMPIRE

The Founding of the Roman Republic

The legendary date for the founding of the city of Rome is 753 B.C.E., and although this is probably not exact, it is approximately correct. According to this legend, beloved by the Romans, Romulus and Remus, twin sons of Mars, the god of War, founded the city at the site where they were rescued from the Tiber River and suckled by a nurturing she-wolf. (See the accompanying Etruscan statue of a she-wolf (p. 164); the suckling

Opposite **Battle line formed with shields by the Romans against the Dacians, from Trajan's Column, Rome, c. 113 C.E. Plaster cast of marble original.** The Romans adapted the Greek phalanx into a more maneuverable, but tightly configured, array of foot soldiers with shields, spears, and daggers. Victory memorials, like Trajan's column, celebrated the resulting successes in battle. (*Museo della Civiltà, Rome*)

republic A state that is not ruled by a hereditary leader (a monarchy) but by a person or persons appointed under the constitution.

centuries The smallest units of the Roman army, each composed of some 100 foot-soldiers and commanded by a centurion. A legion was made up of 60 centuries. Centuries also formed political divisions of Roman citizens.

Capitoline Wolf, *c.* 500 B.C.E. According to legend, Rome was founded by Romulus and Remus, twin sons of Mars, at the spot where they were rescued from the Tiber River and suckled by a she-wolf. The group of she-wolf with twins was adopted as the symbol of Rome, although the children in this particular statue were added almost two thousand years later, in the Renaissance. (*Museo Capitolino, Rome*)

children were added two thousand years later, to represent the legend of Romulus and Remus.)

For two and a half centuries, kings of the neighboring Etruria, the land to Rome's north, ruled the city. The Romans learned much from the Etruscans about city building, art, religion, mythology, and even language. As Rome entered the Mediterranean trade networks of the Etruscans, merchants and craft workers immigrated to the city. The Etruscan king Servius Tullius (578–534 B.C.E.) reformed the military, creating the *comitia centuriata*, a deliberative ruling council organized by hundreds (*centuriae*), representing the soldiers of Rome. This assembly of Roman citizens persisted for centuries after Etruscan rule had ended, reinforcing the connection between the armies of Rome and its government.

About 509 B.C.E., the wealthy, powerful, citizens of Rome—all veterans of military service—drove out the Etruscan kings. They declared Rome a **republic**, a government in which power resides in a body of citizens and consists of representatives elected by them. Although they overthrew the monarchy, the new oligarchs—the small, elite group of rulers—retained many other political institutions. Their armies remained the center of power. Because soldiers provided their own arms, only men with some wealth and property could command and rise in the ranks. They in turn were ordered by class, according to the quality and cost of the weapons they provided, and then divided into military units called **centuries**, or groups of one hundred, as they had been under the Etruscans. The leaders of the centuries continued to meet together in assembly to elect magistrates and decide questions of peace and war.

The magistrates, administrative and judicial officials, administered the Roman Republic. At the lowest level of **quaestor** they had limited financial authority. At the highest level, **consuls** held power that extended over all the lands Rome ruled. As magistrates ended their one-year (renewable) term of office, they automatically entered the Senate of Rome, the highest legislative and consultative body of the government.

At each level, two officials were paired, so that they would have to consult with one another, and neither could seize excessive power. The power of the former kings, for example, was now shared between the two consuls in this new system of checks and balances. (In extraordinary emergencies, one man could be named as dictator for the limited term of six months.)

The Conquest of Italy

The Roman Republic established alliances with other nearby city-states in west-central Italy, and began to challenge the Etruscans. In 396 B.C.E., after a siege of six years, the Romans captured Veii, a principal Etruscan city only 12 miles from Rome. Celtic invaders sacked Rome itself in 390 B.C.E.(see p. 192), but the setback was brief, and Rome's expansion continued.

Its armies, fighting until now in phalanxes, according to the Greek model (see p. 146), were reorganized. Small, flexible units, armed with swords and throwing javelins in place of older spears, lined up with less experienced, younger troops in front, more tested troops behind them, and then, as the final resort, veterans of courage and proved valor. If the front ranks could not hold and fell back into the rear lines, the advancing, over-confident enemy was suddenly confronted by a compact mass of soldiers of the greatest numbers and skill. By 264 B.C.E., Roman armies controlled all of Italy south of the Po valley.

As it expanded, Rome often offered its opponents a choice between alliance and conquest. Subsequently it bestowed various levels of Roman citizenship throughout Italy to induce its residents to support Rome and join its armies.

Rome became a society geared for war. Roman armies, and a new navy created to combat their Mediterranean opponents, continued to expand Roman rule. For the next 140 years its troops were almost constantly on the move. The most bitter and the most decisive of their battles were the three Punic Wars against Carthage.

The Conquest of Carthage and the Western Mediterranean

Carthage, only 130 miles across the narrow waist of the Mediterranean from Italy, had developed as a major trade outpost of Phoenician seafarers. Just as Rome dominated Italy, the Carthaginians controlled the north central coast of Africa and the western Mediterranean. One of their trade networks focused on the mineral wealth of Spain, especially its silver mines. To protect that route, Carthage developed ports and cities in Sicily and Sardinia. It even controlled trade outposts on the Italian mainland in Etruria. Carthage and Rome were set on a collision course.

The three wars that broke out are known as the Punic Wars after the Roman term for Phoenicians, *Punici*. The fighting opened in Sicily in 264 B.C.E. By 241 B.C.E., when the first Punic War ended, Rome was victorious both on land and sea. It took control of Sicily and imposed taxes on the island. Four years later, Rome took advantage of a mutiny among Carthaginian troops in Sardinia to occupy Sardinia and Corsica. In 227 B.C.E., it annexed the islands. For the first time, Rome had provinces outside the Italian peninsula.

quaestor A junior official in ancient Rome. There were originally two, elected annually, but more were appointed as the empire expanded. Most were financial officials.

consul Under the Roman Republic, one of the two magistrates holding supreme civil and military authority. Nominated by the Senate and elected by citizens in the Comitia Centuriata (popular assembly), the consuls held office for one year and each had power of veto over the other.

AT A GLANCE : THE ROMAN EMPIRE

DATE	POLITICAL	RELIGION AND CULTURE	SOCIAL DEVELOPMENT
500 B.C.E.	■ Rome independent of Etruscan rule (509); Republic founded		
450 B.C.E.	■ Rome sacked by Gauls (390)		■ Laws of Twelve Tables promulgated
350 B.C.E.	■ Roman expansion into Italy south of Po (327–304)		
300 B.C.E.	■ 1st Punic War (264–241)		■ Earliest Roman coinage (280–75)
250 B.C.E.	■ 2nd Punic War (218–201) ■ Hannibal invaded Italy ■ Roman conquest of Cisalpine Gaul (202–191)	■ Stoicism – Zeno	
200 B.C.E.	■ Rome annexed Spain (197) ■ Conquest of Macedon (167)	■ Polybius (200–118)	
150 B.C.E.	■ 3rd Punic War (149–146) ■ T. Gracchus tribune (133) ■ G. Gracchus tribune (123 and 122) ■ Gallia Narbonensis a Roman province	■ Carthage destroyed ■ Corinth destroyed	■ Pax Romana led to widespread trade throughout Empire; roads built
100 B.C.E.	■ Sulla conquers Greece ■ Civil war in Rome (83–2) ■ Conquest of Syria (66) ■ 1st Triumvirate (60)		■ Spartacus slave revolt (73–71)
50 B.C.E.	■ Civil war (49) ■ Caesar dictator (47–44) ■ 2nd Triumvirate (43) ■ Annexation of Egypt (30) ■ Augustus Caesar (d. 14 C.E.)	■ Cicero (d. 43) ■ Virgil (d. 19) ■ Augustus deified on his death ■ Forum in Rome ■ Livy (d. 17 C.E.)	

Carthage, however, rebuilt its forces, especially in Spain. When the Spanish city of Saguntum asked for Roman help, the Romans intervened, threatening Carthage's Spanish colonies. The brilliant, twenty-seven-year-old Carthaginian commander Hannibal (247–183 B.C.E.) defeated Rome's troops in 219 B.C.E., and the second Punic War had begun. It continued for almost twenty years.

Hannibal unexpectedly took the offensive by land, marching tens of thousands of troops and thirty-seven elephants 1000 miles along the French coast, over the Alps, into the Po valley, and toward Rome. In two months he overran most of north Italy and destroyed the armies sent against him. But Hannibal could not break the power of Rome. Most of Rome's allies remained loyal and Rome raised new armies. Rome recaptured those cities that had previously gone over to Hannibal, including Capua, Syracuse, and Tarentum. Hannibal did annihilate a Roman army at Cannae in south Italy, but ultimately he was isolated there. Meanwhile, Rome won victories in Spain in 211–206 B.C.E., especially under the general Publius Cornelius Scipio. In 204 B.C.E. Scipio invaded Africa. Hannibal returned to defend his homeland, but Scipio, later named Scipio Africanus for his victory, defeated him at the Battle of Zama (202 B.C.E.). The war was over, and Carthage became a dependency of Rome.

In its treatment of the rebellious city of Capua and its surrounding region of Campania, just to the south of Rome, the Romans exhibited what would become known as their "New Wisdom," a policy of brute force toward their enemies. Roman leaders executed seventy senators, imprisoned three hundred Campanian aristocrats, and put others into the custody of Latin allies. They sold the mass of Campanian citizens into slavery, although they allowed resident aliens, freedmen, and petty tradesmen and artisans to continue to work.

A half-century later, Rome again responded with brute force after Carthage attacked Rome's African ally, King Masinissa of Numidia. Disregarding Carthage's legitimate claims that its land was being encroached upon, Rome sided with its ally and provoked the third Punic War (149–146 B.C.E.). With the aged Cato the Censor calling in the Roman Senate for the complete destruction of Carthage, Rome razed it to the ground, sold its survivors into slavery, and sowed salt into the soil so that it would never again flourish. The Romans annexed all of Carthage into the Roman province of Africa. Rome had become mistress of the Mediterranean.

Rome's brutal use of military power served as a warning to potential foes. Roman generals were not pressed to win quick, brilliant victories, but to defeat the enemy through patient, deliberate preparation, and decisive force. Ideally, the enemy would be so awed by Roman forces that it would never dare oppose them.

Subsequent Expansion

After Rome had eliminated the Carthaginian threat with the end of the second Punic War, in 202–191 B.C.E. it turned to the conquest of the Gauls in northern Italy and annexed their territory. It annexed Spain in 197 B.C.E. but treated that province so harshly that constant revolts simmered until Rome finally crushed them in 133 B.C.E. Rome then turned its power toward Gaul, modern France. In southern Gaul, Rome's

AT A GLANCE : THE ROMAN EMPIRE (continued)

DATE	POLITICAL	RELIGION AND CULTURE	SOCIAL DEVELOPMENT
25 C.E.	■ Christianity reaches Rome ■ Invasion of Britain (43)		
50 C.E.	■ Trajan (98–117)	■ Seneca (d. 65) ■ Destruction of Temple in Jerusalem (70) ■ Pompeii and Herculaneum buried by eruption of Vesuvius (79)	■ Jewish revolt (66–73) ■ Roman women gain new rights
100 C.E.	■ Dacia conquered by Trajan ■ Hadrian (117–38)	■ Tacitus (d. 120) ■ Trajan's column and forum (112–113) ■ Pantheon in Rome ■ Hadrian's Wall	
150 C.E.	■ Marcus Aurelius (161–180)	■ Apuleius (d. c. 170) ■ Galen (d. 199)	
200 C.E.	■ Caracalla (212–217) ■ Decius (249–51)	■ Baths of Caracalla	■ Roman citizenship for all males
250 C.E.	■ Gallienus (253–268)	■ Persecution of Christians	
300 C.E.	■ Constantine (r. 306–337)	■ Edict of Milan (313) ■ Constantinople inaugurated (330)	
350 C.E.		■ St. Augustine (354–430) ■ End of state support for paganism (394)	
400 C.E.	■ Sack of Rome (410)		
450 C.E.	■ End of Roman Empire in West (476)		
550 C.E.			■ Justinian codifies Roman law

The Roman Empire. Rome built its empire on military expansion, first within Italy by overthrowing its neighbors, then across the Mediterranean by defeating the Carthaginians, then northwest to Gaul and Britain and north to the Danube. Rome offered many benefits to the peoples it conquered, but finally its power rested in its armies.

ally Massilia (Marseilles) asked for help against Gallic tribes, and by 121 B.C.E. Rome had annexed most of the region.

Northern Gaul seemed stably divided among various Gallic peoples until the Helvetii, Celts driven out of Switzerland, began to invade. In response, Julius Caesar (100–44 B.C.E.), the Roman commander in north Italy and southern Gaul, moved with his army into central and northern Gaul. Caesar's *Gallic War* tells of his conquests in 58–52 B.C.E. By the time his campaigns ended in 49 B.C.E., all Gaul belonged to Rome.

The Romans were opportunists, seizing land wherever they saw weakness. Even as they conquered territory in the west, they expanded in the east as well. In the eastern Mediterranean, the Romans encountered Macedonians and Greeks, the proud heirs of Alexander the Great, who still ruled the lands that he had conquered and Hellenized. Rome's first battle on Greek soil came in 200 B.C.E., and it began the complete restructuring of political power in the eastern Mediterranean.

At the death of Alexander the Great in 323 B.C.E. his empire had divided into three regional kingdoms. In 203–202 B.C.E. two of these kingdoms, Macedonia and Syria, where the Seleucid dynasty ruled, combined to threaten the third, Egypt, where the Ptolemaic family ruled. Neighboring Greek city-states encouraged Rome to use these divisions to establish its own balance of power in the region. Rome accepted the invitation. It warned Macedonia not to interfere in Greek affairs. When Philip V of Macedon (r. 211–179 B.C.E.) rejected this warning, the Romans attacked and defeated him. In victory, the Romans declared the Greek city-states of the eastern

SOURCE

Artifactual Records

Rome has bequeathed rich material artifacts. Much of the infrastructure of the empire—its roads, aqueducts, stadia, public baths, forums, temples, triumphal arches—as well as substantial parts of many of the military camps and cities it constructed still stand. Roman coinage and statuary are everywhere.

The cities of Pompeii and Herculaneum, comprising a total population of about 20,000, were buried in dust and cinders in the volcanic eruption of Mount Vesuvius in 79 C.E. Archaeologists uncovered these remains, forgotten for almost two millennia, in the late eighteenth century, providing an unparalleled view of the structure and furnishings of these provincial towns. Preserved like time capsules, they reveal their urban design, buildings, furniture, and household objects.

Pompeii was a walled town, with seven gates, a forum, council chamber, offices of magistrates, temples dedicated to Apollo and Jupiter, market buildings, a stock exchange, law court, theater, auditoriums, an amphitheater for gladiatorial contests and wild beast hunts, three Turkish-style baths, workshops, shops, brothels, and homes. Carbonized food, preserved and sealed in hot volcanic mud, suggests that at least some of the inhabitants ate well. Walls, surviving to their full height, have preserved vivid murals from the residences and businesses. At least some Pompeiians had cultivated aesthetic sensibilities. Some of the art in the seven brothels indicates also a cultivated taste for pornography.

In the countryside, archaeologists have also been able to reconstruct latifundia, rural estates that were controlled by rich owners who bought up family farms and ran them as plantations. Off-shore searches have uncovered sunken ships in the Italian Mediterranean that shed light on Roman trade missions and their cargoes.

Archaeological digs have also uncovered the history of the many Gothic, Celtic, and other groups of migrating peoples who lived on the fringes of the empire, later settled within its territories, and finally established their own states on those lands as the empire disintegrated. Their settlements, burial grounds, tools, and artwork yield significant information about their lives, even though they had no writing systems until they learned from the Romans.

With such extensive artifacts complementing the rich documentary record, scholars can reconstruct the rise and fall of the Roman Empire and its relationships with neighboring peoples. Relatively abundant materials provide the sources also to explore new topics such as the extent of slavery, the treatment of women, and patterns of health and disease in ancient Rome.

The young Hercules wrestling with a snake, fresco, House of the Vettii, Pompeii.

The body of a man petrified by ash from the eruption of Mount Vesuvius, Pompeii, 79 C.E.

Mediterranean "free," granting them nominal independence, but, in fact, placing them under Roman control.

Rome had similarly warned Antiochus III, the Great, of Syria (r. 223–187 B.C.E.) to stay out of Europe and Egypt. When Antiochus ignored the warning, Roman forces crushed him, pushed him back to Syria, and forced him to pay a huge indemnity.

In the next generation, Rome decisively defeated Philip V's son Perseus (r. 179–168 B.C.E.) in 168 B.C.E., ending the Macedonian monarchy. In the same year, Rome again protected Egypt from the Seleucids, asserting its own control of the eastern Mediterranean.

Here, too, Rome applied the brutal tactics of the "New Wisdom." In 148 B.C.E., when the Greek city-state of Corinth and its allies flouted Roman wishes, and even attacked Roman envoys, Rome razed Corinth to the ground, sold all its surviving inhabitants into slavery, and carried its artistic works to Rome. Recognizing Rome's power, the king of Pergamum, in Asia Minor, bequeathed his lands to Rome at his death in 133 B.C.E. Throughout the Mediterranean, Rome was now the dominant power.

In the east, the general Pompey (106–48 B.C.E.) added Syria and most of Asia Minor to the empire. In 63 B.C.E. he captured Jerusalem, the capital of Judaea, allowing a Jewish king to rule as a client-monarch. Gnaeus Pompeius Magnus (Pompey the Great) favored such indirect rule through local potentates throughout the east, where sophisticated governmental structures had existed for centuries. He also founded some forty cities as centers of Roman political influence.

Institutions of Empire

Empires are ultimately sustained by military force, but successful empires must also win at least some degree of support from among the conquered peoples. Beginning with its early conquests, Rome had often won such support through several of its political, cultural, economic, and ideological policies, most importantly through the granting of citizenship.

Politically, Rome bestowed benefits on conquered peoples, especially the benefits of citizenship. All free men from Rome were citizens automatically; the rest of the men of Italy, however, were not. In 381 B.C.E., the town of Tusculum, some 15 miles from Rome and surrounded by Roman territory, seemed poised to oppose Rome. The Romans won over the Tusculuns by offering incorporation into Rome and full citizenship. In 338 B.C.E. full citizenship was bestowed on four additional Latin cities; others received partial citizenship with no voting rights but with rights of property, contracts, and the right to marry Roman citizens. They were also freed of property taxes. Roman citizenship also protected its beneficiary from arbitrary arrest and violence.

In 91 B.C.E. Marcus Livius Drusus the Younger was elected **tribune**, one of the most powerful offices in ancient Rome. Drusus proposed extending citizenship and the vote to all the Italian allies, but the Roman Senate rejected the proposal. Drusus was later assassinated, leaving the Italians frustrated and furious. So began the "Social War" or "War of the Allies." After two years, however, Rome did offer full citizenship to all Italians who had remained loyal and even to those who agreed to put down their arms. It extended full citizenship north as far as the Po River, and partial citizenship up to the Alps Mountains. So, grudgingly, citizenship was offered as an inducement to loyalty. In newly annexed lands, the aristocrats, the group to whom Rome usually granted these rights and obligations, regarded even partial citizenship as attractive.

tribune In ancient Rome, a plebeian officer elected by the plebeians and charged to protect their lives and properties, with a right of veto against legislative proposals of the Senate.

Patrons and Clients

Asymmetrical power relationships characterized Roman life—private as well as public—under the Republic. The earliest enduring social structure in Rome was the patron–client relationship. Strong men acted as protectors of the weak; the weak, in turn, provided obedience and services for the strong as requested.

In civilian life, patrons, usually patricians, would provide legal protection and representation for their clients, usually **plebeians**, those without longstanding hereditary

plebeian A citizen of ancient Rome who was not a member of the privileged patrician class. From the later Republican period, the term *plebeian* implied low social class.

HOW DO WE KNOW?

Contemporary Historians Evaluate the History of Rome

During the later Republic historians began consciously to write the history of the city. Their accounts were often ambivalent, revealing a mixture of pride in the conquests and achievements of their empire with skepticism and even hostility toward the abandonment of the earlier republican ideals.

The most famous of the early historians was Polybius (c. 200–c. 118 B.C.E.), a Greek taken to Rome as a political captive. Polybius marveled at the overwhelming event of his own time, Rome's conquest of an empire through its victories over Carthage, Macedonia, and Spain:

There can surely be no one so petty or so apathetic in his outlook that he has no desire to discover by what means and under what system of government the Romans succeeded in less than fifty-three years [220–167 B.C.E.] in bringing under their rule almost the whole of the inhabited world, an achievement which is without parallel in human history. (The Histories I:1; p. 443, cited in Finley)

Livy (59 B.C.E.–17 C.E.) praised the glories of Rome's imperial expansion, but he decried the resulting class conflict between Rome's aristocrats and its common people that was currently ripping apart Rome's self-governing, elected, republican form of government.

Tacitus (c. 56–c. 120 C.E.) continued the story to the height of imperial power. He praised the heroism of the Roman conquerors, but he also understood the anguish and bitterness of the conquered peoples. In Agricola, Tacitus attributes to the Celtic chieftain Calgacus one of the most devastating critiques of imperialism ever articulated. In Tacitus' account, Calgacus condemns

the Romans, whose tyranny cannot be escaped by any act of reasonable submission. These brigands of the world have exhausted the land by their rapacity, so they now ransack the sea. When their enemy is rich, they lust after wealth; when the enemy is poor, they lust after power. Neither East nor West has satisfied their hunger. They are unique among humanity insofar as they equally covet the rich and the poor. Robbery, butchery, and rapine they call "Empire." They create a desert and call it "Peace." (I:129, cited in Andrea and Overfield)

As the empire began to decay, mainstream historians added more critical perspectives. Dio Cassius (c. 150–235 C.E.) nostalgically recalled the rule of Augustus as Rome's golden age and lamented the empire's subsequent decline "from a monarchy of gold to one of iron and rust." Like Tacitus, he cited and sympathized with the frustration and rage of those, like Boudicca, the warrior-queen of the Celts, who led her armies in revolt against the Romans in 61 C.E.:

We have been despised and trampled underfoot by men who know nothing else than how to secure gain. (Lewis and Reinhold, II:334)

Other historians illuminated the empire from its fringes rather than from its center, and they, too, were often critical of the effects of empire on its subjects. For Jewish historians, such as Philo of Alexandria (c. 13 B.C.E.–c. 45 C.E.) and Josephus (c. 37–c. 100 C.E.), and for Christian theologians, such as Tertullian (c. 155–c. 225 C.E.) and St. Augustine, bishop of Hippo in north Africa (354–430 C.E.), the Roman Empire was not the central concern, but it was an inescapable presence. These historians, philosophers, and theologians had to take account of Rome's power in their own teaching, writing, and actions. From their marginal positions, they usually counseled realistic accommodation to Rome's power.

In addition to these formal histories, leading men of the empire left important documents that shed light on their times. The great orator and political leader Cicero (106–43 B.C.E.) left dozens of letters, fifty-seven public speeches, and extensive writings on public affairs. Julius Caesar's account of the Gallic War describes his military organization and strategy, the Roman virtues that characterized his troops, and the lands and peoples against which he fought. It is the only account of a Roman war written by a participant that has endured to today. In part, Caesar was writing a propaganda piece, preparing the path for his later assertion of personal power in Rome.

His accounts are filled with great slaughter. For example, in 58 B.C.E., he reported that his armies slaughtered 226,000 Helvetii, with only some 110,000 surviving. In the same year he reports killing almost an entire German army of 120,000 men and, the next year, almost every soldier in a Belgic army of 60,000 men. He captured the region around Namur in northern France and sold all 53,000 inhabitants into slavery. In 56 B.C.E., he massacred two German peoples, killing as many as 460,000 people, including women and children. By the end of nine years of war in Gaul, Caesar reports a total of 1,192,000 enemy killed and another million captured.

- Which Roman authors and historians saw the expansion of the Roman Empire as unfortunate for the people of Rome? Why? Do you agree? Why or why not?

- Name Jews and Christians whose writings shed light on the Roman Empire. What issues did they address that are useful in understanding empires?

- If you could join archaeologists at a Roman site, which site would you like to explore? Why?

ties to the state, and usually without property. In exchange, clients were expected to help pay fines and public charges levied against their patrons and to help provide dowries for their patron's daughters at marriage. To mark the symbolism of the relationship, the client was to present himself periodically at the residence or office of the patron, and the patron was to give him a small gift at that time. The relationship of ex-masters to ex-slaves was of patron to client, and it was frequently characterized by warm feelings, especially if freedom was granted by gift of manumission rather than by the slave's purchase. These relationships often endured through several generations. Similar patron–client relationships between strong and weak later characterized Rome's imperial control over conquered provinces.

The Roman Family. Patron–client relationships also marked the structure of the family. The father of the family, the ***paterfamilias***, had the right of life and death over his children as long as he lived. In reality, most fathers were not tyrants, and in exercising the right to choose their children's occupations and spouses, and to control their economic possessions, they would normally try to consider their needs and desires. Nevertheless, fathers had the legal power to act as they wished: they continued to have control over their daughters' economic lives even after their marriages, for these rights did not pass to the husbands. These rights were enshrined in the law of *patria potestas*, the right of the head of the household.

According to Roman custom and practice, woman's role was subordinate to man's. A woman was legally subject to her father as long as he lived. After his death, she was required to obey the advice of her husband or a legally appointed guardian in any kind of legal or business transaction. Actual practice was, however, more liberal. If a woman had reached adulthood, she usually gained her independence at the death of her father, as did her brothers. Also, at least as early as the fifth-century B.C.E. *Law of the Twelve Tables*, women could block the legal powers of their husband by absenting themselves from his home for three nights in a row each year.

The families of the bride and groom arranged their marriages. Motherhood was considered the most significant rite of passage for women. Free-born women were exempted from having a guardian after giving birth to three children, and freed women after four children.

People respected women if they lived chastely and more or less contentedly within these guidelines of family, motherhood, and domesticity. The feminine ideal was the faith-ful and loyal *univira*, the "one-man woman." A woman caught in adultery was banished from her home and might well be executed; men apprehended in adultery were not punished. Women found drinking wine could also be punished; men could not. These principles of behavior were, of course, fully applicable only to the upper classes. The masses of lower-class free women entered the working world outside the home, and slaves had little control over their lives. The prevalence of prostitution and brothels further indicate the limited applicability of the Roman female ideal.

Class and Class Conflict. Despite the structure provided by patron–client relationships, class conflict was a staple of Rome's history. The system of government

paterfamilias The head of a family or household in Roman law—always a male—and the only member to have full legal rights. The *paterfamilias* had absolute power over his family, which extended to life and death.

Mosaic of Neptune and Amphitrite (detail), Herculaneum, before 79 C.E. Art sometimes seems to contradict the legal evidence concerning gender relationships in the Roman Empire. The artist responsible for this mosaic of the sea-god Neptune and his wife Amphitrite has accorded the couple an apparent equality.

under the early Republic had included only 7 to 10 percent of the population: the wealthy, the powerful, and some with hereditary ties to Rome. These were the patricians (from the Latin "pater," father). The overwhelming majority, the plebeians, those without long-standing hereditary ties to the state, and usually without property, could not serve as officers in the military and were thus excluded from government, as were slaves and women.

The two classes, patricians and plebeians, had become increasingly polarized under Etruscan rule. The patricians forbade intermarriage with the plebeians and monopolized for themselves the magistracies, membership of the Senate, and even the religious offices of the state. In response, the plebeians had looked to the Etruscan king as their protector. The fall of the monarchy c. 509 B.C.E. reduced the status of the plebeians still further.

The Struggle of the Orders. The first conflict between patricians and plebeians, the Struggle of the Orders, persisted through more than half a century—494 to 440 B.C.E.—of the early Republic. The plebeians relied on their ultimate strengths: their bodies and their numbers. They were the foot soldiers of Rome, and their periodic boycotts of the patricians, by withdrawing to the Aventine Hill, threatened the city of Rome itself. In 451 B.C.E., in an attempt to resolve the conflict, a commission of ten patricians codified Rome's existing customary practices into the *Law of the Twelve Tables*.

The patricians were pleased with their legal accomplishments and apparent liberality, but the plebeians were horrified when they recognized the force of the laws that were imposed upon them. For example, after a thirty-day grace period, debtors could be arrested and brought to court, held in chains or stocks, and, after sixty days, sold into slavery or killed. The financial punishment for bruising or breaking the bone of a freeman was twice that for similar injuries to a slave. The punishment for pasturing animals on someone else's land or for cutting crops from someone else's field secretly by night was death by hanging. The punishment for theft by a freeman was flogging and arranging some form of repayment; for theft by a slave it was flogging and execution by being thrown from the Tarpeian Rock on the Capitoline Hill in Rome. On the other hand, a patron who defrauded a client was subject to execution, later commuted to exile and confiscation of property (Lewis and Reinhold, I:109–113).

Slowly, under pressure, the patricians yielded power, and the first plebeian consul was elected in 360 B.C.E. A series of laws that relieved debt also helped the plebeians, although indebtedness continued to be a problem throughout Roman history.

Imperial expansion exacerbated class conflicts within Rome. The benefits of the conquests went mostly to the rich, while the yeoman farmers, who supplied the troops, were often bankrupted by the wars. After serving in the army for years, they would return home to find that in their absence their wives and children had not been able to maintain the family farms and might even have sold them to owners of large estates, called *latifundia*, and left for the city, impoverished.

Urban Splendor and Squalor. Class divisions were most glaring in the capital. The city of Rome itself grew seemingly without limit and without adequate planning. As Rome came to control Italy and then the Mediterranean, the city's population multiplied, reaching one million by about the first century C.E.

Some of the newcomers were wealthy and powerful, and they adorned the city by adding new examples of Greek architecture and urban design to the earlier Etruscan forms. They replaced wood, mud, and local volcanic rock with concrete and finer stone. Augustus himself boasted that he had found Rome a city of brick and left it one of marble. A modern urban historian has described the private homes of the wealthy patricians as models of comfort:

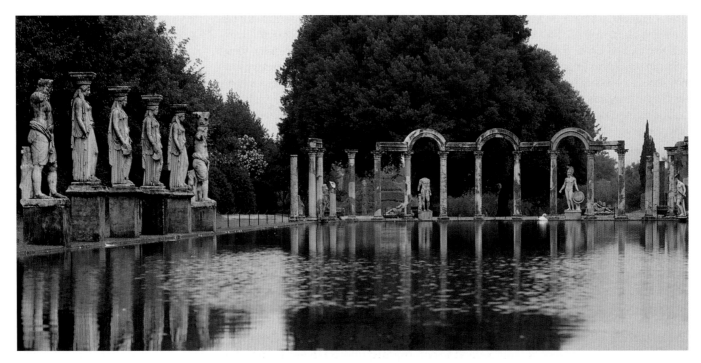

Canopus, Hadrian's Villa, Tivoli, c. 135 C.E. Rome's wealthy and powerful elites commanded private luxuries beyond the imagination of the average Roman. The Villa of the Emperor Hadrian comprised a series of buildings, gardens, and pools—this one representing a well-known Egyptian canal—laid out on the side of a hill in Tivoli. The complex was designed to bring the more sophisticated pleasures of city life to the country.

The houses of the patricians, spacious, airy, sanitary, equipped with bathrooms and water closets, heated in winter by hypocausts, which carried hot air through chambers in the floors, were perhaps the most commodious and comfortable houses built for a temperate climate anywhere until the twentieth century; a triumph of domestic architecture. (Mumford, p. 220)

The poor also came streaming into the city, but from bankrupt family farms. For them, Rome was a nightmare. The contrast was shocking.

Not only were these buildings unheated, unprovided with waste pipes or water closets, unadapted to cooking; not merely did they contain an undue number of airless rooms, indecently overcrowded: though poor in all the facilities that make for decent daily living, they were in addition so badly built and so high that they offered no means of safe exit from the frequent fires that occurred. And if their tenants escaped typhoid, typhus, fire, they might easily meet their death in the collapse of the whole structure. Such accidents were all too frequent …

The main population of the city that boasted its world conquests lived in cramped, noisy, airless, foul-smelling, infected quarters, paying extortionate rents to merciless landlords, undergoing daily indignities and terrors that coarsened and brutalized them, and in turn demanded compensatory outlets. (pp. 220–21)

Attempts at Reform. The most exemplary of the leaders who tried to achieve equity for Rome's poorer citizens were the reforming Gracchi brothers, Tiberius Sempronius Gracchus (163–133 B.C.E.) and Gaius Sempronius Gracchus (153–121 B.C.E.). In 133 B.C.E., while serving as tribune of the people, the office established to protect the interest of the plebeians, Tiberius proposed distributing some public lands among the poor, especially among poor soldiers. Opposed to this liberal proposal and fearing that Gracchus was attempting to gain too much political power for himself, a number of senators, supported by their clients, clubbed Tiberius and 300 of his supporters to death. This was the first political murder over a public policy issue in Rome in nearly 400 years. Despite the murder, the redistribution of public land did take place.

In 123 B.C.E., Gaius Gracchus was elected tribune of the people. He extended his brother's plan for land redistribution by establishing new colonies for the resettlement of some of the poor people of Rome in the regions conquered in the Punic Wars, including Carthage itself. He also introduced subsidized grain sales—later extended into a dole of free bread—to the poor people of Rome. Gaius argued that citizenship should be granted to all Latins and to the local civic officials in all other communities.

He was not equally sensitive to the problems of non-Italians, however, for his legislation exploited the provinces by enabling Roman knights to serve as "publicans" or tax farmers. These tax farmers struck an agreement with the state to turn over a fixed amount of net taxes from their region while retaining the right to collect as much as they were able and to keep the balance for themselves. Tax farming enabled the state to collect taxes without monitoring the process; it enabled the tax farmers to become wealthy; and it exploited the people who were being taxed, leaving them without protection. Gaius auctioned off the collection of taxes in Asia. While this profited the elite and helped to secure their loyalty to him personally, it impoverished the residents of the Roman province of Asia. Many senators became increasingly hostile to Gaius Gracchus, and in 121 B.C.E. he too was assassinated, along with his fellow tribune, Flaccus. Some 3000 of his supporters were executed.

The reforms of the Gracchi brothers seemed blocked, but in fact they laid the foundations for the events that led to the end of the Republic a century later. They challenged the power of the Senate and exposed the problems of the poor and the war veterans, while their enemies employed violence, murder, and thuggery as tools for fashioning and implementing public policy. Julius Caesar and Augustus Caesar, the two men most responsible for finally turning the Republic into a militaristic empire headed by a single person, learned from the experiences of the Gracchi brothers to play on Rome's class divisions by soliciting the support of the lower classes. They created an alliance between the emperor and the urban poor.

"Bread and Circuses." A new method of coping with class conflict developed: "Bread and circuses." Rome bribed the poor, many of them former soldiers from its conquering armies, with a dole of free bread. Up to 200,000 people were served each day. The dole encouraged them to while away their time in public religious festivities, races, the theater, and gladiatorial contests of great cruelty, which pitted man against man and man against beast in spectacles witnessed by tens of thousands. The public arenas of Rome, including Rome's largest race-track and stadia, could accommodate about half of Rome's adult population. On days of gladiatorial contests, as many as 5000 animals, including elephants and water buffalo, were slaughtered. Hundreds of humans, too, were slain in a single day. This combination of spectacle and free food was offered to keep the unemployed urban masses compliant.

Later emperors continued these policies designed to keep the plebeians quiet without actually solving the problems of unemployment and lack of dignity. Until its final collapse, the empire was threatened by unrest and revolt, and one of the reasons for the later popularity of Christianity in Rome was its message of compassion and salvation for the poor and downtrodden (Chapter 10).

Slaves and Slave Revolts

As wealthy Romans assembled vast estates and as Roman armies captured valuable underground mineral resources, they needed labor for farming and mining. Increasingly, they turned to the acquisition of slaves. Through military conquest, piracy, and raids in foreign regions, Rome accumulated slaves numbering perhaps in the millions. Short wars, such as those in Macedonia (197 B.C.E.) and Illyria (177 B.C.E.), yielded thousands; longer conflicts, such as those against the Teutons and Cimbrians (102–101 B.C.E.), hundreds of thousands. In his nine years in Gaul Julius Caesar may have captured nearly half a million. As much as a quarter of Rome's agricultural labor force was slave labor.

"Every slave we own is an enemy we harbor," was a sardonic Roman proverb by the time of Caesar Augustus (Lewis and Reinhold, I:245). That emperor proclaimed in his epitaph that in successful campaigns against pirates, "I turned over to their masters for punishment nearly 30,000 fugitive slaves who had taken up arms against the state" (Lewis and Reinhold, I:569). Three great slave revolts grew into wars. During the Great Slave War in Sicily (134–131 B.C.E.) 70,000 slaves resorted to armed resistance. In 104–100 B.C.E., a second revolt in Sicily broke out when it seemed that Germanic tribes would invade Italy and keep the imperial troops occupied in the north. Finally, Spartacus led a revolt among the gladiators in 73–71 B.C.E. that the Romans crushed. Some 100,000 slaves were killed in the fighting, and 6000 captured slaves were crucified on the roads leading into Rome.

Slaves continued throughout the imperial centuries as a threat within the Roman Empire. As Alaric besieged Rome with an army of Goths in 410 C.E., "Day by day almost all the slaves who were in Rome poured out of the city to join the barbarians, who now numbered about forty thousand" (Zosimus, *New History*, cited in Lewis and Reinhold, II:626).

Military Power

From its beginning, Rome was a military state. According to one legend, its founders, the twin brothers Romulus and Remus, were the sons of Mars, the god of war. An alternative legend, reported in Virgil's *Aeneid*, saw them descended on their mother's side from Aeneas, a pious and devoted warrior-hero from the fallen city of Troy.

Rome's armies were central to its life and they excelled in organization and technology. When necessary they adopted creative innovations. Although at first they copied the Greek hoplite phalanxes (see Chapter 5) in their military deployment, later Roman armies were structured around smaller, more maneuverable units, arrayed together in battle lines from least to most experienced, so that enemies were forced to confront row-on-row of soldiers of increasing skill and valor. Confronting groups of invading Goths, they created new, mobile cavalry units to supplement their more conventional infantry legions of 3000 to 6000 foot soldiers.

Although it had never previously possessed a navy, Rome built one that conquered Carthage, the greatest sea-power of the day. The

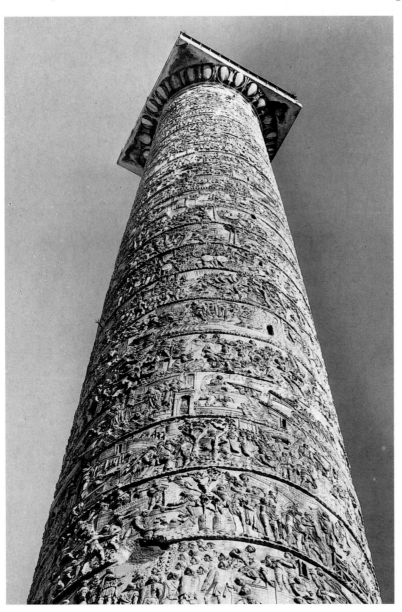

Column of Trajan, Rome. Dedicated 113 C.E. The Romans built tall commemorative columns in order to celebrate the power and military might of the empire. The Column of Trajan is covered by a continuous strip of carving that tells the story of the Emperor Trajan's victories over the barbarian tribes along the Danube.

Arch of Trajan, Benevento, 114–117 C.E.
Triumphal arches are another peculiarly Roman means of celebrating the power of the ruler and his empire. This particular arch, dedicated to Trajan, stands at the point where the road to Brindisi, a port on the east coast, branches off the Appian Way, the first major road in the Romans' strategic network.

Romans learned to build sophisticated warships by capturing one from Carthage and copying it. Confronting great walled towns in the east, Rome developed unprecedented machinery to besiege the walls, catapult firepower into them, and batter them down. The Roman preference for massing overwhelming strength and their willingness to let time work on their side through siege warfare, brought many victories with minimal losses of their own.

To be a free man was to serve in the army. Within Italy, captured city-states were required to supply not gold and taxes but men for the armies. At the time of Julius Caesar, the average Italian male served seven years in the army. Under Augustus, soldiering became more professional: men enlisted for between sixteen and twenty-five years and were paid regular wages. Conquered peoples outside Italy also contributed troops to Rome's armies. The Barbarians who invaded the empire were often encouraged to settle in Roman territories and to enlist in Roman armies. An outward spiral of imperial expansion resulted. As Rome expanded, so did its armed forces; it then expanded further in part to capture the wealth needed to pay its larger armies; this expansion, in turn, enlarged its armies once more.

In the field, the soldiers built their support systems: military camps, administrative towns, strings of fortress watch-towers along the borders, roads, and aqueducts. Roman engineering feats astonished the world in their day, and many of them remain to astonish us as well. Many of the walled military camps were kernels from which sprouted later towns and cities, one of Rome's most distinctive contributions. These urban outposts established Rome's military and administrative rule in the midst of remote rural regions. In the reign of Augustus, these nodes were linked by 50,000 miles of first-class roads and 200,000 miles of lesser roads. The roads facilitated commerce and communication, but their original and fundamental purpose was to enable the swift movement of troops throughout the empire.

Generals in Politics

In this militaristic empire, generals gained power. At first Rome's military leaders were constrained by the aristocratic Senate and the general assembly of Rome. Later, the generals began giving the orders. General Gaius Marius campaigned to have himself elected consul in 107 B.C.E. He broke with the normal practice of recruiting only troops who owned property, and accepted soldiers who were indebted to him personally for their maintenance. Elected consul six times between 107 and 100 B.C.E., Marius restructured the armies to increase their efficiency. He arranged large allotments of land for veteran soldiers in north Africa, Gaul, Sicily, Greece, and Macedonia, a move that solved temporarily one of the great problems of Rome: How to accommodate soldiers returning home after long tours of duty. The armies now depended for their welfare on Marius rather than on the state.

The generals began to compete among themselves for power. At the highest level, the struggle between the generals Lucius Sulla and Gaius Marius precipitated civil war in Rome. To fight against Mithridates VI, king of Pontus (r. 120–63 B.C.E.), the Senate called Sulla. Marius, however, arranged to have the command transferred to himself. In response, Sulla rallied soldiers loyal to him and invaded Rome, initiating the first civil war (83–82 B.C.E.). He declared Marius an outlaw and left with his troops for Greece, where he defeated Mithridates. Meanwhile Marius, joined by another general, Lucius Cornelius Cinna, seized Rome and banned Sulla. Sulla returned with his army, invaded Italy and Rome, had himself declared dictator, a position he held for two years, and then abdicated.

Twenty years later, in 60 B.C.E., two great generals, Julius Caesar and Pompey, and Marcus Licinius Crassus, a wealthy businessman who became a military commander, formed a **triumvirate**, an alliance of the three men to rule. The three competed among themselves until Caesar defeated the others. Caesar ruled as dictator from 47 until 44 B.C.E., when rivals assassinated him because they felt he had usurped too much power.

Born in Rome of an aristocratic patrician family about 100 B.C.E., Caesar felt the hand of the military dictator Sulla as a young man when Sulla ordered him to divorce his wife, Cornelia, daughter of Cinna, one of Sulla's greatest rivals. Caesar refused. Biographers are not sure whether this was because of Caesar's love for Cornelia, exceptional personal pride, an assessment that the alliance with Cinna's faction would, in the long run, prove advantageous, or some combination of calculations. In any case, Caesar's refusal was unusual in a world where aristocratic marriages—and divorces—were usually contracted for political purposes. (Caesar, for example, later married his seventeen-year-old daughter to the forty-seven-year-old Pompey.) No one else, even Pompey, refused Sulla's commands. It was also out of character for Caesar himself, a man who had already begun to earn a growing reputation for marital infidelity, including rumors of some homosexual activity (Grant, *Julius Caesar*, pp. 23–4, 33–9).

triumvirate An unofficial coalition between Julius Caesar, Pompey, and Crassus was formed in 60 B.C.E. After Caesar's murder in 44 B.C.E., a triumvirate that included his heir Octavian (later Augustus), Mark Antony, and Marcus Lepidus was appointed to maintain public order.

To escape Sulla's grasp, Caesar fled into exile in the Greek islands where he studied philosophy and oratory until he was pardoned and returned to Rome. He was elected magistrate in 65 B.C.E., with responsibilities for producing public games. Pouring his own money as well as public and borrowed funds into the task, he won widespread acclaim. His prominence increased when he was elected chief priest, *pontifex maximus*, of the Roman state in 63 B.C.E., a position of greater prestige and patronage than of religious significance. Reaching toward the pinnacle of political power, Caesar was elected **praetor** in 60 B.C.E. and consul—the highest elected position in Rome—in 59. A military man, he sometimes used strong-arm methods to intimidate the Senate, on one occasion having his fellow consul attacked and beaten.

In Rome, military prowess counted most, and in 58 B.C.E. Caesar led his armies on a mission to dominate Gaul (modern France) and protect it from invaders. This move also got him out of Rome at the end of his term as consul, thus escaping legal prosecution for his violent acts while serving in that position. Caesar's *Gallic War* tells of the nine years of military campaigns that brought all of Gaul under Rome. Caesar also briefly crossed the Rhine River, to demonstrate that Rome had the capacity to invade the Germanic territories if it wished, and he twice invaded Britain, also briefly. Caesar was Rome's most successful general and one of its best orators as well.

The triumvirate broke down when Crassus was killed during warfare in Turkey, as he sought to extend Rome's empire in the east. Pompey now saw Caesar as his direct rival, and Rome dissolved into civil war. Pompey was defeated in a series of battles and finally killed while seeking refuge in Egypt. Caesar now ruled Rome alone, but only briefly. Jealous of, and frightened by, his extraordinary powers, senators followed Brutus and Cassius in stabbing him to death on the Ides of March, March 15, 44 B.C.E.

In his three years as dictator, Caesar revised the Roman calendar creating the Julian calendar that lasted for 1500 years; re-organized Rome's city government; extended citizenship to the peoples of many conquered provinces; continued the policy of free bread and circuses; and appointed many of his opponents to public office in an attempt at reconciliation. He resolved one of the most intractable problems of Rome's citizens: the debts that had piled up during the years of civil war. He forced creditors to accept payment in land and property valued at pre-war prices, and he canceled all interest due since the wars began. Caesar selected his sister Julia's grandson, Gaius Octavius (63 B.C.E.–14 C.E.), later called Octavian, as his heir. Following Caesar's assassination, this adopted son avenged his death by murdering 300 senators and 2000 knights; triumphed over Lepidus and Mark Antony, the two rivals who had been for sometime his colleagues in a second triumvirate; and became the unchallenged ruler of Rome for almost half a century.

To avert civil war, Octavian used his sister Octavia as a diplomatic and political tool, marrying her to his rival, Antony (83–30 B.C.E.) in 40 B.C.E. In 36 B.C.E., Antony openly married the alluring and seductive queen of Egypt, Cleopatra (r. 51–30 B.C.E.), even though he was already married to Octavia, and established his headquarters in Egypt, the richest state in the east. By sharing local rule with Cleopatra, Antony betrayed Rome's imperial policies. Eventually, Antony discarded and divorced Octavia, humiliating Octavian personally as well as infuriating him politically. The warfare between the two men became especially bitter. Octavian finally defeated Antony and Cleopatra in the decisive naval battle at Actium (31 B.C.E.), formally annexed Egypt, and seized the Egyptian treasury for himself. Octavian now controlled more wealth than the Roman state.

praetor In ancient Rome, the name was originally applied to the consul as leader of an army. In 366 B.C.E. a further praetor was elected with special responsibility for the administration of justice in Rome, with the right of military command. Further praetors were subsequently appointed to administer the increasing number of provinces.

Augustus of Prima Porta, early 1st century C.E. With the gratitude of the Senate of Rome that was weary of civil warfare among its generals, Augustus transformed Rome into an imperial monarchy under his control. (*Musei Vaticani, Rome*)

SOURCE

The Legacy and Epitaph of Augustus Caesar

Our primary sources on Augustus' life are limited, and almost all of his own autobiography has been lost. Therefore, the Res Gestae Divi Augusti *("Account of the Accomplishments of Augustus") has become a crucial text. Written for the people of Rome by Augustus himself shortly before he died, and inscribed on several temples throughout the empire, it records the emperor's own statement of how he wanted to be remembered. Its thirty-five paragraphs fall into three sections: the offices and honors bestowed on him; his personal donations for public purposes; and his accomplishments in war and peace:*

1. At the age of nineteen, on my own initiative and at my own expense, I raised an army by means of which I liberated the Republic ... the people elected me consul and a triumvir for the settlement of the commonwealth ...

3. I waged many wars throughout the whole world by land and by sea ... and when victorious I spared all citizens who sought pardon ... About 500,000 Roman citizens were under military oath to me.

15. To the Roman plebs I paid 300 sesterces apiece in accordance with the will of my father [Julius Caesar]; and in my fifth consulship [29 B.C.E.] I gave each 400 sesterces in my own name out of the spoil of war, reaching never less than 250,000 persons ... In the eighteenth year of my tribunician power and my twelfth consulship [29 B.C.E.] I gave out of the spoils of war 1000 sesterces apiece to my soldiers settled in colonies ... received by about 120,000 persons ... In my thirteenth consulship [2 B.C.E.] I gave sixty denarii apiece to those of the plebs who at that time were receiving public grain ... a little more than 200,000 persons.

19. I built ... the senate house and ... the temple of Apollo ...

22. I gave a gladiatorial show three times in my own name, and five times in the names of my sons or grandsons; at these shows about 10,000 fought ... Twenty-six times I provided for the people ... hunting spectacles of African wild beasts in the circus or in the Forum or in the amphitheaters ...

23. I turned over to their masters for punishment nearly 30,000 slaves who had run away from their owners and taken up arms against the state.

28. I established colonies of soldiers in Africa, Sicily, Macedonia, in both Spanish provinces, in Achaea, Asia, Syria, Narbonese Gaul, and Pisidia. Italy, moreover, has twenty-eight colonies established by me which grew large and prosperous in my lifetime ...

31. Royal embassies from India, never previously seen before any Roman general, were often sent to me. (Lewis and Reinhold, I:561–72)

By 30 B.C.E., following fourteen years of civil war, Octavian had become master of a re-unified Roman world. A grateful Senate, weary of seemingly endless civil wars, heaped him with honors, including, in 27 B.C.E., the title "Augustus," meaning "sacred" or "venerable." His achievements were immense, and after his death the Romans designated him a god.

Under one name or another, Augustus ruled Rome for fifty-six years until his death in 14 C.E. He fought wars that stabilized the borders of the empire while ensuring peace and facilitating trade, commerce, and economic growth throughout the Mediterranean. He restructured imperial administration into a form that lasted for almost two centuries. He inaugurated public projects that beautified Rome and kept its workers employed. He pacified the Roman masses and won over the aristocracy. He patronized the arts and literature, which flourished in a "Golden Age." He built new roads and cities throughout the length and breadth of the empire.

Augustus instituted conservative policies concerning religion and family life. The growth of urban life, especially in Rome itself in the first century B.C.E., offered new opportunities to a few upper-class Roman women to gain education and even to participate in public life, although usually behind the scenes. New marriage laws enabled them to live as equals of their husbands and gave them the right to divorce and to act without reference to a legal guardian. They could own and control wealth in their own name. Women did not have access to the professions or to public political office, but several exercised great influence over their husbands, brothers, and sons.

Augustus sought to restore the earlier family order. He made adultery a criminal offense, punishable by exile, confiscation of property, and even execution. Indeed, he exiled his own daughter and only child, Julia, a charming and intelligent woman who offended him with her frequent and publicly known affairs. He encouraged marriage and childbearing and punished celibacy. These laws were widely opposed and disobeyed, but they reveal to us the link in Augustus' mind between a well-ordered family and a well-ordered empire, a link that was repeated in the official policies of many empires throughout history. (Compare China and India in Chapters 7 and 8, Britain in Chapter 16, Japan in Chapter 17, and Germany in Chapter 18.) Moreover, despite the general religious skepticism and indifference of the Roman upper classes, Augustus rebuilt temples and encouraged the worship of ancestral gods as a foundation of state morality.

The End of the Republic

With Augustus, Rome became an imperial monarchy, a territorial, political, and economic empire ruled by a single military commander, the *imperator* (from which the term emperor is derived), and his armies. For years generals had wanted this centralized power. Now, in gratitude, the Senate was willing to turn it over to Augustus. Augustus rejected the title of monarch, preferring to be called princeps, or first citizen. This gesture of humility fooled no one. With Augustus' reign, the imperial form of government begins even though the Senate and the consuls and other magistrates survived. From Augustus on, all real power in the Roman state lay in the hands of the emperor.

As the empire continued to expand through military conquests, Rome's generals demanded, and were granted, increasing powers until, with Augustus, they supplanted republican, civilian government with an administration headed by the military commander-in-chief. Before we analyze the significance of this political transformation, however, let us complete our account of the continuing geographical expansion of the empire.

Augustus annexed modern Switzerland and Noricum (modern Austria and Bavaria) in 16–15 B.C.E., and established Rome's historical frontier in central Europe at the Danube River. After an attempt to conquer central Germany failed in 9 C.E., the Rhine became the normal border in the northeast.

In the 40s C.E. the Romans conquered modern England and Wales, which became the Roman province of Britain. Some 2000 miles to the east, the Emperor Trajan (r. 98–117 C.E.) conquered Dacia (modern Romania), and briefly annexed Armenia and Parthia (Mesopotamia).

Trajan's successor, Hadrian (117–138 C.E.), consolidated Roman gains. He permanently withdrew the Roman forces from Mesopotamia back to the Euphrates and built a wall, west to east, across the narrow neck of the northern part of Britain. Twenty-five years later, his successor, Antoninus Pius (r. 138–161 B.C.E.), built another wall some 50 miles further north. The limits of the Roman Empire had been reached.

The policy of granting citizenship to consolidate empire continued on a limited basis as Rome expanded. In 14 C.E. Augustus Caesar announced that there were 4,937,000 citizens in the empire, about 2 million of them in the provinces. At that time, the total population of the empire was between 70 and 100 million. In 212 C.E., the Emperor Caracalla (r. 212–217) officially proclaimed citizenship for all free males in the empire, although ambiguous legal restrictions limited the effect. Provincials could occupy the highest offices in the empire: senator, consul, and even emperor. The Emperor Trajan was from Spain; Septimius Severus (r. 193–211) was from north Africa; Diocletian (r. 284–305) was from Dalmatia (modern Croatia).

The development of international law, the *jus gentium*, the law of nations, also helped to unite and pacify the empire. After its victory in the first Punic War in 241 B.C.E., Rome interacted more than ever with foreigners and with subjects of Rome who did not have citizenship. To deal with legal cases between Romans and others,

HOW DO WE KNOW?

Roman Law: Theory and Practice

Modern historians have generally praised Rome's incipient international legal system as:

one of the most potent and effective ideas that the Romans ever originated ... It demonstrated that a body of law could be established upon a foundation acceptable to the members of different peoples and races at any and every phase of social, economic, and political evolution; and so it brought the laws of the Romans nearer to universal applicability than any others that have ever been devised. *(Grant, pp. 104–5)*

Legal theory and practice, however, did not always coincide in ancient Rome (just as they do not always coincide today). The poor did not receive the same protection and benefits as the rich, soldiers abused their authority, and laws were not always applied consistently. The satirist Juvenal (c. 55–c. 127) ridiculed t he inability of Rome's legal system to curb the arbitrary violence of Roman soldiers:

Your teeth are shattered? Face hectically inflamed, with great black welts? You know the doctor wasn't too optimistic about the eye that was left. But it's not a bit of good your running to the courts about it. If you've been beaten up by a soldier, better keep it to yourself. *(cited in Boardman et al., p. 575)*

In practice, the law was also not always as universal as it claimed, and those challenging the empire might not reap its benefits. Jewish nationalist writers, for example, compared the hypocrisy of Rome's laws to the ambiguous associations of the unclean pig:

Just as a pig lies down and sticks out its trotters as though to say "I am clean" [because they are cloven], so the evil empire robs and oppresses while pretending to execute justice. *(cited in Boardman et al., p. 582)*

Beginning about the second century C.E., preferential treatment for the wealthy and the powerful entered explicitly into the law, deepening class antagonisms, and weakening the empire.

- *On what basis do historians differ when evaluating the quality of the Roman legal system?*
- *The modern historian Michael Grant writes about Rome's system of international law while the satirist Juvenal lived in ancient Rome and wrote about its local criminal law. How is each author's perspective affected by his time and expertise?*
- *What do you think is the effect on society of a legal system that gives preferential treatment to one group over another?*

a new official, the foreign magistrate, was appointed. The *jus gentium* evolved from his judgments. Over time, this law was codified, first by Hadrian, and later, in the East, by the Emperor Justinian (r. 527–565).

Economic Policies of the Empire

The empire brought extraordinary benefits to the rulers, and sometimes to the ruled. Imperial rule and the opening of imperial markets brought opportunities for economic development and profit in the conquered provinces, although most of these went to the local wealthy elites who possessed the capital and skills to take advantage of them. In general, Roman rulers were solicitous of the upper classes in the provinces, both because of a shared class position and because they believed that the loyalty of these elites was crucial to maintaining Roman hegemony.

The cost of this imperial role, however, could also be heavy and eventually became oppressive. The Romans levied tribute, taxes, and rents, and recruited soldiers from the peoples they conquered. They settled their own soldiers in captured lands, turning those lands into Roman estates and enslaving millions of people to work on them. They exploited their political power for the economic advantage of their own traders and military and administrative elites.

As the size and wealth of the empire grew, many Romans felt that they had conquered the world but lost their souls. They spoke not of victory, but of loss. The historian Livy, writing at the height of the age of Augustus, lamented the end of innocence:

with the gradual relaxation of discipline, morals first gave way, as it were, then sank lower and lower, and finally began the downward plunge which has brought us to the present time, when we can endure neither our vices nor the cure. *(cited in Lewis and Reinhold, I:8)*

For an interactive version of this map, go to: **http://www.prenhall.com/spodek/map6.2**

Eurasian trade. The commercial links that bound the ancient world were both extensive and sophisticated. Self-sustaining individual networks—the Saharan caravans, the Arab dhows plying the Indian Ocean, the fleets of Chinese junks coasting east Asia, and most famously the Silk Routes traversing central Asia—linked at key entrepots such as Alexandria and Oc Eo by sea, and Ctesiphon and Kashgar by land, to form a truly intercontinental trading system.

Livy proclaimed the widely held myth of an older, golden age of simplicity and lamented its loss:

> No state was ever greater, none more righteous or richer in good examples, nor ever was where avarice and luxury came into the social order so late, or where humble means and thrift were so highly esteemed and so long held in honor. For true it is that the less men's wealth was, the less was their greed. Of late, riches have brought in avarice, and excessive pleasures the longing to carry wantonness and license to the point of personal ruin and universal destruction. (cited in Lewis and Reinhold, I:8)

This nostalgia had two related, but different versions. One drew on examples from the days of simple, rustic equality before the advent of the Etruscan kings. It condemned the maltreatment of the plebeians and the slaves at the hands of the patricians that had begun under Etruscan rule and intensified under the Republic. The other version wished to re-create the days of the oligarchic, patrician Republic, before the transfer of power from the Senate to the generals.

ROMAN EMPERORS

	Augustus (27 B.C.E.–14 C.E.)
Julio-Claudian dynasty	Tiberius (14–37) Caligula (37–41) Claudius (41–54) Nero (54–68)
Flavian dynasty	Vespasian (69–79) Titus (79–81) Domitian (81–96)
Age of the Antonines	Nerva (96–98) Trajan (98–117) Hadrian (117–138) Antoninus Pius (138–161) Marcus Aurelius (161–180) Commodus (180–193)
Severan dynasty	Septimius Severus (193–211) Caracalla (212–217) Elagabalus (218–222) Severus Alexander (222–235)
The late empire	Philip the Arabian (244–249) Decius (249–251) Gallus (251–253) Valerian (253–260) Gallienus (253–268) Claudius (268–270) Aurelian (270–275) Tacitus (275–276) Florian (276) Probus (276–282) Carus (282–283) Numerianus (283–284) and Carinus (283–285) Diocletian (284–305)

Supplying Rome. Feeding and provisioning the city of Rome, which had a population of about a million by the time of Augustus, called on vast resources throughout the empire. The most important requirement was grain, and Romans imported it from Sicily, Egypt and the north African coast, Spain, and the lands surrounding the Black Sea.

Merchants imported more specialized products from all parts of the empire: olive oil and wine came from within Italy, Spain, and the Mediterranean shores; pottery and glass from the Rhineland; leather from southern France; marble from Asia Minor; woolen textiles from Britain and northern France, Belgium, and the Netherlands; slaves from many lands. For gladiatorial contests in the Colosseum, and for general display in Rome, lions were brought from Africa and Asia, bears from Scotland, horses from Spain, crocodiles and camels from Egypt, and leopards and rhinoceroses from northwest Africa. The transportation of bulk commodities, especially within the empire, was most often by sea.

Building Cities. A few other extremely large cities, such as Alexandria, also needed to import extensively to provide for their hundreds of thousands of inhabitants, but most of the empire was locally self-sufficient. In this pre-industrial age, most people worked on the land, most production was agricultural, and people consumed most produce near the place of production, especially in the newly conquered and settled regions of western Europe.

To incorporate these regions into the empire, the Romans constructed and promoted new cities as administrative, military, and financial centers. These included the cores of modern London, Paris, Lyons, Trier, Nimes, Bruges, Barcelona, Cologne, Budapest, and many other European cities. In an empire that rested on agriculture, Rome laid the foundations of a small but potent ruling urban civilization.

At the height of its power, the empire contained more than 5000 civic bodies. The orator Marcus Tullius Cicero referred to Narbonne, Rome's administrative capital in southern Gaul from about 118 B.C.E., as "a colony of Roman citizens, a watch tower of the Roman people, a bulwark against the wild tribes of Gaul" (cited in Mumford, p. 209). Roman rule especially attracted and benefited the urban upper classes in the conquered regions, and helped to urbanize some leaders of the newly arriving immigrant German settlers.

Luxury Trades. People of wealth and power could command specialty goods. Supplying their demands generated small but significant streams of intercontinental, long-distance, luxury trade. For this commerce to flourish, trade routes had to be protected and kept safe. The Pax Romana secured the Red Sea routes, which allowed the import of frankincense, myrrh, and other spices from the Arabian peninsula and the Horn of Africa and spices and textiles from India, some of them transshipped from China. By the first century C.E., sailors had discovered that by sailing with the summer monsoon winds they could reach India from Egypt in about four months. They could then return with the winter monsoon, completing the round trip within a year.

Rome's repayment in this exchange was mostly precious metals. Hoards of gold coins from Rome have been discovered in south India, with smaller treasuries in China, southeast Asia, and east Africa. The historian Pliny the Elder (23–79) complained that the trade drained Italy's precious metals, but the profits to be made back home were extraordinary: "In no year does India absorb less than 50,000,000 sesterces

The Roman aqueduct at Segovia, Spain, early first or second century C.E. Unlike the Greeks, the Romans are remembered less for their art than for their great engineering feats. The need to improve the water supply to Roman settlements increased along with urban population growth. The popularity of the public bathing houses heightened the demand even more. The Romans developed a massive network of aqueducts to channel water into cities across uneven terrain.

Timgad, North Africa. Timgad, in Algeria, was founded as a military and administrative fortress around 100 C.E. and designed as a perfect square with a grid plan for the streets. The Romans tended to adhere to standard templates of town construction, despite variations in local topography, and Timgad is one of the clearest surviving models of what a provincial headquarters looked like.

of our Empire's wealth, sending back merchandise to be sold with us at a hundred times its original cost" (cited in Lewis and Reinhold, II:120).

Overland routes were also vital. The need for safety and protection was most evident in the silk trade, which prospered when Augustan Rome, Parthian Mesopotamia and Iran, Kushan India, and Han China—the four empires that spanned the silk routes—were at their peaks. Goods from Luoyang and Xian in China crossed the mountains of central Asia, connecting finally at one of the great trading emporia of Begram, Bactra, or Merv. From there, they continued onward into the Mediterranean.

Silk, light and valuable, was the principal export westward, but the caravans also carried lacquerware, bronzes, and other treasures. A storehouse discovered in 1938 in Begram, which stood at the crossroads of China, India, Persia, and the Mediterranean, revealed some of the principal luxury goods of this intercontinental trade: lacquer-work from China; ivory statues and carvings from India; alabaster, bronze, and glass works from the Mediterranean. Astonishingly, many of the carriers of these treasures seem to have been the steppe nomads of central Asia, the Huns and other "barbarians," who at other times attacked and plundered the empires across which they now traded.

Officially, the Roman upper classes scorned trade as beneath their status. Unofficially, they often entered into contracts with freedmen, their own ex-slaves, to front for their commercial enterprises. Trade was lucrative, and the aristocrats did not wish to lose the profits. The preferred methods of earning a livelihood were from land ownership, tax collecting for the state, or military conquest, but even generals, like Julius Caesar, profited from the sale of slaves captured in war.

Roman traders could be very exploitative. Especially when working in Rome's provinces, they often inspired great hatred. When Mithridates VI, king of Pontus in northern Anatolia, invaded the Roman province of Asia in 88 B.C.E. he encouraged Asian debtors to kill their Roman creditors. Eighty thousand Italian and Italian-Greek businessmen were reported murdered (Grant, p. 184).

In the late second century C.E. internal revolts and external attacks by Germanic peoples brought an end to the Pax Romana and introduced major obstacles to this trade. Roads and markets were no longer secure, and only items that could be consumed locally were worth producing. For example, manufacturers cut back sharply the production of glass, metals, and textiles in northern Europe. Provisioning Rome and other cities became more difficult. The population of cities fell and the protection they could offer declined, as did their levels of consumption. They provided less opportunity for making a profit and less incentive to producers. Trade and productivity faltered. As the Pax Romana began to break down politically and militarily, trade declined and became more localized.

Cultural Policies of the Empire

Greco-Roman Culture. To win and secure allies, Rome not only granted citizenship, codified international law, and built a remarkable physical infrastructure of towns and roads for unifying the empire, it also developed a culture that it brought to the people it conquered. Roman cultural achievements had lagged far behind those of

The Colosseum, Rome, c. 72–80 C.E. Built to house spectacular entertainments, such as mock sea-battles and gladiatorial combats, for audiences of up to 50,000 people, the Colosseum combined Greek decorative traditions with Roman engineering ingenuity, epitomized in the advanced use of concrete as a building material.

Greece, but as Rome conquered the Greek city-states, it began to absorb the culture of those it conquered. The Roman aristocratic classes adopted Greek language and literature as well as the architectural, sculptural, and painting traditions of the Greeks. The Romans now borrowed from the Greeks as they had earlier borrowed from the Etruscans.

Rome carried this polyglot culture outward in its conquests in Europe and Asia. Its schools in the provinces spread Greek as well as Latin among the tribal Goths and Gauls. Greek was the language of high culture. Latin, however, became the language of administration. Roman troops constructed amphitheaters, stadia, and baths wherever they went, the Roman invention of concrete making such constructions feasible. In these settings Roman rulers provided theaters and spectacles modeled on those in Rome.

Rome's sense of its own superiority doubtless encouraged its conquest of other peoples, deemed inferior, and was encouraged, in turn, by the success of those conquests. Rome's greatest epic poem, the *Aeneid*, written by Virgil during the reign of Augustus, sings the emperor's praises and celebrates Rome's superiority.

> ... Behold the Romans,
> Your very own. These are Iulus' children,
> The race to come. One promise you have heard
> Over and over: here is its fulfillment,
> The son of a god, Augustus Caesar, founder
> Of a new age of gold, in lands where Saturn
> Ruled long ago; he will extend his empire
> Beyond the Indies, beyond the normal measure
> Of years and constellations, where high Atlas
> Turns on his shoulders the star-studded world.

At the same time, Virgil upholds the concept of *noblesse oblige*, the duty of the superior to help the inferior:

> ... remember Romans,
> To rule the people under law, to establish
> The way of peace, to battle down the haughty,
> To spare the meek. Our fine arts, these, forever.
> (*Aeneid*, VI:822–31, 893–6; trans. Rolphe Humphries)

In the *Aeneid*, Virgil incorporates many of the forms of the earlier Greek epics, especially of Homer's *Odyssey*, but obviously he adds his own notes of an intensely imperialistic triumphalism.

Stoicism. Romans borrowed philosophical as well as literary ideas from the Greeks. Many thoughtful Romans were attracted to Stoicism, a philosophy founded by the Greek Zeno about 300 B.C.E. Stoicism took its name from the *stoa*, the covered walkway, in Athens where he taught. Zeno began with a cosmic theory of the world as a rational, well-ordered, and coherent system. Therefore humans should accept, without joy or grief, free from passion, everything that takes place in this world. Lucius Annaeus Seneca (*c.* 4 B.C.E.–65 C.E.), a Roman Stoic living three centuries later, elaborated:

> What is the principal thing? A heart ... which can go forth to face ill or good dauntless and unembarrassed, paralyzed neither by the tumult of the one nor the glamour of the other. (Seneca, *Natural Questions*, cited in Lewis and Reinhold, II:165–6)

A corollary of Zeno's moral philosophy stated that people should treat one another with decency because we are all brothers and sisters. Marcus Tullius Cicero (106–43

B.C.E.), one of Rome's most important orators, commentators, and statesmen, and much influenced by Stoic beliefs, wrote:

> The private individual ought first, in private relations, to live on fair and equal terms with his fellow citizens, with a spirit neither servile and groveling nor yet domineering. (Cicero, *On Duties*, cited in Lewis and Reinhold, I:273)

How, then, did Stoics address the conditions of slavery in Rome? Although Stoics did not advocate the end of slavery, they did propose more humane treatment. Writing on the treatment of slaves, Seneca proposed a kind of Golden Rule:

> Treat those below you as you would be treated by those above you. (Seneca, *Moral Epistles*, cited in Lewis and Reinhold, II:180)

At this, however, Tacitus accused Seneca, one of Rome's richest citizens, of hypocrisy: "By what wisdom, by what principles of philosophy had he acquired 300,000,000 sesterces within four years of [receiving Emperor Nero's] royal favor? At Rome the childless and their wills are snared in his nets, as it were; Italy and the provinces are drained by his enormous usury" (*Annals* XIII:xlii, cited in Lewis and Reinhold, II:165–6, n. 58).

Stoicism reached the height of its influence in Rome with the selection of Marcus Aurelius Antoninus as emperor (r. 161–180 C.E.). He ruled through two decades of almost continuous warfare, economic upheaval, internal revolts, and plague. Through it all, Marcus Aurelius remained courageous and Stoic. He recorded his thoughts in his *Meditations*, one of the most philosophically reflective works ever written by a man in a position of such power:

> Keep thyself then simple, good, pure, serious, free from affectation, a friend of justice, a worshipper of the gods, and help men. Short is life. The universe is either a confusion, and a mutual involution of things, and a dispersion; or it is unity and order and providence ... If the [latter], I venerate, and I am firm, and I trust in him who governs. (VI:30, 10)

Religion in the Empire. Officially, Rome celebrated a religion centralized on the person of the emperor-god. After the deification of Augustus at his death, the official priesthood offered animal sacrifices to him and later to his successors, adding these to the traditional sacrifices to the major pagan gods, especially Jupiter, Juno, and Minerva. People celebrated the birthdays and death anniversaries of the emperors as holidays.

GREEK AND ROMAN GODS

In the second century B.C.E., Greece was absorbed by the Roman Empire. In the process the Romans adopted and adapted many Greek myths, linking their own gallery of gods to Greek legends and deities.

Greek	Roman	
Aphrodite	Venus	Goddess of love and beauty
Apollo, Phoebus	Apollo, Phoebus	Greek god of sun, god of music, poetry, and prophecy
Ares	Mars	God of war
Artemis	Diana	Virgin huntress, goddess of the moon
Asclepius	Aesculapius	God of medicine
Athena (Pallas)	Minerva	Goddess of wisdom and art
Cronus	Saturn	Father of the supreme god: Zeus or Jupiter
Demeter	Ceres	Goddess of the harvest
Dionysus	Bacchus	God of wine and fertility
Eros	Cupid	God of love
Hades	Pluto, Dis	God of the underworld
Hephaestus	Vulcan	God of fire
Hera	Juno	Queen of heaven, wife of Zeus/Jupiter, goddess of women and marriage
Hermes	Mercury	Messenger of the gods, god of roads, cunning, commerce, wealth, and luck
Hestia	Vesta	Goddess of the hearth
Hymen	Hymen	God of marriage
Irene	Pax	Goddess of peace
Pan	Faunus	God of flocks and shepherds
Persephone	Proserpina	Goddess of corn and the spring, goddess of the dead
Poseidon	Neptune	God of the sea
Zeus	Jupiter, Jove	Supreme ruler of gods and men, king of heaven, and overseer of justice and destiny

Beyond these rituals, however, Roman religious policies allowed a great deal of flexibility. For the most part, as long as people venerated the emperor and did not question the legitimacy of the state, Roman emperors allowed diverse religious practices to flourish. Mithraism, a religion that worshiped the Persian sun god Mithra as mediator between god and man, emphasized discipline and loyalty. It was especially popular within the military, especially among the Germanic and eastern troops who found attractive its message of fighting vigorously against both internal passions and external military opponents.

Two additional religions popular in early imperial Rome centered on female goddesses, and were especially attractive to women. Like Mithraism, both were mystery religions—that is, they had rituals of initiation that defied rational understanding and that were unknown to outsiders. These could include orgies and baptisms. One such faith worshiped Cybele, the venerated earth-mother of Asia Minor. Another worshiped the Egyptian goddess Isis, with her annual promise of rebirth and a variety of dramatic rituals to be observed throughout the year.

Rome did not, however, tolerate sects that challenged the authority of the empire or the emperor. The government cracked down on worship of the god Bacchus, for example, in 186 B.C.E., fearing that lower-class members of this cult might turn against the state. The same antagonism toward potential revolt put Rome on a collision course with the Jews of Judaea, in the eastern Mediterranean.

After conquering the eastern Mediterranean from the Seleucid inheritors of Alexander the Great, the Romans turned their attention to Judaea. For at least a century the region had been fragmented, and often in the throes of open warfare, among contending factions: Seleucids, pagans, and Jews of a wide variety of beliefs and political commitments. In Chapter 10 we shall see how the Jews, from their seventeenth-century B.C.E. roots, developed a religion based on ethical monotheism and a fierce sense of ethnic nationalism. Here, we only note that both of these qualities evoked strong opposition among the Roman rulers. The zealous monotheism of most of the Jews left no room for worship of the Roman emperor as a god, and the ethnic nationalism meant that a spirit of revolt against Roman authority was always simmering. From the time that Rome conquered Judaea and turned it into a subject state, in 63 B.C.E., fighting broke out frequently, not only between Jews and Romans, but also among Jewish political and religious factions that differed on the proper behavior toward the Roman conquerors and toward each other. In response to three major revolts by the Jews—in 66–73 C.E., 115–117 C.E., and 132–135 C.E.—the Romans destroyed Jerusalem and its principal Jewish Temple, established the Roman colony of Aelia Capitolina on its site, destroyed Judaea as a Jewish state, and exiled the Jews from this land, with repercussions that would last for centuries.

One of the religious factions that grew up among the Jews in Judaea was the veneration of the preacher, exorcist, and miracle worker Jesus of Nazareth (c. 4 B.C.E.–c. 30 C.E.). Many of his followers believed him to be divine and later called him Christ, or the Messiah (the anointed one of God). The discussion of his ministry and its emergence from Jewish roots will also wait for Chapter 10 in the unit on religion. Here suffice it to say that the Roman government clashed with the early Christians, followers of Jesus, much as it did with Judaism, on the grounds of its monotheism, resistance to emperor worship, and potential as a force for political revolution. For the first three centuries of its existence, many Romans viewed Christianity as atheistic because it rejected the divinity of the emperor. Some Romans saw the new Christian religion as treasonable because it spoke of a kingdom of heaven that was distinct from the Roman earthly empire. Finally the Roman governor of Judaea, Pontius Pilate, tried and crucified Jesus partly because he was a threat to the religious and political stability of their colony.

Christianity Triumphant. By the time of Marcus Aurelius, however, Christianity was making serious inroads into Roman thought. The Stoic philosophy was not far removed from the Christian concept of an orderly world and concern for social welfare. To these beliefs, Christianity added faith in a god actively intervening in human affairs and, specifically, the doctrines of the birth, life, miracles, and resurrection of Jesus. This combination of beliefs was attractive to increasing numbers of Romans, and despite severe persecution of Christians under several emperors—Nero (r. 54–68), Marcus Aurelius (r. 161–180), Maximinus I (r. 235–238), Decius (r. 249–251), Valerian (r. 253–260), and Diocletian (r. 284–305)—over the course of three centuries Christianity became acceptable in Rome and flourished. At first it attracted the poor, who were moved by Jesus' concern for the downtrodden, but later, more powerful classes also joined, attracted by both the organization and message of Christianity. The new religion promoted greater freedom for women, with a few reaching positions of prominence as deaconesses and abbesses, and it began to incorporate some of the sophistication of Greek philosophy, attracting a new intellectual leadership. By the time of Constantine's legalization of Christianity in 313, estimates suggested that one out of ten inhabitants of the Roman empire was a Christian (Lewis and Reinhold, II: 553).

In 313 the joint emperors, Constantine and Licinius, issued the Edict of Milan, which recognized Christianity as a valid faith, along with polytheism. After 324, when Constantine ruled alone, he favored Christianity as a religion that had brought miraculous benefits to himself personally and to his empire, and he granted it official recognition and legal status. Thereafter Christianity spread freely throughout the conquered lands and peoples of northwestern Europe. The network of roads and towns created to facilitate administration also served to transmit the message of Christianity, and members of the clergy frequently served as a bridge between the religious practices of Christian Rome and those of the "barbarians." After emerging as the official state religion, Christianity succeeded in having government support for polytheistic cults terminated in 394. Even the most widespread of them, Mithraism, with its message of loyalty to the emperor, died out. Christianity emerged triumphant. (For a fuller discussion of early Christianity and its relationship to the Roman Empire, see Chapter 10.)

THE BARBARIANS AND THE FALL OF THE ROMAN EMPIRE

Rome labeled many of its neighbors on its far-flung borders barbarians, including the Celts of central Europe, the various Germanic groups of northern and eastern Europe, and the steppe nomads of central Asia. These peoples spoke unknown foreign languages. They did not have cities, written languages, formal government structures, established geographical boundaries, codified laws, or labor specialization. Some, like the Celts and Germans, lived in villages and carried on settled farming. Nomadic steppe peoples spent their lives riding, herding, and often fighting among themselves in far-off central Asia. Such peoples, the Romans must have thought, could benefit from the civilizing influences of the empire. Perhaps Virgil had this in mind when he was writing the *Aeneid*.

Invaders at the Gates

The Celts had arrived in central Europe as early as 2000 B.C.E. Burials indicate their respect for horse-riding warriors and the slow development among them of iron technology in weapons and tools. The Hallstatt cemetery in Austria reveals a greater use of iron by the eighth century B.C.E. and includes items of Greek manufacture.

A cemetery at La Tène in what is now Switzerland shows continuing Greek and then Roman influences from the fifth century B.C.E. to the first century C.E.

By 400 B.C.E., the Celts were expanding their territory. In 390 B.C.E. they sacked Rome, and by 200 B.C.E. Celtic groups had covered central Europe and were pushing outward toward Spain, the British Isles, the Balkans, and Anatolia. Learning from Greek and Roman examples, they built fortified towns throughout their territories. The largest of these covered more than a half square mile. Celtic women enjoyed more freedom than did the Roman women, and this evoked the scorn of some Roman writers. Tacitus, who seemed to appreciate Calgacus' revolt in 83–84 C.E., was far more critical of the failed Celtic revolt of 61 C.E. in Britain led by the female leader Boudicca at the head of her armies. Ultimately, Rome conquered the Celtic peoples. They were killed, or assimilated, or fled to Ireland, Scotland, and Wales, where, to some degree, they continue today to preserve the Celtic language and culture.

The coming of the Barbarians. Rome's control of northern and western Europe declined in the fourth century C.E. as successive waves of Germanic peoples began to migrate and colonize the outer reaches of the empire. When the Huns began to advance westward from central Asia they pushed before them additional Gothic peoples who increased the pressures on Rome. Other Huns were meanwhile pushing south into India and east into China.

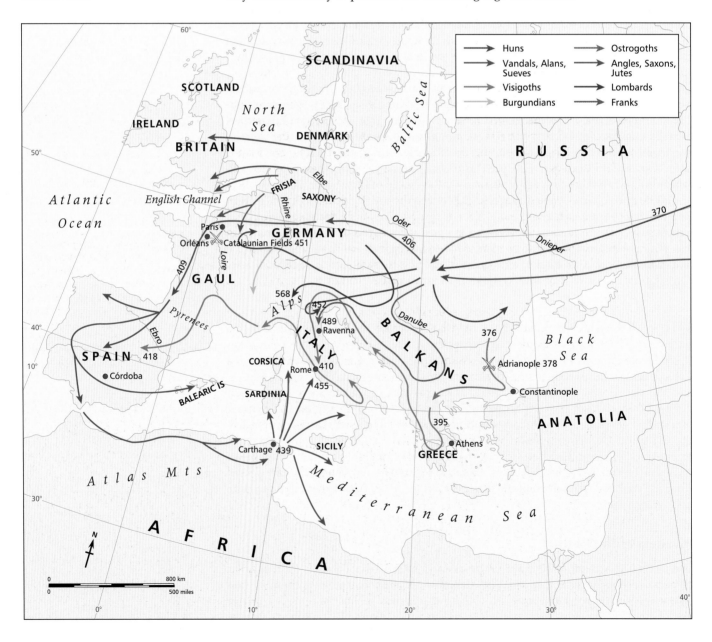

The Goths—an array of Germanic peoples (primarily Visigoths and Ostrogoths), distinguished in part by their use of Germanic languages, in part through their residence in lands that later became Germany—settled at first in northern Europe outside the Celtic and Roman strongholds. Indeed, much of what we know of this early period comes from burials in the bogs of what are now northern Germany and Denmark. By 600 B.C.E. these Germanic peoples had established small villages, and by about 500 B.C.E. they had begun working with iron. With the discovery of richer iron deposits and contact with Greek and Roman technology, the Goths developed more sophisticated tools and weapons.

Romans and Germans had faced each other along the Rhine since Julius Caesar had conquered Gaul, and along the Danube from the time Augustus had secured that border. They had skirmished, traded, and at times penetrated each other's territories. Recent archaeological excavations show that leaders of the Germans adopted for themselves many of the tools, weapons, and luxury goods of the conquering Romans. Roman goods, and some values, spread through imitation as well as by force.

In 370 C.E., steppe nomads began to invade across the thousands of miles from central Asia, bringing pressure to bear on the whole of Europe. In response to this pressure, the Goths began to migrate westward, pushing more vigorously into Roman territories. These massive Germanic invasions upset the rough balance of power that existed between Rome and the Goths, and threatened the stability of the empire. Ultimately, the Goths formed their own states within the imperial territories. A second Germanic emigration occurred about 500 C.E. as a response to floods in the areas of north Germany and Denmark. Among the emigrant Germanic groups, the Saxons sailed across the North Sea and the English Channel to Britain, where they came to form a substantial part of the population.

The Romans called all the steppe peoples who invaded Europe from central Asia in 370 C.E. "Huns." In fact, however, the Huns were only one of the many groups of warrior-nomads who inhabited the flat grasslands from European Russia to Manchuria. They virtually lived on their horses, herding cattle, sheep, and horses as well as hunting. They lived in tents and used wagons to transport their goods as they moved from place to place, especially in their annual shift between summer and winter locations.

Although they lived in tent encampments, the Huns' living arrangements and political structures were by no means random. Many groups had chiefs and even governments, and their leaders lived in the most elaborate of the tents. When the Huns invaded Europe, Romans observed emissaries of various peoples enter the tent of Attila, their leader, to conduct political negotiations.

Funerary bronze couch from the Hallstatt prince's tomb at Eberdingen-Hochdorf, near Stuttgart, Germany, c. 530 B.C.E. This couch demonstrates the remarkable sophistication of some early Celtic art. It was buried in the tomb of a sixth-century B.C.E. Celtic chieftain in Germany, along with other possessions reflecting the wealth and importance of the dead man. (*Württembergisches Landesmuseum, Stuttgart*)

HOW DO WE KNOW?

The "Barbarians"

Chinese Sources

The steppe peoples had no written language, and their nomadic life style has left few archaeological remains. We know about them in part from burials, especially of the Scythians, a group living in southern Russia and in the Altai Mountains of Mongolia. Mostly we know of them from the accounts of the peoples whose lands they invaded: Romans, Greeks, Chinese, and Indians. All these accounts report them as fierce, mobile, swift, and terrifying warriors on horseback, armed with powerful bows, swords, and lances. In more peaceful times, the Huns carried the goods of the overland silk routes through central Asia.

Latin histories did not mention the Huns until Ammianus Marcellinus (330–395 C.E.) described them:

They are without fixed abode, without hearth, or law, or settled mode of life, and they keep roaming from place to place, like fugitives, accompanied by the wagons in which they live; in wagons their wives weave for them their hideous garments, in wagons they cohabit with their husbands, bear children, and rear them to the age of puberty ...

This race of untamed men, without encumbrances, aflame with an inhuman desire for plundering others' property, made their violent way amid the rapine and slaughter of the neighboring peoples as far as the Halani [on the river Don]. (cited in Lewis and Reinhold, II:623)

Five hundred years earlier the Chinese historian Sima Qian had depicted them as coarse warriors:

During the Ch'ien-yuan reign [140–134 B.C.E.] ... the Son of Heaven made inquiries among those of the Hsiung-na [Xiongnu; Huns] who had surrendered and been made prisoners, and they all reported that the Hsiung-na had overcome the king of the Yueh-chih and made a drinking vessel out of his skull. The Yueh-chih had decamped and were hiding somewhere, constantly scheming how to revenge themselves on the Hsiung-na. (Sima Qian, p. 274)

Further elaboration by Sima delineates several groups of steppe nomads who frequently fought among themselves and sometimes invaded China itself. Both his description and that of Ammianus Marcellinus reflect the similar fear with which settled, imperial powers viewed their powerful, nomadic adversaries.

- What examples of barbarism does Ammianus Marcellinus cite from Rome? How do they compare with those cited by Sima Qian from China?
- What advantages did horse-mounted warriors with bows, swords, and lances have against the might of the empires of Rome and China?
- If we had records from the "barbarians" about the "civilized" peoples whose land they were invading, how do you think they would describe them?

At the time Augustus ruled Rome, groups of steppe nomads engaged in battles that would ultimately help to topple the Han dynasty in China. They also launched the attacks on India that would make two of the groups the rulers of north India: the Kushanas, 150–300 C.E., and the Hunas, 500–550 C.E. The Huns arrived in Europe in 370 C.E., defeating and displacing the Alans, Ostrogoths, and Visigoths, and pushing them in the direction of Rome.

The "domino effect" that would ultimately destroy the empire had begun.

The Decline and Dismemberment of the Roman Empire

Rome proved vulnerable to the invaders, especially because of a plague that wiped out up to a quarter of the population of some areas in 165–180 C.E. Historians debate the exact severity and impact of this plague, but it diminished the numbers and undermined the self-confidence of the empire's population. During the reign of Marcus Aurelius (r. 161–180 C.E.), the Marcomanni, a Germanic tribe from Bohemia, began to invade the Danube basin. Some penetrated into Greece, and across the Alps and into Italy. "Barbarian" invasions continued for hundreds of years, ultimately leading to the break-up of the Roman Empire.

For seven years, 168–175, Marcus Aurelius fought against the invaders, but he also recognized that they could be assimilated into the empire for mutual benefit. The Marcomanni wanted to establish settlements, so he offered them land within the borders of the empire that they could farm; they were soldiers, so he also offered them positions in Rome's armies.

Some of the Gothic groups also accepted assimilation into the empire. Others wished simply to plunder and withdraw. Still others wished to seize portions of the empire for themselves and settle.

The Crisis of the Third Century. Invaders repeatedly penetrated the borders represented by the Danube and the Rhine. In 248 the Emperor Decius (r. 249–251) defeated an invasion of Goths in the Balkans but was himself killed by another Gothic group. The Goths continued into the Balkans and beyond into Asia Minor. They took to ships and attacked Black Sea commerce, in the process cutting off large parts of Rome's grain supplies. Meanwhile, further west, Franks and Vandals swept across the Rhine into Gaul, Spain, and as far south as north Africa.

The empire struck back. The Emperor Gallienus (r. 253–268) created a mobile cavalry and moved the imperial military headquarters from Rome to Milan in the north, better to confront invaders into Italy. In a series of battles Roman armies preserved Italy for the empire.

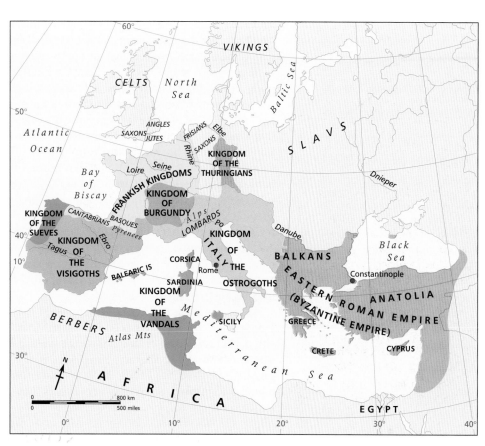

Aurelian (r. 270–275), an even more brilliant and energetic general, succeeded Gallienus as emperor after the latter died in a plague. In a series of battles, Aurelian protected Rome's western and northern borders, although he abandoned Dacia and pulled back to the Danube.

In the east, too, Rome defeated revolts. The greatest challenge came as the new, expansive Sassanian dynasty in Persia confronted Rome in Armenia and Syria. In 260 C.E. the Roman Emperor Valerian (r. 253–260) was captured and held prisoner for the rest of his life in humiliating conditions. (Legend told that after his death he was stuffed and preserved in a Persian temple.) Nevertheless, Rome recaptured its eastern areas, partly because the Sassanians treated the inhabitants of these lands so badly that they revolted. In another revolt against Rome, Zenobia, the widow of the leader of semi-independent Palmyra, declared the independence of Syria and Mesopotamia, and annexed Egypt. Her revolt lasted only a few years, and in 273 Aurelian defeated her, took her back to Rome in chains, and put her on public display, fully bedecked in jewels.

The Fragmentation of Authority. Continuing warfare forced the decentralization of Rome's power from the capital to distant provincial battlefields, and from civilian control by the Senate in Rome to generals in the field. Soldiers in Gaul, Britain, and Spain declared their general Postumus (r. 259–268 C.E.) the independent emperor of those regions, but Aurelian defeated their mutiny in 274 C.E. Militarily, the empire staged an extraordinary comeback.

In the belief that an aura of pomp and majesty would be helpful in asserting central control, the Emperor Diocletian (r. 284–305 C.E.) claimed for himself a sanctity and splendor never before seen in Rome. The expense of his battles and the splendor of his

Rome's successors. Following the sack of Rome by the Ostrogoths in 455 C.E., a new map of Europe emerged. The Roman power base had shifted east to Constantinople, forming the Byzantine Empire. The steppe invaders, keen to emulate the Romans, had created new kingdoms in Italy, Africa, and Iberia, while Germanic peoples were struggling to create a new power balance in the north.

court bankrupted the empire and brought misery to its inhabitants. To cope with the attacks on far distant borders, emperors established regional capitals, and in 330 C.E. Constantine established Constantinople as a secondary capital for ruling the entire eastern region. After 395 C.E., one emperor in Rome and another in Constantinople formally divided the empire, west and east.

"Barbarian" tribes continued to breach the imperial borders and defenses. Valentinian I (r. 364–375) was the last emperor capable of driving them back effectively. From this time on, impelled by the invasion of the Huns, the Germans pushed against Roman defenses in increasing numbers. In 378 Valentinian's brother, the eastern Emperor Valens (r. 364–378), lost two-thirds of the eastern armies—and his life—in battle against the Visigoths at Adrianople. Valens' successor, Theodosius I (r. 379–395), who ruled from Constantinople, settled Visigoths within the empire, requiring them to provide soldiers and farmers for the imperial armies and lands. This "federate" status for Goths and other "barbarians" became a common pattern, with Goths, Franks, Alans, and Vandals settling within the imperial borders in increasing numbers. The empire was Roman in name, but was a mixed enterprise in terms of population, armies, and leadership. Increasingly, emperors avoided Rome and preferred to reside in cities such as Milan and Trier.

Alaric, the Visigoth (c. 370–410), invaded Italy in 401 and, in response, the Emperor Honorius (r. 395–423) removed the capital from Milan to Ravenna, a more defensible city on the east coast of Italy. Alaric invaded Italy again in 407, and in 410 he sacked Rome. At the end of 406, combined armies of Goths, Vandals, Suevi, Alans, and Burgundians crossed the Rhine into Gaul and moved into Spain. At first they sacked, looted, and burned, but within a few years they established their own settlements and local kingdoms, displacing or merging with Roman landlords. The Vandal King Geiseric (r. 428–477) crossed into north Africa, seizing Carthage and its agriculturally rich hinterlands. Gaining control of a fleet, he challenged Roman control of the Mediterranean. The Romans could not defeat him.

The Huns were building up their own imperial confederacy in central Europe. Their most powerful leader, Attila (c. 406–453), commanded them from 434 to 453. His territory stretched from the Baltic to the Danube. He invaded Italy in 451, threatening Rome and withdrawing only on the intervention of Pope Leo I. After Attila's death, his armies dissolved and never again regained their power. In 476, the German general Odoacer deposed the last Roman emperor in the west. Odoacer became the first barbarian king of Italy (r. 476–493), and thus the five-centuries-old Roman Empire came to an end.

In the west, the Roman imperial system continued to function for at least two more centuries, but its leadership and its legions were in the hands of Germans and other invading groups. The groups carved the empire up into several distinct regions. There was no central government. Rome was no longer capital of an empire.

Causes of the Decline and Fall

Structural problems had been visible in the Roman Empire even at the height of its power. Internally, the conflict between the elite and the masses continued, under different names, throughout the history of the Republic and the empire. The cost of sustaining the empire by military force overtaxed the imperial economy, impoverishing the middle classes and the remaining agricultural classes. The yeoman-farmer class, the class that had first built up the Roman Republic, was ruined. Although the rich continued to live off their estates in Italy and elsewhere and the senatorial classes continued to do well, popular support for the imperial ideal had disappeared. In earlier times, an ever-expanding frontier had brought new economic resources to support the empire, but expansion had come to an end in the second century. The empire was overextended.

In addition, the quality of the empire depended on the quality of its emperors, but Rome had no viable system of succession. In the century between Marcus Aurelius and Diocletian, more than eighty men assumed command as emperor, and many of these were assassinated. In the third century C.E., as fighting in the border regions decentralized the empire, competing armies fought to have their generals selected as emperor. The results were devastating to the economy, administration, and morale of the empire.

Rome could no longer win its frontier battles against invaders, but neither could it continue to assimilate Goths and others into its armies and settlements as subordinates. The Roman armies and vast territories of the empire had become heavily Germanic, and when whole tribes of Goths began to serve together in single units under Gothic commanders, questions arose concerning the army's loyalty to the empire. Romans and Germans saw each other as "other," alien, and the Romans even forbade intermarriage. As Germanic peoples began to take over leading positions, the empire effectively ceased to be Roman.

The rise of Christianity as the principal religion and philosophy of the empire (see Chapter 10) also suggested that the Roman desire for earthly political power was evaporating. At first, Christianity was accepted by the poor, who used it as a means of expressing their disaffection from the power of the Caesars. Later, however, when Constantine declared Christianity a legitimate state religion in 313, and the official state religion in 324, more mainstream Romans converted. Christianity offered an alternative focus for human energy. The eighteenth-century English historian Edward Gibbon argued in his classic *History of the Decline and Fall of the Roman Empire* that Christianity turned people against this-worldly attractions and power. Later historians

The Byzantine Empire. Despite the erosion of Roman power in western Europe by 457 C.E., the East Roman or Byzantine Empire survived with varying fortunes for another thousand years—albeit Greek-speaking and Orthodox Christian—until 1453. Centered on Constantinople, its heartland straddled the crossroads between Europe and Asia. Only briefly, under Justinian (483–565), did it recover control of the western Mediterranean.

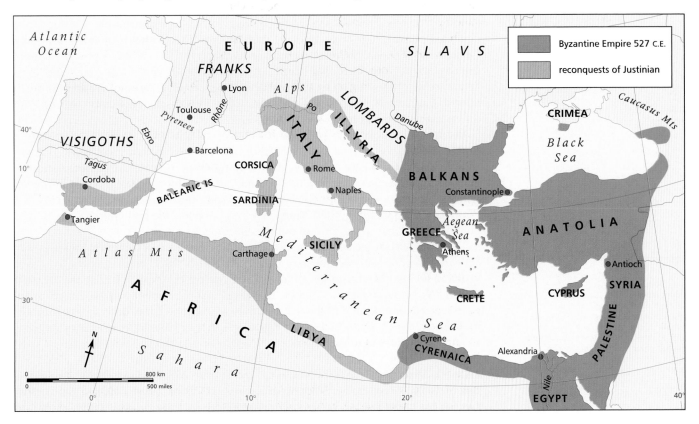

regard this as an overstatement. They point to growing numbers of imperial administrators who converted to Christianity as evidence that the new religion and the Roman empire were compatible. Christianity did preach that eternal salvation was more important than fighting for the empire and it siphoned energy toward more spiritual and humanitarian goals, and toward competition with other religious groups.

More recently, scholars have suggested that climatic change reduced agricultural productivity and hurt the economy. Still others have noted that epidemics killed up to a quarter of the population in some imperial centers between 165 and 180 C.E. and again between 251 and 266 C.E. These diseases sapped the empire of manpower and left it more open to attack. Such biological and ecological arguments complement the more traditional explanations of Rome's fall: overextension; financial and military exhaustion; a failure of leadership; the rise of new, alternative value systems; and the infiltration of Germanic peoples, which fragmented the empire into new, separate, independent states that no longer wished to be subordinated to Rome.

The Empire in the East

On May 11, 330, the Emperor Constantine inaugurated the "New Rome which is Constantinople," to share with Rome, as co-capital, the administration of his huge empire. From its inception three complementary elements characterized the new city: Greek language and culture; Roman law and administration; and Christian faith and organization. While the western half of the empire survived only another century and a half, the eastern empire continued on its own for another thousand years, until 1453. It became an empire in its own right, later called Byzantium after the name of the Greek city around which Constantinople was built.

Resurgence under Justinian. Like the west, the east had to withstand military attack. Germanic tribes crossed the Danube, but found Constantinople impregnable, defended behind huge walls built by the Emperor Theodosius II (r. 408–450). Using German mercenaries, the eastern emperor Justinian I (r. 527–565) recaptured many of the western regions including north Africa, southern Spain, Sicily, Italy, and even Rome itself, but the costs in wealth and manpower crippled his empire. After his death most of these western conquests were lost, while the Persians constantly warred with the remnants of the Roman Empire in the east.

Justinian's legal, administrative, and architectural initiatives produced more lasting results. He had the Roman system of Civil Law codified in four great works, known collectively as the Justinian Code, thus helping to perpetuate an administration of great competence. In time, the Code became the basis for much of modern European law. He adorned Constantinople with numerous new buildings, crowned by the Church of Hagia Sophia, the Church of Holy Wisdom. He had churches, forts, and public works constructed throughout the empire.

Theology was closely intertwined with politics in the eastern empire. Disputes that appeared to concern only theology frequently had political consequences, and here Justinian seemed to over-reach. When many Syrian and Egyptian Christians declared themselves **Monophysites**, believers that Jesus' nature was only divine, not human, Justinian oppressed them in the name of theological conformity and imperial authority. In his religious zeal, he created antagonisms that smoldered for centuries and contributed to the loss of these provinces to the Muslims in the seventh century.

Religious Struggles. Troops burst out of Arabia after 632, inspired with the religious zeal of Islam (Chapter 11). Emperor Heraclius (r. 610–641) had defeated the Persian Empire, but he and his successors could not hold back these new invaders. The Arabs

Monophysites The supporters of a doctrine in the early Christian Church that held that the incarnate Christ possessed a single, wholly divine nature. They opposed the orthodox view that Christ had a double nature, one divine and one human, and emphasized his divinity at the expense of his capacity to experience real human suffering.

captured much of the land of the eastern empire, including Syria and Egypt with their disaffected Monophysites.

By this time, so much had changed in the relationship between Rome and Constantinople that the eastern empire had taken on an identity of its own as the Byzantine Empire. For centuries, the Christian Byzantine empire based in the Balkans and Asia Minor would confront Islam militarily and religiously. The Byzantine Empire organized its armies into **themes**, administrative districts and army units, in which peasants were given farms in payment for their military service. These themes and the impregnable fortifications of Constantinople were the empire's bulwark in confronting Arab armies.

The **iconoclastic** controversy, the bitter battle over the use of images, or icons, in Christian worship, began in 726, in large part as a response, to the Arab invasions. Islam rigorously excluded religious imagery and its armies were hugely successful. Some eastern clergy thought that these two facts might be linked. They became iconoclasts, arguing that Christianity should enforce the biblical commandment against idol worship by also banning icons. They campaigned to break and discard religious images, and the reigning Byzantine emperors supported them. For more than a century, until it was rescinded, this decision split what became known as the Eastern

themes A theme was originally a military unit stationed in one of the provinces of the Byzantine empire, but it later applied to the large military districts that formed buffer zones in the areas most vulnerable to Muslim invasion.

iconoclast An "image-breaker", or a person who rejects the veneration of **icons**, on the grounds that the practice is idolatrous.

Hagia Sophia, Constantinople, 532–7. The Hagia Sophia (Church of the Holy Wisdom), built under the Emperor Justinian, is an imposing visual symbol of the power of the eastern empire. The minarets, or pointed towers at the four corners, were added in the fifteenth century when the Ottomans captured Constantinople and the church was converted into a mosque.

Orthodox hierarchy and positioned its mainstream in opposition to the western Church. It added to the strain in the political-religious relationship between the western Church and the Byzantine Empire.

The great leaders of the Byzantine Empire were known for their combination of military prowess and religious leadership. Basil I (r. 867–886), for example, kept control of the Balkans and crushed the Bulgar invaders; initiated a dynasty which reconquered Crete, Syria, southern Italy, and much of Palestine from the Arabs; and also healed the religious rift with Rome for a time.

Ultimately, however, beginning in the late eleventh century C.E., a combination of religious and political antagonisms contributed to the decline of the Byzantine Empire. Battered from the north by invading Normans and Slavs, the Byzantines turned to the pope in Rome for help against the Islamic Seljuq Turks who had overrun Asia Minor from the east (Chapters 11 and 14). In response, the pope preached the crusades, but in 1204 crusaders—acting against the pope's explicit orders—conquered and sacked Constantinople, poisoning relationships between the eastern and western churches for centuries. The Byzantines recovered the city in 1261, but their empire was irreparably weakened. In 1453 it finally succumbed to the Turks.

A Millennium of Byzantine Strength. How did the Byzantine Empire manage to survive for 1000 years after Rome had fallen? The administrative system of the Byzantines deserved much of the credit, as a modern historian has explained:

> Consisting of a group of highly educated officials trained primarily at the university or, rather "higher school" of Constantinople, the civil service was organized into a hierarchical system of considerable complexity even by today's standards. Taxes were collected regularly, justice was administered, armies were raised and put into the field, and the functions of the state in general were very adequately carried out. It may be said that in its period of greatest power (330–c. 1050) the Byzantine government, despite all its faults (excessive love of pomp and protocol, bureaucratic tendencies, and frequent venality), functioned more effectively, and for a longer period, than virtually any other political organism in history. (Geanakoplos, p. 3)

The ruling classes were never as isolated and alienated from the common people as in the west. The eastern empire was also less geographically overextended. Even when it lost its more distant territories, it could defend its heartland. Its sources of wealth and military manpower were in Thrace and Anatolia, geographically close to its center of political power in Constantinople, which remained an impregnable fortress for almost 1000 years. In these settled lands, the Byzantine Empire had an older and stronger urban tradition than the west, and its cities remained viable centers of commerce long after most cities in the west had all but disappeared. The fiercest of the invading Germanic tribes turned away from these more settled regions and marched westward, toward the more open agricultural lands of the Roman Empire. In all these ways, the east was different from the west and was able to survive as an imperial state for another thousand years.

THE LEGACY OF THE ROMAN EMPIRE
WHAT DIFFERENCE DOES IT MAKE?

The Roman Empire laid foundations that have lasted until today in language, law, urban and regional development, and religious organization. Rome's language, Latin, was the official language of the empire, and it persisted as one of the two languages (with Greek) known by all educated Europeans until the seventeenth century. It survived until the mid-twentieth century as the language of ritual prayer for the Roman Catholic Church. It formed the base of the Romance languages (Italian, Spanish, Catalan, Portuguese, French, and Romanian) and contributed substantially to English.

Roman law, which developed and was codified over several centuries, inspired the transition to modern, codified law in much of Europe. It was the ancestor of the Napoleonic Codes that the French general and emperor institutionalized wherever he ruled in early nineteenth-century Europe (see Chapter 15).

The hundreds of towns that Rome founded and developed as administrative and military centers throughout the empire provided the nuclei around which the urban structure of much of modern Europe and northern Africa developed. The 50,000 miles of well-paved roads that connected the cities of the empire laid the foundation for much of modern Europe's land transportation patterns.

Even after its decline and fall, c. 476, the Roman Empire continued to shape the vision and the administration of hundreds of millions of people. In 330 the Emperor Constantine inaugurated Constantinople as an eastern, sister capital of the Roman Empire, and that city dominated much of the eastern Mediterranean for another thousand years, until 1453.

Meanwhile in western Europe, during that millennium, the Roman Catholic Church adapted the Roman imperial administrative organization for its own uses. This basic organization persists to the present. When the Emperor Constantine gave Christianity legal status throughout the empire, and chose it as his own religion, he opened the gates for its unprecedented growth. What later became known as the Holy Roman Empire, which ruled much of central Europe for some 900 years from 800, also styled itself a successor to Rome, although the comparison was somewhat remote.

Images of the Roman Empire remain powerful even to our own times. The British Empire, which girdled the globe from the eighteenth to the mid-twentieth centuries, proudly described itself as recreating and extending the imperial military power, administration, legal system, and technological superiority that had characterized Rome. Like the early Romans, the British claimed to have stumbled into their imperial possessions rather than to have actively pursued them (see Chapter 16).

They spoke of administering a "Pax Britannica." More recently, many political analysts have referred to the exercise of American political and military power around the globe as the "Pax Americana."

Review Questions

- Why did Rome choose to expand from city-state to empire? What stages marked that expansion?
- What was the policy of the "New Wisdom" in Rome's military strategy? Give examples of its implementation. Do you think it was an appropriate and effective policy? What other strategies did Rome employ to win over its enemies?
- Social hierarchy was fundamental to Roman political and social life at all levels throughout its history. Give examples from domestic life to civic life to imperial life.
- What was the policy of "bread and circuses"? How did it evolve? What do you think were its effects?
- What were the accomplishments in which Roman emperors took the most pride? In our text, the example of Augustus is most fully discussed, but other emperors are also mentioned.

- What changes took place in the Roman Empire and in Christianity that enabled Christianity to become the dominant religion? Please note the stages in this evolution.
- Why might historians say that the Roman Empire was "dismembered," rather than say that it "fell"?
- What factors enabled the eastern, Byzantine Empire to survive for one thousand years after the end of the Roman Empire?

Suggested Readings

PRINCIPAL SOURCES

Boardman, John, Jasper Griffin, and Oswyn Murray, eds. *The Oxford History of the Classical World* (New York: Oxford University Press, 1986). Very useful array of expert articles on Greece and the Roman Empire.

Cornell, Tim and John Matthews. *Atlas of the Roman World* (New York: Facts on File, 1983). The series of atlases in the *Facts on File* series are encyclopedic in their coverage, and extremely accessible as well.

Grant, Michael. *History of Rome* (New York: Scribner's, 1978). Grant is an excellent scholar-writer who leads the reader through the heart of his subject matter. An outstanding introduction to the field. His many other books are also extremely useful. See for example *Julius Caesar* (New York: McGraw-Hill, 1969).

Lewis, Naphtali and Meyer Reinhold, eds. *Roman Civilization: Selected Readings: Vol I: The Republic and the Augustan Age; Vol II: The Empire* (New York: Columbia University Press, 1990). *The* documentary collection. Indispensable.

MacMullen, Ramsay. *Romanization in the Time of Augustus* (New Haven, CT: Yale University Press, 2000). Argues that Roman ways of life were eagerly sought by conquered peoples, especially their leaders, and spread through imitation more than by force. Several of MacMullen's other very readable books illuminate class and religious relationships in imperial and post-imperial Rome. See especially *Roman Social Relations, 50 B.C. to A.D. 284* (New Haven, CT: Yale University Press, 1981).

Time-Life Books. *Time Frame 400 B.C.–200 A.D.: Empires Ascendant* (Alexandria, VA: Time-Life Books, 1988) and *Time Frame A.D. 200–600: Empires Besieged* (Alexandria, VA: Time-Life Books, 1988). These books are more at the advanced high school level than college, but all the books in this series are backed by excellent scholarship, clear and effective prose, and lavish, superb illustrations. These two volumes contain important chapters on Rome.

ADDITIONAL SOURCES

Antoninus, Marcus Aurelius. *Meditations*, trans. by H. G. Long in Whitney J. Oates, ed., *The Stoic and Epicurean Philosophers* (New York: Modern Library, 1940). The classic statement of Stoicism by an emperor of Rome known also for his ruthless military conquests.

Aries, Philippe and Georges Duby, eds. *A History of Private Life: Vol. I: From Pagan Rome to Byzantium* (Cambridge, MA: Harvard University Press, 1987). Life cycle, marriage, family, slavery, the household, architecture, the private attitudes of public officials, work and leisure, wealth, public opinion, pleasure, religion, and community are the subjects of three of the fascinating, lengthy essays in this book.

Bradley, K.R. *Slavery and Society at Rome* (Cambridge: Cambridge University Press, 1994). A comprehensive, accessible, up-to-date review.

Brown, Peter. *The World of Late Antiquity, A.D. 150–750* (New York: Harcourt Brace Jovanovich, 1971) and *The Rise of Western Christendom* (Malden, MA: Blackwell, 1996). Brown's scholarship and clarity of presentation on the world of the late Roman Empire and the rise of Christianity make these excellent introductions.

Carcopino, Jerome. *Daily Life in Ancient Rome* (New Haven, CT: Yale University Press, 1940). Although dated and generalized, Carcopino's introduction to the way in which people actually lived is most useful.

Clark, Gillian. *Women in Late Antiquity: Pagan and Christian Life Styles* (Oxford: Oxford University Press, 1993). Sketchy analysis of gender relations accompanying the introduction of early Christianity.

Fantham, Elaine, *et al. Women in the Classical World* (New York: Oxford University Press, 1994). A collection of essays on gender relations through texts and art work.

Finley, M.I., ed. *The Portable Greek Historians* (New York: Viking Press, 1959).

Frank, Andre Gunder and Barry K. Gillis, eds. *The World System: Five Hundred Years or Five Thousand* (New York: Routledge, 1993). Many new explorations of trade in the ancient world, and new ways of understanding trade as the context of political as well as economic system building, make this a fascinating interpretive study.

Geanakoplos, Deno John. *Byzantium: Church, Society, and Civilization Seen Through Contemporary Eyes* (Chicago, IL: University of Chicago Press, 1984). An excellent analysis of the strengths of the Byzantine empire, stressing its bureaucratic organization.

Gibbon, Edward. *The History of the Decline and Fall of the Roman Empire* (New York: Modern Library, 3 Vols. 1932). Available in several abridgements. This classic, two-century-old, study includes important analyses of the Germanic nations, the Huns, the confrontation with early Islam, and the origins of early modern Europe as well as the fall of Rome. Fascinating for its perspective from the age of the European enlightenment.

Johns, Catherine. *Sex or Symbol? Erotic Images of Greece and Rome* (London: British Museum Press, 1989). An outstanding presentation of selections from the special collections of the British Museum on Greece and Rome introducing an analysis of the function of sexual art in religious rituals, drama, and erotic titillation.

Jones, A.H.M. *Augustus* (New York: W.W. Norton & Co., 1970). The basic introduction to this pivotal emperor and his accomplishments. Jones is another classical master scholar-writer. Among his many other books, note *The Later Roman Empire, 284–602: A Social,* *Economic, and Administrative Survey*, 2 Vols. (Oxford: Basil Blackwell, 1990).

Luttwak, Edward N. *The Grand Strategy of the Roman Empire* (Baltimore, MD: Johns Hopkins University Press, 1976). A fascinating analysis of Rome's military strategy, stressing "The New Wisdom" of application of overwhelming strength.

Mumford, Lewis. *The City in History* (New York: Harcourt, Brace, and World, 1961). Mumford's classic, moralistic analysis of historic urbanization sees Rome, both city and empire, as a catastrophe of the exploitation of the poor and vulnerable by the rich and powerful.

Ramage, Nancy and Andrew Ramage. *Roman Art: Romulus to Constantine* (Englewood Cliffs, NJ: Prentice Hall, 1991). Useful, accessible, basic introductory text. Richly illustrated.

Runciman, Steven. *Byzantine Civilization* (Cleveland, OH: World Publishing Co., 1933). Even after seventy years, Runciman is still a fascinating and readable introduction.

Virgil. *Aeneid*, trans. Rolphe Humphries (New York: Charles Scribner's Sons, 1951). Many translations available. Writing in the age of Augustus, Virgil gives the classic, idealized statement of Rome's mission.

Wells, Peter. *The Barbarians Speak: How the Conquered Peoples Shaped Roman Europe* (Princeton, NJ: Princeton University Press, 1999). Reviews and extends studies of the relationships between Romans and "Barbarians" based on recent archaeological findings.

⊙ World History Documents CD-ROM

CHINA

FRACTURE AND UNIFICATION: THE QIN, HAN, SUI, AND TANG DYNASTIES 200 B.C.E.–900 C.E.

KEY TOPICS
- The Qin Dynasty
- The Han Dynasty
- Disintegration and Reunification
- Imperial China

When we last discussed the north China plain in Chapter 4, the Zhou (Chou) dynasty (1100–256 B.C.E.) was in decline. As the dynasty began to weaken, the powerful, independent states of the region fought among themselves so constantly that China's historians have named the years between *c.* 481 and 221 B.C.E. the Warring States period. In 221 B.C.E., after hundreds of years of warfare, the Qin (Ch'in) dynasty defeated the others, unifying north China and creating the first unified Chinese Empire.

This chapter will consider the Chinese Empire during its first 1100 years, from 221 B.C.E. to 907 C.E. During this time China created political and cultural forms that would last for another thousand years, and, as we shall see in Chapter 21, perhaps even to the present.

We will examine the key accomplishments under China's imperial rulers—the conquest, consolidation, and confirmation of the empire—and the expansion of China to include "outer China," the distant, conquered provinces inhabited by people not ethnically Chinese. In addition, we outline relationships with peoples to the south and southwest, who were ultimately incorporated into China, and with Korea and Japan, whose cultures were influenced profoundly by China. We close by comparing and contrasting the Chinese Empire with that of Rome.

THE QIN DYNASTY

The Qin dynasty expanded from a geopolitical base around the confluence of the Yellow and Wei rivers to control the whole of north China and a segment of the south. The Qin conquest ended centuries of fighting among the warring dynasties of north China that began with the decline of the Zhou dynasty and lasted through the period of the Warring States. The Qin defeated other regional states over the course of perhaps a century, until by 221 B.C.E. they could rightfully claim to have established a unified empire, the first in China's history. Although the dynasty itself lasted only a few years after it succeeded in establishing the empire, the new empire itself persisted with few interruptions to the present.

Military Power and Mobilization

Armed force was fundamental in the Qin's conquest. The *Book of Songs*, dating from the early years of the Zhou dynasty, suggests the constant nature of warfare in early China:

Which plant is not yellow?
Which day don't we march?

Opposite **Great Wall of China. Begun 214 B.C.E., rebuilt repeatedly.** "The seven wonders of the world are not comparable to this work," wrote one awestruck seventeenth-century European observer of this most imposing relic of China's past. Faced with brick and stone and averaging 25 feet high and wide, the 1500-mile-long wall is studded with towers that serve as signaling stations, warning of the approach of mobile enemies.

Which man does not go
To bring peace to the four quarters?

Which plant is not brown?
Which man is not sad?
Have pity on us soldiers,
Treated as though we were not men!

… We are neither rhinos nor tigers
Yet are led through the wilds,
Have pity on us soldiers,
Never resting morn or night.

The Qin not only conquered north China but also defeated the Xiongnu (Hsiung-na), border tribes (probably related to the groups that the Romans called the Huns) to the north and west of China proper. They gained authority over northern Korea, and defeated some of the Yue tribes in the south. The first Qin ruler to govern a unified China was Qin Shi Huangdi (r. 221–210 B.C.E.), "the first august emperor of the Qin," not unlike the title "Caesar Augustus of Rome" that Octavian bestowed upon himself.

In addition to their military efforts, the Qin also mobilized tens of thousands of men for enormous public works projects. After conquering the other states of north China they fortified and linked the defensive walls that had been constructed by local rulers into the 1500-mile Great Wall of China in seven years with a work force of one million laborers. This wall was to keep the northern Xiongnu "barbarians" out of China proper and, with its 40-foot high watch-towers constructed every few hundred yards, to serve as a first warning in case of attempted invasion.

The first emperor also conscripted 700,000 laborers to construct his palace, a complex large enough to hold 40,000 people. But perhaps even more impressive was Qin Shi Huangdi's tomb. In 1974 archaeologists digging near his mausoleum

Terra cotta army from the tomb of Qin Shi Huangdi, Qin dynasty, 210 B.C.E. The vastness of the terra cotta army—it comprised thousands of soldiers, still being uncovered—buried near the tomb of the First Emperor of Qin and the care with which each life-sized figure was molded suggest at once the enormous power of the Qin army and the emperor's concern with the afterlife.

discovered a ceramic army of some 7000 life-sized soldiers and horses, arranged in military formation and armed with bronze weapons, spears, longbows, and crossbows (a Chinese invention). In 1976, a second excavation uncovered an additional 1400 chariots and cavalrymen in four military units. The next year archaeologists discovered a much smaller pit, holding what appeared to be a terra cotta officer corps. These thousands of figures were not mass produced. Craftsmen modeled and painted each figure separately, even down to its elaborate hairstyle, which symbolized its specific military office. The figures apparently represented the elite of the imperial troops and were fashioned to accompany the emperor to his own tomb and afterlife.

Economic Power

The Qin undertook some of the enormous public works projects to increase the economic productivity of the empire. During the centuries of their rise to power, the Qin had built canals and river transport systems in both the Wei River system in the north and the Min River system in Sichuan in west-central China. In Sichuan they irrigated the region around Chengdu, turning it into a granary for the nation. The transportation and irrigation systems they built in the northern state of Shanxi transformed it into an area so rich in agricultural productivity and the means of transporting it that they could control all of north China from this base. As ironworking became increasingly important in Chinese military and economic development, the Qin also captured the richest sources of iron ore and two of China's best ironworking facilities, crucial resources for fashioning both tools and weapons.

Administrative Power

Administratively, Qin Shi Huangdi ruled through a bureaucracy. He did away with the system of personal allegiance by which officials were appointed on the basis of their personal, often family, ties to the court and therefore owed allegiance to the emperor himself rather than to the empire as an institution. Instead, the emperor chose people for office on the basis of ability; their tasks were fixed and governed by systematic, formalized, written rules; and their work was rewarded or punished according to the degree of their efficiency and fidelity. The Qin divided the empire into some forty administrative units called "commanderies." Each commandery was staffed with three leading officials: a civil authority, a military authority, and an inspector representing the emperor. The three officials served as checks and balances on one another: no one individual could assert too much power and threaten the control of the emperor at the center.

The Qin standardized as they centralized. They fixed weights and measures, values of coinage, the size of cart axles and of the roads they traveled. They standardized the legal code. Perhaps most important of all, the Qin standardized the written form of the Chinese language, possibly the most important single act of political and cultural unification in China's history. To this day, despite great variation in the local forms of spoken Chinese, written Chinese is uniform throughout the country, just as the Qin established it.

EARLY ADVANCES IN WEAPONRY	
3000 (B.C.E.)	War chariot invented. In Mesopotamia and southeastern Europe first metal swords and shields made (bronze).
2000	First armor made, from bronze scales, in Mesopotamia.
c. 700	The Phoenicians and Egyptians invent galleys—warships powered by oars.
500	Giant crossbows and catapults used by the Greeks and Carthaginians.
200	Hand-held crossbow now being used in China.
300 (C.E.)	Stirrups used in China.
950	Gunpowder used by Chinese for signaling devices and fireworks.
1250–1300	Bronze and iron cannon probably used by the Chinese; in Europe, first recorded use of cannon is 1326.

AT A GLANCE : CHINA

DATE	POLITICAL	RELIGION AND CULTURE	SOCIAL DEVELOPMENT
500 B.C.E.	■ Warring States period (481–221)	■ Confucius (551–479)	
250 B.C.E.	■ Zhou dynasty ends (256) ■ Qin Shi Huangdi initiates Qin dynasty (221–206) ■ Revolts against Qin (207)	■ Han Feizi (d. 233) ■ Daoism ■ Legalism ■ Great Wall	
200 B.C.E.	■ Liu Bang (206–195) first emperor of Han dynasty		
150 B.C.E.	■ Han Wu (141–87)	■ Confucian Academy established (124)	■ Travels of Zhang Qian
100 B.C.E.	■ Reign of usurper Wang Mang (9–23 C.E.)	■ Sima Qian (145–85) ■ Invention of paper	
50 C.E.		■ First mention of Buddhism in China	
200 C.E.	■ Han dynasty ends (220) ■ Age of Disunity (221–331) ■ Three Kingdoms (220–280)		
300 C.E.	■ Jin dynasty (265–316) ■ Northern Wei dynasty (386–534)	■ Buddhism expands ■ Gu Kaizhi (334–406)	
600 C.E.	■ Sui dynasty (581–618) ■ Tang dynasty (618–907)	■ Invention of block printing ■ Grand canal completed (610) ■ Buddhist cave art	■ Boundaries of empire extended to Mongolia, Turkestan, Afghanistan, Pakistan, and Iran ■ Tang briefly held North Korea and Vietnam
650 C.E.	■ Empress Wu (625–705)		■ First pharmacopoeia
700 C.E.	■ Battle of Talas River (751) ■ An Lushan rebellion (755–63)	■ Wang Wei (701–62) ■ Li Bai (701–61) ■ Du Fu (712–70) ■ Porcelain produced	
800 C.E.		■ Repression of Buddhism	
900 C.E.	■ Collapse of Tang, leading to disunity (907–960) ■ Song dynasty (960–1279)		

Competing Ideologies of Empire

In their public proclamations, Chinese emperors stressed the importance of their philosophy to the actual process of building, sustaining, and guiding their empire. In addition, the official historians who compiled China's records were an elite trained in philosophy. As a result, China's history reflects a profound concern with the conflicts over the philosophy and ideology of empire. These philosophies and ideologies themselves emerged in the late Zhou period and the years historians have called the Period of the Warring States (*c.* 481–221 B.C.E.). The chaos of the times induced some individuals either to search for a solution to Chinese political and social problems or to find tranquility apart from society and politics. The three schools of thought—Confucianism, Daoism (Taoism), and Legalism—that emerged in this period deeply influenced the dynasties that sought to rule the Chinese empire after the Qin established their dynasty.

Confucianism. Kong Fuzi (551–479 B.C.E.), known in Latin as Confucius, a philosopher and political adviser from the small state of Lu in modern Shandong, sought to reform

China by redefining Chinese political and ethical thought. Confucius began his career as a scholar. He mastered the six arts of ritual, music, archery, chariot driving, calligraphy, and arithmetic, and then began his career as a teacher. At a time when China was divided into many states, often in conflict, he formulated principles that he thought would bring peace, contentment, dignity, and personal cultural development at least to the elites of his time. Although Confucius was unsuccessful in finding employment as an adviser in any single state, his disciples kept his vision alive, and it has permeated Chinese thought and, often, government policy.

Confucius felt that good government depended on good officials, men of *jen*, or humanity, benevolence, virtue, and culture. Although he was not much concerned with the supernatural, he did believe that a moral order pervaded the universe and that it could be understood. In contrast to the tumult of his own day, Confucius believed that the early days of the Zhou dynasty had been a golden age of peace and order, wisdom and virtue. In those days, political leaders had understood the importance of social hierarchy, ritual, music, and art. The neglect of these elements of humanism and rationalism and the absence of schools that taught them to new leaders, had reduced China to chaos.

Confucius and his disciples canonized five of China's earliest historical texts as especially fine examples of the philosopher's own thought and his concern for history, music, the arts, and rituals:

- the *Book of Documents*, a collection of various statements of early kings and their ministers;
- the *Book of Changes*, the *I Ching*, which details methods of predicting the future through casting sticks;
- the *Book of Songs*, which contains 305 poems, about half of which relate to the everyday lives of ordinary people, half to issues of court politics and rituals;
- the *Spring and Autumn Annals*, which contains brief chronologies from Lu, Confucius' home state;
- *Rites and Rituals* (three texts, grouped together as one), which combines both philosophies and rituals of the court.

In addition to these five, Confucius' disciples recorded his own teachings in *The Analects* (see p. 210). A large body of interpretation and commentary grew up around each of these texts.

Confucius believed in the essential goodness and educability of each individual, and believed that the virtues of the past could be regained. He believed in the centrality of the "gentleman" (*junzi*), the moral leader who had the vision to move the society toward peace and virtue. Such a gentleman would and should be concerned about political leadership and the proper ordering of the state. For Confucius, however, gentlemen were not born but made, fashioned through proper education. Believing that character, not birth, was important, he taught whoever would come to him, but Confucius' own era was too violent for his teachings to find immediate acceptance.

The Qin dynasty did not welcome his teachings either, but the next dynasty, the Han, did. Under the Han, Confucius' ethical and political values came to dominate the culture and thought of China's scholars and intellectuals, and they continued powerful for most of the following 2000 years, also influencing the political thought of Korea, Japan, and southeast Asia.

Moreover, because Confucius expressed his ideas in such general terms, subsequent disciples could adapt them to particular problems. Thus, Confucianism evolved and often transformed into new forms that sometimes maintained its core values and sometimes changed them. For example, Mencius (Mengzi) (*c.* 371–*c.* 289 B.C.E.) had an optimistic view of human nature and believed that education would function to bring

SOURCE

Confucius and The Analects

We have no record that Confucius wrote down his own teachings. The Analects as a collection of thoughtful perceptions attributed to him, was apparently recorded and compiled by disciples of his disciples. Because these aphorisms—497 verses in twenty chapters—are brief, unelaborated, unorganized, and written in ideographic form, their exact meaning is not always clear, but these same qualities promote the reader's engagement with and interpretation of the text. The Analects have been a part of the education of every Chinese school student for centuries, at least until the communist revolution in 1949. The selections here represent typical issues for Confucius: the importance of formal, humanistic education in forming proper character; teaching and learning by example; focus on the world of here-and-now; and respect for others, especially for parents and elders.

A young man is to be filial within his family and respectful outside it. He is to be earnest and faithful, overflowing in his love for living beings and intimate with those who are humane. If after such practice he has strength to spare, he may use it in the study of culture.

Lead them by means of regulations and keep order among them through punishments, and the people will evade them and will lack any sense of shame.

Lead them through moral force (*de*) and keep order among them through rites (*li*), and they will have a sense of shame and will also correct themselves.

In education there should be no class distinctions.

Shall I teach you what knowledge is? When you know something, to know that you know it. When you do not know, to know that you do not know it. That is knowledge.

The noble person is concerned with rightness; the small person is concerned with profit.

I am not one who was born with knowledge; I am one who loves the past and is diligent in seeking it.

The Three Armies can be deprived of their commander, but even a common person cannot be deprived of his will.

The wise have no doubts; the humane have no sorrows; the courageous have no fears.

Before you have learned to serve human beings, how can you serve spirits …

When you do not yet know life, how can you know about death?

Look at nothing contrary to ritual; listen to nothing contrary to ritual; say nothing contrary to ritual; do nothing contrary to ritual.

What you would not want for yourself, do not do to others.

Zigong asked about government. The Master said, "sufficient food, sufficient military force, the confidence of the people." Zigong said, "If one had, unavoidably, to dispense with one of these three, which of them should go first?" The Master said, "Get rid of the military." Zigong said, "If one had, unavoidably, to dispense with one of the remaining two, which should go first?" The Master said, "Dispense with the food. Since ancient times there has always been death, but without confidence a people cannot stand." (deBary, 1999, pp. 45–60)

Throughout Chinese history, some groups rebelled against Confucius' ethical principles. Peasant rebels, a frequent presence throughout the centuries, condemned Confucius' emphasis on order and harmony. In the late nineteenth and twentieth centuries, as China saw itself fall behind the technological and military achievements of the Western world, Confucian traditions were challenged with renewed vigor (see Chapters 18 and 21). Critics argued that Confucianism was incompatible with equality, scientific education, rebellious youth movements, dignity of physical labor, peasant equity, and equal rights for women. The communist government that has ruled China since 1949 attacked Confucius especially bitterly in 1973 and 1974 during the Cultural Revolution, asserting that in his own day Confucius had served as a representative of the slave-owning aristocracy. As communism has more recently been transformed in contemporary China, the study of Confucianism is returning to China's schools.

out the best in people. He encouraged government leaders to rule in the best interests of the people and society by encouraging harmony according to Confucian principles. Another disciple, Xunzi (Hsün-Tzu) (312–235 B.C.E.), took a more negative view of human nature. Having many years of experience in government, he emphasized different aspects of Confucian thought. Most important, he believed that human nature was inherently bad and that only through education and participation in rituals would people learn to put the needs of society ahead of their private desires. Unlike Mencius, Xunzi believed in an education that would emphasize restraints on human behavior.

Legalism. Rejecting Confucianism, the Qin favored a philosophy of government known as **legalism**, which was characterized by strict laws and strict enforcement, with rewards for those who observed the laws and swift and appropriate punishment for those who broke them. During his reign Qin Shi Huangdi set up inscriptions on stone in various parts of his empire proclaiming his values and policies. For example, after he put down a rebellion in the far northeast, he inscribed on the city walls:

> Then he mobilized armies, and punished the unprincipled, and those who perpetrated rebellion were wiped out.
> Armed force exterminates the violent and rebellious, but civil power relieves the guiltless of their labors, and the masses all submit in their hearts.
> Achievements and toil are generously assessed, and the rewards even extend to cattle and horses, and his bounty enriches the land.
> The August Emperor gave a vigorous display of his authority, and his virtue brought together all the states, and for the first time brought unity and supreme peace.
> City walls were demolished [suggesting that peace had been established so that they were no longer necessary for defense], waterways were opened up, and obstacles were flattened.
> When the physical features of the land had been determined, there was no conscript labor for the masses, and all under heaven was pacified.
> Men take pleasure in their farmland, and women cultivate their tasks, and all matters have their proper arrangement.
> His kindness protects all production, and for long they have been coming together in the fields, and everyone is content with his place. (Sima Qian, p. 74)

In another inscription he wrote:

> When the sage of Qin took charge of his state, he first determined punishments and names, and clearly set forth the ancient regulations.
> He was the first to standardize the system of laws, examine and demarcate duties and responsibilities, so as to establish unchanging practices. (Sima Qian, p. 82)

He proclaimed a code of sexual conduct:

> If a man commits adultery, to kill him is no crime, so men hang on to the standards of righteousness.
> If a wife elopes to remarry, then the son will not have a mother, and so everyone is converted into chastity and purity. (Sima Qian, p. 83)

In his rulings Qin Shi Huangdi followed many of the policies of the political philosopher Han Fei Tzu (d. 233 B.C.E.), a student of the Confucian scholar Xunzi. Han Fei Tzu called himself a Legalist because he believed that strict laws, strictly enforced, were the best assurance of good and stable government. Han Fei Tzu summed up the power of the law:

> To govern the state by law is to praise the right and blame the wrong … To correct the faults of the high, to rebuke the vices of the low, to suppress disorders, to decide against mistakes, to subdue the arrogant, to straighten the crooked, and to unify the folkways of the masses, nothing could match the law.
> The means whereby the intelligent ruler controls his ministers are two handles only. The two handles are chastisement and commendation. (Han Fei Tzu, I:45–7)

Daoism. Daoism (Taoism) was a philosophy of spontaneity in the face of nature and the cosmos. It was a mystical philosophy, not usually directly applicable to government, but often a solace to public men in their private lives, especially after retirement.

legalism A school of Chinese philosophy that came into prominence during the period of the Warring States and had great influence on the policies of the Qin dynasty. Legalists took a pessimistic view of human nature and believed that social harmony could only be attained through strong government control and the imposition of strict laws, enforced absolutely.

Daoism is often seen as an inspiration to artists, and, because it advocates a high regard for nature, it is often seen as an inspiration to natural scientists as well.

The legendary founder of Daoism and the author of its key text, the *Daodejing* ("The Way and its Power"), is Laozi (*c.* 604–*c.* 517 B.C.E.), but the school and the book more likely date to the third or fourth centuries B.C.E. Its teachings are cloaked in paradox and mystery:

> The Way that can be spoken of is not the constant Way;
> The name that can be named is not the constant name.

Rejecting the emphasis on sophisticated learning and education that characterized Confucian thought, Daoists believed that untutored simplicity was powerful:

> Do away with sageliness, discard knowledge,
> And the people will benefit a hundredfold.
> Do away with humaneness, discard righteousness,
> And the people will once more be filial and loving,
> Dispense with cleverness, discard profit,
> And there will be no more bandits and thieves.
> These three, to be regarded as ornaments, are insufficient.
> Therefore let the people have something to cling to:
> Manifest plainness,
> Embrace uncarved wood,
> Diminish selfishness,
> Reduce desires.

> What is softest in the world
> Overcomes what is hardest in the world.
> No-thing penetrates where there is no space.
> Thus I know that in doing nothing there is advantage.
> The wordless teaching and the advantage of doing nothing—there are few in the
>   world who understand them.

Those who followed Daoism believed in a natural order or path (Dao). They taught that government should leave people alone:

> The more prohibitions there are in the world,
> The poorer are the people.
> The more sharp weapons people have,
> The more disorder is fomented in the family and the state.
> The more adroit and clever men are,
> The more deceptive things are brought forth.
> The more laws and ordnances are promulgated,
> The more thieves and robbers there are.
> Therefore the sage says:
> I do nothing (*wuwei*),
> And the people are transformed by themselves.
> (deBary, 1999, pp. 79–90)

This Daoist view of simplicity diminishes the need for government: "Let the state be small and the people be few" (deBary, 1999, p. 94). Nor is there need to travel. Beauty, peace, and joy are to be found at home:

> Though neighboring states are within sight of one another,
> And the sound of cocks and dogs is audible from one to the other,
> People will reach old age and yet not visit one another. (deBary, 1999, p. 94)

For an interactive version of this map, go to: http://www.prenhall.com/spodek/map7.1

Qin Empire c. 206 B.C.E.

Han Empire c. 2 C.E.

■ Qin imperial capital

● Qin state capitals

■ Han imperial centres

● Han trading centres

→ attacks by northern peoples

Daoism can be viewed as a rejection of Confucian principles, but over time many Chinese embraced both Confucianism and Daoism, allowing the former to shape their public lives, while gaining solace from the latter in their private lives. Also, because Daoism allowed the individual to find his or her own path, over time it began to embrace a variety of popular beliefs, alchemy, mysticism, and magic, all reinforced through a variety of rituals. Finally, Daoism may have facilitated the acceptance of Mahayana Buddhism in China, since both stressed the idea of transcending the material world.

The Struggle between Legalism and Confucianism. The philosophies of Legalism and Confucianism collided during the Qin dynasty. In direct contrast to the Confucianists' reverence for the past, the prime minister Li Si (Li Ssu) (c. 280–208 B.C.E.) argued that

Classical China. In 221 B.C.E. two centuries of internecine rivalry—the "Warring States" period—ended with the rise to centralized power of the Qin dynasty, but internal revolt and external pressures on the borders precipitated further civil war. The Han dynasty emerged as the new rulers in 202 B.C.E. They refortified the northern walls, and extended imperial control far to the south and west, deep into central Asia along the silk route, defining a Chinese territorial extent that has been asserted down to the present day.

the administration of the Qin was far superior to the government of any earlier time. The Qin success was the result of its decision to replace personal, *ad hoc* administration with an orderly system of laws and appointment to office on the basis of efficiency in accordance with Legalist principles.

Li Si recommended that the Confucian classics be collected and burned so that the past could no longer be held up as an alternative to present policies. In 213 B.C.E. the Qin burned the books. Subsequently, as Confucian scholars continued to oppose Qin Shi Huangdi, the emperor had 460 scholars buried alive. Sima Qian, the official, Confucian, historian of the Han government, recorded these acts of anti-intellectualism and brutality, which leave the Legalist Qin with a dismal reputation. The cruel intrigues and struggles for succession that helped end the Qin dynasty confirm that view.

The Mandate of Heaven. One of the enduring philosophical concepts of Chinese imperial politics was the Mandate of Heaven. Heaven—not a personal god but the cosmic forces of the universe—underpinned rulers of high moral stature and undercut those who lacked it. An omnipotent heaven conferred its mandate, or authority to rule, on the moral and revoked it from the immoral. Dynasties were thus held accountable for their actions, and they could not expect to rule forever. Their loss of cosmic connection would be made manifest, not only in the usual political and economic strife of a weak administration, but also through nature itself going awry in the form of floods, droughts, or other natural disasters. Throughout Chinese history, rebels against an emperor would claim evidence of his having lost the "Mandate," while those supporting new rulers would proclaim their possession of it.

The Fall of the Qin Dynasty

Qin Shi Huangdi died in 210 B.C.E. and was buried in the enormous mausoleum he had created, accompanied by the vast ceramic army he had ordered. Within four years his apparently powerful, centralized, productive, well-organized dynasty had collapsed. Despite the apparent strengths, the Qin had oppressed to its breaking point the nation and its peasantry, the 90 percent of the population who paid the taxes, served in the armies, built the public works projects, and the women who supported all these projects through their work at home. The final crisis began when the emperor sent several hundreds of thousands of these peasants to fight the Xiongnu in the far north and northwest on both sides of the Great Wall. As the *Han History* later reported,

> For more than ten years they were exposed to the rigors of military life, and countless numbers died … Although the men toiled at farming, there was not enough grain for rations; and the women could not spin enough yarn for the tents. The common people were ruined. (cited in Elvin, p. 27)

In addition to these systemic problems, the fight over the succession to Qin Shi Huangdi's throne destroyed the dynasty. A contest for power broke out among the late emperor's son, the minister Li Si, and another court official, the eunuch Zhao Gao. In the struggle, the emperor's son murdered many of his father's supporters on advice from his minister. Fear and disloyalty flourished. Each contestant seemed concerned only for his own survival and aggrandizement. Qin Shi Huangdi had instituted bureaucracy in place of personal rule throughout the empire, but personal politics still dominated the imperial court. Finally, Zhao forced the emperor's son to commit suicide, but then he himself was assassinated. While the court was convulsed in these internal struggles, rebels broke into the capital at Xianyang and captured power. Warfare continued until, in 206 B.C.E., the rebel leader Liu Bang emerged victorious and established the Han dynasty.

Han historians proclaimed their belief that the Qin dynasty had lost the Mandate of Heaven. Nevertheless, the Qin had brought China to a new stage of political development: the empire had been founded; an effective bureaucratic administration had been established; and careers had been opened to new men of talent. All these innovations were to last, in changing measures, for 2000 years.

THE HAN DYNASTY

When Liu Bang (r. 206–195 B.C.E.) prevailed in the warfare that ended the Qin dynasty, the empire remained intact. One ruling family fell and another took its place and asserted its own control, but the empire itself continued united under a single emperor. The principal Legalist ministers who had guided the Qin were replaced, but the administrative bureaucracy continued to function.

A Confucian Bureaucracy

Change came in the leadership style of the new dynasty. Liu Bang was himself a commoner and a soldier, perhaps illiterate, with many years of warfare still ahead of him—he died in battle in 195 B.C.E.—but as his ministers he chose educated men with Confucian principles. Slowly, a new social and political hierarchy emerged, with scholars at the top, followed by farmers, artisans, and merchants. Legalism still influenced the administrative systems, and Daoism's emphasis on nature and emotion continued to be attractive, but Confucius' ethical teachings captured the imagination of the court.

The influence of Confucianism appeared in four other areas. First, history became more important than ever. The appointment of Sima Tan and then of his son Sima Qian as court historians established the tradition of imperial record keeping (see p. 217). The Confucian notion of the importance of tradition and continuity prevailed over the Legalist idea of discounting the past.

Second, in 124 B.C.E. the most powerful and longest lived of the Han rulers, Wudi or Emperor Wu (r. 141–87 B.C.E.), the Martial Emperor, established an elite imperial academy to teach specially selected scholar-bureaucrats the wisdom of Confucius and its applicability to problems of governance. The emperor also declared that knowledge of the Confucian classics would be a basis for promotion in the imperial civil service. Although the academy could at first educate only fifty men, it multiplied in size until in the later Han period it could accommodate 30,000 men. In Han times, the landed aristocracy still gained most of the places in the bureaucracy, but the principle of appointment and promotion based not on birth but on success in an examination in the Confucian classics was finally established during the Tang dynasty (618–907 C.E.).

Third, an imperial conference of Confucian legal scholars was convened in the imperial palace in 51 B.C.E. to codify and establish the principles for applying case law. This established and consolidated the Chinese legal system for centuries to come.

Jade burial suit of Princess Tou Wan, Western Han dynasty, late second century B.C.E. As a very hard stone, jade was believed to be an effective preservative. When the Princess Tou Wan, daughter-in-law of the Emperor Jingdi, died, a burial suit was created for her using 2160 pieces of jade tied together with gold wire.

SOURCE

Treatises about Women in Han Society

During the Han dynasty, several authors decided to address the subject of women's role in society. Unfortunately, we have far more records on aristocratic women than we do on the peasantry. Ban Zhao (45–116 C.E.), sister of the famous court historian Ban Gu, wrote Admonitions for Women, *a text of advice on the virtues appropriate for aristocratic women, which was divided into seven sections on humility, resignation, subservience, self-abasement, obedience, cleanliness, and industry. Ban Zhao explained:*

In ancient times, on the third day after a girl was born, people placed her at the base of the bed, gave her a pot shard to play with, and made a sacrifice to announce her birth. She was put below the bed to show that she was lowly and weak and should concentrate on humbling herself before others. Playing with a shard showed that she should get accustomed to hard work and concentrate on being diligent. Announcing her birth to the ancestors showed that she should focus on continuing the sacrifices. These three customs convey the unchanging path for women and the ritual traditions.

Humility means yielding and acting respectful, putting others first and oneself last, never mentioning one's own good deeds or denying one's own faults, enduring insults and bearing with mistreatment, all with due trepidation.

Industriousness means going to bed late, getting up early, never shirking work morning or night, never refusing to take on domestic work, and completing everything that needs to be done neatly and carefully. Continuing the sacrifices means serving one's husband-master with appropriate demeanor, keeping oneself clean and pure, never joking or laughing, and preparing pure wine and food to offer to the ancestors. (Ebrey, p. 75)

Placing a similar stress on the virtues of self-sacrificing service, Liu Xiang (79–8 B.C.E.) wrote the Biographies of Heroic Women, *which recounted the virtues of 125 women. He especially praised the mother of the philosopher Mencius, the greatest of the Confucian scholars. Liu Xiang quotes Mencius' mother telling her son of her concept of women's obligations:*

A woman's duties are to cook the five grains, heat the wine, look after her parents-in-law, make clothes, and that is all! Therefore she cultivates the skills required in the women's quarters and has no ambition to manage affairs outside of the house. The *Book of Changes* says, "In her central place, she attends to the preparation of the food." The *Book of Songs* says, "It will be theirs neither to do wrong nor to do good, / Only about the spirits and the food will they have to think." This means that a woman's duty is not to control or to take charge. Instead she must follow the "three submissions." When she is young, she must submit to her parents. After her marriage, she must submit to her husband. When she is widowed, she must submit to her son. These are the rules of propriety.

The pervasive Confucian stress on hierarchy and deference permeates these prescriptions for women's conduct. However, throughout Han times—but not after—women could inherit property, divorce, and remarry after divorce or widowhood. And even the most highly placed women sometimes rebelled against Confucian ideals.

Finally, Confucian scholars, both male and female, began to establish principles of conduct for women. Confucius had spoken of the importance of five relationships in human society: ruler–subject; father–son; husband–wife; older brother–younger brother; and friend–friend. The first four were hierarchical relationships of superior–inferior. Little, however, had been written about the role of women. During the Han dynasty several Confucian scholars addressed the issue. They urged women to be self-sacrificing, serving others, especially the males in their lives: father, brother(s), husband, and son(s). The Source box includes examples of such advice by Ban Zhao, sister of one of the Han court historians, and Liu Xiang, who wrote *Biographies of Heroic Women*.

Military Power and Diplomacy

The Han emperors were no less militaristic than the Qin. Confucian principles of moral rectitude held sway among the educated elites, but the government did not dispense with formal legal systems nor did it forsake offensive or defensive warfare. The standing army numbered between 300,000 and 1,000,000, and all able-bodied men between the ages of about twenty and fifty-six were conscripted, serving for one year of training and one year of duty in the capital or in battle on the frontiers. They could be recalled in case of warfare.

Throughout the Han dynasty, China was engaged in incessant battles with the Xiongnu and other tribes around the Great Wall. Indeed, as we shall see shortly, the Han forced open a corridor through Gansu in the direction of Xinjiang (Turkestan). One reason for this expansion was to open markets for silk in the west. Parthian traders carried goods on this trade route as far as Rome. China also wanted to secure a supply of horses from distant Bactria for the military. As the Chinese Empire expanded, emperors sought new ways of regulating foreign affairs with neighboring peoples, including nomadic groups, such as the Xiongnu. They created a "tributary

HOW DO WE KNOW?

The Grand Historians

The Chinese valued recording the past both for itself and for the moral principles it was believed to teach. China therefore prepared and transmitted the most fully and continuously documented history of any ancient empire. Building on this legacy of historical literature, the Han emperor, Wu (r. 141–87 B.C.E.), created a new official position, the Grand Historian of the Han court, with the responsibility of preparing a comprehensive history of the entire Chinese past.

The first to hold the post was Sima Tan (d. 110 B.C.E.). He was succeeded by his son Sima Qian (145–85 B.C.E.), one of the greatest of all historians. Father and son transformed their task from one of writing dynastic chronologies to one of evaluating the quality of governments and rulers. They created the art of Chinese history as a commentary on politics and ethics.

At the very end of his great work, Shi Qi, 130 chapters recounting the history of China from mythological times almost to his own, Sima Qian includes an autobiographical sketch:

Qian was born at Longmen. He ploughed and kept flocks on the sunny slopes of the mountains near the Yellow River. By the age of ten he was reading aloud the ancient writings. At twenty he journeyed south to the Yangtze and Huai rivers, ascended Kuaiji to search for the cave of Yu, espied Jiuyi, went by water down to Yun and Xiang, journeyed north and crossed the

Wen and Si to investigate the traditions in the cities of Qi and Lu, and observed the customs handed down by Master Kong [Confucius], and took part in the archery competition held at Mount Yi in Cou. He suffered distress in Po, Xie, and Pengcheng, and returned home via Liang and Chu. Afterwards Qian served as a palace gentleman, and received orders to be sent on the western expedition to the south of Ba and Shu. Having gone south and captured Qiong, Ze, and Kunming, they returned and made their report on the mission. (Dawson trans., p. xix)

So his training included farming, literature, travel, adventure, anthropological research, archery, court service, and warfare. If historians improve with their own experience of life, since it enables them to understand more fully the lives of the people they study, then Sima Qian was off to a good start.

The highlight of Sima Qian's historical writing is its emphasis on biography, a traditional Chinese literary form that he developed into a vehicle for commenting on the political and ethical policies of the state not only in the past but also in his own time. His judgments could be fierce, and they sometimes got him into trouble. His support for his friend General Li Ling at a time when the general was in great disfavor in court led to Sima Qian's castration. Later, the Han Emperor Wu was so angered by Sima Qian's account of his father, the Emperor Jingdi, that he had this chapter removed. Eventually, however, imperial feelings mellowed, and Sima Qian won his reputation as the

greatest master of the early Chinese historical tradition.

Sima Qian completed his accounts up to c. 100 B.C.E. A later historian, Ban Biao (3–54 C.E.), added tens of chapters of "Supplementary Chronicles," and his son, Ban Gu (32–92 C.E.), wrote the Han Shu ("History of the Han Dynasty") to 22 C.E. Ban Gu established the tradition of compiling a history of each dynasty, a form continued in the Hou-Han shu ("History of the Later Han") and enduring into the twentieth century.

Because the official histories carry their own Confucian, conservative biases and focus almost entirely on issues of the central government and its court, unofficial materials from the provinces are especially useful in giving additional viewpoints. Grave sites and tombs yield documents, inscriptions, and engravings, and these often include relief sculptures of the activities of the deceased during his or her life. The burial goods represent in miniature the deceased's house, tools, carriages, boats, farms, and equipment. They often included terra cotta figures or painted frescoes of entertainers, musicians, servants, and maids, who had enriched the life of the deceased.

- What were the reasons for recording an official court history of each dynasty?
- What were the reasons for the rise, fall, and return to prominence of Sima Qian?
- How would you evaluate the training of Sima Qian as an historian?

system," in which the neighboring tributary group would acknowledge Chinese dominance and offer gifts (tribute) to the emperor. In exchange the emperor would send gifts to the ruler of the tributary group. On the northern and western borders, where Chinese, Mongol, Tibetan, and Barbarian forces fought, each learned the strengths and weaknesses of the other. A Chinese strength was the crossbow. An important Mongol and Tibetan strength was cavalry, mounted on strong, fast horses. To achieve military parity, the Han emperors sought and found a supply of equivalent horses in central Asia. The Gansu corridor served as an access route, and Emperor Wu garrisoned it with 700,000 soldiers. Administrative records written on wooden strips have survived to tell of the lives of these immigrant soldier-colonizers in some detail.

Population and Migration

In both the south and the northern border regions, the Han established military-agricultural colonies to provide military defense and economic development. The Chinese attempted to win the local populations over to Chinese culture. Often they succeeded, but not always. On the borders and in the southeast they met opposition, and rebellions against the Chinese settlers erupted in 86, 83, and 28–25 B.C.E.

During the later Han dynasty the population of northern China declined dramatically, even as the population of the south was expanding, perhaps from immigration from the north as well as from natural growth. The earliest preserved census in the world, taken in China in the year 2 C.E., shows the Chinese heartland clearly in the north; the southern population was sparse, mostly settled along the rivers. The second preserved census, taken 138 years later in 140 C.E., showed a sharp overall decline of 10 million people from about 58 million to about 48 million. The regional distribution had shifted from 76 percent in the north and 24 percent in the south, to 54 and 46 percent, respectively. In absolute terms the population of the south actually went up by more than 50 percent, from 14 million to 22 million, while the entire north declined from 44 million to 26 million.

Xiongnu and Tibetan massacres along the northern and western borders contributed to population losses, as did the floods caused when the Yellow River broke its banks and twice changed course, in *c.* 4 C.E. and again in 11 C.E. The military and natural turbulence also impoverished China's civilian population. Meanwhile, the imperial government allocated more and more resources to support the army,

Chinese expansion. A substantial shift in Chinese population distribution began during the first two centuries C.E., a fact that can be traced from Han census records. As land-hunger and pressure from the Xiongnu and the Tibetans on the northern border forced migration from the densely populated northeast, and as techniques for rice cultivation in the humid basin of the Yangzi improved, the lands to the south were mastered, and population clusters developed along the river valleys.

expansionism, and the court in the capital city of Chang'an.

In the south, in general, there was little indigenous population and little hostility or resistance to the increase in Han Chinese. The regional Yue or Viet tribes were more often involved in fighting one another, although in 40 C.E. there was a revolt, and violence broke out on at least seven occasions between 100–184 C.E. Perhaps the increased resistance in the later years was evoked by the vast increase in the flow of population from the north to the south.

Economic Power

Han rulers also encouraged the expansion of China's iron industry. They developed the technique of liquefying iron and pouring it into molds to produce cast iron and later steel. In spite of the demographic decline in the north, the economy of Han China grew with the exploitation of new sources of wealth from along the Yangzi River, Sichuan, and the south. New inventions in mining (including salt mining), paper production, the compass, the breast-strap harness for horses, a redesigned plowshare, hydraulic engineering, and the tapping of natural gas increased wealth and productivity.

Inventory written on bamboo, 95 C.E. Government bureaucracy expanded with military and economic power under the Han dynasty, producing an enormous number of documents on wooden and bamboo strips. This inventory lists the equipment of two infantry units. (*British Library, London*)

The road through the Gansu corridor to Xinjiang (Turkestan) brought increased knowledge of distant lands and new trade possibilities. In 138 B.C.E. Emperor Wu dispatched Zhang Qian to inner Asia to seek enemies of the Xiongnu who might serve as allies of the Chinese. Zhang returned twelve years later without new alliances but with precious new information on lands as far west as Bactria, in modern northern Afghanistan. New trade possibilities opened not only in horses but also in silk. Parthian traders served as intermediaries between the Chinese and Roman Empires. By 57 B.C.E. Chinese silk had reached Rome. The first silk route had been opened. Geography and cartography flourished, and gazetteers began to be published.

The cost of military expeditions and garrisons, and the expenses of the self-aggrandizing court ate up the gains, however. Having dramatically lowered the land revenues when they first took office, the Han emperors began to raise them again. They also began to nationalize private enterprise by bringing it under state control, not in order to promote efficiency or honesty but to gain the profits for the state. Although commerce and business were theoretically held in low regard by Confucianists, businessmen flourished under the Han, and Sima Qian praised their enterprise:

> A family with a thousand catties of gold may stand side by side with the lord of a city; the man with a hundred million cash may enjoy the pleasures of a king. Rich men such as these deserve to be called the "untitled nobility," do they not? (Sima Qian, p. 356)

Emperor Wu sought to expropriate some of this wealth to pay for his military ventures and his imperial court. He altered coinage, confiscated the land of the nobility, sold offices and titles, and increased taxes. He established government monopolies in the production of iron, salt, and liquor, and he took over part of the grain trade, arguing that this was a means of stabilizing prices, but actually intending to secure

Stone relief of harnessed cattle found at Mizhi, Shaanxi province.
Technological advancements, such as the development of the animal-drawn plow, went hand in hand with the increase in the area of cultivated land under the Han dynasty.

profits for his government and its border wars. On his death, his successor, the Emperor Zhao, arranged a debate between his chief minister, who advocated continuing the state monopolies on salt and iron, and a number of Confucian scholars, who opposed them. The minister defended and explained the emperor's policy:

He established the salt, iron, and liquor monopolies and the system of equitable marketing in order to raise more funds for expenditures at the borders. … [O]ur critics … would have the men who are defending our passes and patrolling our walls suffer hunger and cold. … Abolition of these measures is not expedient! (deBary, vol. 1: p. 361)

The Confucianists opposed the policy of costly military expansion and the government plan to take over businesses in order to finance it:

Never should material profit appear as a motive of government. Only then can moral instruction succeed and the customs of the people be reformed. But now in the provinces the salt, iron, and liquor monopolies, and the system of equitable marketing have been established to compete with the people for profit, dispelling rustic generosity and teaching the people greed. (deBary, vol. 1: p. 360–1).

The Confucianists also distrusted businessmen as self-seeking and corrupt, and they feared that government-run businesses would increase that corruption. The new emperor came to accept the Confucian argument and relinquished at least some government-run monopolies temporarily.

Fluctuations in Administrative Power

The bureaucracy of the early Han seemed to run well, and the adoption of Confucian principles tempered some of the harshness of the Legalist codes. In addition, the wars that the Qin had pursued to establish China's borders made fighting somewhat less necessary for the Han. For two hundred years even the problems of succession, problems that had ultimately helped destroy the Qin dynasty, were negotiated effectively, if sometimes quite cruelly. Nevertheless, the absence of clear principles of imperial succession continued, and in 9 C.E. the Han temporarily fell from power because there was no clear successor.

An Interregnum. In 1 B.C.E., the eight-year-old Emperor Ping inherited the throne. A regent, Wang Mang, was appointed to run the government during the boy's minority, and when Ping died in 9 C.E., Wang Mang became the *de facto* ruler, declaring himself founder of a new dynasty. His policies, however, alienated virtually everyone. These policies—fighting against the Xiongnu, breaking up large estates, reinstating the prohibition on the sale of land, fixing commodity prices, terminating the status of the Han nobility and reducing them to commoners, cutting bureaucratic salaries, confiscating villagers' gold in exchange for bronze—inflamed rich and poor, nobility and commoners, and urban and rural folk.

To add to his problems, just at the beginning of Wang Mang's regency, the silt-laden, shallow Yellow River again broke its banks and changed course twice in five years, wreaking immense devastation to property, and loss of life. In 23 C.E., a combination of Xiongnu invasions in the north, the rebellion of Han nobles near the capital, and, after 18 C.E., the revolt of the Red Turbans, a mass movement centered in the Shandong peninsula, which had been most devastated by the Yellow River's flooding, brought down Wang Mang and led to the reinstatement of the Han dynasty.

A Weakened Han Dynasty. The later Han dynasty, 23–220 C.E., did not have the same strength as the former Han. To cope with continuing incursions, the later Han made alliances with the barbarians, inviting them to settle within the Great Wall, to provide soldiers for Chinese armies, and even to intermarry with the Chinese, policies that were similar to Rome's actions in its border regions. Although this pattern demonstrated the weakness of the Chinese central government, it also contributed to the **sinicization** of the tribal barbarians, who learned the language, culture, and administrative patterns of the Chinese. Reversing the pattern of tribute of the years of strong government, the later Han gave silk cloth to the border tribes so that they would not invade. Later Han emperors also moved the capital from Chang'an eastward to the less exposed city of Luoyang.

The movement of population to the south increased the wealth of the empire generally, but the increase went largely to merchants and landlords. Peasants continued to be exploited and oppressed by the exactions of both their landlords and the imperial government. As government taxes increased, peasants sold off their private holdings and went to live and farm under the jurisdictions of local landlords, where they sought to evade government taxes and military conscription.

The landlords themselves faced a dilemma. As members of the governing elite, they were to collect and remit taxes to the central government and to turn over their tenants for conscription, but as landlords and local potentates, it was to their advantage to retain the taxes and the tenants' labor for themselves. Strong central governments were capable of demanding loyalty and collection; the later Han, however, frequently failed. Peasants absconded, the government's tax and labor bases diminished, and provincial notables developed independent power bases. Peasant revolts, which would become endemic in most of China, broke out with increasing frequency.

Peasant Revolt and the Fall of the Han. The beginning of the end of the Han is usually dated to 184 C.E., when a revolt of hundreds of thousands of peasants broke out. Zhang Jue, a Daoist healer who proclaimed that a new era would begin with the fall of the Han, launched the rebellion, called the Yellow Turban revolt for the headgear worn by the rebels. It broke out simultaneously in sixteen commanderies throughout the south, east, and northeast of China. Although this specific revolt was suppressed, it triggered a continuous string of additional outbreaks.

At least four factions struggled for power within the palace—the emperor, who, after the death of Emperor Ling in 189, was a child; the bureaucrats, advisers, palace guards, and regent to the young emperor; the eunuchs in the court, about 2000 castrated men chosen primarily for their direct loyalty to the emperor and the women of the court; and the women of the court and their families. Since each emperor had several wives and consorts, competition among them was fierce, both for their own recognition and for recognition of their sons at court, especially in the selection of the heir to the emperor. After the death of an emperor, his widows and his mother often remained embroiled in court politics to defend their own positions and those of their family.

sinicization The adoption and absorption by foreign peoples of Chinese language, customs, and culture.

Gu Kaizhi, two concubines in front of a mirror, *Admonitions* ..., fourth century C.E. As the Han Dynasty collapsed, artists lamented the neglect of the Confucian codes of behavior. Here the court painter Gu Kaizhi (334–406) illustrates the text of the poet Zhang Hua (c. 232–300): "Men and women know how to adorn their faces, but there is none who knows how to adorn his character. ..."

In the last decades of Han rule, 189–220 C.E., the court was buffeted from the outside and divided on the inside. For example, on September 25, 189 C.E., generals in the court murdered hundreds of eunuchs to remove their influence. By the year 220, when the last Han emperor, Xian, abdicated, the court had no center and the lands of the empire had already been divided among numerous, competing warlords.

DISINTEGRATION AND REUNIFICATION

The fall of the Han brought the disintegration of China into three separate states, but the ideal of a united Chinese empire was not lost. The empire was restored for fifty years, 265–316 C.E., then divided again for 273 years until 589 C.E., when a new dynasty introduced a unification that would last for more than three centuries. Even during periods of disintegration, elements of an underlying unity endured, for China has deep and pervasive common cultural traditions, just as, during periods of powerful imperial rule, elements of divisive regionalism persisted, for China is a huge and diverse country.

Ecology and Culture

On the fall of the Han dynasty, China divided into three states: the Wei in the north, ruling over some 29 million people; the Wu in the south, ruling over 11 million; and the Shu in the west, ruling over 7 million. From 265 to 316 C.E. a single dynasty, the Jin (Chin), reunited China briefly. Then, for 273 years, 316–589 C.E., China was divided north from south, more or less by the Huai River Basin, halfway between the Yellow River to the north and the Yangzi River to the south.

This division was characterized by a number of geographical features. To the north, the top soil is a fine yellow dust, called loess. Borne by winds from the west, it is 250 feet deep to the north of Chang'an, a region with little irrigation. The agriculture in this region has been dry-field farming not dependent on massive irrigation projects and mostly carried on by owner-operators. Its principal crops are wheat, millet, beans, and turnips. The region is intensely cold in winter. The south, by contrast, has many waterways, which are useful for both irrigation and navigation. The warmer weather, even subtropical in the far south, makes it possible to grow rice and tea, which were introduced from southeast Asia probably toward the end of the Han dynasty. The area is typically organized into landlord-tenant estates.

During the centuries of imperial division, six successive dynasties governed the south, while a series of non-Chinese barbarian dynasties ruled the north. Warfare and ecological disaster in the north steadily reduced the population, while people moved south, shifting the balance of population to a southern majority by this period. It appeared that the Chinese Empire, like that of Rome, had lost control of its original homeland and divided forever.

While China was divided politically, however, its culture and ethical ideologies persisted, keeping alive its traditions of unity. In the south, especially, the arts, painting, calligraphy, and poetry flourished, frequently with the themes of spiritual survival amid political disarray. The Chinese language, too, continued to unite all literate Chinese as their means of communication.

Chinese technology. Classical Chinese cultures were administratively and technologically sophisticated. They mastered diplomacy, bureaucracy, navigation, architecture, chemistry, mechanics, astronomy, printing, and, most dramatically, hydrology. Terraced farming, intensive irrigation systems, and the construction of thousands of miles of navigable canals harnessed the often unpredictable rivers of eastern China, and opened up the inland cities to commerce.

In the north, China was more open to new social and ethnic syntheses. The Chinese absorbed the barbarians into their continuing cultural life, and, through intermarriage, into China's genetic pool as well. When scholars today note the homogeneity of China's population as "95 percent Han," they are referring to cultural rather than ethnic homogeneity and recognizing the openness of China toward accepting and assimilating neighboring peoples who accept the culture of the "Han." The Chinese themselves echo the importance of this common culture, referring to all who have accepted it as "people of the Han." The nomadic peoples living on the northern borders and settling within the Great Wall at the invitation of the later Han emperors had already begun to absorb Chinese culture. When they became powerful enough to conquer north China, they found that they needed to enlist Chinese bureaucrats to administer their gains. In many regions, the administrators appointed by the new rulers were descended from families whom the Han had employed. Thus, below the surface of foreign rule, a powerful stratum of Chinese elites remained in place.

The most powerful and longest ruling of the nomadic conquerors became the most assimilated. These were the Northern Wei dynasty (r. 386–534), also named the Toba Wei after the tribal group that founded it. The longer they ruled, the more assimilated they became. In 493–494 they moved their capital from the far west to one of the former Han capitals, Luoyang, in order to consolidate their control of the northeast. But in Luoyang they wore Chinese dress, adopted Chinese names, and many intermarried. The Toba also made their own contributions to China's administrative practices, instituting a new pattern of urban organization by wards in Luoyang. Subsequent dynasties used this system in laying out the restored capital of Chang'an. Still later, Japanese imperial planners copied it in Nara. Similarly, in their attempts to keep agricultural populations from fleeing from north China, the Toba took over all land ownership for the state and continued to redistribute it in "equal fields" as each generation of cultivators died and new ones inherited the land. According to the "equal fields" system, all families received some land in return for paying a tribute in goods or in labor.

The developing, new aristocracy of mixed Chinese–Toba blood alienated the unassimilated Toba troops who garrisoned the frontiers. They finally revolted and defeated the Northern Wei government in 534, opening the way to the Sui dynasty, a family of mixed Chinese-foreign (barbarian) parentage, that reunited China.

Buddhism Reaches China

While China was beset by this dynastic turmoil, a new religion was spreading through the country. During the Han dynasty, Buddhism had entered China from its birthplace in India. It is first noted in Chinese historical records in the first century C.E.

Siddhartha Gautama, the Buddha, "the enlightened one" (c. 563–483 B.C.E.), introduced a religion of compassion in the face of a world of pain. Buddhism is discussed at length in Chapter 9. Here, however, we ask why and how this religion, which later died out in its own native soil in India, was able to take root in far-off China, even in the face of early opposition by Confucian scholars and bureaucrats and an institutionalized Daoist establishment.

Over time, Buddhism's very foreignness may have contributed to its success. The nomadic conquerors who succeeded the Han may have felt comfortable accepting, and even sponsoring a religion which, like themselves, came from outside China.

Second, Buddhism arose in India, to a large degree, as an anti-priestly religion favored by the merchant classes. These merchants sponsored Buddhist monasteries, convents, and cave temples along the silk routes between India and China, some of which remain impressive even today. When Buddhism arrived in China with the silk-route merchants, Chinese merchants were already familiar with it and the new religion appeared cosmopolitan rather than exclusively Indian.

Buddhism persevered in China, securing patronage in several regional courts, capturing the hearts of millions of followers, and ultimately becoming one of the unifying elements in Chinese culture. Eventually it mixed with Confucianism and Daoism, bringing popular new spiritual, intellectual, cultural, and ritual innovations (see Chapter 9).

Reunification under the Sui and Tang Dynasties

Despite almost 400 years of imperial fragmentation, many elements of Chinese unity were potentially at hand: language, ideology, culture, administration at the local level, aristocratic families with deep roots, and sufficient imperial prestige and administrative expertise that even China's conquerors were assimilated to it. To reunite the empire required the restoration of military power, economic productivity, and administrative integration. The Sui dynasty (581–618) provided all three.

The Short-lived Sui Dynasty. The Sui dynasty was founded by the Emperor Wen (Yang Chien) (r. 581–604), a general from one of the northern Chinese states, who usurped power in his own state and then succeeded in conquering and unifying all of inner China. Militarily, Wen raised the status of his militia, settled them on their own lands, and gave them property rights. He thus created an effective, committed, and loyal standing army of peasant-farmers. A powerful crossbow, protective body armor, and constant drills to achieve precision in maneuvers and battle made these troops a formidable fighting force.

Ideologically, the first Sui emperor and his son, Yang (Yang Kuang) (r. 604–615), who succeeded him, employed a combination of Confucian, Daoist, and Buddhist symbolism and practice to win popular loyalty. Administratively, they centralized authority, eliminating a layer of local administrators and transferring their own appointees from one jurisdiction to another every three years to prevent them from establishing their own local power base. They drew up a new centralized legal code that still recognized local customs. Economically, the Sui dynasty completed the Grand Canal from Hangzhou in the south to Luoyang in the center. The canal linked the Yangzi and Yellow River systems, and extensions connected it to the rebuilt capital in Chang'an and, later, to Beijing. The canal provided for the transportation of the agricultural produce of the rapidly developing south to the political-military centers of the north.

The expense of mobilizing and dispatching imperial troops and administrators on their far-flung missions depleted the treasury of the Sui dynasty. The Grand Canal produced many economic benefits, but it cost dearly in manpower. Built in seven years, the canal required the labor of 5.5 million people, and to complete some sections, all commoners between the ages of fifteen and fifty-five were pressed into service. As many as 50,000 police supervised the construction, flogging and chaining those who could not or would not work, and ordering every fifth family to provide one person to supply and prepare food. In addition to these public works, three costly and disastrous military campaigns in Korea and in central Asia wasted lives and treasure and sapped the loyalty of the troops. Finally, the leading general of the Sui seized control of the state and under the imperial name Gaozu established the new Tang dynasty in 618 C.E.

When the Sui fell, after over-extending itself militarily and economically, the Tang dynasty (618–907) continued and even strengthened these attributes of empire. Moreover the Sui and Tang extended China's reign to truly imperial dimensions—that is, beyond China proper to "outer China," Mongolia, Turkestan, and central Asia, as far

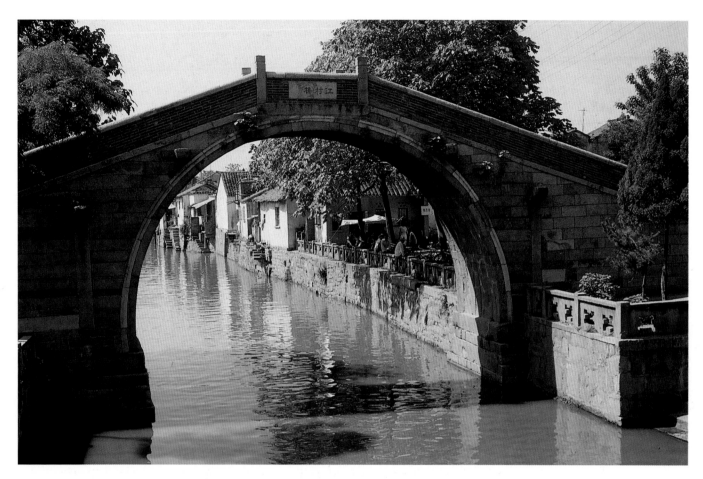

as the frontiers of modern Afghanistan, Pakistan, and Iran. China also held strong cultural sway over Tibet, although without achieving direct political control. These lands were larger than all of "inner China" in area, although they held only perhaps 5 percent of its population. In addition, Tang China held northern Vietnam and, briefly, northern Korea. China's cultural influence at this time was extremely strong in Japan as well (see below).

Arts and Technology under the Tang Dynasty. Tang policies built on those of the Sui, consolidating and improving them where possible. The Tang dynasty relied more than ever on the imperial examination system to provide its administrators, and in 754 the emperor founded a new Imperial Academy, the Han-Lin Yuan (the Forest of Pens).

The arts and technology, often reinforcing one another, flourished under the Tang as never before. The world's first block printing was invented, partly in response to the needs of Buddhists to disseminate their doctrines, for under the Tang the Buddhist religious establishment became increasingly powerful. Buddhist religious art found expression also in further cave sculptures and paintings. New ceramic manufacturing methods led to the production of the first true porcelain, a product of great beauty and durability. For centuries, China alone knew the secret of its manufacture. Millers developed machinery and gears for converting linear and rotary motion, encouraging further development of both water- and windmills. In 659 China produced the world's first pharmacopoeia, which listed the contents and uses of all known medicines.

Finally, Tang era poetry of meditation, nature, politics, fate, suffering, and individual identity transmitted its living legacy even to today's readers in China and beyond.

Bridge over the outer moat, a connecting link of the Grand Canal at Suzhou. The engineering feats of the Sui dynasty made significant contributions to the closer integration of the empire. By digging the Grand Canal and building roads in the north China plain, rulers ensured effective communication and the opening of new trade routes between diverse regions.

The Tang revival. The Sui Dynasty (581–618 C.E.) and its successor, the politically organized Tang, restored the Chinese imperial impulse four centuries after the decline of the Han, extending control along the silk route as far as the Tien Shan mountain range and the arid Ferghana basin. Trade flourished. China finally reached its western limits when its forces were defeated by the imperial armies of the Muslim Abbasid empire at the Talas River in 751.

Each of the three most famous Tang poets has been seen as linked to a different cultural tradition: Wang Wei (701–762) to Buddhism; Li Bai (Li Bo) (701–761) to Daoism; and Du Fu (Tu Fu) (712–770) to Confucianism, although each was influenced by all three traditions. Du Fu's "Autumn Meditation" expresses the tension between the high-stakes, hustle-bustle of the imperial court under stress and his own desire for a life of peace within nature:

I've heard them say Chang'an's like a chessboard;
sad beyond bearing, the happenings of these hundred years!
Mansions of peers and princes, all with new owners now;
in civil or martial cap and garb, not the same as before.
Over mountain passes, due north, gongs and drums resound;
wagons and horses pressing west speed the feather-decked dispatches.
Fish and dragons sunk in sleep, autumn rivers cold;
old homeland, those peaceful times, forever in my thoughts!

(*Du Fu*, Watson translation, p. 134)

Above **Hill of the Thousand Buddhas, Jinan, Tang dynasty.** The increased power of the Buddhist religious establishment in Tang times is reflected in the growth of cave paintings and sculptures. The merchants and missionaries who brought Buddhism to China along the silk route also brought ideas about the iconography of temples and the depiction of the Buddha.

Pottery figure of a Ferghana horse, excavated from a tomb, Tang dynasty (618–907 C.E.). The Tang dynasty opened the Grand Canal, stimulated growth in trade, and expanded the boundaries of the empire. For much of this they were dependent on the mobility of the army, which in turn was dependent for covering great distances on the famed Ferghana horses, immortalized in literature as "the horses that sweated blood." (*Idemitsu Museum of Arts, Tokyo*)

Ceramic model of a group of musicians seated on a camel, Tang dynasty (618–907 C.E.), excavated from a tomb in the suburb of Xian. The beards, facial features, and costumes of some of the musicians in this group suggest that they are from central Asia. Such models, commonly found in the tombs of the Tang elite, are evidence of a taste for the goods that came along the silk route from the west and the central Asian music that accompanied them.

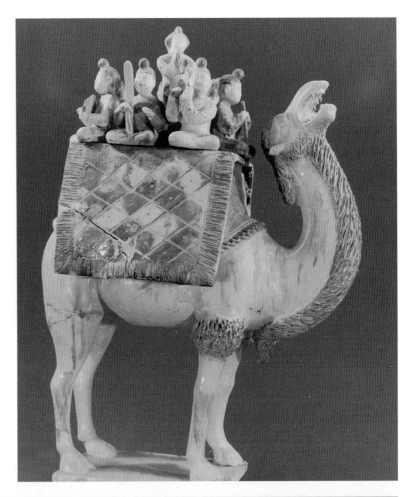

Caravanserai, Kirghizstan, Tang dynasty, (618–907 C.E.). The silk route led traders through hundreds of miles of inhospitable terrain, such as this barren and mountainous region of Kirghizstan in central Asia. This Tang dynasty-era caravanserai, the oldest complete example in existence, would have protected traders from the elements and from preying bandits.

HOW DO WE KNOW?

Poetry as a Source for History

Du Fu's "Ballad of the Army Carts" repeats the heartbreaking pain of war as the troops describe the seemingly endless fighting and dying:

Carts rattle and squeak,
Horses snort and neigh—
Bows and arrows at their waists, the
  conscripts march away.
Fathers, mothers, children, wives run to say
  goodbye.
The Xianyang Bridge in clouds of dust is
  hidden from the eye.

They tug at them and stamp their feet,
  weep, and obstruct their way.
The weeping rises to the sky.
Along a road a passer-by
Questions the conscripts. They reply:
They mobilize us constantly. Sent
  northwards at fifteen
To guard the River, we were forced once
  more to volunteer,
Though we are forty now, to man the
  western front this year.
The headman tied our headcloths for us
  when we first left here.
We came back white-haired—to be sent
  again to the frontier.
Those frontier posts could fill the sea with
  the blood of those who've died,
But still the Martial Emperor's aims remain
  unsatisfied.
In county after county to the east, Sir, don't
  you know,
In village after village only thorns and
  brambles grow,
Even if there's a sturdy wife to wield the
  plough and hoe,

The borders of the fields have merged, you
  can't tell east from west.
It's worse still for the men from Qin, as
  fighters they're the best—
And so, like chickens or like dogs, they're
  driven to and fro.
  Though you are kind enough to ask,
  Dare we complain about our task?
  Take, Sir, this winter. In Guanxi
  The troops have not yet been set free.
  The district officers come to press
  The land tax from us nonetheless.
  But, Sir, how can we possibly pay?
  Having a son's a curse today.
Far better to have daughters, get them
  married—
A son will lie lost in the grass, unburied.
  Why, Sir, on distant Qinhhai shore
The bleached ungathered bones lie year on
  year.
New ghosts complain, and those who died
  before
Weep in the wet grey sky and haunt the ear.
(Seth, pp. 48–9)

Du Fu probably wrote this poem of exhaustion and discontent after two decisive and disastrous military operations. In the first, the Battle of the Talas River, on one of the most distant of China's western frontiers, 2000 miles from Chang'an, Arab armies defeated China in 751. China lost control of its central Asian holdings, and the silk route was opened to the cultural influence of Islam, which displaced Buddhism and Confucianism. Four years later, An Lushan, one of China's frontier generals of Turkish extraction, revolted. Although the Chinese put down the revolt in 763, the cost of the warfare, and the vulnerability it

revealed, weakened the Tang dynasty for the entire century and a half leading up to its fall.

The Tang dynasty had extended China's border farther than any other except the Qing (Manchu) that ruled a thousand years later (1644–1912). Tang holdings in central Asia had flanked and protected the silk route and brought new opportunities for wealth. Ultimately, however, these lands cost more than they brought in economically and militarily. The border groups—Turks, Uighurs, Khitans, and other ethnic groups—no longer accepted Chinese domination, but continually probed the Tang border fortifications. Finally, China ceded control of central Asia to them. In China proper, agricultural and commercial wealth continued to grow, but the central, imperial government could no longer control it. Regional rulers grew in authority and power. In 907 the Tang dynasty finally disappeared, as China splintered into ten separate states. Yet the imperial idea and pattern held. In 960 the Song dynasty arose, ruling all of China until 1127, and the south until 1279.

- What elements of the poem might suggest that Du Fu was influenced by Confucianism?
- Who is the poem's main speaker? What are his feelings about the war?
- How does the poem help us understand the feelings of the Chinese after the battle's defeat and subsequent developments?

The three centuries of Sui and Tang rule consolidated the theory and practice of Chinese imperial rule even to the present (although today there is no emperor). Since 581 China has been divided into two administrations only once, in 1127–75, and fragmented into several regions only twice, in 907–959 and 1916–49. Apart from these three periods, totalling 133 years, China has stood united for a continuous period of more than fourteen centuries.

IMPERIAL CHINA

We opened this unit on empires by noting that the word empire signifies rule by one people over another. Let us examine this definition in relation to China. First, within

assimilation The process by which different ethnic groups lose their distinctive cultural identity through contact with the dominant culture of a society, and gradually become absorbed and integrated into it.

the borders of China, empire frequently meant the **assimilation** of others. In the north, many of the tribal groups against which China fought and against which Chinese rulers constructed the Great Wall, nevertheless came to enlist in China's armies, settle its land, assimilate its culture, adopt its language and calligraphy, and intermarry with its peoples.

Both the ethnic Chinese and the "barbarians" regarded this process as mutually beneficial. Both also understood the dangers: the barbarians might lose their culture and even find themselves in civil war with others of their ethnic group who rejected assimilation; the Chinese might be conquered by their new allies. Indeed, both of these results did occur frequently, and the interchanges transformed the cultures of both the barbarians and the Chinese.

The West and Northwest

The most geographically far-reaching of China's expansions beyond the borders of inner China were to the northwest and west. Emperor Wu's expansion into Gansu and beyond did not survive the early Han dynasty; similarly, the expansion of the Sui and Tang even deeper into central Asia did not survive the Battle of the Talas River and the An Lushan revolt. Nevertheless, China's cultural and symbolic influence over these regions persisted, even after its political, military, and direct economic power was gone. (In the seventeenth century, under the Qing dynasty, China returned to dominate these areas, and rules them today; see Chapter 14.)

The South and Southwest

Processes of assimilation also took place in south China, but they have made much less of a mark in the records. China as an ethnic, cultural, and political entity developed first in the north, around the Yellow River, but as Chinese peoples moved south of the Yangzi they met people of other ethnic groups. As the Chinese encroached, some southern peoples retreated still further south to preserve and develop their own separate national identities. The Vietnamese are the clearest example of this pattern. Other groups of southerners remained as distinct, separate tribal groups, usually in remote areas somewhat difficult to access. Occasionally, these peoples revolted against the Chinese invasion and take-over of their land. The Miao gave the clearest example of this response. Most of the rest assimilated, including some Vietnamese and Miao, without making a lasting impression on the historical records.

Vietnam

For a thousand years China held Annam (northern Vietnam) as a colony. The Han dynasty conquered Annam and incorporated the area as a province of China in 111 B.C.E. It remained part of China until 939 C.E., when, not long after the collapse of the Tang, the Vietnamese rebel Ngo Quyen declared himself the king of the independent state of Dai Viet.

CHINA'S IMPERIAL DYNASTIES

Listed below are all the imperial dynasties, starting with the Qin, and the two major pre-imperial ruling houses. Gaps in the date sequences mark those periods when the country was divided between two or more rulers.

Shang	*c.* 1600–1100 B.C.E.
Zhou	*c.* 1100–256
Qin	**221–206**
Han	**202** B.C.E.–**220** C.E.
Three Kingdoms (Kingdom of Shu Han, Kingdom of Wei, Kingdom of Wu)	**220–65**
Northern and Southern Dynasties	**265–589**
Western Jin	265–317
Eastern Jin	317–419
Northern Wei	386–534
Sui	**581–618**
Tang	**618–907**
Song	**960–1279**
Yuan (Mongol)	**1279–1368**
Ming	**1368–1644**
Manchu (Qing)	**1644–1912**

During and after Chinese colonization, the Vietnamese were locked in a love-hate relationship with Chinese culture and politics. Chinese scholars and officials, many of them fleeing imperial policies in China, brought to Vietnam their own ideographic script, Confucian ethical principles, and the Confucian literary classics. The Vietnamese adopted them all.

Buddhism also arrived in Vietnam by way of China. The rest of southeast Asia absorbed Buddhism in its Theravada form from India; Vietnam adopted Mahayana Buddhism as it had developed in China, after about the fifth century C.E. These cultural innovations appealed primarily to the Vietnamese upper-class aristocracy. At the level of practical technology, the Chinese also introduced a number of valuable agricultural innovations: the construction of a huge network of dams and waterworks that protect against monsoon flooding every year; the use of human excrement as fertilizer; market gardening; and intensive pig farming.

Although they adopted many Chinese customs, the Vietnamese resented foreign hegemony by the colossus to its north. For example, the two Trung sisters led a military revolt in 39 C.E., succeeded in evicting the Chinese, ruled jointly over Vietnam for two years, but committed suicide when their revolt was crushed. They are revered in Vietnam to this day. Leaders of numerous, less dramatic revolts against China are also viewed as national heroes, yet paradoxically, the most profound adoption of Chinese administrative reforms occurred in the fifteenth century, when Vietnam was independent. As a result of Chinese direct rule in the earlier period and Chinese power and proximity during later periods of Vietnamese independence, the country became a Confucian state, with an examination system, an intellectually elitist administration somewhat aloof from the masses, and an intense desire for independence from China.

Korea

Korea came under direct Chinese rule only briefly, but Chinese cultural hegemony profoundly influenced the peninsula. The Han Emperor Wu first conquered northern Korea in 109–108 B.C.E., along with Manchuria. Military garrisons established Chinese control and influence.

Korea, like Vietnam, had borrowed heavily from prehistoric China, including much of Shang technology and, later, iron technology, paper production, printing, lacquerwork, porcelain (although Korean double-fired, greenish, celadon ware had a distinct beauty all its own), wheat and rice agriculture, and the ideographs of written language. In 1446, at the initiative of its king, Koreans created a written system called *han'gul*, based on phonetics, which they proudly describe as the most scientifically formulated of all the world's scripts. Until after World War II, however, Korean elites suppressed the use of the simple *han'gul*, preferring the more prestigious, more elitist, and more difficult Chinese ideographs.

After the collapse of the Han in 220 C.E., Korea broke free of direct control, although it remained a vassal of the Chinese. Some of China's colonies remained in place, but without military capacity. The Sui dynasty sent three expeditions to conquer Korea, but all ended in disaster. The expansive Tang dynasty also tried to retake Korea in the seventh century and succeeded in occupying much of the peninsula in 668–676. Ultimately, however, Korea regained and maintained its independence, although it was often forced to accept tributary status, acknowledging China's regional dominance.

China's power over Korea can be seen far more in terms of cultural hegemony than in political-military rule. Confucianism, law codes, bureaucratic administration, literature, art, and Mahayana Buddhism entered Korean life from China, independent of government pressure. In 935 C.E., after the fall of the Tang, Korea's Silla dynasty also fell. The Koryo dynasty, which took its place, built a new capital at Kaesong, just north of today's South Korean capital at Seoul, and modeled it on Chang'an, the Tang capital in China. Both China and Korea spoke of a "younger brother/older brother" relationship between the two countries.

Japan

China never conquered Japan, but Japan did accept China's cultural hegemony. Indeed, through the seventh and eighth centuries C.E. Japan actively and enthusiastically attempted to model its state, religion, technology, art, and language on those of China. As the Korean peninsula stands between the Chinese mainland and the four major islands of Japan, much of the importation of Chinese forms came to Japan through Korea.

Immigration and Cultural Influences. Although archaeological records show that Japan was populated by the Jomon people of the coastal regions at least as early as 10,000 B.C.E., rice agriculture seems to have begun only about 300 B.C.E., when it was introduced from south China. Bronze tools and weapons arrived about the first century B.C.E. and the technology for making iron tools about 200 years later.

Waves of immigrants from Korea and China arrived in Japan between *c.* 200 B.C.E. and *c.* 500 C.E. By 500 C.E., about one-third of Japan's nobility claimed Korean or Chinese descent, and many artisans and metal workers in Japan had come from Korea. All was not peaceful between Japan and Korea, however, and invasions and raids were launched from both sides. In this period, the Chinese represented the Japanese by an ideograph that signifies "dwarf," presumably suggesting an inferior status.

In 405 C.E., a Korean scribe named Wani traveled to Japan to teach the Chinese script. This became Japan's earliest written language, and Japan's recorded history begins only in the eighth century C.E. Most of our knowledge of these earlier years comes either from archaeological records or from references in the literatures of China and Korea. These archaeological and literary materials tell of the formation of an embryonic Japanese state about the third century C.E., when a clan of people worshiping the sun-goddess established their rule over the Yamato Plain in central Honshu Island. Ultimately, the imperial line of Japan claimed descent from this group. They used Chinese written characters and accepted elements of both Confucianism and Buddhism to

Asian imperial capitals. The Tang capital of Chang'an was grid-planned as a massive rectangle over 5 miles square, focusing on the imperial quarters and housing about a million people within its walls. The newly centralized Japanese Yamato state built Nara in imitation of Chang'an: a grid plan incorporated the Todaiji Temple complexes.

enrich the polytheistic practices of the indigenous religion, Shinto, and its deification of the Japanese emperor.

After China succeeded in re-establishing its own powerful empire under the Sui and Tang dynasties, Japanese rulers dispatched numerous delegations of hundreds of members each to China to learn and adopt Chinese models. The Chinese calendar and many methods of government were introduced. In 604 a new seventeen-point "constitution" was introduced, a guide that was modeled on Chinese practice. The document included reverence for Confucianism and Buddhism, for the sovereign of Japan, and, on a more mundane level, asserted the government's monopoly over the collection of taxes.

Officially, Japanese elites recognized the emperor as the head of Japan, but, in fact, he was little more than a figurehead; real power belonged to those behind the throne. Bloody struggles for control of the court in Japan brought Nakatomi no Kamatari to power in 645. He took the surname Fujiwara, and under this name his family dominated the politics of Japan for centuries to come. (One descendant, Prince Konoe Fumimaro, served as prime minister in 1937–9 and again in 1940–41.) Fujiwara adopted Chinese culture, religion, and government as the way to centralize and unify Japan and to assert his own control. He proclaimed the Taika ("great change") reforms in 646, consolidating provincial administration and constructing an extensive road system. The reforms also abolished private ownership of land and redistributed it at each generational change.

The Nandaimon, or "Great South Gate," of the Todai Buddhist temple, 745–752 C.E. The first Japanese Buddhist temples—modeled on the Buddhist temples of China—are among the oldest surviving timber buildings in the world. So faithful and enduring are they that they have become our best examples of *Chinese* architecture for the period.

In 710 two acts further consolidated centralized rule. First, a new capital, modeled on Chang'an, was built at Nara. Second, the Japanese ruler now claimed to rule through divine mandate, although, unlike the Chinese "Mandate of Heaven", it could never be revoked. (To this day, the same family occupies the imperial throne, although after World War II, its divinity was officially repudiated; see Chapter 19.) At about the same time, again following Chinese models, the Japanese began to record their history for the first time in the *Nihongi*, in Chinese, and their legends in the *Kojiki*, which was written in a mixture of Chinese and Japanese forms.

The emperor served as the chief priest of Japan's Shinto faith, but as Shinto is a religion that worships the gods of nature—streams, trees, rocks—it can be practiced anywhere. Buddhism, by contrast, provides a more centralized form of organization, through monasteries and temples. Many new Buddhist temples were, therefore, constructed in Chinese form at Nara to centralize worship in Japan. From this time onward Buddhism and Shinto have coexisted in Japan, with millions of Japanese declaring themselves devotees of both faiths.

As centuries passed and Japan became more secure in its own political organization and cultural identity, the reliance on Chinese models declined. But in the centuries when its basic cultural and political identity was formed, Japan had followed carefully and devotedly the hegemonic examples of China, without compulsion or force of any sort.

LEGACIES FOR THE FUTURE
WHAT DIFFERENCE DO THEY MAKE?

The Roman and Chinese Empires are among the greatest empires in history in terms of longevity, population, geographical extent, and lasting influence. A comparison between them will help to clarify the characteristics and significance of each and help establish guidelines for thinking about other empires of other times, and our own.

Differences

Not surprisingly, there are important differences between these two huge empires, separated by such great distances.

Geopolitical. China's heartland was far larger and more cohesive, geographically and culturally, than Rome's. Rome had as its heartland only central Italy, and even after conquering Italy, it held just that single peninsula bounded by the Alps Mountains and the Mediterranean Sea. In the time of Augustus in Rome and the Han dynasty in China, the Roman and Chinese empires each held about 60 million people, but in Rome only a few of these millions lived in Italy. In China virtually all inhabited "inner China." Ninety percent of them were in the north China plain.

Ideological. Although Confucian China spoke of a mythological golden age of equality among people living in harmony with each other and with nature, realistically the Confucianists believed that the best possible government was a well-ordered empire. Many philosophers and writers in imperial Rome, on the other hand, believed in an actual, historical republican past (albeit an idealized past) and always looked back to it as a golden age. Roman imperial expansion and stratification were often regarded as violations of the earlier republican ideals.

Longevity and Persistence. Rome's empire rose, fell, and disappeared, although it lived on as a concept. China's empire has lasted for the past 2000 years. Dynasties have come and gone, sometimes the empire has broken into fragments, and sometimes it has been ruled by conquering "barbarians," but finally the empire endured as a single political entity. Today, although there is no emperor, China's geopolitical unity continues.

Policy and Powers of Assimilation. As China moved both north and south, it assimilated a great number of the peoples it invaded and conquered. Non-ethnic Chinese were absorbed culturally and biologically. Many of the 95 percent of today's Chinese population who are called "Han" are descended from ancestors who were not. Confucian and Buddhist ideology held the empire together, supported by the power of the emperor and his armies. Rome's empire was held together by law and backed by military power. Selected non-Romans could gain citizenship under law, but ethnically and culturally the conquered peoples remained "other." Intermarriage with non-citizens was usually forbidden. Romans maintained the cultural distinctions between themselves and those they conquered far more than did the Chinese.

Language Policy. The Chinese language unified the Chinese Empire across space and through time—even today—far more than Latin did the Roman Empire. Chinese was never subordinated to another language and culture, as Latin was to Greek for many years and in many regions. Nor did Chinese compete with regional languages as Latin ultimately did. Indeed, Chinese helped to bring even neighboring countries—Vietnam, Korea, and Japan—together into a single general cultural unit.

Ideology and Cultural Cohesion. China's Confucian bureaucracy provided a core cultural identity throughout the empire and beyond. Even the alternative political-cultural philosophies of China, such as Daoism, Legalism, and later Buddhism, usually (but not always) served to broaden and augment the attraction of Confucianism. Rome's emperor worship did reinforce its cohesion, but its principal philosophies of polytheism, Stoicism, and, later, Christianity did not significantly buttress and augment its imperial rule. The latter two may even have diminished popular loyalty to the empire, except in its later continuation in the east as the Byzantine Empire.

Influence on Neighbors. The Roman Empire influenced the lands it conquered, but had less influence on those outside its boundaries. China exercised lasting hegemonic influence even on neighbors it did not conquer, such as Japan, or conquered only briefly, such as Korea. A considerable part of this legacy was religious and cultural as well as political, economic, and administrative.

Similarities

The many points of similarity between China and Rome reveal some basic truths about the nature of empires.

Relations with Barbarians. Both empires faced nomadic groups from central Asia who threatened and penetrated their boundaries. Indeed, the Huns, who invaded Europe, and the Xiongnu, who invaded China, may have belonged to the same ethnic group. Both empires settled the "barbarians" near their borders and enlisted them in their imperial armies. In both cases, the barbarians came to hold great power. Ultimately, however, they dismembered the Roman Empire, while the Chinese absorbed them.

Religious Policies. Both empires incubated foreign religions, especially in times of imperial disorder. In China, Buddhism was absorbed into Confucianism and Daoism and helped to sustain the national culture in times of political trouble. In Rome, however, Christianity did not save the empire. In fact, by challenging the significance of earthly power it may even have contributed to the empire's weakness.

The Role of the Emperor. Both empires ascribed divine attributes to the emperor, and both frequently had difficulty in establishing rules for imperial succession. The Romans often attempted to choose their best general, while the Chinese selected a man who could control the imperial family and court. Neither empire believed that a single imperial family should rule forever. The Chinese believed that eventually the Mandate of Heaven would pass from one dynasty to another.

Gender Relationships and the Family. The family was extremely important for both empires, and both empires subordinated women to men at all stages of life. Both drew analogies between hierarchies and loyalties in a well-run family and those in a well-run empire. Both empires used marriages as a means of confirming political alliances with foreign powers. Both periodically felt that excessive concern with sexual relationships distracted energy from the demands of sustaining the empire, and both proclaimed strict codes of sexual morality.

The Significance of Imperial Armies. In both empires the army was crucial in creating and sustaining the political structure in the face of domestic and foreign enemies. The Roman Empire was established and ruled by generals, as were the Qin, Han, Sui, and Tang dynasties in China. Both empires were periodically threatened and usurped by rebel generals asserting their own authority. The cost of the armies, especially on distant, unprofitable expeditions, often drained the finances of the government and encouraged its subjects to evade taxes and military service and even to rise in revolt. Both empires established colonies of soldier-colonizers to garrison and develop remote areas while simultaneously providing compensation and retirement benefits for the troops.

Overextension. Both empires suffered their greatest challenges in confronting simultaneously the strains of overexpansion and the subsequent internal revolts that were triggered by the costs. In Rome these dual problems, along with the barbarian invasions, finally precipitated the end of the empire in the west. In China they led to the loss of the Mandate of Heaven and the downfall of dynasties. The external battles against Qin-Jurchen border tribes, for example, combined with the revolt of the Yellow Turbans, brought down the later Han; the loss of the distant Battle of the Talas River, combined with the internal revolt of An Lushan, sapped Tang power.

Public Works Projects. Throughout their empire the Romans built roads, aqueducts, public monumental structures, administrative/military towns, and the great capital cities of Rome and Constantinople. The Chinese built the Great Wall, the Grand Canal, systems of transportation by road and water, public monumental structures, administrative/military towns throughout the empire, and several successive capitals, especially Chang'an and Luoyang.

The Concentration of Wealth. In both empires, the benefits of imperial wealth tended to flow toward the center and to the elites in the capital cities. The capitals grew to unprecedented size. Both Chang'an and Rome housed more than one million people.

Policies for and against Individual Mobility. To maintain power and stability in the face of demands for change, both empires periodically bound their peasantry to the soil and demanded that the sons of soldiers follow their fathers' occupations. Both found these policies difficult to enforce. Both offered some individual mobility through service in their armies. In addition, the Chinese examination system provided for advancement within the imperial bureaucracy.

Revolts. Both empires experienced frequent revolts against the emperor and his policies. In Rome, which housed a much larger slave population, slaves led some of the revolts. In China they were more typically initiated by peasants. Rome attempted to forestall mass revolts in the capital and other large cities through the provision of "bread and circuses." Both empires faced constant challenges from those living on their peripheries.

Peasant Flight. In both empires during times of upheaval, peasants sought to evade taxes and conscription by finding refuge as tenants on large, landed estates. Whenever imperial government was weak, the largest of these estates challenged the power of the central government.

The influence of the early Chinese Empire continues today, not only in China itself, but in east Asia, southeast Asia, and central Asia. Consistent patterns in language, culture, geopolitical organization, and international relations are there to be discovered through the ages. The same is true of Rome throughout the areas it ruled directly in western and southern Europe, the Mediterranean, and North Africa. To a lesser degree, its influence extends to eastern Europe and to the European settler colonies in the Americas, Australia, and New Zealand. The imperial ideals of China and Rome have entranced many who have studied them, and repelled many as well. As we turn to study the empires of ancient India, these models help to guide our thinking.

Review Questions

- Many kinds of standardization accompanied the creation and consolidation of empire in China. What were these forms of standardization, and which do you think were the most important?
- What were the three most prominent philosophies of rule in the Chinese Empire? They seem to have been applied under different circumstances. Under what circumstances do you think each was most appropriate? Why?
- What were the attitudes of Confucianism toward the role of women in society? How did these attitudes compare with those of other Chinese philosophies, and with philosophies from ancient Rome?
- Compare the policies of the Tang dynasty with those of the Han. You might consider the geographical extent of the empire under these dynasties, their administrative mechanisms, philosophies of government, and international relations.
- Why are Vietnam, Korea, and Japan often considered to be daughter civilizations of China?
- How did China regard the barbarians on its borders, in terms of international relations and in terms of assimilation? How did China's policies compare with those of Rome?

Suggested Readings

PRINCIPAL SOURCES

Blunden, Caroline and Mark Elvin. *Cultural Atlas of China* (New York: Facts on File, 1983). Excellent introductory coverage to history and culture, lavishly illustrated with maps, pictures. Excellent as both narrative and reference.

deBary, William Theodore and Irene Bloom, eds., *Sources of Chinese Tradition*, Vol. I: *From Earliest Times to 1600* (New York: Columbia University Press, 2nd ed., 1999). The premier primary source reference to the thought of the elites of ancient China.

Ebrey, Patricia Buckley, ed. *Chinese Civilization: A Sourcebook* (New York: The Free Press, 2nd ed., 1993). This primary sourcebook covers social and economic materials of everyday life of common people.

Elvin, Mark. *The Pattern of the Chinese Past* (Stanford, CA: Stanford University Press, 1973). Most Chinese history has been written dynasty-by-dynasty. Elvin seeks deeper patterns of change in the economy and social life. Introduces new approaches.

Twitchett, Denis and Michael Lowe, eds. *The Cambridge History of China*, Vol. I: *The Ch'in and Han Empires, 221 B.C.–A.D. 220* (Cambridge: Cambridge University Press, 1986). Comprehensive, standard compendium of analysis and narrative.

Twitchett, Denis, ed. *The Cambridge History of China*, Vol. III: *Sui and T'ang China, 589–906*, Part I (Cambridge: Cambridge University Press, 1979). Comprehensive, standard compendium of analysis and narrative.

Waley, Arthur, trans. *The Book of Songs* (New York: Grove Press, 1996). Marvellous collection by master translator.

Watson, Burton, trans. *The Selected Poems of Du Fu* (New York: Columbia University Press, 2002). An excellent selection and translation.

ADDITIONAL SOURCES

Andrea, Alfred and James H. Overfield, eds. *The Human Record:* Vol I (Boston, MA: Houghton Mifflin Co., 3rd ed., 1998). Excellent array of primary sources, arranged and cross-referenced to provide its comprehensive course of study.

Creel, H.G. *Confucius: The Man and the Myth* (Westport, CT: Greenwood Press, reprinted 1972 from 1949 ed.). Little is known about Confucius the man. This classic study tells us what we know and how it has been represented and interpreted.

Fairbank, John K., Edwin O. Reischauer, and Albert M. Craig. *East Asia: Tradition and Transformation* (Boston, MA: Houghton Mifflin, rev. ed., 1989). This is the standard history of the subject, updated from time to time.

Friedman, Edward. "Reconstructing China's National Identity: A Southern Alternative to Mao-Era Anti-Imperialist Nationalism," *Journal of Asian Studies* LIII, No. 1 (February 1994), 67–91. An analysis of continuing differences between China's southern, coastal, commercial regions, and its more bureaucratic and politically oriented interior and north.

Han Fei Tzu. *The Complete Works of Han Fei Tzu,* 2 vols. trans. W.K. Liao (London: Arthur Probsthain, 1959). The basis of the Legalist tradition.

Hughes, Sarah Shaver and Brady Hughes, ed. *Women in World History*, Vol. I (Armonk, NY: M.E. Sharpe, 1995). A reader with materials drawn from all over the world.

Lattimore, Owen. *Inner Asian Frontiers of China* (London: Oxford University Press, 1940). Classic statement of the relationship between China proper and the areas north and west of the Great Wall.

Lockard, Craig A. "Integrating Southeast Asia into the Framework of World History: The Period Before 1500," *The History Teacher* XXIX, No. 1 (November 1995), 7–35. Establishes a point-of-view for understanding southeast Asia as a part of the world. Designed for teaching, but widely useful for its range of subjects and their context.

Murphey, Rhoads. *East Asia: A New History* (Boston, MA: Addison-Wesley, 2nd ed., 2000). Standard textbook history.

Needham, Joseph. *The Shorter Science and Civilization in China*, Vol. I, abridged by Colin A. Ronan (Cambridge: Cambridge University Press, 1978). First volume in Needham's monumental work opening up the scientific accomplishments to an English-reading audience.

Past Worlds: The (London) Times Atlas of Archaeology (Maplewood, NJ: Hammond, 1988). Excellent introduction to the entire subject, including archaeology of ancient China. Lavishly illustrated with maps, pictures, charts.

SarDesai, D.R. *Southeast Asia: Past and Present* (Boulder, CO: Westview Press, 4th ed., 1997).

Schirokauer, Conrad. *A Brief History of Chinese and Japanese Civilizations* (Fort Worth: Harcourt Brace Jovanovich, 2nd ed., 1989).

Schwartz, Benjamin I. *The World of Thought in Ancient China* (Cambridge, MA: Harvard University Press, 1985). Fine analysis of philosophies and policies in ancient Chinese thought and politics.

Seth, Vikram. *Three Chinese Poets: Translations of Poems by Wang Wei, Li Bai, and Du Fu* (New York: HarperCollins, 1993). Translations of classical poetry of classical poets. The insistence on rhyme is sometimes monotonous.

Sima Qian. *Historical Records*, trans. Raymond Dawson (New York: Oxford University Press, 1994). Translation from the works of China's pre-eminent dynastic historian. Clear, readable with introduction to and evaluation of the historian's life and work.

Sima Qian. *Records of the Historian: Chapters from the Shih Chi of Ssu-ma Ch'ien*, trans. Burton Watson (New York: Columbia University Press, 1969). Translation from the works of China's pre-eminent dynastic historian. Places the work in the context of Chinese history and literature.

Sullivan, Michael. *The Arts of China* (Berkeley, CA: University of California Press, 4th ed., rev. 2000). Well illustrated introduction to classical Chinese painting, sculpture, and fine arts.

Sun Tzu [Sunzi]. *The Art of War*, trans. Thomas Cleary (Boston, MA: Shambhala, 1988). Accessible translation of the classic treatise on fighting a war, often through not fighting. A Zen approach. Consulted by Chinese strategists, including Mao.

Waley, Arthur, trans. *Chinese Poems* (New York: Dover, 2000). Marvellous collection by a master translator.

World History Documents CD-ROM

2.7 Sima Qian: The Historian's Historian Writes About the Builder of the Great Wall
2.8 Shi Huang Ti of Qin: A Study in Absolutism
9.1 The Tang Dynasty (618–907): The Art of Government
9.2 Sung (Song) China: Imperial Examination System
9.3 Record of Ancient Matters: Futo No Yasumaro
9.4 Prince Shotoku's Seventeen-Article Constitution
9.5 Pilgrimage to China (840): Ennin
9.6 Thai Civilization: Southeast Asia

INDIAN EMPIRES

CULTURAL COHESION IN A DIVIDED SUBCONTINENT 1500 B.C.E.–1100 C.E.

KEY TOPICS
- New Arrivals in South Asia
- The Empires of India
- Invasions End the Age of Empires
- India, China, and Rome: Empires and Intermediate Institutions

What do we mean by "India"? In this chapter we include the entire subcontinent of south Asia, which includes not only the present-day country of India, but also its neighbors: Pakistan, Bangladesh, Nepal, and Bhutan. Geographers call the entire region a subcontinent because it is so large and so clearly bounded by powerful natural borders. Along its entire southern perimeter it is a peninsula surrounded by oceanic waters: the Arabian Sea to the west and the Bay of Bengal to the east. To the north, the Himalaya Mountains, the highest in the world, form an almost impenetrable barrier. At the eastern and western ends of the Himalayas, rugged spurs of the great range complete the ring of demarcation, but these mountains are lower and more negotiable. Passes such as the Khyber Pass make entrance accessible through the northwest mountains, as does a route through the desert along the western Makran coast.

The peoples who came to India before 3000 B.C.E., for whom we have no historical record, seem to have arrived from a variety of approaches, probably including some by sea voyages from Africa, southeast Asia, and the islands of the Pacific. Since 3000 B.C.E., all the major immigrations have come from the northwest. In modern times British traders and rulers also came by sea (see Chapters 13 and 16). They had an important impact on the subcontinent, but they did not stay.

The geographical area of the subcontinent is equal to about one-fourth the size of Europe. The entire region has been unified into a single empire only once, under British rule in the nineteenth and early twentieth centuries. Asoka Maurya (r. c. 265–238 B.C.E.) was the first person to come close to achieving that goal, but he never captured the far south. Usually, as today, a number of rulers controlled different regions of the subcontinent. It is not surprising, then, that Indian empires did not last more than a few hundred years. Yet unlike Rome, and much more like China, India has maintained a persistent cultural unity over several thousand years. In this chapter we will begin to consider why India dissolved politically into many separate states, and in Chapter 9 we will consider the religious and cultural institutions that nevertheless served to bring a loose unity to the subcontinent. We will consider India as an empire based as much on cultural cohesion as on political and military unity.

NEW ARRIVALS IN SOUTH ASIA

In Chapter 3 we read of the civilization of the Indus valley, which began with the appearance of the first cities in south Asia about 2500 B.C.E. That civilization—the Harappan—began to fade about 1500 B.C.E. for reasons that are not entirely understood. Perhaps simultaneously, perhaps somewhat later, new waves of "Aryan" immigrants arrived.

Opposite **Prince Gautama, Ajanta Cave 1, Maharashtra, India,** *c.* **450–500.** The prince is seated within an ornamental pavilion. Servants are pouring holy water over him.

The Spread of Aryan Settlement

Indo-Aryan A sub-group of the Indo-Iranian branch of the Indo-European group of languages, also called Indic and spoken in India, Sri Lanka, Bangladesh, and Pakistan. The Indo-Aryan languages descend from Sanskrit, the sacred language of Hinduism.

These new arrivals are named not for their race, but for Sanskrit and the other related **Indo-Aryan** languages they spoke. Archaeologists are not certain of the geographical origins of the new arrivals; some claim they came from central Asia, others from the Iranian plateau, while a few suggest Europe. In successive waves of immigration, the nomadic and pastoral Aryans, riding the horses of central Asia and light, spoke-wheeled chariots, mixed with indigenous peoples, migrated slowly eastward, and reached the Ganges valley about the year 1000 B.C.E.

Written Texts

The greatest sources of information for the Aryan immigrations, settlements, and empires are written materials that preserve earlier oral traditions. A special group of bards and chroniclers collected and composed these materials, although they did not attempt to establish a direct chronological, interpretive record of the sort found in Greece or Rome, or in China.

The Vedas. The earliest existing source is one of the four Vedas, the *Rigveda*, 1028 hymns composed in Sanskrit about 1500–1200 B.C.E. at the very time the Aryans were moving into the subcontinent. The Vedas are religious reflections rather than historical accounts, but to the extent that they refer to the life of the Aryan peoples who wrote them, their accounts are probably reliable. They do refer to conquests made by the Aryans in the course of their migrations southward and eastward. Three other Vedas, the *Samaveda*, *Yajurveda*, and *Atharva Veda*, were composed some centuries later. Other religious literature of the Vedic period (1500–500 B.C.E.) include the Brahmanas, which give instructions on rituals and sacrifices, and the Upanishads, which are mystical speculations. These were composed *c.* 700 B.C.E. and afterwards.

The Puranas, or legends and folk tales from earliest times, were finally collected and written down between *c.* 500 B.C.E. and 500 C.E. They contain genealogical lists of rulers from before the first humans were born until historic times, mixing fact and

HOW DO WE KNOW?

Pottery and Philology

Archaeology can tell us comparatively little about the Aryan way of life in the Ganges valley. The valley is a humid, subtropical region, where heavy monsoon rains have not allowed ancient settlements to endure. It is also densely inhabited, making archaeological excavation difficult if not impossible. As a result, we know less about the Aryan settlements along the Ganges than we do about the earlier Indus valley, where the sparsely populated desert sites facilitated relatively easy excavation.

The distribution of pottery—painted grayware dating primarily before 500 B.C.E., and northern black polished ware from after that date—helps us to identify and follow the waves of Aryan

immigration into the Ganges valley. The more recently discovered ocher-colored pottery in the western Ganges valley and the presence of black and red ware further east suggest that by the time the Aryans arrived indigenous peoples had already settled on the land. Since the late 1970s archaeological digs have uncovered small settlement sites dating from 1000–600 B.C.E. throughout the Ganges valley. However, it is difficult to trace in any detail the spread and nature of early Aryan civilization without additional excavations of many other cities and small towns.

Philology helps to establish the dispersion of Indo-Aryan peoples by tracking the spread of their languages. The first known surviving specimens of writing in the Ganges valley are Asoka's rock and

pillar inscriptions in Brahmi script, which date to the third century B.C.E. To track the oral transmission patterns of earlier centuries, anthropologists study texts that recorded them in written form at a much later time, and compare them with the distribution and evolution of today's spoken languages.

- Why is there more archaeological evidence about the Indus valley than the Ganges valley?
- What is the evidence that indigenous peoples preceded the Aryans in the Ganges valley?
- How do the study of pottery and philology complement each other in an analysis of early settlements in the Ganges valley?

fable, human and divine, and making no attempt to distinguish between them. The tales of the Puranas bring the gods of the Aryans into the popular imagination of the multitudes.

The *Mahabharata* and the *Ramayana*. India's two great epics, the *Mahabharata* and the *Ramayana*, recount events that took place between 1000 and 700 B.C.E., although the texts themselves place the action in earlier mythic times. Neither is an historical account, but both provide valuable information on the social structures, the ways of life, and the values of the time in which they were written.

The *Mahabharata* is the longest single poem in the world, some ten times longer than the Bible. Its central story is of a great civil war fought between two branches of the same family. Into its tales, subplots, and asides are woven myth, speculation, folklore, moral teaching, and political reflection that are central to India's living culture. The intermingling of the great themes of life, death, family, warfare, duty, and power give the *Mahabharata* continuing universal appeal. The most famous single segment of the *Mahabharata* is the profound religious meditation and instruction called the *Bhagavad-Gita*, or "Song of God". The *Gita* takes the form of advice given

AT A GLANCE : INDIA

DATE	POLITICAL	RELIGION AND CULTURE	SOCIAL DEVELOPMENT
600 B.C.E.	■ *Janapadas* established		
500 B.C.E.	■ Gandhara and Sind held by Persian Empire (*c.* 518) ■ *Maha-janapadas* established (500–400)	■ Buddha, Siddhartha Gautama (*c.* 563–483) ■ Puranas written (*c.* 500 B.C.E.– 500 C.E.) ■ Vedic period ends (1500–500)	
400 B.C.E.	■ Nanda dynasty in Magadha (*c.* 364–324)		
300 B.C.E.	■ Alexander the Great in south Asia (327–325) ■ Chandragupta Maurya (*c.* 321– *c.* 297) founds Mauryan dynasty (324–185) in Magadha ■ Kautilya wrote *Artha–sastra* (*c.* 300)	■ *Mahabharata* and *Ramayana* (*c.* 300 B.C.E.–300 C.E.)	
250 B.C.E.	■ Bindusara Maurya (*c.* 297– *c.* 272) ■ Asoka Maurya (*c.* 265–238)	■ Rock inscriptions of Asoka ■ Asoka enhances spread of Buddhism ■ Asokan lion column (see p. 250)	■ Mauryan empire extended from Afghanistan to Bay of Bengal to Deccan
200 B.C.E.	■ Sunga dynasty (185–173) ■ Mauryan Empire fractures, along with unity of India (185)	■ Jain influence increases	
150 B.C.E.	■ Menander (Milanda) king of Indo–Greek Empire (*c.* 160–135)	■ Sanchi stupa (p. 288)	■ Trade contacts with S.E. Asia
100 B.C.E.	■ First Shaka king in western India (*c.* 94)	■ Sangam poetry from Tamil culture	
50 C.E.	■ Height of Kushana power under Emperor Kanishka (*c.* 78–*c.* 103)	■ Bhagavad-Gita	
100 C.E.		■ Gandhara Buddha (p. 251) ■ Rise of Mahayana Buddhism	■ Trade flourishes between India and the Central Asian trade routes
200 C.E.		■ Beginning of Hindu–Buddhist influence on southeast Asia	

AT A GLANCE : INDIA (continued)

DATE	POLITICAL	RELIGION AND CULTURE	SOCIAL DEVELOPMENT
300 c.e.	■ Gupta Empire (c. 320–540) established by Chandra Gupta (320–c. 330)	■ Sanskrit used for official business ■ Hindu ascendancy over Buddhism	■ Indian trade contacts with Oc Eo, Funan (300–600)
350 c.e.	■ Samudra Gupta (c. 330–c. 380) expands dynasty throughout north and into south		
400 c.e.	■ Chandra Gupta II (c. 380–c. 415) expands empire to maximum ■ Kumara Gupta (c. 415–455)	■ Cultural "golden age" ■ Panini, Sanskrit grammarian (fl. 400) ■ Faxian, Buddhist pilgrim ■ Ajanta caves (c. 5th–8th C.) (pp. 253, 289)	
450 c.e.	■ Skanda Gupta (455–467) repulses Huna invasion from central Asia (c. 460) ■ Budha Gupta (467–497)	■ Kalidasa composes "Meghaduta" and Shakuntala	■ Sanskrit in S.E. Asia; Indian gods; Buddhism
500 c.e.	■ Hunas gain control of north India	■ Classical urban culture declines	
600 c.e.	■ Pallavas rise to power at Kanchipuram under Mahendravarman I (c. 600–c. 611) ■ Harsha-vardhana (606–647) rules north India from Kanauj ■ Chalukyas rule central India under Pulakeshin II at Badami (608–642)	■ Xuanzang, Buddhist pilgrim	
700 c.e.	■ Arabs conquer Sind (712)	■ Ellora temple complex (p. 283) (757–790) ■ Borobudur, Java (p. 258) (778–824) ■ Khajuraho temple complex (p. 282) (1025–1050) ■ Vedantic philosophy flourishes ■ Angkor Wat, Cambodia (p. 259)	
1100 c.e.	■ Cholas defeat Srivijaya Empire, Sumatra		

to a warrior facing battle, but it expands into professional advice on life, death, and rebirth.

The *Ramayana*, which is much shorter, refers to somewhat later times, and there are many versions. The first known written version in Sanskrit was composed by Valmiki about 700 B.C.E. Its core story tells of the mythical god-king Rama's victory over Ravana, the demon king of Sri Lanka, who had kidnapped his wife, Sita. The diverse versions of the *Ramayana* indicate its great popularity and the variety of its uses. Some focus on the battles between north and south, perhaps a reference to the first Aryan invasions of the south about 800 B.C.E. Some southern versions, however, tend to justify Ravana as defending the south against Rama's invasions from the north. The role of Sita is also told in different ways. Men more frequently praise Sita for her adoration of Rama and her willingness to renounce even her life so that his reputation might remain intact. Women, however, are often critical of Rama for inadequately defending Sita in the first place, then for doubting her fidelity to him during her captivity in Sri Lanka, and, finally, for bowing to public skepticism of her loyalty by exiling her from his royal court.

Indian sailors, merchants, and priests carried their culture to southeast Asia, and the *Ramayana* has become a national epic in several of the countries of that region, especially in Thailand and Indonesia, where it is often dramatized by live actors and through puppetry. In India, the story is retold each year on the holiday of Dussehra, which celebrates the victory of good over evil with great color and pageantry. Broadcast on Indian national television in serialized form for about a year each, the *Mahabharata* and the *Ramayana* drew audiences of hundreds of millions for each weekly episode in the mid-1980s. In this way, modern technology keeps alive and vital the ancient literature of India in tens of millions of eagerly receptive homes. The epics live on in the West also. In 1985 the British theatrical producer Peter Brook staged a nine-hour version of the *Mahabharata* in English and French.

Despite these literary sources and their implicit evidence of major political and social change, there are no purely historical written records for these crucial centuries in Indian history. Gradually, however, other records do begin to appear and cast light on the changes that were taking place. Codes of law and statecraft, such as the *Artha-sastra* from around 300 B.C.E., and Asoka's rock inscriptions about a half-century later illuminate politics and imperial ideology. Many more such codes appeared in later times, together with Buddhist and Jain texts that usually include chronologies and some interpretation.

Visitors from outside also give periodic "snapshot" accounts of India. These include the observations by Megasthenes (*c.* 350–*c.* 290 B.C.E.), a Greek ambassador and historian sent to the court of Chandragupta Maurya about 300 B.C.E., and Menander (Milinda; *fl.* 160–135 B.C.E.), a Greek king of northwest India who became a Buddhist. Later, about 400–700 C.E., Faxian (Fa-hsien; *fl.* 399–414 C.E.) and Xuanzang (Hsuantsang; 602–664 C.E.), Buddhist pilgrims from China, recorded further observations. The travelers' reflections echo their own positions and interests, but in general depict a prosperous country. The earliest of the four visitors, Megasthenes appears to have been most interested in India's geography and history, one that combines many myths with the actual accomplishments of Alexander and Indian forces. He was also fascinated with India's caste system, which he believed to have included seven castes. Like all the travelers, he was impressed by the Indian

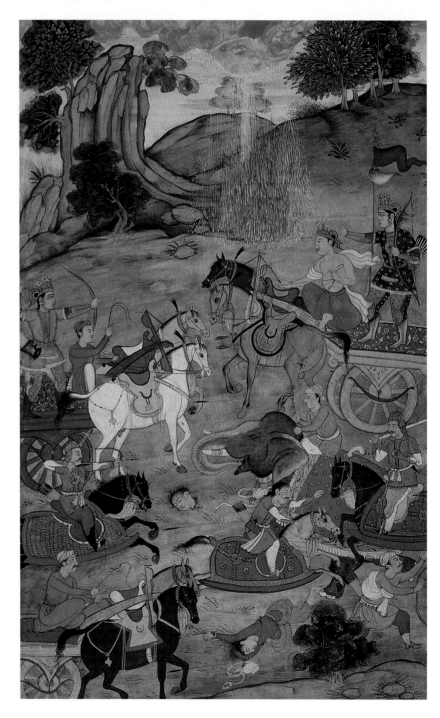

Ahmad Kashmiri, Mughal School, scene from the *Mahabharata*, 1598 C.E. In this illustrated manuscript, a Muslim painter depicts a scene from the great Hindu epic. The god Agni is shown creating fire as a smokescreen to assist his father-in-law, while Arjun quells the flames with magic arrows that release springs of water. (*Oriental & India Office, London*)

Indian School, scene from the *Ramayana*, 1713 C.E. This painting from the *Ramayana* is remarkable for its exquisitely rich gouache illustration. Among the heroes depicted are Rama, his faithful wife Sita, his loyal brother Laxman, and the army of monkey warriors who accompany him in his battle against Ravana, the Lord of Lanka. (*Oriental & India Office, London*)

janapada A large political district in India, beginning about 700 B.C.E.

government's respect for foreigners. Faxian, who came much later, was most interested in visiting places associated with the Buddha's life. He found India a country of rich and prosperous cities, where peace and order prevailed and the wealthy provided for the poor and the disadvantaged.

The Establishment of States

Both archaeological and written sources reveal that, as they settled in India, the Aryans began to build a new urban civilization and to form new states. By 700–600 B.C.E., numerous political groupings, called *janapadas* (populated territories), began to emerge. The leadership of the territories was centered in specific family lineage groups, and as these lineages grew larger and as they cleared more forest land to expand their territorial control, the *janapadas* began to take on the political forms of states with urban capitals and political administrations. Some constituted themselves as republics, others as monarchies. By 500–400 B.C.E., about the time the Persian armies of Darius reached the Indus, sixteen large *maha-janapadas* had emerged in northern India.

By about 300 B.C.E. four of these large states dominated the rest, and one, Magadha, was beginning to emerge as an imperial power over all. As we saw in Chapter 5, Alexander had reached the Indus in 326 B.C.E. and had wanted to continue his sweep all the way across the subcontinent to the ocean that he believed to be at the end of the world. His troops, however, mutinied, refused to proceed further, and forced Alexander to withdraw. Soon thereafter Chandragupta Maurya, the ruler of Magadha, marched his own troops from Magadha into northwest India to fill the power vacuum. With this triumph the Maurya dynasty began to carve out India's first empire.

THE EMPIRES OF INDIA

For the following fifteen centuries, comparatively brief but influential empires alternated with long periods of decentralized and often weak rule. India nevertheless retained a strong sense of cultural unity, based in large part on the intermediate familial, social, economic, and religious institutions that brought cohesion to both ancient and modern India.

In the following pages, therefore, we analyze not only the two major imperial dynasties of ancient India, the Mauryas and the Guptas, but also the more permanent institutions that mediated between the individual and the state. The religious philosophies and social practices of Hinduism that inspire much of the statecraft of these dynasties are discussed briefly here, and are treated much more fully in Chapter 9. Hinduism, as we shall see, is not a specific set of dogmas and rituals, but rather the variety of religious beliefs and practices of the peoples of India—excluding only those who explicitly reject them in favour of a different religion. This separation in the discussion of political and religious practices is somewhat artificial, but it allows us to recognize the importance of each system separately as well as to see them interacting in support of one another.

The Maurya Empire

The Maurya family dynasty succeeded to the throne of Magadha in 324 B.C.E. Its founder, Chandragupta Maurya (r. *c.* 321–*c.* 297 B.C.E.), may have first imagined an India-wide empire from a possible meeting with Alexander the Great, and he conquered much of northern India between 321 and 297 B.C.E. His son, Bindusara (r. *c.* 297–*c.* 272 B.C.E.), expanded still further the empire that his father had created, and Bindusara's son, Asoka (r. *c.* 265–238 B.C.E.), brought the empire of the Mauryas to its greatest extent, ruling from modern Afghanistan in the northwest to the Bay of Bengal in the east and well into the Deccan peninsula in the south. By this time India may have held as many as 100 million people.

Government under the Maurya Dynasty. The Maurya dynasty created an imperial government that ruled over or displaced earlier political structures based only on family lineage. Hereditary family lineage did not cease to be important—after all, the imperial ruling dynasty itself was a lineage—but a new state apparatus stood above it in authority and power. The *Mahabharata* told of a large family of cousins falling into intra-family war over issues of inheritance of power, but by the time of the Mauryas, the state stood above such individual families and lineages.

The new empire expressed its theory of politics in the *Artha-sastra*, or manual of politics and economics, which has been attributed to Kautilya, the minister of Chandragupta Maurya. (The date of composition is not certain, and the text may actually have been written down later, but its ideas were current under the Mauryas. The *Artha-sastra* text had been lost to historians and was rediscovered only in 1909.) The text spoke of *danda niti*, translated into English alternatively and provocatively as the "policy of the scepter" or the "policy of the big stick." It had a cut-throat view of inter-state competition. Even in the earlier age of the *janapadas* (smaller political groupings), Indian political thought had already

Mauryan India. A contemporary of Alexander the Great, Chandragupta Maurya seized control of the kingdom of Magadha and annexed lands to the west, eventually controlling by 300 B.C.E. the strategic trade routes of the Ganges and Indus basins. His grandson Asoka extended the empire west into Seleucid Persia, and south via the wealthy kingdom of Kalinga to gain control of the Deccan by 250.

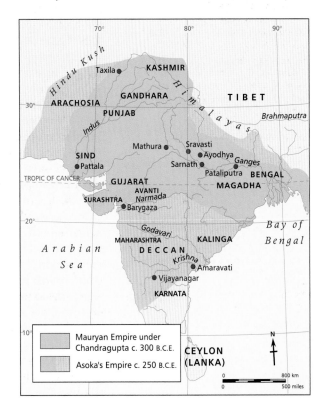

expressed itself in terms of the "justice of the fish"—that is, larger states swallowed smaller ones. The *Artha-sastra* postulated that every state must be on constant guard against all its neighbors, for all were potential enemies. It counseled that strong states be hedged in through mutual treaties among their neighbors, providing a balance of power, while weak states should be attacked and conquered. The *Artha-sastra* regarded the immediate circle of neighbors as potential enemies but the next circle beyond them as potential allies, in keeping with the doctrine that the "enemy of my enemy is my friend." Kautilya's advice included suggestions for collecting taxes and encouraging trade. He was also obsessed with using spies. In this competitive world of constant warfare, the state had come into its own.

The state had many internal regulatory functions as well. First among these was the requirement to provide a powerful setting in which people had the opportunity to seek the four major goals of life in accord with Hindu philosophy: *artha* (wealth), *kama* (sensual pleasure), *dharma* (the fulfillment of social and religious duties), and *moksha* (the release from earthly existence and union with the infinite power of the universe, achieved, if at all, at the time of death).

The state helped to enforce rules of behavior between males and females. This relationship charged men with power over women and the responsibility for protecting them, while women were expected to run the household in accordance with the wishes of men and to be available for the pleasure of men. As the *Kama Sutra* explained, "By a girl, by a young woman, or even by an aged one, nothing must be done independently, even in her own house." Women's property rights were always very limited, and in some periods they had none. On the other hand, some professions, notably weaving, were open to women. Hindu views of women's proper role and behavior are discussed briefly on page 257.

The state also regulated the behavior of its subjects in terms of the rules of the caste. In Hindu belief each person has a social, economic, and ritual position, which was inherited at birth directly from his or her parents. Although this status may, in practice, be changed with difficulty, in theory it remains for life and on into future generations. Caste status not only governs private behavior, it also gives people different, unequal status under law. (The origins, rationale, and functions of the caste system as part of Hindu religious belief are discussed in detail on pages 257–8.) It was the task of the state to enforce these caste distinctions, especially their differential rankings, liabilities, and rights in legal proceedings.

The state also regulated religious establishments. The larger Hindu temples and Buddhist monasteries developed considerable economic and political power based on the land and resources that devout followers, especially wealthy landlords, businessmen, and often kings themselves, donated to them. They also influenced a wide range of public and private decisions made by their devotees, and the state attempted to regulate the use of this wealth and power.

guild A sworn association of people who gather for some common purpose, usually economic. In the towns of medieval Europe, guilds of craftsmen or merchants were formed in order to protect and further the members' professional interests and for mutual aid.

The state also enforced rules developed by India's **guilds**, associations of businessmen and producers. Closely associated with the *jati*, or subcastes, these mostly urban groups convened to set work rules, prices, and weights and measures, and to enforce quality control. Independent of the state, the guilds could nevertheless call on the state to enforce the regulations they had agreed upon.

Some students of Indian social structures have asked why the business guilds seem never to have attempted to gain direct control of the government in India as they did in medieval Europe. The answer is not entirely clear, but caste distinctions designated some people for government and military careers, and others for business, separating those who were permitted to take up the bow and the sword in using force to gain government control from those who could wield influence only through wealth. In Europe businessmen both armed themselves and hired troops; in India, it seems, they did

SOURCE

Asoka, India's Buddhist Emperor

Until just over a hundred years ago, little was known about Asoka, the Mauryan emperor who held sway over the bulk of the Indian subcontinent from 265 to 238 B.C.E. In the nineteenth century, however, inscriptions that Asoka had made on pillars and rocks to spread his name and ideals were deciphered, and for the first time in modern history Asoka's identity and teachings were understood.

Asoka had constructed at least seven pillar edicts and had inscribed at least fourteen major and numerous minor rock edicts which have been discovered and excavated across many regions of India. Most are written in Brahmi script and are the oldest existing writing in India. The script, although an early variant of Sanskrit, had been lost for centuries until a British official, James Prinsep, redeciphered it in 1837. He also analyzed the collective significance of the rock and pillar edicts discovered up to his time along with materials on Asoka found in early chronicles in Ceylon (modern-day Sri Lanka).

Asoka's famed conversion to Buddhism, a dramatic turning-point in his life, is described in the Thirteenth Major Rock Edict. The carnage he had created in his military victory at Kalinga and the suffering of his victims had left Asoka with a terrible sense of remorse. As reparation for his actions, he proclaimed his renunciation of violence and acceptance of Dhamma, *the teachings of the Buddha that promote compassion, tolerance, and honesty.*

A hundred and fifty thousand people were deported, a hundred thousand

Asoka, as depicted in a nineteenth-century engraving.

were killed and many times that number perished. Afterwards, now that Kalinga was annexed, the Beloved of the Gods [Asoka] very earnestly practiced *Dhamma*, desired *Dhamma*, and taught *Dhamma*. (Thapar, *Asoka*, p. 255)

He did not however renounce the conquest and annexation of Kalinga, and while he disavowed violence as a general principle, he seemed to retain it as an option of state policy, especially in dealing with the tribal people of the hills.

the Beloved of the Gods conciliates the forest tribes of his empire, but he warns them that he has power even in his remorse, and he asks them to

repent, lest they be killed. (Thapar, *Asoka*, p. 256)

To spread his message and promote a universal faith, Asoka dispatched missionaries throughout his empire and beyond. He also made his own journeys to practice Dhamma *and help alleviate suffering, especially in rural areas. The Sixth Major Rock Edict proclaims Asoka's dedication to public welfare:*

I consider that I must promote the welfare of the whole world, and hard work and the dispatch of business are the means of doing so. Indeed there is no better work than promoting the welfare of the whole world. And whatever may be my great deeds, I have done them in order to discharge my debt to all beings. (Thapar, *Asoka*, p. 253)

Projects implemented by Asoka to improve the welfare of his people included the founding of hospitals, the planting of medicinal plants and trees, and the building of some 84,000 stupas (Buddhist burial mounds) and monasteries. In his bid to create a more tolerant, compassionate society, Asoka granted religious groups outside of Buddhism the freedom to worship, but at the same time encouraged them to respect the beliefs and practices of other sects. The sacrificial use of animals was banned.

Asoka's active contribution to the spread of Buddhism had a lasting impact. His inscriptions offer us tangible evidence of the great influence Buddhism had not only on his own life but on Indian life and thought as a whole.

neither. They sought to influence the warrior classes, but not by taking up arms against them.

With so many responsibilities for regulating the interests of conflicting groups internally, and recognizing the need to remain constantly vigilant against powerful neighbors, Chandragupta Maurya and his son Bindusara attempted to build a highly centralized administration with a group of well-paid central ministers and bureaucrats, a powerful military, and an efficient system of spies dispersed throughout the empire.

Asoka, India's Buddhist Emperor. At first Asoka followed similar policies, and he was especially effective at enlarging the empire through military force, but nine years into his administration, he abruptly changed course. In 260 B.C.E. Asoka defeated Kalinga (now Orissa), incorporating this eastern kingdom into his empire. The killing and chaos required to win the victory soured his heart, and he determined to become a different person and a different ruler. He converted to Buddhism, a religion firmly committed to nonviolence, and began to dispatch missionaries throughout his realm as well as to parts of south India beyond his own borders, and to Syria, Greece, Egypt, and, probably, southeast Asia. He sent his own son on a mission to Sri Lanka and the island kingdom permanently converted to Buddhism.

For thirty years after the battle of Kalinga Asoka's reign brought general peace to India and the further expansion of a new, more universalist ethic for a people who were increasingly settling down from nomadism into stable agricultural and urban life. Buddhism, diminishing the importance of the brahmin castes, was especially attractive to merchant castes and guilds, and Asoka's patronage was apparently also good for business.

Successor States Divide the Empire. Following Asoka's death in 238 B.C.E., no emperor was strong enough to maintain centralized power, and the Mauryan Empire went into a half century of decline. One of his military commanders assassinated the last Maurya king in 184 B.C.E. The Mauryan dynasty came to an end, and with it the unity of India. The subcontinent subsequently divided among many regional rulers, including some rulers who invaded and seized control of large territories.

The Mauryas had always depended on the power of their lineage as the core of their rule, but they had not continued to produce emperors of the power and charisma of Chandragupta, Bindusara, and Asoka. The Maurya lineage had not institutionalized its state into a permanent form. India dissolved again into a variety of contesting states.

The Sunga dynasty, 185–173 B.C.E., ruled the core region that remained from Magadha. With Indian governments faltering, Indo-Greeks, the inheritors of Alexander's empire stationed in Afghanistan and Bactria, invaded in 182 B.C.E., capturing the northwest all the way south to the coastal cities of Gujarat. They produced a hybrid culture with the Indians they conquered. King Menander (*fl.* 160–135 B.C.E.), an Indo-Greek, carried on a profound conversation with the Buddhist monk Nagasena, who introduced the king to his religion. Their dialogue is still studied today as the *Questions of King Milinda*. Gandharan art, synthesizing Greek and Indian contributions, flourished in this period, as did the city of Taxila, the great center of trade, culture, and education in the northwest. Finally, large caches of Indo-Greek coinage reflect the importance of trade routes running through the northwest and linking India to the great silk routes of central Asia.

Lion capital of the pillar erected by Asoka at Sarnath, Mauryan, c. 250 B.C.E. The polished sandstone columns erected by the Emperor Asoka at places associated with events in the Buddha's life, or marking pilgrim routes to holy places, are of special interest for their 7-foot-tall capitals. These provide us with the best remaining examples of Mauryan imperial art and are rich in symbolism. For instance, the Buddha was spoken of as a "lion" among spiritual preachers, whose sermon penetrated to all four corners of the world, just as the lion's roar established his authority in the forest.

Indo-Greek coins (obverse and reverse), central Asia. The Indian subcontinent was linked to the silk route by trade routes that passsed through Afghanistan and the Kushan Empire and continued westward. These economic connections account for the large quantity of Indo-Greek coinage, like this example showing the Macedonian king Demetrius I (c. 337–283 B.C.E.). (*British Museum, London*)

"The Bimaran reliquary." Gandhara, first century C.E. The central figure of the Buddha is flanked by the Hindu gods Indra and Brahma. This mixed grouping reflects the crossroads nature of the Gandhara region, the border between today's Pakistan and Afghanistan.

New invaders conquered and displaced the old. In Chapter 7 we read of tribal wars in east Asia, on the borders of China, which pushed Mongol groups westward to Rome. The Shakas, who invaded and ruled parts of northwest and western India for about a century, *c.* 94 B.C.E. to *c.* 20 C.E., were one of these tribal groups. They, in turn, were displaced by yet another, larger nomadic tribal group from east Asia, known in India as the Kushanas. The geographical extent of Kushana rule is not entirely known, but it seems to have included today's Afghanistan, Pakistan, Kashmir, and India as far south as Gujarat and its ports. The most outstanding Kushana king, Kanishka (r. *c.* 78–*c.* 103 C.E.), seems also to have promoted Buddhism and may have adopted it himself. With a single ruler controlling all these lands, trade between the subcontinent and the central Asian silk routes flourished.

The Gupta Empire

In 320 C.E. a new dynasty began its rise to power in the Ganges valley, apparently through a fortunate marriage. The founder came from a dynasty of no historical fame, but he married a princess of the powerful Licchavi lineage. Reflecting a deep sense of history and a desire to gain legitimacy, he deliberately named himself after the founder of the Mauryan Empire and became Chandra Gupta I (r. 320–*c.* 330). His son, Samudra Gupta (r. *c.* 330–*c.* 380), earned a reputation as one of India's greatest military conquerors. The record of his battles, inscribed on an already existing Asoka pillar at Allahabad, touches all regions of India: the far south, the east to Bengal and even Assam, the north to Nepal, and the mountain kingdoms of central India, which had often remained independent because of their inaccessibility.

Samudra's son and successor, Chandra Gupta II (r. *c.* 380–*c.* 415), conquered the Shakas and annexed western India, including prosperous Gujarat and its Arabian Sea

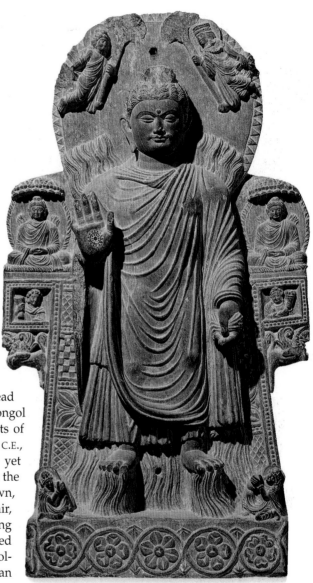

Buddha of the "great wonders." Gandhara, third to fourth century C.E. The Hellenistic draping of the Buddha's clothing again represents the crossroads nature of the Gandhara region. The Buddha's right hand is raised in the *abhaya mudra*, or hand position expressing reassurance. His palm is marked with the Wheel of the Buddha's Doctrine of Enlightenment.

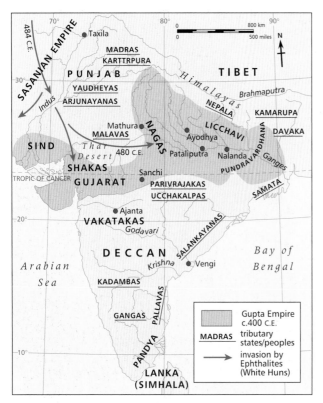

Gupta India. In the fourth century C.E. the indigenous Gupta dynasty gained control of the middle Ganges and rapidly built an empire straddling the subcontinent from Sind to the Ganges delta, augmented by a web of treaty and tributary arrangements with neighboring powers. This classical age of Indian civilization was destroyed by invasions of central Asian peoples in the fifth century.

ports, for the first time in five centuries. By marrying his daughter to the head of the Vakataka lineage, he cemented an alliance with his kingdom in central India. Other Gupta alliances were established through marriages with other powerful lineages in the Deccan. The fourth Gupta emperor, Kumara Gupta (r. *c.* 415–455), presided over a great empire now at peace.

Gupta rule was often indirect. Following many of their distant military victories, the Gupta emperors abdicated the tasks of administration and withdrew, demanding only tribute payments. Nor did their alliances with other kingdoms and lineages call for direct rule. In the Ganges valley heartland of the empire, the Gupta emperor himself appointed governors at provincial levels, and sometimes even at the district level. At the most local level of the village and the city, however, the Guptas allowed considerable independence to local administrators. The area they administered directly was much smaller than the Mauryan Empire, and the two centuries of Gupta rule and influence are considered India's "golden age" more for their cultural brilliance than for their political power.

A Golden Age of Learning. The Guptas presided over a resurgence of Sanskrit literature and Hindu philosophy. The great playwright Kalidasa (fifth century C.E.) composed two epic poems, a lyrical poem "Meghaduta," and the great drama *Shakuntala*, the first Sanskrit drama translated into a Western language in modern times. Much of the important literature that had been transmitted orally was now transcribed into writing, including the Purana stories of legend and myth. Further emendations were made to the great epics, the *Mahabharata* and *Ramayana*.

Plaque of musician with lyre, central India, fifth century C.E. During the Gupta period terra cotta plaques, such as this cross-legged lyre-player, were used to adorn the exterior of temples. It comes from one of the few surviving examples of free-standing brick temples decorated in this way at Bhitargaon in the Gupta heartland. (*British Museum, London*)

The Gupta Empire began to use Sanskrit for its official correspondence. The great grammarian Panini (*fl. c.* 400 B.C.E.) had fixed the essentials of Sanskrit grammar in his *Astadhyayi* (perhaps the most systematic grammar ever produced in any language), but the Mauryas and most other earlier rulers had used Prakrit, a variant of Sanskrit that was closer to the common language of the people. Now Sanskrit law codes, such as the *Laws of Manu*, and manuals of statecraft, such as Kautilya's *Artha-sastra*, were studied, revised, and further codified. Many locally powerful officials patronized scholars, humanists, and artists. Important academic centers for Buddhist learning flourished at Taxila in the northwest and Nalanda in the Ganges valley. Chinese Buddhist scholars visited and described these academies, although their descriptions of Hindu academies have not been preserved to the present.

The Resurgence of Hinduism. This was especially an age of the resurgence of Hindu religious authority, and major systems of Hindu philosophy were articulated. The most influential, Vedanta (the culmination, or end, of the Vedas), expanded upon the teachings of the Upanishads. Vedanta philosophy posed a powerful, attractive alternative vision to Buddhism, and Hinduism began to regain ascendancy over Buddhism in India.

Wall-painting illustrating the *Vishvantara Jataka,* **Cave 17, Ajanta. Gupta period, fifth century** C.E. The rock-cut sanctuaries of Ajanta in northwest Deccan were abandoned for centuries until they were rediscovered in 1817 by British soldiers hunting tigers. The twenty-nine cave temples contain some of the earliest surviving Indian painting and mark the last true flowering of Buddhist art in the subcontinent prior to the ascendancy of Hinduism. This erotic fresco, taken from a folk tale, portrays Prince Vishvantara informing his queen that he has been banished from his father's kingdom.

The caste system was elaborated and enforced in more detail. Rulers, high-level administrators, and wealthy landlords gave patronage to brahmins in the form of land grants and court positions. Brahmin priests also asserted their role in ritual performance. Buddhism, which had flourished through the patronage of earlier empires, and the support of business classes, ceded the performance of many of its own rituals to brahmin priests, and began to decline.

Despite its military and cultural achievements, the Gupta dynasty's power began to wane in the late fifth century C.E. The subcontinent was once again politically divided and subject to one wave of invader-rulers after another. These internal divisions and conquests by outsiders continued until the modern independence of India and Pakistan in 1947, and of Bangladesh in 1971.

INVASIONS END THE AGE OF EMPIRES

In the fifth century, new conquerors came through the passes of the northwest, overthrowing the Gupta Empire and establishing their own headquarters in Bamiyan, Afghanistan. These invaders were the Hunas, a branch of the Xiongnu, the nomadic Mongol tribes that roamed the regions north of the Great Wall of China and sometimes invaded. In previous expansions, they had driven other groups west, even into the Roman Empire, as we saw in Chapter 6. Domino fashion, these groups pushed one another westward. The Shakas had invaded India as a result of this sequence in about 94 B.C.E. The Kushanas followed about a century later. Now the Hunas themselves arrived in force. These same ethnic peoples were called Huns in the Roman Empire, which they invaded under Attila in 454 C.E.

The Hunas and their Legacy

Skanda Gupta (r. 455–467) repulsed the first Huna invasions, which occurred about 460 C.E. But the continuing Huna presence across India's northwest border seems to have disrupted international trade and reduced Gupta wealth. Skanda's successor apparently could not hold the empire together, and regional strongmen began to assert their independence. With central control thus weakened, Huna armies invaded again in about 500 C.E., and for the next half-century they fought in, and controlled much of, northern and central India.

From their capital in Bamiyan, Afghanistan, the Hunas ruled parts of India as their own imperial provinces. As in Rome, they earned a reputation for great cruelty, reported not only by Indians but also by Chinese and Greek travelers who visited the region. Huna rule proved brief, however. In 528 C.E. Indian regional princes drove them northwest as far as Kashmir. About a generation later Turkic and Persian armies defeated the main Huna concentrations in Bactria, removing them as a force in India.

Although it was short-lived, the Hunas' impact on India was considerable. Their invasion further weakened the Gupta Empire, enabling regional powers to dismember it and to declare their own independence. Except for a brief reign by Harshavardhana or Harsa (r. 606–647), king of the north Indian region of Kanauj, no further unification of all of India was ever seriously attempted from inside the subcontinent until the twentieth century. (The Moghul and British Empires, discussed in Chapters 14 and 16, were created by invasions from outside, although the Moghuls later settled within the subcontinent.)

The urban culture of north India dimmed. The Buddhist monasteries, which the Hunas attacked with especial force, never recovered. On the other hand, by opening up their invasion routes the Hunas indirectly enriched India's population pool.

Gurjaras and Rajputs entered western India more or less along with the Hunas and settled permanently. The modern Indian states of Gujarat and Rajasthan are named for them and their descendants.

The legacies of the Hunas in India—the destruction and dismemberment of the Gupta Empire, the reduction in inter-regional trade, the decline of culture, and the introduction of new nomadic groups into already settled imperial lands—quite closely mirror those of their Hun brothers in the Roman Empire. Even the timings were similar, products of the same emigration from central Asia. Of the great empires of the ancient world, only China was capable of defeating or assimilating these invaders without losing its own coherence and identity.

Regional Diversity and Power

The history of the Indian subcontinent tends to be written from the perspective of the Ganges valley as the center of political power and influence. (The settlements of the central Indus valley discussed in Chapter 3 did not endure, and the region is now a desert.) The Aryans established their centers in the Ganges region; the Mauryas continued the pattern; so did the Guptas; the later Moghuls established their capitals there; the British ultimately followed Moghul patterns by also placing their capital at Delhi; and today's government of independent India has followed suit. But other regions of India have always been important, too. Even at times when India has been unified, regional powers have regularly challenged the supremacy of the Ganges heartland. In periods such as the millennium from 500 C.E. to 1500 C.E., when India had no central empire, the outlying regions asserted their status as independent states.

The major regions of India speak different languages from one another, although imperial rulers have usually introduced a unifying link language for inter-regional communication: Prakrit under Asoka; Sanskrit under the Guptas; Persian under the Moghuls; and English under the British. Today, India uses two

For an interactive version of this map, go to: http://www.prenhall.com/spodek/map8.3

Classical South Asia. As kingdoms rose and fell, India had no centralized empire for almost a thousand years. Local powers grew up, often based on different languages and ethnicities. More powerful groups occupied the richest lands, while the weaker were forced into the hills. The roots of today's separate states of India lie in some of these early ethnic kingdoms.

Earthenware sculpture, Nilgiri Hills, south India, early centuries C.E. The Tamil culture of southern India generated not only a separate language and an expressive literary tradition, but also distinctive artifacts. A buffalo cult among the Todas, the largest of the Nilgiri Hills tribal groups, led to the creation of this characterful figurine, made to decorate the lid of an urn containing ashes. (*British Museum, London*)

official languages, Hindi and English. Pakistan uses Urdu and English, and Bangladesh, Bengali.

The peoples of different regions have immigrated into the subcontinent from different places and at different times, some preceding the Aryans, others following them. In regions dominated by Aryans, many of these non-Aryans (people who spoke other languages) found a place within the social system of the Aryans. The highly stratified Aryan society—marked by caste and *jati*—could make room for the absorption of various groups by creating new categories for them within the hierarchy. When not consolidated into larger empires, these diverse groups have created their own political-cultural administrations. The peoples of Gujarat in the west and of Bengal and Orissa in the east have all seen themselves as distinct ethnic groups, even when they were ruled from the north, and as independent when that rule was broken. Regional dynasties came and went.

The indigenous tribal peoples whose immigration predates any historical records, referred to today as *"adivasis"*—that is, "original inhabitants," or **tribals**—generally inhabit less accessible areas, frequently in hilly tracts not easy to farm. They have attempted to protect their independence from outside exploitation by maintaining their inaccessibility.

The most distinct and separate region was the far south. Here, several lineage and ethnic groups fought to maintain their independence: the Pandyas in the extreme southeast; the Pallavas just north of them along the coast; and then the Cholas and the

tribals The aboriginal peoples of the Indian sub-continent, who are outside the **caste** system and live quite separately from the rest of society, generally in remote places.

SOURCE

Tamil Culture in Southeast India

The dominant language of the southeast was Tamil, and it developed an especially expressive literature. The poetry of the southern Tamilian academies, called sangam *poetry and written 100 B.C.E.– 250 C.E., set in counterpoint the private, bittersweet play of love against a public atmosphere of warfare and strife. This poetry was lost until scholars rediscovered it in the later decades of the nineteenth century. It has been brought to the attention of the English-speaking world especially by the efforts of the late A.K. Ramanujan.*

A King's Double Nature

His armies love massacre,
he loves war,

yet gifts
flow from him ceaselessly.

Come, dear singers,
let's go and see him in Naravu

    where, on trees
    no axe can fell,
    fruits ripen, unharmed
    by swarms of bees,
    egg-shaped, ready
    for the weary traveller
    in the fields of steady, unfailing harvests;
    where warriors with bows
    that never tire of arrows
    shiver
    but stand austere
    in the sea winds
    mixed with the lit cloud
    and the spray of seafoam.

There he is,
in the town of Naravu,
tender among tender women.

Harvest of War

Great king,

you shield your men from ruin,
so your victories, your greatness
are bywords.

Loose chariot wheels
lie about the battleground
with the long white tusks
of bull-elephants.

Flocks of male eagles
eat carrion
with their mates.

Headless bodies
dance about
before they fall
to the ground.

Blood glows,
like the sky before nightfall,
in the red center
of the battlefield.

Demons dance there.
And your kingdom
is an unfailing harvest
of victorious wars.

      (trans. by A.K. Ramanujan, pp. 131, 115)

HOW DO WE KNOW?

Coins and Excavations

About 50 C.E., a Greek merchant wrote of the Roman trade with Malabar, the southwest coast of India, in his great compendium of trade in the Indian Ocean, The Periplus of the Erythrean Sea:

> They send large ships to the market-towns on account of the great quantity and bulk of pepper and [cinnamon]. There are imported here, in the first place, a great quantity of coin; topaz, thin clothing, not much; figured linens, antimony, coral, crude glass, copper, tin, lead, wine, not much, but as much as at Barygaza [the flourishing port of Gujarat, further north] ... There is exported pepper, which is produced in quantity in only one region near these markets ... Besides this there are exported great quantities of fine

pearls, ivory, silk cloth, spikenard from the Ganges, [cinnamon] from the places in the interior, transparent stones of all kinds, diamonds and sapphires, and tortoise shell. (cited in Kulke and Rothermund, p. 106)

Numerous hoards of Roman gold coins throughout south India provide archaeological evidence of trade between Rome and India. In 1945, the British archaeologist Sir Mortimer Wheeler discovered the remnants of a Roman trading post at Arikamedu, a fishing village adjacent to Chennai (formerly Madras), and he excavated the brick foundations of large halls and terraces, cisterns, fortifications, and ceramics that had been produced in Italy between 30 B.C.E. and 35 C.E. This outpost suggests that the traders actually

carrying the goods across the Arabian Sea were foreign rather than Indian: Arabs, Jews, and Romans. The Roman historian Pliny complained that Rome was sending around 50 million sesterces a year to India to buy its luxuries, although he also noted that they sold in Rome for one hundred times that amount.

- What seems to have been the main item exported from Europe to pay for Indian goods?
- Why was this pattern of exports disturbing to the Roman Pliny?
- Is it surprising to you that India's import-export trade with Rome was apparently not carried by Indians, but by Arabs, Jews, and Romans? Why or why not?

Chalukyas. Along the southwest coast, the Perumal and Cera lineages dominated. The place of their origin and the time of their immigration are not clearly known, but their languages form a linguistic family called Dravidian, not related to the Sanskritic family of languages of the north.

Sea Trade and Cultural Influence: From Rome to Southeast Asia

Imperial governments based inland in the Ganges valley and even further to the north-west tended to draw their economic power from their control over those rich lands and from trade through the mountain passes connecting to the silk routes. Many of the regional, coastal powers, on the other hand, traded by sea. This gave them wide-ranging external connections, from the Roman Empire in the west to southeast Asia in the east.

Under the Roman emperor Caesar Augustus (r. 27 B.C.E.–14 C.E.), Rome annexed Egypt, thereby opening up a trade route to the east by way of the Red Sea. Rome controlled enormous wealth, which generated a powerful economic demand for goods from Asia. Roman traders learned from the Arabs to sail with the southwest monsoon winds from the Red Sea to the west coast of India; about six months later they could sail back with the northeast monsoon.

Southeast Asia: "Greater India"

Some of the luxuries shipped to Rome were first brought to India from southeast Asia. Indian sailors traveled to all the coastal countries of modern southeast Asia: Myanmar (formerly Burma), Thailand, Cambodia, Vietnam, Malaysia, and Indonesia. To anchor this trade, they established settlements in port cities such as Oc Eo in Funan, in the southernmost part of modern Vietnam. Brahmin priests and Buddhist monks settled along with the traders, serving the Indian expatriates and attracting local converts at the same time.

Long before any of these trade ventures, in the third century B.C.E. King Asoka had dispatched missionaries to Sri Lanka and to Myanmar to begin the process of converting these lands to Buddhism. Local mythology and Chinese historical records tell (quite different) stories of the arrival of a brahmin priest named Kaundinya. As a result of his activities, Funan adopted Sanskrit as the language of the court and encouraged Hinduism.

Funan remained an independent state, not an Indian province. Indeed, in the third century C.E. Funan extended its own rule to southern Vietnam, Cambodia, central Thailand, northern Malaya, and southern Myanmar from its capital at Vyadhapura, near present-day Phnom Penh. Wherever Funan expanded, it encouraged the adoption of Indian culture.

Ironically, Funan later infused Indian culture even among those who conquered it. When Champa expanded southward into Funan lands, the kings of Champa began to adopt the cultural, linguistic, and architectural styles of the Pallavas of south India that were then current in Funan. Bhadravarman, a Champa king, built the first Champa temple to the Hindu god Shiva.

Two additional areas under Funan hegemony later established independent states with strong Hindu and Buddhist cultural elements: Java, which was ruled by the Sailendra lineage, and the kingdom of Srivijaya in Sumatra. In Java, the Sailendras built an extraordinary Buddhist temple at Borobudur in 778–824. When the Sailendras

Borobudur, Java, late eighth century. This monument, the supreme example of Buddhist art in southeast Asia and Indonesia, is a fantastic microcosm, reproducing the universe as it was known and imagined in the Mahayana school of Buddhist theology. The relief sculptures, of which there are some 10 miles, represent the doctrine of karma, the cycle of birth and rebirth, of striving, and release from the Wheel of Life.

attacked the Khmer peoples of present-day Cambodia, the Khmers unified their defenses under King Jayavarman II (r. 790–850). He established a new capital and introduced Hindu temples and philosophies into the whole region around it at Angkor, which later became the location of one of Hinduism's greatest temples constructed by Jayavarman VII (r. 1181–1219).

The diffusion of Indian religious and cultural forms continued for centuries throughout southeast Asia. It proceeded almost entirely peacefully, spread by priests and traders. A few exceptions, however, stand out. The Pallava king Nandivarman III (r. c. 844–866) supported a military camp on the Isthmus of Siam to protect a group of south Indian merchants who were living and working there. The Chola king Rajendra I (r. 1014–47) dispatched a fleet to Sumatra and Malaya and defeated the Srivijaya Empire. It appears that his goal was to keep the trade routes open and to support India's shippers on the competitive sea lanes; he claimed no territory. In 1068–9, the Cholas apparently intervened in a dispute among rival claimants to rule in Malaya, conquered a large part of the region, but then turned it over to their local client.

Angkor Wat, Angkor, Cambodia, early twelfth century C.E. Dedicated to the Hindu god Vishnu, this huge, jungle-bound temple complex once served as the centerpiece of the Khmer Empire, originally founded in 880. Decorated with extensive relief sculpture, the temples of Angkor Wat were intended to emulate mountains in dressed stone.

INDIA, CHINA, AND ROME: EMPIRES AND INTERMEDIATE INSTITUTIONS

Chapter 7 ended with a comparison of the long-lived and far-flung Roman and Chinese empires. The following section extends that comparison to include the Indian empires. The comparison alerts us to the need to analyze empires not only from the top-down perspective of the central administration but also from the bottom-up—from their foundations in local regions and institutions.

Sources

Comparing India, China, and Rome is not straightforward. To begin with, India lacks the detailed political, military, economic, administrative, and personal records that would facilitate comparison in any detail. Rome and China compiled official histories, and a wide variety of personal accounts have also survived to the present. For India, on the other hand, we must often rely on the observations of foreign visitors for our best accounts. Even the life, writings, and policies of Asoka, now regarded as ancient India's greatest emperor, were lost from historical consciousness for centuries until his rock and pillar edicts were deciphered in the nineteenth century.

Administration

Second, both Rome and China built institutionalized bureaucracies and systems of administration, lasting for centuries in Rome and millennia in China. By contrast, India's states and empires generally seemed to be extensions of family lineages. Even the most powerful of ancient India's empires, the Mauryan and Gupta, were family holdings. Despite the administrative rigor suggested by Kautilya's *Artha-sastra*, even Chandragupta Maurya's dynasty began to weaken after the death of his grandson Asoka. In India, power remained more personal than institutional.

International Relations

The *Artha-sastra* characterized inter-state relations by the law of the fish, the large swallow the small: "When one king is weaker than the other, he should make peace with him. When he is stronger than the other, he should make war with him." Despite Asoka's renunciation of the excessive use of force, the constant rise and fall of kingdoms and small empires throughout India suggest that Kautilya's view generally prevailed. We do not have records of internal revolts against states and empires in India. Instead, dissidents would abscond to a neighboring state where they felt they could live more freely and where they might join the official military to fight against their former ruler.

Invasion of the Hunas

Indian empires did not expand beyond the borders of the subcontinent. Indian trade missions in southeast Asia exported cultural and religious innovations along with their material cargo, but they made little attempt to establish political rule there. On the other hand, outsiders frequently invaded the subcontinent.

Remarkably, the one political experience that the empires of India, Rome, and China shared was invasion and at least partial conquest by the Hunas (Huns, Xiongnu) and by the peoples they displaced. Indeed, the last three chapters point to the great importance of the Hunas/Huns in world history, especially from the third through the sixth centuries C.E. Historical records include not only the builders and sustainers of sedentary empire, but also their nomadic challengers. (We will explore this issue further in considering the Mongols in Chapters 12 and 14.)

Local Institutions and the State

In Rome and China, government touched much of the population directly, through taxes, military conscription, imperial service, and aggressive bureaucracies. The state was fundamental to all areas of life. In India, on the other hand, the state seemed to preside over a set of social institutions that had previously existed, were more deeply rooted, and were more persistent through time. These institutions included family lineages, aware and proud of their histories; caste groups, each presiding over its own occupational, ritual, and ethnic niche; guild associations, overseeing the conditions of economic production and distribution; local councils, providing government at the village and town level; and religious sects, which gave their members a sense of belonging, identity, and purpose. The state was important in overseeing the activities of all of these groups, but it existed only in the context of their existence. States and empires came and went, but these varied, pervasive institutions carried on in their own rhythms. In India political authority was intimately connected, and sometimes subordinated, to familial, cultural, and religious power. In the next chapters on religion in world history, and especially in Chapter 9 on Hinduism and Buddhism, we will explore these connections.

INDIAN EMPIRES
WHAT DIFFERENCE DO THEY MAKE?

Ancient Indian empires shed light both on the later history of India and on the structure of empires generally. Modern India is a direct descendant of its ancient empires and shares their diversity, their many languages and ethnic groups incorporated into the whole, their "unity in diversity." The ancient texts—philosophical, political, and epic—continue to provide a common cultural imagery to the majority of Indians today, and their influence extends to large parts of southeast Asia. Questions concerning the ethics of rule, answered quite differently by such practitioners of politics as Emperor Asoka and such political advisers as Kauṭilya, author of the *Artha-sastra*, continue to be debated. Most of all, the power of the subdivisions of empire—regions, castes, guilds, village organizations—retain their importance in modern India and in its south Asian neighbors as well.

The tensions between center and periphery, between centralized bureaucracy and regional interest groups, that mark all empires to some degree were—and are—especially prominent in India. While China and Rome draw most attention for their ability to build the central institutions of empire and impose them on their subjects, India teaches more lessons in imperial structures that integrate and balance already existing local forms of organization. This is more a matter of degree than of complete difference in philosophy of government: Asoka was willing to use brute force to conquer and subdue enemies of his empire even after his adoption of Buddhism; Rome and China were willing to accommodate local interests if they did not threaten imperial control. Nevertheless, more than Rome or China, India gives us an example of empire built up by integrating its constituent parts rather than by defeating them or completely assimilating them.

Because these patterns continue to re-appear in empires throughout history and around the globe, these early explorations of Rome, China, and India give us some of the tools we need to analyze the successes—and the failures—of imperial structures down to our own times.

Review Questions

- India is almost always described as "diverse." Why? What are the bases of its diversity?
- Modern historians sometimes complain that too much attention is paid to Aryans and not enough to other groups in early India. What are some of these other groups, and why do you think they may not receive adequate attention?
- Asoka has gained a reputation as perhaps the greatest of all Indian emperors. What do you think is the basis of that judgment?
- What were the most important consequences of the successful invasion of India by the Hunas?
- Discuss the overseas influences of India on the broader world from the time of the Emperor Asoka until about 1000 C.E.
- Compare the power of the Maurya and Gupta Empires in India with the Roman Empire and the Chinese Empire under the Qin and Han Dynasties.

Suggested Readings

PRINCIPAL SOURCES

Basham, A.L. *The Wonder That Was India* (New York: Grove Press, 1954). Graceful, comprehensive, standard introduction to early Indian history. Dated on Indus valley, but still valid on imperial India.

Embree, Ainslee, ed. and rev. *Sources of Indian Tradition*, Vol. I: *From the Beginning to 1800* (New York: Columbia University Press, 2nd ed., 1988). The principal source for materials on ancient India, especially on high culture, philosophy, and politics.

Kulke, Hersmann and Dietmar Rothermund. *A History of India* (Totowa, NJ: Barnes and Noble Books, 1986). Brief, accessible, excellent introductory history. Kulke brings his considerable expertise on ancient India to the section on empires.

Thapar, Romila. *Ancient Indian Social History* (New Delhi: Orient Longman, 1978). Principal introduction to the institutions of ancient India.

Thapar, Romila. *Asoka and the Decline of the Mauryas* (Delhi: Oxford University Press, 1963). Principal introduction to the empire of the Mauryas.

Thapar, Romila. *A History of India*, Vol. I (Baltimore, MD: Penguin Books, 1966). Principal general introduction to ancient Indian history.

Thapar, Romila. *Early India: From the Origins to A.D. 1300* (Berkeley, CA: University of California Press, 2003).

Thapar, Romila. *Interpreting Early India* (New York: Oxford University Press, 1992). Philosophy of studying ancient India, opposing the use of history to advance political programs.

ADDITIONAL SOURCES

Allchin, F.R., *et al. The Archaeology of Early Historic South Asia: The Emergence of Cities and States* (Cambridge: Cambridge University Press, 1995). Somewhat dated, but very accessible, wide ranging introduction for a non-specialist.

Craven, Roy C. *A Concise History of Indian Art* (New York: Oxford University Press, n.d.).

Green, Peter. *Alexander of Macedon, 356–323 B.C.* (Berkeley, CA: University of California Press, 1991). For Alexander at the threshold of India.

Hughes, Sarah Shaver and Brady Hughes, eds. *Women in World History*, Vol. I: *Readings from Prehistory to 1500* (Armonk, NY: M.E. Sharpe, 1995). Good readings on India.

Lockhard, Craig A. "Integrating Southeast Asia into the Framework of World History: The Period Before 1500," *The History Teacher* XXIX, No. 1 (November 1995), 7–35. Designed for preparing syllabi, with good conceptual scheme for understanding southeast Asia.

Hammond Atlas of World History (Maplewood, NJ: Hammond, 5th ed., 1999). Indispensable world history atlas.

Past Worlds: The (London) Times Atlas of Archaeology (Maplewood, NJ: Hammond, 1988). Fascinating introduction to history through archaeological finds. Lavishly illustrated with maps, pictures, charts.

Ramanujan, A.K., ed. and trans. *Poems of Love and War: From the Eight Anthologies and the Ten Long Poems of Classical Tamil* (New York: Columbia University Press, 1985). An outstanding modern poet and scholar translating classical Tamil poetry.

Richman, Paula, ed. *Many Ramayanas: The Diversity of a Narrative Tradition in South Asia*

(Berkeley, CA: University of California Press, 1991). The Ramayana has many interpretations and uses. Richman provides an astonishing, scholarly array of them.

Rowland, Benjamin. *The Art and Architecture of India: Buddhist/Hindu/Jain* (New York: Penguin Books, 1977). Still a useful introduction.

SarDesai, D.R. *Southeast Asia: Past and Present* (Boulder, CO: Westview Press, 1994). A standard introduction to an understudied field.

Schwartzberg, Joseph E., ed. *A Historical Atlas of South Asia* (Chicago, IL: University of Chicago Press, 1978). A scholarly, encyclopedic coverage of history through geography. Superb research tool.

Spodek, Howard and Doris Srinivasan, eds. *Urban Form and Meaning in South Asia: The Shaping of Cities from Prehistoric to Precolonial Times* (Washington D.C.: National Gallery of Art, 1993). Papers from an outstanding international scholarly seminar.

Thapar, Romila. *Cultural Pasts: Essays in Early Indian History* (New Delhi: Oxford University Press, 2000). Principal introduction to the institutions of ancient India.

Tharu, Susie and K. Lalita, eds. *Women Writing in India 600 B.C. to the Present*, Vol. I (New York: The Feminist Press, 1991). Beginning of the movement to include women's materials in the history of ancient India. Wide-ranging subjects.

◉ World History Documents CD-ROM

3.7 "King Milinda": The Greek World's Incursion Into India
3.8 Fa-Hsien: A Chinese Perspective on Gupta India

Politics and Religion

R eligions, the subject of our next unit, have at least two faces: the personal and the public. As a personal experience, religion is a search for meaning and purpose in the life of each individual. When whole societies seek meaning and purpose, however, the path can lead to the union of religion and politics. This union has existed through most of human history. The separation of religion and politics—the separation of Church and state—that we find in the United States and other modern nations, marks a turning point in world history. From earliest times, priests of religion and political rulers usually made common cause. Often high priest and ruling king would be united in a single person. We have seen examples in Gilgamesh of Mesopotamia, the pharaohs of ancient Egypt, and, at least in name, the emperors of Rome following Augustus Caesar. The authority and power of the ruler and of the priest reinforced one another.

Even in the ancient world, however, there were occasions when religious leaders would challenge and confront political rulers, accusing them of transgressing the will of god. Most notably, the Hebrew prophets confronted their kings with these accusations, as we will see in Chapter 10.

Religion reinforced the powers of legislation as well as those of administration. About 1750 B.C.E., when Hammurabi composed one of the earliest known legal codes, he did so in the name of the gods of Babylonia. The stele on which the code was inscribed is topped by a relief showing the god of justice, the sun-god Shamash, commissioning Hammurabi to write down his law code. The inscription itself opens with the words

> ... lofty Anum, king of the Anunnaki,
> (and) Enlil, lord of heaven and earth ...
> named me
> to promote the welfare of the people,
> me, Hammurabi, the devout, god-fearing prince,
> to cause justice to prevail in the land,
> to destroy the wicked and the evil,
> that the strong might not oppress the weak.
>   (Pritchard, p. 164)

Hammurabi's Code, Susa, c. 1700 B.C.E. Diorite stele. (*Louvre, Paris*)

The stele itself was carried from Babylon to Susa apparently as a spoil of war about 1200 B.C.E., and in the winter of 1901–2 French archaeologists moved it to Paris.

Many subsequent legal codes were also said to be the word of god, delivered in person or through a supernatural presence. In the Jewish tradition, for example, Moses ascended Mount Sinai to receive directly from God the Ten Commandments engraved in stone, and, orally, the remainder of the earliest Jewish code of laws. As the biblical Book of Exodus describes the process, Moses became the ethical, legislative, executive, judicial, and inspirational leader of the Jewish people, largely through his constant contact with God. Moses' brother Aaron served as high priest, performing the ritual celebrations of the nation.

Michelangelo's famous sculpture of Moses descending Mount Sinai with the engraved tablets of the Ten Commandments in his hands captures this sense of merged religious and political authority. The commandments themselves are a mixture of religious rules—"Thou shalt have no other gods before me"—with civil laws—"Do not murder. Do not steal." But several of the commandments seem to lie somewhere between these two spaces, such as "Observe the Sabbath Day. Honor Thy Father and Thy Mother. Do not covet."

Christianity was transformed from an often-persecuted religion, mostly of the downtrodden, to the dominant religion of the Roman Empire by the conversion of the Emperor Constantine. Jesus' sermons, addressed primarily to the humble, meek, and poor, condemned the power of the wealthy and preached aloofness from political power. St. Paul, as he went on his missionary voyages to spread the new faith, often ran afoul of Roman authorities. Several emperors launched campaigns against the early Christians. But after Constantine accepted Christianity, in 313 C.E., formally converting on his deathbed, the Roman government began withdrawing its

Michelangelo Buonarroti, Moses, Tomb of Pope Julius II, Rome, 1513. Marble. (*San Pietro in Vincoli, Rome*)

support from pagan religious groups and transferring funds instead to Christian churches. With this imperial backing, Christianity soon triumphed over all the other religions contesting for recognition and followers to begin its reign as the dominant religion of Europe and, subsequently, the largest religious group in the world.

Islam merged political and religious authority even more fully. Muhammad was both the prophet of the message of God and the political commander of the *umma*, the international community of Muslim believers. Indeed, it was only after he assumed political leadership of the city-state of Medina, that Muhammad's teachings were recognized as authoritative. Until that time in his life, unsympathetic observers, seeing him enter a cave on a mountainside and return with tales of receiving truths—ultimately written down in the Quran—thought of Muhammad as somewhat deranged. Only after his successful political leadership was joined to his religious vision in Medina, and then after his return to Mecca as conqueror of that city, was he widely received as the final Prophet of God. From Muhammad's time onward, Islam saw religious law and political authority united in one institution headed by one person, the caliph. Not until the twentieth century did this union of religion and politics come under serious attack.

Hinduism, with its many deities, portrayed gods intervening in political and military activity on a regular basis. The most famous and best-loved Hindu religious text, the *Bhagavad-Gita*, tells of a civil war between two branches of the same family. The Lord Krishna serves as the chariot driver and military and spiritual guide to Arjuna, leader of the Pandava branch. As Arjuna despairs of a war in which either he dies or he kills members of his own family, Lord Krishna teaches him lessons to guide him to a deeper understanding of life and death.

On a more mundane level, earthly Hindu kings were in charge not only of the secular administration of their

Krishna instructs Arjuna, India, 10th century C.E.

realm, but also of the administration of temple estates, which could be quite large and quite wealthy, and of ensuring that the rules of social order, including the rules of caste hierarchy, were enforced. In effect, that meant that while brahmins might be the leading caste group in theory, it was only the supporting force of the king-rulers that secured their position in practice. In exchange for this royal support, brahmins were expected to endorse the kings' authority.

The Buddha, son of a king, left his father's palace to seek truths about life and suffering. His discoveries through meditation led him on a path that diverged from both the warrior-ideal of his family and the Hinduism of his youth. He became instead a great and compassionate teacher of many monk-disciples. His message became the basis of a major religion, only three centuries after his death, however, when it was adopted by King Asoka, ruler of India. When Asoka found that rule meant warfare, killing, and suffering, he found solace in the Buddha's message of nonviolent compassion toward all creatures. He tried to live this message himself, to the extent that it was consistent with the demands of government, and he spread it throughout his kingdom. According to tradition, he dispatched missionaries to give instruction in Buddhist ethics throughout east Asia, and sent his own son to spread the message to Sri Lanka. Within India, he erected numerous pillars and rock edicts inscribed with references to the influence of the Buddha's teaching on his own administration. Many later kings—and merchant-princes as well—followed Asoka's example in adopting Buddhism. They may have been attracted not only by its message of compassion, but also by its emphasis on equality among castes; this equality reduced the prestige of the brahmins and raised their own.

The next section will discuss the evolution of world religions in terms of their doctrines, organization, cultural contributions, and their impact on individuals. It will also point out the importance of the relationship between government and religion in the evolution of both.

Marble head of Constantine, Palazzo dei Conservatori, Rome, 313 C.E.

QUESTIONS

1. To what degree is the importance of religions related to their spiritual and ethical messages?
2. To what degree is the importance of religions related to their cultural contributions to the arts and the humanities?
3. To what degree is the importance of religions related to their alliances with political and economic institutions?

PART

4

The Rise of World Religions

2500 B.C.E. –1500 C.E.

NOT BY BREAD ALONE: RELIGION IN WORLD HISTORY

Religion is the sense of human relationship with the sacred, with forces in and beyond nature. Throughout history people have felt the need to establish such relationships with powers that they believed capable of protecting and supporting them and capable of providing a deeper sense of significance to life and the possibility of some form of existence after death. Some people have thought of these forces as abstract and remote; others have regarded them as having personalities, as gods. Some people, of course, do not believe in such powers at all, or they are skeptical.

Mircea Eliade (1907–86), perhaps the leading historian of religion in the mid- and late twentieth century, wrote:

> In the most archaic phases of culture, *to live as a human being* was in itself *a religious act*, since eating, sexual activity, and labor all had a sacramental value. Experience of the sacred is inherent in man's mode of being in the world.
>
> When we think of the sacred we must not limit it to divine figures. The sacred does not necessarily imply belief in God or gods or spirits ... it is the experience of a reality and the source of an awareness of existing in the world ... The sacred cannot be recognized "from outside." It is by means of internal experience that each individual will be able to recognize it in the religious acts of a Christian or a "primitive" man. (Eliade, *Ordeal by Labyrinth*, p. 154)

From the earliest human records we have encountered such religious needs. More than 100,000 years ago Neanderthals buried their dead in anticipation of their journey to an afterlife. Archaeologists have found Neanderthal burials with flint tools, food, and cooked meat at Teshik-Tash in Siberia; the burial of a man with a crippled right arm at the Shanidar cave in the Zagros Mountains of Iraq; and graves covered with red ocher powder, including some group burials, in France and central Europe. With the evolution to modern humans, far more elaborate burials appear. Perhaps the most extraordinary yet uncovered are at Sungir about 100 miles east of Moscow, in Russia. Dating back 32,000 years, the five skeletons uncovered there include one—apparently an adolescent boy—buried with about 5000 beads, 250 canine teeth of foxes, and carved ivory statues and pendants, and another—apparently an adolescent girl—with 5274 beads in addition to other objects.

Burial rituals—the formal recognition of our common mortality—suggest that the earliest humans thought about the significance of their lives. They hoped that life might

Stonehenge, Salisbury Plain, England, Neolithic period. Stonehenge was once believed to be a temple of Druids or Romans, but even its third phase, about 2000 B.C.E., preceded these groups in England.

continue in some form, even after death, and they must also have dedicated a part of their energies to transmitting values that would continue after they died and to creating institutions to perpetuate those values.

In Part 2 we saw that many early cities and states were dedicated to particular gods or goddesses, sometimes even carrying their names. Gilgamesh, builder of the city of Uruk in Mesopotamia, was two-thirds a god and sought eternal life. In Babylon, Hammurabi transmitted his legal code in the name of the god Shamash. Egyptian hymns proclaimed the divinity of the pharaohs. Chinese of the Shang dynasty used oracle bones to augur the will of transcendent powers. Athens was named for the goddess Athena.

The empires we discussed in Part 3 sought the validation provided by religious leaders and, in exchange, gave financial and political backing to religious institutions. The emperors of Rome and China served also as high-priests for their people. When the Roman emperor Constantine believed that he had been miraculously assisted by Jesus, he transferred his allegiance from paganism to the embattled Christian church. Hinduism and its caste system provided India with a sense of unity and continuity. In several states of south and southeast Asia, Buddhist priests were called upon to validate the authority of rulers. Confucianism, which was discussed in

Chapter 7 as one of the pillars of the Chinese imperial system, presents a profound theory of ethical human relationships. Unlike the religions just mentioned, however, Confucianism has very little otherworldly focus.

This part focuses in greater depth on the role of religion in human history. Chronologically, the part spans the entire period, from earliest humans to about 1500 C.E. Its key focus, however, is from *c.* 300 C.E. to *c.* 1200 C.E. In this period Hinduism became more fully defined and systematized throughout India; Buddhism rose to great importance in China, Japan, and southeast Asia; Judaism, exiled from its original home in Israel, spread with the exiles throughout much of west Asia, the Mediterranean basin, and northern Europe; Christianity grew into the great cultural system of Europe; and Islam radiated outward from the pivotal center of Afro-Eurasia to the far corners of the eastern hemisphere. These five religions often confronted one another, sometimes leading to syncretism, the borrowing and adaptation of ideas and practices; sometimes to competition; and sometimes to direct conflict.

HINDUISM AND BUDDHISM

THE SACRED SUBCONTINENT: THE SPREAD OF RELIGION IN INDIA AND BEYOND
1500 B.C.E.–1200 C.E.

9

KEY TOPICS

- Examining Religious Beliefs
- Hinduism
- Buddhism
- Comparing Hinduism and Buddhism

This chapter begins with a definition of religion and a description of early religious practices. It proceeds to a brief history of early Hinduism, the most ancient of existing major religions, and analyzes its evolution as the principal cultural system of the Indian subcontinent. Buddhism emerged out of Hinduism in India and spread throughout central, eastern, and southeastern Asia, defining much of the cultural and religious life of this vast region. Its history concludes this chapter.

EXAMINING RELIGIOUS BELIEFS

Organized religious groups usually build on the religious experiences proclaimed by their founders and early teachers. All five of the religions we study in this part grew from such experiences, and many of these experiences were called miraculous—that is, they are contrary to everyday experience, and they can be neither proved nor disproved. For example, most Hindus believe that gods have regularly intervened in human life, as Krishna is said to have done at the Battle of Kurukshetra. They also believe in the reincarnation of all living creatures, including gods. Buddhists believe in the revelation of the Four Noble Truths and the Eightfold Path to Siddhartha Gautama (the Buddha) under the bodhi (bo) tree at Bodh Gaya in northern India; most also believe that Siddhartha was a reborn soul of an earlier Buddha and would himself be born again. Most Jews have believed in special divine intervention in the lives of Abraham and his descendants, a special divine covenant with the Jewish people, and a revelation of divine law at Mount Sinai. Most Christians have believed in the miracle of Jesus' incarnation as the Son of God and his resurrection after death. Most Muslims believe that God revealed his teachings to Muhammad through the angel Gabriel.

Historians, however, cannot study miracles. Historical study seeks proof of events, and such proof is not usually available for miracles. Almost by definition, a belief in miracles is a matter of faith, not of proof. Moreover, history is the study of the regular processes of change over time, and miracles, again by definition, are one-time-only events, which stand outside and defy the normal processes of change.

What can be studied are the manifestations and effects of religious beliefs on people's behavior. Sincere believers in religious miracles restructure their lives accordingly, creating and joining religious organizations to spread the word about these miracles and about their own experiences with them. These new organizations formulate rules of membership, and they infuse their beliefs into everyday life by establishing sacred time, sacred space, sacred liturgy, and sacred literature and culture. Historically,

Opposite **Shiva with the corpse of the goddess Sati, southern India, 17th century. Bronze.** Lord Shiva, one of the most revered of all the gods of Hinduism, is usually portrayed in awe-inspiring forms because he is the god of destruction, but that destruction sets the stage for later rebirth and reconsruction. (*Trivandrum, Government Museum*) when religious identity combined with political power, group boundaries became even more important, marking in-group from out-group, separating "us" from "them," sometimes even leading to violent conflict. Historians do study these manifestations and effects of religious beliefs:

- **The sanctification of time** Each religion creates its own sacred calendar, linking the present with the past by commemorating each year the key dates in the history of the religion and in the life of its community. It marks dates for the performance of special rituals, celebrations, fasts, and community assemblies. In addition to the community calendar, members of religious organizations create their own individual and family calendars to mark the rites of passage—the great life cycle events of birth, puberty, marriage, maturity, and death—so that each event has its own ritual observance. Religions especially formulate rules of marriage in an attempt to channel the raw, powerful, mysterious, and often indiscriminate forces of youthful sexuality to conform to the norms of the group.

- **The sanctification of space** Each religion creates its own sacred geography by establishing shrines where miraculous acts are said to have occurred; where saints had been born, flourished, or met their deaths; and where relics from the lives of holy people are preserved and venerated. The most sacred of these sites become centers of pilgrimage. As we have seen in earlier chapters, whole cities, and especially their sacred quarters, were dedicated to gods and goddesses, and thought to be under their special protection.

- **The sanctification of language and literature** Each religion shapes its own use of language, literature, and artistic imagery. The Hebrew Bible, the Greek New Testament, the Arabic Quran, the Sanskrit Veda and epics, and the Pali Buddhist Tripitaka have provided linguistic and literary canons across the millennia. In translation these texts have given character to new languages. For example, translations of the Bible by St. Jerome (*c.* 347–419), William Tyndale (*c.* 1494–1536), and Martin Luther (1483–1546) have enriched Latin, English, and German, respectively. The retelling in Hindi by Tulsidas (*c.* 1543–1623) of the Sanskrit Ramayana helped to establish the importance of that modern language in north India. This religious literature usually provides the core of religious liturgy and thus becomes part of the daily expression of faith of the common people. Part 4 quotes religious scriptures extensively because of their centrality to the world's languages, literatures, and imagery.

- **The sanctification of artistic and cultural creativity** Religious sensibilities often inspire specific creative efforts, and religious groups often encourage the creation of art and music to express and enhance their message.

- **The sanctification of family and ancestors** Many religions not only celebrate events of the life cycle, but they also link living generations to those that have gone before. Through prayers and periodic ritual performances such as visits to graves and shrines, current generations are informed that even ancestors who are no longer living still deserve, and require, respect and reverence. Ancestor remembrance and worship situate current life into a deeper historical context and may promote a more conservative outlook on life.

- **The creation of religious organization** As religion moves from individual experience to group membership, organization develops. At one extreme this may be a hierarchical structure with a single leader at the apex and an array of administrative and spiritual orders down to the most local level, the form of the Roman Catholic Church. At another extreme there may be no formal overall organization, and no formal set of rules and regulations, but instead a loose association of local communities related to one another through common beliefs and social structures, the form of Hinduism.

HINDUISM

Hinduism began before recorded time. The other major religions of the world claim the inspiration of a specific person or event—Abraham's covenant; the Buddha's enlightenment; Jesus' birth; Muhammad's revelation—but Hinduism emerged through the weaving together of many diverse, ancient religious traditions of India, some of which precede written records. Hinduism evolved from the experience of the peoples of India.

The Origins of Hinduism

Because Hinduism preserves a rich body of religious literature written in Sanskrit, the language of the Aryan invaders of 1700–1200 B.C.E., scholars believed until recently that Hinduism was a product of that invasion. Even the excavations at Mohenjo-Daro and Harappa, which uncovered a pre-Aryan civilization (see Chapter 3), did not at first alter these beliefs. But as excavation and analysis have continued, many scholars have come to believe that the Indus valley civilization may have contributed many of Hinduism's principal gods and ceremonies. Excavated statues seem to represent the

AT A GLANCE : HINDUISM AND BUDDHISM

DATE	POLITICAL/SOCIAL EVENTS	LITERARY/PHILOSOPHICAL EVENTS
1500 B.C.E.	■ Caste system	■ *Rigveda* (1500–1200)
900 B.C.E.		■ Brahmanas (900–500)
800 B.C.E.		■ Upanishads (800–500)
500 B.C.E.	■ Siddhartha Gautama (Buddha) (*c.* 563–483) ■ Mahavir (b. 540), Jain teacher	■ Buddha delivers sermon on the Four Noble Truths and the Noble Eightfold Path
300 B.C.E.		■ *Mahabharata* (*c.* 300 B.C.E.–300 C.E.) ■ *Ramayana* (*c.* 300 B.C.E.–300 C.E.)
200 B.C.E	■ Buddhism more widespread than Hinduism in India (until 200 C.E.); spreading in Sri Lanka ■ Mahayana Buddhism growing in popularity	
10 C.E	■ 4th general council of Buddhism codified Theravada doctrines ■ Buddhist missionaries in China (65 C.E.)	■ Nagarjuna (*c.* 50–150 C.E.), philosopher of Mahayana Buddhism
300 C.E	■ Spread of Hinduism to southeast Asia	
400 C.E.	■ Hindu pantheon established ■ Buddhism declining in India	■ Puranas written (400–1000) ■ Faxian's pilgrimage to India ■ Sanskrit; Hindu gods, temples, and priests in southeast Asia; Buddhism in southeast Asia
500 C.E.	■ Bhakti begun in south India ■ Buddhist monks to Japan	
600 C.E.	■ Buddhist monks to southeast Asia ■ Buddhism flourishes under Tang dynasty (618–907)	■ Xuanzang's pilgrimage to India
700 C.E.	■ Hindu temples and shrines begin to appear in India ■ Buddhism begins to decline in China ■ Buddhism becoming established in Japan	■ Hindu philosopher Shankaracharya (788–820) ■ Saicho (767–822), Japanese Buddhist priest ■ Kukai (774–835), Japanese Buddhist priest
800 C.E.	■ Hindu priests in southeast Asia ■ Emperor Wuzong attacks Buddhism in China	■ Earliest printed book (*The Diamond Sutra*) (868)
1000 C.E.	■ Muslim invasion of India (1000–1200) ■ Buddhist institutions close in India	■ Hindu philosopher Ramanuja (*c.* 1017–1137)

god Shiva (see p. 270), the sacred bull Nandi on which he rides, a man practicing yogic meditation, a sacred tree, and a mother goddess. Archaeologists increasingly argue that the invading Aryans absorbed religious beliefs and practices, along with secular culture, from the Indus valley and from other groups already living in India when they arrived.

Contemporary anthropological accounts support this idea that Hinduism is an amalgam of beliefs and practices. These accounts emphasize Hinduism's remarkable ability to absorb and assimilate tribal peoples and their gods. Today, about 100 million people, about 10 percent of India's population, are officially regarded as "tribals." These peoples were living in India before the arrival of the Aryans, and they have largely attempted to escape Aryan domination by retreating into remote hilly and forested regions, where they could preserve their own social systems. Hindus have, however, pursued them and their lands, building temples in and around tribal areas. These temples recognize tribal gods and incorporate them with the mainstream deities in an attempt to persuade the tribals to accept Hindu religious patterns. Indeed, one of Hinduism's most important gods, Krishna, the blue/black god, was apparently a tribal god who gained national recognition.

As India's peoples have been diverse, so its evolving religious system is diverse. The concept of "Hinduism" as a unified religion comes from outsiders. Greeks and Persians first encountering India spoke of India's belief systems and practices collectively as "Hinduism," that is, the ways of the peoples on the far side of the Indus River. When Muslims began to arrive in India, beginning in the eighth century C.E., they adopted the same terminology.

Hindu south Asia. Hinduism is the oldest of the world's leading religions, although its geographic range is confined to the peoples of south Asia. Here its impact has been profound, exemplified by the sacred geography of the subcontinent; rivers, mountains, and regions associated with divine mythology are important, and networks of pilgrimage centers and temples provide cultural unity.

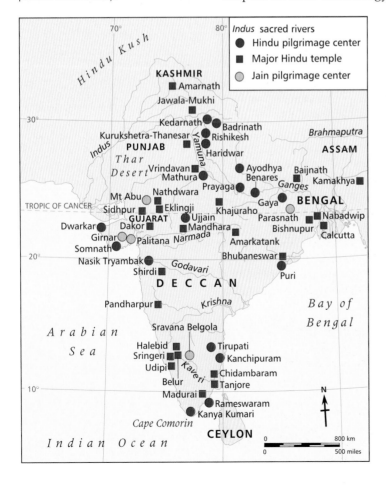

Sacred Geography and Pilgrimage

Hinduism is closely associated with a specific territory, India. Almost all Hindus live in India or are of Indian descent. Within India itself a sacred geography has developed. Places visited by gods and by saints, as well as places of great natural sanctity, have become shrines and pilgrim destinations. Pilgrims traveling these routes have created a geography of religious/national integration, and modern transportation, in the form of trains, buses, and airplanes, has increased the pilgrim traffic throughout India. Some of the most important shrines are at the far corners of India, such as Somnath on the far west coast, Haridwar and Rishikesh in the far north on the upper Ganges, Puri on the east coast, and Kanya Kumari (Cape Comorin) at the extreme southern tip. Travel to all of these shrines would thus provide the pilgrim with a "Bharat Darshan," a view of the entire geography of India. Such pilgrimage routes have helped to unify both Hinduism and India.

Each locality in city and village is also knit together by religious shrines, ranging from the simple prayer niche, containing pictures and statues of the gods of the kind found in even the most humble home; through neighborhood shrines, nestled perhaps into the trunk of an especially sacred tree; to local and regional temples.

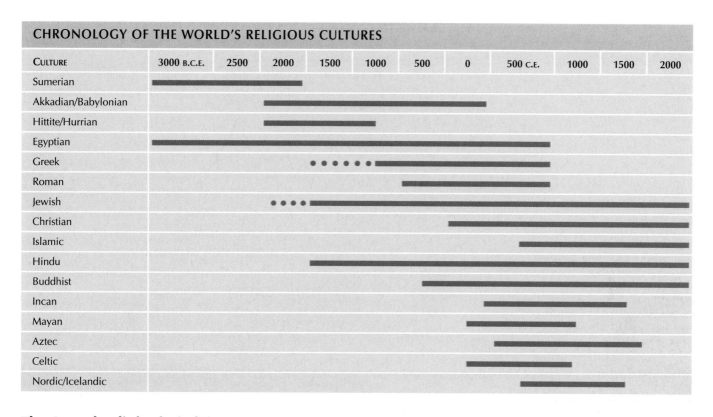

CHRONOLOGY OF THE WORLD'S RELIGIOUS CULTURES

CULTURE	3000 B.C.E.	2500	2000	1500	1000	500	0	500 C.E.	1000	1500	2000
Sumerian											
Akkadian/Babylonian											
Hittite/Hurrian											
Egyptian											
Greek											
Roman											
Jewish											
Christian											
Islamic											
Hindu											
Buddhist											
Incan											
Mayan											
Aztec											
Celtic											
Nordic/Icelandic											

The Central Beliefs of Hinduism

Hinduism has none of the fixed dogmas of most other-worldly religions, and great flexibility and variety of beliefs exist under the general term "Hindu." Nevertheless, sacred texts do provide a set of beliefs and orientations toward life that are very widely shared. Over time, the introduction of new texts to the Hindu legacy marked the evolution of Hinduism as a living, changing system of beliefs and practices.

The *Rigveda*. Between *c.* 1500 and 1200 B.C.E. brahmin priests of the nomadic pastoralist Aryan peoples entering India composed the *Rigveda*, a collection of 1028 verses of Sanskrit poetry, the oldest and most venerated of the four books called, collectively, Vedas. These verses invoke many early gods, including Agni, the god of various kinds of fire; Indra, a phallic god of rain and fertility; Surya, god of the sun; and Varuna, the sovereign of the world who assures that the cosmic law is maintained. They include references to music, dance, and acting as modes of worship. Vedic worship also takes the form of animal sacrifice offered on sacred altars. The *Rigveda* speculates on the creation of the world and on the significance of life in this world, but it does not pretend to offer conclusive answers:

> Who really knows? Who shall here proclaim it? whence things came to be, whence this creation. … This creation, whence it came to be, whether it was made or not—he who is its overseer in the highest heaven, he surely knows. Or if he does not know …?
> (X:129, Embree, p. 21)

Caste. The *Rigveda* also introduces the mythic origin and rationale of the caste system, one of the most distinctive features of Hindu life. Caste began, the *Rigveda* suggests, in a primeval sacrifice of a mythical creature, Purusha. He was carved into four sections, each symbolizing one of the principal divisions of the caste system:

When they divided Purusha, in how many different portions did they arrange him? What became of his mouth, what of his two arms? What were his two thighs and his two feet called? His mouth became the *brahman* [priest]; his two arms were made into the *rajanya* [or *kshatriya*, warrior]; his two thighs the *vaishyas* [business people and farmer/landlords]; from his two feet the *shudra* [person of the lower working class] was born. (X:90 Embree, pp. 18–19)

Apparently, the Aryan invaders were even then thinking of a social system that separated people by occupation and sanctioned that separation through religion. The caste system that developed in India was probably the most rigidly unequal and hierarchical of any in the world. Caste status was hereditary, passing from parent to child at birth. Each caste was subject to different local legal rules, with upper castes being rewarded more generously and punished less severely than lower. Only upper castes were permitted to receive formal education, and the separate castes were not to intermarry nor to even dine with one another. Their vital fluids were distinct and different, and the blood and semen of one group were not to mingle with those of another. The food fit for one group was not necessarily appropriate for others: brahmin priests were to be vegetarians, but *kshatriya* warriors were to eat meat.

Commentators throughout the centuries have searched for additional roots of the caste system, more grounded in social, economic, and political rationales. Many have seen India's caste system as a means of ordering relationships among the multitude of

Gouache illustration from Bhanudatta's *Rasamanjari*, 1685. Krishna, the eighth *avatar* (incarnation) of Vishnu, is always depicted with blue/black skin and is renowned for his prowess as a warrior and a lover. In this scene from one of his amorous adventures, a woman hinders a forester from felling the tree under which she has arranged to meet Krishna for a romantic tryst.

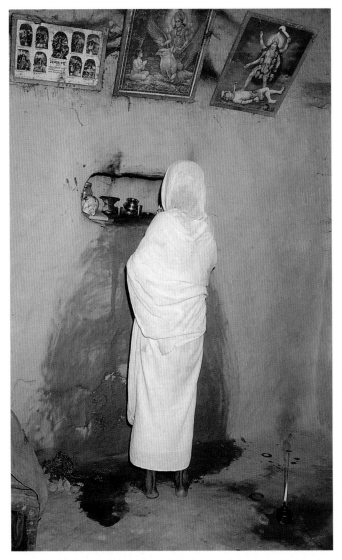

Prayer room and shrine, India. Nearly every Hindu home in India has a shrine with pictures or small statues of various deities, and many have a special prayer room set aside for their worship. For *puja*, or worship, which is observed every day, ritual purity is emphasized; the time for offerings to the gods is after the morning bath or evening wash.

MAJOR RELIGIONS OF THE WORLD, 2002

Religion	Number of followers	Percentage of world population
Christians	2,019,052,000	32.9
Roman Catholics	1,067,053,000	17.4
Protestants	345,855,000	5.6
Orthodox	216,314,000	3.5
Anglicans	80,644,000	1.3
Independents	391,856,000	6.4
Unaffiliated Christians	111,689,000	1.8
Muslims	1,207,148,000	19.7
Hindus	819,689,000	13.4
Nonreligious	771,345,000	12.6
Chinese folk religionists	387,167,000	6.3
Buddhists	361,985,000	5.9
Ethnic religionists	230,026,000	3.8
Atheists	150,252,000	2.5
New-religionists	102,801,000	1.7
Sikhs	23,538,000	0.4
Jews	14,484,000	0.2
Baha'is	7,254,000	0.1
Confucianists	6,313,000	0.1
Jains	4,281,000	0.1
Shintoists	2,732,000	0.0
Zoroastrians	2,601,000	0.0

(Encyclopedia Britannica Book of the Year 2002)

immigrant groups in India's multi-ethnic population, consolidating some at the top and relegating others to the bottom. Others have seen caste as the result of a frozen economic system, with parents doing all they could to make sure that their children maintained at least the family's current occupational status. They sacrificed the possibility of upward mobility in exchange for the security that they would not fall lower on the social scale.

Many suggested that the system was imposed on the rest of the population by an extremely powerful coalition of brahmin priests and *kshatriya* warrior-rulers. Such a dominant coalition is common in world history, and the Indian situation was simply more entrenched than most.

MAJOR HINDU GODS AND GODDESSES

A shrine with images of one or more of the thousands of gods in the pantheon can be found in every devout Hindu home. The most widely worshiped gods are probably Shiva with his consort Parvati, and Vishnu with his consorts Lakshmi and Saraswati. But most Hindus offer at least some form of devotion to more than one god.

Brahma	The creator god, whose four heads and arms represent the four vedas (scriptures), castes, and yugas (ages of the world).
Ganesh	The elephant-headed god, bringer of good luck.
Kali	Shiva's fierce consort—the goddess of death—is shown as a fearsome, blood-drinking, four-armed black woman.
Krishna	The eighth avatar (incarnation) of Vishnu, depicted with blue or black skin. He is honored for his skills as a lover and a warrior; with his consort **Radha**.
Rama	The personification of virtue, reason and chivalry; with his consort **Sita**, revered for her loyalty.
Shiva	God of destruction, whose dancing in a circle of fire symbolizes the eternal cycle of creation and destruction.
Sitala	Mothers traditionally pray to this goddess to protect their children from disease.
Vishnu	The preserver, a kindly god, who protects those who worship him, banishes bad luck, and restores good health; with his consorts **Lakshmi**, the goddess of wealth, and **Saraswati**, the goddess of wisdom and the arts.

Historians employ the insights of anthropologists as they attempt to understand the historical origins and basis of the caste system. Anthropological observation shows that the four generalized castes of the Veda are not the actual groupings that function in practice today. Instead, India has tens of thousands of localized castes, called *jatis*—indeed, there are thousands of different brahmin groups alone. In practice, caste is lived in accordance with the accepted practices of these local groupings, in the 750,000 villages, towns, and cities of India. From customary law to dining patterns to marriage arrangements, caste relationships are determined locally, and there is no national over-arching religious system to formulate and enforce rules. Residents of any given village, for example, may represent some twenty to thirty castes, including all the various craftspeople and artisans. There may be more than one caste claiming brahmin status, or *kshatriya*, or *vaishya*, or *shudra*. Anthropologists therefore differentiate between the mythological four *varna* groups of the Vedic caste system and the thousands of *jati* groups through which caste is actually lived in India. Both historians and anthropologists are convinced that the same multitude of castes that they find "on the ground" today existed also in the past. Eventually, "outcastes," or "untouchables" emerged, people who were outside the caste system because of the "polluting" work they performed, which might include dealing with dead animals or handling those who died.

Throughout Indian history there have been revolts against the hierarchy of the caste system. In the twentieth century and into the present century the government of India has acted assertively to eliminate the historic discrimination of the caste system, as we shall see in Chapter 20. Nevertheless, through the millennia, caste has usually been more important than government in determining the conditions of life of most people. Personal identity and group loyalty were formed far more by caste locally than by government, which tended to be remote.

The Brahmanas and Upanishads. A second collection of Sanskrit religious literature, dating from *c.* 900–500 B.C.E., sets out rules for brahmins, including procedures for sacrifice and worship. These scriptures, the Brahmanas, include discussions of the origins of various rituals and myths of the immortal gods.

The Upanishads, composed 800–500 B.C.E., are devoted primarily to mystical speculation and proclaim the oneness of the individual and the universe. The universal spirit, Brahman, and the soul of each individual, *atman*, are ultimately the same substance, just as individual sparks are the same substance as a large fire. In time, each *atman* will be united with the universal Brahman. To reach this unity, each soul will experience reincarnation (*samsara*) in a series of bodies, until it is purged of its attachments to the physical world and achieves pure spirituality. Then, at the death of this final body, the *atman* is released to its union with the Brahman.

The Upanishads introduce several concepts fundamental to almost all strands of Hinduism. *Dharma* is the set of religious and ethical duties to which each living creature in the universe is subject. These duties are not the same, however, for each creature; they differ according to ritual status. *Karma* is the set of activities of each creature and the effects that these activities have on its *atman*. Each action has an effect on the *atman*; activities in accord with one's *dharma* purify the *atman*; activities in opposition to one's *dharma* pollute it. "Good *karma*," the good effects brought about by actions in accord with *dharma*, will finally enable the *atman* to escape *samsara*, or reincarnation, and reach *moksha*, release from the travails of life on earth and ultimate union with the Brahman. Thus Hinduism sees reward and punishment in the universe as a natural consequence. Good, *dharmic* actions carry their own reward for the *atman*; activities opposed to *dharma* carry their own negative consequences. Activities in this life earn good or bad *karma*.

The Upanishads also introduce the concept of the life cycle, with its different duties at each stage. The first stage, *brahmacharya*, is the youthful time of studies and celibacy; the second, *gruhasta*, the householder stage, is for raising a family; the third, *vanaprastha*, literally forest-wandering, is for reflection outside the demands of every-day life; and the last, *sannyasin*, is for total immersion in meditation in preparation for death and, ideally, for *moksha*.

These early scriptures established a set of principles that constitute the core of Hindu belief: caste, *dharma*, *karma*, life stages, *samsara*, and, ultimately, *moksha*, the union of *atman* and Brahman. They represent a rational system of order in the universe and in individual life. They teach the importance of dharmic activities in this world in order to reach *moksha* in the deeper reality beyond. They are transmitted from *guru*, or teacher, to *shishya*, or student. The codification of many of these specific behavioral norms for each caste in *The Law of Manu* attempted to institutionalize the position of the priests and to elaborate on core Hindu beliefs. Written in the first or second century B.C.E., the treatise almost certainly reflected earlier practices, spelling out the appropriate relationships between social classes and between men and women.

Although it reveres the brahmin priest (not to be confused with the Brahman spirit of the universe), Hinduism is ultimately accessible to each individual, even to those of low caste. Despite the hierarchy of the caste system, Hinduism allows enormous spiritual scope to each individual. It has no core dogma that each must affirm. Each individual Hindu may claim his or her own unique sense of spirituality. This universal accessibility of Hinduism is most clear in three later forms of literature that have become a kind of folk treasury (in contrast to the Vedas, Brahmanas, and Upanishads, which are the province of the brahmin priests).

The Great Epics. In the last chapter we discussed India's two great epic poems, the *Ramayana* and the *Mahabharata*. The latter's central story revolves around the civil war between two branches of the family of the Bharatas (from whom India derives its current Hindi name, Bharat). The *Mahabharata* presents moral conflicts, the dilemma of taking sides, and the necessity of acting decisively. At its center stands the *Bhagavad-Gita* ("Song of God"), a philosophical discourse on the duties and the meaning of life and death.

The *Bhagavad-Gita* opens on the field of Kurukshetra before the final battle between the two branches of the Bharata family. Arjun, leader of one branch, despairs of his choices: if he fights, he kills his cousins; if he does not fight, he dies. He turns to his chariot driver, the Lord Krishna, for advice. Krishna's reply incorporates many fundamental principles of Hindu thought.

SACRED WRITINGS OF HINDUISM	
Veda	The most sacred of the Hindu scriptures, meaning "divine knowledge." They consist of collections of writings compiled by the Aryans: *Rigveda* (hymns and praises), *Yajurveda* (prayers and sacrificial formulas), *Samaveda* (tunes and chants), and *Atharva-Veda* (Veda of the Atharvans, the priests who officiate at sacrifices).
Upanishads	Philosophical treatises, centering on the doctrine of Brahma.
Brahamanas	Instructions on ritual and sacrifice.
Ramayana	An epic poem, telling how Rama (an incarnation of the god Vishnu) and his devotee Hanuman, the monkey god, recover Rama's wife, Sita, who has been abducted by the demon king Ravana.
Mahabharata	("Great Poem of the Bharatas") It includes the *Bhagavad-Gita* ("Song of God") and consists of eighteen books and 90,000 stanzas. The central narrative of civil war, and the innumerable sidebars, emphasize the struggle to do one's duty faithfully.

Actor in the *Ramayana* festival, 1996.
Dressed in the classical Yogya style, the actor portrays the enemy of Lord Rama, Ravana, in this tale of the battle of good versus evil.

First, Krishna speaks of the duty of Arjun, a *kshatriya* by caste, to fight: "For a *kshatriya* there does not exist another greater good than war enjoined by *dharma*" (II:31). Each person has a unique *dharma*, largely determined by caste. In this philosophy, changing one's vocational duty is no virtue:

> Better is one's own *dharma* that one may be able to fulfill but imperfectly, than the *dharma* of others that is more easily accomplished. Better is death in the fulfillment of one's own *dharma*. To adopt the *dharma* of others is perilous. (III:35)

The *Bhagavad-Gita* summarizes many of the key doctrines of Hinduism. Lord Krishna promises to help people who do their duty, and points the way toward spiritual fulfillment. The text demonstrates considerable assimilation within Hinduism, for the Lord Krishna is dark-skinned, usually represented as blue-black in color. He appears to be originally a non-Vedic, non-Aryan tribal god, perhaps from the south. His centrality in this most revered Sanskrit text suggests the continuing accommodation

SOURCE

The Bhagavad-Gita *from the* Mahabharata

Lord Krishna counsels Arjun to do his duty in leading the fighting of a civil war, even though the warrior has no desire to shed the blood of his relatives. Krishna continues with additional advice—on the importance of proper action for its own sake regardless of praise or condemnation, on reincarnation, and on Lord Krishna's grace upon those who seek him—much of which has been accepted by many Hindus then and now as key principles of life.

Krishna counsels Arjun to action. He notes three kinds of yoga, or discipline, which bring people to spiritual liberation: the yoga of knowledge; the yoga of devotion; and the yoga of action. (The yoga of physical discipline and meditation, known widely today in the West, is yet another form.) In this case, Krishna tells Arjun, the yoga of action is required:

> Do your allotted work, for action is superior to nonaction. Even the normal functioning of your body cannot be accomplished through actionlessness. (III:8)

The key, however, is performing the action because it is right, without concern for its results or rewards.

> Action alone is your concern, never at all its fruits. Let not the fruits of action be your motive, nor let yourself be attached to inaction … Seek refuge in the right mental attitude. Wretched are those who are motivated by the fruits of action. (II:49)

Non-attachment is the ideal:

> He who feels no attachment toward anything; who, having encountered the various good or evil things, neither rejoices nor loathes—his wisdom is steadfast. (II:59)
>
> He who behaves alike to foe and friend; who likewise is even-poised in honor or dishonor; who is even-tempered in cold and heat, happiness and sorrow; who is free from attachment; who regards praise and censure with equanimity; who is silent, content with anything whatever; who has no fixed abode, who is steadfast in mind, who is full of devotion—that man is dear to me. (XII:18–19)

In reply to Arjun's specific anxiety about killing his cousins, Krishna reminds him of the doctrine of reincarnation:

> As a man discards worn-out clothes to put on new and different ones, so the disembodied self discards its worn-out bodies to take on other new ones.
>
> Death is certain for anyone born, and birth is certain for the dead; since the cycle is inevitable, you have no cause to grieve! (II:22, 27)

Krishna also assures Arjun of his abiding concern for him, and of the god's power to help him: "If I am in your thought, by my grace you will transcend all dangers" (XVIII:58). Arjun does fight, and wins, and in the end all the warriors who die are reborn.

---

between the Aryans and the indigenous peoples of India. The *Gita* provided the basis for the continuing emphasis in Hinduism on *bhakti*, mystical devotion to god. "No one devoted to me is lost … Keep me in your mind and devotion, sacrifice to me, bow to me, discipline your self toward me, and you will reach me," (IX:31,34) is one of many statements in the *Gita* that called for this devotion. Bhakti was a revolt within Hinduism against formality in religion, against hierarchy, and against the power of the brahmin priesthood. Bhakti continues today in the hymns and poetry of the common people and in the multitudes of devotional prayer meetings in every corner of India.

The two epics generally also reflect greater prestige for women than did earlier Sanskrit texts. In the *Ramayana*, Sita appears as a traditionally subordinate wife to Rama, but her commitment to honor and duty surpasses even his; she defends Rama's honor even when he fails to defend hers. She is more heroic than he, although her heroism is defined by her role as dutiful wife. Rama is implicitly criticized for his inability to defend her both from Ravana and from the gossip of his own subjects. In some versions, the criticism is made explicit. In the *Mahabharata* Draupadi is the wife of five noble brothers, and she protects, defends, and inspires them in their struggles, going far beyond the subservient role that women play in the majority of Aryan literature. In the epics, the female force, *shakti*, has gained recognition.

The Puranas. The most popular of the gods of Hinduism, Vishnu and Shiva, appear in the Puranas, a collection of ancient stories. Here, too, appear female goddesses, often as consorts of the principal gods, such as the goddesses Lakshmi and Saraswati with the lord Vishnu; and the goddesses Parvati, Durga, and Kali with the lord Shiva. These goddesses also help to balance the rather suppressed position of females evident in the earlier Aryan literature.

Temples and Shrines

By the seventh century C.E. fundamental changes had taken place in the form of Hindu worship. Personal prayer, often addressed to representations of the gods in statues and pictures, displaced sacrifice. Hindus built temples of great beauty. The caves at Ellora in western India were fashioned into temples in the eighth century, reflecting the early importance of caves in Hindu worship. Within the cave-temples, sculpture and painting demonstrate the artistic development in religious worship.

Bronze sculpture of Vishnu, early Chola period, first half of tenth century. Vishnu is beloved as the tender, merciful deity—the Preserver—and as the second member of the Hindu trinity he complements Brahma the Creator and Shiva the Destroyer. He is said to come to earth periodically as an *avatar*, an incarnation in various forms, to help humankind in times of crisis. (*Metropolitan Museum of Art, New York*)

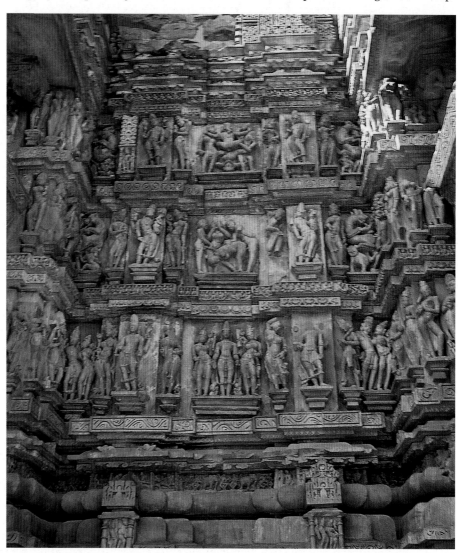

Kandariya Mahadeo Temple at Khajuraho, Chandela, c. 1025–1050 C.E. The twenty surviving temples at Khajuraho, though maimed by time, are still among the greatest examples of medieval Hindu architecture and sculpture in north India. Beneath the soaring towers, multilayered bands of sculptures writhe in a pulsating tableau of human and divine activity. The depictions of athletic lovemaking, which so scandalized nineteenth-century European travelers, can be linked to tantric sects of Hinduism, then prevalent in the Chandela region.

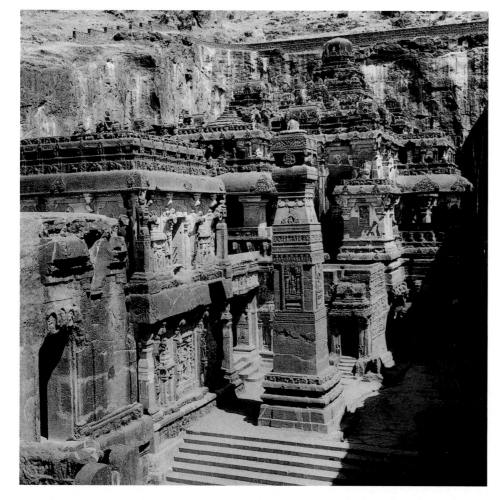

Kailasanatha Temple at Ellora, Rashtrakuta, c. 757–790 C.E. Carved into an escarpment of volcanic stone, the thirty-three shrines of Ellora have for centuries been a pilgrimage center for Hindus, Buddhists, and Jains. The monolithic stone shaft in the foreground, 60 feet high, would have originally supported a trident symbol of Shiva, to whom this temple is dedicated.

The bas reliefs and artwork in the temples at Kanchi and Mahabalipuram in the south, also built in the eighth century, continue to dazzle viewers today. Magnificent temples flourished everywhere in India, but especially in the south of the subcontinent. Sexual passion and the union of male and female entered into forms of worship, symbolically representing passion for, and union with, god, as the temple sculptures at Khajuraho in north India about 1000 C.E. illustrate.

Religion and Rule

Wealthy landowners and rulers, who sought validation of their power and rule through the prestige of brahmin priests, often patronized temples. As in many religions, rulers supported priests, while priests affirmed the authority of the rulers. This was especially true in the south. At least as early as the eighth century, new rulers who seized lands occupied by indigenous tribal peoples often imported brahmin priests to overawe the tribals with their learning, piety, and rituals, and to persuade the tribals of the proper authority of the king. To pacify the tribals, their gods might be incorporated into the array of gods worshiped in the temple by the priests, just as the tribal peoples would begin to worship the major gods of Hinduism. Anthropologists describe this process as an interplay between the "great" national tradition and the "little" local tradition. As new lands were opened, and tribals were persuaded to accept the new ruling coalition, the temples grew larger and more wealthy.

In exchange for their support, kings rewarded priests with land grants, court subsidies, and temple bequests. Brahmin priests and Tamil rulers in south India prospered together as temples took on important economic functions in banking and money-lending for the villages in their region. Hindu colleges, rest-houses for pilgrims, centers of administration, and even cities grew up around some of these temples.

Hinduism in Southeast Asia

Hinduism did not generally attract, nor seek, converts outside of India, but southeast Asia was an exception. Here, the initiative for conversion grew out of politics, as it had in southern India. The powers of the Hindu temple and the brahmin priesthood were imported to validate royal authority in southeast Asia from as early as the third century C.E. to as late as the fourteenth century.

Trade contacts between India and southeast Asia date back to at least 150 B.C.E. Indian sailors carried cargoes to and from Myanmar, the Straits of Malacca, the

Asian trade. Ports along the Indus and Ganges served Arab maritime traders for many centuries, and provided links to the kingdoms of southeast Asia and the South China Sea. To the north, roads following river valleys and passes through the towering Himalayas and the Hindu Kush provided contact with China and the silk route respectively.

HOW DO WE KNOW?

Hinduism in Southeast Asia

Evidence for the influence of Hinduism in southeast Asia comes from a variety of sources. Even today, the historical stamp of Hinduism endures in southeast Asia in the names of cities, including Ayuthia in Thailand, derived from Ayodhya in northern India; in the influence of Sanskrit on several southeast Asian languages; in the popularity of the Ramayana and other Hindu literature in the folklore and theater of the region. Moreover, Hindu temples still stand, most spectacularly the Angkor Wat temple complex in Cambodia.

Evidence of Hindu influence in southeast Asia appears also in early reports of Chinese visitors, archaeological remains, and epigraphy (inscriptions on metal and rock). These records are, nevertheless, sparse. Brahmin priests appear in the southeast-Asian records only after 800 C.E. It is, therefore, difficult to answer the question: "What brought Indian power and prestige into southeast Asia from about the third century to about the fourteenth century?"

Three theories explaining the appearance of Indian influence in southeast Asia have been suggested. One theory argued that Indians initiated contact and attempted to introduce their religion and culture into southeast Asia. This theory, which stressed the use of military might, is no longer accepted. As noted in Chapter 8, there is very little record of Indian military action in the area, and none suggesting a desire for conquest. A second theory—that Indian traders brought their culture with them— has wider acceptance, but it also encounters serious opposition. Trade connections between India and southeast Asia were numerous, long-standing, and intense. Some cultural and religious influence must have accompanied them, but these contacts were by sea, while much of the Hindu influence was found inland.

A third theory argued that local rulers invited brahmin priests to come from India to southeast Asia to build temples, to promote agricultural development on land specially granted to them, to invoke the Hindu gods to validate their authority, and to convince the local population of this divine validation. In the words of one historian, these priests were to serve as "development planners." They brought with them from India principles of government, religious law, administration, art, and architecture. In promoting these religious/political practices through the priests, southeast-Asian rulers were emulating the policies of the Pallava and Chola kings of southern India. But Hinduism did not survive in southeast Asia. It was superseded by Buddhism and, later, by Islam.

Local kings and southeast-Asian rulers also invited Buddhist monks as well as Hindu priests to southeast Asia to help establish and consolidate their power, and they found the Buddhist monks to be as useful as the Hindu brahmins, for they served similar political and administrative functions, but in the name of Buddhism. For example, the ruler of the Srivijaya Empire in the East Indies welcomed 1000 Buddhist monks to his kingdom in the late seventh century C.E. Jayavarman VII, the Buddhist ruler of the Khmer kingdom at the end of the twelfth century, added Buddhist images in the great temple of Angkor Wat, which had been built earlier in the century to honor the Hindu god Vishnu.

By about the fourteenth century, Hinduism had died out in southeast Asia, while Buddhism continued to thrive. In fact, Buddhism became an enormously successful proselytizing religion throughout Asia. In India, on the other hand, Buddhism withered away, while Hinduism flourished.

- Of the theories explaining the spread of Hinduism in southeast Asia, why does the theory of the priest as "development planner" seem the most convincing?
- What is the evidence for the co-existence of Hinduism and Buddhism, for a time, in southeast Asia?
- What was the functional relationship between priests and rulers in southeast Asia?

Kingdom of Funan in modern Cambodia and Vietnam, and Java in modern Indonesia. By the third century C.E., Funan had accepted many elements of Indian culture, religion, and political practice. Chinese envoys reported a prosperous state with walled cities, palaces, and houses. Sanskrit was in use, as was some Indian technology for irrigation and farming. By the fifth century it appears that Sanskrit had spread, Indian calendars marked the dates, and Indian gods, including Shiva and Vishnu, were worshiped, as were representations of the Buddha (see below). Hindu temples began to appear with brahmin priests to staff them.

BUDDHISM

Buddhism was born in India, within the culture of Hinduism, and then charted its own path. Like Hinduism, it questioned the reality of this earthly world and speculated on the existence of other worlds. Unlike Hinduism, however, Buddhism had a founder, a set of originating scriptures, and an order of monks. In opposition to Hinduism, it renounced hereditary caste organization and the supremacy of the brahmin priests. Buddhism spread to southeast Asia, gaining acceptance as the principal religion of Myanmar (Burma), Thailand, Cambodia, Laos, and Vietnam until today. It won multitudes of adherents throughout the rest of Asia as well, in Sri Lanka, Tibet, China, Korea, and Japan. Yet in India itself, Buddhism lost out in competition with Hinduism and its priesthood, virtually vanishing from the subcontinent by about the twelfth century C.E.

The Origins of Buddhism

All we know of the Buddha's life and teaching comes from much later accounts, embellished by his followers. While there is much doubt about almost every aspect of the Buddha's life and teachings, the accounts that exist tell the following story.

The Life of the Buddha. Siddhartha Gautama was born *c.* 563 B.C.E. in the foothills of the Himalayan mountains of what is now Nepal. His father, a warrior chief of the *kshatriya* caste, received a prophecy that Siddhartha would become either a great emperor or a great religious teacher. Hoping that his son would follow the former vocation, the chief sheltered him as best he could so that he would experience neither pain nor disillusionment.

When he was twenty-nine years old, Siddhartha started to grow curious about what lay beyond the confines of his father's palace. Leaving his wife, Yasadhara, and their son, Rahula, he instructed his charioteer to take him to the city, where he came across a frail, elderly man. Never having encountered old age, Siddhartha was confused. His companion explained that aging was an inevitable and painful part of human experience. As Siddhartha took further excursions outside the palace, he soon came to see that pain was an integral part of life, experienced in illness, aging, death, and birth. The search for a remedy for this pervasive sorrow became his quest.

On his fourth and final trip he met a wandering holy man who had shunned the trappings of wealth and material gain. Siddhartha decided to do likewise. Bidding farewell to his family for the last time, he set out on horseback in search of an antidote to sorrow and a means of teaching it to others.

For six years Siddhartha wandered as an ascetic. Nearing starvation, however, he gave up the path of asceticism. Determined to achieve enlightenment, he began to meditate, sitting under a tree at Bodh Gaya near modern Patna, in India. Mara, the spirit of this world, who tempted him to give up his meditation with both threats of punishment and promises of rewards, tested his concentration and fortitude. Touching the ground with his hand in a gesture, or *mudra*, repeated often in sculptures of the Buddha, Siddhartha revealed these temptations to be illusions. On the forty-ninth day of meditation he reached enlightenment, becoming the Buddha, He Who Has Awakened. He had found an antidote to pain and suffering. He proceeded to the Deer Park at Sarnath, near Banaras, where he delivered his first sermon, beginning by setting forth the Four Noble Truths of suffering. Its source, he taught, was personal desire and passion:

> This is the [first] Noble Truth of Sorrow. Birth is sorrow, age is sorrow, disease is sorrow, death is sorrow, contact with the unpleasant is sorrow, separation from the pleasant is sorrow, every wish unfulfilled is sorrow—in short all the five components of individuality are sorrow. This is the [second] Noble Truth of the Arising of Sorrow. [It arises from] thirst, which leads to rebirth, which brings delight and passion, and seeks pleasure now here, now there—the thirst for sensual pleasure, the thirst for continued life, the thirst for power. (Basham, p. 269)

Teaching Buddha, **from Sarnath, India, Gupta dynasty, fifth century C.E.** Siddhartha Gautama sought to understand the causes of and remedy for human suffering. After many trials, he finally found his answer on the forty-ninth day of intense meditation. As the Buddha, the Enlightened One, he began to teach his new message. The *mudra*, the hand gesture, here represents the Buddha teaching. (*Archaeological Musem, Sarnath*)

SOURCE

The Address to Sigala: Buddhism in Everyday Life

Much of the Buddha's moral and ethical instruction is directed to the monks of the Sangha. In the Address to Sigala, however, he speaks to laypeople about their relationships and responsibilities toward one another. The address includes practical advice to husbands and wives, friends, employers, and employees. The lengthy address is translated and summarized here by A.L. Basham.

Husbands should respect their wives, and comply as far as possible with their requests. They should not commit adultery. They should give their wives full charge of the home, and supply them with fine clothes and jewelry as far as their means permit. Wives should be thorough in their duties, gentle and kind to the whole household, chaste, and careful in housekeeping, and should carry out their work with skill and enthusiasm.

A man should be generous to his friends, speak kindly of them, act in their interest in every way possible, treat them as his equals, and keep his word to them. They in turn should watch over his interests and property, take care of him when he is "off his guard" [i.e.,

intoxicated, infatuated, or otherwise liable to commit rash and careless actions], stand by him and help him in time of trouble, and respect other members of his family.

Employers should treat their servants and workpeople decently. They should not be given tasks beyond their strength. They should receive adequate food and wages, be cared for in time of sickness and infirmity, and be given regular holidays and bonuses in times of prosperity. They should rise early and go to bed late in the service of their master, be content with their just wages, work thoroughly, and maintain their master's reputation. (Digha Nikaya, iii:161; cited in Basham, p. 286)

Its antidote followed from this analysis:

> This is the [third] Noble Truth of the Stopping of Sorrow. It is the complete stopping of that thirst, so that no passion remains, leaving it, being emancipated from it, being released from it, giving no place to it. And this is the [fourth] Noble Truth of the Way which Leads to the Stopping of Sorrow. It is the Noble Eightfold Path—Right Views, Right Resolve, Right Speech, Right Conduct, Right Livelihood, Right Effort, Right Recollection and Right Meditation. (Basham, p. 269)

A new consciousness could be achieved by a combination of disciplining the mind and observing ethical precepts in human relationships. In the face of continuing rebirths into the pain of life, the Buddha taught that right living could bring release from the cycle of mortality and pain, and entry into *nirvana,* a kind of blissful nothingness. On the metaphysical plane, the Buddha taught that everything in the universe is transient; there is no "being." There exists neither an immortal soul nor a god, neither *atman* nor Brahman. The Buddha's teachings about the illusion of life and about rebirth and release were consistent with Hindu concepts of *maya, samsara,* and *moksha,* but the Buddha's denial of god put him on the fringes of Hindu thought. His rejection of caste as an organizing hierarchy and of the Hindu priests as connoisseurs of religious truth, won him powerful allies—and powerful opponents.

Although much of the Hindu priesthood opposed the Buddha's teachings, the kings of Magadha and Koshala, whose territories included most of the lower Gangetic plain, befriended and supported him and the small band of followers gathered around him. The Buddha taught peacefully and calmly until about 483 B.C.E., when, at the age of eighty, he died, surrounded by a cadre of dedicated monks and believers, the original Buddhist Sangha (order of monks). The three-fold motto of all devout Buddhists became, "I seek refuge in the Buddha; I seek refuge in the Doctrine; I seek refuge in the Sangha."

The Sangha. The Sangha was open to all men regardless of caste and thus drew the antagonism of brahmins, although some did join. For a time, women were permitted to form their own convents, but only under special restrictions. Today Buddhist nuns exist only in Tibet.

The monks wore saffron robes and shaved their heads. They practiced celibacy and renounced alcohol, but did not have to take a vow of obedience to the order. The monks were intellectually and spiritually free. Decisions were made through group discussion, perpetuating the pattern of the early republics of the north Indian hills. Monks studied, disciplined their spirits, meditated, and did the physical work of their monasteries. At first, they wandered, begging for their living, except during the rainy months of the monsoon. But as monasteries became richer, through donations of money and land, the monks tended to settle down. They also tended to give up begging, which diminished their contact with the common people to some degree.

The Emergence of Mahayana Buddhism

A series of general councils began to codify the principles, doctrines, and texts of the emerging community. The first council, convened shortly after the Buddha's death, began the continuing process of collecting his teachings. The second, about a century later, began to dispute the essential meaning of Buddhism. The third, convened at Pataliputra, Asoka's capital, revealed more of the differences that would soon lead to a split over the question of whether the Buddha was a human or a god.

By this time an array of Buddhist *caityas*, or shrines, was growing. In addition to monasteries, great stupas, or monuments filled with Buddhist relics, were built at Barhut, Sanchi, and Amaravati. Between 200 B.C.E. and 200 C.E. there were more

Great Stupa, Sanchi, third century B.C.E.–first century C.E. With its four gloriously carved gates and majestic central hemisphere, the Great Stupa of Sanchi is the most remarkable surviving example of the 84,000 such Buddhist shrines reputedly erected by the emperor Asoka during the Mauryan Empire. This "world mountain," oriented to the four corners of the universe, contained a holy relic, the object of pilgrims' devotion, and is topped by a three-tiered umbrella representing the Three Jewels of Buddhism: the Buddha, the Law, and the community of monks.

SACRED WRITINGS OF BUDDHISM

Tripitaka	"The Three Baskets": **Vinaya**, on the proper conduct of Buddhist monks and nuns; **Sutta**, discourses attributed to the Buddha; and **Abhidhamma**, supplementary doctrines. Written in Pali.
The Mahayanas	(Mahayana is Sanskrit for "Greater Vehicle.") The body of writings associated with the school of Buddhism dominant in Tibet, Mongolia, China, Korea, and Japan. Includes the famous allegory, the Lotus Sutra, the Buddhist Parable of the Prodigal Son.
Milindapanha	Dialogue between the Greek king Milinda and the Buddhist monk Nagasena on the philosophy of Buddhism.
Buddha's Four Noble Truths	Suffering is always present in life; desire is the cause of suffering; freedom from suffering can be achieved in nirvana (perfect peace and bliss); the Eightfold Path leads to nirvana.

Seated Buddhas, Cave 2, Ajanta, Maharashtra, India, fifth century C.E. While the original Theravada Buddhism saw the Buddha as a human being of great enlightenment, later forms of Buddhism, especially Mahayana Buddhism, taught that there had been many Buddhas who had lived at different times and continued to live on in various heavens, and that others would follow.

Buddhist than Hindu shrines in India. Theological discussion flourished, with a heavy emphasis on *metta*, or benevolence; nonviolence; *dharma*, or proper behavior (although not related to caste, since Buddhism rejected hereditary caste); and tolerance for all religions.

The fourth general council, convened in the first century C.E. in Kashmir, codified the key doctrines of Buddhism as they had developed from earliest times. These were the principles of the Theravada ("Doctrine of the Elders") branch of Buddhism, which we have been examining and which is today the prevailing form in Sri Lanka and southeast Asia, except for Vietnam.

By now, however, a newer school of Mahayana Buddhism had been growing for perhaps two centuries and had become a serious challenge to Theravada. Mahayana means "the Greater Vehicle," and its advocates claimed that their practices could carry more Buddhists to nirvana because they had bodhisattvas to help. A bodhisattva was a "being of wisdom" on the verge of achieving nirvana but so concerned about the welfare of fellow humans that he postponed his entrance into nirvana to remain on earth, or to be reborn, in order to help others.

In addition, Mahayana Buddhism taught that religious merit, achieved through performing good deeds, could be transferred from one person to another. It embellished the concept of nirvana with the vision of a Mahayana heaven, presided over by Amitabha Buddha, a Buddha who had lived on earth and had now become a kind of father in heaven. Subsequently, Mahayanists developed the concept of numerous heavens with numerous forms of the Buddha presiding over them. They also developed the concept of the Maitreya Buddha, a suffering servant who will come to redeem humanity.

Some theologians note the similarity of the concept of this Maitreya Buddha to the Christian Messiah, and some suggest that the Buddhists may have borrowed it. They also suggest that Christians may have borrowed the narratives of the virgin birth of the Buddha and of his temptation in his search for enlightenment, and applied them to Jesus. There are significant similarities in the stories of these two men/gods and their biographies. Further, Mahayanists spoke of three aspects of the Buddha: Amitabha, the Buddha in heaven; Gautama, the historical Buddha on earth; and the most revered of all the bodhisattvas, the freely moving Avalokiteshvara. Theologians ask: To what degree do these three Buddhist forms correspond to the Father, Son, and Holy Spirit of Christianity as it was developing at the same time? How much borrowing took place between India and the Mediterranean coast, and in which direction?

Within India, Mahayana Buddhism began to challenge Hinduism more boldly than Theravada had. Wishing to compete for upper-caste and upper-class audiences, Mahayanists began to record their theology in Sanskrit, the language of the elite, rather than the more colloquial Pali language, which Theravada had preferred. Mahayana theologians, most notably Nagarjuna (*fl. c.* 50–150 C.E.), elaborated Buddhist philosophy and debated directly with brahmin priests. Buddhist monasteries established major educational programs, especially at Nalanda in Bihar, where the Buddha had spent much of his life, and at Taxila, on the international trade routes in the northern Punjab.

The Decline of Buddhism in India

From its beginnings in India, Buddhism's strongest appeal had been to *kshatriya* rulers and *vaishya* businessmen, who felt that brahmin priests did not respect them. The Buddha himself came from a *kshatriya* family, and his early friendship with the *kshatriya* kings of Magadha and Koshala had ensured their support for his movement. Later kings and merchants also donated huge sums of money to support Buddhist monks, temples, and monasteries. Many people of the lower castes, who felt the weight and the arrogance of all the other castes pressing down on them, also joined the newly forming religion. They were especially attracted by the use of the vernacular Pali and Magadhi languages in place of Sanskrit, and the absence of the financial demands of the brahmins.

Buddhism began to lose strength in India around the time of the decline of the Gupta Empire (*c.* 320–550 C.E.). Regional rulers began to choose Hinduism over Buddhism, and alliances with priests rather than with monks. At the popular level, lower castes—who had found the anti-caste philosophy of Buddhism attractive—apparently also began to shift their allegiances back toward more orthodox Hinduism as an anchor in a time of political change. Also, without imperial assistance, merchants' incomes may have decreased within India, reducing their contributions to Buddhist temples. By the fifth century C.E., the Chinese Buddhist pilgrim Faxian noted weaknesses in Indian Buddhism.

Mahayana Buddhism, with its many god-like Buddhas and bodhisattvas inhabiting a multitude of heavens, seemed so close to Hinduism that many Buddhists must have seen little purpose in maintaining a distinction. Finally, Buddhists throughout their history in India had relied upon Hindu brahmin priests to officiate at their life cycle ceremonies of birth, marriage, and death, so Hindu priests could argue that they always had a significant claim on Buddhist allegiance.

Readers who are accustomed to the monotheistic pattern of religions claiming the undivided loyalty of their followers will recognize here a very different pattern. Many religions, especially polytheistic religions, expect that individuals will incorporate diverse elements of different religions into their personal philosophy and ritual. We

For an interactive version of this map, go to: http://www.prenhall.com/spodek/map9.3

Legend:
- origin of Buddhism
- • Buddhist center
- ▲ pagoda
- ○ stupa
- ■ rock-carved temple

Buddhist Asia. Radiating from the site of Buddha's enlightenment at Bodh Gaya in northeast India, Buddhism spread through Asia in three directions following established trade routes: north across the Hindu Kush and along the silk route to Xinjiang, China, and Korea, eventually reaching Japan; south to Sri Lanka; and east through Burma to the kingdoms and islands of southeast Asia.

will see more examples of this personal syncretism and loyalty to multiple religions as we examine Buddhism's relationship with Confucianism in China and with both Confucianism and Shinto in Japan.

As Hinduism evolved, it became more attractive to Buddhists. Theologians like Shankaracharya (788–820) and Ramanuja (c. 1017–1137) advanced philosophies based on the Vedic literature known to the common people and built many temples and schools to spread their thought. At the same time, Hinduism, following its tradition of syncretism, incorporated the Buddha himself within its own polytheistic universe as an incarnation of Vishnu. A devotee could revere the Buddha within the overarching framework of Hinduism. Finally, neither Buddhism nor Hinduism gave much scope to women within their official institutions of temples, schools, and monasteries. For Hinduism, however, the home was much more central than the public institution, and here women did have a central role in worship and ritual. Buddhism was much more centered on its monasteries and monks. The comparative lack of a role for women, and the comparative uninterest in domestic life generally, may have impeded its spread.

Buddhism in India began to wane when Muslim traders gained control of the silk routes through central Asia. The final blow came with the arrival of Muslims during the first two centuries of their major invasions into India, between 1000 and 1200 C.E. Muslims saw Buddhism as a competitive, proselytizing religion, unlike Hinduism, and did not wish to coexist with it. Because Buddhism was, by this time, relatively weak and relatively centralized within its monasteries and schools, Muslims were able to destroy the remnants of the religion by attacking these institutions. Buddhist monks were killed or forced to flee from India to centers in southeast Asia, Nepal, and Tibet. Hinduism survived the challenge because it was much more broadly based as the religion of home and community and far more deeply rooted in Indian culture.

In the 1950s, almost a thousand years after Buddhism's demise in India, about 5 million "outcastes" revived Buddhism in India in protest at the inequalities of the caste system and declared their allegiance to the old/new religion. These "neo-Buddhists" are virtually the only Buddhists to be found in India today (see Chapter 20).

Jainism

Jainism is another religion of India, with many similarities to early Buddhism. At about the time of the Buddha, the teacher Mahavir (c. 540 B.C.E.), the twenty-fourth in

Jainist nuns on their way to worship. Although most Jains are laypersons, important monasteries house priests and nuns. These nuns wear mouth-cloths to prevent injury to insects that might otherwise be inhaled.

a long lineage of Jain religious leaders, guided the religion into its modern form. The religion takes its name from Mahavir's designation *jina*, or conqueror. Like Theravada Buddhists, Jains reject the caste system and the supremacy of brahmin priests, postulating instead that there is no god, but that humans do have souls that they can purify by careful attention to their actions, and especially by practicing nonviolence. If they follow the eternal law of ethical treatment of others and devotion to the rather austere rituals of the faith, Jains believe they will reach nirvana, which is an end to the cycle of rebirths rather than a rewarding afterlife.

Jainism's emphasis on nonviolence is so powerful that Jains typically do not become farmers lest they kill living creatures in the soil. In a country overwhelmingly agricultural, Jains are usually urban and often businessmen. Jainism did not spread outside India, and its 4 million adherents today live almost entirely in India. Because Jains, like earlier Buddhists, employ brahmin priests to officiate at their life cycle events, and because Jains intermarry freely with several Hindu *vaishya* (business) subcastes, some consider them a branch of Hinduism, although they do not usually regard themselves as Hindus. One of the regions of Jain strength in India is western Gujarat, the region where Mahatma Gandhi grew up (see Chapter 20). The Mahatma attributed his adherence to nonviolence in large part to the influence of Jainism.

Buddhism in China

Because of its decentralization and vast geographical diffusion, Buddhism has taken on different forms from place to place, time to time, and state to state. It arrived in new locations in foreign form, but over time each regional culture put its own stamp on Buddhism. We must, therefore, examine the faith and practice of Buddhism in each region separately, by studying the works of the monks, missionaries, poets, architects, and sculptors who spread the faith.

Arrival in China: The Silk Route. The long, thin line of communication over which pilgrims and missionaries carried the message of the Buddha from India to China and beyond was the silk route, the same route that carried luxury products between China and India and then on to the West. The first Buddhist missionaries are mentioned in Chinese records about 65 C.E. They established their first monastery at Luoyang. Over the centuries, many more were built within China and along the silk route.

Chinese pilgrims traveled the silk route in the opposite direction to visit and study in the land of the Buddha, and some, most notably Faxian, who visited in 399–414, left important records of their observations. Thousands came to study at Taxila and Nalanda.

Several of the pilgrims who traveled these routes, especially Faxian, in the early years of the fifth century C.E., and Xuanzang, in the early years

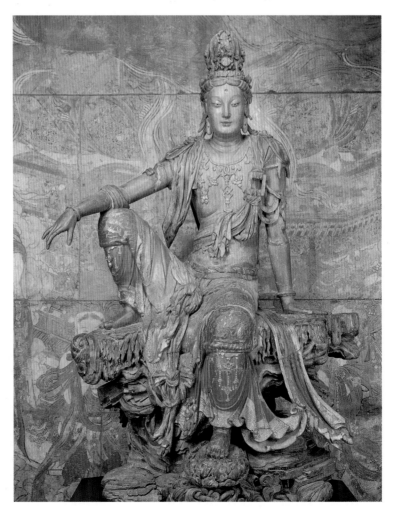

Guanyin, Buddhist deity, Northern Song dynasty, China, c. 1200 C.E. Guanyin, a bodhisattva, or enlightened being, who remains in this world to relieve human suffering, was a very popular subject in Chinese art: this painted-wood example is particularly sensuous and refined. Buddhist deities are considered to have the spiritual qualities of both genders and by this date the feminine qualities were accentuated. (*Nelson-Atkins Museum of Art, Kansas City, Missouri*)

of the seventh, brought back both Buddhist texts and important first-hand information from India and the lands along the silk routes. Turning north from India through Kashgar, and then east to Khotan, Turfan, Dunhuang, and on to Chang'an in the heart of China, Buddhist pilgrims improved these trade routes with rest-houses, temples, and monasteries, some of them built into caves.

Relations with Daoism and Confucianism. Although Buddhism first appeared in China in the first century C.E., at the height of the Han dynasty, it took firmer root after the dynasty eventually fell. Confucianism, China's dominant philosophy, was intimately tied to the fate of the imperial government, and only after this central political structure collapsed could Mahayana Buddhism find a place. The mystical character of Mahayana Buddhism especially attracted Daoists. To some degree, the two beliefs competed, but some of the competition eventually led to each validating the other. For example, some Daoists claimed that the Buddha was actually Laozi as he appeared in his travels in India. Many Buddhists, in turn, accorded to Laozi and Confucius the status of bodhisattva. In this way, competition sometimes turned into mutual recognition.

As a foreign religion, Buddhism also had special appeal for some of the rulers of northern China in the third through the sixth centuries, since they, too, were outsiders. The Toba rulers of the Northern Wei dynasty (386–534) occasionally persecuted Buddhists as a threat to the state, but mostly they felt some kinship to this religion of outsiders. They patronized Buddhist shrines and monks, but they also regulated them.

In the south, with its abundance of émigrés from the northern court, Confucianism was crippled by the severance of its connection with the government. In contrast, newly arriving Buddhists won followers by proposing an organized, aesthetic philosophy for coping with the hazards of life in semi-exile. In southern China Buddhist arts of poetry, painting, and calligraphy flourished, and monasteries in the south offered refuge to the men who might have been part of the governing Confucian aristocracy in other times. In the southern state of Liang, the Emperor Wu (r. 502–549) declared Buddhism the official state religion, built temples, sponsored Buddhist assemblies, and wrote Buddhist commentaries.

Doctrinally, Buddhism had important differences from Confucianism, but the two world perspectives seem to have reached mutual accommodation. For example, Confucianism encouraged family cohesion and the veneration of ancestors, while Buddhist monks followed lives of celibacy; but Buddhist laypeople also valued family, and the monks themselves venerated the Buddha and bodhisattvas as their spiritual ancestors. Nevertheless, tension between the two belief systems and organizations never completely dissipated. Confucians thought in terms of government order and control, while Buddhists tended toward decentralized congregational worship within a loose doctrinal framework. In many areas of China, as Buddhist monasteries became wealthy from the donations of local magnates and landlords, Confucian governments moved to regulate their power.

Buddhism's network of pilgrims and monks crisscrossed China, helping to integrate the nation. Through almost four centuries of division in China, from the fall of the Han (220 C.E.) to the rise of the Sui (581), Buddhism continued to grow in both north and south. Indeed, the founder of the Sui dynasty, a Buddhist himself, also patronized Confucianism and Daoism, seeing all these belief systems as vital to earning legitimacy for his government. The Tang extended this veneration.

Buddhism under the Tang Dynasty. For most of the Tang dynasty (618–907), the intellectual, spiritual, and artistic life of Buddhism flourished. Eight major sects developed, each with a different interpretation of the original message of the Buddha, the

SOURCE

The Transience of Life: A Woman's Perspective from the Tang Dynasty

This anonymous poem of the Tang dynasty, discovered in the Dunhuang cave and translated by Patricia Ebrey and Lily Hwa, illuminates the Buddhist sense of the transience of life as experienced by a woman of high status.

A Woman's Hundred Years

At ten, like a flowering branch in the rain,
She is slender, delicate, and full of grace.
Her parents are themselves as young as the rising moon
And do not allow her past the red curtain without a reason.

At twenty, receiving the hairpin, she is a spring bud.
Her parents arrange her betrothal; the matter's well done.
A fragrant carriage comes at evening to carry her to her lord.
Like Xioshi and his wife, at dawn they depart with the clouds.

At thirty, perfect as a pearl, full of the beauty of youth,
At her window, by the gauze curtain, she makes up in front of the mirror.
With her singing companions, in the waterlily season,
She rows a boat and plucks the blue flowers.

At forty, she is mistress of a prosperous house and makes plans.
Three sons and five daughters give her some trouble.
With her lute not far away, she toils always at her loom.
Her only fear that the sun will set too soon.

At fifty, afraid of her husband's dislike,
She strains to please him with every charm.
Trying to remember the many tricks she had learned since the age of sixteen.

No longer is she afraid of mothers- and sisters-in-law.

At sixty, face wrinkled and hair like silk thread,
She walks unsteadily and speaks little.
Distressed that her sons can find no brides,
Grieved that her daughters have departed for their husbands' homes.

At seventy, frail and thin, but not knowing what to do about it,
She is no longer able to learn the Buddhist Law even if she tries.
In the morning a light breeze
Makes her joints crack like clanging gongs.

At eighty, eyes blinded and ears half-deaf,
When she goes out she cannot tell north from east.
Dreaming always of departed loves,
Who persuade her to chase the dying breeze.

At ninety, the glow fades like spent lightning.
Human affairs are no longer her concern.
Lying on a pillow, solitary on her high bed,
She resembles the dying leaves that fall in autumn.

At a hundred, like a cliff crumbling in the wind,
For her body it is the moment to become dust.
Children and grandchildren will perform sacrifices to her spirit.
And clear moonlight will forever illumine her patch of earth.   (Ebrey, p. 104)

importance of rules and regulations, rituals, meditation, scholarship, disciplinary exercises, and devotion. Among the larger and more significant schools was the Pure Land Sect. Its devotees believed that anyone could reach the Pure Land of paradise after death through faith in the Buddha Amitabha, the presiding authority in that realm. Members of the sect demonstrated their faith by continuously repeating the name Amitabha. Devotees also meditated on the Bodhisattva Guanyin, the bodhisattva of mercy (see picture, p. 293).

Another sect, Chan Buddhism, taught the importance of meditation. Some followers believed in lengthy disciplines of meditation, which would gradually lead to enlightenment; others in spontaneous flashes of insight, which would lead to the same goal. Both Pure Land and Chan were adopted in Japan as well, where the meditative exercises of Chan became known as Zen.

Buddhists are credited with inventing woodblock printing as a means of reproducing their sacred texts. The earliest woodblock print known is an illustrated copy of the *Diamond Sutra* from 868 C.E., discovered in the Dunhuang Caves. Most of the Buddhist

Diamond Sutra, 868 C.E. This superb frontispiece, showing the Buddha preaching to an elderly disciple, comes from the *Diamond Sutra*, a Sanskrit tale transmitted along the silk route and translated into Chinese in the fifth century. Produced by woodblock to a high standard of technical and artistic achievement, the 17-foot-long sutra is the world's earliest dated printed book. (*British Library, London*)

art and architecture of Tang China was destroyed in later persecution, confiscation, and warfare. Its leading representations are now seen in Japan, which at just about this time adopted much of Chinese Buddhism as its own and then modified it (see pp. 297–301).

The only woman ever to rule China in her own name, the "Emperor" Wu (625–705), was a great patron of Buddhism. First ruling indirectly through the Emperor Gaozong (d. 683), whose concubine she was, and then, after his death, through two of their sons, in 690 she proclaimed herself the emperor of a new dynasty, which she named the Zhou (not to be confused with the earlier Zhou dynasty discussed in Chapter 3). She patronized Buddhism as a means of legitimizing her rule, declaring herself a reincarnation of Maitreya, the Buddha of future salvation. The empress built temples in every province of China. Before she was deposed in 705, she had overseen the warfare that expanded the Tang to its greatest geographical extent, including Xinjiang and Tibet.

Dying Buddha, Cave 428, Dunhuang, China, early sixth century C.E. The monastery at Dunhuang was one of the most important of those along the Silk Route, and the paintings in its 460 caves are spectacular. Here, bodhisattvas attend the Buddha at his death, appearing rather ascetic, abstract, and enchanted. Compare the scene from Japan on p. 297.

Buddhism's Decline in China. Political and military defeats started Buddhism on its decline during the late Tang period in China. In far-off central Asia, Muslim forces defeated Chinese forces in the decisive Battle of the Talas River in 751. Four years later, the revolt of General An Lushan in northeast China occupied the imperial armies for eight years. China's power in central Asia was broken, and with it the power of Buddhism in these regions. Islam would become the world religion of most of central Asia (see Chapter 11). In these vast regions, Buddhism remained powerful, and was supported by state power, only in Tibet. It was carried there from eastern India about the eighth century in a newly emerging form called *vajrayana* Buddhism, "the vehicle of the thunderbolt," or tantric Buddhism, for its *tantras*, or scriptures advocating magic rituals. Tantric Buddhism venerated not only buddhas, bodhisattvas, and other divinities, but also their wives or feminine counterparts, new additions to the growing array of sacred personalities. Tantric rituals were secret, esoteric, sometimes sexual, and only for the initiated.

Almost a century later, the Tang emperor Wuzong (r. 840–846) attacked Buddhism and its monasteries. Wuzong was a Daoist, personally opposed to Buddhism. He feared the power of the Buddhist establishment, and the wealth and influence of its various monasteries, especially when the Tang had been weakened by external defeats and internal revolts. Wuzong confiscated the lands and wealth of the Buddhist monasteries. He forced monks and nuns to leave the monasteries, claiming that he personally had defrocked 260,500 monks and nuns. He destroyed sacred texts, statues, and shrines, leaving only 49 monasteries and 800 monks in all of China. Later rulers alternated between reversing and re-imposing Wuzong's policies. Although Buddhism has remained a presence in China, even to today, it has never recovered its numbers, vitality, or influence.

Buddhism in Japan

Long before Buddhism arrived in Japan, the people of Japan followed "The Way of the *Kami*," later called Shinto. *Kamis* were the powers and spirits inherent in nature. Found everywhere, they could be called upon to help in time of human need. Shrines to the *kami* were built throughout the land, always including a mirror in tribute to the sun-goddess, a sword, and a jewel.

Accounts of the *kami* appear in the earliest Japanese records, the *Kojiki* (712 C.E.) and *Nihon shoki* (720 C.E.). These semi-mythological records give a basic history of early Japan, but these documents—and all accounts of Buddhist saints—must be read with some caution, because they blend myth with factual record. According to the *Kojiki* and *Nihon shoki*, the highest of the *kami* were Amaterasu, the sun-goddess, and her obstreperous brother Susa-no-o. Amaterasu's grandson, Niniqi, descended to earth and set out to conquer Japan. He established himself as Japan's first emperor in 660 B.C.E., and all subsequent emperors trace their lineage directly back to this mythological founder.

With the later arrival of Buddhism, the *kami* continued to have a distinguished and venerated position, often as minor Buddhas or bodhisattvas. Conversely, the Buddhas and bodhisattvas were accepted as especially powerful and exalted *kami*, capable of helping those in adversity. The royal family in Japan knew that the Emperor Asoka in India had adopted Buddhism and they emulated his decision.

Buddhism's Arrival in Japan. Buddhism first came to Japan from China in 552 C.E. via the Paekche kingdom of southwest Korea. The *Nihon shoki* tells of the Paekche king sending Buddhist texts and statues and asking help in a war against another Korean kingdom, the Silla.

From the beginning, Buddhism had political as well as religious implications. Clans close to the Japanese emperor were divided in their reception of the foreign religion. Those who accepted it regarded Buddhism as a force for

Dying Buddha, Japanese scroll, seventeenth to eighteenth century C.E. Here the dying Buddha is attended by human disciples, bodhisattvas, grieving animals, and representatives of other worlds. From across the river, another disciple leads the Buddha's mother and her retinue down from heaven to attend his last teaching.

Horyuji Temple, Nara, Japan, 670 C.E.
Through the seventh and eighth centuries the Japanese court enthusiastically welcomed Chinese political and artistic forms (see Chapter 7). This is Japan's earliest surviving example of Buddhist architecture, which was adopted along with Chinese writing, painting, and sculpture. It became a central shrine for all of Japan.

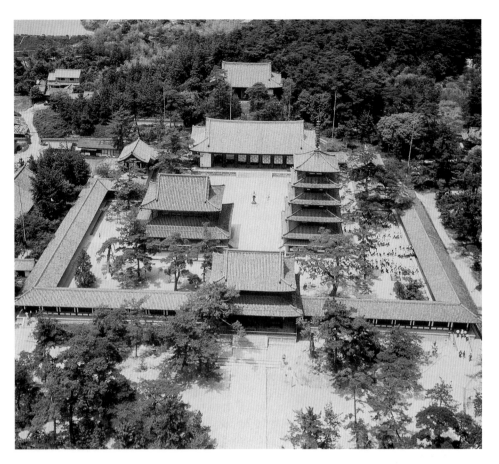

performing miracles, especially healing the sick, and many Buddhist monks were especially skilled in medicine. A minority, however, thought the new religion ought to be banned.

Buddhism found acceptance at a political level in Japan a half century later under Prince Shotoku Taishi (573–621). The prince effectively ruled the country as the regent to the ruler of the Yamato Plain, the western region of Japan. An enthusiastic Buddhist, Shotoku built many temples, including the Horyuji in the capital city of Nara. A scholar of Buddhist theology, he invited Buddhist clergy from Korea, and he dispatched four Japanese missions to Sui China to learn more about Buddhism, both as a religious system and as a model for centralizing his political rule. At this time China was the premier state of eastern Asia, and Buddhism was seen as one of the principal constituents of its power. In 604, Prince Shotoku introduced a kind of constitution to centralize and strengthen the Japanese government. Among its seventeen articles, the first promoted Confucian principles of social organization and the second declared that the Japanese people should, "Sincerely reverence the three treasures ... the Buddha, the Law, and the Monastic orders" (Embree, p. 50).

Buddhism's Role in Unifying Japan. A century later, in 710, the ruling clans of Japan moved their capital to Nara, then called Heijo. Continuing to regard China as the model state of their day, the Japanese rulers copied much of the Chinese structures of authority and administration. They used Chinese ideographs as their written language and adopted Chinese patterns of bureaucracy, taxation, architecture, and land reforms. They modeled their new capital on the city plan of Chang'an, building a smaller version of that Chinese capital at Nara.

Within Nara, Japan's rulers built numerous Buddhist temples, including several of national significance. They encouraged the creation of a system of monasteries and convents throughout the provinces, with the Todaiji monastery, built by the Emperor Shomu (r. 715–749), at the apex. Inside that great temple is one of the world's great repositories of art, holding several thousand treasures from the eighth century, including painting, sculptures, calligraphy, textiles, ceramics, jade, metal and lacquer work, masks for drama, and musical instruments.

Buddhism became a pillar in the structure of Japanese national unity and administration. Buddhism did not replace Shinto, the indigenous worship of spirits, especially spirits of nature. Rather, it complemented the indigenous system. The emperor performed the official rituals of both Shinto and Buddhist worship.

Buddhism introduced a measure of centralization. Shinto, a looser system of belief and worship, had spread throughout all of Japan with no need of a central shrine for its worship of nature. By contrast, the Horyuji Temple near Nara became a central shrine for all of Japan. In 741 the emperor ordered that a Buddhist temple and pagoda be established in each province. Buddhism and Shinto coexisted in Japan in a pattern that continues today.

As in China, the power and wealth of Buddhist monasteries and temples in Japan, and especially in Nara, alarmed some members of the court. To reduce the power of the Buddhist clergy and to increase the power of his own lineage, Emperor Kammu (r. 781–806) moved the capital again, from Nara to Heian (modern Kyoto) in 794. This move initiated the Heian period in Japanese history and coincided with the decline of the Tang Empire in China. The Japanese government dispatched its last official mission to China in 838. With Japan on the ascendant and China in decline, Japan's Buddhism developed along its own paths, helped by substantial imperial patronage. The emperor himself patronized two young Japanese monks who founded the Tendai and Shingon schools of Buddhism, the two most powerful and enduring Buddhist movements in Japan.

Japanese Buddhism Develops New Forms. The Buddhist priesthood itself became increasingly Japanese, no longer reliant on priests from the Chinese mainland. It also entered more profoundly into politics. The priest Saicho (767–822) studied Tiantai (Tendai in Japanese) Buddhism in China and introduced it into Japan. Based on the Lotus Sutra, Tendai taught that each person could achieve enlightenment through sincere religious devotion. On Mount Hiei, northeast of Kyoto, Saicho built the Enryakuji monastery, which grew rapidly and steadily into one of the most important temple communities in Japan.

Saicho had intended his monastery to remain aloof from politics, and he therefore built it far from the national capital in Nara. Ironically, however, when the capital was moved to Kyoto, the monastery again found itself geographically close to the national political center. Saicho encouraged the monks to add teaching, administration, and social work in the service of the nation to their religious duties, merging Confucian and Buddhist value systems. His monastery grew to house tens of thousands of monks in some 3000 buildings. By the eleventh century, an era of deep and violent political fissures in Japanese political life, many Shinto and Buddhist temples supported standing armies to protect themselves and their extensive land holdings and branch temples. Troops from the Mount Hiei monastery began to enter the capital, demanding additional lands and thus completely reversing Saicho's original wishes. The Buddhist clergy thereafter became increasingly intertwined with Japanese politics.

Kukai (774–835), another Japanese Buddhist priest who had studied in China, also returned home to preach a new form of Buddhism. He became abbot of the monastery

Hoodo (Phoenix Hall), Byodoin Temple, Uji, Japan, eleventh century. The Phoenix Hall of the Byodoin Temple, with its jauntily uplifted roof-corners, indicates how over time the Buddhist style took on a distinctively Japanese flavor and shed its Chinese influence (contrast with picture, p. 286).

mantra A formula of utterances of words and sounds that are believed to possess spiritual power, a practice of both Hinduism and Buddhism.

mandala A symbolic circular diagram of complex geometric design used as an instrument of meditation or in the performance of sacred rites in Hinduism and Buddhism.

syllabary A writing system in which each symbol represents the syllable of a word (cf. ideogram).

ideogram (alternative: ideograph) A character or figure in a writing system in which the idea of a thing is represented rather than its name.

of the great Toji temple at Kyoto, where he introduced Shingon ("True Word") Buddhism. Shingon emphasizes the repetition of mystic incantations or **mantras**; meditation on colorful, sometimes stunning, geometrically ordered religious paintings, called **mandalas**, of Buddhas and bodhisattvas in their heavens; complicated rituals; music; and ecstatic dancing. Because the transmission of these forms was closely guarded among believers, Shingon was also called Esoteric Buddhism. Creating more accessible forms as well, Kukai introduced rituals, such as the austere and beautiful tea ceremony, in which a formal ritual surrounding the serving and drinking of tea invites deep meditation. Kukai is also credited with inventing the *kana* **syllabary**, a Japanese script in phonetic letters rather than **ideograms**. These innovations, in addition to mysterious, secret rituals, use of herbal medicines, and the elegant pageantry of Shingon, gave Kukai's monastery great popularity and power.

Another Chinese form of Buddhism that deeply influenced Japan was dedicated to Amida, or, in Sanskrit, Amitabha, the Buddha of the Infinite Light. In the tenth century, two priests, Kuya (903–972) and Genshin (942–1017), popularized this sect, which taught the importance of chanting the mantra *nembutsu*, "Praise to Amida Buddha." Amidism grew in subsequent generations through the organizational abilities of a series of monks, including Ryonin (1072–1132), who taught the counting of rosary beads to accompany the repetition of the *nembutsu*, a practice that spread to most sects of Japanese Buddhism. By the late twelfth century, Amidism established its independence from other Buddhist sects and at last reached a mass audience for whom its message of uncomplicated, universal access to salvation had great appeal.

Chan Buddhism, Zen in Japanese, appeared in Japan during the seventh century, but began to flourish only after the twelfth century. Much of Zen's popularity resulted from the teachings of Eisai, a Buddhist monk who believed that in addition to meditation, Zen should defend the state. Its emphasis on martial arts made Zen Buddhism particularly attractive to the increasingly powerful warrior class. Since then it has deeply influenced Japanese culture and remains important in Japan today.

Lasting Buddhist Elements in Japanese Society. Three other elements gave Buddhism a prominence and significance in Japanese life that has continued till today. First, Japanese Buddhism cultivated an especially pure aesthetic dimension, which we have seen here in the representations of the Buddha and bodhisattvas and of the architecture and art of the Japanese Buddhist temples. This appreciation of artistic creativity is apparent throughout Japan in formal gardens, in painting and calligraphy, and in the art of presentation of everything from self, to gifts, to tea, to food. Second, Buddhism's emphasis on the transience of all life has inspired much of the greatest Japanese literature, from the *Tale of Genji*, written by Lady Murasaki (*c.* 978–*c.* 1015) at the Japanese court a thousand years ago, to the novels of Mishima Yukio (1925–70), who committed *seppuku*, ritual suicide, immediately after completing his last novel. Third, Buddhism has coexisted and even merged to some degree with indigenous Shinto worship and belief.

By the twelfth century Japan had entered its Buddhist Age. Despite occasional attacks on Buddhism as a foreign religion and as an excessively wealthy and powerful organization, Buddhism has remained one of the two national religions of Japan. Most Japanese continue to mingle Buddhism and Shinto in their aesthetic and spiritual lives as well as in their ritual practices.

COMPARING HINDUISM AND BUDDHISM

Hinduism and Buddhism have undergone enormous transformations through their thousands of years of history. Geographically, Hinduism spread across the Indian subcontinent from its roots in the encounter between Aryan invaders and the indigenous peoples of the Indus valley and north India. It extended briefly even to southeast Asia (where a single Hindu outpost still remains on the Indonesian island of Bali). Buddhism spread from the Buddha's home region in the Himalayan foothills throughout India, where it subsequently died out, and most of east and southeast Asia, where it flourishes. Buddhism's array of monasteries and temples, and its veneration of the homeland of the Buddha himself, mark its sacred geography.

Both religions established their own sacred calendars and their control over life cycle events. In this, Hindu priests took a commanding position since even Buddhists (and Jains) employed them to officiate. Within India this continuing role of the brahmin priests ultimately helped Hinduism to absorb Buddhism. Outside India, where no other major religion was already in place, Buddhist priests performed their own rituals and came to predominate.

Both groups developed sacred languages. Buddhists felt that Sanskrit was narrowly limited to Hindu priests and so used Pali, a language closer to the vernacular. Over time, as the common people expressed their own religious feelings in their own languages, the leaders of both religions responded by also using the vernacular. Both religions inspired extensive literatures, including philosophy, mystical poetry, drama, and folk tales. Both generated their own artistic traditions in painting, sculpture, and temple architecture.

Organizationally, Buddhism, especially in its early Theravada form, was seen as a religion of its monks. Many common people found comfort and meaning in their philosophy and supported them, but ultimately they turned to brahmin priests for their ritual needs. Within Hinduism the caste system structured all classes and occupations into a single framework of relationships, with brahmins, *kshatriyas*, and sometimes *vaishyas*, predominating. Buddhism's later Mahayana form, with its multitudes of gods, bodhisattvas, and heavens, reached out to more people ritually as well as emotionally.

The evolution of Hinduism and Buddhism demonstrates the flexibility of great world religions. A small sect may define itself narrowly, proclaiming a core set of principles and practices and adhering to them rigidly. For its small membership, these restrictions may be the very attraction of the sect. But for a religion to grow in numbers, it must be open organizationally, doctrinally, and ritually to the varied spiritual, psychic, and social needs of diverse peoples. Like the empires we studied in Part 3, a world religion must be able to accommodate, satisfy, and absorb people of various languages, regions, classes, and previous spiritual beliefs and practices. World religions expand their theologies and practices to incorporate ever more members, until they reach the limits of their flexibility.

Finally, religions and governments have been historically interdependent. Buddhism flourished thanks to the early support of the Buddha's royal allies and later through the backing of the Emperor Asoka. It spread to southeast Asia and to Japan as kings offered their support in exchange for Buddhist legitimation. In China, Buddhism found its opening after Confucian dynasties fell and people searched for new belief systems and new leaders. Hinduism flourished as kings in India struck their own agreements with brahmin priests. Conversely, when governments turned against particular religious groups, they could devastate them. And when sizable religious groups shifted their support away from a ruler, they undermined his authority. We shall find more examples of this mutual antagonism in the next chapters.

HINDUISM AND BUDDHISM
WHAT DIFFERENCE DO THEY MAKE?

Hinduism keeps alive a major religion of active polytheism. Although many Hindus would argue that behind all of the gods a single reality pervades the world, others would argue, more literally, that there are indeed many very different gods with influence over the world and its creatures. These advocates of polytheism find a consistency between the diversity of life forms and life experiences and the multitude of gods of existence.

Hinduism has given a general cultural unity and depth to much of south Asia, in its arts and literature, its complex and sophisticated philosophical systems, and its hierarchical social, economic, and political order, which is based on caste forms. Today, the government and people of India cope with these legacies in a world that generally proclaims publicly the equality of all people. As a result, many political and religious questions regarding the relationships between the historic claims of hierarchy and the contemporary demands for equality confront India, and there are conflicting arguments about the most appropriate direction for future development, as we shall see in Chapter 20.

Buddhism also continues as the basis of the culture and religion of hundreds of millions of people, most of them in east and southeast Asia. The religion takes many different forms, from the relative austerity of the Theravada Buddhism of Sri Lanka, to the more elaborated and otherworldly Mahayana forms of southeast Asia, and the more mystical and isolated forms of Tibetan Buddhism. In many lands Buddhism is practiced freely, often in conjunction with other religions, as in Japan. In China, however, especially in Tibet, Buddhism struggles for survival against a hostile government, as we shall also see in Chapter 20. To understand religions in history, we must see them in the context of the political, social, and economic systems in which they are embedded.

We turn in the next chapters to three religions—Judaism, Christianity, and Islam—that have been militantly monotheistic. Although Judaism has remained relatively limited in its numbers, Christianity and Islam have been aggressive in their desire to win converts and are now the largest of the world's religions, with about 2 billion and 1.2 billion followers, respectively. Their relationships with the governments alongside which they exist have been checkered. Their impact on spiritual, cultural, social, and aesthetic life has been immense.

Review Questions

- What is the difference between studying a religion and studying about a religion? How does this compare to the differences between the studies of theologians and of historians?
- In what ways is Hinduism especially related to the land of India?
- Beginning with the emergence of Buddhism out of early brahminic beliefs and practices, what were the key turning points in the evolution of Buddhism?
- Describe the key elements in the competition between Hinduism and Buddhism, including such issues as principal beliefs, role of the clergy, role of the home, social hierarchy, and support of the government.
- What are the geographical distributions of Hindus and Buddhists? How and why have they changed over time?
- What have been the relationships between Buddhism and Confucianism in China? In Japan?

Suggested Readings

PRINCIPAL SOURCES

Basham, A.L. *The Wonder That Was India* (New York: Grove Press, 1954). Graceful, comprehensive, standard introduction to early Indian history. Dated on Indus valley, but still valid on imperial India.

Bhagavad Gita, trans. Barbara Stoler Miller (New York: Bantam Books, 1986). A fine, readable, clear translation of one of the greatest classics of Hinduism.

deBary, William Theodore and Irene Bloom, eds., *Sources of Chinese Tradition*, Vol. I: *From Earliest Times to 1600* (New York: Columbia University Press, 2nd ed., 1999). The best available repository of primary sources from the literature.

Ebrey, Patricia Buckley, ed. *Chinese Civilization: A Sourcebook* (New York: The Free Press, 2nd ed., 1993). An excellent sourcebook, drawn much more from the lives of common people.

Embree, Ainslee, ed. and rev. *Sources of Indian Tradition*, Vol. I: *From the Beginning to 1800* (New York: Columbia University Press, 2nd ed., 1988). The best available repository of primary sources from the literature.

Tsunoda, Ryusaku, William Theodore deBary, and Donald Keene, comps. *Sources of Japanese Tradition* (New York: Columbia University Press, 1958). The best available repository of primary sources from the literature.

ADDITIONAL SOURCES

Allchin, F.R., *et al. The Archaeology of Early Historic South Asia: The Emergence of Cities and States* (Cambridge: Cambridge University Press, 1995). Accessible, wide-ranging introduction, for non-specialists.

Andrea, Alfred and James Overfield, eds. *The Human Record*, Vol. I (Boston, MA: Houghton Mifflin Company, 3rd ed., 1998). Excellent collection of primary sources on world history.

Appadurai, Arjun. *Worship and Conflict under Colonial Rule* (Cambridge: Cambridge University Press, 1981). Demonstrates the interweaving of the major temples with the politics, economics, and social structures of their region.

Berger, Peter L. *The Sacred Canopy* (New York: Anchor Books, 1967). A classic introduction to the importance of religion and religious organizations in society.

Blunden, Caroline and Mark Elvin. *Cultural Atlas of China* (New York: Facts on File, 1983). Superb introduction to China, with fine interpretive essays, maps, pictures. Especially strong on geography and its implications.

Bodde, Derk. *Essays on Chinese Civilization*, ed. Charles Le Blanc and Dorothy Borei (Princeton, NJ: Princeton University Press, 1981). A classic set of essays on the significance of Chinese civilization.

Britannica Book of the Year 2002 (Chicago, IL: Encyclopedia Britannica, Inc., 2001) Updates a great deal of basic information, especially quantitative information on societies around the world.

Conze, Edward. *Buddhist Scriptures* (New York: Penguin Books, 1959). Basic source readings.

Craven, Roy C. *A Concise History of Indian Art* (New York: Oxford University Press, n.d.). Excellent introduction to Indian art, especially of the classical period.

The Dhammapada, trans. by Juan Mascaro (New York: Penguin Books, 1973). Fine translation and introduction to this Buddhist literary and religious classic.

Dimmitt, Cornelia and J.A.B. van Buitenen, ed. and trans. *Classical Hindu Mythology* (Philadelphia, PA: Temple University Press, 1978). An exposition of Indian mythology and texts by masters of the field.

Eberhard, Wolfram. *China's Minorities: Yesterday and Today* (Belmont, CA: Wadsworth Publishing, 1982). Fills in the picture for non-Han Chinese, a subject often overlooked.

Eliade, Mircea. *Ordeal by Labyrinth* (Chicago, IL: University of Chicago Press, 1982). Elegant exposition of the role of religion in society.

Eliade, Mircea. *The Sacred and the Profane* (New York: Harper Torchbooks, 1959). Thought provoking introduction to the way in which religion moves people and encourages them to create institutions.

Eliade, Mircea. *Yoga: Immortality and Freedom* (Princeton, NJ: Princeton University Press, 1969). The philosophy of yoga presented clearly and profoundly.

Elvin, Mark. *The Pattern of the Chinese Past* (Stanford, CA: Stanford University Press, 1973). Elvin explores especially the economy of China, its highs and lows.

Hall, Kenneth R. *Maritime Trade and State Development in Early Southeast Asia* (Honolulu: University of Hawaii, 1985). Especially good on the relationships between India and southeast Asia in trade and in political evolution.

Hall, Kenneth R. and John K. Whitmore, eds. *Explorations in Early Southeast Asian History: The Origins of Southeast Asian Statecraft* (Ann Arbor, MI: Center for South and Southeast Asian Studies, University of Michigan, 1976). Set of outstanding seminar papers.

Hammond Atlas of World History (Maplewood, NJ: Hammond, 5th ed., 1999). Indispensable world history atlas.

Hughes, Sarah Shaver and Brady Hughes, eds. *Women in World History*, Vol. I: *Readings from Prehistory to 1500* (Armonk, NY: M.E. Sharpe, 1995). Includes short, but interesting sections on husbands and wives, Sita and Rama, and Buddhist nuns.

Kulke, Hermann and Dietmar Rothermund. *A History of India* (Totowa, NJ: Barnes and Noble Books, 1986). Brief, accessible, excellent introductory history.

Lewis-Williams, David. *The Mind in the Cave: Consciousness in the Origins of Art* (London: Thames and Hudson, 2002). Exploration of meaning in earliest art includes religious speculations.

Lockard, Craig A. "Integrating Southeast Asia into the Framework of World History: The Period Before 1500," *The History Teacher* XXIX, No. 1 (November 1995), 7–35. Concern with pedagogy leads also to good conceptual scheme for understanding southeast Asia.

Martin, Rafe. *The Hungry Tigress: Buddhist Legends and Jataka Tales* (Berkeley, CA: Parallax Press, 1990). Classic legends and tales as means of transmitting the essential moral lessons of Buddhism.

Murphey, Rhoads. *A Brief History of Asia* (New York: HarperCollins, 1992). Useful especially for its cross-regional explorations.

Needham, Joseph. *The Shorter Science and Civilization in China*, Vol. I, abridged by Colin A. Ronan (Cambridge: Cambridge University Press, 1978). The classic study of Chinese science, demonstrating its methods, findings, and significance.

Nelson, Lynn and Patrick Peebles, eds. *Classics of Eastern Thought* (San Diego, CA: Harcourt Brace Jovanovich, 1991). Fine collection of basic texts.

Past Worlds: The (London) Times Atlas of Archaeology (Maplewood, NJ: Hammond, 1988). Fascinating introduction to history through archaeological finds. Lavishly illustrated with maps, pictures, charts.

Ramanujan, A.K., ed. and trans. *Poems of Love and War: From the Eight Anthologies and the Ten Long Poems of Classical Tamil* (New York: Columbia University Press, 1985). An outstanding modern poet and scholar translating classical Tamil poetry.

Ramanujan, A.K., trans. *Speaking of Síva* (Harmondsworth, England: Penguin Books, 1973). Further translations specifically on the Lord Shiva in the imagination of India.

Richman, Paula, ed. *Many Ramayanas: The Diversity of a Narrative Tradition in South Asia* (Berkeley, CA: University of California Press, 1991). The Ramayana has many interpretations and uses. Richman provides an astonishing, scholarly array of them.

Rowland, Benjamin. *The Art and Architecture of India: Buddhist/Hindu/Jain* (New York: Penguin Books, 1977). Indian religion can be understood only with reference to its art and architecture. A fine introduction.

SarDesai, D.R. *Southeast Asia: Past and Present* (Boulder, CO: Westview Press, 3rd ed., 1994). Good on the context of the spread of Buddhism.

Schwartzberg, Joseph E., ed. *A Historical Atlas of South Asia* (Chicago, IL: University of Chicago Press, 1978). A scholarly, encyclopedic coverage of history through geography. Superb research tool.

Smart, Ninian. *The World's Religions* (Cambridge: Cambridge University Press , 1989). Fine, comprehensive introduction to the major religions.

Stein, Burton. *Peasant State and Society in Medieval South India* (New Delhi: Oxford University Press, 1980). Provides context for understanding religion and religious institutions in the life of the society.

Thapar, Romila. *Ancient Indian Social History* (New Delhi: Orient Longman, 1978). Thapar's works are the most accessible, clear, comprehensive introduction to ancient India, its politics, institutions, leaders, economy, social groups, and religions.

——. *Asoka and the Decline of the Mauryas* (New Delhi: Oxford University Press, 1963).

——. *A History of India*, Vol. I (Baltimore, MD: Penguin Books, 1966).

——. *Early India: From the Origins to AD 300* (Berkeley, CA: University of California Press, 2003).

——. *Interpreting Early India* (New York: Oxford University Press, 1992).

Tharu, Susie and K. Lalita, eds. *Women Writing in India 600 B.C. to the Present*, Vol. I (New York: The Feminist Press, 1991). Includes writings from various regions of India, and puts them into context.

Twitchett, Denis and Michael Lowe, eds. *The Cambridge History of China*, Vol. I: *The Ch'in and Han Empires, 221 B.C.–A.D. 220* (Cambridge: Cambridge University Press, 1986). Comprehensive, scholarly, helps understand early Buddhism in China.

Twitchett, Denis, ed. *The Cambridge History of China*, Vol. III: *Sui and T'ang China, 589–906*, Part I (Cambridge: Cambridge University Press, 1979). Comprehensive, scholarly, follows Buddhism through its flourishing in China.

Zimmer, Heinrich. *Philosophies of India* (New York: Meridian Books, 1956). Classic introduction to the texts and concepts.

⊚ World History Documents CD-ROM

3.1 *Rig Veda*
3.2 *Bhagavad Gita*: Hinduism
3.3 The Foundation of the Kingdom of Righteousness
3.4 Dhammapada: Buddhism
3.5 Mahavira: The "Great Hero" of the Jain Religion
3.6 Asoka: How a Life Was Turned Around

JUDAISM AND CHRISTIANITY

PEOPLES OF THE BIBLE: GOD'S EVOLUTION IN WEST ASIA AND EUROPE 1700 B.C.E.–1100 C.E.

KEY TOPICS
- Judaism
- Christianity
- Christianity in the Wake of Empire

Into a world that believed in many gods who often fought with one another and interfered capriciously in human life, the Hebrews introduced and perpetuated the concept of a single god whose rule was both orderly and just. In contrast with the many gods of polytheism, each with his or her own temperament and judgment, the new monotheism provided a more definitive statement of right and wrong. At the same time it demanded much greater conformity in both faith and action, calling for adherence to a strict code of ethics within a community governed by laws proclaimed by a single god. The Hebrews' belief in one god was not simply a reduction in the number of gods from many to one. Their god represented a new religious category of a god above nature and free of compulsion and fate. Their belief in only one god, however, also confronted them with a fundamental theological dilemma, a dilemma for all monotheistic religions: If there is only one god, and if the god is both all-powerful and caring, then why does human life on earth often appear so difficult and unjust?

The Hebrews' early home was in the Middle East, and other peoples in that region sometimes expressed similar ideas. In Egypt, for example, Akhenaten also proclaimed a belief in one god. His declaration of faith, however, came several centuries after that of the Hebrews. More importantly, his new faith did not survive his death and had no lasting effects on his country. Later pharaohs rejected Akhenaten's beliefs and his style of worship. In Mesopotamia, Hammurabi of Babylon issued a law code in the name of his god Shamash, by the year 1750 B.C.E., some 500 years before Hebrew sacred texts record a similar gift of a legal system from their god YHWH, through their leader Moses. Over time, however, the code of Hammurabi was forgotten in Mesopotamia while the Hebrew people kept their legal codes alive as they evolved into the Jewish people.

In their early years the "Hebrews" were known as the people whose legendary founder, Abraham, came from "eber," meaning "the other side" of the Euphrates River. Later they took on the name of Jews, in honor of one of their tribes, Judah, and of the new territory that they claimed in Judaea, in the modern land of Israel and Palestine.

Today there are only about 14 million Jews worldwide, but their role in history has been disproportionate to their numbers. Many of their core beliefs were incorporated into Christianity and Islam, the two great monotheistic faiths that have come to include half the world's population today. Meanwhile Judaism itself adapted to changing conditions over time and space, maintaining its own core beliefs, traditions, and identity as an independent religious community. We begin this chapter with a study of Judaism and then proceed to Christianity, which emerged from it, and challenged it. In the next chapter we explore Islam and the interactions among all three of these closely related, but often bitterly antagonistic, monotheistic religions.

Opposite **The four evangelists, from the *Gospel Book of Charlemagne*, early ninth century.** With the exception of the cross, the best-known symbols in early Christianity were associated with the four gospels. Based on a text in the Book of Revelation (4:7), Matthew was represented by a man, Mark by a lion, Luke by a winged ox, and John by an eagle. (*Cathedral Treasury, Aachen, Germany*)

AT A GLANCE : JUDAISM AND CHRISTIANITY

DATE	POLITICAL/SOCIAL EVENTS	LITERARY/PHILOSOPHICAL EVENTS
1700 B.C.E.	■ Abraham travels from Mesopotamia to Israel (*c.* 1750)	
1600 B.C.E.	■ Hebrew slavery in Egypt	
1200 B.C.E.	■ Moses (?1300–?1200) ■ Exodus from Egypt; legal codes formulated; return to Palestine; tribal government under Judges	
1000 B.C.E.	■ Period of Kings begins with Saul, David, and Solomon ■ First temple in Jerusalem	
900 B.C.E	■ Jewish kingdom divides into Israel and Judaea	
800 B.C.E.	■ Prophets exhort Jewish nation (800–500) ■ Assyrians conquer Israel and exile Jews (721)	■ Numbers (850–650) ■ Genesis (mid 5th–8th century) ■ Prophets Isaiah, Amos, Micah
700 B.C.E.		■ Josiah begins to write down Torah (640) ■ Deuteronomy (mid 7th century) ■ Leviticus (mid 7th century) ■ Jeremiah
600 B.C.E.	■ Babylonians conquer Judaea, exile the people, and destroy the first temple (586) ■ Jews permitted to return to Judaea and rebuild the temple (538)	■ Book of Job (600)
300 B.C.E.		■ Books of TaNaKh (the Torah) edited and canonized
100 B.C.E.	■ Birth and death of Jesus (*c.* 4 B.C.E.–*c.* 30 C.E.)	
10 C.E.	■ Rome captures Jerusalem (63) ■ Christianity emerges from Judaism ■ St. Paul, Saul of Tarsus, organizes early Christianity (d. *c.* 67) ■ Rome destroys second temple (70)	■ Gospels (70–100) ■ Acts (70–80) ■ Epistles of Paul (50–120)
100 C.E.	■ Rome exiles Jews from Judaea; Jewish diaspora throughout Mediterranean basin and west Asia (135) ■ Rabbinical tradition developed (1st to 4th century)	
200 C.E.	■ Christians persecuted under Severus, Decius, and Diocletian	■ Babylonian and Jerusalem Talmuds edited and published (200–500)
300 C.E.	■ Christianity legalized (313) and then declared the official religion of the Roman Empire (392) ■ Council of Nicaea (325) ■ Georgia and Armenia convert to Christianity (*c.* 330)	■ Augustine's *The City of God* and *Confessions*
400 C.E.	■ Council of Chalcedon (451)	
500 C.E.	■ Monasticism in Europe ■ Clovis converted to Christianity ■ St. Benedict founds monastery of Monte Cassino	
600 C.E.	■ England converted to Christianity	■ Venerable Bede, Ecclesiastical *History of the English People*
700 C.E.	■ Iconoclastic controversy	
800 C.E.	■ Coronation of Charlemagne (800) ■ St. Cyril and St. Methodius convert Russia, translate the Bible, and create the Cyrillic alphabet	■ Einhard, *Life of Charlemagne*
900 C.E.	■ Missionaries proliferate among the Vikings	

AT A GLANCE : JUDAISM AND CHRISTIANITY (continued)

DATE	POLITICAL/SOCIAL EVENTS	LITERARY/PHILOSOPHICAL EVENTS
1000 C.E.	■ Christians capture Toledo from Muslim control and begin *reconquista* (1085) ■ Split of Western and Eastern Christianity (1054) ■ 1st Crusade (1095–9)	
1100 C.E.	■ 2nd Crusade (1147–9) ■ 3rd Crusade (1189–92)	
1200 C.E.	■ 4th Crusade (1202–04) ■ Children's Crusade (1212) ■ Crusaders capture Constantinople (1204–61) ■ 5th–8th Crusades (1218–91)	
1300 C.E.	■ Monastic orders	
1400 C.E.	■ Christians capture Granada, Spain, complete the *reconquista* (1492), expel Jews and Muslims	

JUDAISM

The story of Judaism, as recorded in Hebrew scriptures, begins some 3800 years ago with one man's vision of a single, unique God of all creation. They tell us that God and Abraham sealed a covenant stating that Abraham's descendants would forever revere and worship that God, and God, in return, would forever watch over and protect them. From then until now Judaism has remained a relatively small, family-based religion, with branches throughout the world, but focused in part in Israel, the land that Jews believe God promised to Abraham.

The Sacred Scriptures

Our knowledge of early Jewish history comes from the scriptures known collectively as the **TaNaKh**: Torah (the Five Books of Moses), Nevi'im (the Books of the Prophets), and Ketuvim (additional historical, poetic, and philosophic writings). Christians have incorporated the entire TaNaKh into their Bible, referring to these scriptures collectively as the "Old Testament." Because the New Testament is written in Greek and the Old Testament in Hebrew, the TaNaKh is often referred to as the Hebrew Bible.

The narratives of the five books of the Torah abound with miracles, as God intervenes continuously in the history of the Jews. The Torah begins with God's creating the world and contracting his covenant with Abraham. Over the next several generations, the Torah continues, famine struck Israel (then called Canaan), the land God promised to Abraham. Abraham's grandson and his family traveled to the Nile valley of Egypt in search of food. At first invited by the pharaoh to remain as permanent residents, they were later enslaved. About 1200 B.C.E., after 400 years of slavery, the Jews won their freedom and escaped from Egypt under the leadership of Moses through the miraculous intervention of God. During their journey back to Israel through the wilderness of the Sinai Desert, the contentious group of ex-slaves was forged into a small but militant nation. The Torah records a dramatic miracle at Mount Sinai in which God revealed a set of religious and civil laws for them to follow.

For centuries, Jews and Christians believed that these earliest books of the Bible, which describe the creation of the world and the earliest history of the Jewish people, were the literal word of God. During the past two centuries, scholarship has given us a new sense of the historical place of these books. Today historians ask: When and

TaNaKh A Hebrew term for the books of the Bible that are written in Hebrew. The word is composed of the initial letters of the words Torah (first five books of the Bible, traditionally attributed to Moses), Nevi'im (the books of the Prophets) and the Ketuvim (additional historical, poetic, and philosophic writings). These are the three sections of the Hebrew Bible.

The Kingdom of Israel. The first unified Jewish state in Palestine emerged around 980 B.C.E. under King David. He united the tribes of Israel during a period of decline among their more powerful neighbors—Egypt and the Hittites. After the death of his son Solomon (926 B.C.E.), tribal rivalries divided the empire into the kingdoms of Judah and Israel, but the sense of cultural unity survived.

where were the books of the Hebrew Bible composed and how valid are they as historical documents?

Modern scholarly analysis of the TaNaKh texts became a prominent academic enterprise in Germany during the early nineteenth century. The founders of "biblical criticism" noted certain inconsistencies in the biblical texts. For example, the first chapter of Genesis reports that God created man and woman simultaneously, "male and female he created them," while the second chapter reports that God first created man and then removed one of his ribs and created woman from it. The critics noted also that different names are used for God in the Hebrew text—most notably YHWH and Elohim—and they suggested that the different names represent the stylistic preferences of different authors. They noted similarities between the stories and laws of the Bible and those in the literature of other peoples of the region, and they suggested that some of the external stories had found their way into the biblical accounts. Through rigorous analysis, the biblical scholars argued persuasively that Josiah (r. 640–609 B.C.E.), the king of the Jewish state of Judaea, first made the decision to begin to edit and write down the definitive edition of oral texts that had been passed from generation to generation.

The story of Josiah's reign is told in the biblical book of 2 Kings, chapters 20–21. Struggling to survive in the face of the powerful Assyrian Empire, Josiah was anxious to promote allegiance to the state and its religion. He centralized Jewish worship in the national temple in Jerusalem and collected and transcribed the most important texts of his people. Josiah regarded adherence to the laws laid down in these scriptures as fundamental to the maintenance of the Jewish religion, the Jewish people, and his own Jewish kingdom. From existing literary fragments, folk wisdom, and oral history he had the book of Deuteronomy, the fifth book of the TaNaKh, written down. Soon, additional literary materials from at least three other major interpretive traditions were also woven together to create the books of Genesis, Exodus, Leviticus, and Numbers. Together with Deuteronomy, these books formed the Torah or "Five Books of Moses."

With the ravages of time, older copies of the Torah, written in Hebrew on parchment scrolls, began to perish and new ones were copied. The oldest existing Hebrew manuscripts of the entire Torah date only to the ninth to the eleventh centuries C.E., but fragments dating to as early as the second century B.C.E. have been discovered. Stored in caves near the Dead Sea in Israel, these Dead Sea Scrolls have been rediscovered only since 1947. Another very early edition of the Torah is a Greek translation from the Hebrew, the Septuagint. It was prepared for the Greek-speaking Jews of Egypt in the third and second centuries B.C.E. It still exists and is consistent with the Hebrew texts of our own time. In short, the written text of the Torah appears to have been preserved with great fidelity for at least 2600 years. The oral texts on which the written scriptures were based date back much further.

The Torah remains one of the greatest examples of myth-history. Although its stories should not necessarily be read as literal, historical records, their version of events gave birth to the Jewish people's concept of itself and helped to define its character and principal beliefs. The stories of the Torah tell us what the Jewish people, and especially its literate leadership, have thought important about their own origins and mission. They also define images of God that have profoundly influenced the imagination and action of Jews, Christians, and Muslims for millennia.

Essential Beliefs of Judaism in Early Scriptures

The Torah fixes many of the essential beliefs and principles of Judaism:

- A single caring God, demanding obedience, who administers rewards and punishments fairly and in accordance with his fixed laws:

  Hear, O Israel, the Lord is our God, the Lord alone. You shall love the Lord your God with all your heart, and with all your soul, and with all your might. (Deuteronomy 6:4–5)

  Know therefore that the Lord your God is God, the faithful God who maintains covenant loyalty with those who love him and keep his commandments, to a thousand generations, and who repays in their own person those who reject him. (Deuteronomy 7:9–10)

- A God of history, whose power affects the destiny of individuals and nations:

  I am the Lord your God who brought you out of Egypt, out of the land of slavery. (Exodus 20:2–3)

- A community rooted in a divinely chosen family and ethnic group:

  Now the Lord said to Abram, "Go from your country and your kindred and your father's house to the land that I will show you. I will make of you a great nation, and I will bless you, and make your name great, so that you will be a blessing." (Genesis 12:1–2)

- A specific, "promised," geographical homeland:

  When Abraham reached Canaan, God said to him: "Raise your eyes now, and look from the place where you are, northward and southward and eastward and westward; for all the land that you see I will give to you and to your offspring forever." (Genesis 13:14–15)

- A legal system to guide proper behavior: religious, familial, sexual, commercial, civic, ethical, and ritual. The introduction to this code was the Ten Commandments, revered as the heart of the revelation to Moses at Mount Sinai.

Dead Sea Scrolls, Isaiah scroll 1Q Is. 9 verses 58.6–63.4. The five hundred or so documents that make up the Dead Sea Scrolls—which date between about 250 B.C.E. and 70 C.E.—appear at one time to have formed the library of a Jewish community. As well as providing evidence of the accuracy of Hebrew biblical texts, they give information about the life of the community itself. (*Israel Museum, Jerusalem*)

SOURCE

The Ten Commandments

The Torah contains legal codes governing many aspects of life, including family rules concerning marriage, divorce, and inheritance; civil laws regulating business practices and responsibilities; criminal law mandating rules of evidence and of punishment; rules commanding ethical and charitable behavior especially toward the weak and helpless, strangers, orphans, and widows; and extensive rules concerning ritual practices of prayer, sacrifice, food, and priestly behavior. At the center of the codes are the Ten Commandments, given, according to the Torah account, directly by God to Moses atop Mount Sinai amidst terrifying thunder, lightning, clouds, and trumpet blasts. These commandments dictate behavior toward God, parents, and fellow humans. They also proclaim the importance of observing a Sabbath day once a week.

I am the Lord your God who brought you out of Egypt, out of the house of slavery.

You shall have no other gods before me.

You shall not make for yourself an idol, whether in the form of anything that is in heaven above, or that is on the earth beneath, or that is in the water under the earth.

You shall not bow down to them or worship them; for I the Lord your God am a jealous god, punishing children for the iniquity of parents, to the third and fourth generation of those who reject me, but showing steadfast love to the thousandth generation of those who love me and keep my commandments.

You shall not make wrongful use of the name of the Lord your God, for the Lord will not acquit anyone who misuses his name.

Remember the Sabbath day, and keep it holy. Six days you shall labor and do all your work. But the seventh day is a Sabbath to the Lord your God; you shall not do any work—you, your son or your daughter, your male or female slave, your livestock, or the alien resident in your towns. For in six days the Lord made heaven and earth, the sea, and all that is in them, but rested the seventh day; therefore the Lord blessed the Sabbath day and consecrated it.

Honor your father and your mother, so that your days may be long in the land that the Lord your God is giving you.

You shall not murder.

You shall not commit adultery.

You shall not steal.

You shall not bear false witness against your neighbor.

You shall not covet your neighbor's house; you shall not covet your neighbor's wife, or male or female slave, or ox, or donkey, or anything that belongs to your neighbor. (Exodus 20:2–17; see also Deuteronomy 5)

- A sacred calendar: Jewish religious leaders reconstituted earlier polytheistic celebrations of nature into a calendar of national religious celebration. A spring festival of renewal was incorporated into Passover, the commemoration of the exodus from Egypt; an early summer festival of first harvest was subsumed into Shavuot, a rejoicing in the revelation of the Ten Commandments at Sinai; and an early fall harvest festival became part of Sukkot (Succoth), a remembrance of the years of wandering in the desert. All these festivals were to be celebrated, if possible, by pilgrimage to the central, national temple in Jerusalem. Celebrations of nature, history, and national identity were fused together.

To ground the mystical beliefs and forge the Jewish people into a "kingdom of priests and a sacred nation," rules issued in the name of God forbade intermarriage with outsiders; prohibited eating animals which do not have cloven hooves and chew their cud, and fish that do not have scales and fins (Deuteronomy 14 and Leviticus 11); and centralized worship in the hands of a priestly aristocracy. Animal sacrifices were to be offered, but only by the hereditary priests and only in a single national temple in Jerusalem.

The Later Books of Jewish Scripture

The later volumes of the TaNaKh, the books of Nevi'im and Ketuvim, carry an account of the history of the Jewish people from about 1200 B.C.E. to about the fifth century B.C.E. God continues as a constant presence in these narratives, but he intervenes less openly and less frequently. These later records can generally be cross-checked against

Moses, mosaic in San Vitale, Ravenna, Italy, sixth century C.E. After he had led the Israelite slaves out of Egypt by the miracle of parting the Red Sea), Moses ascended Mount Sinai. There he received from God the Torah, or sacred teachings, beginning with the two tablets of the Ten Commandments. He led his quarrelsome people across the Sinai desert but died at the border of the promised land.

the archaeology of the region and the history of neighboring peoples, and they seem generally consistent.

The Book of Joshua begins the story about the year 1200 B.C.E., as the Jews returned to Canaan, or Israel, the land promised to them, and made it their home. This biblical account tells of continuous, violent, political and religious warfare between the invading Jews and the resident Canaanite peoples. Modern scholarship suggests, however, that re-entry into the land of Israel was a gradual process, with fewer, more localized battles and considerably more cultural borrowing among all the groups in the region.

Rule by Judges and by Kings. Arriving in Canaan, the Jews first organized themselves in a loose tribal confederacy led by a series of "Judges," *ad hoc* leaders who took

Map of the world by Heinrich Bunting, 1585. Many peoples believed that their capital city was the cosmo-magical axis of the universe. This map, shaped like a clover leaf, places Jerusalem at the center, uniting Africa, Asia, and Europe.

command at critical periods, especially at times of war. Later, despite warnings that a monarchy would lead to increased warfare, profligate leaders, extortionate taxes, and the impressment of young men and women into royal service, the Jews anointed a king. For three generations (c. 1020–950 B.C.E.), strong kings, Saul, David, and Solomon, are said to have ruled and expanded the geographic base of the people. They established a national center in Jerusalem, where they united political and religious power by building both palace and temple, exalting both king and priest. The earlier warnings against royal excesses, however, proved correct. Unable to sustain Solomon's legendary extravagances in expenditure and in his relationships with 700 wives, many of them foreign princesses, and 300 concubines, the kingdom split in two, the kingdom of Judah and the kingdom of Israel.

The Teachings of the Prophets: Morality and Hope. Continuing despotism by their kings and greed on the part of their wealthier citizens ripped apart the social fabric of the two splinter kingdoms. A group of prophets emerged, demanding reform. In powerful and sublime language, these men called for a reinstitution of justice, compassion, and ethics. Speaking in the name of God and of the people, they cried out against the hypocritical misuse of religious and political power.

The prophet Isaiah, in the eighth century B.C.E., led the charge:

When you stretch out your hands, I will hide my eyes from you; even though you make many prayers, I will not listen; your hands are full of blood.
Wash yourselves; make yourselves clean; remove the evil of your doings from before my eyes; cease to do evil,
Learn to do good; seek justice, rescue the oppressed, defend the orphan, plead for the widow. (Isaiah 1:15–17)

A century later, Jeremiah continued in the same spirit of moral outrage, rebuking the rulers and people of Judah, the southern kingdom:

You keep saying, "This place is the temple of the Lord, the temple of the Lord, the temple of the Lord!" This catchword of yours is a lie; put no trust in it. Mend your ways and your doings, deal fairly with one another, do not oppress the alien, the orphan, and the widow, shed no innocent blood in this place, do not run after other gods to your own ruin. (Jeremiah 7:4–6)

So even at the time that Israel and Judah developed into powerful kingdoms, the prophets remembered that the beginnings of the Jewish people were in slavery and that a significant part of its mission was to identify with and help the downtrodden. When destruction came, the prophets interpreted it as punishment not *of* their God, as earlier peoples had often done, but *by* their God. Destruction of a corrupt nation indicated not the weakness of its God, but his ethical consistency.

Finally, the prophets not only harangued, blamed, and condemned, they also held up visions of a future to inspire their listeners. They saw God transforming human history. He offered rewards as well as punishments. He offered hope. Micah's prophecy in the eighth century B.C.E. is one of the most exalted, and perhaps utopian:

He shall judge between many peoples, and shall arbitrate between strong nations far away; they shall beat their swords into plowshares, and their spears into pruning hooks; nation shall not lift up sword against nation, neither shall they learn war any more; but they shall all sit under their own vines and under their own fig trees, and no one shall make them afraid; for the mouth of the Lord of hosts has spoken. (Micah 4:1–4)

Micah closed with a vision of great Jewish religious commitment, balanced by equally great appreciation for the diversity of others:

For all the peoples walk each in the name of its god, but we will walk in the name of the Lord our God forever and ever. (Micah 4:5)

The Evolution of the Image of God

The Torah portrays God as an evolving moral force in dialogue with humans. In God's early interactions with humans, his nature is still malleable. Disgusted at human disobedience, he destroys almost all humankind through a flood, but he then pledges never to be so destructive again, creating a rainbow as a kind of treaty of peace with humanity (Genesis 6–8). Still fearful of the collective power of humanity, God confounds their inter-communication by dividing them into separate language groups at the Tower of Babel (Genesis 11). While deciding the fate of the sinful cities of Sodom and Gomorrah, God listens to Abraham's plea for the defense: "Far be it from thee to do this—to kill good and bad together; for then the good would suffer with the bad. Far be it from thee. Shall not the judge of all the earth do what is just?" (Genesis 18–19). God apparently bans child sacrifice when he stops Abraham from killing his son Isaac. (The Muslim Quran reports this to be Abraham's son Ishmael.)

When asked by Moses to identify himself by name, God replies enigmatically and powerfully, "I am who I am" (Exodus 3:14). The Hebrew designation for God's name is YHWH, "Being." English-speaking readers have usually rendered it either Jehovah or Yahweh.

In Jewish theology, God is almighty but still directly accessible to every human being through prayer and even through dialogue. Indeed, humans and God come to understand each other by arguing with one another in a process that the contemporary rabbi Arthur Waskow has called "Godwrestling." If Jews are to be God's people and to follow his will, he, in turn, is expected to be a compassionate and attentive ruler.

This view challenged the polytheistic beliefs in self-willed gods, but it left Judaism with no strong answer to the eternal problem of evil in the universe: If there is a single God, and if he is good, why do the wicked often prosper and the righteous often suffer? One biblical response is found in the Book of Job (c. 600 B.C.E.). To the questions of the innocent, suffering Job, God finally responds with overwhelming power:

> Who is this whose ignorant words cloud my design in darkness?
> Brace yourself and stand up like a man; I will ask the questions, and you shall answer.
> Where were you when I laid the earth's foundations? Tell me, if you know and understand.
> Who settled its dimensions? Surely you should know …
> Is it for a man who disputes with the Almighty to be stubborn?
> Should he that argues with God answer back? (Job 38:2–5; 40:2)

But while God lectures Job for his brashness in questioning his authority and power, he understands Job's anguish at the apparent injustice in the world and ultimately rewards Job with health, a restored family, and abundance for his honesty in raising his questions.

Crossing the Red Sea, c. 245 C.E. Fresco, synagogue at Dura Europos, Syria. The Old Testament tells of God's miraculous intervention in helping Moses and the people of Israel escape enslavement in Egypt. Hotly pursued by pharaoh's soldiers to the banks of the Red Sea, Moses saw the waves draw back in front of him to allow the Jews to pass. When the Egyptians tried to follow, the sea engulfed them and they were drowned. (*National Archaeological Museum, Damascus, Syria*)

Patriarchy and Gender Relations

The Torah grants women fewer civil and religious rights (and obligations) than men. By conventional interpretation, women were expected to be responsible for nursing and child care, tasks that know no time constraints, and they were therefore freed of all ritual obligations that had to be performed at specific times, for instance prayers at specific times of day.

The regulation of sexuality is a fundamental issue in biblical Jewish law, as it is in most religions. Women are regarded as ritually unclean each month at times of menstruation and in childbirth. Men may be ritually unclean as a result of wet dreams or sexual diseases (Leviticus 15), but these occurred with less regularity. Marriage is regarded as the norm, with a strong emphasis on bearing children. Homosexual behavior is strongly rejected. (Today, however, many branches of Judaism have revised gender rules and discarded prohibitions on homosexuality.)

Jewish scriptures credit a few women with heroic roles. Sarah, Abraham's wife, forced him to choose her son as his proper successor, and she gained God's approval (Genesis 16). Deborah led Israel in peace and war during the period of conquering the land of Israel (Judges 4–5). Ruth, a convert, taught the importance of openness to the outside world; she became an ancestor of King David and, therefore, in Christian belief, of Jesus (Book of Ruth). Esther was married to the Persian king and used her position to block the attempts of a court minister to kill the Jews of the Persian Empire (Book of Esther). Although none of these stories can be authenticated externally nor dated exactly, they speak to the significance of individual, exceptional women at turning points in Jewish history, and in the collective mind of the Jewish people.

JEWISH FESTIVALS AND FAST DAYS		
Hebrew date	Gregorian date	Name of festival
1–2 Tishri	Sept–Oct	Rosh Hashana (New Year)
10 Tishri	Sept–Oct	Yom Kippur (Day of Atonement)
15–21 Tishri	Sept–Oct	Sukkot (Feast of the Tabernacles)
22 Tishri	Sept–Oct	Shemini Atzeret (8th Day of the Solemn Assembly)
23 Tishri	Sept–Oct	Simchat Torah (Rejoicing of the Law)
25 Kislev–2–3 Tevet	Nov–Dec	Hannukah (Feast of Dedication)
14–15 Adar	Feb–Mar	Purim (Feast of Lots)
14–20 Nisan	Mar–Apr	Pesach (Passover)
5 Iyar	Apr–May	Israel Independence Day
6–7 Sivan	May–Jun	Shavuot (Feast of Weeks)
9 Av	Jul–Aug	Tisha be–Av (Fast of 9th Av)

Defeat, Exile, and Redefinition

Jews represent both an ethnic community and a universal religion. This dual identity became especially clear when foreign conquerors exiled part of the Jewish population from Israel as part of a plan to encourage their assimilation and to open the land to foreign immigration. This dispersion of Jews to various lands ruled by other peoples is known as the **diaspora**.

First, Sennacherib of Assyria dispersed the Jews of the northern kingdom of Israel in 721 B.C.E. These exiles drifted into assimilation and were subsequently referred to as the "Lost Ten Tribes of Israel." In 586 B.C.E., Babylonian conquerors destroyed the temple in Jerusalem and exiled thousands of Jews from the southern kingdom of Judah to Babylon, but these Jews remained loyal to their unique identity as a separate community, remembering their homeland:

diaspora A dispersion of peoples. Most commonly used to refer to the dispersion of Jews among the gentiles, which began with the Babylonian captivity of the sixth century B.C.E.

By the rivers of Babylon—there we sat down and wept when we remembered Zion …
Our captors asked us for songs: "Sing us one of the songs of Zion!"
How could we sing the Lord's song in a foreign land?
If I forget you, O Jerusalem, let my right hand wither!
Let my tongue cling to the roof of my mouth if I do not remember you, if I do not set
   Jerusalem above my highest joy. (Psalm 137)

The second (Herod's) temple (model), 20 B.C.E. The temple at Jerusalem was originally built in the tenth century B.C.E. by King Solomon as a symbol of national unity and as a religious pilgrimage center. Razed by the Babylonians in 586 B.C.E., it was rebuilt sixty years later. It was finally destroyed by the Romans in 70 C.E. as part of the campaign to crush Jewish rebellion.

When the emperor Cyrus permitted the Jews to return to Judaea some sixty years later, many Jews left Babylonia, returned to Judaea, rebuilt their temple, and reconstructed national life. But many did not. Those who stayed behind did not assimilate into the Babylonian culture, however. Instead, they reconstituted their religion, replacing the sacrificial services of the temple with meditation and prayers offered privately or in synagogues. They replaced the hereditary priesthood with teachers and rabbis, positions earned through study and piety. In academies at Sura and Pumbeditha, towns adjacent to Babylon, rabbis continued the study of the Torah. They interpreted and edited Jewish law, and they elaborated Jewish stories and myths, which often conveyed moral principles. The multi-volumed record of their proceedings, the Babylonian Talmud, was completed about 500 C.E. So distinguished was the Jewish scholarship of Babylonia, that this Talmud was considered superior in coverage and scholarship to the Jerusalem Talmud, which was produced about the same time in academies in Israel.

Jews lived in substantial numbers both in Israel and in the diaspora. Many had chosen to remain in Babylonia even after they were permitted to return to Judaea. Many others traveled by free choice throughout the trade and cultural networks that were established by the Persians in the sixth century B.C.E., enhanced by Alexander the Great in the fourth century B.C.E., and eventually extended by the Roman Empire.

A census of the Roman Empire undertaken by the Emperor Claudius in 48 C.E. showed 5,984,072 Jews. This figure suggests a total global Jewish population of about 8 million. At the time, the population of the Roman Empire was perhaps 60 million, while that of the Afro-Eurasian world was about 170 million. Most Jews outside Israel continued to look to Jerusalem as a spiritual center, and they sent funds to support the temple.

Judaea itself passed from one conqueror to another, from the Persians to Alexander the Great and his successors, and then to the Roman Empire in 63 B.C.E. As noted in Chapter 6, struggles simmered continuously under Roman rule, not only between Jews and Romans, but also among Jewish political and religious factions. Three major revolts broke out and Roman authorities responded with overwhelming force in suppressing them. In 70 C.E. they destroyed the Jewish temple in Jerusalem, exiled all Jews from the city, and turned it into their regional capital. In 135 C.E. they dismantled the political structure of the Jewish state and exiled almost all Jews from Judaea.

Unlike earlier exiles, this Roman dispersion fundamentally and permanently altered Jewish existence, removing all but a few Jews from the region of Israel until the twentieth century. This final exile established the principal contours of Jewish diaspora existence from then on: life as a minority group; dispersed among various peoples around the world; with distinct religious and social practices; united in reverence for sacred texts and their teachings, as interpreted by rabbi-scholars; usually dependent on the widely varying policies of the peoples among whom they lived; and sometimes forced to choose between religious conversion, emigration, or death. Jews preserved their cohesion through their acceptance of the authority of the TaNaKh and the importance of studying it, and their persistence in seeing themselves as a special kind of family even in dispersion.

Menorah procession, Arch of Titus, Rome, c. 81 C.E. The Romans put down the Jewish revolt of 70 C.E. by recapturing Jerusalem, destroying the temple, and looting its sacred objects. This relief from Emperor Titus' triumphal arch shows Roman soldiers with the temple *menorah*, a seven-branched candelabrum, which today serves as an official emblem of the state of Israel.

Minority–Majority Relations in the Diaspora

In general, Jews remained socially and religiously distinct wherever they traveled. This identification was imposed partially from the outside by others, partially by internal discipline and loyalty to the group, its traditions, and its laws. Jewish history becomes a case study also of tolerance and intolerance of minorities by majority peoples around the world.

In some civilizations, Jewish life in the diaspora survived and even flourished. For example, Rabbi Benjamin of Tudela, Spain, visited Muslim Baghdad in 1160–70 C.E. and reported: "In Baghdad there are about 40,000 Jews, and they dwell in security, prosperity, and honor under the great Caliph, and amongst them are great sages, the heads of Academies engaged in the study of the law. In this city there are ten Academies … and twenty-eight Jewish synagogues" (Andrea & Overfield, Vol. I, pp. 248–9).

There were contrary examples, however. The Book of Esther, written about (and probably during) the Persian diaspora, 638–333 B.C.E., captures the vulnerability of minority existence. A royal minister sees his chance to advance his career and profit and argues to the king:

For an interactive version of this map, go to: http://www.prenhall.com/spodek/map10.2

The Jewish diaspora. Following the Jewish Revolt in 66 C.E., the Roman destruction of the temple in Jerusalem in 70, and the defeat of the Bar-Cochba revolt in 135, the Roman government expelled the Jews from Judaea. These migrations spread Judaism north into Mesopotamia and Anatolia, followed trade routes throughout the Mediterranean and the Red Sea, and eventually resulted in Jewish communities being established as far afield as northwest Europe and Ethiopia.

There is a certain people, dispersed among the many peoples in all the provinces of your kingdom, who keep themselves apart. Their laws are different from those of every other people; they do not keep your majesty's laws. It does not befit your majesty to tolerate them. If it please your majesty, let an order be made in writing for their destruction; and I will pay ten thousand talents of silver to your majesty's officials, to be deposited in the royal treasury. (Esther 3:8–9)

The king agrees: "The money and the people are yours; deal with them as you wish" (Esther 3:11). On this occasion, according to Jewish traditions, the actions of Esther saved these Jews from destruction. But the biblical account captures a pattern of official xenophobia and greed, repeated frequently in Jewish history—and in the history of many minorities.

CHRISTIANITY

Christianity Emerges from Judaism

At the height of Roman rule over Judaea, a splinter group within the Jewish people was forming around the person and teachings of Jesus of Nazareth. External histories indicate that the times were turbulent and difficult. As a colony of the Roman Empire, Judaea was taxed heavily and suppressed economically and politically. The Romans also demanded emperor worship from a people who were devoted to monotheism. Religious and political antagonisms were closely intertwined in an explosive mixture. The Jewish prophets of the Old Testament had promised a final end to such anguish, and many of Jesus's followers believed that he was the "servant" that had been promised to lead them into a brighter future.

In the face of Roman colonialism, the Jews were divided into at least four conflicting groups. The largest of these groups, the Pharisees, identified with the masses of the population in resenting the Roman occupation, but, seeing no realistic alternative to it, found some comfort in keeping alive and reinterpreting Jewish religious traditions. The more elite Sadducees, the temple priesthood and their allies, had become servants of the Roman state and preached accommodation to it. A much smaller, militant group of Zealots sought, quixotically, to drive out the Romans through violence. A fourth, still smaller group, the Essenes, lived a prayerful existence by the shores of the Dead Sea, stayed aloof from politics, and preached the imminent end of the world as they knew it.

Into this volatile and complex society, Jesus was born to Joseph, a carpenter, and Mary, his betrothed, about the year 4 B.C.E., in the town of Bethlehem, about 10 miles southwest of Jerusalem. (The year of Jesus' birth is not recorded. The Christian calendar places it at the beginning of the year 1, but it must have taken place no later than 4 B.C.E., for Herod, king at the time of Jesus' birth, died that year.) Biblical accounts report little about his early life, except that his parents took him to Jerusalem to celebrate the Passover holiday when he was twelve years old, and he entered there into probing discussions of religion with teachers sitting in the temple, astonishing onlookers and his parents. Jesus next emerges, at about the age of thirty, as a powerful preacher, attracting multitudes to his sermons that are filled with allegories and parables concerning ethical life, moral teachings, and predictions of the future.

In his calls for rapid and radical religious reform, Jesus found himself in opposition to the more conservative Pharisees, whom he frequently referred to as hypocrites. Like the Essenes, he spoke often of an imminent day of divine judgment of the whole world. He promised eternal life and happiness to the poor and downtrodden people of colonial Judaea if only they would keep their faith in God. Similar predictions had also been common among the Jewish prophets centuries before, and Jesus' emphasis on the coming of the kingdom of God resonated strongly with the earlier voices as well as with the Essenes. Jesus' message, however, stressed a future not on earth during people's lifetimes, but in heaven after their deaths. In this he differed from most Jewish beliefs of his time. In addition to his preaching, according to biblical accounts Jesus also performed exorcisms and miracles, fed multitudes of people, cured the blind and lame among his followers, and even brought the dead back to life. He pursued his unorthodox search for truth in the Galilee, the beautiful and lush northern region of Judaea, only recently converted to Judaism. There he continued his preaching, angering both the Jewish religious establishment, which viewed him as a heretic, and the Roman imperial government, which feared the revolutionary potential of his rabble rousing.

Jesus' followers, however—mostly common people—revered him as one specially chosen and anointed by God (*Messiah* in Hebrew, *Christos* in Greek). They proclaimed

Silver crucifix from Birka, Sweden, c. 900 C.E. The cross—signifying Christ's crucifixion—was adopted by Christians as a symbol of their faith as early as the second century. Making "the sign of the cross" was believed powerful in warding off evil, and, in later centuries, crusaders were said to "take the cross" when they set off on crusade (a word itself derived from the Latin for cross, *crux*). (*Historiska Museet, Stockholm*)

Palestine at the time of Jesus.
Christianity first emerged as a sect within Judaism when Roman control of Palestine was increasing. Shortly before Jesus' birth, Rome had granted Herod the Great the Kingdom of Judaea as a client ruler. Upon his death in 4 B.C.E. the kingdom was divided among his sons, and Judaea itself came under direct Roman military rule.

Jesus to be the source of eternal life and accepted him as a miracle-worker and the son of God. They believed, according to the biblical accounts, that his birth had been a miracle, that he had been conceived by the Holy Spirit of God and born to Mary, who was a virgin.

Jesus said that he had come "not to abolish the Jewish law but to fulfill it," and his followers accepted much of the moral code of Jewish teachings, but they rejected most parts of its legal and separatist covenant. Beginning in a few towns at the eastern end of the Mediterranean Sea, Jesus' followers built an entirely new organizational structure for sustaining and spreading their new faith in this man whom they called Christ, God's anointed representative.

As Jesus' fame spread, the fears of the Jewish religious authorities and the Roman colonial administrators increased. To prevent any potential rebellion, the Roman government seized him when he once again returned to Jerusalem to preach and to celebrate the Passover, and executed him by crucifixion when he was thirty-three years old.

But death did not stop Jesus' message. His followers believed that he arose from the grave in a miraculous resurrection and triumph over death, and ascended to heaven to join God the Father. Their belief contained equal measures of admiration for his message of compassion and salvation and for his ability to perform miracles. Jesus' disciples took his message of compassion, salvation, and eternal life to Rome. The proud upper classes of Rome scoffed at first, but more and more of the simple people believed. Despite early persecution, Christianity increased in influence, until, in the fourth century, it became the official religion of the empire.

Spread through the networks of the empire, the Christian Church ultimately became the most important organizing force in post-Roman Europe. The message of Christianity and the organization of the Church expanded throughout the world. Today almost 2 billion people, one-third of the world's population, distributed among numerous different churches and denominations, declare themselves followers of Jesus, the simple preacher from Judaea.

HOW DO WE KNOW?

The Search for the Historical Jesus

The only records of Jesus's life are the four gospels, "the good news accounts," the first four books of the New Testament, which is the second section of the Christian Bible. Named for their authors—Matthew, Mark, Luke, and John—the gospels are neither unbiased nor contemporary. Mark, probably the oldest of the four, dates to 70 C.E., forty years after Jesus' death. As with the early literature of Hinduism, Buddhism, and Judaism, the gospels represent written recordings of oral traditions. They bring together traditions surrounding Jesus's life as they were transmitted among his followers. Although individual names are associated with them, the actual authors of the gospels are unknown. Mark, for example, was the most common name in the Roman Empire at the time. Moreover, it appears that they were written for different audiences and therefore tell their stories somewhat differently. Mark, for example, addressed his beliefs in a future life to Christians who were being persecuted in Rome.

Fifty-two additional texts, called by scholars the Gnostic gospels, were discovered near the town of Nag Hammadi in upper Egypt in 1945, and have been subject to intense study ever since. Scholars believe that these texts were transcribed at about the same time as the four gospels of the Christian Bible, but that they contain accounts of Jesus'

teachings that were inconsistent with them and that they were therefore banned by Church leaders and hidden away.

According to the most important of the Gnostic gospels, The Secret Gospel of Thomas, Jesus taught that each individual could find the light of God within him or herself, without the necessity of belief in Jesus. "The kingdom is inside of you, and it is outside of you. When you come to know yourselves, then you will become known, and you will realize that it is you who are the sons of the living father." The search for meaning is most important: "Jesus said, 'Let him who seeks continue seeking until he finds. When he finds, he will become troubled. When he becomes troubled he will be astonished, and he will rule over the all.'"

The Gnostic gospels also give a greater place to women in the search for religious truth, and they suggest that Jesus had some measure of physical relationship with Mary Magdalene, a prostitute whom he brought back to respectable society. These somewhat mystical gospels, with their message of a greater sexuality for Jesus, were suppressed as heresies in the wake of theological struggles within the Church in the late second century.

The four biblical gospels themselves also present additional problems for historical analysis. They begin with the story of the birth of Jesus told as a miracle. According to the gospels, Jesus was the son of God, born miraculously through Mary, a virgin betrothed to Joseph, a carpenter from Nazareth in the region of the Galilee. Believers certainly

accept such an account, but it is not subject to historical verification. Moreover, despite the gospels' accounts of Jesus' multitudes of followers, and his political and religious influence, neither Roman nor Jewish records of the time take note of his life or his teachings. Tacitus, although scornful of the early Christians, does take note of Jesus' death.

Modern scholars who have attempted to reconstruct the life of Jesus have reached very different conclusions about his essential character, depicting Jesus as political revolutionary, magician, Galilean charismatic, Galilean rabbi, proto-Pharisee, Essene, prophet of the end of days, exorcist, miracle worker, and marginal Jew. All the research, however, no matter how scholarly and how inventive, remains inconclusive. The four biblical gospels, despite their richness as religious teachings, have serious shortcomings as religious texts, and the historical validity of the Gnostic gospels is clouded by their official suppression.

- What are the shortcomings of the gospels as historical texts for understanding the life of Jesus? What are their strengths?
- Historians attempting to characterize the life of Jesus, have reached very different conclusions. What kinds of sources do you think they used?
- If the Gnostic gospels had not been suppressed by powerful theologians, do you think the Church might have developed differently? If so, how? If not, why not?

Jesus' Life, Teachings, and Disciples

Whatever the reality of the miracles associated with Jesus, clearly a new religion, Christianity, emerged from earlier Jewish roots, and in this process, a number of adaptations and innovations took place.

Adapting Rituals to New Purposes. As we have seen, newly forming religions often adapt rituals and philosophies from already existing religions, as, for example, Buddhism adapted the concept of *dharma* from Hinduism. This borrowing and adaptation can be attractive to members of the existing religion who wish to join the new one, for it assures them that their spiritual customs will be maintained. At the same time, a new interpretation gives the ritual a new meaning for the new faith. Jesus' form of prayer and much of his preaching were fully in accord with Jewish tradition. When he accepted baptism from the desert preacher John the Baptist, however, Jesus prepared the way for adapting an existing practice and giving it new meaning for his followers. A minor practice within Judaism, baptism would later become in Christianity a central **sacrament** of purification enjoined on all members.

Another example of adaptation is Jesus' "last supper," a Passover ritual meal. Jesus ate unleavened, flat bread as a symbol of slavery in Egypt, and he drank the wine that accompanies all Jewish festivals as a symbol of joy. Then he offered the bread and wine also to his disciples with the words, "This is my body ... this is my blood." Thus he transformed the foods of the Passover meal into the **Eucharist**, or Holy Communion, another central sacrament, a mystery through which Christians believe the invisible Christ grants communion to them.

Overturning the Old Order. In his teachings, Jesus also addressed political and social issues, staking out his own often ambiguous positions in relationship to the different and competing philosophies of the day. When Jesus, following John the Baptist, taught, "Repent; for the kingdom of heaven has come near" (Matthew 4:17), he was not explicit in describing that kingdom or its date of arrival. But in metaphor and parable he preached that life as we know it on earth would soon change dramatically, or even come to an end.

sacrament In Christian theology, a rite or ritual that is an outward sign of a spiritual grace conveyed on the believer by Christ through the ministry of the Church.

Eucharist From the Greek *eucharistia*, thanksgiving. The central **sacrament** and act of worship of the Christian Church, culminating in Holy Communion.

SOURCE

The Beatitudes from the Sermon on the Mount

Jesus' teaching—powerful in direct address, in parable, and in allegory—established his identification with the poor and oppressed, his disdain for the Roman authorities, and his scorn for the Jewish religious leadership of his time. He sounded much like a latterday Jewish prophet calling his people to reform. The Beatitudes, a list of promises of God's rewards for the simple, righteous people, the first of Jesus' great sermons recorded in the New Testament, was delivered from the top of a hill in Galilee.

Blessed are the poor in spirit, for theirs is the kingdom of heaven.
Blessed are those who mourn, for they will be comforted.
Blessed are the meek, for they will inherit the earth.
Blessed are those who hunger and thirst for righteousness, for they will be filled.
Blessed are the merciful, for they will receive mercy.
Blessed are the poor in heart, for they will see God.
Blessed are the peacemakers, for they will be called children of God.
Blessed are those who are persecuted for righteousness' sake, for theirs is the kingdom of heaven. (Matthew 5:3–10)

Jesus' words must have been especially welcome to the poor, as he spoke repeatedly of the "Kingdom of Heaven" in which the tables would be turned:

> It will be hard for a rich person to enter the kingdom of heaven. Again I tell you, it is easier for a camel to go through the eye of a needle than for someone who is rich to enter the kingdom of God. (Matthew 19:23–4)

Jesus declared that the most important commandment was to "Love the Lord your God with all your heart, and with all your soul, and with all your mind," and the second was "Love your neighbor as yourself," both directly cited from the TaNaKh (Deuteronomy 6:7 and Leviticus 19:18). Indeed, he projected these principles into new dimensions, declaring "Love your enemies and pray for your persecutors" (Matthew 5:44). But he also warned that the coming apocalypse would be violent:

> Do not think that I have come to bring peace to earth; I have not come to bring peace, but a sword. (Matthew 10:34)

Jesus and the Jewish Establishment. The gospels depict Jesus' attitude toward Jewish law as ambivalent but often condescending, and his relationship toward the Jewish religious leadership as confrontational. He scoffed at Jewish dietary laws: "It is not what goes into the mouth that defiles a person, but it is what comes out of the mouth that defiles" (Matthew 15:11). He constantly tested the limits of Sabbath restrictions, declaring that: "The Sabbath is made for man, not man for the Sabbath" (Mark 2:27). He restricted divorce, announcing that: "If a man divorces his wife for any cause other than unchastity he involves her in adultery; and anyone who marries a divorced woman commits adultery" (Matthew 5:32). Many of his teachings may have reflected his desire to return to earlier beliefs in faith and spirituality and his belief that the future lay in heaven, not on earth.

Miracles and Resurrection. The gospels describe Jesus' ministry as filled with miracles—healing the sick, restoring sight to the blind, feeding multitudes of followers from just a few loaves and fishes, walking on water, calming storms, and even raising the dead. Reports of these miracles, perhaps even more than his ethical teachings, brought followers flocking to him. The gospel narrative of Jesus' suffering on the cross, presenting him at the final moment of his life as both human and divine in one personage, and finally his miraculous resurrection from the grave, his appearances to his disciples, and his ascent to heaven, complete the miracle and the majesty of his life and embody his promise of eternal life for those who believe in his power.

The stories of Jesus's life and death, message and miracles, form the basis for Christianity, at first a new sect located within Judaism. Although different followers attributed more or less divinity and greater or lesser miracles to him, apparently all accepted Jesus as a new, reforming teacher. Many saw him as the long-awaited "Messiah," a messenger and savior specially anointed by God. His apostles, especially Paul of Tarsus (d. 67), now refocused Jesus's message and built the Christian sect into a new, powerful religion. The apostles' preaching, organizational work, and letters to fledgling Christian communities fill most of the rest of the New Testament.

The Growth of the Early Church

At first, the followers of Jesus functioned as a sect within Judaism, continuing to meet in synagogues and to identify themselves as Jews. Peter, described in the gospels as Jesus' chosen organizational leader, first took the Christian message outside the Jewish community (Acts 10). Declaring circumcision unnecessary for membership, he

Paul's missionary journeys. Following Jesus' trial and crucifixion, about 29 C.E., his disciples, notably the Roman convert Paul, set out to convert non-Jews or gentiles. Paul's journeys took him throughout the Greco-Roman east Mediterranean, and beyond. These journeys and the epistles Paul wrote began to weave struggling Christian groups into a new religious organization, the Christian Church. Paul died in Rome, apparently a martyr to the Emperor Nero.

welcomed gentiles, people who were not Jewish, into the new Church. James, Jesus' brother and leader of the Christian community of Jerusalem, abrogated most of the Jewish dietary laws for the new community (Acts 15). These apostles believed that the rigorous ritual laws of Judaism inhibited the spread of its ethical message. Instead, they chose to emphasize the miraculous powers of Jesus and his followers. They spoke little of their master's views on the coming apocalypse but stressed his statements on the importance of love and redemption.

Paul Organizes the Early Church. Tensions continued to simmer between mainstream Jewish leaders and the early Christians. One of the fiercest opponents of the new sect was Saul from the Anatolian town of Tarsus. Saul was traveling to confront the Christian community in Damascus when he experienced an overpowering mystical vision of Jesus that literally knocked him to the ground. Reversing his previous position, Saul now affirmed his belief in the authenticity of Jesus as the divine Son of God. In speaking within the Jewish community, he had preferred his Hebrew name, Saul. Now, as he took his new message to gentiles, he preferred his Roman name, Paul. Jewish by ethnicity and early religious choice, Roman by citizenship, and Greek by culture, Paul was ideally placed to refine and explicate Jesus' message. He became the second founder of Christianity and dedicated himself to establishing Christianity as an independent, organized religion.

To link the flourishing, but separate, Christian communities, Paul undertook three missionary voyages in the eastern Mediterranean, and he kept in continuous communication through a series of letters, Paul's "Epistles" of the New Testament. He advised the leadership emerging within each local church organization: the presbyters, or elders; the deacons above them; and, at the head, the bishop. He promised eternal life to those who believed in Jesus' power. He declared Jewish ritual laws an obstacle to spiritual progress (Galatians 5:2–6). Neither membership in a chosen family nor observance of laws or rituals was necessary in the new religion. Paul proclaimed a new equality in Christianity:

> There is no longer Jew or Greek, there is no longer slave or free, there is no longer male or female; for all of you are one in Christ Jesus. (Galatians 3:28)

Paul formulated a new concept of "original sin" and redemption from it. Jews had accepted the story told in Genesis of Adam and Eve's disobedience in the Garden of Eden as a mythical explanation of some of life's harsh realities: the pain of childbirth, the struggle to earn a living, the dangers of wild beasts, and, most of all, human mortality. Paul now proclaimed that Adam and Eve's "original sin" could be forgiven. Humanity could, in a sense, return to paradise and eternal life. Jesus' death on the cross atoned for original sin. According to Paul, those who believed in Jesus and accepted membership in the new Christian community would be forgiven by God and "saved." Although they would still be mortal, at the end of their earthly lives they would inherit a life in heaven, and, much later, would even be reborn on earth (Romans 5–6).

Christmas The Christian feast celebrating the birth of Jesus Christ.

Easter The principal feast of the Christian calendar celebrating the resurrection of Christ.

Pentecost This festival commemorates the descent of the Holy Spirit on the Apostles of Christ and the beginning of their preaching mission on the fiftieth day after the resurrection of Christ at **Easter**.

The Christian Calendar. Like other religions, Christianity established a sacred calendar. People had long celebrated the winter solstice; in the fourth century Christians fixed the observance of Jesus' birth, **Christmas**, at that time of year, although no one knew the actual date of his birth. Good Friday, at about the time of Passover, mourned Jesus' crucifixion and death; three days later his resurrection was celebrated in the joyous festival of **Easter**. Corresponding to the Jewish holiday of **Pentecost**, the anniversary of receiving the Ten Commandments fifty days after the Passover, Christianity introduced its own holiday of Pentecost. It commemorates the date when, according to Acts 2, the "Holy Spirit," the third element of the Trinity along with God the Father and Jesus the son, filled Jesus' disciples and they "began to talk in other tongues, as the Spirit gave them power of utterance," enabling them to preach to the various peoples of the world. (Modern-day Christian Pentecostals "speak in tongues," praying and uttering praises ecstatically, healing through prayer and laying on of hands, and speaking of experiencing spiritual miracles.)

Over time, special saints' days were designated to mark the lives and deaths of people who helped to spread the new religion. The new Christian calendar, which has become the most widely used in the world, fixed its first year at the approximate date of Jesus' birth. The Jewish Sabbath, a weekly day of rest and reflection, was transferred from Saturday to Sunday.

Gender Relations. Jesus attracted many women as followers, and women led in the organization of several of the early churches. Paul welcomed them warmly and treated them respectfully at first, but women gradually lost their influence as Jesus' disciples institutionalized the Church. Although they taught spiritual equality, early Christians allowed gender and social inequalities to remain. Paul had proclaimed that in Jesus "There is no longer male or female," but he seemed to distrust

MAJOR CHRISTIAN FESTIVALS

January 6	Epiphany
February–March	Shrove Tuesday, or Mardi Gras (day before Ash Wednesday)
February–March	Ash Wednesday (first day of Lent)
February–April	Lent
February 2	Candlemas Day
March–April	Easter
March 25	Feast of Annunciation
April–June	Ascension (40 days after Easter)
May–June	Pentecost/Whit Sunday (50 days after Easter)
May–June	Trinity Sunday (Sunday after Pentecost)
November–December	Advent
December 24	Christmas Eve
December 25	Christmas Day

sexual energies. Like Jesus he was unmarried. He recommended celibacy and, for those unable to meet that standard, monogamous marriage as a means of sexual restraint:

> It is well for a man not to touch a woman. But because of cases of sexual immorality, each man should have his own wife and each woman her own husband. The husband should give to his wife her conjugal rights, and likewise the wife to her husband. (1 Corinthians 7:1–3)

In addition, Paul moved to subordinate women, first at home:

> I want you to understand that Christ is the head of every man, and the husband is the head of the wife … he is the image and reflection of God; but woman is the reflection of man. Indeed, man was not made from woman, but woman from man. Neither was man created for the sake of woman, but woman for the sake of man. (1 Corinthians 11:3–9)

Then in church:

> Women should be silent in the churches. For they are not permitted to speak, but should be subordinate, as the law also says. If there is anything they desire to know, let them ask their husbands at home. (1 Corinthians 14:34–35)

Paul had also declared that spiritually "There is no longer slave or free," but in practice he accepted slavery, saying, "Slaves, obey your earthly masters with fear and trembling." He did urge masters to be kind to slaves and to "stop threatening them for you know that both of you have the same Master in heaven, and with him there is no partiality" (Ephesians 6:5–9).

From Persecution to Triumph

Having established the central doctrines of the new religion and stabilized its core communities, both Peter and Paul moved to expand its geographical scope. They saw Rome as the capital of empire and the center of the international communication network of the time, and they traveled there to preach and teach. Tradition holds that both were martyred there in the persecutions of the Emperor Nero, about 67 C.E., and that both are entombed and enshrined there.

In this capital of empire, Christianity appeared as one of several mystery religions, all of which were based on beliefs in supernatural beings. They included the religion of Mithra, a Persian sun-god; Demeter, a Greek goddess; YHWH the god of the Jews; and an eclectic mixture of beliefs called Gnosticism. Romans seemed to be in search of a more inspiring, otherworldly faith than paganism provided, but at the time of the deaths of Peter and Paul, Christianity was still a relatively weak force.

The first Christians, Jews by nationality, were scorned as provincial foreigners. Some Roman authorities thought that Christian beliefs in resurrection and an afterlife undermined pride in citizenship and willingness to serve in the army. About the year 100, the historian Tacitus wrote of:

> a class of persons hated for their vices whom the crowd called Christians. Christus, after whom they were named, had undergone the death penalty in the reign of Tiberius, by sentence of the procurator Pontius Pilate, and the pernicious superstition was checked for a moment only to break out once more, not only in Judaea, the home of the disease, but in the Capital itself, where everything horrible or shameful in the world gathers and becomes fashionable. (Tacitus, *Annales* XV:44)

Paradoxically, because they refused to worship the emperor or to take oaths in his name, official Rome viewed Christians as atheists. Their emphasis on otherworldly salvation and their strong internal organization were seen as threats to the state's authority. Roman leaders also mocked the sacrament of the Eucharist, in which Christians consumed consecrated wafers and wine as the body and blood of Christ, as a sign of cannibalism. Official treatment of Christianity was erratic but often marked by severe persecution. Nero (r. 54–68) scapegoated the Christians, blaming them for the great fire in 64, apparently executing both Peter and Paul among his victims, and sending hundreds of Christians to die in public gladiatorial contests and by burning. Edicts of persecution were issued by Emperors Antoninus Pius (r. 138–161), Marcus Aurelius (r. 161–180), Septimius Severus (r. 193–211), Decius (c. 201–251), and Diocletian (r. 284–305). In 257 the Emperor Valerian (r. 253–260) was prepared to launch a major persecution of Christians, but he was captured in battle by Persians. In these early years of persecution, thousands of Christians suffered martyrdom.

Despite the scorn and the persecution, Christianity continued to grow. Its key doctrines and texts were written, edited, and approved by leaders in the network of Christian churches. After years of debates, Christian leaders and scholars agreed on the contents of the New Testament by about the year 200, and by 250 the city of Rome alone held about 50,000 Christians among its million inhabitants. Most were of the lower classes, attracted by Jesus' message to the poor, but middle- and upper-class Romans had also joined. In particular, Christianity proved attractive to the wives of Roman leaders, who often contributed to their husbands' conversions. By the reign of Constantine, estimates reported that one out of ten inhabitants of the Roman Empire was Christian.

The Conversion of Constantine. In 313, Constantine (r. 306–337) had a vision in which a cross and the words *in hoc signo vinces*, "in this sign you will be victorious," appeared to him the night before he won the critical battle that made him sole emperor in the western empire. He immediately declared Christianity legal. He funded Christian leaders and their construction of churches, while he withdrew official support from the pagan churches, making Christianity the *de facto* official religion of the Roman Empire. On a personal level, Constantine encouraged his mother Helena to embrace Christianity, which she did enthusiastically. Helena had churches built in Asia Minor and the Holy Land, and traveled to Jerusalem seeking the cross on which Jesus died. After her death, she was canonized as a saint in the Catholic Church.

As emperor, Constantine took a leading part in Church affairs. He sponsored the Council of Nicaea in 325, the largest assembly of bishops of local Christian churches up to that time. He convened the council primarily to establish the central theological doctrines of Christianity, but it also established a Church organization for the Roman Empire, a network of urban bishoprics grouped into provinces, with each province headed by the chief bishop of its largest city. In 337, on his deathbed, Constantine accepted baptism.

In 392, Emperor Theodosius (r. 379–395) declared Christianity to be the official religion of the Roman Empire. He outlawed the worship of the traditional Roman gods and severely restricted Judaism, initiating centuries of bitter Christian persecution of both traditions.

How Had Christianity Succeeded? How had Christianity, once scorned and persecuted, achieved such power? Christian believers attributed the success to divine assistance. Historians seek more earthly explanations. Let us consider one of the major historians to tackle the topic, Edward Gibbon (1737–94).

In 1776, Gibbon began the publication of his six-volume masterpiece, *The History of the Decline and Fall of the Roman Empire*. A child of the Enlightenment philosophy of his time, which rejected supernatural explanations (see Chapter 15), Gibbon rather

HOW DO WE KNOW?

Explanations for the Spread of Christianity

Many historians of our own time accept the thrust of Gibbon's explanations, but tend to emphasize more the importance of community within the Church.

"From the outset, the major goal of the Jesus movement was to call into existence a new kind of inclusive community that might arch over all the ordinary human distinctions of race and religion," writes Howard Clark Kee (1991, p. 2). Kee analyzes five different kinds of community that were active in the Roman world during the first two centuries of the Christian era and suggests that Christianity developed an appeal to each of them: The community of the wise, seeking special knowledge of the future; the community of the law-abiding, seeking appropriate rules of guidance in the present; the community where God dwells among his people, seeking assurance that it was specially selected and cared for; the community of mystical participation, influenced by the mystery religions of the time; and the ethnically and culturally inclusive community, outsiders seeking a place of belonging. Different aspects of the Christian message, developed by different Church leaders, spoke to each of these communities and succeeded in drawing them in (Kee, 1995).

Historical sociologist Michael Mann cites the psychological and practical rewards of the growing Christian "ecumene," the worldwide community of the Church, with its comprehensive philosophy for living and organizing. Although much of Christianity's message targeted the poor, Mann notes that the religion also drew a large following of urban artisans, whom the aristocratic Roman Empire devalued. Excluded from political power, these working-class people were in search of a comprehensive and welcoming community. They wanted to recreate an earlier, simpler, more participatory era, and they became Christians. As imperial power became increasingly centralized, remote, insensitive, and, later, unstable, "In many ways Christianity represented how Rome liked to idealize its republican past" (Mann, p. 325).

- Jesus and St. Paul promised life after death to Christians. Do Kee and Mann cite this as a reason for Christianity's success in winning new adherents? If so, what terms do they use to indicate this promise? If not, why do you think they omit it?
- Gibbon suggests that a large part of the appeal of early Christianity was the miracles that Christ and his disciples were said to have performed. Kee and Mann don't emphasize miracles. Why?
- Both Kee and Mann suggest that different groups were attracted to Christianity for different reasons. Give examples. Based on people's motivations for joining religious groups, with which of their reasons would you agree? Disagree?

Neoplatonic A philosophical system founded by Plotinus (205–270 C.E.) and influenced by Plato's theory of ideas. It emphasizes the transcendent, impersonal, and indefinable "One" as the ground of all existence and the source of an eternal world of goodness, beauty, and order, of which material existence is but a feeble copy.

sarcastically presented five reasons for Christianity's victories. But beneath his sarcasm Gibbon revealed the profound strengths of the new religion:

- Its "inflexible and intolerant" zeal, derived from its Jewish roots.
- Its promise of resurrection and a future life for believers, soon augmented by the threat of eternal damnation for nonbelievers.
- Its assertion of miraculous accomplishments.
- The austere morals of the first Christians. The Christian search for spiritual perfection, a monogamous sexual code, the rejection of worldly honor, and a general emphasis on equality attracted many converts. In the extreme case, martyrdom won admiration, sympathy, and followers. Later commentators noted that the simplicity and self-sacrifice of the early Christians reminded some Romans of the ideals of the early Republic.
- The Church gradually generated a state within a state through the decentralized leadership of its local bishops and presbyters, the structure Paul had begun to knit together. As imperial structures weakened, Christianity provided an alternative community. This Christian community distributed philanthropy to needy people, Christian and non-Christian alike. It also publicized its message effectively—in Greek, the language of the eastern part of the empire.
- Many later commentators noted that the Christian community included a local church in which to share the joys and sorrows of everyday life, celebrate life-cycle events, and commemorate major events in the history of the group. At the same time it provided membership in a universal Church that extended to the entire known world, and suggested participation in a life that transcended earthly concerns altogether.

Doctrine: Definition and Dispute

As it grew after receiving official recognition, institutional Christianity refined its theology. The most influential theologian of the period, St. Augustine (354–430), bishop of Hippo in north Africa, wrote *The City of God* (413–426) to explain Christianity's relationship to competing religions and philosophies, and to the Roman government with which it was increasingly intertwined.

Despite Christianity's designation as the official religion of the empire, Augustine declared its message to be spiritual rather than political. Christianity, he argued, should be concerned with the mystical, heavenly City of Jerusalem rather than with earthly politics. Although Augustine encouraged the Roman emperors to suppress certain religious groups, some elements of his theology supported the separation of Church and state.

Augustine built philosophical bridges to Platonic philosophy, the dominant system of the Hellenistic world of his time and place. Christianity envisioned Jesus, God's son, walking the earth and suffering for his people. He was, literally, very down-to-earth. God, the Father, had more transcendent characteristics, but they were less emphasized in Christian theology at the time. Plato (*c.* 428–348 B.C.E.) and later **Neoplatonic** philosophers, however, provided the model of a more exalted, more remote god, a god that was more accepted among the leading thinkers of Augustine's time. According to Augustine, Plato's god was:

> the maker of all created things, the light by which things are known, and the good in reference to which things are to be done; ... we have in him the first principle of nature, the truth of doctrines, and the happiness of life. (p. 253)

In addition, Plato's god existed in the soul of every person, perhaps a borrowing from Hinduism (see Chapter 9).

Augustine married these Platonic and Neoplatonic views to the transcendent characteristics of God in Christian theology. This provided Christianity with a new intellectual respectability, which attracted new audiences in the vast Hellenistic world. He also encouraged contemplation and meditation within Christianity, an important element in the monastic life that was beginning to emerge among Christians (as it had among Buddhists). Augustine himself organized a community of monks in Tegaste (now Souk-Ahras), the city of his birth.

In his earlier *Confessions* (*c.* 400), Augustine had written of his personal life of relatively mild sin before his conversion to Christianity. Now he warned Christians that Adam and Eve's willfulness had led to original sin; sin had unlocked the forces of lust, turning the flesh against the spirit; and lust had called forth a death sentence on all humans in place of the immortality originally intended for them:

> As soon as our first parents had transgressed the commandment, divine grace forsook them, and they were confounded at their own wickedness ... They experienced a new motion of their flesh which had become disobedient to them, in strict retribution of their own disobedience to God ... Then began the flesh to lust against the Spirit

El Greco, *St. Augustine*, c. 1580. Oil on canvas. El Greco's painting captures the formal power of Augustine's position within the early Church as Bishop and theologian. Augustine emphasized spiritual rather than worldly issues, encouraged contemplation and meditation, and incorporated Platonic and Neoplatonic concepts of a transcendent god into Christianity. (*Museo de Santa Cruz, Toledo*)

> ... And thus, from the bad use of free will, there originated the whole train of evil ... on to the destruction of the second death, which has no end, those only being excepted who are freed by the grace of God. (pp. 422–3)

For Augustine as for Paul, and thus for early Christianity, sexuality was perilous and woman suspect. In early Christian theology, profane flesh and divine spirit confronted each other uneasily.

Augustine also believed that Christians should subordinate their will and reason to the teachings and authority of the Church. Although it is usually associated with the development of Protestant religions much later, the idea of predestination—that is, that individuals could do nothing through their own actions to obtain salvation and entrance to heaven—dominated Augustine's theology. Some Christian theologians, such as Pelagius (c. 354–after 418), rejected Augustine's argument about original sin and taught that human beings could chose between good and evil to determine their own fate. They feared that the growing acceptance of Augustine's beliefs would devalue both public service for the poor and private initiative by less disciplined Christians. Ultimately, Augustine's views prevailed, and popes at the time labeled those of Pelagius heresy.

Battles over Dogma. Some theological disputes led to violence, especially as the Church attempted to suppress doctrinal disagreement. The most divisive dispute concerned the nature of the divinity of Jesus. The theologian Arius (c. 250–336) taught that Christ's humanity limited his divinity, and that God the Father, wholly transcendent, was more sacred than the son who had walked the earth. The Council of Nicaea, which was convened in 325 to resolve this dispute, issued an official statement of creed affirming Jesus' complete divinity and his indivisibility from God. The Arian controversy continued, however, especially on the fringes of empire, where Arian missionaries converted many of the Gothic tribes to their own beliefs. Wars between the new Arian converts and the Roman Church ensued, until finally Arianism was defeated in armed battle. Of these struggles, the historian Ammianus Marcellinus (c. 330–395) wrote: "No wild beasts are such enemies to mankind as are most of the Christians in the deadly hatred they feel for one another."

In the eastern Mediterranean, too, bitter and violent conflicts broke out among rival Christian theological factions, again over the precise balance between Jesus' divinity and his humanity. Persecution of dissidents by the Orthodox Church in Carthage, Syria, and Egypt was so severe that the arrival in the seventh century of Muslim rule, which treated all the Christian sects equally, was often welcomed as a respite from the struggles.

By the sixth century Christians far surpassed Jews in numbers, geographical spread, power, and influence. Christian missionaries continued their attempts to convert Jews, often by coercion. In 576, for example, a Gallic bishop gave the Jews of his city the choice between baptism and expulsion, a pattern that was repeated periodically, although Jews had not yet immigrated into western Europe in large numbers.

CHRISTIANITY IN THE WAKE OF EMPIRE

Christianity spread to western and northern Europe along the communication and transportation networks of the Roman Empire. Born in Judaea under Roman occupation, Christianity now spread throughout the empire, spoke its languages of Greek and Latin, preached the gospel along its trade routes, and constructed church communities in its cities. Thanks to official recognition and patronage, the Church grew steadily. As the Roman imperial government weakened, it enlisted the now official Church as a kind of department of state. While the empire weakened and dissolved, Christianity emerged and flourished.

The Conversion of the Barbarians

During the first millennium C.E. bishops in the western Church came "from the ranks of the senatorial governing class ... they stood for continuity of the old Roman values ... The eventual conversion of the barbarian leaders was due to their influence" (Matthew, p. 21). "None of the major Germanic peoples who entered the Roman provinces in the fourth and fifth centuries remained pagan for more than a generation after they crossed the frontier" (Mann, p. 335). About 496 Clovis, chief of the Merovingian Franks, rejected Arianism and converted to Roman Christianity, the first barbarian to accept the religion of the empire. He established his capital in Paris and had thousands of his tribesmen converted, for, in general, followers accepted the religion of their leader. Clovis' acceptance of Christianity brought him the support of the Roman ecclesiastical hierarchy, including the pope, and insured the triumph of this version of Christianity in Gaul.

Decentralized Power and Monastic Life

In western Europe, Christianity developed a multitude of local institutions. Churches, monasteries, and convents were established, and leadership was decentralized. In regions that lacked organized government and administration, local Church leaders and institutions provided whatever existed of order, administration, and a sense of larger community. For several centuries, "Christendom was dominated by thousands of dedicated unmarried men and women" (McManners, p. 89), the clergy of the Church. Missionary activity continued enthusiastically, but now turned northward toward the Vikings and the Slavs, as other geographical doors had been forcibly shut.

Pope Gregory I (r. 590–604) saw the usefulness of the monasteries and monks in converting and disciplining the barbarians, and he began to encourage the monastic movement. By the year 600 there were about 200 monasteries in Gaul alone, and the first missionaries dispatched by Rome arrived in England c. 597. By 700 much of England had been converted. In the ninth, tenth, and eleventh centuries, missionary activity was directed toward the "Northmen," the Vikings from Scandinavia, who raided and traded for goods and slaves from North America and Greenland, through the North Sea and the Baltic, down the Volga River, across the Caspian Sea, and on as far as Baghdad. The Vikings came into the Christian fold with only a tenuous link to Rome and a strong admixture of pagan ritual.

Although the pope in Rome had nominal authority over Christian affairs in the west, the Church's power was, in fact, fragmented and decentralized between 500 and 1000. Christianity spread in urban areas through its bishops in their large churches. In rural and remote areas, monks, acting as missionaries, carried the message.

Monasteries, which were small, isolated communities, each under the local control of a single abbot, modeled the spirituality and simplicity of the earliest Christian communities. Because sexual activity was ruled out, monasticism became as accessible to women in convents as to men in monasteries, and was equally valued by both. Many monasteries contained both men and women, each living in celibacy.

The most famous of the early monastics, St. Benedict (c. 480–547), founded a monastery at Monte Cassino, about 100 miles southeast of Rome. The writings of Pope Gregory I give us the most detailed information on the life, regulations, and discipline of that exemplary institution, although each monastery had its own variations in administration and practice.

Monastery of St. Catherine, Mount Sinai, 557 C.E. According to the Torah, Moses received the tablets of the law from God on Mount Sinai. It was for this reason that the Byzantine emperor Justinian I (r. 527–565) chose to found the monastery of St. Catherine here. The remote beauty of the place also made it ideal for spiritual meditation.

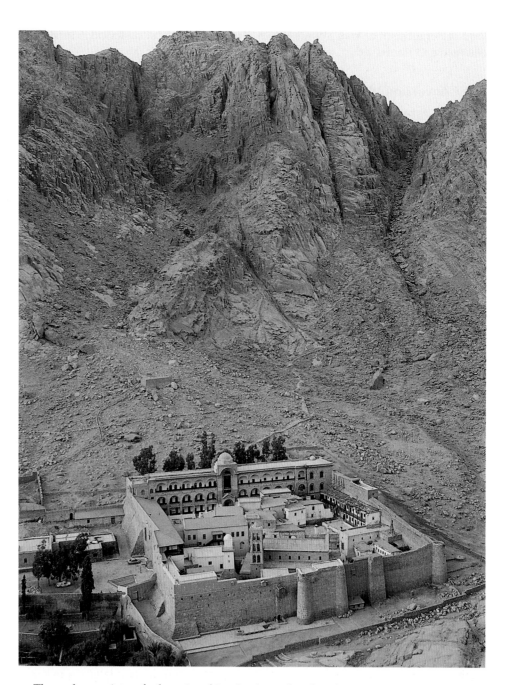

Through a variety of educational institutions, the churches, monasteries, convents, and bishops kept Rome's culture alive in northern and western Europe. In much of rural western Europe, local authorities valued the monks not just as the only literate people in the region but also as the most capable persons in administering land and agriculture. These authorities also sought an alliance with the prestige and power of the Church. They granted land and administrative powers to nearby monasteries, transforming them into important local economic forces. (Compare the administrative roles of Hindu priests and Buddhist monks in south and southeast Asia; Chapter 9.) Monks became courtiers and bishops as well as missionaries as they expanded the geographic, social, and economic dimensions of the Church. Until the Fourth Lateran Council (1216) under Pope Innocent III (r. 1198–1216), monasteries could form and dissolve at local initiatives, so we have no record of their exact numbers in the early centuries.

A history of the very decentralized Church of this time would have to be written from the bottom up. The Church in the west was decentralized partly because the Roman Empire was decentralized, having lost its administrative power. There was no longer an emperor in Rome. The Church and what was left of the government in western Europe groped toward a new mutual relationship.

The Church Divides into East and West

In the far more literate and sophisticated Byzantine Empire, political leaders did not relinquish their power to Church authorities. Indeed, the emperor at Constantinople served as administrative head of the Church, a pattern that had been set by Constantine when he presided over the Council of Nicaea, outside Constantinople.

Today, Eastern Orthodoxy and Roman Catholicism share the same fundamental faith and scripture and they maintain official communication with each other, but they developed many historic differences over Church organization, authority, and language. Doctrinally, at the Council of Chalcedon (451) both Eastern Orthodoxy and the Roman Church accepted the belief that Jesus was simultaneously an historical person and one with God. Organizationally, however, the Eastern Church remained far more urban. The west had so few roads and so little trade that it was held together organizationally by its military and ecclesiastical strongholds. The Council of Chalcedon recognized four centers of Church organization, or sees, in the east—Antioch, Jerusalem, Alexandria, and Constantinople—with Constantinople predominating and having the same leadership role in the east as Rome had in the west. Rome, once one of the patriarchates, and the only one in the west, was now deemed an entirely separate administrative center, still under its own emperor and with its own bishop.

The Split between Rome and Constantinople. Rome and Byzantium have remained divided over the authority of the bishop of Rome to the present. From the sixth century, he has claimed to be pope, *pappa*, father of the (Roman) Catholic Church and the direct organizational successor of the apostle Peter. Eastern Orthodox Christianity, however, has never recognized the pope's claim to pre-eminent authority, accepting as their principal authority the patriarch or bishop of Constantinople. Also, unlike the Roman practice, all but the highest clergy in Eastern Orthodoxy are permitted to marry, so here again the two clergies have not accepted each other's authority. The language of Rome is Latin, while the East uses Greek and the various Slavic languages of eastern Europe.

When Leo IX became pope in 1048, he aimed to expand his influence over all of Europe and sponsored the writing of a treatise that emphasized the pope's power. He sent one of his more zealous reformers to Constantinople to argue against the patriarch of Constantinople's claims to be independent of Rome's control. After failed negotiations, the reformer excommunicated the patriarch; in response, the patriarch excommunicated the reformer. Through this mutual rejection, called the Great Schism of 1054, the two Churches divided definitively

Icon of Mary, Jesus, and SS. Theodore and George, St. Catherine's Monastery, Israel, sixth to seventh century C.E. The dispute over the use of icons in worship divided the Eastern Orthodox Church for over a century, 726–843, between iconoclasts who wanted them banned and iconodules who continued to venerate them.

**Icon of the "Triumph of Orthodoxy,"
Constantinople, late fourteenth/early
fifteenth century C.E.** In 843 the
Empress Theodora restored the use of
icons, an event still celebrated in the
Eastern Church on the first Sunday in
Lent.

into the Latin (later Roman Catholic) Church, which
is predominant in western Europe, and the Greek
Orthodox Church, which prevailed in the east. Friction between the two groups has waxed and waned
over time, with the most direct confrontation coming
in 1204, when crusaders dispatched by Rome to fight
against Muslims in Jerusalem turned northward and
sacked Constantinople instead.

New Areas Adopt Orthodox Christianity. As in the
west, monastic life flourished in the Byzantine
Empire, with exemplary institutions at remote,
starkly beautiful sites such as Mount Sinai and Mount
Athos. The greatest missionary activity of the Orthodox monks came later than in the west. Hemmed in
by the Roman Church to the west and by the growing
power of Islam to the east after about 650, Byzantium
turned its missionary efforts northward, toward
Russia. The brothers St. Cyril (c. 827–869) and St.
Methodius (c. 825–884) translated the Bible into
Slavonic, creating the Cyrillic alphabet in which to
transcribe and publish it. When Russia embraced
Orthodox Christianity in the tenth century it also
adopted this alphabet. In the late fifteenth century,
after the fall of Constantinople to the Turks (1453),
Moscow began to refer to itself as the "Third Rome,"
the spiritual and political heir to the Caesars and the
Byzantine Empire.

In other regions of east-central Europe, Rome and
Byzantium competed in spreading their religious and cultural messages and organi-
zations. Rome won in Poland, Bohemia, Lithuania, and Ukraine; the Orthodox Church
in Bulgaria, Romania, and Serbia. Other national Churches also grew up beyond
Rome's jurisdiction, including the Coptic in Egypt, the Armenian, and the Ethiopian.
They also asserted their independence from Constantinople, creating a pattern of dis-
tinct national Churches that the Protestant Reformation would later adopt (see
Chapter 13).

Christianity in Western Europe

The abrupt, dramatic rise of Islam throughout the Middle East and into the Mediterranean, which we will examine in the next chapter, had an immediate and profound
influence on Christianity. By the year 700, Muslim armies had conquered the eastern
Mediterranean and the north coast of Africa, key regions of both Christianity and the
former Roman Empire. The Muslim Umayyad dynasty pushed on into Spain and
crossed the Pyrenees. Stopped in southern France by the Frankish ruler Charles Martel
(c. 688–741) at the Battle of Tours in 732, the Umayyad forces withdrew to Spain.
Muslim troops captured segments of the southern Italian peninsula, Sicily, and other
Mediterranean islands. These Muslim conquests cut Christianity off geographically
from the lands of its birth and early vigor. As a result, Christianity became primarily a
religion of Europe, where many of its members were recently converted "barbarian"
warrior nobles.

For an interactive version of this map, go to: http://www.prenhall.com/spodek/map10.5

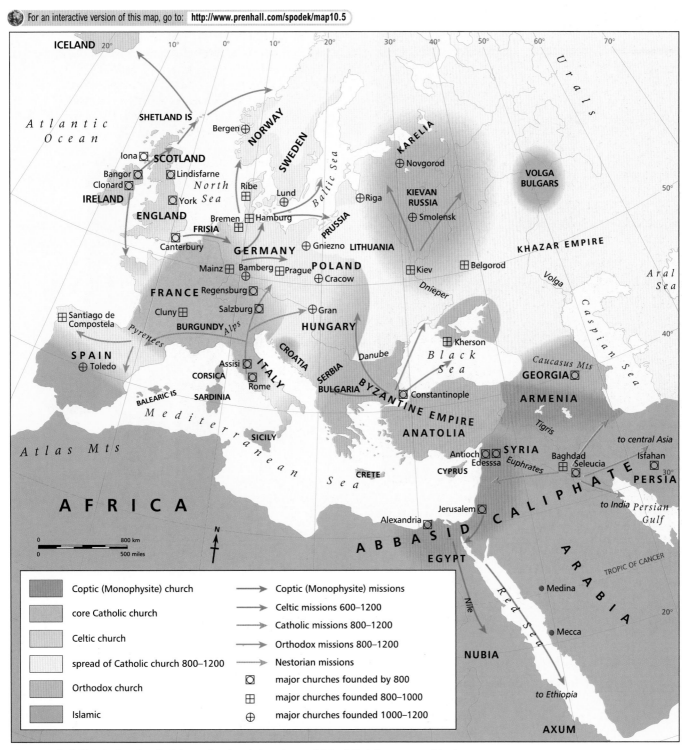

Legend:

- Coptic (Monophysite) church
- core Catholic church
- Celtic church
- spread of Catholic church 800–1200
- Orthodox church
- Islamic

- → Coptic (Monophysite) missions
- → Celtic missions 600–1200
- → Catholic missions 800–1200
- → Orthodox missions 800–1200
- → Nestorian missions
- ◎ major churches founded by 800
- ⊞ major churches founded 800–1000
- ⊕ major churches founded 1000–1200

The spread of Christianity. The disciples and early missionaries established Christian communities in southwest Asia, Greece, Italy, north Africa, and India. On the other hand, Roman persecution, the decline of western Rome, and the rise of Islam hindered its dissemination. The Orthodox Church of Constantinople converted eastern Europe, penetrating Russia; Rome became reestablished as a powerful center; and Celtic missionaries traveled throughout northwest Europe.

Christ triumphing over evil, Frankish terra cotta plaque, *c. 500–750* C.E. It was not unusual for western Europeans to represent Christ in contemporary local costume. Here, dressed as a member of the German warrior nobility, he treads the serpent, an emblem of the devil, underfoot. (*Musée des Antiquités, St-Germain-en-Laye, France*)

Bronze and gilt statuette of Charlemagne, *c. 860–870* C.E. Charlemagne's ceaseless warfare spread Christianity and Frankish rule across western Europe, while repelling barbarian intruders and enemies of Rome. In 800 C.E. Pope Leo III showed his gratitude by crowning him Holy Roman Emperor. (*Louvre, Paris*)

The Pope Allies with the Franks. In Rome, the pope felt surrounded by the hostile powers of Constantinople and Islam to the east and south, and several Gothic kings to the north and west. Seeking alliances with strong men, he turned to a Frank, Charles (Carolus) Martel, who gave his name to the Carolingian family. As we have seen, Martel had repulsed the Muslims at Tours in 732. In 754 his son, Pepin III (r. 751–768), answered the call of Pope Stephen II (r. 752–757) for help in fighting the Lombards who were invading Italy and threatening the papal possessions. Pepin secured a swath of lands from Rome to Ravenna and turned them over to papal rule. In exchange, the pope anointed Pepin and his two sons, confirming the succession of the Carolingian family as the royal house ruling the Franks.

SOURCE

Charlemagne and Harun-al-Rashid

Charlemagne spent his lifetime fighting in the name of the pope and on behalf of Christianity. In 777 he invaded Muslim Spain and by 801 had captured Barcelona. (His campaigns in Spain gave rise to the epic poem The Song of Roland *about the defeat of his rearguard in the pass of Roncesvalles. This became the most celebrated poem of medieval French chivalry.)*

Yet Charlemagne carried on a valued diplomatic friendship with the most powerful Muslim ruler of his day, Harun-al-Rashid, Caliph of Baghdad (r. 786–809). Charlemagne's adviser, friend, and biographer Einhard (c. 770–840) describes the friendship:

With Harun-al-Rachid [*sic*], King of the Persians, who held almost the whole of the East in fee, always excepting India, Charlemagne was on such friendly terms that Harun valued his goodwill more than the approval of all the other kings and princes in the entire world, and considered that he alone was worthy of being honoured and propitiated with gifts. When Charlemagne's messengers, whom he had sent with offerings to the most Holy Sepulchre of our Lord and Saviour and to the place of His resurrection, came to Harun and told him of their master's intention, he not only granted all that was asked but even went so far as to agree that this sacred scene of our redemption should be placed under Charlemagne's own jurisdiction. When the time came for these messengers to turn homewards, Harun sent some of his own men to accompany them and dispatched to Charlemagne costly gifts, which included robes, spices and other marvels of the lands of the Orient. A few years earlier Harun had sent Charlemagne the only elephant he possessed, simply because the Frankish King asked for it. (Einhard, p. 70)

Einhard does not note what gifts Charlemagne might have sent to Baghdad in return, nor does he comment on the political benefits of this interfaith diplomacy between the two great empires—empires that flanked, and confronted, the Byzantine Empire lying between them.

Charlemagne Revives the Idea of Empire. Pepin's son Charles ruled between 768 and 814, achieving the greatest recognition of his power when Pope Leo III (r. 795–816) crowned him Roman Emperor on Christmas Day, 800. In spite of this seeming unity of interests, Charles, who became known as Charles the Great or Charlemagne, rejected the title throughout most of his life and was often at odds with the various popes as he sought to expand an empire of his own. To achieve his goal, Charlemagne spent all his adult lifetime in warfare, continuing the military expeditions of his father and grandfather. He reconquered the northeastern corner of Spain from its Muslim rulers, defeated the Lombard rulers of Italy and relieved their pressure on the pope, seized Bavaria and Bohemia, killed and looted the entire nobility of the Avars in Pannonia (modern Austria and Hungary), and subdued the German Saxon populations along the Elbe River after thirty-three years of warfare. Himself a German Frank, Charlemagne offered the German Saxons a choice of conversion to Christianity or death.

With Charlemagne's victories, the borders of his kingdom came to match the borders of the dominance of the Church of Rome, except for the British Isles, which he did not enter. The political capital of western Europe passed from Rome to Charlemagne's own palace in Aachen (Aix-la-Chapelle) in modern Germany. Although Charlemagne was barely literate, he established within this palace a center of learning that attracted Church scholars from throughout Europe, initiating what historians call the Carolingian Renaissance.

THE CAROLINGIAN DYNASTY

751	Pepin III "the Short" becomes King of the Franks
755	Franks drive Lombards out of central Italy; creation of Papal States
768–814	Charlemagne rules as King of the Franks
774	Charlemagne defeats Lombards in northern Italy
800	Pope Leo III crowns Charlemagne
814–840	Louis the Pious succeeds Charlemagne as "emperor"
843	Treaty of Verdun partitions the Carolingian Empire
870	Treaty of Mersen further divides Carolingian Empire
875–950	New invasions of Vikings, Muslims, and Magyars
962	Ottonian dynasty succeeds Carolingian in Germany
987	Capetian dynasty succeeds Carolingian in France

Laon Cathedral, west front, c. 1190–95. Gothic architecture was the dominant style in Europe after the twelfth century and was based on northern European models. Gothic churches were built to communicate, announcing the glories of heaven with their confident mastery of space and light and, at the same time, heralding the wealth and power of the Church.

Charles persuaded the noted scholar Alcuin of York (c. 730–804), England, to come to Aachen as head of the palace school and as his own personal adviser. The goals of the school were Christian and basic: reading and writing of biblical texts in Latin, chanting of prayers, knowledge of grammar and arithmetic. This training would prepare missionaries for their work among the peoples of northern Europe. Scribes at the school prepared copies of prayers and biblical texts for the liturgical and scholarly needs of churches and scholars. In the process they created a new form of Latin script that forms the basis of the lower-case (small) letters we use today. Charlemagne also fostered the arts by bringing to his capital sculpture from Italy and by patronizing local artisans and craftspeople. Alcuin himself had the ear of the emperor, criticizing him for using force in converting the Saxons and convincing him not to repeat the practice by invading England.

Charlemagne's coronation challenged the authority of the eastern emperor in Constantinople, but during the next years Charlemagne managed, through negotiation and warfare, to gain Constantinople's recognition of his title. There were once again two emperors, east and west.

The Attempt at Empire Fails. The Carolingian family remained powerful until about the end of the ninth century. But then they could no longer fight off the new invasions of the western Christian world by Magyars (Hungarians), Norsemen, and Arabs. Regional administrators, emboldened by the Carolingian emperor's weakness, began to act independently of his authority. Only after yet another century would militarily powerful leaders begin once again to cobble together loosely structured kingdoms in northwestern Europe. Meanwhile, political leadership in Europe was generally decentralized in rural manor estates controlled by local lords.

Religious leadership in the cathedrals, churches, monasteries, and convents filled the gap, providing a greater sense of overall community and order. In this era, 600–1100 C.E., the Church gave Europe its fundamental character and order. The Magyar and Norse invaders, like the Germans before them, converted to Christianity. By the end of the eleventh century, the Roman Church, as well as the political authorities of western Europe, were preparing to confront Islam.

EARLY CHRISTIANITY
WHAT DIFFERENCE DOES IT MAKE?

Christianity completed its first millennium during the High Middle Ages in Europe. It had originated in the eastern Mediterranean and spread throughout Europe. It had begun with the teachings of one man preached by a handful of disciples and institutionalized through the zeal of a single missionary, and had flowered into two separate, far-flung Church hierarchies and several localized structures. It had begun with a membership of downtrodden Jews, added middling-level gentiles, attracted some of the elites of Rome, and finally converted multitudes of Europe's invading barbarians. It had expanded its own organizational establishment via the network of transportation, communication, and trade put in place by the Roman Empire. And when that empire dissolved and contracted, the Church maintained and consolidated its position within the remains of those old Roman administrative and market centers. As European society became more rural, Christian monasteries and convents were founded in the countryside and often took on administrative and developmental roles alongside their spiritual missions. In short, the Church, like the empire, was much transformed. By the year 1000 it had become the most important organizational and cultural force in western Europe.

The transformations of both the Christian religious world and the European political world continued after 1000 with extraordinary developments in crusading vigor, trade and commerce, urbanization, intellectual and artistic creativity, and religious reform. We will explore these transformations in Chapter 12. First, however, we turn to equally startling and revolutionary developments that had created another world religion, originating in the Arabian peninsula only a few hundred miles from the birth place of both Judaism and Christianity. By the year 1000 it had spread across north Africa, northward into Spain, throughout the Middle East, and on through Iran and Afghanistan into India. Our study of Islam in Chapter 11 will complete our introduction to the origins and early life of the three major monotheistic religions.

Review Questions

- In what ways did the Judaism of the prophets differ from the Judaism of the Torah? In what ways were they similar?
- Early Judaism was very closely associated with the land of Israel. How did exile force the Jewish people to restructure their religion in order to survive?
- What were the reasons for Christians and Muslims to treat their Jewish minorities respectfully? What were the reasons for treating them spitefully?
- What elements from Judaism were incorporated into Christianity? What elements were rejected?
- How did St. Paul take the original teachings and organization created by Jesus and build them into a Christian Church?
- Christianity began in Judaea and became the dominant religion in Europe. What were the key steps in making and consolidating that geographical move?

Suggested Readings

PRINCIPAL SOURCES

The New English Bible with the Apocrypha. Oxford Study Edition (New York: Oxford University Press, 1970). Clear, readable, authentic text produced by interfaith team of scholars.

Brown, Peter. *The Rise of Western Christendom* (Malden, MA: Blackwell Publishers, 1996). Brown brings to bear expertise on the Roman empire at the time of Christ to provide context to early Christianity.

Crossan, John Dominic. *The Historical Jesus. The Life of a Mediterranean Jewish Peasant* (San Francisco, CA: HarperCollins, 1991). One of the clearest interpretations of Jesus in his time.

Kee, Howard Clark, *et al. Christianity: A Social and Cultural History* (New York: Macmillan Publishers, 1991). Excellent, scholarly analysis and narrative of early Christianity.

Pagels, Elaine. *The Gnostic Gospels* (New York: Random House, 1979). Clear, concise explanation of the significance to our understanding of early Christianity of the Gnostic manuscripts discovered at Nag Hammadi in 1945.

Smart, Ninian. *The World's Religions* (Cambridge: Cambridge University Press, 1989). Useful general survey, clearly written.

Smeltzer, Robert M. *Jewish People, Jewish Thought* (New York: Macmillan Publishing Co., Inc., 1980). Excellent general history.

ADDITIONAL SOURCES

Andrea, Alfred and James Overfield, eds. *The Human Record*, Vol. I (Boston, MA: Houghton Mifflin Company, 3rd ed., 1998). Superbly chosen selections.

Armstrong, Karen. *A History of God* (New York: Knopf, 1993). Concise history of the evolution of the three major monotheistic religions.

Augustine. *The City of God*, trans. Marcus Dods (New York: Modern Library, 1950). A central work of Christian theology from the late Roman Empire.

Baron, Salo Wittmayer. *A Social and Religious History of the Jews*, Vol. 1 (New York: Columbia University Press, 1952). First in a multivolume series by one of the leading Jewish historians of his time.

Holy Bible. New Revised Standard Version (Grand Rapids, MI: Zondervan Publishing House, 1989). Another excellent, standard translation.

de Lange, Nicholas. *Atlas of the Jewish World* (New York: Facts on File, 1984). Excellent text, helpful maps. Beautiful illustrations.

Einhard and Notker the Stammerer. *Two Lives of Charlemagne*, trans. Lewis Thorpe (Harmondsworth, England: Penguin Books, 1969). The standard primary source on Charlemagne.

Eliade, Mircea. *Ordeal by Labyrinth* (Chicago, IL: University of Chicago Press, 1982). The leading religious historian of the early twentieth century explains principles of his view of religious history.

———. *The Sacred and the Profane* (New York: Harper Torchbooks, 1959). Explains his view of religion in history.

Gibbon, Edward. *The History of the Decline and Fall of the Roman Empire*, 3 vols., abridged by D.M. Low (New York: Washington Square Books, 1962). The classic from the age of the Enlightenment. Follows and projects the story through the fall of Constantinople to the Turks.

Grant, Michael. *History of Rome* (New York: Charles Scribner's Sons, 1978). Readable, basic text.

———. *Jesus: An Historian's Review of the Gospels* (New York: Touchstone, 1995). Does the best he can to reconstruct Jesus' life and teachings based on the gospels.

Halpern, Baruch. *The First Historians: The Hebrew Bible and History* (San Francisco, CA: Harper and Row, 1988). Attempts to demonstrate the extent to which Hebrew stories from the Bible can be authenticated.

Honour, Hugh and John Fleming. *The Visual Arts: A History* (Englewood Cliffs, NJ: Prentice-Hall, 4th ed., 1995). Excellent textbook approach to the history of art.

Hopfe, Lewis M. *Religions of the World* (New York: Macmillan Publishing Company, 5th ed., 1991). Useful textbook survey.

Kaufmann, Yehezkel. *The Religion of Israel* (Chicago, IL: University of Chicago Press, 1960). Fascinating analysis of biblical Judaism, stressing the inability of the early Jews even to comprehend the significance of images in worship.

Kee, Howard Clark. *Who Are The People of God: Early Christian Models of Community* (New Haven, CT: Yale University Press, 1995). Kee stresses the importance of the community of believers in the success of the early Christian Church.

Mann, Michael. *A History of Power from the Beginning to A.D. 1760* (Cambridge: Cambridge University Press, 1986). Mann searches for the success of early Christianity in its sociological composition and appeal.

Matthew, Donald. *Atlas of Medieval Europe* (New York: Facts on File, 1983). Excellent text. Useful maps. Beautiful illustrations.

McManners, John, ed. *The Oxford Illustrated History of Christianity* (New York: Oxford University Press, 1990). Outstanding set of basic introductory articles by major scholars, highly illustrated.

Meier, John P. *A Marginal Jew: Rethinking the Historical Jesus* 2 vols. (New York: Doubleday, 1991, 1994). Meier emphasizes Jesus' abilities as a magician and exorcist in attracting followers.

Momigliano, Arnaldo. *On Pagans, Jews, and Christians* (Hanover, NH: University Press of New England for Wesleyan University Press, 1987). Compares the attractions of each of these perspectives, and their confrontations with one another in the early years of Christianity.

Pagels, Elaine. *Beyond Belief: The Secret Gospel of Thomas* (New York: Random House, 2003). Pagels' analysis of the most significant of the Gnostic gospels, and its meaning for her.

Palmer, R.R. and Joel Colton. *A History of the Modern World*, 8th ed. (New York: Knopf, 1984). Eurocentric and mostly centered on the period since 1500, nevertheless an excellent, readable text, strongest on the French Revolution.

Pritchard, James B., ed. *Ancient Near Eastern Texts Relating to the Old Testament* (Princeton, NJ: Princeton University Press, 3rd ed., 1969). Basic compendium of the most important documents. Indispensable for the subject.

Rosenberg, David and Harold Bloom. *The Book of J* (New York: Grove Weidenfeld, 1990). Analyses the four major editorial strands in the composition of the Torah, stressing the one that refers to god by his Hebrew name of JHWH.

Rubenstein, Richard L. *When Jesus Became God* (New York: Harcourt Brace, 1999). An account of the armed battle and victory of the Roman Church over the theologian Arius who declared that Christ's human nature diminished his divine nature.

Smart, Ninian and Richard D. Hecht, eds. *Sacred Texts of the World: A Universal Anthology* (New York: Crossroad Publishing, 1982). Useful selection of religious texts.

World History Documents CD-ROM

1.9 Hebrew Scriptures
6.1 The Acts of the Apostles
6.2 Pliny the Younger on the Vesuvius Eruption and the Christian "Controversy"
6.3 Julian Imperator: The Ultimate Pagan
6.4 Bishop Synesius of Cyrene: A Lukewarm Churchman
6.5 Leo I: The Man Who Laid the Foundations for the Medieval Papacy
6.6 St. Augustine of Hippo: *The Just War*
6.7 Paulus Orosius: *History Against the Pagans*
6.8 St. Benedict
7.4 Einhard
7.5 The Missi Dominici (802)
7.6 Launching the Crusades (1095): "It Is the Will of God!"

ISLAM

SUBMISSION TO ALLAH: MUSLIM CIVILIZATION BRIDGES THE WORLD 570 C.E.–1500 C.E.

KEY TOPICS
- The Origins of Islam
- Successors to the Prophet
- Spiritual, Religious, and Cultural Flowering
- Relations with Non-Muslims

Islam, in Arabic, means "submission." Islam teaches submission to the word of God, called "Allah" in Arabic. Muslims, "those who submit," know God's word primarily through the Quran, the Arabic book that records the teachings of God as they were transmitted to the Prophet Muhammad (570–632). Stories of Muhammad's life, words, and deeds (*hadith*), carefully collected, sifted, and transmitted over many generations, provide Muslims with models of the righteous life and how to live it. According to Islam's holy book, the Quran, Muhammad was the most recent prophet of God's message of ethical monotheism. Devout Muslims declare this belief in prayers, which are recited five times each day: "There is no God but God, and Muhammad is his Prophet."

For Islam the teachings of the Quran and of Muhammad's life are fulfilled only with the creation of a community of believers, the *umma*, and its proper regulation through political structures. Through its early centuries, Islam established administrative and legal systems in the areas to which it spread: Arabia, western Asia, northern Africa, and Spain. As Islam spread later to eastern Europe, central Asia, south Asia, and sub-Saharan Africa, it arrived sometimes with government backing, sometimes without. After the twelfth century, Islam expanded into China and southeast Asia as a religious and cultural system without government support.

Islam is considered here as a world religion, but because it often unified government and religion into a single system, it may also be compared with the materials in Part 3 on the expansion of world empires. In this chapter, we shall trace the growth and spread of Islam as a religious, governmental, and cultural system. We shall also examine its encounters with other religions and empires.

umma The community of believers in Islam, which transcends ethnic and political boundaries.

THE ORIGINS OF ISLAM

Islam emerged in the Arabian peninsula, an area largely inhabited by nomadic Bedouin tribes. The Bedouins organized themselves as clans. Inhabiting the desert, they lacked the sources of water so crucial for the emergence of cities and civilizations in the ancient world, although a few cities, such as Mecca, grew up alongside major oases. Mecca flourished as a trading center in the seventh century, but the region, in general, lacked the governmental institutions and the powerful emperors that supported the emergence of major religions elsewhere. Religiously, the region was polytheistic, worshiping many gods. Mecca held an especially prominent role in this worship. It held the Ka'aba, a rectangular building that housed a cubical black stone structure, and the sacred tokens of all the clans of Mecca and of many of the surrounding tribes as well. Serving as a center of pilgrimage and trade, Mecca brought enormous economic benefits to the traders of the Quraysh tribes who controlled the city and its shrine.

Opposite Niche (*Mihrab*) with Islamic calligraphy. Islamic design features a meandering pattern made up of repetitive motifs and a suggestion of infinite extension. (*Metropolitan Museum, New York*)

AT A GLANCE : ISLAM

DATE	POLITICAL/SOCIAL EVENTS	LITERARY/PHILOSOPHICAL EVENTS
500 C.E.	■ Muhammad (570–632)	
600 C.E.	■ Hijra (622) ■ Muslim conquest of Mecca ■ Orthodox or Rightly Guided Caliphs (632–661) ■ Muslim conquest of Iraq, Syria, Palestine, Egypt, western Iran (632–642), Cyprus (649), and Persian Empire (650s) ■ Umayyad caliphate (661–750); capital in Damascus ■ Muslim conquest of Carthage (698) and central Asia (650–712) ■ Husayn killed at Karbala (680); Sunni–Shi'ite split	■ Revelation of the Quran to Muhammad (610) ■ Persian becomes second language of Islam
700 C.E.	■ Muslim conquest of Tunis (700), Spain (711–716), Sind and lower Indus valley ■ Muslim defeat at Battle of Tours (732) ■ Muslims defeat Chinese at battle of Talas River (751) ■ Abbasid caliphate (750–1258) ■ Baghdad founded (762)	■ Biography of Muhammad by Ibn Ishaq (d. 767) ■ Formulation of major systems of Islamic law
800 C.E.	■ Divisions in Muslim Empire (833–945) ■ Fez founded (808)	■ al–Tabari, *History of Prophets and Kings* ■ al–Khwarazmi develops algebra ■ Abbasid caliphate establishes "House of Wisdom" translation bureau in Baghdad ■ Sufi tariqat
900 C.E.	■ Persians seize Baghdad (945) ■ Cairo founded (969)	■ Ferdowsi, *Shah Nama* ■ al–Razi, *Encyclopedia of Medicine* ■ Turkish becomes third language of Islam ■ Mutazilites challenge Islamic orthodoxy
1000 C.E.	■ Seljuk Turks dominate Abbasid caliphate (1038) ■ Almoravid dynasty in north Africa and Spain (1061–1145) ■ Battle of Manzikert (1071) ■ 1st Crusade (1095–9)	■ Ibn Sina (Avicenna), philosopher, produces "Canon of Medicine" ■ al–Biruni writes on mathematics and astronomy (d. 1046)
1100 C.E.	■ Almohad dynasty rules north Africa and Spain (1145–1269) ■ 2nd Crusade (1147–9) ■ Salah al-Din (Saladin) recaptures Jerusalem (1187) ■ 3rd Crusade (1189–92)	■ al–Ghazzali (d. 1111), Muslim philosopher and theologian ■ Ibn Rushd (Avarroes; 1126–98) ■ Maimonides (1135–1204), Jewish physician, philosopher, and theologian
1200 C.E.	■ 4th Crusade (1202–04) ■ Sultanate of Delhi (1211–1526) ■ Children's Crusade (1212) ■ 5th–8th Crusades (1218–91) ■ Crusaders driven from west Asia (1291) ■ Fall of Baghdad to Mongols (1258); end of Abbasid Caliphate	■ Jalal al–Din Rumi, *Mathnawi* ■ al–Juvaini, *History of the World Conquerors* ■ Rashid al–Din, *World History*
1300 C.E.	■ Mansa Musa's pilgrimage to Mecca (1324) ■ Conversion of Malayans and Indonesians to Islam	■ Ibn Battuta (1304–c. 1368), traveler ■ Ibn Khaldun, *Universal History*
1400 C.E.	■ Ottoman Turks conquer Constantinople (1453) ■ Christians capture Granada, complete *reconquista* (1492)	

The Prophet: His Life and Teaching

Born in 570 to parents eminent in the Quraysh tribe, Muhammad was orphaned at an early age, and he was raised by his grandfather and later his uncle. He became a merchant, employed by a wealthy widow named Khadija. When he was twenty-five years old, he married her and they had four children together.

Muhammad was a deeply meditative person, retreating regularly to a nearby hill to pray and reflect. In 610, when he was forty years old, his reflections were interrupted, according to Islamic teachings, by the voice of the angel Gabriel, who instructed him: "Recite: In the name of the Lord who created Man of a blood-clot." Over the next two decades, according to Islamic theology, God continued to reveal his messages to Muhammad through Gabriel. Muhammad transmitted these revelations to professionals whose task it was to commit them to memory. The verses were also transcribed on palm leaves, stone, and other material. Soon after Muhammad's death, during the rule of Umar I, the second leader of the Islamic community (r. 634–644), scribes and editors compiled the entire collection of written and oral recitations into the Quran, which in Arabic means recitations. Umar's successor, Uthman (r. 644–656), issued an officially authorized edition of the Quran.

Approximately the length of the Christian New Testament, the Quran is considered by Muslims to be the absolute, uncorrupted, word of God. Composed in poetic form, the Quran helped to define the literary standards of the Arabic language. Muslims chant and study its text in Arabic, considering each syllable sacred. Even today many Muslims reject translations of the Quran into other languages as inadequate.

In the next century, new technologies led to broader dispersion of the Quran. During the middle eighth century, as Arab armies defeated Chinese forces in central Asia, the Muslim victors learned from their prisoners-of-war the technology of papermaking. By the end of the eighth century Baghdad had a paper mill; Egypt by 900; Morocco and Spain by 1100. Turks brought the art of papermaking to north India in the twelfth century. One use of paper was, of course, in the administration of the government bureaucracy. Another, perhaps even more important, was in the copying and diffusion of the Quran.

Trumpet call of the archangel Gabriel. Muhammad's religious career as a prophet seems to have been inspired by his early supernatural experiences. Once, he encountered a mighty being, the archangel Gabriel, on the horizon, who commanded him to recite ... This was the first *surah* (section from the Quran) revealed to humanity, and is symbolized here by Gabriel's blowing on a trumpet. (*British Library, London*)

The Five Pillars of Islam

The Quran reveals the "five pillars" of Islam, the five ritual expressions that define orthodox Muslim religious belief and practice:

- Declaring the creed, "There is no god but God, and Muhammad is his Prophet."
- Praying five times daily while facing Mecca (2:144), and, if possible, praying also in public assembly at midday each Friday.

- Giving alms to the poor in the community, especially to widows and orphans (2:212 ff.), later recommended at 2½ percent of income.
- Fasting each day during the month of Ramadan, the ninth month of the lunar year, although eating is permitted at night, with a major feast marking the month's end (2:179–84).
- Making the *hajj*, a pilgrimage to Mecca, at least once in a lifetime, if possible (2:185 ff.).

Jihad, or sacred struggle, is sometimes called a "sixth pillar" of Islam. It was less stringently required and has been interpreted in different ways. Some scholars interpret *jihad* as a call to physical warfare to preserve and extend the **dar al-Islam**, the "abode of Islam," the lands under Muslim rule, or, later, the lands in which Islam could be practiced freely, even if not under Muslim political rule. Even in this interpretation, however, *jihad* should be practiced only in self-defense, for "God loves not the aggressors" (2:187). Other scholars understand *jihad* as a personal call to the individual, internal, spiritual struggle to live Islam as fully as possible. The Quran gives a capsule description of this proper life:

> true piety is this: to believe in God, and the Last Day, the angels, the Book, and the Prophets, to give of one's substance, however cherished, to kinsmen, and orphans, the needy, the traveller, beggars, and to ransom the slave, to perform the prayer, to pay the alms. And they who fulfil their covenant, and endure with fortitude misfortune, hardship and peril, these are they who are true in their faith, these are the truly godfearing. (2:172–3)

Finally, the Quran promises repeatedly that those who observe Islam faithfully will find their reward in paradise, described as "gardens underneath which rivers flow … a shelter of plenteous shade" (4:60). On the other hand, those who reject the opportunity to fulfill the teachings of Islam will burn in a fiery Hell forever. Humans must choose between doing good and evil, but the Quran asserts that ultimately free will is limited: "God has power over everything" (4:87).

The Quran emphasized many of the same principles as those of Judaism and Christianity, including the importance of worshiping a single God—Allah in Arabic—and the obligation of the rich to help the poor. As in Christianity, the Quran taught that there would be a final Judgment Day. Many of the Quran's practices, too, were consistent with the existing rituals of Christians, Jews, and Zoroastrians living in Arabia at the time, and this made acceptance of the new religion easier. For example, regular prayer times and recitals of creed were also central to Judaism and Christianity, as was institutionalized charity. Animal sacrifice was a part of pagan and Zoroastrian religions, and had once been central to Judaism as it was now of Islam. Ritual slaughter of animals for food mirrored Jewish practice, as did male circumcision. Ritual washing before public prayers was also practiced by Zoroastrians.

Responses to Muhammad

In Mecca, Muhammad created the nucleus of the *umma*, or community of Muslims, as people converted to his message. Some were successful business people, some slaves, some tribeless people, some were family members. His wife Khadija became his first disciple, his cousin, Ali, seems to have been the second.

Most Meccans, however, found Muhammad's moral teachings too demanding, and, when he told them of the physical state—resembling an epileptic fit—in which he received some of the revelations from the angel Gabriel, many questioned his stability. On more practical grounds, they feared that his teachings threatened their own beliefs,

dar al-Islam The literal meaning of the Arabic words is "the abode of peace." The term refers to the land of Islam, or the territories in which Islam and its religious laws (**shari'a**) may be freely practiced.

Opposite **"Celebration of the End of Ramadan,"** from *The Maqamat (The Meetings)*, c. **1325–50** C.E. At the end of Ramadan, the month of fasting, Muslims don new clothes, throng the congregational mosques, and share their mingled senses of joy, relief, and achievement. Here a cavalcade, brandishing flags bearing religious inscriptions, unites in celebration. (*Bibliothèque Nationale, Paris*)

HOW DO WE KNOW?

Sources on Early Islam

Much of the historical writing on Islam is based on orthodox Islamic sources or, conversely, on the writings of their opponents. Such sources are not unbiased. In addition, several key documents were written down long after the events they describe, allowing possible alterations in the text. The Quran itself, for example, was compiled some fifty years after Muhammad received his first revelation. Muhammad ibn Ishaq (c. 704–767) wrote the first Arabic biography of the Prophet more than a century after his death.

Moreover, Islam suffered three civil wars in its first 120 years and considerable internal fighting thereafter, and many of the "official" histories were prepared in support of one position or another. Finally, as Islam confronted other religious civilizations, the accounts of its history were frequently tendentious, again supporting one side or another.

In their search for unbiased information, recent historians have made use of sources that were not recorded as historical narratives but that provide data from which history can be written:

> The new generation of historians thus uncovered an impressive variety of sources: commercial documents, tax registers, official land grants, administrative seals, census records, coins, gravestones, magical incantations written on bowls, memoirs of pilgrims, archeological and architectural data, biographical dictionaries, inscriptional evidence, and, more recently, oral history. (Eaton in Adas, p. 4)

From these records has emerged a deeper understanding of the culture of Muhammad's homeland in Arabia and of the adjacent Byzantine and Sasanid Persian Empires. These records suggest that Islam did not develop within a national vacuum. It incorporated religious, cultural, and social structures that were already present among its neighbors. As it grew and expanded, it incorporated aspects of Arab, Greek, Roman, and Persian civilizations.

- What are some issues in the early history of Islam that have led to the creation of primary source documents with conflicting interpretations?
- What use are tax registers, official land grant documents, and census records in interpreting the early history of Islam?
- If you were to study the degree to which Islam adopted practices from either the Greco-Roman or Persian civilizations, what primary sources would you seek?

especially the idol worship in their homes and in the Ka'aba. Some Meccans were already monotheists, especially the Jews and Christians who lived in the city, but most of them also rejected his message for they did not believe that their own religions needed the purification that Muhammad proposed. Despite this intense opposition, including apparent threats on Muhammad's life, his family and his branch of the Quraysh tribe stood by him, including some who did not accept his message but trusted his integrity.

After Khadija and some others of his early supporters died, however, Muhammad's position in Mecca became more precarious. Some members of the Muslim community began to leave Mecca in search of a home more accepting of the new teachings.

The Hijra and the Islamic Calendar. Largely rejected by his own tribe and the inhabitants of Mecca, Muhammad, too, sought a place that would be more receptive. He welcomed an invitation from the elders of the city of Medina to come with his followers to their oasis city some 200 miles to the north to adjudicate bitter disputes that had arisen among local tribes and to take over the reins of government. Muhammad may also have been attracted because Medina had a large Jewish population. As monotheists, they shared the most central principle of his faith, and he may have thought that he could ultimately convert them.

hijra The "migration" or flight of Muhammad from Mecca, where his life was in danger, to Medina (then called Yathrib), where he was welcomed as a potential leader in 622 C.E. The Islamic era (A.H.: After Hijra) is calculated from this date.

Known as the **hijra**, Muhammad's flight under pressure to Medina became a central moment in Islamic history. As Christians begin the year 1 of their calendar with an event in the life of Jesus—his birth—so Muslims begin theirs with the *hijra* and Muhammad's assertion of governmental leadership in Medina, a year that corresponds to the year 622 on the Christian calendar.

Though he failed to convert many Jews, Muhammad found many other inhabitants of Medina who did accept his religious message. This allowed him to consolidate the *umma* as the unified religious community of Muslims. He believed that for Islam to survive, he needed to create an Islamic government, a *dar al-Islam* ("an abode of Islam"), that included institutions that would protect the faith. In Medina he promulgated codes of business ethics as well as family laws of marriage, divorce, and inheritance, all based on the teachings of the Quran.

Muhammad Extends his Authority. After establishing his authority in Medina, Muhammad sought to gain converts in Mecca and ended up in skirmishes with the Quraysh tribes that opposed him. In 624 he and his followers successfully raided a large Meccan caravan train in the Battle of Badr, reducing Mecca's prosperity by cutting important trade routes and winning local fame for themselves. In 625 the Meccans fought back, defeating Muhammad and his forces at Uhud. In 627 the two sides fought to a draw at the Battle of the Ditch, but Muhammad's reputation grew as he stood up to the proud and powerful Meccans. In 630, following a dispute between the tribes of the two cities, Mecca surrendered to Medina. Muslims gained control of the Ka'aba, destroyed the Meccan idols, and turned the building with its sacred black rock into an Islamic shrine. By the time he died in 632, Muhammad was well on his way to creating from the warring tribes an Arabia-wide federation dedicated to the faith and the political structure of Islam.

Connections to Other Monotheistic Faiths. According to the Quran, Muhammad was only a messenger of God, not the originator of a new doctrine. Indeed, he was not even the founder of Islam: Several prophets came before him, including Adam, Noah, Abraham, Ishmael, Moses, and Jesus:

> We believe in God, and in that which has been sent down on us and sent down on Abraham, Ishmael, Isaac and Jacob, and the tribes, and that which was given to Moses and Jesus and the Prophets, of their Lord; we make no division between any of them, and to Him we surrender. (Quran, 2:130–32)

Muslims claim the Hebrew Abraham, whom Jews see as the father of Jewish monotheism, as the first Muslim: "Abraham in truth was not a Jew, neither a Christian; but he was a Muslim and one of pure faith" (Quran, 3:60). For this reason, Muslims often refer to Jews, Christians, and Muslims collectively as "children of Abraham."

The teachings of each of the earlier prophets, Muslims believe, were corrupted over time by their followers. Muslims challenged the Christian belief in Jesus as the son of God and maintain that the Christian doctrine of Jesus' divinity conflicts with the fundamental concept of pure monotheism. The Quran deplored this heresy, declaring, "It is not for God to take a son unto Him" (19:36). The Jews' error was in refusing to accept the Quran as a revised and updated version of the truth already given to them:

> When they were told, "Believe in that God has sent down," They said, "We believe in what was sent down on us"; and they disbelieve in what is beyond that. (2:85)

Muhammad and his followers came to believe that the revelations he received were final, uncorrupted, and true. Muhammad did not formulate this message; he only transmitted it as received. For Muslims, in the chain of prophets, Muhammad is the last and final link.

Christian Arabs remained largely aloof from Muhammad's alliances, while some Jews actively opposed his political goals and rejected his claims to religious prophecy. Disappointed in his wish to unite the members of the two monotheistic religions of the region under his leadership, and especially infuriated that some Jewish families had joined his Meccan enemies in war, he had the Jewish men of the Banu Qurayza clan executed, and the women and children enslaved. Elsewhere in Arabia, however, Jews and Christians, though subject to a special tax, were free to practice their religion.

HOW DO WE KNOW?

Gender Relations in Islam

Although many readers might consider the relationships between men and women a private matter, in fact in each religion—and empire—that we have studied some official doctrines attempted to regulate gender relationships. In general, they placed women under the authority of men and granted men more legal rights than they accorded to women. Although they often gave women greater importance than men in the private realm of house and hearth, they vested more public power and responsibility with men. Islam also follows this general pattern. The Quran states:

> Men have authority over women because God has made the one superior to the other, and because they spend their wealth to maintain them. Good women are obedient. They guard their unseen parts because God has guarded them. As for those from whom you fear disobedience, admonish them and send them to beds apart and beat them. Then if they obey you, take no further action against them. God is high, supreme. (4:34)

According to the Quran, women are to satisfy men's sexual desires and to bear children:

> Women are your fields: go, then, into your fields whence you please. (2:223)

Although, as in Judaism and Hinduism, sexual intercourse is forbidden during a woman's menstrual period:

> Keep aloof from women during their menstrual periods and do not touch them until they are clean again. (2:222)

It might appear that men are the initiators of sexual relations, but women are considered sexually seductive, and the Quran therefore urges the Prophet to:

> Enjoin believing women to turn their eyes away from temptation and to preserve their chastity; to cover their adornments (except such as are normally displayed); to draw their veils over their bosoms and not to reveal their finery except to their husbands, close relatives, and the very old and very young. (24:31)

As witnesses in legal matters, the testimony of two women equals that of a single man (2:282). Similarly in matters of inheritance, "A male shall inherit twice as much as a female" (4:11).

Despite these regulations that apparently limit the status of women, some modern scholars assert that Islam actually introduced "a positive social revolution" (Tucker, p. 42) in gender relations. Compared to what came before, Islam introduced new rights for women and gave them greater security in marriage. Islamic law, shari'a, safeguarded the rights of both partners in marriage through contractual responsibilities: it insisted on the consent of the bride; it specified that dowry, or bridal gift, go to the bride herself and not to her family; and it spelled out the husband's obligations to support his wives and children, even wives that he might divorce. Although men were allowed to take up to four wives, the Quran added, "But if you fear that you cannot maintain equality among them, marry one only or any slave-girls you may own. This will make it easier for you to avoid injustice" (4:3); so, in practice, only one wife was normally permitted.

These scholars note also that in the life of Muhammad, three women played exemplary roles: his first wife, Khadija, who supported him economically and emotionally when the revelations he received brought him scorn from others; Aisha, the most beloved of the wives he took after Khadija's death; and Fatima, the daughter of the Prophet and wife of the fourth caliph, Ali. Nevertheless, these women drew their importance from their service to prominent men, and were criticized when they asserted more independent roles.

Other scholars, on the other hand, have argued that Islam made the plight of women worse than it had been. These scholars argue that in pre-Islamic Arabia, women could initiate marriage, they could have more than one husband, they could divorce their husbands, they could remain in their parents' home area and have their husbands come to live with

them, and they could keep custody of their children in case of divorce. In pre-Islamic Arabia, some, like Allat, al-Uzza, and Manat were worshiped with great honor, suggesting there was considerable respect for females.

Of those scholars who feel that the position of women declined under Islam, some put the blame on Islam itself, but others suggest that the teachings of Islam were actually comparatively liberal. These scholars argue that it was contact with the Byzantine and Sasanid Empires that reduced women's status. They argue that tribal, nomadic Arabia had treated women with relative equality, but the neighboring empires, with their settled, urban civilizations, veiled women and kept them mostly at home under male domination. The Arabs adopted these practices. In effect, this group of scholars is also saying that the more liberal Quranic rules regarding women were reinterpreted after contact with societies outside Arabia. Whatever the rules of the Quran, in practice gender relations varied widely in different parts of the world of Islam.

Ibn Battuta (1304–c. 1368), a famous Berber (North African) traveler whose adventures took him to much of the known world, learned his concepts of gender relations in the Arab heartland of Islam. As he traveled, he was often astonished, and sometimes shocked, by the status of women in other Islamic countries. In the Turkish and Mongol regions between the Black and Caspian Seas, wives of local, ruling khans (sultans) owned property. When the senior wife appeared at the khan's residence, Ibn Battuta observes, the khan (sultan)

> advances to the entrance to the pavilion to meet her, salutes her, takes her by the hand, and only after she has mounted to the couch and taken her seat does the sultan himself sit down. All this is done in full view of those present, and without any use of veils. (Dunn, p. 168)

In the Maldive Islands, in the Indian Ocean, Ibn Battuta was even more scandalized:

Divorce proceedings. A scribe records the accusations of a husband and wife as they petition for a divorce in front of a *qadi*, or judge. A woman had limited rights to divorce her husband, but a man could divorce his wife without stipulating a reason, though in practice matters were rarely this simple. A *qadi* would bring to bear the combined wisdom of scriptural knowledge, local custom, and his own judgment in making an adjudication. (*Bibliothèque Nationale, Paris*)

HOW DO WE KNOW? (continued)

Their womenfolk do not cover their hands, not even their queen does so, and they comb their hair and gather it at one side. Most of them wear only an apron from their waists to the ground, the rest of their bodies being uncovered. When I held the qadiship [judge] there, I tried to put an end to this practice and ordered them to wear clothes, but I met with no success. No woman was admitted to my presence in a lawsuit unless her body was covered, but apart from that I was unable to effect anything. (McNeill, p. 276)

In Mali, west Africa, female slaves and servants went publicly into the ruler's court completely naked. When Ibn

Battuta found a scholar's wife chatting with another man, he complained to the scholar. But the scholar quickly put Ibn Battuta in his place:

The association of women with men is agreeable to us and a part of good conduct, to which no suspicion attaches. They are not like the women of your country. (Dunn, p. 300)

Ibn Battuta left immediately and never returned to the man's home.

● *In terms of gender relationships, to what degree is Islam concerned with*

regulating biological, sexual relations? Family relationships? Social and legal relationships outside the family? How do regulations in Islam compare with those from other religions?

● *What is the evidence that Islam in its early years was more egalitarian toward women than were either the other groups in Arabia or the Byzantine and Sasanid Empires outside Arabia? What is the evidence that it was less egalitarian?*

● *Ibn Battuta was surprised that the treatment of women varied quite widely in the various lands of Islam. Are you surprised? Why or why not?*

SUCCESSORS TO THE PROPHET

When the Prophet died leaving no male heir, the Muslim community feared that the *umma* and its political organization would break up. To preserve them, the Muslim leadership elected Abu Bakr (r. 632–634), one of Muhammad's closest associates and the father of his wife Aisha, as **caliph**—that is, successor to the Prophet and head of the Muslim community. The next three caliphs were similarly elected from among Muhammad's relatives and companions, but amidst much more dissension.

Abu Bakr mobilized to prevent Muslims from deserting their new religion and the authority of its government, attacking those who tried. Arabia was convulsed in tribal warfare. The contending tribes fought for power and looted one another, as they had traditionally. Their battles spilled over the borders of the Arabian peninsula, as did their search for allies. The Byzantine and Sasanid Empires saw the Arab troops encroaching on their territories and fought back, but at the Battle of Ajnadayn (634), in southern Palestine, the Arab clans combined to form a unified army and defeated the Byzantine army. With their victory at Ajnadayn, the Arab warriors were no longer simple raiders in search of plunder. They were now at war for the control of settled empires.

Conquest followed conquest—Damascus in 636, Jerusalem in 638—but the northward march stopped as Byzantine troops held fast at the borders of the Anatolian peninsula. The Byzantine Empire defended its Anatolian borders for another four

caliph The spiritual head and temporal ruler of the Muslim community.

The expansion of Islam. The Muslim faith spread with astonishing speed from its center at Mecca, exploiting the weakness of the Byzantine and Sasanid Empires. Within a century of the death of the Prophet Muhammad in 632 C.E., Arab armies had reached the Atlantic coast in the west, and the borders of India and China in the east.

For an interactive version of this map, go to: **http://www.prenhall.com/spodek/map11.1**

centuries, and its Balkan territories for eight. But the Sasanid Empire collapsed almost immediately. In 637 Arab armies defeated the Persians in battle, seized their capital, Ctesiphon, and forced the last emperor to flee. Meeting little opposition, Arab armies swept across Iraq, Iran, Afghanistan, and central Asia. Other Arab armies now turned toward northern Africa, taking Egypt in 641–643 and Tripoli in 643.

The second caliph, Umar I (r. 634–644), established the early principles of political administration, as a "rightly guided" caliph, in the conquered territories. The troops were not to interfere with the way of life of the conquered populations. The early caliphs did not encourage conversion to Islam, lest the political and social status of conqueror and conquered become confused. Also, since Muslims were exempted from land taxes and poll taxes, the conversion of conquered peoples would cause considerable loss of tax revenue to Umar's government.

To prevent the armies and the administrators from interfering with the economy and the social traditions of the newly conquered territories, Umar ordered the occupiers to live somewhat apart from the conquered populations. Muslim armies built new garrison cities, such as Basra, Kufa, Fustat, and Merv, and added new neighborhoods to existing cities for their troops and administrators. They largely left local systems of taxation and administration in place, and incumbent personnel often kept their jobs, but the new government confiscated lands that had been owned by the state and its officials and claimed them for itself.

These new arrangements proved unstable. In the new garrison cities, conqueror and conquered lived side by side, and they could not effectively be segregated socially and culturally. In addition, the troops soon argued that their pay was not adequate. Their incomes lagged, even as the new conquests enriched the top-level administrators. What had become of Islam's call for a more egalitarian society? In essence, the imperial aims of the ruling class and the religious goals of Islam were pulling in opposite directions.

Civil War: Religious Conflict and the Sunni-Shi'a Division

The jockeying for power among various political, economic, tribal, and religious interest groups precipitated a series of civil wars. A contingent of Arab troops from Egypt assassinated the third caliph, Uthman (r. 644–656), complaining that under his administration their local governors were cruel, their pay was inadequate, and class divisions were destroying Arab unity.

Uthman's successor, Ali (r. 656–661), was elected despite considerable opposition. Supporting his election most strongly was the *shiat Ali*, "the party of Ali," usually referred to simply as the Shi'a or Shi'ites. This group felt that the caliph should be chosen from the family of the Prophet. They had opposed the election of the first three caliphs. Ali, as the cousin and also the son-in-law of Muhammad, having married his daughter Fatima, was the first caliph to fit their requirement. In opposition, members of Uthman's family, the Ummayad clan, preferred one of their own. They argued for acceptance of the first three caliphs as legitimate since they were chosen by the *umma* and reflected the *sunna*, or example, of the Prophet. They and their followers called themselves Sunnis. Finally, a third group, who had long opposed the Umayyad for their own reasons, feared that Ali might reach an accommodation with their rivals, and assassinated him.

After Ali's assassination, the Umayyad leader, Mu'awiya (r. 661–680), declared himself caliph. Moving the capital out of Arabia to Damascus in Syria, Mu'awiya distanced himself from the original Muslim elite of the Arabian peninsula. He opened Islam to more cosmopolitan influences and a more professional style of imperial administration.

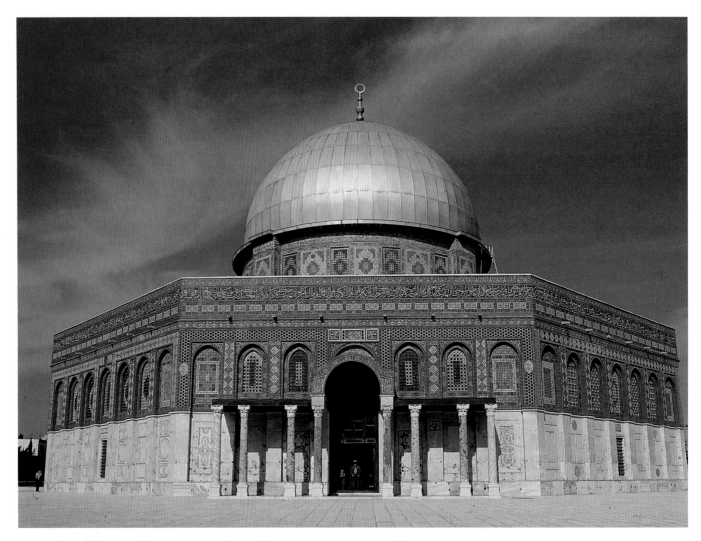

The exterior of the Dome of the Rock, Jerusalem, first constructed in 692 C.E. The first Umayyad caliph, Abd al-Malik (r. 685–705) built this shrine as the first major monument in Islamic history. It celebrates the triumphal conquests of the Umayyad dynasty as it emerged from Arabia and defeated both the Byzantine and Persian Empires to carve out a new empire of its own.

imam In Islam, a title for a person whose leadership or example is to be followed.

mahdi According to Islamic tradition, a messianic leader will appear to restore justice, truth, and religion for a brief period before the Day of Judgment.

Tension remained high among the various religious and tribal factions, however, and civil war broke out again on Mu'awiya's death in 680. His son, Yazid I (r. 680–683), claimed the caliphate, but Husayn, son of the assassinated Ali, took the field against him. When Husayn was killed in battle at Karbala, Iraq, in the year 680, he joined his father as the second martyr of the Shi'a branch of Islam.

The Shi'as stressed the importance of religious purity and they wanted the caliph to represent Islam's religious principles rather than its imperial aspirations. They felt that Ali, in addition to his heritage as a member of the family of the Prophet, represented that purer orientation, and they would recognize only descendants of Ali as **imams**, religious leaders who were also rightful caliphs. From 680 onward, Shi'as went into battle for the appointment of their imams to fill the position of caliph.

One after another, all of the first eleven Shi'a imams are believed to have died as martyrs, either in battle or through assassination. After the death of the eleventh imam in 874, and the disappearance of his son, the hereditary line ended. From that time onward, "twelver" Shi'as have looked forward to the reappearance of the "hidden" twelfth imam, referred to as the **mahdi**, or the "rightly guided one," a messiah, to usher in a new age of Islam, truth, and justice. Meanwhile, they have usually been willing to accept the authority of the current government, while stressing matters of the spiritual rather than the temporal world.

The great majority of Muslims, however, regarded the caliph as primarily a political official, administering the empire of Islam. They accepted the rule of the Umayyads, based on *sunni* teachings and the importance of the *umma* in making political decisions.

The division between Sunni and Shi'a, which began over the proper succession to the caliphate, has continued to the present, long after the caliphate has ceased to exist, as the principal sectarian division within Islam. Some 83 percent of the world's Muslims today are Sunnis, 16 percent Shi'as. The split is largely geographical with Shi'as forming 95 percent of the population of Iran and about 60 percent of Iraq. Ismailis, a branch of Shi'as, are found mostly in Pakistan and India. Elsewhere Sunnis are the overwhelming majority.

The Sunni-Shi'a division is the most significant in Islam, but it is not the only one. At the death of the sixth imam in 765, there was another conflict over acceptance of the seventh. The majority chose the imam's younger son, but a minority followed the elder son Ismail. The Ismailis proselytized actively and led frequent rebellions against the caliphate. Later the Ismailis also divided. One branch lives on today, revering the Aga Khan as its leader.

Clay figurine of a female slave from Khirbat al-Mafjar, Syria, *c.* eighth century. Female slaves had their place in the world of the Umayyad dynasty and beyond. Often the objects of passionate love, many were accomplished singers and highly educated.

The Umayyad Caliphs Build an Empire

After the succession struggle on Mu'awiya's death, the Umayyads consolidated their rule and embarked on wars of imperial conquest. To symbolize their imperial power, the Umayyad caliphs constructed elegant, monumental mosques in Jerusalem in 691 (the Dome of the Rock); in Medina, 706–710; Damascus, 706–714; and, again, Jerusalem (the al-Aqsa Mosque), 709–715. They began also to create an imperial bureaucracy which owed its allegiance to the state rather than to the current ruler personally.

Life in the cities eroded the solidarity of tribal society. A new social structure was developing that was dividing the Arab upper and lower classes while mixing together the Arab and non-Arab elites. The Umayyad caliphs looked to Islam as the glue that could hold the splintered society together. They sought actively to convert the conquered peoples and assimilate them into a single Muslim *umma*. By the middle of the eighth century, conversions to Islam were increasing among the urban populations, as was the use of Arabic as the language of administration, literature, and everyday speech.

The Umayyads quickly expanded their empire through a series of enormously successful imperial conquests. Arab armies conquered the entire northern coast of Africa by 711. In north Africa, after initial resistance, most of the conquered Berber tribes converted to Islam. At one extreme, conversion was accompanied by intermarriage, and some of the Arab conquerors and Berber peoples intermingled to the point where it was no longer possible to distinguish among them ethnically. In other cases, whole tribes converted. They became part of the Islamic world but remained in their tribal groupings. Often they conducted their own internal administration as if they were a small state. Other Muslim armies marched eastward, capturing large parts of central Asia, and raiding repeatedly in the Indus valley region of Sind.

Between 711 and 756, Arab and Berber forces crossed the Straits of Gibraltar and completed the conquest of Spain. Muslim raiders also moved into France, but Charles Martel and Frankish armies pushed them back south of the Pyrenees in 732 after the Battle of Tours.

Muslim governments continued to rule at least parts of Spain for seven and a half centuries, until 1492. During those years the relationships between Muslims, Christians, and Jews were sometimes severe. Sometimes, however, they were very fruitful.

The Umayyads copied the imperial structures of the Byzantine and Persian Empires: wars of imperial conquest, bureaucracy in administration, monumentality in architecture, and regal opulence at court. They used Arabic as their language of administration and encouraged conversion to Islam.

However, Umar's successors were not so committed to the program of equality under Islam as earlier caliphs had been. Their implementation was inconsistent, and various interest groups were frustrated by the vagaries of their changing fortunes. Many Sunni religious leaders, although pleased with the new emphasis on Islam, were offended by the imperial pomp of the Umayyads and their use of religion for blatantly political purposes. Many Shi'as continued to nourish the hope that one of their imams would displace the Umayyads and take his rightful place as caliph. In Kufa, Iraq, Shi'as revolted in 740, but the revolt was suppressed, and its leaders were executed.

The Ummayads had raised conflicting expectations. Non-Arab Muslims, whose taxes were not lowered or were lowered only temporarily, railed against the government for not delivering on its promises. Arabs were unhappy that their own taxes were being raised to compensate for the reductions offered to others.

The Umayyad armies, which were overextended and exhausted, began to lose major battles. The Turks drove them from Transoxiania in central Asia; the Khazars stopped them in Armenia in 730; Charles Martel halted the Umayyad advance in France in 732; the Greeks destroyed a major Muslim army in Anatolia in 740; in north Africa Berber rebels, although defeated in 742, destroyed an Umayyad army of 27,000 in the process. Umayyad forces did win the critical Battle of the Talas River in 751, halting the advance of Chinese forces westward and opening central Asia and its silk routes to Islamic religious and cultural missions, but they did not push forward. Military advances stopped. Pulled in many conflicting directions, without the strength to reply, the caliphate was drawn into a third civil war.

Portrait of Mahmud of Ghazni, from Rashid al-Din's *World History*, 1306–7. Mahmud (998–1030), a Sunni Muslim prince, is shown putting on the traditional diplomatic gift of a robe of honor, bestowed by the Abbasid caliph. Regional rulers sometimes declared their independence from central control, but Mahmud of Ghazni was careful to include the caliph's name on his coinage, thereby presenting himself as a loyal subject. (*Edinburgh University Library*)

The Third Civil War and the Abbasid Caliphs

The Abbasid clan in northern Iran—descended from an uncle of Muhammad named Abbas and also claiming support from descendants from the line of Ali—revolted against the Umayyads. Supported by Arab settlers in Iran who were protesting against high taxes, by Shi'as who were seeking their own rule, and also by a faction from Yemen, the Abbasid clan overthrew the Umayyad caliphate. In 750, Abu al-Abbas al-Saffah initiated the new Abbasid caliphate, which ruled in reality for a century and a half but held power in name until 1258. Signaling new policy directions, the Abbasid caliph built a new capital at Baghdad, 500 miles east of Damascus, along the banks of the Tigris River, in the heart of the historic fertile crescent.

The Abbasid caliphs continued the tasks of the Umayyads in trying to bring order and unity to an empire of heterogeneous peoples, and they followed many of the principles set forth by Umar II. They used Arabic as a unifying language of official communication and administration, and continued to urge non-Muslims to convert. They recruited widely among all the peoples of the empire to fill administrative and military positions, and as the bureaucracy expanded, Nestorian Christians, Jews, Shi'as, and numerous ethnic groups became prominent in the Abbasid administration.

For a century the Abbasids succeeded—to a surprising degree—in solving the problems of administering large empires. They kept their administration cosmopolitan and centralized, yet at the same time in touch with local communities. They rotated their officers so that none could become entrenched and semi-independent in a distant posting. They regularized taxes. They employed spies as well as troops of soldiers and armed police. They also attempted to maintain good relations with local notables, such as village headmen, large landowners, *qadis* (judges), officials of local mosques, religious teachers, moneylenders, accountants, merchants, and family patriarchs, who were the critical sources of information and power in the villages and towns.

The Weakening of the Caliphate

Inevitably, however, the Abbasid caliphate, too, encountered difficulties. The process of choosing a successor to the caliph remained unresolved. At the death of Caliph Harun-al-Rashid (r. 786–809), his two sons fought for the throne, provoking a fourth civil war. Recruiting troops proved an even bigger problem. Throughout the empire, local strongmen were invited to ally their troops to the caliph's armies, but these military contingents naturally owed their allegiance not to Baghdad but to the local potentate.

The caliphs expanded sharply the use of slave troops in their armies. Slave troops, mostly from central Asia, were often poorly disciplined, and sometimes various contingents turned on one another. At the same time the civilian bureaucracy became more corrupt and more distant from the general population, and tax collection was increasingly turned over to exploitive, semi-independent tax farmers. Corruption and reliance on slaves isolated the caliphs from their own civilian populations. The rulers became increasingly remote from the people they ruled—the more imperial the caliphate, the more distant it became from the original Islamic ideals of equality and simplicity.

The Emergence of Quasi-independent States. As a consequence, revolts struck the caliphate. In 868 a Turkish commander established a virtually independent dynasty that included Egypt and Syria, until the caliph regained them in 905. The slaves in the salt mines of southern Iraq waged a successful revolt for fifteen years, 868–883. In 867, frontier troops in central Iran revolted and won control of southern and western Iran.

Ismaili and Shi'a religious leaders organized revolts throughout the empire. Denying the legitimacy of Abbasid claims to rule and highlighting the exploitation of the village and tribal masses by the distant and corrupt administration in Baghdad, they won many victories in the name of their own views of Islam. Inspired by the Ismailis, peasant and Bedouin raiders attacked Mecca, briefly carrying away the sacred Ka'aba stone, the most venerated shrine in the holy city.

The Fatimid clan, claiming to be the rightful successors of the Prophet, conquered Egypt and much of northern Africa. They broke openly with Baghdad, declaring themselves the legitimate caliphs. In Iraq, other rebels took control first of the regions around Baghdad and then, in 945, of Baghdad itself. The caliph was permitted to continue to rule in name, but in effect the empire as a unified, centralized administration was finished. The unity of the Abbasid state dissolved, although the nominal authority of the caliph was still accepted everywhere.

Seljuk Turks and their Sultanate. Meanwhile, in the seventh and eighth centuries, the consolidation of the Tang dynasty in China had revived the pressure on the pastoral, nomadic peoples of inner Asia, pushing them westward, just as the Han had done centuries before (see Chapter 7). This time the pastoral nomads encountered peoples who had been converted to Islam. As a result of contacts with Muslim scholars and mystics, many of the nomadic peoples converted as well.

One of these groups, the Turkish-speaking Qarluq peoples, gained control of Bukhara (992) and Samarqand (999) in modern Uzbekistan. They propagated Islam and began to sponsor the development of the Turkish language and a Turkish-Islamic civilization.

Another Turkish-speaking group, led by the Seljuk (or Saljuq) family, entered central Asia, conquered Afghanistan and Iran, and seized Baghdad in 1055. In Baghdad, the Seljuk Turks kept the Abbasid caliph on his throne and ruled in his name.

Byzantium and Islam. The Byzantine Empire remained the bastion of Christian political power in Asia Minor for a thousand years after the fall of Rome. A powerful new force for Islam, the Seljuk Turks, appeared out of central Asia in the eleventh century. After invading Persia and Syria, they defeated a Byzantine army at Manzikert in 1071 and began to infiltrate the Byzantine heartland.

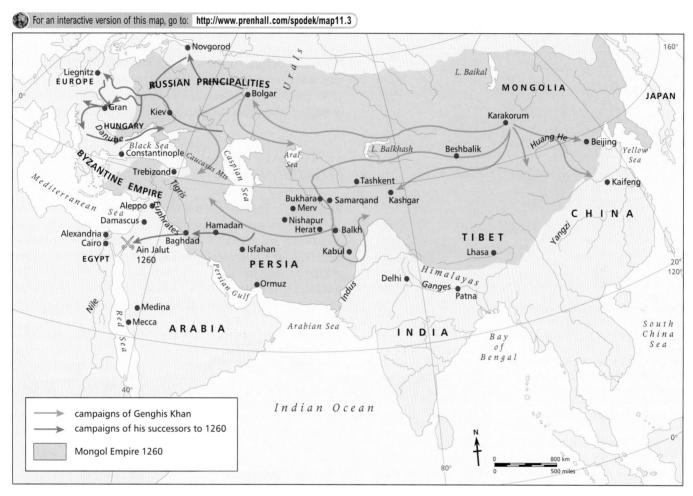

For an interactive version of this map, go to: http://www.prenhall.com/spodek/map11.3

campaigns of Genghis Khan
campaigns of his successors to 1260
Mongol Empire 1260

They titled themselves sultans, claiming authority over the secular side of government, while leaving the administration of religious affairs to the caliph.

The Mongols and the Destruction of the Caliphate. In the twelfth century, a new threat destabilized empires from China to Europe, including the areas under Muslim rule. In Karakorum, Mongolia, Temujin (*c.* 1162–1227), later called Chinngis (Genghis) Khan ("Universal Ruler"), forged a confederation of Mongol and Turkish peoples, who rode outward, east and west, creating the largest land-based empire in history. The story of the Mongol expansion is told in Chapter 12.

Muslims whose lands the Mongols conquered felt devastated. An eyewitness observer, Ibn al-Athir, records his response to the early waves of invasions in 1220–21:

> For some years I continued averse from mentioning this event, deeming it so horrible that I shrank from recording it. To whom, indeed can it be easy to write the announcement of the death-blow of Islam and the Muslims, or who is he on whom the remembrance thereof can weigh lightly? O would that my mother had not born me, or that I had died and become a forgotten thing ere this befell … These [Mongols] spared none, slaying women and men and children, ripping open pregnant women and killing unborn babes. (McNeill and Waldman, pp. 249–51)

In 1258, Chinngis' grandson Hülegü (*c.* 1217–65) conquered Baghdad and executed the caliph, ending the Abbasid empire. The Mongols might have continued further on

The Mongol world. The irruption across Eurasia of the Mongols, an aggressive steppe nomad people, remains one of the most successful military undertakings of all time. Within thirty years the campaigns of Genghis Khan took the Mongol cavalry east to the Chinese heartland and west to Kievan Russia, the Caucasus, and Persia. His immediate successors consolidated China, entered Europe, and went on to establish a network of trans-Asian empires.

The Empire of Timur. The final stage of Mongol power was inspired by Timur's ambitions. Originating in Samarqand, his armies struck southeast to India, north to the Khanate of the Golden Horde, and west against the Ottoman and Egyptian Mameluke empires. Despite brilliant, brutal, early successes, the empire was unable to sustain its internal dynamics, and its collapse saw the exit of Mongol power from the world stage.

their conquests in west Asia, but the death of Hülegü's brother in China diverted their attention. Meanwhile, the sultan in Cairo defeated the Mongol troops at the Battle of Ain Jalut (1260), near Nazareth, ending their threat of further advance. Mongol rule in west Asia continued, however, until 1336. Significantly, even after it lost its political power to the Mongols, Islam continued to expand and gain converts.

SPIRITUAL, RELIGIOUS, AND CULTURAL FLOWERING

When the caliphate fell, the universal Muslim community, the *umma*, seemed to fall with it. Its central political focus was destroyed. Earlier historians have therefore characterized 1258 as a downward turning point, ushering in a protracted decline. More recent writers, however, emphasize the continuing growth of Islam outside the Arab world. The descendants of the Mongols themselves converted to Islam

Delivering a lecture. A traditional saying—"Kings are the rulers of the people, but scholars are the rulers of kings"—indicates the esteem in which learning is traditionally held by Muslims. Moreover, the transmission of knowledge was deemed a major act of piety. A well-stocked library serves as the backdrop for a lecture, in which a teacher would first dictate a text, then discourse upon it. (*Bibliothèque Nationale, Paris*)

within a century of their arrival in Islamic lands. Muslim scholars, mystics, and merchants carried Islam throughout the entire region of the Indian Ocean by sea, and along the length of the silk routes by land.

When Timur the Lame (Tamerlane or Tamburlane; 1336–1405) led his Turkish invaders along many of the routes and in many of the same kinds of campaigns as Genghis Khan had done, sacking or capturing Delhi (1398), Aleppo (1400), Damascus (1401), Ankara (1402), and Bukhara (1402), he had the support of Islamic scholars, *ulama* and mystics, **Sufis**. Timur's descendants patronized Islamic scholarship, and within a century Samarqand and Bukhara had become major capitals of Islamic culture. They also patronized Turkish as a literary language, encouraging its development as the third language of Islam along with Arabic and Persian.

Today, approximately 17 percent of the world's Muslim population lives in southeast Asia, an area never subject to the rule of the caliphate; 30 percent lives in south Asia, where conversion took place almost entirely after its fall; 12 percent lives in sub-Saharan Africa, again virtually untouched by the caliphate. In short, some 60 percent of today's Muslims are descended from peoples who had no connection to the Abbasid caliphate in Baghdad. In the following pages we consider the factors that enabled Islam to flourish and spread as a religion and a civilization even after its historic political center collapsed.

Islam Reaches New Peoples

The end of the caliphate did not mean the end of the spread of Islam. Quite the contrary. Regional rulers, finding themselves more independent, pursued policies of political and military expansion while proclaiming the religion and culture of Islam as their own.

India. A Muslim government run by slave soldiers who had earned their freedom had established itself in Ghazni, Afghanistan, as early as 962. From that base, Muslims launched raids into India and established their rule over the Punjab. In 1211, the Muslim general who conquered Delhi declared himself an independent sultan, initiating a series of five dynasties, which are known collectively as the Sultanate of Delhi (1211–1526). By 1236 they controlled north India; by 1335, almost the entire subcontinent.

When Delhi's power dimmed, numerous Muslim rulers controlled other regions of India. These regional governments, in particular, stayed close to their subjects, encouraged the development of regional languages, and provided new opportunities to Sufis, Muslim mystics and teachers, to introduce and practice Islam in new areas. In 1526, temporarily, and in 1556, more permanently, a mixture of Mongol and Turkish Muslim invaders conquered India, heralding the start of a new era, the Mughal Empire.

Most, but not all, of the Muslim rulers recognized the importance of a respectful religious accommodation with the overwhelming Hindu majority. The first Muslim invaders in Sind in the eighth century extended a protected status to Hindus usually granted only to monotheists. They argued that behind the many forms of god in Hinduism there was just one reality They also recognized that warfare against so

ulama The theologians and legal experts of Islam.

Sufi In Islam, a member of one of the orders practicing mystical forms of worship that first arose in the eighth and ninth centuries C.E.

The rise of the Delhi Sultanate. The Muslim Afghan Ghaznavid Empire was the first of a number of Afghan and Turkic powers who, exploiting divisions among local Hindu rulers, established their hegemony in northern India. Based at Delhi, six successive Muslim dynasties commanded varying territorial extents, but only briefly in the mid-fourteenth century did they completely control the Deccan.

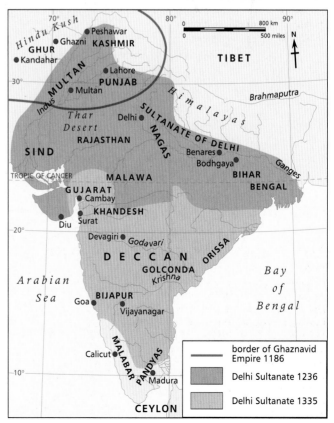

large a majority of Hindus was impossible. They allowed Hindus the right to practice their own religion as long as they accepted Islamic rule. Usually they protected Hindu temples, although in some instances they defaced shrines as a means of asserting their own supremacy. For example, they destroyed the famous Shaivite temple at Somnath, western India, in 1024. The Turkish forces occupying Bengal and Bihar also destroyed the last remaining libraries and monasteries of Buddhism in that region, delivering the final death blow to a religion that had already seen most of its following in India disappear.

The Muslim conquest of India opened the subcontinent to Persians, Afghans, Turks, and Mongols seeking jobs with the new governments (see Chapter 14). This immigration brought a variety of Islamic practices to India, where no single orthodoxy prevailed. Diverse Muslims coexisted with diverse Hindus, venerating some saints and sharing some devotions in common. India's population became 20–25 percent Muslim. Many were descendants of Muslim immigrants near the top of the social hierarchy;

Islam in south and southeast Asia. The disruption of centralized political power in the Muslim world did not stop the expansion of Islam in Africa and southern Asia. Arab maritime traders carried their faith to the shores of India and onward throughout maritime southeast Asia. The Indian heartland was conquered by successive waves of Muslim invaders, who, by 1400, secured the key Indo-Gangetic plain.

others were converts, escaping untouchability at the bottom of the caste system. The majority of India's population, however, remained Hindu.

Southeast Asia. The beginning of mass conversions of southeast Asians to Islam came in the fourteenth and fifteenth centuries, and today, Malaysia and Indonesia are overwhelmingly Muslim. Ocean traders and Sufis from India seem to have accomplished most of the missionary work. The traders offered increased economic opportunities to local people who would adopt Islam, while the Sufis and the regional kings of southeast Asia exchanged support for one another in a familiar pattern of interdependence between religious and political leaders. We will consider this further in Chapter 12.

Sub-Saharan Africa. As in southeast Asia, Islam was first carried to sub-Saharan Africa by traders and Sufis. They came from three directions: from Mediterranean north Africa across the Sahara to west Africa; from Egypt up the Nile to east Africa; and from India and Arabia across the Indian Ocean to the coast of east Africa.

The Arab conquest of north Africa in the seventh and early eighth centuries set the scene for increasing contacts between Arab and Black Africans. As traders, and sometimes as warriors, the Arabs began to cross the Sahara. When they arrived, they found flourishing kingdoms in place, their power derived from control of the desert trade routes and the taxes they imposed on this trade. Founded (according to legend) about 300 C.E., Ghana was the largest of these sub-Saharan kingdoms. (This Ghana is located approximately in the area of modern Mali, and is not to be confused with modern Ghana to the southeast.) By the ninth century Ghana was both a partner and a rival of the northern Berbers for control of Saharan trade. Along these routes, gold, slaves, hides, and ivory were transported northward in exchange for copper, silver, metal goods, horses, dried fruit, cloth, and salt transported southward.

By the eleventh century, a network of Islamic traders extended from the Atlantic Ocean in the west to modern-day Nigeria in the east, from the Sahara in the north to the fringes of the forested areas in the south. The traders included people of the Mandingo, Jakhande, and Dyula ethnic groups. Traders from the north invited their southern counterparts to adopt their religion, and Sufis came to establish new communities of faith and good works. Although the common people were not much affected until the nineteenth century, leading traders and rulers began to convert to Islam.

Trade connections were not the only source of converts. A wave of conversions also followed the domination of Ghana in the eleventh century by the Almoravid dynasty of Morocco. The Almoravids and their Berber allies waged a holy war to convert the Ghanaians, although many of the new converts continued to participate in indigenous religious practices even while officially accepting Islam. The Almoravids fought among themselves, as well as against the Ghanaians, and their cattle degraded the ecology of the region. Groups that had been ruled by, or allied with, the kingdom of Ghana began to assert their autonomy, until about 1235 the Keita kings of Mali, with greater access to the Niger River, surpassed Ghana in importance. Mali's founding king, Sundiata, is commemorated in the national epic of his nation, the *Sundiata*, as a great hunter and warrior possessed of magical powers. Although he himself observed African religious practices along with Islam, he encouraged his people to accept Islam.

About a century later, a more orthodox Muslim came to rule Mali. Mansa Musa (r. 1307–1332) made the *hajj* (pilgrimage) to Mecca in 1324, disbursing legendary amounts of gold along the way. He and subsequent rulers of Mali sought prestige through public affiliation with, and support for, Islamic institutions. They made improvements in Timbuktu, the most important trading city on the Niger River, at its northern bend

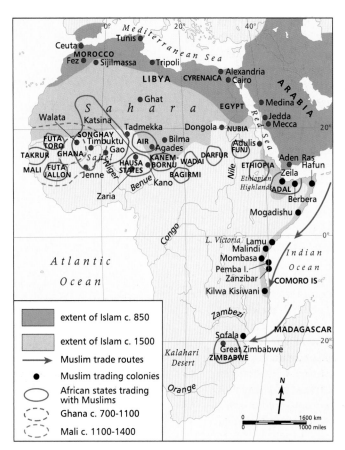

extent of Islam c. 850

extent of Islam c. 1500

→ Muslim trade routes

● Muslim trading colonies

◯ African states trading with Muslims

⌒ Ghana c. 700-1100

⌒ Mali c. 1100-1400

Islam in Africa. Islam entered sub-Saharan Africa as a result of trade. Trans-Saharan caravans from Egypt, Libya, and Morocco gradually introduced the faith overland among the trading kingdoms of west Africa, while the Arab traders of the Indian Ocean carried the message south by sea along the east coast of the continent.

near the Sahara, transforming the city into a major center of Arabic and Islamic studies. In the late fifteenth century, however, Sonni Ali (1464–1492), king of the Songhay people, slightly to the east, destroyed the empire of Mali and diminished its connection to the Islamic world of north Africa. Mali's rulers and people resumed the kind of halfway position between Islam and traditional African religions that Sundiata had held. Islam continued to be important in the private life but not the governance of the country. Mosques, for example, were treated as sanctuaries, so long as they were not used for political meetings. Ironically, at the death of Sonni Ali, one of his former generals, al-Hajj (the informal title often given to a person who has completed the *hajj* pilgrimage) Muhammad Askia (1493–1528) helped to restore connections with major Islamic centers in north Africa. Timbuktu resumed its growth. By the mid-sixteenth century, when it was under the rule of Songhay, Timbuktu held between 150 and 180 Quranic elementary schools that, in turn, laid the foundations for more advanced education. Timbuktu's scholarship matched that of Morocco, and leading scholars of Morocco came to learn from Timbuktu's leading scholar, Ahmad Baba (1556–1627). In 1591, however, the power of the city and its trading networks were undercut by the conquest of the region by Moroccan forces. Although the Moroccans were also Muslims, they acted as conquerors rather than as members of the same community, and the status of Muslims actually declined.

From Ghana, Mali, and Songhay, Islam was spreading eastward across Africa. For example, in the beginning of the twelfth century, the king of Kanem converted to Islam, made a pilgrimage to Mecca, and constructed a religious school in Cairo for students from Kanem. His subjects followed him in converting to Islam. When his Saifawa ruling dynasty was forced militarily to leave Kanem in the mid-fourteenth century, they reestablished their Muslim state in nearby Bornu. Islamic influences from Kanem and Bornu, in turn, reinforced the religious message that the *ulama* accompanying traders from Mali brought to the neighboring Hausa people in Kano in modern northern Nigeria. In these lands, too, Islamic practices and local religious practices ofter blended, with the people choosing whichever seemed most efficacious in their personal lives. Kings often responded similarly, following the practices that seemed most associated with their military victories, and abandoning those that seemed to accompany defeats. Still farther east, the upper Nile valley had been mostly Christianized by the time Muslim traders, gold miners, and slave traders arrived. As Muslim governments in Egypt began to push southward, however, they defeated the Nubian Christian kingdom and Islam began to take root, with the first Islamic states in Nubia dating to around 1500. The state of Sinnar, ruled by the Funj dynasty, became the most important of these states, in part because its subjects were expected to accept the Islamic religion of its rulers, and it gave special privileges to Islamic holy men and scholars.

Islam arrived on Africa's east coast by the eighth century. As Islam crossed from Arabia and the Yemen into east Africa, it met fierce resistance in Ethiopia, which had become staunchly Christian. Nevertheless, about 1630, a Portuguese missionary estimated that Muslims made up one-third of Ethiopia's population. A mosque at Shanga, off the east coast of Kenya, dates to about the beginning of the ninth century.

At about the same time, al-Masudi, an Arab historian and sailor, reported Muslim settlers on the east coast of Africa. Much larger growth appeared in the thirteenth century, and by the fourteenth century more than thirty communities, with mosques, lined the east African coast. Kilwa in southeastern Tanzania was the most important settlement and port, and modern archaeologists have been busy excavating its medieval remains along with those of other coastal towns. Philologists also study the interaction between the Arabic language of the overseas traders with the Swahili language of the African coast as trading necessities brought the two languages—and the two peoples—together.

Law Provides an Institutional Foundation

One of the central features of Islamic society that survived the fall of the caliphate was the law. The legal systems of Islam, *shari'a*, lived on and flourished. For Muslims, as for other populations, law expresses in formal terms the standards of proper conduct. Law supports the fundamental Islamic duty of *hisba*, "to promote what is right and to prevent what is wrong" (Musallam in Robinson, p. 175). Muslims encounter their legal system in the regulation of public life; in family matters of marriage, divorce, parental responsibilities, and inheritance; and in the *shari'a*'s advice on daily activities such as eating, dressing, and housekeeping.

As the early caliphs and the Abbasids began to confront legal questions, they appointed *qadis* (judges) to resolve them. The *qadis* searched the classical texts of the Quran, the **hadith** (quotations from Muhammad), and biographies of the Prophet for their core teachings, and then relied on a combination of local custom and their own deliberation and judgment (*ijtihad*) in rendering final decisions.

hadith Traditional records of the deeds and utterances of the prophet Muhammad, and the basis, after the Quran, for Islamic theology and law.

Seeking to overcome wide differences in local practices, four great legal scholars of the eighth and ninth centuries formulated the major systems of Islamic law that endure today: the system of Abu Hanifah (699–767) is in use mostly in the Arab Middle East and south Asia; of Malik ibn Anas (*c.* 715–795) in north, central, and west Africa; of Muhammad al-Shafii (767–820) in east Africa, southern Arabia, and southeast Asia; and of Ahmad ibn Hanbal (780–855) in Saudi Arabia. Although most localities have followed one or another of these systems since about the tenth century, the existence of multiple systems has allowed flexibility in interpretation. Under certain circumstances, local legal experts have the option of drawing on any of the four texts. Because Shi'ites maintain different traditions of authority, encompassing the teachings of Ali and the early imams, they have also developed different schools of law. The most widespread is that of Jafar al-Sadiq (d. 765).

The personnel of the legal system are the *ulama* (singular *alim*), the religiously trained scholars of Islam who interpret and implement the law. The *ulama* constitute a class that includes *qadis* and their assistants, Quran reciters, prayer leaders, and preachers. The *ulama* are sometimes trained in formal theological schools or, more frequently, are simply apprenticed to senior *ulama*. Islam has no formal hierarchical, bureaucratic institution of *ulama*—indeed, it has no official Church. Informal networks of respected *ulama* have provided cohesion, stability, and flexibility within Islam, regardless of the changing forms of government.

Ideally, *ulama* and ruler worked together to decide and implement religious policy, but when Caliph al-Mamun (r. 813–833) proclaimed that he had the right to give authoritative interpretations of the Quran, the *ulama* mobilized the population of Baghdad against him. He responded with an inquisition to root out these opponents. The only major leader who stood up to him was Ahmad ibn Hanbal, the greatest *hadith* scholar of his generation, who argued that only the scholars had the authority to interpret Quranic text. The people supported him, and to escape the continuing popular protest, Caliph al-Mutasim (r. 833–842) moved his capital from densely populated Baghdad to Samarra, 60 miles away.

In 848–849 the Caliph al-Mutawakkil (d. 861) withdrew the claim of caliphal authority in religious matters. The *ulama* had won, but the battle had so embittered relations between caliph and *ulama* that their spheres of influence were forever separated: the caliph had authority over matters of state; the *ulama* over matters of religion. The caliphs came to represent the imperial aspirations of the state, while the *ulama* represented the everyday needs and wishes of the people. Over time, such departures from popular accountability cost them the caliphate. But the *ulama* endured, in touch with the people, and serving as their guides.

Sufis Provide Religious Mysticism

Law brings order to life. It makes concrete the responsibilities of one individual to another and to society in general. In Islam it also fixes the formal obligations due to God. The *ulama* conveyed and interpreted this message, carrying it to people in vastly different societies. Sufis also spread Islam to many parts of the world, but were much less interested than the *ulama* in strict religious doctrine and emphasized devotion to Allah instead.

The Role of Mysticism. As the Umayyad empire weakened, many people inhabiting it began to reject the materialism of its leaders and turned to a pious asceticism. For these spiritual seekers, Sufis revealed Islam's inner, mystical path to God. Early Sufis found and transmitted the inner disciplines of mind and body, the purifications of the heart

Whirling Dervishes. Sufism represents the mystical, contemplative strand of Islam—a strand that is captured vividly by the "Whirling Dervishes," a religious order closely linked to the teachings of the thirteenth-century Persian poet Jalal al-Din Rumi. Their slow, revolving dance helps to create higher states of consciousness, while being a ceremonial ritual in its own right.

SOURCE

Al-Ghazzali, "the Renewer of Islam."

The more solemn ulama *and the more emotional Sufis were often suspicious of one another. Deeply disturbed by the tension between the two perspectives, the revered scholar Abu Hamid Muhammad al-Ghazzali (1058–1111) finally formulated a synthesis of the intellectual and the mystical sides of Islam that has proved satisfying to Muslims ever since.*

Born and educated in Iran, al-Ghazzali was appointed at the age of thirty-three to teach philosophy at the leading madrasa, *or theological institute, in Baghdad. During four years there, Ghazzali began to doubt the role of rationality in life and searched for more holistic ways of experiencing the world. Torn between holding his prestigious tenure at the* madrasa *or giving it up to pursue new roads toward truth, Ghazzali was on the verge of breakdown:*

> For nearly six months … I was continuously tossed about between the attractions of worldly desires and the impulses towards eternal life. In that month the matter ceased to be one of choice and became one of compulsion. God caused my tongue to dry up so that I was prevented from lecturing. One particular day I would make an effort to lecture in order to gratify the hearts of my following, but my tongue would not utter a single word nor could I accomplish anything at all. This impediment in my speech produced grief in my heart, and at the same time my power to digest and assimilate food and drink was impaired; I could hardly swallow or digest a single mouthful of food. (al-Ghazzali, p. 57)

In 1095 Ghazzali resigned his post. He traveled to Damascus, Jerusalem, and Mecca, and then returned to his home town, where he lived the monastic life of a Sufi mystic, for ten years:

> I learnt with certainty that it is above all the mystics who walk on the road of God; their life is the best life, their method the soundest method, their character the purest character. (p. 60)

During his time of contemplation, Ghazzali wrote a great number of philosophical and theological works, including the influential Revival of the Religious Sciences, *exploring the relationship between religion and reason. He asserted the importance of mystical experience and a direct, personal understanding of God, while at the same time defending the doctrine and authority of the Islamic faith.*

In 1106 Ghazzali was persuaded to return to teaching, now proclaiming the complementarity of Sufism and rationality:

> Just as intellect is one of the stages of human development in which there is an "eye" which sees the various types of intelligible objects, which are beyond the ken of the senses, so prophecy also is the description of a state in which there is an eye endowed with light such that in that light the unseen and other supra-intellectual objects become visible. (p. 65)

By the end of his life, Ghazzali's reconciliation of Sufism and rationality within Islam had earned him the title "Renewer of Islam."

---

that enabled their followers to feel that they experienced God directly as the ultimate reality. They usually disdained worldly pleasures. One of the earliest of the Sufis, Hasan al-Basri (643–728), concluded: "This world has neither worth nor weight with God, so slight it is" (Esposito, p. 102). Though most Sufis were men, some, like Rabi'a al-Adawiyya (d. 801), were women. Rabi'a, like the Hindu Mirabai, rejected marriage to devote herself to God: "Love of God hath so absorbed me that neither love nor hate of any other thing remain in my heart" (Embree, p. 448).

As we have seen throughout this part, every theistic religion has an aspect of devotional love of god, expressed through spontaneous prayer, private meditation, fasting and asceticism, and, often, of physical disciplines, music, dance, and poetry. In Islam these aspects were adopted by the Sufis, who also absorbed influences from the mystics of other religions, especially monasticism from Christianity and Buddhism, and ecstasy in prayer from Hinduism.

Through their lives of exemplary devotion to God and people, the Sufis enhanced the message of Islam. They attracted people through the simplicity of their piety, their personal love of God, and their dedication to the needs of others. Some developed reputations for magical powers. The mosques where they lived and prayed, and the mausolea in which they were buried, were revered as sacred shrines. A sixteenth-century folk ballad of eastern Bengal tells of one such Sufi saint:

> At that time there came a Mahomedan *pir* [Sufi] to that village. He built a mosque in its outskirts, and for the whole day sat under a fig tree ... His fame soon spread far and wide. Everybody talked of the occult powers that he possessed. If a sick man called on him he would cure him at once by dust or some trifle touched by him. He read and spoke the innermost thoughts of a man before he opened his mouth ... Hundreds of men and women came every day to pay him their respects. Whatever they wanted they miraculously got from this saint. Presents of rice, fruits, and other delicious food, goats, chickens, and fowls came in large quantities to his doors. Of these offerings the *pir* did not touch a bit but freely distributed all among the poor. (Eaton in Adas, pp. 21–2)

tariqa In Islam a generic term meaning "path," referring to the doctrines and methods of mysticism and esoterism. The word also refers to schools or brotherhoods of mystics, which were often situated at a mosque or the tomb of a Muslim saint.

Individual mystics appeared in Islam from its earliest days, drawing their inspiration directly from the Quran. Centuries later, they began to form **tariqas**, or mystical brotherhoods, often located at the mosque or mausoleum of an especially revered saint. Some *tariqas* emphasized ecstatic practices; others were more sober and meditative. The *tariqa mawlawiya* was founded by Jalal-al-Din Rumi (1207–73) in Konya, Turkey. Rumi is most famous for his expression of ecstatic worship through the dance of the "whirling dervishes." Rumi's Persian language text, the *Mathnawi*, expressed in rich and evocative lyrics his love of God: "The result of religion is nothing but rapture" (Rumi, *Mathnawi* 1:312, Vitray-Meyerovitch, p. 83).

Intellectual Achievements

As the *ulama* provided order to the social structures of Islam, and the Sufis spread its spiritual powers, other intellectuals further enriched its cultural depth.

History. The historian and theologian al-Tabari (*c.* 839–923) introduced formal historical writings with his *History of Prophets and Kings*. The segment on prophecy recorded the contributions from Abraham through Muhammad; the record of kings covered rulers from biblical times to his own and included eyewitness reports of relatively recent events.

With the conquest of Iran in the mid-seventh century, Persian became the second language of Islam. (The arrival of the Turks in 923 introduced Turkish as the third.) The Persian poet Ferdowsi (940–1020) wrote an epic poem on the mythical origins of the Persian peoples, in which one of his central themes is the tragedy that befalls "a good man whose king is a fool."

The Mongols also supported historical writing, including al-Juvaini's (1226–83) *History of the World Conquerors*, which told of Chinggis Khan's conquests, especially in Iran. Rashid al-Din (1247–1318) wrote *World History*, which many regard as the first attempt at a history of humanity, as it integrates Chinese, Indian, European, Muslim, and Mongol history into a single cosmopolitan perspective.

Although others, notably Rashid al-Din, had attempted to write comprehensive, narrative histories before him, Ibn Khaldun (1332–1406) of Tunis is often viewed as the first to apply social science theory to the study of history. His *Universal History* stressed a cyclical theory of history, in which vigorous nomadic peoples regularly conquered urban peoples who were settled, cultured, and contented, took over their cities, settled into lives of luxury, and then themselves fell prey to the next round of invasion from more robust nomads. The theory seemed to fit the comings and goings of nomadic invaders from Arabia, Mongolia, and central Asia that characterized his times. Among Ibn Khaldun's other interpretive themes that still seem insightful today are: "The differences between Easterners and Westerners are cultural [not innate]"(p. 51); "The differences between peoples arise principally from the differences in their occupations" (p. 80); and, perhaps, "Scholars are of all men those least fitted for politics and its ways" (p. 64).

Philosophy. Theology and philosophy had been regarded as inferior to revelation in early Islam, but as Muslims came into contact with the philosophies of the Hellenistic and Indian worlds, they were drawn to concepts of Platonism and Neoplatonism in particular. The caliphate established in Baghdad a "house of wisdom," a translation bureau under Hunayn ibn Ishaq (803–873). In the next 200 years some eighty Greek authors were translated, including Aristotle, Plato, Galen, and Euclid. So, too, were writings from Syriac, Sanskrit, and Persian.

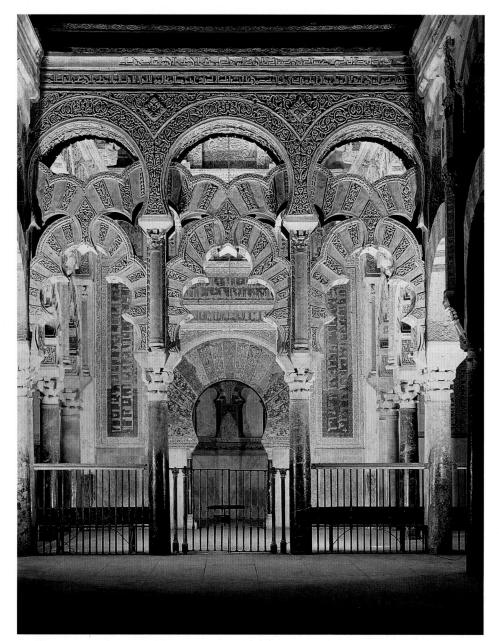

Mihrab in the Great Mosque, Cordoba, Spain, c. 961–976. Under the Umayyads, Cordoba grew to be by far the most prosperous city in western Europe, second only to Baghdad in the Islamic world. At its height, the city is said to have contained some 300 public baths and 3000 mosques within its walls. Shown here is the most important surviving example. Great attention was lavished on the decoration of the Great Mosque, and the *mihrab*, a small domed chamber indicating the direction of Mecca, is considered unique for its horseshoe-shaped doorway, a stylistic innovation of the Muslims in Spain.

A group of Islamic philosophers, called *Mutazilites,* "those who keep themselves apart," began to challenge orthodox Islamic belief, arguing that the attributes of God in the Quran were not literal but metaphorical, that human actions and life were not pre-determined, and that the Quran had not existed eternally. Al-Farabi (*c.* 870–950) argued that philosophical knowledge gained through study and thought was of higher value than revelation from God. Similar notions of the supremacy of philosophy were expressed by al-Kindi (d. 870), Ibn Sina (Avicenna; d. 1037), and Ibn Rushd (Averroes; 1126–98). Such philosophical speculation was marginal to mainstream Islamic thought and actually found more resonance among Christian and Jewish philosophers of the time.

Christian thinkers in Europe were indebted to the Muslims for keeping alive the Hellenistic traditions, for with the fall of the Roman Empire in the west the intellectual traditions and resources of Christianity had been neglected and forgotten. Now, thanks to Arabic translations and Islamic thought, Christian and Jewish philosophers grappled both with the original texts from Greece and India, and with the newer concepts introduced by Muslim thinkers.

Mathematics, Astronomy, and Medicine. The intersection of intellectual traditions also enriched mathematics, astronomy, and medicine. Indian scholars brought their texts on astronomy to Baghdad as early as 770. The caliph had them translated into Arabic, which was becoming the common language of scholarship throughout the empire. Arabs adopted and transmitted Hindi numerals and the decimal system, including the zero, throughout the empire and into Europe, where they were (mis)named "Arabic" numerals. A few decades later, al-Khwarazmi (d. *c.* 846) used Indian texts in conjunction with scholarship from Greece and Iran to develop algebra (from the Arabic *al-jabr,* "restoration"). (The word *algorithm* comes from al-Khwarazmi's name.) Al-Biruni (d. 1046) wrote extensively on number theory and computation, and later scholars developed the trigonometry we study today.

Al-Biruni also wrote *al-Qanun al-Mas'udi,* a compendium of Islamic astronomy, which incorporated findings from throughout the empire. Arabic mathematical and astronomical theories apparently informed Copernicus as he proposed a **heliocentric** universe in the sixteenth century (see Chapter 13).

Medical wisdom and herbal remedies were transmitted from one end of the empire to the other. Al-Razi (Rhazes; *c.* 865–*c.* 935) compiled an encyclopedia of medicine giving the views of Greek, Syrian, Indian, Iranian, and Arab writers on each disease, and including his own clinical observations and opinions. Ibn Sina, noted above for his contributions to philosophy, produced the even more encyclopedic *Qanun fi'l-tibb* ("Canon of Medicine"), which included volumes on the pharmacology of herbs, the functioning of organs, fevers, and surgery. The *Qanun* was translated into Latin and dominated medical thinking for 300 years.

The Extension of Technology

By 751, at the end of the Umayyad dynasty, Islam served as a network of communication that linked all the major civilizations of Eurasia. For example, as we noted above, Muslims learned papermaking from the Chinese and transmitted the technology throughout their domain. European Christians learned the art from Muslims in Spain.

Exchanges of information on agriculture and crops also enriched the world of Islam. Between the eighth and tenth centuries, Arabs brought from India hard wheat, rice, varieties of sorghum, sugarcane, bananas, sour oranges, lemons, limes, mangoes, watermelon, coconut palm, spinach, artichokes, eggplants, and the key industrial crop, cotton. All these crops were introduced throughout the empire, wherever climatic

heliocentric A system in which the sun is assumed to be at the center of the solar system—or of the universe—while Earth and the planets move around it.

conditions were favorable. This may well have been the largest agricultural exchange in world history up to that time. Because most of these crops from India were warm-weather crops, many of them facilitated summer cropping in areas that had previously lain fallow in that season. To replicate the monsoon climate of India, Muslim officials improved existing forms of irrigation (underground water canals and water-lifting mechanisms) and invented new ones (certain kinds of cisterns). Agricultural productivity diversified and increased, encouraging population increase in general and urban growth in particular.

City Design and Architecture

Muslim governments built great cities and adorned their public spaces lavishly and often exquisitely. The largest of the cities were the political capitals. Baghdad was built along the west bank of the Tigris River in 762 to serve as the capital of the Abbasid dynasty, and it served that purpose for almost 500 years. In the ninth century, with between 300,000 and 500,000 people in 25 square miles, Baghdad became the largest city in the world outside China.

As the caliphate declined, and Baghdad with it, regional capitals grew in importance: Bukhara, Nishapur, and Isfahan in the east, and Cairo, Fez, and Cordoba in the west. The Fatimid rulers of Egypt began their administration in Fustat and expanded

The Great Mosque and minaret of al-Mutawakkil, Samarra, Iraq, 848–52. Though now only a shadow of its former glory, this 1150-year-old mosque remains the largest of its kind in the world. The three essential elements of simple mosque architecture emerge clearly through the ruins: a central courtyard or atrium, a (formerly) covered sanctuary inside the perimeter walls, and a minaret, or tower, from which the *muezzin* (crier) summons the community to worship.

that already existing city into al-Qahira (Cairo) in 969. In Morocco, King Idris II (r. 791–828) built Fez in 808 as the capital of the Idrisid dynasty, which had been founded by his father. A later dynasty, the Almoravids built their capital Marrakesh in 1070. In Andalusia, southern Spain, the Umayyads developed Cordoba into one of the most cosmopolitan cities of the Islamic world. It achieved its greatest splendor in the mid-tenth century, but was sacked by Berbers in 1013 and never fully recovered. The architecture of these cities proclaimed the splendor of Islam and the power of the Muslim ruler.

Although the daily prayers in Islam may be performed privately, Friday noon prayers require collective assembly, so all cities and most neighborhoods within cities also constructed mosques for public services. Wealthy rulers proclaimed their power and piety by building monumental central mosques, as they did early on in Jerusalem, Medina, and Damascus. The Abbasids constructed an enormous central mosque in Baghdad, and during the years that Samarra served as their capital (848–852) a huge mosque was constructed there, too. Great mosques were also built at Qayrawan in Tunisia, Fez in Morocco, and Cordoba in Spain.

As the Seljuk Turks conquered and then joined the world of Islam, they built an especially monumental mosque at Isfahan in the late eleventh century, and then rebuilt it fifty years later after Ismaili Shi'as burned it down. Ottoman architects, most notably Hoja Sinan (1490–1578), constructed magnificent mosques, such as the Selimiye at Edirne and the Sulaymaniye in Istanbul, and other public buildings that incorporated Byzantine and Islamic forms. When Islam crossed the Sahara desert, a new architectural form developed: the Sahelian mosque. When Mansa Musa returned from his trip to Mecca in 1325, he brought with him an Arab architect to supervise the construction of mosques and madrasas (theological schools) especially in Timbuktu.

Because Islam teaches that all the dead should be honored, and some believe that the saintly among them could confer blessings, mausolea have a special significance and sanctity. The followers of Timur (Tamerlane), for example, built for him an enormous tomb at Samarqand in 1405. Some burial shrines reveal extraordinary personal love and devotion. In 1632–49 the Emperor Shah Jahan built perhaps the best known of all Islamic buildings, the Taj Mahal in Agra, India, as a mausoleum for his wife Mumtaz Mahal, who died giving birth to their fifteenth child. At a more humble level, simple tombs of local holy men are found throughout the Islamic world, attracting followers, especially women, who pour out their hearts in prayer, trusting that the sanctity of the saint will carry it to God.

The public architecture of mosques, mausolea, and, to a lesser extent, the royal and governmental

Bronzesmith, Isfahan bazaar, Iran. In Islam, religion and business are integrally linked, in that the land adjoining mosques is often leased to market traders whose rents support the buildings and their activities. Here a bronzesmith works outside his shop in the bazaar at Isfahan, which has been thriving since the third century C.E.

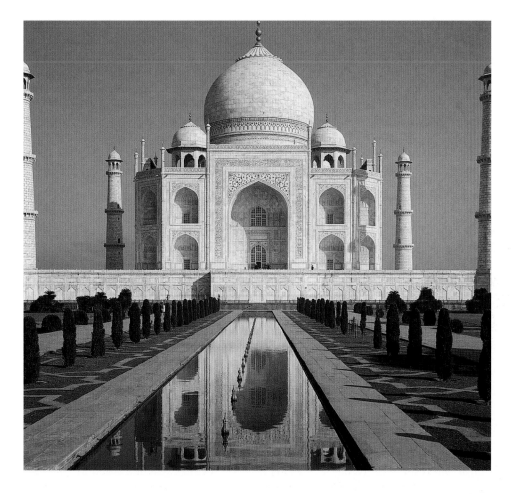

The Taj Mahal, Agra, India, 1632–48. Perhaps the best known of all Islamic buildings, the Taj Mahal was built by India's Emperor Shah Jahan as a mausoleum for his beloved wife Mumtaz Mahal, who died giving birth to their fifteenth child.

buildings that frequently adjoin them, anchored the formal religious and political institutions of the Islamic city. The bazaar, or market area, was home to business activities. Business in Islam was an honored profession. Muhammad himself had been a caravan operator, and his first wife, Khadija, had been a businesswoman. Even today mosques often control the land immediately adjacent to them and lease it out to businesses so that the rents can support the mosques.

Islamic cities were, in effect, nodes on international trade routes linking the Islamic world from China to Morocco and Spain. These trade routes enabled the movement not only of goods but also of people and ideas from one end of Eurasia to the other (see Chapter 12). The *hajj* (pilgrimage) to Mecca was also instrumental in creating a communication network among the regions and peoples of Islam.

The *Rihla* or travelogues of Ibn Battuta demonstrate the opportunities for travel open to a person of culture. In thirty years of traveling from his home in Tangier, he traversed approximately 73,000 miles of territories that today belong to some fifty different countries. Thanks to his mastery of Arabic and his knowledge of *shari'a*, he found a welcome reception, and frequently temporary employment and gifts of wives and wealth in the lands he traversed. Muhammad Tughluq, sultan of Delhi, appointed him a *qadi* and, later, his envoy to China.

Ibn Battuta's tales of adventure reflect the unity of the Islamic world. Despite its diversity, this world was held together by reverence for the Quran, the *shari'a*, the Arabic language (supplemented by Persian and Turkish), the political officials who ruled in its cities, and the scholars and merchants who traveled through them.

RELATIONS WITH NON-MUSLIMS

Early Islamic governments spread their worldly power by the sword. As a result, popular belief in the West has held that the religion of Islam spread in the same way. Although conversion by force was practiced occasionally (just as it was by Christianity), by and large forced conversion to Islam was unusual. For example, the early "rightly guided" caliphs and the early Umayyads did not seek to convert the people they conquered. They preferred to rule as Arab Muslim conquerors over non-Arab, non-Muslim subjects. Only when the later Umayyads feared that they could not continue minority rule over so large a majority, did they decide actively to seek conversion of, and alliance with, the conquered peoples.

Dhimmi Status

Non-Muslims were offered three choices. The first was to convert to Islam. The second was to accept "protected," *dhimmi*, status as worshipers of one God who accepted Muslim rule. All the monotheistic "peoples of the book" were eligible for this status, including Christians, Jews, and Zoroastrians. Later, Islamic governments in India also extended *dhimmi* status to Hindus. The *dhimmi* were often required to pay a special poll tax, but they could follow their own religion and their own personal law regarding marriage, divorce, and inheritance, and they were to be protected by the Muslim government. The third option was to fight against the Muslim state, an option that few chose.

The status of the *dhimmi* was spelled out in "The Pact of Umar," a document ascribed to Umar I (r. 634–644). This document prescribed second-class status for the *dhimmi*. They were not to build new houses of worship nor to reconstruct old ones. They were not to convert anyone to their religion. They were not to wear the same clothing as Muslims, but to wear distinguishing garments. The sounds of their prayers, their calls to prayer, and their funeral processions were to be muted. Their houses were not to be higher than the houses of Muslims. The poll tax, however, was not mentioned in this document. Perhaps designed to encourage non-Muslims to gain first-class citizenship by converting, these rules were nevertheless not crippling to life, and, indeed, they were often unenforced. Travelers throughout the Muslim world noted that Jews and Christians often held some of the highest positions in public and private life, and were self-governing in their religious life.

A principal goal of conquest, however, remained the creation of a *dar al-Islam*, "an abode of Islam," a land with a government under which Islam could be practiced freely. This did not mean that the people of the land were forced to become Muslims, only that the Muslims among them must have the freedom to practice their religion and sustain their culture.

Later, when many Muslims lived under non-Muslim governments, the *ulama* declared that any government that permitted freedom of religion to Muslims could be a *dar al-Islam*. The alternative was a *dar al-Harb*, an "abode of war," which had to be opposed because it restricted the practice of Islam.

The Crusades

At opposite ends of the Mediterranean, Muslims and Christians fought each other in war. The crusades (1095–1291) were as much political and economic as religious in their motivation. After Arab armies captured Jerusalem in 638, they built new, glorious mosques to indicate their own dominance, but they allowed Christians to continue their religious practices without hindrance and permitted Jews to return to Jerusalem officially for the first time since their exile by the Romans in 135 C.E.

Only centuries later, after Muslim Turkish armies won the Battle of Manzikert in 1071 and opened Anatolia to conquest, did the Byzantine emperor Alexius I call on Pope Urban II to help fight the Muslims and to recapture Jerusalem and the "Holy Land." The pope seized this opportunity to unite western Europe and its various rulers under his own banner in the name of religion. For those who would undertake the crusades, he promised indulgences that would reduce the time that they would serve in purgatory—before entering heaven—after their death. On a more earthly level, the pope promised that their property and assets would be protected in their absence. Many pious Christians responded to his call: rich and poor, men and women, old people and children. Christian rulers, knights, and merchants joined in, driven not only by religious inspiration but also by their own political and military ambitions, and by the promise of trade opportunities that would accompany the establishment of a Latin kingdom in the Middle East. In the course of the first four crusades—the major crusades—more than 100,000 people participated.

At first, the European Christian crusaders were successful—and brutal. In 1099 they captured Jerusalem, killing its Muslim residents, men, women, and children. They turned the Dome of the Rock into a church and the adjacent al-Aqsa mosque into an official residence. The savagery of the crusaders—reported in both Christian and Muslim sources—ushered in centuries of confrontation far more bitter than ever before. At the time, Muslim leadership in the region was divided, however, and did not respond. Then Salah al-Din (Saladin) (c. 1137–93), who had established a new dynasty in Egypt, recaptured Jerusalem in 1187. Records show that he treated the crusaders reasonably and humanely. But more crusades followed. When Richard I of England, called the Lion-Heart (r. 1189–99), captured Acre on the Mediterranean coast in the Third Crusade (1189–92), he also massacred its men, women, and children. By 1291, however, Muslim forces had reconquered Acre and all other crusader outposts. Although four minor crusades followed, none succeeded in capturing and holding any outposts in the Holy Land.

The crusader soldiers themselves were largely mercenaries with worldly motives who attacked many in their path for their own profit. As early as 1096, *en route* overland to Jerusalem on the First Crusade, crusaders paused to slaughter Jews. In 1204, during the Fourth Crusade, Roman Catholic armies, acting against the direct orders of the pope, attacked the city of Zara in Croatia and Constantinople, the capital of the Byzantine Empire, their presumed ally. Instead of uniting Christianity and defeating the Muslims, the crusaders had divided Christianity and were defeated by the Muslims.

THE CRUSADES	
First Crusade (1095–9)	Proclaimed by Pope Urban II, the crusade was motivated by the occupation of Anatolia and Jerusalem by the Seljuk Turks. The crusaders recaptured Jerusalem and established several Latin kingdoms on the Syrian coast.
Second Crusade (1147–9)	Led by Louis VII of France and the Holy Roman Emperor, Conrad III, this was a disaster from the crusaders' point of view.
Third Crusade (1189–92)	Mounted to recapture Jerusalem, which had been taken by Saladin in 1187. Personal rivalry between the leaders, Philip II Augustus of France and Richard I of England, undermined the crusaders' unity.
Fourth Crusade (1202–04)	This crusade against Egypt was diverted, at the instigation of the Venetians, to sack and divide Constantinople, which led to half a century of western rule over Byzantium.
Children's Crusade (1212)	Thousands of children crossed Europe on their way to Palestine. Untold numbers were sold into slavery in Marseilles, France, or died of disease and malnutrition.
Fifth Crusade (1218–21)	King Andrew of Hungary, Cardinal Pelagius, King John of Jerusalem, and King Hugh of Cyprus captured, then lost, Damietta, Egypt.
Sixth Crusade (1228–9)	The Holy Roman Emperor, Frederick II (r. 1212–50), led the crusade that, through negotiation with the sultan of Egypt, recovered Jerusalem. The city was finally lost in 1244.
Seventh Crusade (1249–54) and Eighth (1270–91)	Both led by Louis IX of France (r. 1226–70), who was inspired by religious motives, but both were personal disasters. Louis was later canonized.

Illustration of the Second Crusade (1147–9). Lance-bearing Christian forces face a Muslim army in this scene from the Second Crusade. The fleur-de-lys emblem, here sported on his shield by the French king, Louis VII, was adopted at almost the same time by his opponent, the ruler of Aleppo. (*British Library, London*)

A Golden Age in Spain

At the other end of the Mediterranean, in Spain, Islam flourished and coexisted with the Christian and Jewish communities of the peninsula. Through a century of immigration, conquest, administration, and intermarriage, beginning in 711, Umayyad and Berber invaders brought Islam to a central position in Spain. They also revitalized trade by breaking the monopoly of Byzantine control over the western Mediterranean. They introduced new crops and new irrigation techniques from west Asia. Abd al-Rahman III (r. 912–961) asserted his separation from the Abbasids by declaring himself a caliph rather than just a sultan. A series of rulers expanded the ornate mosque at Cordoba, making it one of the architectural showcases of Islam.

Eastern scholars of law and philosophy immigrated to the flourishing court. Poets developed new styles, based in Arabic but also influenced by local Spanish and Latin styles. Greek philosophical and medical treatises were translated into Latin as well as Arabic, thus opening intellectual communication with the educated classes in Christendom. Although some Christians revolted against Islamic and Arabic inroads, and were killed in battle (850–859), many more adopted Arabic lifestyles.

By 1030, the caliphate in Spain had disintegrated. Various armed struggles broke out between the provinces and the capital, between townsmen and rural Berber immigrants, and between converts and Arabs. The conflicts did not, however, impede the spread of Islam. As in the eastern Mediterranean, provincial administrations replaced the central caliphate and brought the culture of their courts closer to the general population. Sufis spread their ascetic and devotional teachings.

The vacuum in the central government did, however, provide an opening to various Christian forces to begin the *reconquista*, the Christian reconquest of Spain. In 1085 Alfonso VI (r. 1065–1109), king of Leon, then king of Leon and Castile, captured Toledo. By the mid-thirteenth century all of Spain with the exception of Granada was in Christian hands.

During the years of the *reconquista*, culture continued to flourish. Until the mid-thirteenth century, Christian rulers in Spain patronized the rich, hybrid culture. They translated the Bible, the Talmud, and the Quran into Castilian. Arabic texts on astrology and astronomy, and the philosophical works of Muslim thinkers, including al-Kindi, al-Farabi, and Ibn Sina (Avicenna), were translated into Castilian and Latin, as was the philosophy of the Jewish thinker Moses Maimonides and his codification of Jewish religious law. Spain was the entry-way into western Europe for classical writings and their reworking through the prism of Islamic civilization.

With the fall of Seville to the Christian *reconquista* in 1248, Granada remained as the only Islamic kingdom in Spain. Nestled on a spur of the Sierra Nevada mountains in the south, the city flourished thanks to an influx of talented Muslims fleeing the advancing Christian armies, and the enterprise and vigor of its rulers. Two of the kings of the Nasrid dynasty, Yusuf I (1333–54) and Muhammad V (1354–9, 1362–91), built a complex of buildings called in Arabic "Qalat al-hamra," or the Alhambra. This red citadel served as their home, a city within a city. Their legacy is today the best-preserved palace of medieval Spain.

By the fourteenth century, Christianity had become triumphal and intolerant. Jews and Muslims were forced to accept baptism and convert to Christianity, although many of them continued to practice their original religions in secret. In 1478, at the request of the Spanish rulers, the Roman Catholic Church established the Spanish Inquisition to hunt down those suspected of being insincere converts, whether Jewish (called Marranos) or Muslims (called Moriscos). The first Grand Inquisitor, Tomás de Torquemada, began his work in 1483, and brought people to trial not only for apostasy and heresy, but also for sorcery, sodomy, polygamy, blasphemy, and usury. Under Torquemada's direction, about 2000 people were burned at the stake, making his name a watchword for the fanatical misuse of religious authority.

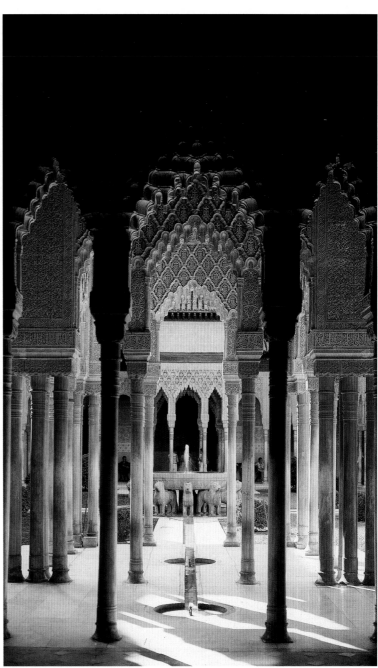

The Court of Lions, Alhambra Palace, Granada, 14th century. The elegance of this courtyard, with its central fountain and a dozen stone lions whose mouths are waterspouts, testifies to the power and aesthetic taste of the last Islamic kingdom left in Spain as the Christian reconquista was completed in 1492.

HOW DO WE KNOW?

Conversion and Assimilation

Only in the last two decades has serious research been done on conversion to Islam, asking exactly how the process worked. For example, Nehemia Levtzion edited a set of studies on Conversion to Islam in 1979 examining the motives of converts. Levtzion argued that "assimilation" was a better term than "conversion" for describing the process of becoming a Muslim. People in conquered areas, especially, were not so much overwhelmed by political conquest as they were impressed with the richness of the culture that Islam brought to them. They found that their lives were enriched by the rituals, philosophy, art, and sense of belonging to a world system that came with joining the umma, the Islamic community.

Richard Bulliet's Conversion to Islam in the Medieval Period: An Essay in Quantitative History demonstrates that conversion took place at different rates of speed in each of the six societies he examines: Arabia, Egypt, Iraq, Syria, Iran, and Spain. He notes the problems of finding data to understand the process,

since "medieval Islam produced no missionaries, bishops, baptismal rites, or other indicators of conversion that could be conveniently recorded by the Muslim chronicler" (p. 4). For data, Bulliet examines the speed of adoption of Muslim names in each of the six societies. He concludes that rapid acceptance of Islam went hand in hand with a breakdown in central political rule. As centralized Islamic rule broke down, paradoxically, Sufis carried the word of Islam more freely and with more backing from local governments.

We also know of the very large-scale assimilation to Islam by the Mongol successors of Genghis Khan and of the followers of Timur the Lame (Tamerlane). These ruling groups were assimilated by Islam because the new civilization they encountered offered them cultural, political, social, economic, and spiritual rewards that were not available in the religions and cultures of their birth.

Finally, the great assimilation that took place outside the heartlands of Islamic conquest, in sub-Saharan Africa and southeast Asia, was carried by traders and

later supported by Sufis and ulama. In both these huge areas, the trade networks by land and sea were so densely worked by Muslims that indigenous traders began to assimilate Islam into their lives, either from religious conviction or from the promise of trade advantage. They stayed to join in one of the world's richest and most widespread civilizations, the umma of Islam.

- Nehemia Levtzion prefers the term "assimilation" rather than "conversion" to describe the process by which people adopted Islam. What does he mean by each term? Do you agree with his argument? Why or why not?
- Besides political rulers, what other groups successfully encouraged large numbers of people to accept Islam? In what geographical regions of the world were they most effective?
- What was the problem faced by Richard Bulliet in determining thow many people accepted Islam? How did he attempt to solve this problem? Do you think his solution appropriate? Why or why not?

Granada fell in 1492 to the Catholic rulers Ferdinand and Isabella. Muslim rule in Spain was broken. In 1492 Ferdinand and Isabella expelled the Jewish population from Spain. After an unsuccessful revolt of 1499–1500, Muslims, too, had to choose between exile and conversion to Christianity. In 1566 use of the Arabic language was banned in Spain. The golden age of religious tolerance and cultural exchange was over.

JUDAISM, CHRISTIANITY, AND ISLAM WHAT DIFFERENCE DO THEY MAKE?

Judaism, Christianity, and Islam shared many common ancestors. They all were monotheistic religions and believed in divinely given written scriptures. Each of them had common rituals and practices. These included encouraging regular prayer, providing charity for the poor, and valuing pilgrimages to sacred holy places. Each also promised that behavior will receive its proper rewards and punishments in the future, on earth and in an afterlife. Finally, all balanced and integrated strands of mysticism, legalism, and pious devotion. Given these commonalities, the three religions of Judaism, Christianity, and Islam would appear to be naturally suited to coexistence and even to mutual reinforcement. And indeed at times, notably in Spain for many years, the three faiths did coexist and gladly learned from one another. But such warm, reciprocally beneficial coexistence has been the exception rather than the rule.

Perhaps two factors can explain the friction that has often characterized the relationships among these religions. First, all three have been proselytizing religions—although Judaism abandoned this practice early in the Christian era—and their very closeness has made them bitterly competitive. Each has had some feeling that it has come the closest to the essential truths of God and the world, and that the others have somehow failed to recognize this. Both Christianity and Islam, for example, accuse Judaism of stubbornly refusing to accept later revelations that modify and update its original truths. Both Judaism and Islam accuse Christianity of a kind of idolatry in claiming that God begat a son who was actually a form of God and who walked the earth in human form. Both Judaism and Christianity argue that God did not give a special, final revelation to Muhammad. In each case these religions have looked at one another and said that, despite elements of deep commonality, there exist also fundamental antagonisms. Indeed within each of these religions, at various times, internal divisions have turned one group against another amid cries of heresy and calls to armed opposition. Truth was to be maintained, asserted, and defended through the force of arms. (Religions with less insistence on doctrinal correctness, such as Hinduism and Buddhism, have had fewer, and less violent, religious wars.)

Second, as each religion developed, it sought the support of government. It often sought to *be* the government. Truth was to be reinforced by power. Basic competition over spiritual and philosophical truths spilled over into competition also for tax monies, office, land, and public acceptance of specific ritual and architectural symbols, and suppression of opposition. When they could, these religions marched through the world armed. Until recently, in the lands where these three religions predominated, the state and religion were usually intimately bound up with one another, and in many places the leader of the state expected that his subjects would accept his religion as their own, or at least give it preferential treatment.

Historically, Christianity came to dominate the European lands formerly held by the Roman Empire and, as we shall see, traveled with its European faithful to the New World. Islam dominated north Africa and the Asian lands formerly held by the Persian and Alexandrine Empires, and it traveled with armies, saints, and traders to India and southeast Asia. Judaism, which lost out to its younger successors both in numbers and in gaining the support of governments, remained everywhere a minority religion, dependent on the tolerance of others. This identification of different religions with particular geographical parts of the world was typical also of Hinduism, identified with India and, to a much lesser extent, with southeast Asia; and of Buddhism, identified with the Indian subcontinent, east and southeast Asia, and the routes connecting them.

Nevertheless, amid the carving up of the world into zones of religious dominance backed by supportive governments and frequent warfare among religious groups, there were also times of mutually beneficial coexistence, sharing of cultures, and recognition of the commonalities of these religions and of the common humanity of their faithful. In many regions, like the Middle East, and in cities along the various trade routes all over the world, members of different religions lived side-by-side, often developing mutual understanding, respect, and trust. And always the voice of the mystic, like that of Jalal al-Din Rumi, called out for recognition of the oneness of God and the unity of God's universe:

What is to be done, O Moslems? for I do not recognize myself.
I am neither Christian, nor Jew, nor Gabr [Zoroastrian], nor Moslem.
I am not of the East, nor of the West, nor of the land, nor of the sea;
I am not of Nature's mint, nor of the circling heavens.
I am not of earth, nor of water, nor of air, nor of fire;

I am not of the empyrian, nor of the dust, nor of existence, nor of entity.
I am not of India, nor of China, nor of Bulgaria, nor of Saqsin;
I am not of the kingdom of Iraqain, nor of the country of Khorasan.
I am not of this world, nor of the next, nor of Paradise, nor of Hell;
I am not of Adam, nor of Eve, nor of Eden and [the angel] Rizwan.
My place is the Placeless, my trace is the Traceless;
'Tis neither body nor soul, for I belong to the soul of the Beloved.
I have put duality away, I have seen that the two worlds are one;
One I seek, One I know, One I see, One I call. (McNeill and Waldman, p. 242)

Review Questions

- What is the *umma* in Islamic philosophy and practice? Why did Muhammad and later Muslim leaders think that it was important? What did they do to construct and preserve the *umma*?
- To what degree did the philosophy and practices of Islam appear to be new in Arabia? To what extent did they fit into existing philosophies and practices?
- Why have scholars disagreed as to whether early Islam improved the lives of women or made them more difficult?
- What is the basis for the division in Islam between Shi'a and Sunni groups?
- The political capital of Islam was moved from Medina to Mecca to Damascus to Baghdad. When did each of these moves occur, and for what reason?
- As between Sufis and the *ulama*, which group do you think did more to promote Islam in the world? Why do you hold this opinion? How did they do it?
- What were the ways in which Muslims preserved, enhanced, and transmitted knowledge and technology throughout their own domains and beyond?
- Give some historical examples of tensions and warfare between Muslims and Christians. Other examples of peaceful, mutually beneficial coexistence? Some historical examples of tensions and warfare between Muslims and Hindus? Other examples of peaceful, mutually beneficial coexistence?

Suggested Readings

PRINCIPAL SOURCES

Esposito, John. *Islam: The Straight Path* (New York: Oxford University Press, 1991). Clear, basic, exposition of the development and significance of Islam by a lifelong, non-Muslim scholar.

Esposito, John, ed. *The Oxford History of Islam* (New York: Oxford University Press, 1999). Brings together an array of clear, well-illustrated essays by outstanding scholars on the origin and evolution of Islam, including materials on law, society, science, medicine, technology, philosophy, and Islam and Christianity.

Hodgson, Marshall G.S. *The Venture of Islam*, 3 vols. (Chicago, IL: University of Chicago Press, 1974). Hodgson's classic reinterpretation of Islam, seeing it not only in alliance with political power, but also as an attractive global culture.

Keddie, Nikki R. and Beth Baron, eds. *Women in Middle Eastern History* (New Haven, CT: Yale University Press, 1991). Presents a wide variety of feminist perspectives on women in Islamic cultures.

Lapidus, Ira M. *A History of Islamic Societies* (Cambridge: Cambridge University Press, 1988). A comprehensive, even encyclopedic account by a single scholar.

Lewis, Bernard, ed. and trans. *Islam from the Prophet Muhammad to the Capture of Constantinople*, 2 vols. (New York: Oxford University Press, 1987). Outstanding anthology of primary sources, grouped as politics, war, religion, and society.

McNeill, William H. and Marilyn Robinson Waldman, eds. *The Islamic World* (Chicago, IL: University of Chicago Press, 1983). Outstanding anthology of primary sources.

Watson, Andrew. *Agricultural Innovation in the Early Islamic World* (Cambridge: Cambridge University Press, 1983). An account of the major crops of India transplanted westward to the very ends of the Islamic world. A kind of precursor to the later Columbian exchange.

ADDITIONAL SOURCES

Adas, Michael. *Islamic and European Expansion* (Philadelphia, PA: Temple University Press, 1993). Contains excellent interpretive historiographic articles on Islam in world history.

Ahmed, Leila. *Women and Gender in Islam* (New Haven, CT: Yale University Press, 1992). Demonstrates the variety of practices chronologically around the world.

Bulliet, Richard W. *Conversion to Islam in the Medieval Period: An Essay in Quantitative History* (Cambridge, MA: Harvard University Press, 1979). An innovative assessment of the rate of conversion through a study of name change.

E.J. Costello, trans. (from Gabrieli Francesco, trans. from Arabic), *Arab Historians of the Crusades* (Berkeley, CA: University of California Press, 1969). Through the eyes of Arab histori-ans, the Crusades appear less religious, more brutal and cruel, and much more concerned with money, than in most western accounts.

Dunn, Ross E. *The Adventures of Ibn Battuta* (Berkeley, CA: University of California Press, 1986). An interpretive study of the great Muslim traveler as an introduction to the culture and lands of his travels.

Eaton, Richard M. "Islamic History as Global History," in Adas, *op. cit.*, 1–36. Brings new social-science sources to bear in interpreting the rise and significance of Islam.

Eaton, Richard M. *The Rise of Islam and the Bengal Frontier, 1204–1760* (Berkeley, CA: University of California Press, 1993). Innovative assessment of how the region of modern Bangladesh became Islamic.

Eaton, Richard M. *Essays on Islam and Indian History* (New York: Oxford University Press, 2000). Important revisionist views of Muslim-Hindu interaction, usually emphasizing the achievement of accommodation.

Embree, Ainslee T., ed. *Sources of Indian Tradition, Volume I: From the Beginning to 1800* (New York: Columbia University Press, 2nd ed., 1988). The outstanding anthology of primary sources.

Ferdowsi. *The Legend of Seyavash* (London: Penguin Books, 1992). Classic tales of the early rulers of Persia.

al-Ghazzali. *The Faith and Practice of al-Ghazali*, trans. W. Montgomery Watt (London: Allen and Unwin, 1953). Tells of the tribulations of the master as he painfully sought a synthesis between legalism and mysticism in Islam.

Grabar, Oleg. *The Alhambra* (Cambridge, MA: Harvard University Press, 1978). A beautiful, scholarly account of the architectural marvel.

Hodgson, Marshall G.S. *Rethinking World History: Essays on Europe, Islam, and World History*, ed. Edmund Burke III (Cambridge: Cambridge University Press, 1993). A re-assessment of Hodgson's classic scholarship on Islam to demonstrate its relevance to world history.

Ibn Khaldun. *An Arab Philosophy of History*, ed. Charles Issawi (London: John Murray, 1950). An abridgement of this fourteenth-century classic of contemporary social science.

Johns, Jeremy. "Christianity and Islam," in John McManners, ed. *The Oxford Illustrated History of Christianity* (Oxford: Oxford University Press, 1990), 163–95. A basic sketch of the interaction of these religions, positive and negative.

The Koran trans. N.J. Dawood (London: Penguin Books, 1990). Probably the most readable translation.

The Koran Interpreted trans. A.J. Arberry (New York: Macmillan Publishing Co., 1955). The most acceptable translation to Muslim scholars.

Levtzion, Nehemia, ed. *Conversion to Islam* (New York: Holmes and Meier, 1979). Argues that conversion to Islam was at least as much a cultural process of assimilation as a sudden change in belief.

Levtzion, Nehemia. "Islam in Africa to 1800s: Merchants, Chiefs, and Saints," in Esposito (1999), 475–507. Very useful overview of many of the states and regions of sub-Saharan Africa.

Lewis, Bernard. *Islam and the West* (New York: Oxford University Press, 1993). Basic, but controversial interpretive account of cultural and political interaction, by a master.

Morony, Michael. *Iraq after the Muslim Conquest* (Princeton, NJ: Princeton University Press, 1984). Account of the conquests of Genghis Khan, his successors, and their legacies.

Nashat, Guity. "Women in the Middle East, 8000 B.C.–A.D. 1800," in *Expanding the Boundaries of Women's History: Essays on Women in the Third World*, eds. Cheryl Johnson-Odim and Margaret Strobel. (Bloomington, IN: Published for the Journal of Women's History, 1992). An introductory bibliographic survey of existing literature.

Niane, D.T. *Sundiata: an Epic of Old Mali* (Harlow, Essex, England: Longman, 1965). The classic epic of the founder-ruler of Mali.

Riley-Smith, Jonathan, ed. *The Oxford Illustrated History of the Crusades* (New York: Oxford University Press, 2001). A dozen articles by experts mostly from Western, Christian perspectives.

Robinson, Francis, ed. *The Cambridge Illustrated History of the Islamic World* (Cambridge: Cambridge University Press, 1996). Beautifully produced, one volume scholarly introduction to the Islamic world, lavishly illustrated.

Trimingham, John S. *Sufi Orders in Islam* (Oxford: Oxford University Press, 1971). An account of several different Sufi tariqas, their leadership, history, and commitments.

Tucker, Judith. "Gender and Islamic History," in Adas, op. cit., pp. 37–74. A succinct, provocative historiographical assessment of various interpretations of the status of Muslim women through the ages and around the world.

Vitray-Meyerovitch, Eva de. *Rumi and Sufism* (Sausalito, CA: Post-Apollo Press, 1987). Basic introduction to Rumi, his poetry, and his place in the Sufi movement.

◉ World History Documents CD-ROM

8.1 Muhammad: Koran
8.2 Al-Tabari: An Early Biography of Islam's Prophet
8.3 Orations: The Words of the Prophet Through His Speeches
8.4 Islam in the Prophet's Absence: Continuation Under the Caliphate
8.5 Harun al-Rashid and the Zenith of the Caliphate
8.6 Al-Farabi: The Perfect State
8.7 Islamic Science and Mathematics
8.8 The Caliphate in Decline: Al-Matawwakil's Murder
8.9 Shiism and Caliph Ali: Controversy Over the Prophetic Succession
12.1 Sunni versus Shi'ite: "We Exhort You to Embrace the True Faith!"
12.2 Süleyman "The Lawgiver" and the Advantages of Islam: Oigier de Busbecq
12.3 Women in Ottoman Society: Oigier de Busbecq
12.4 The Ottomans: Empire-builders at the Crossroads of Three Continents
12.5 The Safavid Shi'ite Empire of Persia
12.6 Shah Abbas the Great: The Resurgence of the Persian Empire
12.7 Moghul Apogee: Akbar the Enlightened

Religion to Trade

Moving from the theme of religion in Part 4 to the theme of trade in Part 5 may seem a big jump. Are not matters of the spirit quite separate from matters of commerce? In Christianity, did not both the Gospel of Matthew (6:24) and of Luke (16:13) quote Jesus as saying, "No servant can be the slave of two masters … You cannot serve God and Money"? Did not Matthew quote Jesus as saying, "It is easier for a camel to pass thorough the eye of a needle than for a rich man to enter the kingdom of God" (Matthew 19: 23-24). Christian clergy were sworn to lives of poverty.

As the Church became wealthy at various times in its history, reformers lamented its departure from the ascetic standards of its early years. Martin Luther proclaimed his reformation of the Church in the mid-fifteenth century in part as a protest against the Church's sale of "indulgences," documents granting forgiveness of sin in exchange for donations to the Church. Luther argued that money could not take the place of honest penance.

Lucas Cranach the Elder, The Pope's Selling of Indulgences, 1521. Woodcut.

A bishop blessing the annual market, St. Denis, near Paris, 14th century. Miniature. (*Bibliothèque Nationale, Paris*)

Church might bless their economic interests. See for example the illustration (*left*) depicting a bishop blessing the annual market at St. Denis, near Paris.

Other religions generally began with a more accommodating view of the relationship of religion and trade. The Book of Genesis portrays Judaism's founder, Abraham, as a semi-nomadic owner of flocks of sheep and goats, and a man who bargained actively in purchasing a burial site for his wife. In more systemic terms, the rabbis interpreted the Biblical injunction against taking interest as applying to loans among friends and family members; they devised methods of allowing modest interest to be taken on commercial loans. Islam, which views Abraham also as the first Muslim, worked out similar practical methods of discriminating between personal loans and business loans. Islam's great Prophet, Muhammad, was himself a businessman married to a businesswoman. Many mosques are constructed with business properties adjacent to them, the rent of which goes to support the mosque. See the illustration below.

Large and popular religions must, however, have some flexibility in their belief systems, and we find in Christianity many examples of the accommodation of spiritual and financial interests. The Church became wealthy because many people tithed, they gave ten percent of their earnings to the Church. In exchange, the

H. Griffiths, *Mosque of Bajazet with the Seraskier's Gate*, Istanbul, c. 1850. Engraving. (*Stapleton Collection, England*)

Hinduism designates the pursuit of "artha," wealth and power, as an important life goal, and sets aside the longest stage of the life cycle to the practicalities of administering a household. One whole caste category, the vaishyas, is composed of business people. In parts of India, especially Gujarat, at New Year's time, businessmen invite brahmin priests to bless their account books for the coming year in an elaborate ceremony called chopada puja, or the worship of the account books. The illustration on this page indicates that as Hindu businessmen have traveled overseas in modern times, they have continued this custom of integrating business practice with religious ritual.

His Holiness Pramukh Swami Maharaj sanctifying books of account during the Chopada Puja ceremony at the Shri Swaminarayan Mandir, Neasden, London.

QUESTIONS

1. To what degree have religious and business leaders accommodated one another – or failed to find such accommodation?
2. What have been the terms of the accommodation?
3. How have the members of each group benefited or lost out from the accommodation or the failure of accommodation?

5

The Movement of Goods and Peoples 1000–1776

CHANNELS OF COMMUNICATION: THE EXCHANGE OF COMMODITIES, DISEASES, AND CULTURE

We have frequently noted the importance of trade in regional and world economies. Trade linked the oldest centers of urban civilization—Mesopotamia, the Indus valley, and the Nile valley—as we noted in Part 2. In Part 3 we saw that empires sought to protect the principal transportation routes and that emperors sought to capture their profits. In Part 4 we noted that world religions spread along the same routes as trade and that religions were often carried by merchants. Both Buddhism and Islam spread to eastern Asia via the overland silk routes, and to Southeast Asia via the shipping lanes of the Indian Ocean. The exchange of ideas and cultures went hand-in-hand with the exchange of commodities.

In this Part trade is our central focus. In Chapter 12 we explore the role of traders and their relationships with political rulers from about 1100 to about 1500. We study the geography of the principal trade routes. They were not yet fully unified, and certainly not yet global, but they were linked together and capable of delivering goods from one end of Afro-Eurasia to the other. The transportation networks of those days required considerable coordination by merchants from various parts of the world, and considerable off-loading and re-loading of merchandise to move it from one region to the next—but they could deliver the goods.

Epidemics sometimes accompanied trade missions. The most devastating of them, the "Black Plague" of the mid-fourteenth century, wiped out more than one-third of the population in many places from China to western Europe, dramatically restructuring relationships of wealth and power in its wake. Security was critically important along the trade routes, as were the Mongol descendants of Chinggis Khan in providing that security along the silk routes of Central Asia. We read personal accounts of great traders and travelers like Marco Polo and Ibn Battuta. We close with an examination of the expansion of trade in Europe, the growing importance of traders, the resurrection of cities and trade routes and the cultural renaissance that these movements inspired.

Chapter 13 explores some of the oceans and seas of the world. For thousands of years, the Indian Ocean, the Red Sea, the Persian Gulf, the Arabian Sea, the Bay of Bengal the Mediterranean Sea, and the South China Sea, had been principal highways of seaborne trade. But the Atlantic and Pacific Oceans had not. Some evidence suggests that an occasional, rare voyage might have crossed these vast bodies of water, but establishing regular contact awaited Columbus' four voyages across the Atlantic 1492–1504, and Magellan's circumnavigation of the earth, 1519–22. The chapter charts the background of the voyages that provided the first continuous linkage of the three continents of North and South America, and Australia, to the core area of Afro-Eurasia and examines the astonishing results of these voyages.

Chapter 14 describes trade becoming global and the rulers of nation-states encouraging their merchants to participate in it. The Spanish and Portuguese came first, followed by the Dutch, French, and English. The search for wealth inspired the creation of new economic institutions and the reform of cultural and religious thought. In 1776 the Scottish philosopher and economist Adam Smith published *The Wealth of Nations*, signaling the arrival of a new philosophy of economic organization called capitalism, an economic system in which the means of production are privately owned and goods and services are exchanged according to levels of supply and demand in markets. Smith applauded the work of private businesspeople who pursued their own profit, and proclaimed them the chief engine of progressive change in world history. He opposed both governmental and religious control of trade—the existing system—and

Marco Polo, from *Romance of Alexander, c.* 1340. The great world traveler is shown setting sail for China from Venice in 1271. Europe was eager for news of the Mongol Empire—potential allies against the ancient Muslim enemy—and a steady stream of intrepid merchants and missionaries brought back amazing reports of the Khan's court. The exotic reminiscences of Marco Polo are, however, by far the most famous. (*Bodleian Library, Oxford*)

proposed instead free trade, mostly unregulated markets, and independent merchant-capitalists.

Smith's word was not final, and the market-based, supply-and-demand philosophy of capitalism is still debated today—reviled by some, extolled by others—significant to virtually all considerations of economic systems and to many questions of politics, culture, and religion as well. The final section of chapter 14 indicates how the economic and political leadership of a variety of countries, from Russia in the west to Japan in the east, responded to the new wealth and power of western Europe.

ESTABLISHING WORLD TRADE ROUTES

THE GEOGRAPHY AND PHILOSOPHIES OF EARLY ECONOMIC SYSTEMS
TRADE AND TRADERS: GOALS AND FUNCTIONS
1000–1500

KEY TOPICS
- World Trade: An Historical Analysis
- Trade Networks
- Trade in the Americas before 1500
- Trade in Sub-Saharan Africa
- Muslim and Jewish Traders
- Asia's Complex Trade Patterns
- The Mongols

Today, long-distance, international trade forms a substantial part of the world's commerce and includes even the most basic products of everyday food and clothing. In earlier times, however, long-distance trade represented only a small fraction of overall trade, mostly supplying luxury goods—silks, gold, spices, and the like—for the wealthy upper classes. Because these goods were extremely valuable relative to their weight, merchants could carry them over hundreds or even thousands of miles and still sell them for handsome profits. Some commercial goods, like raw wool and cotton, were also traded over medium distances, a few hundred miles. The transportation costs were justified because these raw materials became more valuable after importation and manufacture into finished products.

Before 1500, by far the largest share of trade was local—food crops traded for local hand manufactures or raw materials. These goods were necessities, but they had little value in relationship to their weight: the cost of transportation was a substantial part of their final price. They were, therefore, traded over only short distances. Often, they were bartered in exchange for other local goods rather than sold for money in more distant markets. This local exchange of goods is a fundamental part of local and regional history, but the study of world history focuses on long-distance trade and its importance in knitting together distant regions of the world.

Trade provides an index of economic vitality. It stimulates economic growth; people produce goods and provide services only if markets exist for them. Anyone who has ever looked for a job has experienced this economic truth. If jobs exist, people can find work; if jobs do not exist, they remain unemployed and economically unproductive. Similarly, both production and consumption are limited by the availability of markets. If markets are easily accessible, products can be bought and sold easily; if not, then trade, production, and consumption stagnate.

WORLD TRADE: AN HISTORICAL ANALYSIS

Historians studying world trade seek to understand its purposes, conditions, and regulations. We ask about social as well as economic values. For example: What benefits have different systems of trade achieved? Which systems have benefited which

Opposite **Boucicault Master, Trade in the Gulf of Cambay (detail), India, 1410. Vellum.** As the main port of northeastern India, Cambay excited the wonder of painters and artists in far-off Europe. This illustration from the *Livre des Merveilles* (*The Book of Wonders*) (1410) represents Cambay's ships and traders in European guise, not surprisingly because the artist had never been to the city. (*Bibliothèque Nationale, Paris*) members of society? Which systems have harmed which members of society? What have been the trade-offs in benefits and losses under each system? These questions, of course, are not only historical. The present-day debates over the "globalization" of trade—the opening of more and more countries of the world, and more and more products, to import and export trade—demonstrate their enduring significance. The street demonstrations in Seattle in 1999, and subsequently in other cities around the globe, against the World Trade Organization, which attempts to expand, facilitate, and regulate international trade, reveal the intense passions underlying these debates today.

To what degree do governments regulate or control economic markets? To what degree should they? In a completely **free market economy**, conditions of trade would not be regulated at all. Prices would vary only in terms of the relationship between the **supply** of goods and the economic **demand** for them, and business-people would be free to seek their fortune as they choose. Societies, however, do regulate trade to some degree in order to serve the greater good of the society. For example, governments may wish to ensure that everyone has enough food for survival. They may therefore decide that agricultural production should be expanded and industrial production limited. In time of scarcity—in wartime, for example—governments may ration food and essential commodities to ensure that everyone has access to at least minimum quantities. By taxing some items at high rates and

free market economy An economic system in which the means of production are largely privately owned and there is little or no government control over the markets.

supply and demand In economics, the relationship between the amount of a commodity that producers are able and willing to sell (supply), and the quantity that consumers can afford and wish to buy (demand).

AT A GLANCE : MEDIEVAL WORLD TRADE

DATE	POLITICAL/SOCIAL EVENTS	TRADE DEVELOPMENTS	EXPLORATION
1050 C.E.	■ Almoravids destroy Kingdom of Ghana (1067)		
1100 C.E.		■ Age of Great Zimbabwe in southern Africa	
1150 C.E.		■ Paper-making spreads from Muslim world to Europe	
1200 C.E.	■ Foundation of first Muslim empire in India ■ Chinggis Khan establishes Mongol Empire (1206–1405) ■ Collapse of Mayan civilization in Central America; rise of Incas in Peru ■ Rise of Mali, west Africa		
1250 C.E.	■ Osman I founds Ottoman dynasty in Turkey (1290–1326) ■ Emergence of Empire of Benin ■ Mongols fail to conquer Japan (1281)		■ Marco Polo arrives in China (1275)
1300 C.E.	■ Height of Mali (Mandingo) Empire under Sultan Mansa Musa		■ Ibn Battuta's travels in East Asia and Africa (c. 1330–60)
1350 C.E.	■ Ming dynasty in China (1368)		
1400 C.E.	■ Ottoman Turks establish foothold in Europe at Gallipoli	■ China reconstructs and extends Grand Canal	
1450 C.E.		■ Decline of Kilwa and Great Zimbabwe in southeast Africa (c. 1450)	
1500 C.E.	■ Zenith of Songay Empire of the middle Niger region (1492–1529) ■ Hernán Cortés and Spanish conquistadors defeat Aztecs and seize Mexico (1519–21) ■ Francisco Pizarro and Spanish conquistadors defeat Incas and seize Peru		

others at low rates, governments promote or limit various kinds of production and trade. Business may be more regulated or less regulated, but it is never completely unregulated.

In the earliest societies, such as Egypt, Mesopotamia, and China, government officials, often in alliance with priests, had more power than did private merchants, and trade was highly regulated. Nevertheless, considerable evidence suggests that market economies based on private profit did exist from earliest times. This trade for private profit was embedded in deeper political, social, religious, and moral structures of society. Long-distance private trade flourished most profitably in major port cities around the world. The merchants who carried on this port-city trade were often foreigners, with some independence from local political and social structures. They tended to occupy marginal positions in the host society, but central positions in the international trade networks.

TRADE NETWORKS

These long-distance merchants encouraged and brokered trade between the society in which they were living and far-flung networks of international merchants. They formed "trade diasporas," networks of interconnected commercial communities living and working in major trade cities throughout Africa, Europe, and Asia. As historians of trade have pointed out, trade diasporas appear in the archaeological record as early as 3500 B.C.E.

World trade routes. Between 1100 and 1500 a relay system of trade by land and sea connected almost all populous regions of Eurasia, as well as north and east Africa. Long-distance traders carried goods along their own segments of these routes, and then turned them over to traders in the next sector. The western hemisphere was still separate, and had two major trade networks of its own.

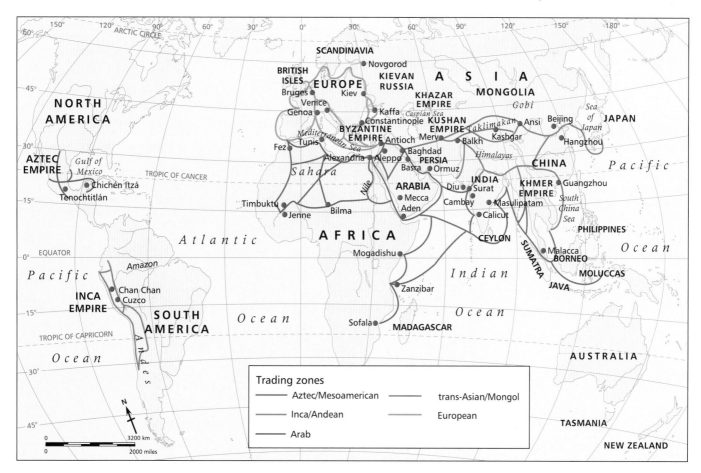

Some of them have endured for millennia. During the height of the Roman Empire, for example, traders from Rome sailed the waters of the Mediterranean Sea and the Indian Ocean. On rare occasions they continued all the way to China. Usually, these traders were not ethnically Roman. Most frequently they were descendants of the major trading communities of the eastern Mediterranean: Jews, Greek-speaking Egyptians, and Arabs. Roman trade left a heritage of these diaspora traders—in the form of small religious communities of Jews, Christians, and Muslim Arabs—living along the southwest coast of India long after the sack of Rome in 410.

Typically, the visiting merchants who carried the trade were marginal to their host societies rather than embedded within them. They were not unregulated by the hosts, nor were they totally subordinated. They were expected to take a reasonable profit in exchange for the benefits they brought to the port city.

TRADE IN THE AMERICAS BEFORE 1500

In the western hemisphere, two major trade networks had developed. The northern network served primarily the area that is Mexico today, although in those years it was ruled by several different groups. The southern network ran north–south both along the Pacific Coast and inland along the spine of the Andes Mountains. East–west routes rose to altitudes of 15,000 feet, linking the coastal settlements with those of the mountains. There was little traffic between North and South America, and virtually none between the eastern and western hemispheres, except for rare voyages, such as that of Leif Eriksson, the Viking explorer who reached Newfoundland about the year 1000 (see Chapter 13).

Trade in the Inca Empire

In the Andes Mountains of South America, a significant and long-lasting hub of civilization grew up after 600 C.E. By the time the Incas consolidated their empire in the early fifteenth century, the mountain peoples generated extensive trade, connecting

Photograph of a *quipu.* In the Inca empire, which extended from Ecuador to central Chile, trading was facilitated by an extensive road network. This *quipu,* a device of knotted string used to record dates and accounts, would have been a handy aid to the traveling South American businessman in the early 1400s.

Pre-Columbian America. Pre-Columbian America had two great regions of trade and political power. In the north, the Aztec kingdom, centered on Tenochtitlán, dominated. The adjacent Maya of Central America were in decline. In South America, about 1500, the Inca dominated the Andes mountain regions, linking them together through an extensive system of roads.

settlements over hundreds of miles north to south and linking together some 32 million people.

Trade was important up and down the mountainsides. With peaks rising up to 20,000 feet, these mountain slopes hosted several different ecological zones, encouraging product differentiation and trade. The valleys below provided sweet potatoes, maize, manioc, squash, beans, chili peppers, peanuts, and cotton. The hills above produced white potatoes, a cereal grain called quinoa, coca, medicines, feathers, and animal skins. The highland people specialized in manufacture and crafts, including gold working.

The state and its semi-divine rulers controlled this trade between the ecological zones. Under Inca rulers, from the early 1400s until the Spanish conquest in 1535, many of the best of the 15,000 miles of roads through the Andes were open only to government officials.

Trade in Central America and Mexico

In the Yucatán peninsula of Central and North America, the Mayan peoples had flourished from 200 B.C.E. to 900 C.E. Mayan traders flourished relatively independently, amassing a disproportionate share of wealth. Archaeologists suggest that the increasing wealth of the traders created social tensions and that ultimately the traders were brought under the control of the hierarchical state, creating a new set of unequal relations dominated by kings rather than merchants.

By the time the Spanish arrived in the 1520s, the Maya had weakened in the Yucatán, and the Aztecs dominated the valley of Mexico. The Spanish conquistadors wrote vivid accounts of the great marketplace of the Aztec capital, Tenochtitlán. As the Spanish leader Hernán Cortés summarizes in one of his letters:

> This city has many squares where trading is done and markets are held continuously. There is also one square twice as big as that of Salamanca, with arcades all around … There are streets of herbalists where all the medicinal herbs and roots found in the land are sold. There are shops like apothecaries', where they sell ready-made medicines as well as liquid ointments and plasters. There are shops like barbers', where they have their hair washed and shaved, and shops where they sell food and drink. (*The Second Letter*, pp. 103–104)

The market met every fifth day, with perhaps 40,000 to 50,000 merchants swarming in, rowing their canoes across the lake to the island on which Tenochtitlán was built. In many ways, the market was like the great fairs that were held in medieval Europe, drawing merchants from distant corners of the kingdom and beyond.

But how independent were these Tenochtitlán merchants? The Spanish described the city's market as being under tight government control. In addition to officers who kept the peace, collected taxes, and checked the accuracy of weights and measures, a court of twelve judges sat to decide cases immediately.

A guild of traders, called *pochteca*, carried on long-distance trade, which expanded steadily through the fifteenth century. They led trade expeditions for hundreds of miles, exchanging city-crafted obsidian knives, fur blankets, clothes, herbs, and dyes for such raw materials as jade, seashells, jaguar skins, feathers from forest birds, and, in the greatest volume, cotton from the Gulf coast. They were to marry only within the guild, and, though they were commoners, they could send their sons to temple schools and they had their own courts.

Because the American Indians had not invented the wheel, goods were carried by pack animals—and by humans. Boats were used on streams and rivers. Along the South American coast, near the equator, the Incas sailed boats constructed of balsa wood, while the Mayans paddled canoes through the river systems of the Yucatán.

The traders often gathered both goods and military intelligence for the ruling Aztec families. Royal troops protected them and sometimes used attacks on traveling *pochteca* as a justification for punishing the attackers and confiscating their lands. The *pochteca* lived in their own wards in the towns, had their own magistrates, and supervised the markets on their own. Their main god, Yiacatecutli, seemed akin to the Toltec god Quetzalcoatl, and this, too, suggests that they were to some degree foreigners living in a trade diaspora, with a high degree of independence from the state and temple.

The two major civilizational hubs functioned independently of one another and both were, of course, virtually completely cut off from Afro-Eurasia. When Europeans arrived in the sixteenth century brandishing new weapons, commanding new military organizations, and transmitting new diseases, the American residents were unprepared for the challenges.

TRADE IN SUB-SAHARAN AFRICA

Africa south of the Sahara was also well-integrated into webs of trade relationships. In West Africa, traders dispatched caravans of goods on camel back across the Sahara, linking the forest cultivators and miners in the south with the merchants and rulers of the Mediterranean coast. In East Africa traders along the coast procured gold and ivory from the interior of the continent and sold them to the seafaring merchants of the Indian Ocean.

West Africa

The domestication of the camel in the second to fifth century C.E. opened the possibility of regular trans-Saharan trade. Oases provided the necessary rest and watering points for caravans, as well as producing dates, a major commodity of trade. The

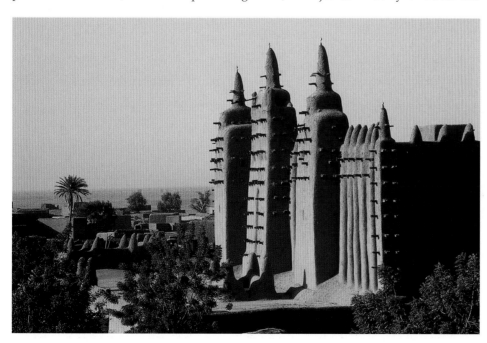

Mosque at Jenne, Mali, first built fourteenth century C.E. The spectacular mud-brick mosques found in the major towns of the African savanna states, such as Jenne and Timbuktu, point to the acceptance of Islam by the merchant and ruling classes in the thirteenth and fourteenth centuries. The mud, which washes away in the rain, needs continual renewal—hence the built-in "scaffolding" of the structure.

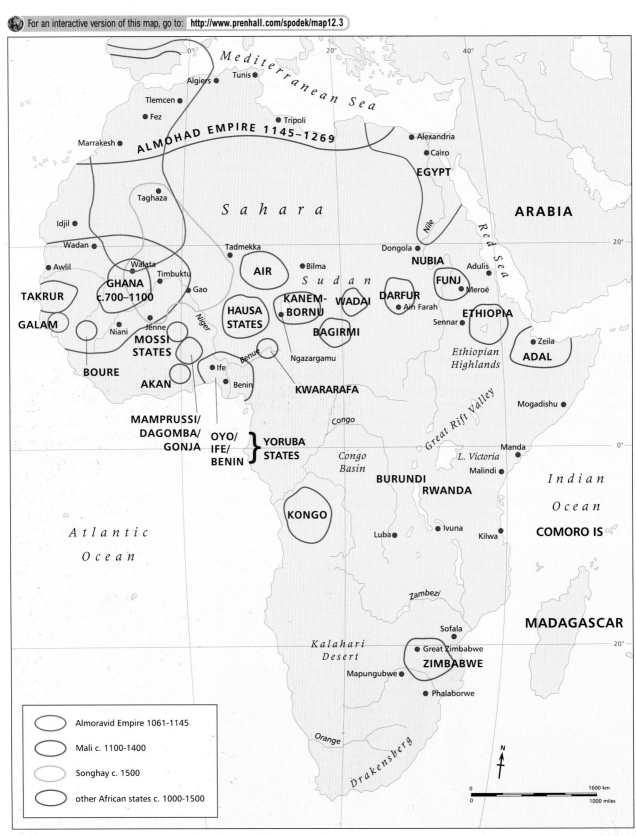

For an interactive version of this map, go to: **http://www.prenhall.com/spodek/map12.3**

African kingdoms. Many states appeared in 1000–1500 in northern and western Africa, their power based on control over long-distance trade—gold, ivory, and slaves moving north; metalware, textiles, and salt carried south. Ghana, Mali, and Songhay are discussed in the text. These states, protected from marauders by the Sahara, could usually maintain their independence.

earliest written records of this trans-Saharan trade begin with the arrival of Muslim traders in the eighth century.

For the most part, African political units were local, but three large empires in succession arose around the northern bend in the Niger, near Timbuktu, where the **sahel**, the arid fringe of the desert, meets the vast Sahara itself. These three empires—Ghana (about 700 to about 1100), Mali (about 1100 to about 1400), and Songhay (about 1300 to about 1600)—kept the trade routes open and secure. In contrast with most governments in other parts of the world that amassed wealth and power by controlling land and agriculture, these empires drew their power from control over trade, traders, and trade routes.

Gold, slaves, cloth, ivory, ebony, pepper, and kola nuts (stimulants) moved north across the Sahara; salt, dates, horses, brass, copper, glassware, beads, leather, textiles, clothing, and foodstuffs moved south. Gold was the central attraction. In the fourteenth century, the gold mines of West Africa provided about two-thirds of the gold used to finance trade in the eastern hemisphere. In 1324, when the Muslim emperor of Mali, Mansa Musa (r. 1307–32), passed through Cairo on his way to Mecca, he dispensed so much gold in gifts to court officials and in purchases in the bazaar that local prices in Cairo were inflated for years to come. A European map of 1375 showing a seated Mansa Musa as ruler of Mali is noted as follows: "So abundant is the gold found in his country that he is the richest and most noble king in all the land."

There were many natural break-points for the north–south trade: From the Mediterranean coast to the northern fringe of the desert, trade was borne by pack horse; across the desert, via oases, by camel; across the arid sahel and the grassy savanna lands south of the Sahara again by pack animal; and finally, through the tropical forest, impenetrable to larger animals and afflicted with the lethal tsetse fly, it was borne by human porters. For the most part, locally dominant trade groups carried the trade from one market center to the next in short relays. A few trading communities, however, notably the Soninke and, especially, their Mande-speaking Dyula branch, established trade diasporas that negotiated with the rulers.

East Africa

In the fourth century, the kingdom of Axum in Christian Ethiopia dominated the trade of the Red Sea and to some extent the Arabian Sea. With the rise of Islam, however, Arab traders gained control of the flow of merchandise and Arab armies began restricting Ethiopian power. After the ninth century, and south of the Horn of Africa, Arab merchants provided the main trading link between East Africa and the Indian Ocean. The first major port to spring up had been Manda, followed in the thirteenth century by Kilwa. The ruling Arab dynasty along the coast also seized control of the port of Sofala further to the south. Through local African merchants they exchanged goods with the peoples of the interior, especially at the trading post of

sahel "Shore"—the northern and southern edges of the Sahara Desert. A semi-arid region of Africa, extending from Senegal eastward to the Sudan.

Great Zimbabwe. The biggest and most celebrated of several stone enclosures in east Africa dating from the tenth to fifteenth centuries, Great Zimbabwe provided raw materials for trade at the coastal settlements, especially gold, copper, tin, and iron, and was also a trading post for luxury goods—Islamic pottery and cowrie shells were dug up at the site.

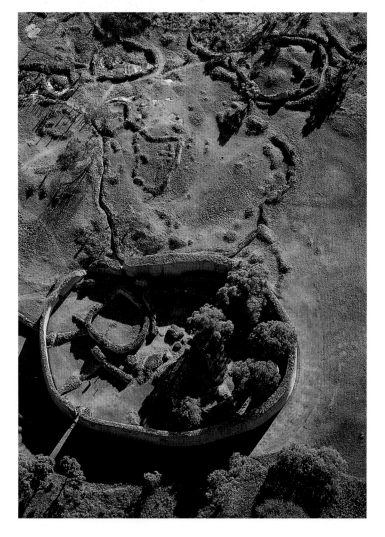

Great Zimbabwe. Here they found abundant supplies of valuable metals such as gold and copper (often cast into ingots) and animal products: ivory, horns, skins, and tortoise shells. Slaves were also an important commodity. Great Zimbabwe was the largest and most remarkable of all the developing towns. Architecturally, it featured a 100-acre stone enclosure and another 100 smaller enclosures in the surrounding region.

From these inland sources, goods were transported to the coastal ports and shipped onward to Arabia and India in exchange for spices, pottery, glass beads, and cloth. In the port cities of Africa's east coast, the Swahili language of the nearby African peoples received from these Indian Ocean traders a strong admixture of Arabic vocabulary, enriching Swahili and ensuring its place as the dominant language of the coastal trade.

MUSLIM AND JEWISH TRADERS

Muslim Arab traders played critical roles in the development of African trade networks, from north to south across the Sahara and overseas from the East African coast to various ports along the shores of the Indian Ocean. Their religion and ethnicity formed the basis of community and trust necessary for conducting business in a world that had no international courts or legal systems. A much smaller group, Jews, too, were able to carry on international trade across the entire eastern hemisphere from China to western Europe and Africa. For Jews, like Arabs, religion and ethnicity were the underlying basis of their trade diaspora. Within their overseas communities they quickly learned whom they could trust and this enabled them to establish highly efficient trade networks. Other groups of global traders also formed commercial networks on the basis of shared religion and ethnicity, although they were generally less extensive geographically, for example Christian Armenians, Jain and Hindu Gujaratis from western India, and Fukienese from the southeast coast of China. Small overseas Muslim trade communities also often attracted local traders to assimilate to Islam, as happened especially in Indonesia and southeast Asia. The other trading communities generally stayed within their own social and religious networks, enjoying trade relations with local groups, but not encouraging their conversion.

Jewish Traders

During the period of Tang-Abbasid control over the silk route—the eighth and early ninth centuries—Jews had once again emerged as a preeminent trading community throughout the diaspora linking Europe and China. The emigration of Jews to many far distant points of settlement facilitated their trade connections. Their religious diaspora supported their trade diaspora. Charlemagne's ninth-century European empire employed them to carry trade in southern Europe. Baghdad, astride many of the key trade routes in western Asia, held the most prominent Jewish community in the world at the time, but there were also small Jewish communities in Calicut and Cochin in south India and in Kaifeng, China. When the Portuguese explorer Vasco da Gama reached Calicut in 1498, a local Jewish merchant was able to serve as interpreter. Cairo, Egypt, one of the world's great trade centers, also sheltered a very significant Jewish community.

Statuette of Semitic trader, Chinese, 10th century. Traders from the Roman Empire traveling the silk routes were likely to be Jews from the Fertile Crescent, Greek-speaking Egyptians, and other Levantines. They and their descendants eventually settled along the trans-Asian routes, which most likely explains the Chinese derivation of this glazed porcelain Semitic peddler, made during Tang dynasty times. (*The Seattle Art Museum*)

Muslim Traders

With the rise of Islam (see Chapter 11), and especially after the Abbasid caliphs shifted their capital to Baghdad in 762, Muslim traders dominated the routes through the Indian Ocean. Ethnically, most were Arabs and Persians. In the thirteenth century, as the Muslim sultanate of Delhi came to rule most of India, many of the Hindu ocean-going traders, especially those in the western Indian region of Gujarat, converted to Islam. Along with their trade goods, they carried their culture and religion. Distant merchants who encountered them in order to trade, slowly also absorbed elements of Islam. In regions as distant as Malaysia and Indonesia local merchants began to assimilate to the religion of these oceanic traders. When the ruler of Malacca converted to Islam, about 1400, the trading circuit of Muslim merchants was complete.

Islam encouraged trade. The *hajj* (pilgrimage), advocated for every Muslim at least once during his or her lifetime, demanded international travel; trade connections flourished with the *hajj*. A Muslim trade colony had operated in Sri Lanka from about 700 C.E. Arab traders sailed with the monsoon winds first to India, then on to Southeast Asia, and some even on to the southeast coast of China. Catching the proper seasonal winds in each direction and using their **lateen** (triangular) sails to maximum effect, sailors could complete a round trip from Mesopotamia to China in less than two years. Carried not by military power but by traders, Islam came to be the dominant religion in Indonesia (the most populous Muslim country in the world today), and to attract tens of millions of Chinese adherents. The entire length of the Indian Ocean

lateen A triangular sail affixed to a long yard or crossbar at an angle of about 45 degrees to the mast, with the other free corner secured near the stern. The sail was capable of taking the wind on either side.

Anon., *King Edward I Returns from Gascony*, 1470. Miniature. This is an example of a ship with lateen sails. Europeans adapted these sails from Arab models because they enabled ships to tack against the wind as well as run with it. (*British Library, London*)

HOW DO WE KNOW?

The Records in the Cairo Genizah

Information on Mediterranean cultures and their trade connections into the Indian Ocean, from the tenth through the thirteenth centuries, has come to historians from the Cairo Genizah (Hebrew for a repository of old papers), studied by Solomon Goitein from the 1950s through the 1980s. Jewish law requires that the written name of "God" not be destroyed but stored for later burial; the Genizah was the storage point in Cairo for such documents for several centuries. Because paper was scarce and often re-used, the manuscripts in the Genizah include massive bundles of notes and manuscripts on secular as well as sacred aspects of life: on trade and commerce, on social organization in general, and on the Jewish community in particular. Marriage contracts "state in detail and with great variety the conditions regulating the future relations of the newly married, and thus constitute a precious source for our knowledge of family life" (I:10). Wills and inventories of estates are "veritable mines of information" (I:10). Letters of correspondence, both personal and business, "form the largest and most important group [of manuscripts]. They are our main source not only for our knowledge of commerce and industry, but also for various other subjects, such as travel and seafaring" (I:11). "There are hundreds of letters addressed to various authorities containing reports, petitions, requests for help, demands for redress of injustice, applications for appointments, and a great variety of other matters" (I:12). Religious responsa are frequent, questions and answers between commoners and sages concerning religious philosophy, doctrine, and practice. Most women were illiterate, but they dictated many letters to scribes: "We hear the female voice guiding the male pen" (I:12). For the most part the writing is in Arabic, but transcribed in Hebrew letters. These centuries-old manuscripts have proven to be a gold mine for historians studying the life of Cairo, its citizens, and their external connections throughout the Mediterranean Sea and the Indian Ocean.

- Given the nature of the Genizah repository, what kinds of records do you think would be most fully represented? Least well represented?
- How might records of family life and records dictated by women help to fill out the records of business transactions?
- How important was Cairo as a trade center at this time?

littoral, from East Africa through India and on to Indonesia, housed a Muslim, largely Arab, trading diaspora.

ASIA'S COMPLEX TRADE PATTERNS

As the largest continent, with the largest population and the oldest civilizations, it is not surprising that Asia developed complex trade networks thousands of years ago. As early as 1250, a set of interlinked trade networks connected the main population and production centers of Asia, Africa, and Europe. The earlier map (p. 377) illustrates their vast and comprehensive geographic coverage. From east to west, Japan and China were linked by land routes to Central Asia and by sea lanes to the Indian Ocean. Both land and sea routes continued westward to Arabia, western Asia, and on to the Mediterranean and Europe. Well-developed sea traffic linked also to the East African coast, where land routes extended into the African continent. North–south routes ran through China, Central and West Asia, and Europe, and from the Mediterranean across the Sahara by camel. At this time there was not yet any central transportation headquarters or company that could carry goods all the way from East Asia to western Europe, for example, but arrangements could be made for even this long voyage to be completed stage by stage.

The Polynesians of the South Pacific

The Polynesians are Austronesian-speaking peoples who migrated from south China and Southeast Asia perhaps 6000 years ago to Taiwan, the Philippines, and eastern Indonesia (see Chapter 1). Those who settled in the islands adjacent to these areas became known as Melanesians. Those who continued on eastward became known as

Polynesians. These Polynesians continued to sail eastward in single and double canoes, 100 to 150 feet long, made of wooden components fitted together and held in place by ropes and cords of fiber. These ships, with their single, square, woven-mat sails, could carry not only men and women but also food supplies and even live animals. In these simple, elegant craft, the Polynesians began vast ocean voyages that would take them as far northeastward as Hawaii (400 C.E.), as far southeastward as Easter Island (400 C.E.), and as far southwestward as New Zealand (750 C.E.). They became the greatest seafaring peoples of pre-modern times. Students of Polynesian history marvel both at the enormous stone statues erected on some of the Polynesian islands, most spectacularly on Easter Island, and at the accomplishments of their sea voyages. Polynesians apparently visited every island within the huge triangle of Hawaii, Easter Island, and New Zealand. Nevertheless, despite traveling through thousands of years and thousands of miles, the Polynesians preserved several remarkably similar elements of culture throughout their domains. Anthropologists note the similarities across the islands of Polynesia of tools, names of plants, terms of kinship, and artistic styles.

Were Polynesians capable of sailing across the Pacific and establishing contact with the Americas? Apparently so. The Hawaiian Islands are closer to the Americas than to Asia, and Easter Island is only 2200 miles off the coast of South America. Indeed, many scholars argue that this contact was accomplished, citing the sweet potatoes and manioc of Polynesia as their evidence. But, whatever the capabilities of the Polynesians and their canoes, and whatever the source of these food supplies, the Polynesians did not establish permanent connections to the Americas. Apparently they were not interested in sailing for the sake of exploration, but only to find places in which to settle, raise families, and obtain necessary food supplies. Although they were among the greatest sailors in human history, they apparently did not sail just for the excitement of the voyage, but rather for more specific and immediate needs.

Malay Sailors in the South China Sea and the Indian Ocean

Extraordinary as the Polynesian sailors were, apparently they adopted their sails from the Malay sailors of the South China Seas probably late in the first millennium B.C.E. These sailors left four major legacies to world seafaring, one primarily in their own neighborhood, the other three of much wider significance. The first was the most important: cargo ships—*jongs*, or junks as they are usually called in English. These ships with multilayered hulls, two to four masts, two rudders, and a normal capacity of 400 to 500 tons, seem to have inspired the junks used by Chinese merchant sailors to the north. Second, their balance-lug square sails seem to have inspired a series of adaptations and inventions, from the sails used by the Polynesians, to the sails used by Arab sailors, later modified to triangular sails, called lateen sails. (Other authorities believe that the balance-lug sail developed on the Nile River, also in the first millennium B.C.E., and they argue that this Egyptian invention was the background source for the Arab lateen

Johannes Baptista van Doetechum, *A Chinese Junk*, from *Jan Huyghen van Linschoten: His Discourse of Voyages into the East and West Indies*, 1579–92. **Engraving.** Apparently first an invention of the Malay sailors of the South China Sea, and adapted by the Chinese, these ships could carry more than a thousand tons of cargo and hundreds of sailors. (*Private Collection*)

sails.) These lateen sails were subsequently copied by European sailors in the Mediterranean and used for their voyages in the Atlantic. The balance-lug sail could be turned to face into the wind or to tack against it, allowing sailors to set their course with much greater maneuverability. As the sail was turned, from an angle it appeared to be triangular, and sailors learned that a triangular sail would work equally well. Thus the lateen sail was born and ultimately carried to the sailing paths of the world.

Third, the Malay sailors learned the patterns of the seasonal monsoon winds of the Indian Ocean and learned to sail with them. The rain-laden monsoon winds are attracted from the Indian Ocean inward toward Central Asia during the summer months, when the continental interior is much hotter than the oceans around it, and blow outward from the continent toward the ocean in the cooler months, when the ocean is warmer than the interior. The Greeks, too, learned how to use the monsoon winds of the Indian Ocean effectively in the first few centuries B.C.E. Whether from the Malays or the Greeks, the knowledge of the wind patterns soon reached all the sailors of the Indian Ocean, including the Europeans when they arrived in 1498.

Finally, using their ship technology and knowledge of the winds, Malay sailors made regular voyages of 3000 miles across the Indian Ocean—probably via the Maldive, Seychelles, and Comoro islands—to the large island of Madagascar, 250 miles off the coast of East Africa, where they established themselves as the majority population, as they remain to this day. The Malay sailors brought to Madagascar bananas, coconuts, taro, and their language, which also continues as the dominant language of the island.

Along with their settlements, the Malay sailors established sea routes from East Africa to China. They carried frankincense and myrrh from East Africa, Arabia, southwest Iran, and the Makran Coast of India to present day Vietnam and China. From Timor, 1800 miles to the southeast of Vietnam, they brought aromatic woods, especially sandalwood. From the "Spice Islands," the Moluccas, 1000 miles east of Java, they brought cloves, nutmeg, and mace. For more than a thousand years they were the master sailors of the South China Sea.

Sailors and Merchants of the Indian Ocean

The great crossroads of the world's shipping lanes in the period 1100–1500 was the Indian Ocean. Its waters encompass three distinct geographical sectors, each with its own cultural orientation. The western sector sweeps from the East African coast across Arabia and continues on to the west coast of India. From the time of Alexander the Great and the Roman Empire, Greek sailors participated in this trade. By the first century B.C.E. Greek sailors had learned to use the monsoon winds to navigate these waters swiftly and effectively. From the fourth to the eighth centuries, following the decline and fall of the Roman Empire, two new groups dominated this western region of the Indian Ocean: sailors from Axum (modern Ethiopia and Eritrea), and its Red Sea port of Adulis, and sailors from Sassanian Persia, an empire that was in the ascendant in western Asia at the time.

From the eighth to the sixteenth century, Arab Muslim traders and sailors became masters of the western Indian Ocean sea lanes. This was the area made famous by the legendary exploits of Sinbad the Sailor. As Islam inspired the people of Arabia to undertake expeditions of conquest by land beginning in the seventh century (see Chapter 11), Arab sailors also began to assume prominence in the Indian Ocean trade. Among the Arabs living at the southern end of the Arabian peninsula, some had experience with sea trade, but those to the north, the majority, did not. As Arab armies moved still further north, however, they came into contact with, conquered, and learned from previous masters of the Indian Ocean, the Sassanians of Iran. Mastering

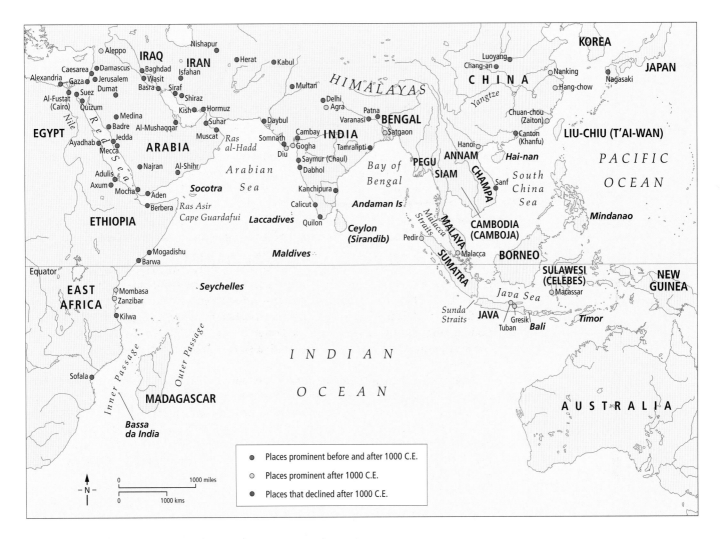

Trading ports and cities, Indian Ocean, 618–1500 C.E. The Indian Ocean was the pivot of long-distance seaborne trade from the Mediterranean to the South China Sea. Each of its port cities housed a rich diversity of merchants of many ethnicities and cultures.

these new skills, and inspired by their own expansionism, Arab sailors displaced the Sassanians. In 762 C.E. the new Abbasid dynasty built a new capital in Baghdad, in the heartland of Mesopotamia. In this land that had participated in sea trade for millennia, the Arabs' concern for oceanic trade increased further.

As they increasingly participated in sea trade, Arab sailors became true masters of the Indian Ocean trade. Lacking wood in Arabia, they depended on others to build their ships, or obtained teak from southern India to build their own. For reasons that remain unclear, they did not use metal nails in ship construction, but "stitched" the wooden planks together with coir—the fiber of coconut husks—or other fibers. Like the Malay and the Greek sailors before them, they learned to sail with the monsoon winds. The Arab Muslim Ahmad Ibn Majid included extensive recommendations on travel dates appropriate to the monsoon winds in his comprehensive fifteenth-century guide to navigation throughout the Indian Ocean. For example:

> Travelling from Bengal and connected regions [begins] in the 40th day of the year [1st January] and its end is the 70th day [31st January]: it is no good travelling later than that if bound for Hormuz or Yemen or the Hijaz. Travelling to Ceylon and the Maldives is possible until the 70th and 80th days although it is a gamble in some years by the 80th and the same from Malacca, Pegu, and Siam. But from Java, Sumatra, Malacca, and Tanasari to Bengal, sailing takes place from the 90th to the 140th days.

The pattern of emporia trade in the Indian Ocean, c. 1000–1500. Trade goods did not travel on a single ship the whole length of this region. Rather, they would be loaded at a port in one of the three regions, off-loaded and reloaded in the next for shipment to the third region.

The rise of Arab Muslim sea traders was a remarkable transformation for this ethnic and religious group. The Arabs had been quite accustomed to trade—Muhammad himself was a camel driver and leader of caravans—but trade by sea was different. They took to this new way of life eagerly and came to dominate the sea lanes from the Mediterranean coast in the west all the way east to Guangzhou (Canton) and Hangzhou in China, frequently displacing previous communities of sailors.

In the eastern waters of the Indian Ocean, for example—from India and the Bay of Bengal to Indo-China and the Malacca Straits—Indian sailors and merchants, largely Hindu, had predominated. East of the Malacca Straits, these sailors entered into the South China Sea, attracted by China's wealth and luxury products. Despite the geographical distance of their homes from this region, they came to surpass in importance the more local Chinese and East Asian merchants.

Until the tenth century, much of the cultural influence in this region came from India, as evidenced in the many astonishingly large and beautiful temple complexes of this region—for example, Borobudur and Prambanan in Java, Angkor Wat in Cambodia, Pagan in Burma, and the Cham Shaivite temple of central Vietnam. These Buddhist and Hindu temples marked centers of cultural as well as political and economic dominance. From the seventh to the tenth century, south Sumatra was home to the Buddhist Srivijayan maritime empire, the largest and most powerful of the Indian-influenced Southeast Asian kingdoms.

Boucicault Master, Trade in the Gulf of Cambay, India, 1410. Vellum. Merchants and travelers carried exciting tales of their adventures, but when European painters sought to represent these wonders they could only fill in their imagination with scenes from their own experience. Hence this illustration looks more like a European town than an Indian city port. (*Bibliothèque Nationale, Paris*)

By the end of the thirteenth century, however, Muslim traders, mostly from India, began their trade and proselytization through the entire Southeast Asian archipelago of islands—today's Indonesia, Borneo, Celebes, the Moluccas, and the Philippines. By the fourteenth century, most of the ocean-going merchants appear to have been Muslims, either Arabs or Indian converts from Hinduism, and their descendants. On the basis of their economic strength as traders they attracted local peoples and encouraged them to assimilate to Islam. When the ruler of Malacca converted, about 1400, Muslim supremacy in Indian Ocean trade reached its zenith. From west to east, Muslim merchants dominated the major ports. In Indonesia and the Malaysian

SOURCE

The Arabian Nights

Arab Muslim traders of the Indian Ocean fill the pages of some of the best loved tales of world literature. The Thousand Nights and One Night, *also called the* Arabian Nights, *fables originally written in Persian during the years of the Abbasid Empire (750–1258), include the tales of the seven voyages of Sinbad (Sindbad) the Sailor, who won a fortune through a series of hazardous (if unbelievable) adventures at sea. The adventures, supposedly told night after night by Scheherazade to the emperor, Haroun al-Rashid (r. 786–809), as a ploy to postpone her scheduled execution, are fanciful, but Sinbad's descriptions of his departures on each of his voyages are based on the reality of Indian Ocean shipping. This translation from the beginning of the third voyage is by Richard F. Burton who brought the complete tales to the English-speaking world in the late nineteenth century.*

I returned from my second voyage overjoyed at my safety and with great increase of wealth, Allah having requited me all that I had wasted and lost, and I abode awhile in Baghdad-city savouring the utmost ease and prosperity and comfort and happiness, till the carnal man was once more seized with longing for travel and diversion and adventure, and yearned after traffic and lucre and emolument, for that the human heart is naturally prone to evil. So making up my mind I laid in great plenty of goods suitable for a sea voyage and repairing to Bassorah [Basra], went down to the shore and found there a fine ship ready to sail, with a full crew and a numerous company of merchants, men of worth and substance; Faith, piety and consideration. I embarked with them and we set sail on the blessing of Allah Almighty and on His aidance and His favour to bring our voyage to a safe and happy issue and already we congratulated one another on our good fortune and bon voyage. We fared on from sea to sea and from island to island and city to city, in all delight and contentment, buying and selling wherever we touched, and taking our solace and our pleasure, till one day … [and here begin the fabulous adventures of the third voyage]. (*The Thousand Nights and One Night*, Vol. 4, pp. 2031–2)

Arab trader, illustration from the *Maqamat* of al-Hariri, 12th century. Regional shipping routes linked into the oceanic, intercontinental routes. This ship, with Arab passengers and Indian, and perhaps African, crew, sailed the Persian Gulf connecting Mesopotamia and the Indian Ocean.

peninsula Islam displaced the Hindu and Buddhist cultures that had already taken root, and today both Malaya and Indonesia are primarily Muslim countries.

Arabs did not sail further, into the Atlantic or Pacific Oceans, simply because they had no need. They sailed at will throughout the most valued seas of the world that they knew. They had no problem of access. While Europeans were beginning to attempt to find new routes to India and China in the fifteenth century, the Arabs were already there.

China

By 1500 China was the most economically advanced region in the world, a magnet for world trade. China is so huge, however, that its internal trade far outweighed its external trade. It is so rich and varied in its productivity that others came to China to obtain its products far more regularly than the Chinese traveled abroad in search of the products of others. China's policies towards trade have, nevertheless, altered through the centuries we are considering here, partly as a result of changes in imperial leadership, partly in response to external pressures. Even though it created a highly integrated system of internal markets and reached extraordinary levels of agricultural and industrial productivity under the Song Dynasty, China was defeated by Mongol invaders and had to abandon a large part of its territories, relocate to the south, and reconstruct its economy. The Ming Dynasty overthrew the Mongols and undertook a series of spectacular ocean voyages. Then, in another change of policy, later Ming emperors forbade the Chinese to trade overseas. Nevertheless, overseas merchants continued to pour in, eager to do business with the Central Kingdom.

International Trade. As early as the fourth century C.E. the Chinese also participated in the trade of the South China Sea and the Indian Ocean, although probably only as far west as Sri Lanka. Their oceanic trade activity increased with the rise of the Tang dynasty (618–907 C.E.). During much of this period, the Abbasid Empire (750–1258) was at its height, and helped to protect the sea lanes of the Indian Ocean. But with the decline of both empires in the ninth century, the Chinese largely withdrew from this oceanic trade and concentrated instead on inland issues, in accord with their geographical position centered on the Yellow River valley and the north. After 1127, however, they returned to oceanic enterprise, when the Song dynasty was driven from north China by the invasions of the Tatars and other northern peoples. As they moved south, establishing a new capital at Hangzhou, about 100 miles from the modern-day port-metropolis of Shanghai, they turned their attention back to the sea. With various northern groups in control of the old overland silk routes, sea-borne trade was an obvious transportation and communication alternative. For this purpose, the Chinese mastered the craft of building large ships and merchants created new patterns of commercial exchange, including sophisticated credit systems. In addition to a merchant marine, China constructed a powerful navy.

伴語隔墙 晚來得少休女 好轉軸頭緒長 探湯上盆額色 意媚窻拍、手 事誰家娘盈、 連邨煮繭香解 練絲

In 1368, a new dynasty, the Ming, came to power. Especially in the early years of the dynasty, Ming emperors adopted policies of expansionism by land and self-assertion by sea. The Ming Emperor Yung-lo (r. 1402–24) dispatched a series of seven spectacular ocean voyages under the Muslim eunuch, Admiral Zheng He. The first voyage set out in 1405 with sixty-two large junks, 100 smaller ships, and 30,000 crew. The largest ships were 450 feet long, displaced 1600 tons, held a crew of about 500, and were the largest ships built anywhere up to that time. They carried silks, porcelains, and pepper. The first expedition sailed as far as Calicut, near the southwest tip of India. In six further missions between 1407 and 1433, Zheng He sailed to ports all along the Indian Ocean shores, at least twice reaching the East African ports of Mogadishu, Brava, Malindi, and Kilwa. Interested in exotic treasures that could not be found in China, Emperor Yung-lo seemed most pleased with a giraffe sent to him by the sultan of Malindi on the fourth voyage, in 1416–19. These colossal expeditions demonstrated both the skill of Admiral Zheng He and the vision of Emperor Yung-lo. On the basis of these accomplishments, many historians believe that the Chinese would have been able to cross either the Atlantic or the Pacific Ocean—had they wished. But they did not push their expeditions any further and, in 1433, the Ming emperor terminated the great, state-sponsored Indian Ocean voyages.

Why did the emperor terminate these voyages? Why did China not dispatch its own missions to Europe, and even to the western hemisphere? It appeared to have the

SOURCE

Chinese Ships in South Indian Harbors: An Account by Ibn Battuta

The fourteenth-century traveler Ibn Battuta (1304–68) did not usually comment on ships and sailors. He was far more interested in his encounters with people on land. In the south Indian port of Calicut, however, he was so impressed with the capacity and design of the Chinese ships in the harbor that he gave a remarkable description. He notes that while the Chinese allowed only Chinese ships to dock in their ports, the pilots and crew were not necessarily Chinese:

We traveled to the city of Calicut, which is one of the chief ports in Malabar [the southwest coast of India], and one of the largest harbors in the world. It is visited by men from China, Sumatra, Ceylon, the Maldives, Yemen, and Fars [Persia], and in it gather merchants from all quarters ... there were at the time thirteen Chinese vessels, and we disembarked. Every one of us was lodged in a house and we stayed there three months as the guests of the infidel [Zamorin ruler of Calicut], awaiting the season of the voyage to China. On the Sea of China traveling is done in Chinese ships only, so we shall describe their arrangements.

The Chinese vessels are of three kinds; large ships called *chunks* [junks], middle-sized ones called *zaws* [dhows], and small ones called *kakams*. The large ships have anything from twelve down to three sails, which are made of bamboo rods plaited like mats. They are never lowered, but turned according to the direction of the wind; at anchor they are left floating in the wind. A ship carries a complement of a thousand men, six hundred of whom are sailors and four hundred men-at-arms, including archers, men with shields and arbalests, who throw naphtha. Each large vessel is accompanied by three smaller ones, the "half," the "third," and the "quarter." These vessels are built only in the towns of Zaytun and Canton. The vessel has four decks and contains rooms, cabins, and saloons for merchants; a cabin has chambers and a lavatory, and can be locked by its occupant, who takes along with him slave girls and wives. Often a man will live in his cabin unknown to any of the others on board until they meet on reaching some town. The sailors have their children living on board ship, and they cultivate green stuffs, vegetables and ginger in wooden tanks. The owner's factor [representative] on board ship is like a great *amir* [nobleman]. When he goes on shore he is preceded by archers and Abyssinians with javelins, swords, drums, trumpets, and bugles. On reaching the house where he stays they stand their lances on both sides of the door, and continue thus during his stay. Some of the Chinese own large numbers of ships on which their factors are sent to foreign countries. There is no people in the world wealthier than the Chinese. (Ibn Battuta, pp. 234–6)

technological capability to do so. Why did Chinese emperors choose only to receive European shipping—rather than to dispatch their own ships—beginning with the Portuguese in 1514?

Many answers appear plausible. The Ming turned their energies inward, toward consolidation and internal development. At first they pushed the Mongols further north from the Great Wall, but an invasion of Mongolia failed in 1449. Thereafter, the Ming limited their military goals, rebuilt the Great Wall, and restricted their forces to more defensible borders.

In 1411 the Ming reconstructed and extended the Grand Canal from Hangzhou in the south to Beijing in the north. The canal was the cheapest, most efficient means of shipping the grain and produce required by the northern capital. The man-made inland waterway also reduced the importance of coastal shipping, enabling the Ming emperors to turn their backs on the seas and ocean. The faction of eunuchs, dedicated court servants like Zheng He, who urged the government to continue its sponsorship of foreign trade, lost out in palace competition to other factions that promoted internal development. International private shipping was also curtailed.

The Ming government limited contacts with foreigners and prohibited private overseas trade by Chinese merchants. In 1371, coastal residents were forbidden to travel overseas. Recognizing the smuggling that resulted, the government issued further prohibitions in 1390, 1394, 1397, 1433, 1449, and 1452. The repetition of this legislation reveals that smuggling did continue, but, for the most part, private Chinese sailors were cut off from foreign trade. The government defined the expeditions of Zheng He as political missions that sought tribute to China from outlying countries. Although products were exchanged on these voyages, officially trade was not their goal. So, while both private and government trade flourished in the interior of China, and while thousands of Chinese emigrated to carry on private businesses throughout Southeast Asia, China's official overseas trade virtually stopped. Zheng He's expeditions stand out as spectacular exceptions to generally restrictive policies.

These decisions to limit China's international trade, both official and private, proved enormously costly. Chinese society became introverted and, although economic growth continued, innovation stagnated. Under the Song dynasty (960–1279) Chinese technology had been the most innovative in the world. Creativity continued under the Mongols, but by about the beginning of the Ming dynasty, China became more conservative. Military technology improved but then it, too, stagnated. China had invented gunpowder before 1000 C.E., but used it only sporadically. Ming cannon in the early fifteenth century were at least equal to those anywhere in the world, but metal was in short supply, limiting further development. The Ming fought few battles against fortress cities, where cannon were most useful, so they also saw little need to invest further in developing this heavy weaponry. No enemies appeared against whom they needed such weapons. In fighting against invasions from the north, the crossbow was of more importance to the infantrymen, who made up China's armies of a million and more soldiers. At first, when China was itself very advanced, these decisions to limit further military innovation seemed not so consequential. Later, however, they would render the country vulnerable to newly rising powers.

Internal Trade. When Marco Polo arrived in China in 1275, the splendor and wealth of the country overwhelmed him. He described its ruler, Kublai Khan, as "the mightiest man, whether in respect of subjects or of territory or of treasure, who is in the world today or who ever has been, from Adam our first parent down to the present moment." Polo correctly informed the West that China in the late 1200s was the richest, most technologically progressive, and largest politically unified country in the world.

The foundations of China's wealth had been in place for centuries. We have already read in Chapter 7 of China's generally growing population, territory, power, and wealth through its successive dynasties from Qin to Tang. Under the Song dynasty (Northern Song, 960–1126; Southern Song, 1127–1279), China underwent an economic revolution. A revolution in agriculture underpinned the advance: better soil preparation and conservation; improved seeds that often allowed more than one crop per season; better water control and irrigation; and more local specialization of crops. The new techniques were implemented most intensively in the lower Yangzi valley, as the Song moved south from China's historic northern base around the Yellow River. Indeed, they maintained regional capitals, two of which served as national capitals: Kaifeng in the north and Hangzhou in the south, near the mouth of the Yangzi. Thanks to the invention of woodblock printing in the ninth century under the Tang dynasty, ideas could spread in China more rapidly than anywhere else. One of the first uses of print had been to conserve and spread religious concepts; the oldest printed book extant in the world is a copy of the Buddhist *Diamond Sutra* from 868. Now the new method of printing was put into the service of disseminating the new farming methods.

Agricultural improvements—plus China's traditional excellence in textile production and remarkable innovations in the most advanced coal and iron industry in the world—inspired a trade revolution. Common people became involved in the mass production of goods for sale. Domestically this included the production of military goods for the Song army of over one million men; internationally it emphasized traditional silks and porcelain ceramics now supplemented with the export of iron and steel products. Trade became monetized, with copper as the principal currency. Chinese currency was so popular in Japan at this time that it became the most important medium of trade. Chinese ships sailed as far as East Africa, returning with exotic goods, such as gold, ivory, tortoise-shell, rhinoceros horns (regarded as aphrodisiacs), leopard skins, ambergris, and some slaves. Large numbers of Song coins were excavated in Zanzibar in 1888. Ships returning from Southeast Asia also brought luxuries: aromatic herbs and spices, rhinoceros horns, pearls, and camphor. From Arabian lands came frankincense.

In 1024, in Sichuan province, China, paper money was printed for the first time in the world. (Sometimes the government printed an excess of paper money, giving rise to inflation.) Merchants invented new credit mechanisms to facilitate trade. Government control of trade, quite marked under the Tang, was sharply reduced in favor of greater market freedom and trade made up an increasing share of government revenue. Customs offices in the nine official ports, especially the largest, Canton and Zaitun (Quanzhou), collected import taxes of 10 to 15 percent of the value of goods. In 1128, maritime trade brought in 20 percent of China's total cash revenues. Merchants were valued for the taxes the state could collect from them. Those who paid the most were rewarded with official rank.

The great luxury products of China—silk, porcelain, and tea—continued to attract thousands of foreign merchants as they had since Tang times. Many were Muslim Arabs. A few Lombards, Germans, and French were also present. They were treated as welcome guests, and special quarters in the port cities were set aside for them. In issues that involved no Chinese but only these foreigners, they could apply their own laws. Shops with foreign goods and foreign schools catered to their interests. Nevertheless, these merchants followed Chinese commercial rules, and many became quite Sinicized in their manners. When they ended their sojourn in China, they were feted with large farewell feasts.

The international merchants were at the peak of a highly integrated national system of trade and commerce, a system that was built on domestic and international water transport. To integrate the system of waterways, portage of goods was arranged at points of dangerous rapids and cataracts. To ensure smooth passage, double locks were installed on the man-made Grand Canal, which extended from Hangzhou in the

River traffic at Qing Ming festival, Kaifeng, by Zhang Zeduan, Song dynasty scroll. The multitude of Chinese junks on the Yellow River suggest the well-developed channels of trade in northern China. (*National Palace Museum, Taiwan*)

SOURCE

River Trade in China

Just as the vast and profitable trade in silk depended ultimately on the hard work of millions of spinners and weavers and their families, so river trade in China depended, at least partially, on the investments of common people. The three sources below support that assertion. The first is from Marco Polo attesting to the abundance of river trade in China. The second is from Pao Hui, writing in the thirteenth century about the financing of overseas river trade. The third is a Song dynasty scroll illustrating the multitude of Chinese junks sailing on the Yellow River at Kaifeng.

First, Marco Polo writing of the Yangzi River:

I assure that this river runs for such a distance and through so many regions and there are so many cities on its banks that truth to tell, in the amount of shipping it carries and the total volume and value of its traffic, it exceeds all the rivers of the Christians put together and their seas into the bargain. I give you my word that I have seen in this city [I-ching] fully five thousand ships at once, all afloat on this river. Then you may reflect, since this city, which is not very big has so many ships, how many there must be in the others. (cited in Elvin, pp. 144–5)

Then compare Pao Hui on the financing of river trade in Southern Song China:

All the people along the coast are on intimate terms with the merchants who engage in overseas trade, either because they are fellow countrymen or personal acquaintances. Leakage [of copper currency] through entrusting occurs when the former give the latter money to take with them on their ships for the purchase and return conveyance of foreign goods. They invest from ten to a hundred strings of cash, and regularly make profits of several hundred per cent. (Shiba Yoshinobu, p. 33)

Finally, examine Zhang Zeduan's twelfth-century scroll painting, Going on the River at the Qingming Festival. *At this time, the city of Kaifeng, situated on the Yellow River and at the crossroads of some of China's most important canals, was the hub of water-borne traffic for all of northern China. Inland Kaifeng and Hangzhou, on the coast, were China's most important regional capitals. They formed the apex of a regional system of urbanization that unified the whole country.*

Market towns sprang up throughout China, enabling virtually every rural family to sell its products for cash and to buy city goods. In turn, the small market towns were linked to larger cities, which provided more specialized products and access to government administrators. Here, families could buy and sell, arrange a marriage, determine the latest government rulings, hear about new farming possibilities, learn the dates and the results of academic examinations. These towns were so widespread that nearly every farm family lived within reach of one.

At the base were the rural families, struggling to survive by producing commodities demanded by the traders. Hand manufacture, especially of cotton and silk cloth, often supplemented farm production in rural areas. Invention made the process more productive. In particular a reeling machine, invented around the eleventh century, drew several silk filaments at once from silkworm cocoons immersed in boiling water. It then drew the filaments through eyelets and hooks and finally banded them into silk thread.

The rural producers were integrated into the market system either through direct, personal access or through brokers who supplied raw materials and bought the finished product. Women were the chief producers in this supplemental rural industry. They also carried the finished product to market. Conditions of production and of marketing could be savage. Xu Xianzhong's "Prose Poem on Cotton Cloth" presents the harshness of both aspects. It is not clear whether the women in the marketplace are selling their cloth, or themselves, or both:

Why do you ignore their toil? Why
  are you touched
Only by the loveliness that is born
  from toil?
…
Shall I tell you how their work
  exhausts them?
By hand and treadle they turn the
  rollers of wood and iron,
Feeling their fibre in between their
  fingers;
The cotton comes out fluffy and the
  seeds fall away.
The string of the cotton bow is
  stretched so taut
It twangs with a sob from its pillar.
They draw out slivers, spin them on
  their wheels
To the accompaniment of a medley
  of creakings.
Working through the darkness by
  candlelight,
Forgetful of bed. When energy ebbs,
  they sing.
The quilts are cold. Unheard, the
  waterclock flows over.
…
When a woman leaves for market
She does not look at her hungry
  husband.
Afraid her cloth's not good enough,
She adorns her face with cream and
  powder,
Touches men's shoulders to arouse
  their lust,
And sells herself with pleasant
  words.
Money she thinks of as a beast its
  prey;
Merchants she coaxes as she would
  her father.
Nor is her burden lifted till one buys.
  (Elvin, pp. 273–4)

south to administrative centers, including Beijing, in the north; this system helped to link the agricultural wealth of the south with the administrative cities of the north. Tugboats with human-powered paddle-wheels serviced the main ports. Chinese oceangoing ships, equipped with axial rudders, watertight bulkheads, and magnetic compasses, gained a reputation as the best in the world.

THE MONGOLS

The Song dynasty (960–1279) developed the waterways of China, but the great Central Asian overland silk routes had declined after the ninth century along with the Abbasid and Tang dynasties that had protected and encouraged them. Under the Mongol Empire (1206–1405), the largest land empire ever known, traffic on the silk routes revived.

The two million Mongols who inhabited the plateau region of Central Asia were divided into several warring tribes, each led by a *khan*. The land was poor and the climate harsh. The Mongols shepherded their cattle, sheep, and goats in a circular pattern of migration called transhumance: in the brief summers they moved their herds northward to pasture; in winter they turned back south. They spent most of their waking hours on horseback and mastered the art of warfare from the stirrups, with bow and arrow as well as sword by their side.

The "Pax Mongolica"

Cultural historians credit the Mongols with little permanent contribution because they were absorbed into other, more settled and sophisticated cultures. But they did establish, for about a century, the "Pax Mongolica," the Mongolian Peace, over a vast region, in which intercontinental trade could flourish across the reopened silk route. Reports from two world travelers, Ibn Battuta (1304–68) of Morocco and Marco Polo (1254–1324) of Venice, give vivid insights into that exotic trade route.

During his thirty years and 73,000 miles of travel, Ibn Battuta commented extensively on conditions of travel and trade. For example, in Central Asia Ibn Battuta encountered a military expedition of Oz Beg Khan (d. 1341), the ruler of the khanate of the Golden Horde:

> We saw a vast city on the move with its inhabitants, with mosques and bazaars in it, the smoke of the kitchens rising in the air (for they cook while on the march), and horse-drawn wagons transporting the people. (Dunn, p. 167)

yurts A portable dwelling used by the nomadic people of Central Asia, consisting of a tentlike structure of skin, felt, or hand-woven textiles arranged over wooden poles, simply furnished with brightly colored rugs.

The tents of this camp/city were Mongol **yurts**. Made of wooden poles covered with leather pelt, and with rugs on the floor, the yurts could be disassembled quickly for travel.

Later, Ibn Battuta was granted his request to travel with one of Oz Beg Khan's wives along the trade route as she returned to her father's home in Constantinople to give birth to her child. Ibn Battuta reported that the princess traveled with 5000 horsemen under military command, 500 of her own troops and servants, 200 female slave girls, 20 Greek and Indian pages, 400 wagons, 2000 horses, and about 500 oxen and camels. They crossed from Islamic Mongol territory to Christian Byzantium.

Marco Polo was a merchant in a family of merchants, and his account of his travels to and in China was thus particularly attuned to patterns of trade. His numerous descriptions of urban markets support the idea of an urban-centered trade diaspora. For example, consider Marco Polo's description of Tabriz in northwest Persia:

HOW DO WE KNOW?

The Mongol Empire

Because it was the largest contiguous land empire in history, understanding the entire Mongol Empire requires language competence in Mongolian, Chinese, Persian, Arabic, Turkish, Japanese, Russian, Armenian, Georgian, and Latin. No scholar can be expected to master all of these languages, but serious scholars are expected to know at least one or two of them and to use others in translation. Surprisingly, Mongolian may not be the most important. Before Chinggis Khan, the language was not written and there are no archives of the Mongol Empire, at least none that have survived. The only major historical text in Mongolian is The Secret History of the Mongols, and, although some scholars think it inauthentic, it is our principal source for the biography of Chinggis Khan. Another text from the days of Chinggis Khan, the Altan Debter, or Golden Book, is lost, but Persian and Chinese historians mention it, and their references show the book to be consistent with, although not the same as, The Secret History.

Chinese and Persian texts are the next most important, discussing Mongol rule over the two empires flanking, and captured by, the Mongol Empire. In China, the major text is the official dynastic history of the Yuan, or Mongol, dynasty. In Persia, several authors are important, most notably Rashid al-Din. Until his time, the Mongol conquest posed a problem for Muslim historians: The conquest of the Abbasid Empire was not supposed to happen. Muslims were to conquer others, as they had done with great consistency; they were not supposed to be conquered themselves. During Rashid al-Din's time, however, the Mongols converted to Islam. Rashid al-Din must have understood this well, since he himself had converted from Judaism. Rashid al-Din wrote the history of the Mongol Empire which, he said, marked a new era in world history. Later, he wrote Jami' al-tawarikh, a Collection of Histories, recording the history of all the peoples touched by the Mongols from the Chinese in the east to the Franks in the west. It was the first example of the form of a world history. For the last twenty years of his life, until he was assassinated as the result of a court intrigue in 1318, Rashid al-Din served as principal adviser to the Il-Khan ruler of Persia.

Distant Europe held relatively little importance for the Mongols, but a number of European sources discuss their conquests. These included men such as Giovanni de Piano Carpini, who was sent by Pope Innocent IV to visit the Khans, and William of Rubruck, who visited the Mongols at the behest of the king of France, Louis IX. The most comprehensive account is by Matthew Paris, who chronicled European reactions to the Mongol advances from his post at St. Albans, England, but the most popular came from travelers, of whom the most famous was Marco Polo.

- Mongolian may not be the most important language in the study of the Mongolian empire, yet the most important biography of Chinggis Khan is in Mongolian. How do you explain this paradox?
- Why are Chinese and Persian important languages for studying the Mongol Empire?
- Would you consider Rashid-al-Din's Collection of Histories a history of the world? Why or why not?

The people of Tabriz live by trade and industry; for cloth of gold and silk is woven here in great quantity and of great value. The city is so favourably situated that it is a market for merchandise from India and Baghdad, from Mosul and Hormuz, and from many other places; and many Latin merchants come here to buy the merchandise imported from foreign lands. It is also a market for precious stones, which are found here in great abundance. It is a city where good profits are made by traveling merchants. The inhabitants are a mixed lot and good for very little. There are Armenians and Nestorians, Jacobites and Georgians and Persians; and there are also worshippers of Mahomet, who are the natives of the city and are called Tabrizis. (Marco Polo, p. 57)

Central Asian routes challenged travelers and their animals. Despite the Pax Mongolica, merchants still had to be prepared to defend themselves from attack. As Marco Polo recounts:

Among the people of these kingdoms there are many who are brutal and bloodthirsty. They are forever slaughtering one another; and, were it not for fear of the government … they would do great mischief to traveling merchants. The government imposes severe penalties upon them and has ordered that along all dangerous routes the inhabitants at the request of the merchants shall supply good and efficient escorts from district to district for their safe conduct on payment of two or three groats for each loaded beast according to the length of the journey. Yet, for all that the government can do, these brigands are not to be deterred from frequent depredations. Unless the merchants are well armed and equipped with bows, they slay and harry them unsparingly. (Polo, p. 61)

For those merchants and statesmen who did reach Beijing, the Khan maintained a massive service industry to provide hospitality. Polo noted, in particular, an army of prostitutes:

I assure you that there are fully 20,000 of them, all serving the needs of men for money. They have a captain general, and there are chiefs of hundreds and of thousands responsible to the captain. This is because, whenever ambassadors come to the Great Khan on his business and are maintained at his expense, which is done on a lavish scale, the captain is called upon to provide one of these women every night for the ambassador and one for each of his attendants. They are changed each night and receive no payment; for this is the tax they pay to the Great Khan. (Polo, p. 129)

Almost everything we know about Marco Polo's life is based on the colorful account he left us of his travels through Asia. Little is known of his childhood years in Venice or his education. Marco's father and uncle, both Venetian merchants, traveled from their home in 1260 on a trade mission as far as the northern end of the Caspian Sea. Then war broke out, and their route back home was blocked. But the route eastward was open, so the brothers traveled on to Beijing, where Chinggis Khan's grandson, Kublai Khan (1215–94), ruled.

The Great Khan invited the men to return with more information on Christianity and a delegation from the pope. The information and delegation never materialized, but in 1271 the two brothers, along with the seventeen-year-old Marco, set out for China again. They arrived in 1275 and remained there for seventeen years. How exactly they occupied themselves during this time is unclear from Marco's account, but it was not uncommon for foreigners to find employment in the Mongol state. Kublai Khan, it appears, was so enchanted by Marco's tales of foreign lands that he sent him on repeated reconnaissance trips throughout the empire. The Polos eventually set off for home in about 1292, reaching Venice in 1295 and reuniting with relatives and friends who had believed them long-since dead.

Soon after his homecoming, Marco was captured in battle by Genoese sailors and imprisoned. He dictated the tales of his travels to his fellow prisoner Rustichello, a writer of romances. Europe now had its most complete and consistent account up to that date of the silk route and of the fabulous Chinese empire of Kublai Khan. Marco's *Travels* was soon translated into several European languages, introducing to Christian Europe a new understanding of the world.

For seven centuries scholars have hotly debated the authenticity of Marco Polo's account. No original copy of *The Travels* exists, and scholars have been faced with some 140 manuscript versions that were copied in various languages and dialects from scribe to scribe before the invention of printing. Frances Wood, head of the China Department at the British Library, has asked, *Did Marco Polo Go to China?* (1996). Wood emphasizes the arguments against. Polo did not mention any of the phenomena that should have caught his attention during his reported time in China: Chinese writing, tea, chopsticks, foot binding, the Great Wall. Despite his claims to frequent meetings with Kublai Khan, Marco Polo is not mentioned in any Chinese records of the time. Wood concludes that Polo's work is actually based on materials gathered from others and that he himself never traveled beyond the Black Sea. As a travel narrative, Wood asserts, the book was a fabrication, but as an account of what was known of China at the time, it was a very rich and very influential source of information. Many commentators are therefore equally adamant that Polo did complete all the travels that he claimed, and the debate over the extent of Marco Polo's own travels continues.

Chinggis Khan

Chinggis (Genghis) Khan Temujin, later called Chinggis (Genghis) Khan, was born about 1162 into one of the more powerful and more militant Mongol tribes. His father, chief of his tribe, was poisoned by a rival tribe. About three generations before Temujin's birth, one of his ancestors, Kabul Khan, had briefly united the Mongols, and Chinggis made it his own mission to unify them once again. He conquered the surrounding tribes, one by one, and united them at Karakorum, his capital. Although skilled at negotiation, Chinggis was also infamous for his brutality. Historian Rashid al-Din (1247–1318), writing almost a century after his conquests, reports Chinggis Khan's declaration of purpose, emphasizing women as the spoils of warfare:

> Man's greatest good fortune is to chase and defeat his enemy, seize all his possessions, leave his married women weeping and wailing, ride his gelding, and use the bodies of his women as a nightshirt and support, gazing upon and kissing their rosy breasts, sucking their lips which are as sweet as the berries of their breasts. (cited in Ratchnevsky, p. 153)

Chinggis defeated the Tartars and killed all surviving males taller than a cart axle. He defeated the rival Mongol clans and boiled alive all their chiefs. In 1206, an assembly of all the chiefs of the steppe regions proclaimed him Chinggis Khan—"Universal Ruler." He organized them for further battle under a pyramid of officers leading units of 100, 1000, and 10,000 mounted warriors, commanded, as they grew older, by his four sons. Promotion within the fighting machine was by merit. Internal feuding among the Mongols ended and a new legal code, based on written and recorded case law, called for high moral standards from all Mongols.

Chinggis turned east toward China. On the way he captured the Tangut kingdom of Xixia, and from Chinese engineers he mastered the weapons of siege warfare: the mangonel and trebuchet, which could catapult great rocks; giant crossbows mounted on stands; and gunpowder, which could be launched from longbows in bamboo-tube rockets. In 1211 Chinggis pierced the Great Wall of China, and in 1215 he conquered the capital, Zhongdu (modern Beijing), killing thousands.

Chinggis departed from China to conquer other kingdoms. His officials and successors continued moving south, however, until they

Chinggis Khan, from Rashid al-Din's world history, 13th century. Chinggis Khan's conquests had as much impact on West Asia as they did on China. This Persian illustration of Chinggis pursuing his enemies comes from a history, which some consider to be the first world history, written by Rashid al-Din (1247–1318), a Persian administrator employed by Mongol Il-Khans in Iran. (*Bibliothèque Nationale, Paris*)

captured all of China, establishing the Mongol dynasty, 1276–1368. They conquered Korea, large parts of Southeast Asia as far as Java, and attempted, but failed, to take Japan as well. The planned assault on Japan in 1281 was stopped by *kamikaze*, divine winds, which prevented the Mongol fleet from sailing.

Chinggis himself turned west, conquering the Kara-Khitai Empire, which included the major cities of Tashkent and Samarkand. He turned southward toward India, reaching the Indus River and stationing troops in the Punjab, but he was unable to penetrate further. Turning northwest, he proceeded to conquer Khwarizm. In the great cities of Bukhara, Nishapur, Merv, Herat, Balkh, and Gurgan, millions were reported killed, an exaggeration, but still an indication of great slaughter. Chinggis went on to capture Tabriz and Tbilisi.

After Chinggis's death in 1227, his four sons continued the expansion relentlessly. In the northwest they defeated the Bulgars along the Volga and the Cumans of the southern steppes and then entered Russia. They took Moscow, destroyed Kiev, overran Moravia and Silesia, and set their sights on the conquest of Hungary. To the terrified peoples in their path, it looked as if nothing could stop the Mongols' relentless expansion. But in 1241, internal quarrels did what opposing armies could not: they brought the Mongol advance in Europe to a halt. During the dispute over succession that followed the death of Chinggis's son Ogedei (1185–1241), the Mongols withdrew east of Kiev. They never resumed their westward movement, and central and western Europe remained untouched.

The Mongol successor states. After the death of Chinggis Khan's grandson Mongke in 1259, the Mongol world devolved into four successor states. Kublai Khan's emerged as the most powerful, but only after a long struggle with Song China. In Central Asia, the Chagatai dominated the eastern steppe; the Golden Horde became established in southwest Russia; and the Il-Khan in Persia ruled from Kabul to Anatolia.

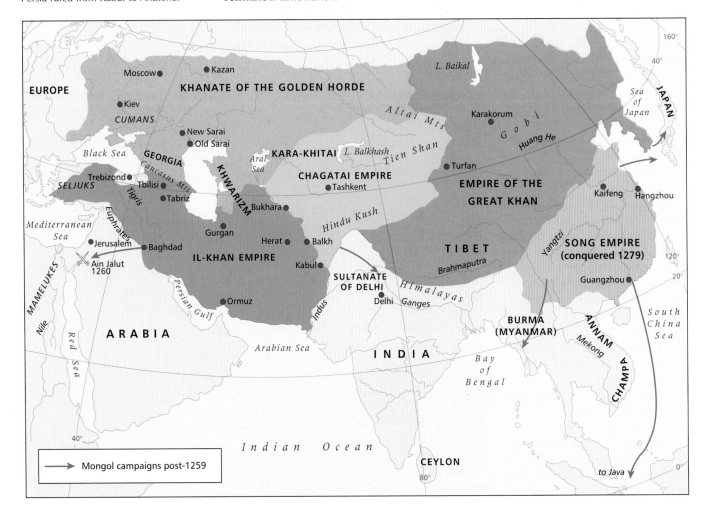

Mongol campaigns post-1259

In the southwest, under Chinggis's grandson Hulegu (*c.* 1217–65), the Mongols captured and destroyed Baghdad in 1258, ending the five-century-old Abbasid dynasty by killing the caliph. But in the next year, Mongke, Chinggis's grandson and the fourth and last successor to his title as "Great Khan," died while campaigning in China, and many of the Mongol forces withdrew to attend a general conclave in Karakorum to choose his successor. In 1260, Mongol forces were defeated by a Mamluk army at the battle of Ain Jalut, in modern Jordan, and never again pushed further to the southwest.

The End of the Mongol Empire

Mongol rule was extensive but brief. At their apogee, 1279–1350, the Mongols had ruled all of China, almost all of Russia, Iran, Iraq, and Central Asia. The huge empire was administered and ruled through four separate geographical *khanates*, or sub-empires, each under the authority of a branch of Chinggis Khan's family. Over time central authority declined and the four khanates separated, each becoming an independent empire.

The Mongols could not govern their empire from horseback, and they were soon absorbed by the peoples they had conquered. They intermarried freely with the Turks who had joined them as allies in conquest. In Russia, Mongols and Turks merged with Slavs and Finns in a new Turkish-speaking ethnic group, the Tartars. In Persia and China they assimilated into local culture, converting to various religions, including Christianity, Buddhism, and Confucianism. In most of the areas inhabited by Muslims, the Mongols and their Turkish allies typically converted to Islam.

As the four segments of Chinggis's empire went their own separate ways, slowly they were driven from their conquests. By 1335 the male line of Chinggis and his grandson Hulegu died out in the Il-Khan Empire in Persia. The Ming dynasty defeated and evicted the Mongol (or Yuan) rulers in 1368. The Chagatai khanate was destroyed by Timur the Lame (Tamerlane) after 1369. The Russians pushed out the Golden Horde (named not, as one might think, for their numbers, but for their tents, *Ordu* in Turkish) more slowly. The last Mongol state in the Crimea was conquered only in the eighteenth century.

Plague and the Trade Routes

In addition to commerce and religion, disease also followed the trade routes. An unexpected side effect of the Pax Mongolica was the spread of a plague—called the Black Death—that devastated Eurasia's population in the 1300s. Until recently this mortal disease was believed to be the bubonic plague, but research within the last decade suggests that it may have been a different, unknown, disease. Whatever the disease was, it apparently followed the Mongols from Central Asia into China in 1331 and decimated its population. China's population, estimated at 123 million in 1200, dropped to 65 million in the census of 1393. Part of the decrease was caused by warfare between Chinese and Mongols, but a large part must also have been caused by the plague.

Along the silk routes, after the mid-fourteenth century, the presence and the role of the Mongols declined, probably also as a result of plague deaths. The plague reached the Crimea in 1346. There, plague-infested rats boarded ships, disembarking with the disease at all the ports of Europe and the Near East.

Within the next five years, in Europe, where the plague was new and people had no natural immunity, one-third of the population died. The ravages of the plague fore-shadowed further, even worse epidemics that would sweep across the continents of

The routes of the plague. The central and east Asian stability imposed by Mongol rule—the "Mongol Peace"—brought mixed benefits. Trade flourished, and travelers such as Ibn Battuta and Marco Polo were able to write remarkable accounts of the lands they visited. At the same time, however, vectors for other travelers, such as the rats that carried bubonic plague, also opened up. The Black Death, originating in Central Asia, was one of a succession of plagues that followed the trade routes by land and sea, decimating parts of Europe and China.

the New World, as groups of people who had not previously been exposed to one another's diseases began to meet for the first time (see Chapter 14).

From Mongol to Ming: Dynastic Transition

During the ninety years of Mongol rule, 1279–1368, China's population plummeted from a high of 100 million to just over 50 million. Despite the splendor of Kublai Khan in his capital at Beijing, the Chinese economy did not serve everyone equally well. Marco Polo told of especially bitter poverty and class division in south China where the Han Chinese of the Southern Song dynasty experienced Mongol rule as cruel and exploitative:

> In the province of Manzi almost all the poor and needy sell some of their sons and daughters to the rich and noble, so that they may support themselves on the price paid for them and the children may be better fed in their new homes. (Polo, p. 227)

Revolution simmered until 1368, when the Ming dynasty overthrew the Mongols and ruled for almost three centuries, until 1644.

Under the Ming dynasty, the population increased sharply. By 1450 it had reached 100 million again, and by 1580 the population was at least 130 million. Plagues and rebellions again caused the population to fall back to 100 million by 1650, but from that trough it rose consistently into present times.

The population settled new territories as it grew. The origins of the Chinese Empire had been in the Yellow River valley in the north (see Chapter 4). At the time of the Han dynasty, more than 80 percent of the population of China lived north of the Yangzi valley. Under the late Tang dynasty, the population was divided about equally between north and south. Warfare with the Mongols in the north drove more migrants south, and at the height of the Mongol dynasty up to 90 percent of the population lived in the south. Economically, the south produced rice, cotton, and tea, three of China's most valuable products, not available in the northern climate. Closer to the sea lanes of Southeast Asia and the Indian Ocean, the south also developed China's principal ports for international commerce. The Song built a powerful navy and Chinese merchants carried on regular trade with Southeast Asia, India, and the Persian Gulf. After the Mongols were defeated, however, migration began to reverse. By about 1500, 75 percent lived in the south, and movement back to the north was continuing.

LEGACIES TO THE PRESENT
WHAT DIFFERENCE DO THEY MAKE?

The years shortly before and after 1500 marked a turning point in world trade patterns. Before 1500 trading routes criss-crossed Africa, Europe, and Asia. These routes connected with one another, but they were not unified into a single system of trade. Long-distance trade goods would travel in stages from one set of routes to the next, carried first by one set of traders and then transferred to another, as goods were transported to their final destination. The most important long-distance traders were the Muslim Arab sailors and merchants of the Indian Ocean routes and beyond to the ports of China. Chinese traders dominated the East Asian waterways and occasionally, and spectacularly, sailed into and across the Indian Ocean. At this time, few European traders journeyed into Asia. In the thirteenth century, Mongol rulers provided protection along the old silk routes, reopening these land passages through Central Asia.

The western hemisphere had two sets of regional routes—mostly unconnected with each other—one centering on Mesoamerica, the other on the Andes Mountains of South America. Except for rare voyages, the American routes and the Afro-Eurasian routes remained separated from each other by the vast expanses of the Atlantic and Pacific Oceans.

As European traders grew more powerful after 1500, they attempted to subordinate pre-existing regional systems to their own centralized control from European headquarters. Within a single generation they seized control of the Americas. Asian powers, however, were much less vulnerable and they tended to pay little attention to the newly arriving Europeans. China and Japan mostly kept them out. European control increased as northwestern Europe industrialized after 1750 (see Chapter 16). Then the European traders, and their governments, supported by new productivity at home, as well as new ships and new guns, began to declare supremacy in global trade. They challenged the legacies of Arab and Chinese supremacy in the east, and Native American isolation in the west, and began to introduce new regimes of trade and domination into world history.

Review Questions

- What is a "trade diaspora"? What was the importance of trade diasporas to the spread of world trade before 1500? What advantages did Jews and Muslims have for exercising world trade in the period 1000–1500?
- What were the principle inter-regional trading networks in 1300?
- What is a lateen sail? Where did it originate? What is its significance?
- How would you compare the relative importance of inland and overseas trade for China in the fifteenth century?
- How did the Mongol Empire facilitate world trade?

● Trace the rise of Arab seafaring to show how it came to be predominant in the Indian Ocean and South China Sea.

Suggested Readings

PRINCIPAL SOURCES

Abu-Lughod, Janet L. *Before European Hegemony: The World System A.D. 1250–1350* (New York: Oxford University Press, 1989). A résumé of the principal trade routes around 1250. Unfortunately omits African routes.

Adas, Michael, ed. *Islamic and European Expansion* (Philadelphia: Temple University Press, 1993). Key collection of historiographical essays on major topics in world history, 1200–1900. Articles by Eaton and Tucker on Islam, and McNeill on "gunpowder empires" are especially helpful for this unit.

Chaudhuri, K.N. *Trade and Civilization in the Indian Ocean: An Economic History from the Rise of Islam to 1750* (Cambridge: Cambridge University Press, 1985). A survey of goods, traders, ships, regulations, and competition among those who sailed and claimed to control the Indian Ocean.

Cortés, Hernán. *Letters from Mexico*, trans. from the Spanish and ed. by Anthony Pagden (New Haven: Yale University Press, 1986). Newest edition of Cortés' letters.

Curtin, Philip. *Cross-Cultural Trade in World History* (Cambridge: Cambridge University Press, 1984). Classical statement of the significance and ubiquity of trade diasporas.

Dunn, Ross. *The Adventures of Ibn Battuta* (Berkeley: University of California Press, 1986). Dunn uses Ibn Battuta and his travels as the center-point of an analysis of Islamic life throughout the Islamic ecumene in the fourteenth century.

Elvin, Mark. *The Pattern of the Chinese Past* (Stanford: Stanford University Press, 1973). Primarily economic history, focused heavily on the central questions of why China did so well economically until about 1700, and then why it did so badly after that time.

ADDITIONAL SOURCES

The Book of the Thousand Nights and a Night: A Plain and Literal Translation of the Arabian Nights Entertainment, 6 vols. in 3, trans. by Richard F. Burton (New York: Heritage Press, 1946).

Bentley, Jerry H. *Old World Encounters* (New York: Oxford University Press, 1993). Survey of the range of cross-cultural, long-distance encounters—especially through trade, religion, and culture—throughout Afro-Eurasia from earliest times to about 1500. Engaging.

Chaudhuri, K. N. *Asia Before Europe* (Cambridge: Cambridge University Press, 1990). Survey of the economic and political systems of Asia before the impact of colonialism and the industrial revolution. Comprehensive, comparative, and thoughtful.

Columbia College. Columbia University. *Introduction to Contemporary Civilization in the West*, Vol. I (New York: Columbia University Press, 2nd ed., 1954). Very well-chosen, long source readings from leading thinkers of the time and place. Vol. I covers *c.* 1000 to 1800.

Crosby, Alfred W. *Ecological Imperialism: The Biological Expansion of Europe, 900–1900* (Cambridge: Cambridge University Press, 1986). The biological—mostly destructive—impact of European settlement around the world, a tragedy for native peoples from the Americas to Oceania.

Frank, Andre Gunder and Barry K. Gills, eds. *The World System: Five Hundred Years or Five Thousand?* (London: Routledge, 1993). In this somewhat tendentious, but well argued, account, globalization is nothing new.

Ghosh, Amitav. *In an Antique Land* (New York: Knopf, 1993). A novel, travelogue, historical fiction of Indian Ocean exchanges in the twelfth century and today. Captivating. Much of the tale is based on the research in Goitein's study, below.

Goitein, Shelomo Dov. *A Mediterranean Society: The Jewish Communities of the Arab World as Portrayed in the Documents of the Cairo Genizah*, 6 vols. (Berkeley: University of California Press, 1967–83). Extraordinary research resulting from the examination of a discovered treasury of about ten thousand documents from about 1000–1300. Despite the title, gives insight into a variety of communities of the time.

Hanbury-Tenison, Robin. *The Oxford Book of Exploration* (New York: Oxford University Press, 1994). An excellent collection of primary sources on exploration.

Hourani, George Fadlo. *Arab Seafaring in the Indian Ocean in Ancient and Early Medieval Times* (Princeton: Princeton University Press, 1951, reprinted 1995). The standard introduction. Examines the trade routes and the ships prior to and after the coming of Islam.

Ibn Battuta. *Travels in Asia and Africa 1325–1354*, trans. and selected from the Arabic by H.A.R. Gibb (New Delhi: Saeed International, edition 1990). Selections from the writings of one of the greatest travelers in history.

Ibn Majid, Ahmad. *Arab Navigation in the Indian Ocean Before the Coming of the Portuguese*, trans., introduced, and annotated by G.R. Tibbetts (London: Royal Asiatic Society of Great Britain and Ireland, 1971). Translation of Ibn Majid's classic fifteenth-century guide for navigators, along with very extensive discussion by Tibbetts placing the author and work in context and discussing contemporary theories of navigation.

Komaroff, Linda and Stefano Carboni, eds. *The Legacy of Genghis Khan: Courtly Art and Culture in Western Asia, 1256–1353* (New York: Metropolitan Museum of Art and New Haven: Yale University Press, 2002). Lavishly illustrated catalogue of blockbuster art exhibit, with numerous interpretive essays as well.

Levathes, Louise. *When China Ruled the Seas: The Treasure Fleet of the Dragon Throne, 1405–33* (New York: Oxford University Press, 1996). Scholarly study of the expeditions of Zheng He.

Ma, Laurence J.C. *Commercial Development and Urban Change in Sung China (960–1279)* (Ann Arbor: Department of Geography, University of Michigan, 1971). Careful, scholarly, detailed research monograph.

Menzies, Gavin. *1421: The Year China Discovered America* (New York: William Morrow, 2003). Menzies brings together many scraps of evidence in concocting the argument that Zheng He actually did sail to America. The evidence does not hold.

Polanyi, Karl, Conrad M. Arensberg, and Harry W. Pearson, eds. *Trade and Market in the Early Empires* (Chicago: The Free Press, 1957). Fundamental argument by historical anthropologists that early trade was mostly regulated by rulers and priests.

Polo, Marco. *The Travels*, trans. from the French by Ronald Latham (London: Penguin Books, 1958). One of the most fascinating and influential travelogues ever written.

Ratchnevsky, Paul. *Genghis Khan: His Life and Legacy*, trans. and ed. by Thomas Nivison Haining (Oxford: Blackwell, 1991). The current standard biography of the personally elusive Chinggis Khan.

Raychaudhuri, Tapan and Irfan Habib, eds. *The Cambridge Economic History of India*. Vol. 1: *c. 122–c. 1750* (Cambridge: Cambridge University Press, 1982). Collection of articles of fundamental significance.

Risso, Patricia. *Merchants and Faith. Muslim Commerce and Culture in the Indian Ocean*. (Boulder: Westview Press, 1995). Among the questions explored: "What difference did it make to be a Muslim?"

Schele, Linda and David Freidel. *A Forest of Kings: The Untold Story of the Ancient Maya* (New York: William Morrow and Co., 1990). The story of the deciphering of the Mayan ideographs and the histories of warfare that they reveal, by two of the leading researchers.

Shaffer, Lynda Norene. *Maritime Southeast Asia to 1500* (Armonk, NY: M.E. Sharpe, 1996). Useful survey on the voyages, trade goods, markets, towns, and government of the region—from earliest times.

Shiba Yoshinobu. *Commerce and Society in Sung China*, trans. by Mark Elvin (Ann Arbor: Michigan Abstracts of Chinese and Japanese Works on Chinese History, 1970). Scholarly source materials with annotations from the economic transformation of the Song dynasty.

Skinner, G. William. "Marketing and Social Structure in Rural China," *Journal of Asian Studies* XXIV, No. 1 (November 1964), 3–43. Classic account of the interlocking structure of urban development in China from local market towns through national capitals of trade.

Toussaint, Auguste. *History of the Indian Ocean*. Trans. from the French by June Guicharnaud (Chicago: University of Chicago Press, 1966). Broad historical sweep of exploration, trade, cultural exchange, fighting, and rule in and of the Indian Ocean from earliest times to the 1960s. Very useful survey.

Wood, Frances. *Did Marco Polo Go to China?* (Boulder, CO: Westview Press, 1996). One of the more recent, and lucid, statements of the controversy.

◎ World History Documents CD-ROM

ILLE DE MAGELLAM

MER DV SV

EUROPEAN VISIONS

ECONOMIC GROWTH, RELIGION AND RENAISSANCE, GLOBAL CONNECTIONS 1100–1776

KEY TOPICS
- The Atlantic
- The Decline of Trade in the Mediterranean
- Trade and Social Change in Europe
- The Renaissance
- A New World
- Oceania

Until 1492 no continuous links connected the eastern and western hemispheres although there had certainly been some voyages between them. The expeditions of Leif Eriksson and other Vikings from Scandinavia around the year 1000 are well known, documented, and authenticated in the artifacts they left behind in their temporary settlements on the northeast coast of North America. Some of the foods of Polynesia—sweet potatoes and manioc—that apparently came from South America present evidence of other contacts, even more fleeting, across the Pacific. Permanent contact between the two major continental landmasses of the world was established, however, only with Christopher Columbus' conquest of the Atlantic Ocean in 1492. The consequences for the people of both hemispheres were enormous.

We have seen that three groups had the capacity to cross the oceans prior to Columbus' expedition. Polynesians and South Americans apparently made contact in some fashion, but neither felt the need to continue their brief encounter. Arab traders of the Indian Ocean probably had the shipping capacity to make the voyage to the Americas, but they also had no need. The Indian Ocean with its neighboring Mediterranean Sea and South China Sea provided all the trading opportunities they required. The Chinese, who were capable of dispatching fleets as far as East Africa, had the capacity, but the imperial decision to terminate these voyages ended their explorations. The Europeans, except for the Vikings, also did not venture out so long as the ports of the Middle East provided access to the great markets of Asia. Only when that access was reduced and profits were curtailed, and when their own economies and technologies grew stronger, did their imaginations expand. Even then, the western Europeans who set off exploring were not looking for new lands, but only for new routes to well-known markets. Columbus did not realize that he had discovered two new continents. In this chapter we discuss the great voyages of exploration of Columbus, Vespucci, Magellan, Tasman, and Cook, who opened new oceanic perspectives to an incredulous world.

THE ATLANTIC

From the eighth until the twelfth century, the European north Atlantic was primarily the province of marauding sailors and raiders from the north. These Vikings were the ancestors of today's Norwegians, Swedes, and Danes. They were also colonizers, fishermen, and traders. One group from Norway began to settle Iceland around 870 and Greenland about 982. Under Leif Eriksson they reached Newfoundland in North America about 1000 and established a settlement there as well, but it did not endure. Danes and Norwegians plundered along the entire Atlantic coast of Europe, with

Opposite **French caravel, 1555. Watercolor on paper.** The sturdy caravel, adapted by Europeans from the Arab ships of the Indian Ocean, became the ship of choice for oceanic exploration. Columbus and Vasco da Gama both sailed in caravels. By arming his caravel with cannon, Gama transformed it into a weapon of war.

The Arrival of King Sweyn and Danish Troops in England, 11th century. Vellum. Sweyn Forkbeard (*c.* 987–1014), a formidable Viking warrior from Denmark, created a Danish North Sea empire, gaining control over Norway (1000) and conquering England (1013). He is shown here disembarking from his warship.

especially early and devastating attacks on Lindisfarne off the northern coast of England (793), Dorestad in Frisia (834), and Nantes in France (842), where they murdered the bishop and all his clergy. In 859 they sailed through the Strait of Gibraltar and attacked ports along the Mediterranean. Arabs from North Africa and Spain were launching similar attacks in the Mediterranean at about the same time.

These Vikings were also traders and colonizers who often fostered urban development and trade in the places they conquered. They founded the town of Dublin, in Ireland, in 841, and they conquered much of northern England, establishing the kingdom of York in the 870s. Vikings also conquered the French territory of Normandy in the late eighth century, from where in 1066 their leader, William of Normandy (William the Conqueror), conquered England. The Normans, as these "Northmen" came to be known, also founded a kingdom in southern Italy and Sicily and established a principality in Antioch.

The Swedes turned eastward across the Baltic Sea and founded trading cities along the river systems of Russia, establishing their capital first at Novgorod in the early ninth century and in Kiev in 882. They proceeded all the way south to the Black Sea, where they traded with the Byzantine Empire. The Swedish settlements became catalysts for the formation of the political and economic organization of the Slavic people in whose midst they were established. Kiev became the capital of the first Russian state; its people were called the "Rus." Historians continue to debate whether that term refers to the Vikings, the Slavs, or the hybrid group that emerged as the Slavic majority assimilated the Viking minority. By about 1000 the fierce Vikings became more peaceful, and their raids ceased as their home regions of Scandinavia developed into organized states and accepted Christianity. They lost interest in further exploration westward across the ocean.

Voyages across the north Atlantic, except those of the Vikings, are not recorded historically and are unlikely to have occurred. In the south Atlantic even less travel took place. There is no known crossing of the south Atlantic. Africans carried on only limited coastal shipping and Europeans were frightened of the unknown hazards of the west African coast, especially south of Cape Bojador. In addition, they recognized that the prevailing winds on the African coast blew from north to south and they feared that while they might be able to proceed to the south they might not be able to return north.

THE DECLINE OF TRADE IN THE MEDITERRANEAN

As Arab armies swept across the Middle East and North Africa, they hesitated before taking to sea battles in the Mediterranean Sea. Nevertheless, in 643 they captured

Scandinavian and Arab Muslim, and East Slav invasions, 9th–10th centuries. Europe was subjected to repeated invasions that temporarily weakened the continent but then increased its power. The Vikings settled and developed Scandinavia, and their interaction with the Slavs gave shape to Russia. The Muslims brought with them an understanding of the culture of ancient Greece and Rome that Europeans had forgotten. (Adapted from *The Times Atlas of World History*, 5th edition. London. Times Books.)

Alexandria, the most important port in the eastern Mediterranean, and in 655 they engaged and defeated a fleet of the Byzantine Empire at Dhat al-Sawari, off the southwestern coast of modern Turkey. They established their dominion by land along the eastern and southern coasts of the Mediterranean and had enough sea power in the eastern Mediterranean to hold their own against the Byzantine Empire, and even to expand. By about 950 they held parts of southern Italy as well as major islands in the Mediterranean: Cyprus, Crete, and Sicily. The southern and southeastern Mediterranean had become a "Muslim lake." The Byzantine Empire continued, however, to control the northeastern shores of the Mediterranean, and various Frankish and Germanic Christian powers held the north-central coast. The Mediterranean Sea, and its coastline, were divided into three major cultural and political spheres of control: Muslim to the south and southeast, Byzantine to the northeast, and Roman Catholic to the northwest. The Mediterranean is so large and so diverse that such divisions seem natural enough. (Look carefully at the accompanying map of the Mediterranean Sea on page 429 to see the many islands and peninsulas and the many smaller seas that mark its inlets.)

Three developments followed these divisions. First, the Mediterranean once again became a war zone. Battles between the Christians of southern Europe and the Muslims of the Middle East and North Africa persisted from the eighth century until 1571, when the naval Battle of Lepanto, in Greek waters, fixed generally accepted zones of control between them. Second, trade continued but oscillated with the fate of Europe's internal economy and with warfare in the Mediterranean. Finally, in the southeastern Mediterranean, where land separated the Mediterranean Sea from the Indian Ocean—where today the Suez Canal provides that link—the European merchants felt blocked. The valuable and profitable merchandise coming from the Indian Ocean basin—the spices of India and Indonesia; the silk and porcelain of China; and the gold and ivory and slaves of East Africa—were controlled by Middle Eastern Muslim traders. The eastern Mediterranean trade blockage is often seen as a religious confrontation. On several occasions, for example, popes forbade Catholics to trade with Muslims. But

AT A GLANCE : MEDIEVAL WORLD TRADE

DATE	POLITICAL/SOCIAL EVENTS	TRADE DEVELOPMENTS	EXPLORATION
1050 C.E.	■ Normans under William I invade England (1066) ■ Seljuk Turks take Baghdad ■ Franks invade Anatolia and Syria and found Crusader states	■ Venice dominates Adriatic; trading ports set up throughout eastern Mediterranean (1000–1100)	
1100 C.E.		■ Wool trade flourishing between England and Flanders	
1150 C.E.	■ Salah al-Din, sultan of Turkish Syria and Egypt, retakes Jerusalem (1187) ■ St. Francis of Assisi (1181–1226) ■ St. Dominic (1170–1221) ■ St. Clare of Assisi (1194–1253)	■ Market fairs in the Champagne region, France	
1200 C.E.		■ Rise of craft guilds in towns of western Europe ■ Foundation of Hanseatic League (1241)	
1250 C.E.		■ Increasing Venetian links with Central Asia and China (1255–95) ■ Revolt of craftspeople in Flanders	
1300 C.E.	■ Hundred Years War between England and France (1337–1453) ■ Bubonic plague in Europe (1346–50)	■ West Africa provides two-thirds of the gold of the eastern hemisphere	
1350 C.E.	■ Ghettoization of Jews in western Europe ■ Ashigawa Shoguns dominate Japan (1338–1573)	■ Revolts of urban workers in Italy and Flanders	
1400 C.E.	■ Ottoman Turks establish foothold in Europe at Gallipoli	■ Great Chinese naval expeditions reach east coast of Africa and India under Zheng He	■ Portugal's Prince Henry the Navigator sponsors expeditions to West Africa
1450 C.E.	■ Printing of Gutenberg's Bible (1455) ■ War of the Roses in England (1453–85) ■ Turks capture Constantinople (1453) ■ Jews driven from Spain (1492) ■ Treaty of Tordesillas (1494)	■ Medici family in Florence: Giovanni, Cosimo, Lorenzo	■ Bartholomeu Dias sails round Cape of Good Hope (1488) ■ Columbus reaches the Americas (1492) ■ Vasco da Gama reaches the Malabar coast, India (1498)
1500 C.E.	■ Machiavelli, The Prince (1513) ■ Muslims in Spain forced to convert or leave	■ Portugal sets up trading port of Goa, in India (1502); Portuguese ships armed with cannon	■ Ferdinand Magellan's voyage round globe (1519–22)

For an interactive version of this map, go to: http://www.prenhall.com/spodek/map13.2

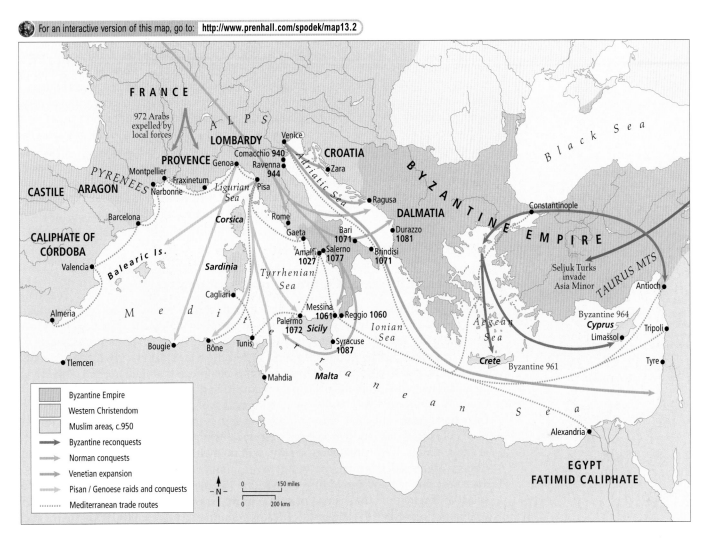

these prohibitions were generally disregarded. More critical was the competition for profits among the many different groups of traders. The Muslim traders themselves were not a unified group. Most were Arabs, but many of the Egyptian traders were Mamluks, and later Seljuk and Ottoman Turks invaded the area as well. Among the European trading communities, many felt that the city-state of Venice, with its skilled merchants and sailors, controlled the eastern Mediterranean trade in spices, cotton, and silk textiles for its own advantage. Religious and ethnic differences may have exaggerated the tensions among the traders, but the main contest was the competition for profits.

In search of higher profits and easier access to trade commodities, some merchants and some princes began seeking alternative routes to the Indian Ocean. This search took on special intensity in western Europe, which was geographically farther from the Middle East and closer to the Atlantic. Beginning in 1277, a maritime route between Italy and Spain in the Mediterranean and England and Flanders in northwestern Europe brought regular trade to the north Atlantic seacoast of Europe. Also, European trade generally was picking up in the early fifteenth century, as the continent recovered from the devastation of the plague. One search now began to explore the southern Atlantic Ocean for routes around the coast of Africa to India; another sought routes directly across the north Atlantic.

European resurgence in the Mediterranean, c. 1000. After centuries of attacks from Vikings and Muslims, the Europeans of the Mediterranean began to fight back effectively, but the Mediterranean continued as a zone of intermittent warfare between Christians and Muslims until the Battle of Lepanto, 1571. (Adapted from *The Times Atlas of World History*, 5th edition. London. Times Books.)

TRADE AND SOCIAL CHANGE IN EUROPE

The popularity of Marco Polo's accounts of his travels reflects the increasing interest of western Europeans in international trade. The Vikings and others were opening a new world of trade in the eastern fringes of Europe by the mid-1200s, and at about this time western Europeans were beginning to emerge from localized, agrarian, manorial economies and from the localized political systems of administration and order that had marked the Middle Ages. This was a period in which agricultural productivity increased and additional lands were brought under the plow as forests were cut down. New wealth enriched the towns and stimulated trade within Europe, while the crusades brought new opportunities for renewed commerce across the Mediterranean to ports of the Middle East and the merchandise that arrived there from Asia. This rebirth of long-distance trade in Europe aggravated the frustrations of the traders of western Europe with the problems of doing business in the Middle East and the eastern Mediterranean generally.

Guilds and City-states Confront Rural Aristocrats

As business increased, local traders and manufacturers formed trade organizations called **guilds**. These guilds regulated prices, wages, the quality and quantity of production and trade, and the recruitment, training, and certification of apprentices, journeymen, and masters. The guilds also represented their members in town governments and thus helped to keep industrial and commercial interests at the forefront of the civic agenda. The guilds were the principal organization through which the merchants successfully confronted the landed aristocrats and won legal rights and privileges for their businesses and their cities. Guild members were mostly males, but widowed heads of households and workshops were also included among the voting members.

Most guilds were organized locally, within their hometowns, but international traders organized international guilds corresponding to their commercial interests. The most famous and powerful of them, the Hanseatic League, though lacking the social and religious dimensions of a true guild, was founded in the mid-thirteenth century to represent the interests of leading shippers of the cities of Germany and the Baltic Sea. Headquartered in the city of Lübeck, the League established its own commercial trading posts as far west as London and Bruges (modern Belgium), and as far east as Novgorod in Russia. Throughout the region, it lobbied for legal systems that favored its members. Ships belonging to the League carried grain, timber, furs, tar, honey, and flax westward from Russia and Poland, and woolen goods eastward from England. From Sweden they carried copper and iron ore. In the fourteenth century about 100 towns were affiliated with the League. As states such as the Netherlands (United Provinces), England, and Sweden grew powerful, they asserted their control of the Baltic and the League began to die a natural death after dominating the commerce of its region for almost two centuries.

Economic and Social Conflict within the City

In two regions of western Europe, north Italy and Flanders, the manufacture of textiles came to dominate the urban economies. In Florence, between 200 and 300 workshops provided a livelihood for one-fourth of the city's population, producing a total of 100,000 pieces of woolen cloth each year. Other cities of northern Italy, though smaller, had similar workshops. The economies of Flanders and the neighboring regions of northern France and what is now Belgium were increasingly dominated by the production of textiles.

guild A sworn association of people who gather for some common purpose. In the towns of medieval Europe, guilds of craftsmen or merchants were formed in order to protect and further the members' professional interests and for mutual aid.

Opposite **Italian School, The Oar Makers, 18th-century painting of a medieval guild sign.** By the thirteenth century, as the advantages of corporate organizations over individual enterprise loomed larger, specific craftsmen's guilds began to appear—in this case, that of the oar makers. Guilds issued regulations that covered everything from protecting the welfare of deceased members' families to ensuring quality of production. (*Museo Correr, Venice*)

HOW DO WE KNOW?

Fernand Braudel Begins the Historical Study of Oceans

Fernand Braudel (1902–1985) was studying for his doctorate in Paris in the 1920s, specializing in the Mediterranean foreign policy of Phillip II of Spain, when he decided to change course:

I was already beginning to move outside the traditional bounds of diplomatic history when I began to ask myself finally whether the Mediterranean did not possess ... a history and a destiny of its own, a powerful vitality, and whether this vitality did not in fact deserve something better than the role of a picturesque background ... (The Mediterranean, p. 1)

Braudel left his studies of diplomatic history and joined the group of young Parisian scholars—the "Annales" School—that was transforming the study of history from narrowly political questions to encompass much broader issues of geography, ecology, social structures, and "mentalités," or attitudes. As his work progressed, he became one of the school's most prominent leaders.

Braudel's first great historical work was The Mediterranean and the Mediterranean World in the Age of Phillip II, in two volumes, first published in 1949. Here Braudel worked out in practice his concept of three time frames always operating simultaneously: most deeply rooted, the longue durée, extending back even to geologic times and establishing the fundamental conditions of material life, states of mind, natural environment, and geography; the middle time frame of social, economic, and political organization; and the short term, the time of an individual life, the time frame of most conventional historical study of events. Implementing this concept of diverse time frames, Braudel began with the physical and human geography of the Mediterranean basin, went on to its political systems, and ended with the specific policies of Philip II and other rulers of his time. He examined general population figures, the everyday food that people ate, the houses they lived in, the clothes they wore, the fashions they affected, the technology they used, their money and media of exchange, and the cities they built and used. His work revolutionized the way many historians understood their discipline.

Two generations later, K.N. Chaudhuri encountered Braudel and his work. Chaudhuri explains the impact of that meeting on his own historical research and writing:

The idea that the study of a civilization might be named after a sea originated with Fernand Braudel. Arab geographers were aware a thousand years ago of the relationship between different oceans and the Bilad al-Islam [the lands of Islam]. In our own times, Braudel remains one of a select group of French historians and geographers who have perceived with rare clarity the connection between the sea and the people who lived around its shores. For him the interaction between space, the passage of solar time, and the identity of civilizations constitutes one of the most important latent forces of history ... a whole generation of historians have learnt their craft from this great teacher. (Trade and Civilization, p. 1)

Chaudhuri then began writing Trade and Civilisation in the Indian Ocean, which he named in tribute to Braudel's pioneering work on the Mediterranean. Other scholars have followed this lead, and its comprehensive perspective has influenced many more.

- What was Braudel's motivation for leaving his studies of diplomatic history to study the Mediterranean Sea?
- What was new about his work?
- In light of Chaudhuri's comments, what questions that Braudel was asking about the Mediterranean might be useful to ask about other great bodies of water?

Left **Aerial view of present-day Delft, west Netherlands.** Here, gabled medieval townhouses are seen surrounding the bustling market square in Delft. Since the late 1500s the town has been famous for its pottery and porcelain known as delftware. Dutch products began to compete in European markets with porcelain imports from China.

Right **Painting of Hertogenbosch, Netherlands, 1530.** Compare today's photograph of a medieval square on market day *(left)* with this view of a cloth market in another Dutch town painted in 1530. The layout and construction of the stalls are virtually identical.

The new organization of textile production created a complex class structure with some possibility of upward mobility. Capitalist traders organized the manufacture. They estimated the market demand for production and supplied workers with the raw materials and equipment necessary to meet it. Below them, guild masters and the aspiring journeymen and apprentices within the guilds held the best positions among the manual workers: shearing the sheep; fulling the cloth (that is, shrinking and thickening it by moistening, heating, and pressing it); and dyeing the wool. Weavers, carders, and combers were lower on the pay and social scales, and of these, only the weavers were likely to organize a guild. Below all these, an army of poor people washed, warped, and spun the wool. Female and child laborers, employed at even lower pay and in worse conditions than the men, enabled working families to survive. Latent class antagonisms between employer and employee occasionally broke out in open conflict.

Revolts broke out in the Flemish cities of Douai, Tournai, Ypres, and Bruges at the end of the thirteenth century. The leaders were usually craftsmen, and they usually demanded that guild members be allowed to participate in government. The proletariat, the workers outside the guild organizations, could hope only that increased wages, shorter hours, and better conditions of work might trickle down to their level as well.

In the fourteenth century, class antagonisms increased. Increasingly impoverished workers, suffering also from plagues, wars, and bad harvests, confronted increasingly wealthy traders and industrialists. Workers were forbidden to strike and, in some towns, forbidden even to assemble. Nevertheless, a limited class consciousness was growing, especially in Florence, the greatest industrial center of western Europe. In 1345 ten wool-carders were hanged for organizing workers.

New Directions in Philosophy and Learning

On the basis of merchant wealth in the cities, a Renaissance—a rebirth in thought, literature, art, manners, and sensibilities—arose throughout central and western Europe. Most historians see the Renaissance emerging in the fourteenth century with the rise of trade and the increasingly favorable emphasis placed upon the profit motive in western Europe. Historians of the Church, however, detect the roots of this transformation as early as the mid-eleventh century—a period usually referred to as the High Middle Ages—when a shift occurred in religious as well as secular values.

Philosophers in the eleventh century began to suggest that pure faith was not enough to attain salvation. They spoke of additional values that opened the way to a new understanding and experience of the world. St. Anselm (1033–1109) stressed the need for an intellectual basis for faith. Peter Abelard (1079–1142) emphasized the need for a rational approach to the interpretation of texts. St. Bernard of Clairvaux (1090–1153) sought to combine love and spirituality with faith. Meanwhile, the new wealth and power of their Church offended some Roman Catholics, and they challenged the Church to live up to its early ideals of compassion for the poor and simplicity in everyday living. New orders of priests and nuns began to form as a way of returning to these early ideals: Franciscans followed the teachings of St. Francis of Assisi (1181–1226), Dominicans followed St. Dominic (1170–1221), and the "Poor Clares", an order of nuns, followed St. Clare of Assisi (1194–1253).

The same era witnessed an intellectual opening to the Arab world, especially through links in Spain. Christian scholars began the systematic translation of Arabic texts into Latin, reestablishing the link with the ancient Roman and Greek texts that the Arabs had preserved and developed, and that the European world had lost. The works of Avicenna (Ibn Sina) (980–1037), Averroes (Ibn Rushd) (1126–98), and the Jewish philosopher Maimonides (1135–1204) helped restore the emphasis upon logic and philosophy that Aristotle had taught.

Universities were founded to preserve, enhance, and transmit knowledge. Most emphasized practical disciplines: medical studies at Salerno and legal studies at Bologna; theological studies at Paris. All were founded before 1200. Later, students and professors from Paris crossed the English Channel and founded the University

Simone Martini, *St. Francis*, c. 1320. Fresco. Church of S. Francesco, Assisi. St. Francis of Assisi (*c.* 1182–1226) gave away all his possesssions to the poor. When his father disowned him, he stripped naked and, cloaked in a robe given by the Bishop of Assisi, went from place to place begging for food, offering service, and preaching. The religious order that he founded became the largest in Europe.

French School, *Avicenna,* **18th century. Oil on canvas.** Ibn Sina, called Avicenna by Christian Europeans, was one of the foremost Islamic students of Aristotle's work. He influenced Church scholars, who re-learned Greek scholarship through him. (*Bibliothèque de la Faculté de Médecine, Paris*)

of Oxford about 1200, with Cambridge following afterward. By 1300 there were about a dozen universities in western Europe; by 1500, nearly one hundred.

Curricula usually centered on theology, but they included grammar, dialectic, rhetoric, arithmetic, music, geometry, and astronomy. The theology curriculum, in particular, required the approval of the Church. This could be problematic, as illustrated by the case of St. Thomas Aquinas (1225–74). St. Thomas was the greatest Christian theologian of his age and paved the way for the new ideas of the Renaissance. Contentiously, he also welcomed the rationality of Aristotle. While many Church leaders rejected Aristotelian logic as contradicting the teachings of the Church, Aquinas saw no conflict. Instead, he declared that logic and reason, as taught by Aristotle, and faith, as taught by the Church, were complementary. In places where they did

Theological lecture at the Sorbonne, Paris, 15th century. Ms illumination. Sponsored by the Church, universities were founded primarily for the study of theology, but some included specializations in medecine and law. All the students were male and most were quite serious-minded. (*Bibliothèque de Troyes*)

Islamic Influences on the European Renaissance

Arab thinkers, their translations of classical Greek works, and their comments on them, helped inspire the European Renaissance. Ibn Rushd's (Averroes') Arabic translations of and commentaries on Aristotle revealed that philosopher's works to western Europeans who had lost contact with the originals. In addition to his philosophy, Ibn Sina's (Avicenna's) Qanun (Canon) of medicine remained central to European medical thought for centuries. Al-Khuwarizmi's work in mathematics remained influential for centuries, and lives on in our lexicon today in the word algorithm, based on his name. From the tenth to the twelfth century Arabs, Christians, and Jews lived in such proximity, and even harmony, in parts of Spain—the home of these three scholars—that linguistic borrowing back and forth became common. Poetic and prose forms were also borrowed, especially from Arabic literature to Latin and the Romance languages. European scholars, such as Gerard of Cremona, sought out the best in Arabic thought in order to translate it. We have also seen that Europeans adapted Arab technology, such as the caravel, which gave them access to the oceans of the world.

Despite this rich harvest of culture and technology from the Arab world, we have the harsh, even hysterical judgment of Petrarch (1304-1374), one of the greatest Italian poets of the Renaissance, often called "the father of humanism":

I implore you to keep these Arabs from giving me advice about my personal condition. Let them stay in exile. I hate the whole lot ... You know what kind of physicians the Arabs are. I know what kind of poets they are. Nobody has such winning ways; nobody, also, is more tender and more lacking in vigor, and, to use the right words, meaner and more perverted. The minds of men are inclined to act differently; but, as you used to say, every man radiates his own peculiar mental disposition. To sum up: I will not be persuaded that any good can come from Arabia. (Cassirer, et al., p. 142.)

What has happened between the early welcome given to Arabic learning and its bitter, summary rejection by Petrarch? Several interpretations are possible: First, Arabic influence was always greatest in Spain, where Muslims ruled much of the country for centuries, in some regions for almost eight centuries. Other European countries were less influenced. Even in Spain, as Christians began to reconquer the country, they began to focus on Muslims as political and religious enemies rather than as cultural colleagues. A similar change over time occurred throughout the Christian world as the launching of the crusades, after 1095, crystallized a new political antagonism between the two religious communities. The passing of time also brought new cultural currents to Europe, the development of new vernaculars especially in the Romance languages, such as Spanish, Italian, and French, broadening and deepening the base of culture, and making it more nationalistic. The Western Europeans also developed their own intellectual competences and institutions, reducing their reliance on others. The European Renaissance took Western Europeans in new directions.

Scholars sometimes designate three different periods as "renaissances" in Western Europe. The first was the Carolingian Renaissance, initiated by Charlemagne, about 800; the second was the Renaissance of the High Middle Ages, about the middle of the eleventh to the middle of the thirteenth centuries, significantly influenced by Muslim scholarship and learning; the third was the best known, and most influential, the Renaissance of the mid-fourteenth to the mid-sixteenth centuries. Each of the later renaissances built on the earlier ones, but also discarded some of their qualities. In Petrarch's dismissal of Arabic poetry and of Arabs generally we see a dramatic transformation in the attitudes of Christian thinkers, as their own religious and philosophical traditions become less open, and more hostile, to the influences of other cultures.

- The fourteenth century Renaissance took place primarily in Italy and in northwestern Europe. Why do you think it did not take place in Spain, where so much earlier cultural development took place?
- Petrarch turned against Arabic learning, but not against the early Greek philosophers. Would such a division have been possible in twelfth-century Spain? Why or why not?
- Arabic learning could be seen as more successful because it continued to hew to traditional paths, whereas Western Christian scholarship could be seen as a failure for turning in new directions. Would you accept such a characterization?

appear to conflict, however, he conceded that divine truths must take precedence: "Some divine truths are attainable by human reason, while others altogether surpass the power of human reason." Clerics should attempt to reach truth through reason, but when that proved too difficult, divine truths as revealed through the Church were the most reliable guide in showing the true path in life.

Aquinas was ahead of his time. For more than fifty years, the Franciscan order banned the reading of his works. Universities at Paris and Oxford condemned many of his doctrines. But within a century, Aquinas' synthesis of logic and faith, of Aristotle and the Church, became the standard orthodoxy of Roman Catholicism. Although Aquinas gave divine revelation precedence over human reason, on the eve of the

Renaissance he opened the door of the Church to the importance of reason in all human endeavors.

No matter how rigorous the rules and regulations of the universities, the assembly of dozens of inquisitive and exuberant young male students led to challenges to authority and quests for individualism. The "Golliard Poets" took their name from the biblical Goliath, a kind of early anti-Christ. These poets reveled in the pleasures of youth and ridiculed the conventions of sobriety, solemnity, and sanctity. They wrote parodies that were usually irreverent and sometimes obscene, for example, a *Drunkard's Mass*, a *Glutton's Mass*, and an *Office of Ribalds*. They mocked the most sacred beliefs of their time, declaring "I believe in dice ... and love the tavern more than Jesus." They declared their blessings for one another: "Fraud be with you."

Today most scholars agree that these many changes in religious and philosophical attitudes opened the way to the European Renaissance, a philosophical and artistic movement that reached its greatest creativity in the two centuries stretching from the mid-1300s through the mid-1500s.

Disasters of the Fourteenth Century: Famine, Plague, and War

Paradoxically, the Renaissance was ushered in not only by an increase in scholarship and cultural borrowing, but also by extraordinary disasters that afflicted Europe in the fourteenth century. The area was plunged into famine, civil upheavals, and, worst of all, a plague that halted its general economic prosperity and its population growth for a century. These catastrophes led to a reshuffling of classes and a reevaluation of values, which provided receptive soil for a renaissance.

For some four hundred years, beginning about 900, Europe's rural population had been increasing in size and density as farmers chopped down forests and brought new land under the plow. However, scarcity of resources then resulted, and by the mid-thirteenth century parts of central Italy, for example, began to suffer depopulation. In addition, in the fourteenth century the climate turned wetter and colder, the winters more severe, reducing harvests. Consequently, the resistance to disease was reduced among populations everywhere.

The plague had begun in Asia and China's population had dropped from about 123 million in 1200 to about 65 million in 1393. When the plague reached Europe by way

Sheep in pen being milked, Luttrell Psalter, 14th century. Woolen-cloth merchants had congregated in Flanders from an early stage, and by the twelfth century the industry there needed English wool to function to capacity. Prior to medieval times overland traders could transport only small and valuable objects over long distances; by the fourteenth century the emergence of sea routes meant that bulk goods, such as wool and grain, could be traded internationally. (*British Museum, London*)

SOURCE

Giovanni Boccaccio Describes the Plague

Giovanni Boccaccio (1313–75) captured the horror of the plague in the introduction to his otherwise droll and humanistic classic of the era, The Decameron:

In the year of Our Lord 1348 the deadly plague broke out in the great city of Florence ... At the onset of the disease both men and women were afflicted by a sort of swelling in the groin or under the armpits which sometimes attained the size of a common apple or egg. Some of these swellings were larger and some smaller, and all were commonly called boils. From these two starting points the boils began in a little while to spread and appear generally all over the body. Afterwards, the manifestation of the disease changed into black or livid spots on the arms, thighs, and the whole person ... Neither the advice of physicians nor the virtue of any medicine seemed to help ... almost everyone died within three days of the appearance of the signs—some sooner, some later ...

The calamity had instilled such horror into the hearts of men and women that brother abandoned brother, uncles, sisters, and wives left their dear ones to perish and, what is more serious and almost incredible, parents avoided visiting or nursing their very children, as though these were not their own flesh. (xxiii–xxiv)

of trading ships in 1348, it killed off a third of Europe's population, reducing it from 70 million in 1300 to only 45 million in 1400.

The Triumph of Death, **French, 1503.** This sixteenth-century work recalls the enormous loss of life caused by the Black Death of 1348. Brought back from East Asia by Genoese merchants, the bubonic plague is estimated to have killed between 20 and 50 percent of Europe's inhabitants. Contemporary medicine was impotent in the face of the disease, whose onset meant almost certain death. (*Bibliothèque Nationale, Paris*)

Social Unrest Follows the Plague

Peasants who survived the plague benefited from the labor shortages that followed, gaining higher wages and access to more land, freedom from labor services, and geographical mobility. They began to form a new class of property-owning farmers. Together with urban industrial workers and guild members, they rioted more frequently and boldly against kings and nobles who attempted to raise taxes to fund their wars.

In urban areas, too, the new scarcity of workers encouraged those who survived to demand higher wages, better working conditions, and more civic rights. In industrialized Florence, the *Ciompi* (the lowest class of workers, named for the neighborhood of Florence in which they lived), revolted, supported by lower level artisans. In 1378 they presented their demands to the officials of Florence. They wanted open access to the guilds, the right to unionize, a reduction of worker fines and punishments, and the right "to participate in the government of the City." They gained some of their goals, but the powerful business leaders of the city ultimately triumphed. By 1382 the major guilds were back in control, and soon a more dictatorial government under the Medici family was installed. Similar revolts occurred in Flanders, but on a smaller scale, and with no more success. The dissolution of the norms of everyday life, and the certainties of the class structure, inspired a reassessment of fundamental values and institutions that may have helped carry Renaissance values of individualism and a humanistic perspective to the common people as well as the elites.

THE RENAISSANCE

The central motivating philosophy of the Renaissance was **humanism**, the belief that the proper study of man is man. Renaissance humanism held strongly to a belief in God, but assigned Him a less overwhelming, less intimidating role in human life and action. Asserting the importance of the individual, it challenged the monopoly of the Church over the interpretation of cultural life. In his *Oration on the Dignity of Man*, Giovanni Pico della Mirandola (1463–94) places in the mouth of God Himself the most succinct statement of this humanistic perspective of the Renaissance:

I have given you, Adam, neither a predetermined place nor a particular aspect nor any special prerogatives in order that you may take and possess these through your own decision and choice. The limitations on the nature of other creatures are contained within my prescribed laws. You shall determine your own nature without constraint from any barrier, by means of the freedom to whose power I have entrusted you … I have made you neither heavenly nor earthly, neither mortal nor immortal so that, like a free and sovereign artificer, you might mold and fashion yourself into that form you yourself shall have chosen.

According to this typical Renaissance perspective, God gives mankind the power to shape its own destiny.

New Artistic Styles

Renaissance art continued to emphasize religious themes, but it also began to reveal the influence of humanistic and commercial values. Masaccio's painting of *Trinity with the Virgin* (1427) demonstrates the evolution of geometric perspective in painting, suggesting not only a new artistic technique but also a new relationship of individuals to space.

Renaissance in Italy, 1300–1570. From 1300–1570 in Italy, artists and intellectuals worked to fuse the Christian tradition (originating in antiquity but developed during the Middle Ages) with the Greco-Roman tradition in a movement fundamental for the later evolution of the modern civilization of the West: the Renaissance. This map shows the principal places that are associated with the names of important figures.

By the fifteenth century, artistic and commercial sensibilities had joined together. *The Arnolfini Wedding Portrait*, painted in 1434 in Flanders by Jan van Eyck, depicts in a realistic setting and clothing the marriage of a businessman, probably an Italian stationed in Flanders, and his perhaps already pregnant wife. Renaissance artists frequently merged their concerns for secular business affairs with their concerns for a spiritual life.

The richest fruits of Renaissance creativity matured in Florence, where the illustrious Medici family provided lavish patronage. The family's fortune had been built by

humanism A term applied to the intellectual movement initiated in Western Europe in the fourteenth century by such men as Petrarch and Boccaccio and deriving from the rediscovery and study of Classical, particularly Latin, literary texts.

Left **Masaccio, *Trinity with the Virgin, St. John, and Donors*, 1427.** During the Renaissance, people began to rethink their relationship to God and the world around them; at the same time, artists were developing a new means of depicting reality. According to some art history scholars, Masaccio's monumental fresco is the first painting created in correct geometric perspective (the single vanishing point lies at the foot of the cross). (*S. Maria Novella, Florence*)

Below **Jan van Eyck, *The Arnolfini Wedding Portrait*, 1434.** Giovanni Arnolfini, an Italian merchant living in Flanders, commissioned this pictorial record of his marriage. On the far wall, van Eyck has written in Latin "Jan van Eyck was here," much as a notary would sign a document. (*National Gallery, London*)

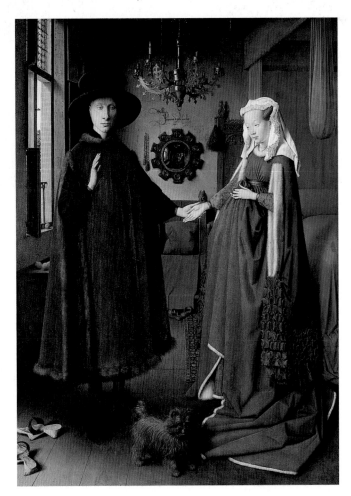

Right **Michelangelo Buonarroti, Sistine Chapel Ceiling (post restoration), 1508–12. Fresco.** Renaissance humanism praised the ability of human beings to be creative and original, yet it continued to be anchored in classical, religious imagery. Pope Sixtus IV commissioned Michelangelo to use his imagination in painting the Sistine Chapel ceiling in the Vatican, Rome, with biblical scenes. (*Vatican Museums and Galleries, Vatican City*)

Leonardo da Vinci, *Vitruvian Man*, c. 1492. Pen and ink on paper. Renaissance artists studied the proportions of the human body carefully and represented it accurately. Leonardo's drawing suggests the geometric perfection of the body, relating it both to the circle and the square, and thus to a perfect and harmonious cosmos. (*Galleria dell'Accademia, Venice*)

the merchant-banker Giovanni de' Medici (1360–1429), and was enhanced by his son Cosimo (1389–1464) and grandson Lorenzo (1449–92). In this supportive environment creative artists developed and expressed their genius. They included Michelangelo (1475–1564), the sculptor of such masterpieces as *David*, *Moses*, and the *Pietà*, and the painter of the Sistine Chapel ceiling in Rome; Leonardo da Vinci (1452–1519), scientific inventor and painter of the *Mona Lisa*; and Niccolò Machiavelli (1469–1527), author of *The Prince*, a harsh, and hard-nosed philosophy of government. At the same time, the general population of the city of Florence enjoyed high standards of literacy and expressiveness.

Developments in Technology

Creativity flourished in the practical arts as well as the fine arts, and it contributed substantially to the rise of merchant power. In 1317 merchants in Venice established regular commercial voyages through the Strait of Gibraltar and northward along the Atlantic coast to France and Flanders. Many innovations resulted from amalgamating local techniques with those encountered in the course of trade, especially with Arab civilization. Improvements in sailing technology included a new design in the ships themselves. In the thirteenth century the caravel of the Mediterranean, with its triangular, or lateen (Latin) sails, used mostly by Arab sailors, was blended with the straight sternpost and stern rudder of northern Europe. The caravel could also be rerigged with a square sail for greater speed in a tail wind. The astrolabe, again an Arab invention, helped sailors determine their longitude at sea. The rediscovery in the early fifteenth century of Ptolemy's *Geography*, written in the second century C.E., and preserved in the Arab world, helped to spark interest in proper mapping. (An error in longitude in Ptolemy's map led Columbus to underestimate the size of the globe by about one-third and to think that he could reach East Asia by sailing across the Atlantic.)

Cannon, especially when mounted on ships, gave European merchants firepower not available to others. Although the Chinese had invented gunpowder centuries before, the Europeans put it to practical use in warfare in the fourteenth century to become the masters of gunmaking. By the early 1400s they were firing cannonballs. The Ottoman Turks employed western European Christians to build and operate the cannons they used in 1453 to besiege and conquer Constantinople. The Turkish rulers of Persia also employed European gunners and gun manufacturers, and copied their works. By the late 1400s European warring powers were competing energetically in an "arms race" to develop the most powerful and effective cannons and guns. Leonardo and others worked on the mathematics of the projectiles. When Portuguese ships began to sail into the waters of the Indian Ocean after 1498, claiming the right to regulate commerce, their guns and cannons sank all opposition. Some historians have designated this era the Age of Gunpowder Empires.

The Chinese had also invented the principle of movable type and the printing press, but, again, European technology surpassed them in implementation. Movable type was better suited to Europe's alphabetic languages than to Chinese ideographs. By 1455, in Mainz, Germany, Johannes Gutenberg (*c.* 1390–1486) had printed the first major book set in movable type, the Bible. By the end of the century at least 10 million individual books in some 30,000 different editions had been produced and distributed.

In fourteenth-century Italy, two centuries after the decimal system had been absorbed from India via the Arab world, businesspeople began to develop double-entry bookkeeping. This facilitated the accurate accounting of transactions and the efficient tracking of business profits and losses. In 1494 Luca Pacioli (*c.* 1445–*c.* 1514), a Franciscan friar and mathematician, first published the method in systematic form.

The cannon. From the 1450s, innovations in weapons changed the nature of warfare. The most dramatic changes affected the cannon, as shown here in *Four Books of Knighthood*, 1528.

The Church Revises its Economic Policies

In establishing its independent power, the urban business community confronted not only landed aristocrats on the one hand and organizations of urban workers on the other, but it also faced an often hostile clergy. From its earliest times, the Church had taken a dim view of the quest for private profit and wealth. St. Augustine perpetuated the disdain. In the High Middle Ages theologians seriously debated whether it was possible for a merchant to attain salvation.

The Church forbade Christians to take and give interest on loans. For this reason, Jews carried out much of the business of moneylending. In fact, Jews were so much a part of the merchant classes in early medieval northern Europe that a traditional administrative phrase referred to "Jews and other merchants." Church laws forbidding Jews to own land also pushed them into urban life and commerce. By the end of the thirteenth century, Christian rulers forced Jews to live in ghettos, specific areas of the cities to which they were confined each night. In European society, Jews were stigmatized four times over: alien by religion, foreign by ancestry, moneylenders by occupation, and segregated by residence. Nevertheless, Jews were tolerated as an economically vital trade diaspora until local people mastered the intricacies of business. After that, Jews

Rodrigo Aleman, *The Conquest of Granada on January 2, 1492*, Toledo Cathedral, late 15th century. The conquest of Granada by the Catholic King Ferdinand II and Queen Isabella I of Spain marked the final victory of the *reconquista*, the Christian recovery of all of Spain from Muslim rule. Here the Moorish king Boabdil is handing over the keys to the town.

were often persecuted, sometimes murdered, and repeatedly exiled—from England in 1290, from France in 1394, from Spain in 1492, and from many German cities.

As commerce increased, the Church began to revise its opposition to business and businessmen. St. Thomas Aquinas addressed the issue directly in his *Summa Theologica*. Aquinas justified commerce: "Buying and selling seem to be established for the common advantage of both parties." He wrote of a "just" price, determined by negotiation between buyer and seller. Neither Church nor government needed to regulate prices: "The just price of things is not fixed with mathematical precision, but depends on a kind of estimate, so that a slight addition or subtraction would not seem to destroy the equality of justice." Profit was allowed if its uses were deemed appropriate: "Nothing prevents gain from being directed to some necessary or even virtuous end, and thus trading becomes lawful." Traders were allowed compensation for their labor: "A man may take to trade ... and seek gain, not as an end, but as payment for his labor." Aquinas elaborated similar interpretations to allow interest on commercial loans.

Most of the dynamism of western European trade through the fifteenth century emanated from the relatively secular city-states of Flanders and Italy, but in the Iberian peninsula, Portugal and Spain created a powerful new merger of the desire to spread missionary Catholicism with the desire for economic profit. The Portuguese crown dispatched sailing missions along the African coast that ultimately reached the Cape of Good Hope, turned north into the Indian Ocean and onward to India, and were poised to continue on to China. The newly unified government of Spain commissioned Christopher Columbus to sail westward in search of a new route to the Indies. Instead he discovered a "New World."

A NEW WORLD

Portugal was particularly well situated geographically to explore the Atlantic coast of Africa as the opening step in finding an alternative route to India. At first, however, the main goal was to achieve supremacy over the Muslims who controlled the southern shores of the Mediterranean. King John I (*c.* 1385–1435) launched a crusade to capture at least part of North Africa from Muslim control. In 1415 he succeeded in taking Ceuta, a local trading center on the African side of the Strait of Gibraltar. John thought he would achieve both spiritual and economic gain, but once the trans-Saharan caravans saw that Ceuta had fallen to Christians, they turned their trade to other coastal cities.

John's third son, Prince Henry (1394–1460), later called the Navigator, expanded on his father's goals. He, too, wished to defeat Muslim power, but he thought the best

Spanish explorers:
→ Columbus 1493-94
---▸ Columbus 1498
······▸ Columbus 1502-04
·····▸ Ponce de León 1512-13
→ Magellan & Elcano 1519-22
---▸ Saavedra 1527

Portuguese explorers:
→ Dias 1487-88
→ da Gama 1497-98
→ Coelho & Vespucci 1501

English explorers:
→ Cabot 1497
→ Hudson 1610

French explorers:
→ Cartier 1534-35

Dutch explorers:
→ Barents 1596-97

── major civilizations c.1500
▨ Portuguese possessions c.1600
▨ areas of Portuguese sugar cane plantations
▨ Spanish possessions c.1600

policy was to outflank the Muslims by sailing down the coast of Africa and striking them from the south. Legends of a Christian king, Prester John, sometimes said to rule in Mesopotamia, sometimes in Africa, led Henry, first, to believe that he would find an ally. Second, Henry was curious about the possibility of oceanic exploration. Finally, he believed that it might be possible to reach India by sailing around Africa, although no-one in Europe had any idea of the size and shape of that continent. At the south-western tip of Portugal he established a center for the study of navigation and the building of ships. He gathered a staff of experts, who tested existing navigational tools, such as the magnetic compass, astrolabe, and compass, and created new geographical and mathematical tables. They constructed caravels modeled on Arab ships, with lateen sails, which could sail with the wind or tack against it, so they would be able to return, no matter what the direction of the prevailing wind. Caravels with lateen sails

European exploration, 1450–1600.
Spanish and Portuguese explorers and traders had established settlements in South America and the Caribbean by 1600, and commercial depots on the coasts of Africa, India, the Pacific islands, China, and Japan—at a time when English, Dutch, and French explorations of North America had just begun.

Portuguese School, *Vasco da Gama,* *c.* **1524.** Gama's 1497–9 expedition on behalf of the Portuguese Crown completed the sea link from Europe around Africa to India. On his next voyage, 1502–3, he established the policy of using military force to create Portuguese power in the Indian Ocean.

became standard for voyages of Atlantic exploration, including those of Christopher Columbus almost a century later.

Slowly, Prince Henry's men attempted a series of explorations, each reaching just a little further down the African coast. They feared the shoals of the coast, and so sailed out to the west, farther out into the ocean, and allowed the northern winds to blow them south, further down the coast. On an expedition in 1444 they captured some 200 Africans and brought them back to Portugal for sale as slaves. Prince Henry died in 1460, but the project continued. As the Portuguese expeditions rounded the hump of west Africa, they proved their profitability as they reached what they called the grain coast, the ivory coast, the gold coast, and the slave coast—each named for its principal exports to Portugal. In 1488, Bartolomeu Dias (*c.* 1450–1500) reached the southern tip of Africa and turned northward for 300 miles. He would have continued onward—toward India—with his two caravels, but his crew refused to go further. The route, however, now lay open.

Dias' career intersected with that of Christopher Columbus (1451–1506). Columbus was in Lisbon seeking support for his intended exploration westward across the Atlantic just as Dias returned. Dias' report made clear that an alternative route to India had been found: there was no need to risk the transatlantic attempt. The Portuguese crown rejected Columbus' appeal, and so he went to Spain, where he was successful. In 1492 he discovered a transatlantic passage, which he thought had carried him to Japan (Cipangu), or at least its vicinity. Meanwhile, disputes at court and domestic problems delayed further Portuguese sailing, and it was not until 1498 that Vasco da Gama (*c.* 1460–1524) made his epic voyage around the coast of Africa to India. In sailing around Africa, Gama chose not to hug the coast but to sail far out into the Atlantic, as far as the Cape Verde Islands, and ride the winds back to the southern tip of Africa. Once he began the voyage northward, there was another touch of irony. The sea captain who guided him from East Africa to India was, according to legend, Ahmad Ibn Majid, the most famous navigator of his day. Thus, Ibn Majid, quite unknowingly, conveyed to India the first of the European Christians, who would soon displace the Arab Muslim merchants and sailors of the Indian Ocean.

Gama made a triumphal return to Lisbon, although he brought back only two of his four ships and only 55 of his 170 men survived. On his return visit in 1502, Gama initiated the policies of destroying ships, persons, and property, and of seizing goods that marked the early centuries of Portuguese conduct in Asia. His ships were armed with cannon, and he was prepared to use them. For example, he confronted a large dhow carrying pilgrims to Mecca. He burned the ship, apparently killing all the people on board, and seized from it 12,000 ducats and goods worth another 10,000. When Gama returned to Lisbon this time, he left behind a permanent armed naval force of five ships to begin to claim control of the waters of the Indian Ocean. In India and the Indian Ocean, Portuguese navies subsequently destroyed the Muslim fleet in 1509, conquered Hormuz at the entrance to the Persian Gulf, established Goa as the capital of Portuguese activities in Asia, captured Malacca in 1511, and opened oceanic trade with the lands of east and Southeast Asia. Wherever they went, they actively sought converts to Christianity, often by force. By establishing its new trade routes to the east, Portugal achieved its economic goals. In 1503 the price of pepper in Lisbon was one-fifth the price in Venice, and thus trade in the eastern Mediterranean between Venice and Alexandria was undermined.

By 1488, when Columbus' plea to the Portuguese court for support was aborted by Dias' voyage, Columbus had already been trying for three years to gain backing for his venture. He was known in Portugal, for he had sailed on various Portuguese ships as far north as the Arctic Circle, south almost to the equator, east to the Aegean, and west to the Azores. Finally, in Spain he received from the newly merged thrones of Ferdinand of Castile and Isabella of Aragon the backing he needed. In his voyage, Columbus depended on two geographical estimates and he got both wrong. He underestimated the total circumference of the earth and he overestimated the total east–west span of the Eurasian continent. The globe was bigger than he thought, and so was the oceanic distance that he had to traverse. And nowhere in his figures was there the space for two continents of which he and the people of Europe knew nothing, despite Leif Eriksson's voyages. When Columbus arrived in the New World, he thought he had reached islands off the eastern coast of Asia. Although he found only a little gold, he believed—and promised his patrons—that an abundance of it yet awaited him. He promised also a virtually limitless supply of cotton, spices and aromatics, timber, and slaves. He characterized the people of the lands he had come upon as ready for conversion to Christianity. He reported all these observations in a letter addressed to Ferdinand and Isabella.

Six months later Columbus embarked on a much larger expedition with seventeen ships, 1200 men, including six priests to carry on the work of conversion, and enough supplies to establish a permanent settlement. The expedition, however, yielded no serious commercial gains and it took Columbus two years to gain support for a third expedition, in 1498, with only six ships. For the first time, he landed on the continental landmass, in what is today Venezuela. Even at the end of his life, after yet another, fourth voyage that brought him to Central America, Columbus recognized neither the enormity of his mistake nor the enormity of his discovery. He never realized that he had not found China, Japan, India, or islands off the coast of Asia. Nor did he realize that he had discovered a "New World."

Amerigo Vespucci (1454–1512) of Florence was the first person clearly to recognize Columbus' error and his success. In 1499, sailing with a Spanish fleet after Columbus' third expedition, Vespucci traveled some 1200 miles along the coast of South America. He recognized clearly that this was a continental landmass, but he did not yet realize which one. In a second voyage, 1501–2, this one under the flag of Portugal, he traveled some 2400 miles down the coast of South America. He reported carefully on all that he saw: humans and their customs and tools, animals, plants, and hints of great treasures. Unlike Columbus, however, Vespucci was cautious: "The natives told us of gold and other metals and many miracle-working drugs, but I am one of those followers of Saint Thomas, who are slow to believe. Time will reveal everything" (Boorstin, p. 250). On his return to Spain, Vespucci was asked by Queen Isabella to establish a school for pilots and a clearing house for information brought back from the New World. In 1507 the clergyman and mapmaker Martin Waldseemüller published a new map of the world as known at the time, and on it he named the new western areas "America." In 1538, Gerardus Mercator published his large and influential map of the world designating two new continents as North America and South America. Vespucci himself died in 1512 of malaria, contracted on his voyages.

Only the eastern coast of the Americas was known to Europeans when Vasco Nuñez de Balboa (1474–1517) followed the guidance of one of his Native American allies, crossed the Isthmus of Panama, climbed a peak, and, in 1513, became the first European to see the Pacific Ocean. Four years later, Balboa was falsely accused of treason toward the king of Spain and was beheaded. With the recognition that the Americas

SOURCE

The Journal of Columbus' First Voyage to the Americas

Columbus kept a day-by-day journal of his first voyage. Columbus' original has been lost, but fortunately the priest Bartolomé de Las Casas (1474–1566) prepared an abstract that he used in writing his own Historia de las Indias. Columbus' leading biographer in English, Samuel Eliot Morison, calls the abstract, "The most important document in the entire history of American discovery." This account of what Columbus saw and how he related to it is written sometimes in the first person of Columbus, sometimes in the third person, as the voice of Las Casas. Note especially the overwhelming importance given to religion:

Prologue: Your Highnesses, as Catholic Christians and Princes devoted to the Holy Christian Faith and the propagators thereof, and enemies of the sect of Mahomet and of all idolatries and heresies, resolved to send me, Christopher Columbus, to the said regions of India, to see the said princes and peoples and lands and the disposition of them and of all, and the manner which may be undertaken their conversion to our Holy Faith, and ordained that I should not go by (the usual way) to the Orient, but by the route of the Occident, by which no one to this day knows for sure that anyone has gone …

12 October 1492: At two hours after midnight appeared the land, at a distance of two leagues … Presently they saw naked people, and the Admiral went ashore in his barge, and [others] followed. The Admiral broke out the royal standard, and the captains [displayed] two banners of the Green Cross, which the Admiral flew on all the vessels as a signal, with an F and a Y, one at one arm of the cross and the other on the other, and over each letter his or her crown … and said that they should bear faith and witness how he before them all was taking, as in fact he took, possession of the said island for the King and Queen …

15 October: It was my wish to bypass no island without taking possession, although having taken one you can claim all …

22 October: All this night and today I was here, waiting to see if the king here or other people would bring gold or anything substantial, and many of this people came, like the others of the other islands, as naked and as painted, some of them white, others red, others black, and [painted] in many ways … any little thing I gave them, and also our coming, they considered a great wonder, and believed that we had come from the sky …

1 November: It is certain that this is the mainland and that I am before Zayto [Zaytun] and Quisay [Hangzhou], [two great port cities of China] 100 leagues more or less distant the one from the other …

6 November: If they had access to devout religious persons knowing the language, they would all turn Christian, and so I hope in Our Lord that Your Highnesses will do something about it with much care … And after your days (for we are all mortal) … you will be well received before the eternal Creator …

12 November: Yesterday came aboard the ship a dugout with six young men, and five came on board; these I ordered to be detained and I am bringing them. Afterwards I sent to a house which is on the western bank of the river, and they brought seven women, small and large, and three boys. I did this because the [Indian] men would behave better in Spain with women of their country than without them …

27 November: Your Highnesses ought not to consent that any foreigner does business or sets foot here, except Christian Catholics, since this was the end and the beginning of the enterprise …

22 December: The Indians were so free, and the Spaniards so covetous and overreaching, that it was not enough that for a lace-tip or a little piece of glass and crockery or other things of no value, the Indians should give them what they asked; even without giving anything they [the Spaniards] wanted to get and take all, which the Admiral had always forbidden …

23 December: In that hour … more than 1000 persons had come to the ship, and that all brought something that they owned, and that before they come within half a crossbow shot of the ship, they stand up in their canoes with what they brought in their hands, saying "Take! Take!" (Morrison, pp. 41–179)

were continental in size, and that another ocean lay between them and Asia, Charles V of Spain commissioned Ferdinand Magellan (*c.* 1480–1521) to sail west, find a passage around the southern tip of South America, and proceed across the Pacific—no matter how big it was—and reach the Spice Islands of East Asia. Magellan set out in 1519 with five ships and about 250 sailors from several different European countries. The voyage became the first circumnavigation of the globe, yielding the first accurate picture of the full magnitude of the planet and completing the picture of most of its main contours. It took just twelve days less than three years. Only eighteen men completed the trip. Magellan himself was killed in a skirmish with Mactan tribal warriors in the Philippine island of Cebu.

OCEANIA

One inhabited continent remained unmapped. Europeans had touched on the northern and western coasts of Australia, but without gaining a clear idea of the continent's size, shape, or character. In 1642, the Dutch East India Company commissioned Abel Tasman (c. 1603–59), a Dutch navigator, to explore the continent. On two voyages, Tasman circumnavigated Australia without actually exploring it. In the process, he also discovered the island later named Tasmania. In 1768, the British government commissioned James Cook (1728–79) to carry out astronomical observations in Tahiti as well as to explore the south Pacific in search of a Great Southern Continent which had been rumored to exist, but whose existence was not proved. He sailed on the *Endeavour*, a sturdy 368 ton, 98 feet long ship, of the sort used to carry coal. He took along with him the young scientist Joseph Banks (1743–1820), who made vast contributions to botany and zoology on the basis of his findings on this voyage. Indeed because of Banks' discoveries, one of the most important harbors in southeast Australia was named Botany Bay. Cook charted the coasts of New Zealand and explored the eastern coast of Australia, but he found no other continent. His voyage of two years and eleven months became the second circumnavigation of the earth. On a second, even more adventuresome voyage, 1772–5, Cook saw the mist, fogs, and icebergs of the Antarctic Ocean, but never landed on or even saw the continent, although he reached within 75 miles of its coast. With these major oceanic adventures, and others, the main contours of the world's oceans and landmasses became known, and, at least geographically speaking, all humanity had come to live in a single, interconnected world.

LEGACIES TO THE FUTURE
WHAT DIFFERENCE DO THEY MAKE?

Voyages of exploration, trade, conquest, and settlement evoke a sense of wonder at the courage, daring, and skill of the captains and sailors who embarked on them, and the governments and businesspeople who organized and financed them. Each participant was called by a different set of values: the desire to chart the unknown; the pressure to find a new home; the quest for profit; the urge to proselytize; the lust for conquest; the competition for superiority. Often, many of these motives were mixed together. Their legacy has left us with admiration for the conquest for the skill of individual European captains to sail into the unknown with such limited ships and equipment. The legacy of these people is the achievement of a geographically known and integrated globe. It is not, however, a single, simple legacy, but a variegated set of mixed legacies that includes competition, greed, self-righteousness, and violence in the achievement of global integration. Few participants prepared for oceanic voyages with the greater good of the entire world at heart. Most, instead, sought benefits for themselves, their region or nation, or their religious group. They looked out on a huge and diverse world from relatively narrow and often self-interested perspectives.

By 1500 European traders had established a permanent connection between the eastern and western hemispheres for the first time, following Columbus' voyages across the Atlantic and Magellan's circumnavigation of the world. Inspired by the early explorations of Prince Henry the Navigator around the west coast of Africa, Portuguese sailors rounded the Cape of Good Hope and opened new routes into the Indian Ocean. These explorations followed centuries of western European economic expansion, national consolidation, and intellectual renaissance. Explorers were motivated by their mixed desire for knowledge, profit, national aggrandizement, and Christian proselytizing.

Review Questions

- Of the groups—Polynesians, Malays, Indians, Chinese, Arabs, and Europeans—discussed in this chapter and in Chapter 12, why do you think that the Europeans were the first to circumnavigate the globe?
- How did the Portuguese displace the Arabs as the predominant maritime power in the Indian Ocean?
- Why do you think that Columbus could not, or did not, recognize that he had not reached East Asia? (There is no single correct answer to this question.)
- What were the demographic, economic, and social effects of the plague in the fourteenth century?
- What was the European Renaissance? To what did degree did it develop from contacts with non-European peoples?

Suggested Readings

PRINCIPAL SOURCES

Adas, Michael, ed. *Islamic and European Expansion* (Philadelphia: Temple University Press, 1993). Key collection of historiographical essays on major topics in world history, 1200–1900. Articles by Eaton and Tucker on Islam, and McNeill on "gunpowder empires" are especially helpful for this section.

Boorstin, Daniel J. *The Discoverers* (New York: Random House, 1983). Extremely well-written, engaging history of four kinds of invention and discovery. One is maritime, mostly European explorers and cartographers 1400–1800.

Chaudhuri, K.N. *Trade and Civilization in the Indian Ocean: An Economic History from the Rise of Islam to 1750* (Cambridge: Cambridge University Press, 1985). A survey of goods, traders, ships, regulations, and competition among those who sailed and claimed to control the Indian Ocean.

Crosby, Alfred W. *Ecological Imperialism: The Biological Expansion of Europe, 900–1900* (Cambridge: Cambridge University Press, 1986). The biological—mostly destructive—impact of European settlement around the world: a tragedy for native peoples from the Americas to Oceania.

Curtin, Philip. *Cross-Cultural Trade in World History* (Cambridge: Cambridge University Press, 1984). Classical statement of the significance and ubiquity of trade diasporas.

SECONDARY SOURCES

Aquinas, St. Thomas. *Summa contra Gentiles* and *Governance of Rulers* (excerpts) in *Introduction to Contemporary Civilization in the West*, cited below. Aquinas defined the field of thirteenth-century Roman Catholic theology—and beyond.

Bloch, Marc. *Feudal Society*, 2 vols. (Chicago: University of Chicago Press, 1961). Classic, if dated, comprehensive view of the workings of feudalism in western Europe.

Boccaccio, Giovanni. *The Decameron*, trans. by Frances Winwar (New York: Modern Library, 1955). Delightful tales, set against the background of the plague raging through western Europe in the 1340s.

Braudel, Fernand. *Capitalism and Material Life, 1400–1800*, trans. from the French by Miriam Kochan (New York: Harper and Row, 1973). Comprehensive survey of the beginnings of the modern capitalist system in Europe.

——. *The Mediterranean and the Mediterranean World in the Age of Phillip II*, 2 vols, trans. Sian Reynolds (New York: Harper and Row, 1973). Comprehensive survey of the beginnings of the modern capitalist system in Europe.

Cassirer, Ernst, Paul Oskar Kristeller, and John Herman Randall, jr. eds. *The Renaissance Philosophy of Man* (Chicago, IL: University of Chicago Press, 1948).

Chaudhuri, K. N. *Asia Before Europe* (Cambridge: Cambridge University Press, 1990). Survey of the economic and political systems of Asia before the impact of colonialism and the industrial revolution. Comprehensive, comparative, and thoughtful.

Cohn, Samuel K., Jr. *The Black Death Transformed: Disease and Culture in Early Renaissance Europe* (London: Arnold, 2002). Studies and summarizes the research on the nature of the plague and its longer term effects.

Columbia College. Columbia University. *Introduction to Contemporary Civilization in the West*, Vol. 1 (New York: Columbia University Press, 2nd ed., 1954). Very well-chosen, long source readings from leading thinkers of the time and place. Vol. I covers about 1000–1800.

Fernandez-Armesto, Felipe. *Columbus* (New York: Oxford University Press, 1991). Careful, sensitive biography of the man and his times.

Frank, Andre Gunder and Barry K. Gills, eds. *The World System: Five Hundred Years or Five Thousand?* (London: Routledge, 1993). In this somewhat tendentious, but well argued, account, globalization is nothing new.

Gabrieli, F. "The Transmission of Learning and Literary Influences to Western Europe,' in Holt, P.M., Ann K.S. Lambton, and Bernard Lewis, eds. *The Cambridge History of Islam, Vol. 2B: Islamic Society and Civilization* (Cambridge, MA: Cambridge University Press, 1970, pp. 851–89). Comprehensive summary of the influence of Islamic learning on Europe, especially good on contrasting different time periods.

The Hammond Atlas of World History ed. Richard Overy (Maplewood, NJ: Hammond, 1999). Excellent, standard historical atlas.

Havighurst, Alfred F., ed. *The Pirenne Thesis: Analysis, Criticism, and Revision* (Lexington, MA: D.C. Heath, rev. ed. 1969). Well-selected pieces from Pirenne, his critics, and supporters. Well introduced, supported, and summarized, although mostly European in orientation.

Hohenberg, Paul M. and Lynn Hollen Lees. *The Making of Urban Europe, 1000–1950.* (Cambridge: Harvard University Press, 1985). Brief, but comprehensive text on the significance of cities to the history of Europe. Special attention to the social development of cities and their residents.

Kee, Howard Clark, *et al. Christianity: A Social and Cultural History* (New York: Macmillan, 1991). An accessible and insightful introduction to a huge subject.

Lindberg, Carter. "The Late Middle Ages and the Reformations of the Sixteenth Century," in Kee, *et al. Christianity*, pp. 257–423. Excellent survey.

Levenson, Jay A. *Circa 1492: Art in the Age of Exploration* (Washington: National Gallery of Art, 1991). Catalogue of an astounding art exhibit, covering the arts in all the major regions in the world at the time of Columbus' voyages.

Morison, Samuel Eliot, trans. and ed. *Journals and Other Documents on the Life and Voyages of Christopher Columbus* (New York: The Heritage Press, 1963). The crucial documents.

Nicholas, David. *The Evolution of the Medieval World* (New York: Longman, 1992). Useful survey.

Pirenne, Henri. *Medieval Cities: Their Origins and the Revival of Trade*, trans. from the French by Frank D. Halsey (Princeton: Princeton University Press, 1925). Classic statement of the importance of free merchants to the rise of commercial cities and the development of the modern world. Dated, and more limited than claimed, but pathbreaking and enormously influential.

——. *Mohammed and Charlemagne*, trans. from the 10th French edition by Bernard Miall (New York: W.W. Norton, 1939). Key revisionist text citing the Islamic victories in the Mediterranean as the end of Roman Europe and the beginning of rebirth in the north under Charlemagne.

Polanyi, Karl, Conrad M. Arensberg, and Harry W. Pearson, eds. *Trade and Market in the Early Empires* (Chicago: The Free Press, 1957). Fundamental argument by historical anthropologists that early trade was mostly regulated by rulers and priests.

Reynolds, Susan. *Fiefs and Vassals* (Oxford: Clarendon Press, 1994). Scholarly, influential examination of "feudalism," arguing that the word is misused to cover too wide a variety of regional and temporal patterns.

Subrahmanyam, Sanjay. *The Career and Legend of Vasco da Gama* (Cambridge: Cambridge University Press, 1997). The most thorough available account of the man, his contributions, and the historical puzzles surrounding them, presented in overwhelming scholarly detail.

Tuchman, Barbara. *A Distant Mirror: The Calamitous Fourteenth Century* (New York: Knopf, 1978). Engaging history of a century filled with war and plague.

Wills, John E., Jr. "Maritime Asia, 1500–1800: the Interactive Emergence of European Domination," *American Historical Review* XCVIII, No. 1 (February 1993), 83–05. Survey of European entrance into and domination of Indian Ocean and Chinese sea lanes.

◉ World History Documents CD-ROM

13.1 *Oration of the Dignity of Man* (1486)

13.2 *The Soul of Man* (1474)

13.3 Castiglione's *Courtier*: Prosperity Makes a Gentleman

14.4 "Cut off Their Ears, Hands and Noses!": Gaspar Correa

14.5 Christopher Columbus

14.6 Bernal Diaz de Castillo

14.7 Bartolomé de Las Casas: Persecutor Turns Protector

14.8 The British Encounter Maoris: A Sailor's Impression

14.9 The Prospects of Christian Conversion: Saint Francis Xavier

15.1 The "Black Legend" of Spain: Bartolomé de Las Casas

15.2 "Our Kingdom Is Being Lost": Nzinga Mbemba

15.3 Olaudah Equiano, *The Life of Olaudah Equiano*

15.4 Commerce, Slavery, and Religion in North Africa

15.5 Thomas Nelson, Slavery and the Slave Trade of Brazil

GLOSSARY

Pronunciation guides for selected terms are enclosed in parentheses, with the stressed syllable appearing in capital letters.

Abhidhamma (Ub-ih-DUM-eh) One of the three principal divisions of the Buddhist scriptures, or Tripitaka, the others being the **Sutta** and the **Vinaya**. It comprises a logical analysis of the Buddha's teachings, arranged systematically, and is more impersonal and abstract than the Sutta. Its aim is meditational, and an important element involves an examination of states of consciousness.

agora (AG-o-rah) A central feature of ancient Greek town planning. Its chief function, like the Roman forum, was as a town market, but it also became the main social and political meeting place. Together with the acropolis, it normally housed the most important buildings of the town.

anthropology The scientific study of human beings in their social and physical aspects. Physical anthropologists study fossil remains to explain the origins and biological evolution of humans and the distinctive features of different races. Cultural anthropologists are concerned with the evolution of human society and cultures, especially through language. Social anthropologists have typically confined their work to "primitive" societies; they seek to analyze social norms, customs, belief, and ritual.

assimilation The process by which different ethnic groups lose their distinctive cultural identity through contact with the dominant culture of a society, and gradually become absorbed and integrated into it.

balance of power In international relations, a policy that aims to secure peace by preventing any one state or alignment of states from becoming too dominant. Alliances are formed in order to build up a force equal or superior to that of the potential enemy. Such a policy was practiced in the ancient world, for example by the Greek city-states.

bas relief (bah reh-LEEF) In sculpture, relief is a term for any work in which the forms stand out from the background, whether a plane or a curved surface. In bas (or low) relief, the design projects only slightly from the background and the outlines are not undercut.

Bible From the Greek *biblia*, books. The Jewish bible, written in Hebrew, comprises the thirty-nine books of the Old Testament (a Christian designation), the canon of which was probably established by 100 C.E. Regarded as divinely inspired, these scriptures are made up of three parts: the Torah (Law), the first five books—Genesis to Deuteronomy—whose authorship is attributed to Moses; the Prophets; and the Writings (the Psalms, etc.). The Christian Church incorporated these books, together with the Apocrypha (supplementary books written in Greek) and the **New Testament** writings, into its bible, the form of which was fixed by the end of the fourth century C.E.

bourgeoisie (boor-ZHWA-zee) A French word that originally applied to the inhabitants of walled towns, who occupied a socio-economic position between the rural peasantry and the feudal aristocracy. With the development of industry, it became identified more with employers, as well as with other members of the "middle class," including professionals, artisans, and shopkeepers. (In Marxist theory, the word refers to those who own the tools of production and do not live by the sale of their labor, as opposed to the proletariat.)

caliph (KAY-lif) The spiritual head and temporal ruler of the Muslim community. As successor to the prophet Muhammad, the caliph is invested with absolute civil and religious authority, providing that he rules in conformity with the law of the Quran and the **hadith**.

caste (KAST) An element in a hierarchical social system in which the ranks are strictly defined, usually according to descent, marriage, and occupation. In more rigorous caste systems, such as that of Hinduism in India, mobility from one caste (Sanskrit: *varna*) to another is prohibited, and traditions and ritual dictate rules for social intercourse as well as such matters as education, diet, and occupation.

centuries The smallest units of the Roman army, each composed of some 100 foot-soldiers and commanded by a centurion. A legion was made up of 60 centuries. Centuries also formed political divisions of Roman citizens; they met in assembly to elect the chief magistrates and had some judicial powers.

Christmas The Christian feast celebrating the birth of Jesus Christ. The day of his actual birth is unknown, but the early Church probably chose this date because it coincided with pagan festivals of sun worship associated with the winter solstice. Pagan cults seem to have been the source of some popular customs connected with Christmas.

consul (KON-sul) Under the Roman Republic, one of the two magistrates holding supreme civil and military authority. Nominated by the Senate and elected by citizens in the Comita Centuriata (popular assembly), the consuls held office for one year and each had power of veto over the other. Their power was much restricted after the collapse of the Republic in 27 B.C.E., when the office fell under the control of the emperors.

cuneiform (kyoo-NEE-uh-form) A writing system in use in the ancient Near East from around the end of the fourth millennium to the first century B.C.E. It was used for a number of languages in the area, but the earliest examples, on clay tablets, are in Sumerian. The name derives from the wedge-shaped marks (Latin: *cuneus*, a wedge) made by pressing the slanted edge of a stylus into soft clay. The signs were abstract versions of the earlier **pictograms**, and represented whole words or the sounds of syllables.

Daoism (Taoism) (DAO-iz-um) A religio-philosophical system of ancient China, which emerged in the sixth century B.C.E. Daoism rejected the activism of Confucianism, the other great Chinese philosophical tradition. It emphasized spontaneity and individual freedom, a *laissez-faire* attitude to life and government, simplicity, and the importance of mystical experience. True happiness could be attained only by surrendering to the Way or principle (Chinese: *dao*) of Nature. The principle texts of Daoism are the *Laozi* or *Classic of the Way and Its Power*, traditionally attributed to the philosopher Laozi, and the *Zhuangzi* of Zhuang Zou.

dar al-Islam (DAHR ahl-is-LAHM) The literal meaning of the Arabic words is "the abode of peace." The term refers to the land of Islam, or the territories in which Islam and its religious laws (**shari'a**) may be freely practiced.

deme (DEEM) A rural district or village in ancient Greece, or its members or inhabitants. The demes were a constituent part of the **polis** but had their own corporations with police powers, and their own cults, officials, and property. Membership of the deme was open only to adult males, and was hereditary; it also guaranteed membership of the polis itself.

dhimmi (dim-MEE) A person who belongs to the class of "protected people" in the Islamic state, who could not be forcibly converted to Islam. They originally comprised the followers of the monotheistic religions cited in the Quran, the "People of the Book" (e.g., Jews and Christians), to whom scriptures had been revealed, and the principle has in some instances been extended to followers of other religions.

diaspora (die-AS-pur-uh) A dispersion of peoples. Most commonly used to refer to the dispersion of Jews among the Gentiles, which began with the Babylonian captivity of the sixth century B.C.E.; the Hebrew term for diaspora is *Galut*, "exile." Because of the special relationship between the Jews and the land of Israel, the term refers not only to their physical dispersion but also has religious, philosophical, and political connotations. The African diaspora refers to the settlement of people of African origin to new locations around the world. "Trade diaspora" has been used to refer to centers of trade in which traders from many different countries live and work.

diffusion The spread of ideas, objects, or traits from one culture to another. Diffusionism is an anthropological theory that cultural similarities among different groups can be explained by diffusion rather than **innovation**, and, in its most radical form, that they derive from a common source.

dominance The imposition of alien government through force, as opposed to **hegemony**.

Easter The principal feast of the Christian calendar celebrating the resurrection of Christ. It is preceded by the penitential season of Lent, which culminates in the solemnities of Holy Week and Good Friday, commemorating Jesus' crucifixion. The date varies, and can fall on any Sunday between March 22 and April 25. The feast was associated by the early Christians with the Jewish Passover, and in some Churches a vigil is held on the night of Holy Saturday.

ecumene (EK-yoo-MEEN) A Greek word referring to the inhabited world and designating a distinct cultural-historical community.

epigraphy (eh-PIG-reh-fee) Inscriptions, usually on stone or metal, or the science of interpreting them.

Eucharist (YOO-kah-rist) From the Greek *eucharistia*, thanksgiving. The central **sacrament** and act of worship of the Christian Church, commemorating the Last Supper of Christ with his disciples, his sacrifice on the cross, and the redemption of mankind, and culminating in Holy Communion, when his Body and Blood in the form of water and wine are conveyed to the believer.

exogamy (adj. exogamous) The practice by which a person is compelled to choose a marital partner from outside his or her own group or clan, the opposite of endogamy, the choice of partner from within the group. Sometimes the outside group from which the partner is to be chosen is specified.

feudal (FEW-dull) Refers to both a social, military, and political system organized on the basis of land tenure and the manorial system of production. Property (the fief) was granted to a tenant (vassal) by a lord in exchange for an oath of allegiance and a promise to fulfill certain obligations, including military service, aid, and advice; in return, the lord offered protection and justice. Originally bestowed by investiture, the fief later became hereditary. Within the system, each person was bound to the others by a web of mutual responsibilities, from the king or emperor down to the **serfs**. Feudalism is particularly associated with medieval Europe, and with China and Japan. (*See* **manorial economy**.)

free market economy An economic system in which the means of production are largely privately owned and there is little or no government control over the markets, which operate according to **supply and demand**. The primary aim is to maximize profits, which are distributed to private individuals who have invested capital in an enterprise. The system is also known as a free enterprise economy or capitalism.

guild (GILD) A sworn association of people who gather for some common purpose. In the towns of medieval Europe, guilds of craftsmen or merchants were formed in order to protect and further the members' professional interests and for mutual aid. Merchant guilds organized trade in their locality and had important influence on local government. Craft guilds were confined to specific crafts or trades; they set and maintained standards of quality, regulated production and controlled recruitment through the apprenticeship system; they also had important social and religious functions. In India the guilds were associations of businessmen and producers who regulated weights and measures and prices and enforced quality control.

hadith (huh-DETH) Traditional records of the deeds and utterances of the prophet Muhammad, and the basis, after the Quran, for Islamic theology and law. The hadith provide commentaries on the Quran and give guidance for social and religious life and everyday conduct.

hegemony (hih-JEM-o-nee) The predominance of one unit over the others in a group, for example one state in a confederation. It can also apply to the rule of an empire over its subject peoples, when the foreign government is exercised with their substantial consent. Hegemony usually implies exploitation but, more positively, it may connote leadership (*see* **dominance**).

heliocentric A system in which the sun is assumed to be at the center of the solar system—or of the universe—while Earth and the planets move around it. Ptolemy of Alexandria's geocentric or Earth-centered system dominated scientific thought in the Western world from the second century C.E. until the publication of Copernicus's *De revolutionibus orbium coelestium* in 1543. There was much religious and scientific controversy before his thesis was shown to be essentially correct.

hieroglyphs (HIGH-ur-o-glifs) The characters in a writing system based on the use of **pictograms** or **ideograms**. In ancient Egypt, hieroglyphics were largely used for monumental inscriptions. The symbols depict people, animals, and objects, which represent words, syllables, or sounds.

hijra (HIJ-reh) The "migration" or flight of Muhammad from Mecca, where his life was in danger, to Medina (then called Yathrib) in 622 C.E. The Islamic era (A.H.: After Hijra) is calculated from this date, which coincides with the establishment of the first Islamic state.

historiography The writing of history, or the theory and history of historical writing.

Homo erectus The most widespread of all prehistoric hominids, and the most similar to humans. Evolved about 2 million years ago and became extinct 100,000 years ago.

hoplite A heavily armed foot soldier of ancient Greece, whose function was to fight in close formation, usually in ranks of eight men. Hoplites were citizens with sufficient property to equip themselves with full personal armor, which consisted of a helmet with nasal and cheek pieces, a breastplate and greaves of bronze. Each soldier carried a heavy bronze shield, a short iron sword, and a long spear for thrusting.

humanism A term applied to the intellectual movement initiated in Western Europe in the fourteenth century by such men as Petrarch and Boccaccio and deriving from the rediscovery and study of Classical, particularly Latin, literary texts. The humanist program of studies included rhetoric, grammar, history, poetry, and moral philosophy (the humanities); the humanist scholar aimed to emulate Classical literary achievements. The examination of Classical civilization formed the inspiration for the **Renaissance**. Although humanism attached prime importance to human qualities and values, unlike its twentieth-century counterpart it in no way involved the rejection of Christianity.

icon (I-kon) A representation of Christ, the Virgin Mary, or other sacred personage or saint, usually a painted image on wood but also wrought in mosaic, ivory, and other materials. The term is usually applied to the sacred images of Eastern, particularly Byzantine and Orthodox, Christianity, where they are regarded as channels of grace. (*See also* **iconoclast**.)

iconoclast (I-kon-o-klast) An image-breaker, or a person who rejects the veneration of **icons**, on the grounds that the practice is idolatrous. Strong disagreements over the cult of images in the Byzantine Empire led to attacks on the images themselves, and the use of icons was forbidden during the Iconoclastic Controversy (726–843 C.E.), when many were destroyed.

ideogram (ID-ee-o-gram) (alternative: ideograph) A character or figure in a writing system in which the idea of a thing is represented rather than its name. Languages such as Chinese use ideograms, but they cannot easily represent new or foreign words and huge numbers of symbols may be required to convey even basic information.

imam (ih-MAHM) In Islam, a title for a person whose leadership or example is to be followed, with several levels of meaning. In a general sense, it can refer to a leader of prayer in a mosque, or the head of a community or group. Among Shi'a Muslims, the title has special significance as applying to the successors of Muhammad, who were regarded as infallible and exercised absolute authority in both temporal and spiritual spheres (*see* **caliph**).

Indo-Aryan (in-DOH-AIR-ee-un) A sub-group of the Indo-Iranian branch of the Indo-European group of languages, also called Indic and spoken in India, Sri Lanka, Bangladesh, and Pakistan. The Indo-Aryan languages descend from Sanskrit, the sacred language of Hinduism; they include Hindi, a literary language, the more colloquial Hindustani, and the widely spoken Sindhi, Bengali, Gujarati, Punabi, and Sinhalese.

Indo-European The largest family of languages, believed to be descended from a single unrecorded language spoken more than 5000 years ago in the steppe regions around the Black Sea, which later split into a number of dialects. The languages were carried into Europe and Asia by migrating peoples, who also transmitted their cultural heritage. The family includes the following sub-groups: Anatolian (the earliest recorded language, now extinct), Indo-Iranian, Armenian, Greek, Albanian, Tocharian, Celtic, Italic, Germanic, Baltic, and Slavic.

innovation The explanation that similar cultural traits, techniques, or objects found among different groups of people were invented independently rather than spreading from one group to another, as in **diffusion**.

interregnum An interval between reigns (Latin: "between reigns"). The term may refer to the period of time between the death of a monarch and the accession of his successor, to a suspension of the usual government, or to the period of rule of an usurper.

janapada (juh-nah-pah-dah) A Sanskrit word that occurs in ancient texts with reference to a large political district.

lateen (lah-TEEN) A triangular sail affixed to a long yard or crossbar at an angle of about 45 degrees to the mast, with the free corner secured near the stern. The sail was capable of taking the wind on either side. The rig, which was developed by the Arabs, revolutionized navigation because it enabled vessels to tack into the wind and thus to sail in almost any direction; with a square sail, ships could only sail with the wind behind them.

Legalism A school of Chinese philosophy that came into prominence during the period of the Warring States (481–422 B.C.E.) and had great influence on the policies of the Qin dynasty (221–207 B.C.E.). Legalists took a pessimistic view of human nature and believed that social harmony could only be attained through strong government control and the imposition of strict laws, enforced absolutely. The brutal application of this political theory under the Qin led to the fall of the dynasty, and Legalist philosophy was permanently discredited in Confucian philosophy.

madrasa (mah-DRASS-ah) A traditional Islamic school of higher education, principally of theology and law, literally a "place of study." The madrasa usually comprised a central courtyard surrounded by rooms in which the students resided and with a prayer room or mosque, where instruction took place. Tuition, board, and lodging were free. Studies could last for several years and primarily consisted of memorizing textbooks and lectures.

mahdi (MAH-dee) An Arabic word meaning "the right-guided one." According to Islamic tradition, a messianic leader will appear to restore justice, truth, and religion for a brief period before the Day of Judgment. Some Shi'a Muslims believe that the twelfth imam (ninth century C.E.) will reappear as the Mahdi. Several impostors have claimed the title.

mandala (MUN-dull-eh) A symbolic circular diagram of complex geometric design used as an instrument of meditation or in the performance of sacred rites in Hinduism and Buddhism. Mandalas can be drawn, painted, wrought in metal, or traced on the ground. Buddhist examples are usually characterized by a series of concentric circles, representing universal harmony and containing religious figures, with the Buddha in the center.

mantra (MUN-tra) A formula of utterances of words and sounds that are believed to possess spiritual power, a practice of both Hinduism and Buddhism. The efficacy of the mantra largely depends on the exacting mental discipline involved in uttering it correctly. Repetition or meditation on a particular mantra can induce a trancelike state, leading to a higher level of spiritual consciousness.

medieval A term coined in fifteenth-century Italy to describe the "middle ages," the period between antiquity and the contemporary Renaissance. It originally had negative connotations, for the Middle Ages were regarded as a period of artistic and cultural decline as compared to the lost glories of ancient Rome and the Renaissance attempts to emulate and surpass those achievements.

Monophysites (moh-NOF-ih-sites) The supporters of a doctrine in the early Christian Church that held that the incarnate Christ possessed a single, wholly divine nature. They opposed the orthodox view that Christ had a double nature, one divine and one human, and emphasized his divinity at the expense of his capacity to experience real human suffering. The doctrine survived in the Coptic and some other Eastern Churches.

myth An interpretive story of the past that cannot be verified historically but has a deep moral message.

Neolithic (NEE-o-lith-ick) "New Stone Age"—the last division of the Stone Age, immediately preceding the development of metallurgy and corresponding to the ninth–fifth millennia B.C.E. It

was characterized by the increasing domestication of animals and cultivation of crops, established agricultural communities, and the appearance of such crafts as pottery and weaving. Although tools and weapons were still made of stone, technological improvements enabled these to be ground and polished rather than flaked and chipped.

Neoplatonic (nee-o-PLAH-ton-ick) A philosophical system founded by Plotinus (205–270 C.E.) and influenced by Plato's theory of ideas. It emphasizes the transcendent, impersonal, and indefinable "One" as the ground of all existence and the source of an eternal world of goodness, beauty, and order, of which material existence is but a feeble copy. By cultivating the intellect and rejecting the material world, humans may become mystically united with the One. Neoplatonism, the last school of Greek philosophy, influenced both Christian theology and Islamic philosophy.

New Testament The second part of the Christian bible, written in Greek and containing the writings attributed to the first followers of Jesus. The twenty-seven books fall into four parts: the four Gospels, dealing with life of Christ; the Acts of the Apostles, concerning the early life of the Church; the Epistles (or letters), written mainly by St Paul; and the Book of Revelation. The canon was established by the end of the fourth century C.E.; the title indicates the Christian belief that Christ's life, death, and resurrection fulfilled prophecies in the Hebrew scriptures, the Old Testament.

paleoanthropologist A student of the earliest humans and the setting in which they lived.

Paleolithic (PAY-lee-o-lith-ick) "Old Stone Age"—the first division of the Stone Age (the earliest phase in a system devised in the nineteenth century to classify human technological development). The Paleolithic (c. 1.5 million B.C.E.–10,000 B.C.E.) extends to the end of the last Ice Age and is associated with the emergence of humans, the use of rudimentary tools of chipped stone or bone, and the practice of hunting and gathering. Evidence of painting and sculpture survives from the later, or Upper Paleolithic, period.

paradigm A model of reality representing one viewpoint.

paterfamilias (pay-ter-fuh-MILL-ee-us) The head of a family or household in Roman law—always a male—and the only member to have full legal rights. The *paterfamilias* had absolute power over his family, which extended to life and death. The family included not only direct descendants of the *paterfamilias* through the male line, unless emancipated by him, but also adopted members and, in certain cases, wives. On his death, each son would become a *paterfamilias* in his own right.

patrician (puh-TRISH-un) A member of the elite class of ancient Roman citizens. In the early days of the Republic, patricians held a monopoly of state and religious offices, but this privileged position was gradually eroded with the admission of other social classes to office (see **plebeian**).

Pax Romana (PAKS roh-MAHN-uh) The "Roman Peace," that is, the state of comparative concord

prevailing within the boundaries of the Roman Empire from the reign of Augustus (27 B.C.E.–14 C.E.) to that of Marcus Aurelius (161–180 C.E.), enforced by Roman rule and military control.

Pentecost The Greek name for a Jewish festival that falls on the fiftieth day after Passover. The name was adopted by the Christian Church to commemorate the descent of the Holy Spirit on the Apostles of Christ and the beginning of their preaching mission on the fiftieth day after the resurrection of Christ at **Easter**.

philology The study of languages, or comparative linguistics. Philologists identify common characteristics in languages, study their relationships and trace their origins.

pictogram (alternative: pictograph) A pictorial symbol or sign representing an object or concept. Prehistoric examples have been found all over the world. Because of the difficulty of representing words other than concrete nouns, writing systems using pictograms generally evolved into those using **ideograms**.

plebeian (plih-BEE-un) A citizen of ancient Rome who was not a member of the privileged patrician class. Plebeians were originally excluded from state and religious offices and forbidden to marry patricians, but from the early fifth century B.C.E. they gradually achieved political equality, gaining admission to all Roman offices. From the later Republican period, the term *plebeian* implied low social class.

polis (POE-lis) The city-state of ancient Greece. It comprised not only the town, which was usually walled with a citadel (acropolis) and a market place (**agora**), but also the surrounding countryside. Ideally, the *polis* comprised the citizens, who could reside in either town or country; they participated in the government of the state and its religious affairs, contributed to its defense and economic welfare, and obeyed its laws.

praetor (PREE-tor) In ancient Rome, the name was originally applied to the consul as leader of an army. In 366 B.C.E. a further praetor was elected with special responsibility for the administration of justice in Rome, with the right of military command. Around 242 B.C.E. another praetor was created to deal with lawsuits involving foreigners. Further praetors were subsequently appointed to administer the increasing number of provinces. Under the Empire, the position eventually became an honorary appointment.

pre-history The period of time before written records began, which varied from place to place. In this period the study of human development is dependent on the evidence of material remains, such as stone tools or pottery.

primary source Original evidence for an event or fact, as opposed to reported evidence (*see* **secondary source**).

Puranas (poo-RAH-nuz) A collection of poetic tales in Sanskrit, relating the myths and legends of Hinduism. The Puranas expound such topics as the destruction and creation of the world, the genealogy of the gods and patriarchs, the reigns and times of the heroes, and the history of royal dynasties.

quaestor (KWESS-ter) A junior official in ancient Rome. There were originally two, elected annually, but more were appointed as the empire expanded. Most were financial officials. The minimum age was twenty-five, and on completion of the tenure membership of the Senate was automatically conveyed.

Quran (koo-RAHN) The holy book of Islam, believed to contain the direct and authentic word of God as communicated to his prophet Muhammad in a series of revelations by the angel Gabriel. According to tradition, these were collected in the Quran under the caliph Uthman (d. 656) after Muhammad's death. Written in classical Arabic, the Quran is regarded as infallible and is the principal source of Islamic doctrine and law.

radiocarbon dating A method of estimating the age of organic matter, also known as Carbon-14 dating. Carbon dioxide contains a small proportion of the radioactive isotope carbon-14, which is produced in the upper atmosphere by cosmic rays. It is absorbed by green plants, and passes to animals via the food chain. When the organism dies, the amount of carbon-14 in its tissues steadily decreases, at a known rate. The date of death can thus be estimated by measuring the level of radioactivity. The method is mostly used for dating wood, peat, seeds, hair, textiles, skin, and leather.

realpolitik (ray-AHL-poe-lee-teek) A German term meaning practical politics, that is, a policy determined by expediency rather than by ethical or ideological considerations.

Renaissance (REN-ay-sahnz) Literally "rebirth," a French term applied to the cultural and intellectual movement that spread throughout Europe from the fourteenth century. It was characterized by a new interest in Classical civilization, stimulated by the Italian poet Petrarch, and a response to the challenge of its models, which led to pride in contemporary achievement and renewed vigor in the arts and sciences. The new concept of human dignity found its inspiration in **humanism**.

republic A state that is not ruled by a hereditary leader (a monarchy) but by a person or persons appointed under the constitution. The head of state may be elected and may or may not play a political role.

sacrament In Christian theology, a rite or ritual that is an outward sign of a spiritual grace conveyed on the believer by Christ through the ministry of the Church. In the Orthodox and Roman Catholic Churches seven sacraments are recognized: baptism, confirmation, penance, the Eucharist, marriage, ordination, and anointing of the sick. The two most important of these, baptism and the **Eucharist**, are the only sacraments recognized by most Protestant Churches.

sahel (sah-HAYL) "Shore"—the northern and southern edges of the Sahara Desert. A semi-arid region of Africa, extending from Senegal eastwards to the Sudan and forming a transitional zone between the Sahara desert to the north and the belt of **savanna** to the south. The area is dry for most of the year, with a short and unreliable rainy season, and is subject to long periods of drought. Low-growing grasses provide pasture for camels, pack oxen, cattle and sheep.

satrapy (SAY-truh-pee) A province or colony in the Achaemenid or Persian Empire ruled by a satrap or governor. Darius I completed the division of the Empire into provinces, and established 20 satrapies with their annual tributes. The term satrapy can also refer to the period of rule of a satrap.

savanna (sah-VAN-ah) The grassland areas of the tropics and sub-tropics adjacent to the equatorial rain forests in each hemisphere and bordered by arid regions of desert. Savannas cover extensive parts of Africa, South America, and northern Australia. The natural vegetation is mainly grass with scattered shrubs and trees, the latter low and often flat-topped. The land is particularly suitable for cattle rearing.

serf An agricultural worker or peasant bound to the land and legally dependent on the lord, characteristic of the manorial economy and the feudal system. Serfs had their own homes, plots, and livestock but they owed the lord labor, dues, and services. These services could be commuted to rent, but serfs remained chattels of the lord unless they were emancipated by him or her, or escaped. Serfdom declined in western Europe in the late medieval period, but persisted in parts of eastern Europe until the nineteenth century.

shaman (SHAH-men) In the religious beliefs of some Asian and American tribal societies, a person capable of entering into trances and believed to be endowed with supernatural powers, with the ability to cure the sick, find lost or stolen property, predict the future, and protect the community from evil spirits. A shaman may act as judge or ruler, and as a priest a shaman directs communal sacrifices and escorts the souls of the dead to the next world.

sinicization (sigh-ne-sigh-ZAY-shen) The adoption and absorption by foreign peoples of Chinese language, customs and culture.

sophist (SOF-ist) An itinerant professor of higher education in ancient Greece, who gave instruction for a fee. The subjects taught, which included oratory, grammar, ethics, mathematics, and literature, had the practical aim of equipping pupils for successful careers. The sophists were criticized for their ability to argue for any point of view regardless of its truth and for their emphasis on material success. They were prominent in the fifth and early fourth centuries B.C.E.

Sufi (SOO-fee) In Islam, a member of one of the orders practicing mystical forms of worship that first arose in the eighth and ninth centuries C.E. Sufis interpret the words of Muhammad in a spiritual rather than a literal sense. Their goal is direct personal experience of God, achieved by fervent worship (*see* **tariqa**).

supply and demand In economics, the relationship between the amount of a commodity that producers are able and willing to sell (supply), and the quantity that consumers can afford and wish to buy (demand). The price fluctuates according to a product's availability and its desirability. Supply and demand thus controls a **free market economy**. In practice it is usually subject to some degree of regulation.

Sutta (SOOT-eh) The second section of the Buddhist scriptures or **Tripitaka**, the others being the **Abhidhamma** and the **Vinaya**. It contains the basic teachings of Buddhism, attributed to the Buddha himself, and expounded in a series of discourses in a lively and engaging style, employing allegories and parables. It also includes birth stories of the Buddha and other material.

syllabary (SIL-eh-ber-ee) A writing system in which each symbol represents the syllable of a word (cf. ideogram). The system appears to have been used for some ancient Near Eastern languages, but Japanese is the only modern-day language to use a syllabary.

syncretism (SING-kri-tiz-ehm) The attempt to combine or harmonize doctrines and practices from different philosophical schools or religious traditions, or the absorption of foreign elements into one particular religion.

TaNaKh (tah-NAKH) A Hebrew term for the books of the Bible that are written in Hebrew. The word is composed of the initial letters of the words Torah (first five books of the Bible, traditionally attributed to Moses), Nevi'im (the books of the Prophets) and the Ketuvim (additional historical, poetic, and philosophic writings). This threefold division of the Bible is commonly found in the Talmud.

tariqa (tah-REE-cah) In Islam a generic term meaning "path," referring to the doctrines and methods of mysticism and esoterism. The word also refers to schools or brotherhoods of mystics, which were often situated at a mosque or the tomb of a Muslim saint.

teleology (tay-lee-OHL-o-gee) From the Greek word *telos*, "end," the philosophical study of final causes or purposes. A "final cause" is an event in the future for the sake of which an occurrence takes place. Teleology refers especially to any system that interprets nature or the universe as having design or purpose. It has been used to provide evidence for the existence of God.

themes A theme was originally a military unit stationed in one of the provinces of the Byzantine empire, but it later applied to the large military districts that formed buffer zones in the areas most vulnerable to Muslim invasion. By the ninth century the system was extended throughout the empire. Soldiers were given farms in the themes in exchange for military service, but they were later able to commute this for tax, which led to the decline of the system.

thermoluminescence A dating technique used for pottery or other fired material. Electrons produced by radiation will be trapped in the flaws of a crystal lattice, but will be liberated in the form of light when heated. The light emissions occur at a constant rate and can be measured when the substance is reheated, and correlated to the duration of exposure to radiation. The period of time that has elapsed since the crystal was last heated can then be estimated.

transhumance (trans-YOO-menz) A form of pastoralism or nomadism organized around the seasonal migration of livestock, practiced in areas that are too cold or wet for winter grazing. The animals are moved to mountain pastures in warm seasons and to lowland ones in winter, or between lower and upper latitudes, or between wet- and dry-season grazing areas.

trebuchet (TRAY-boo-shay) A military engine for hurling heavy missiles, operated by counterpoise, on the principle of the seesaw. Developed in China, the trebuchet first appeared in Europe in the twelfth century.

tribals The aboriginal peoples of the Indian sub-continent, who are outside the **caste** system and live quite separately from the rest of society, generally in remote places. They are thought to have migrated to India in pre-historic times, probably before the emergence of Hinduism.

tribune (TRIB-yoon) In ancient Rome, a **plebeian** officer elected by the plebeians and charged to protect their lives and properties, with a right of veto against legislative proposals of the Senate. The office was instituted during the fifth century B.C.E. and had great political influence under the Republic, but it lost its independence and most practical functions in the time of Augustus (27 B.C.E.–14 C.E.). Military tribunes were senior officers of the legions, elected by the people.

triumvirate (try-UM-vihr-ate) In ancient Rome a board of three men appointed for special administrative duties. An unofficial coalition between Julius Caesar, Pompey, and Crassus

was formed in 60 B.C.E. After Caesar's murder in 44 B.C.E., a triumvirate that included his heir Octavian (later Augustus), Mark Antony, and Marcus Lepidus was appointed to maintain public order; it held almost absolute powers and lasted until 36 B.C.E.

ulama (OO-leh-ma) The theologians and legal experts of Islam. The *ulama* form a body of scholars who are competent to decide on religious matters. They include the imams of important mosques, teachers in religious faculties in universities, and judges.

umma (UM-ma) The community of believers in Islam, which transcends ethnic and political boundaries.

Vedas (VAY-duz) Sacred Hindu hymns or verses composed in Sanskrit around 1500–1000 B.C.E. Many Vedas were recited or chanted during rituals; they are largely concerned with the sacrificial worship of gods representing natural and cosmic forces. The foremost collection is the *Rigveda*, followed by the *Samaveda*, *Yajurveda*, and *Atharvaveda*; the *Brahmanas*, *Aranyakas*, and *Upanishads* are later commentaries but are also considered canonical.

Vinaya (VIN-eh-yeh) The first part of the Buddhist scriptures, or **Tripitaka**. It concerns the early history, regulations, and discipline of Buddhism, focusing in particular on rules for

monks and nuns and on such practical subjects as ordination, holy days, dress, food, and medicine.

Yurts (YOORTZ) A portable dwelling used by the nomadic people of Central Asia, consisting of a tentlike structure of skin, felt or hand-woven textiles arranged over wooden poles, simply furnished with brightly colored rugs.

ziggurat (ZIG-gu-rat) A temple tower of ancient Mesopotamia, constructed of square or rectangular terraces of diminishing size, usually with a shrine on top built of blue enamel bricks, the color of the sky. They were constructed of mud brick, often with a baked brick covering, and ascended by flights of steps or a spiral ramp. The sloping sides and terraces were sometimes planted with shrubs and trees. There were ziggurats in every important Sumerian, Babylonian, and Assyrian center.

zimbabwes (zim-BAHB-ways) Stone-walled enclosures or buildings built during the African Iron Age in the region of modern Zimbabwe and Mozambique. The structures were the courts of local rulers. They have been associated with foreign trade, integrated farming and animal husbandry, and gold production. The Great Zimbabwe is the ruins of the former capital of the Monomatapa Empire, situated in Zimbabwe and occupied from around the thirteenth to the sixteenth century C.E.

INDEX

SINGLE PC LICENSE AGREEMENT AND LIMITED WARRANTY

READ THIS LICENSE CAREFULLY BEFORE OPENING THIS PACKAGE. BY OPENING THIS PACKAGE, YOU ARE AGREEING TO THE TERMS AND CONDITIONS OF THIS LICENSE. IF YOU DO NOT AGREE, DO NOT OPEN THE PACKAGE. PROMPTLY RETURN THE UNOPENED PACKAGE AND ALL ACCOMPANYING ITEMS TO THE PLACE YOU OBTAINED THEM (FOR A FULL REFUND OF ANY SUMS YOU HAVE PAID FOR THE SOFTWARE). *THESE TERMS APPLY TO ALL LICENSED SOFTWARE ON THE DISK EXCEPT THAT THE TERMS FOR USE OF ANY SHAREWARE OR FREEWARE ON THE DISKETTES ARE AS SET FORTH IN THE ELECTRONIC LICENSE LOCATED ON THE DISK:*

1. GRANT OF LICENSE and OWNERSHIP: The enclosed computer programs and data ("Software") are licensed, not sold, to you by Pearson Education, Inc. publishing.as Prentice Hall ("We" or the "Company") and in consideration of your purchase or adoption of the accompanying Company textbooks and/or other materials, and your agreement to these terms. We reserve any rights not granted to you. You own only the disk(s) but we and/or our licensors own the Software itself. This license allows you to use and display your copy of the Software on a single computer (i.e., with a single CPU) at a single location for academic use only, so long as you comply with the terms of this Agreement. You may make one copy for back up, or transfer your copy to another CPU, provided that the Software is usable on only one computer.

2. RESTRICTIONS: You may not transfer or distribute the Software or documentation to anyone else. Except for backup, you may not copy the documentation or the Software. You may not network the Software or otherwise use it on more than one computer or computer terminal at the same time. You may not reverse engineer, disassemble, decompile, modify, adapt, translate, or create derivative works based on the Software or the Documentation. You may be held legally responsible for any copying or copyright infringement that is caused by your failure to abide by the terms of these restrictions.

3. TERMINATION: This license is effective until terminated. This license will terminate automatically without notice from the Company if you fail to comply with any provisions or limitations of this license. Upon termination, you shall destroy the Documentation and all copies of the Software. All provisions of this Agreement as to limitation and disclaimer of warranties, limitation of liability, remedies or damages, and our ownership rights shall survive termination.

4. LIMITED WARRANTY AND DISCLAIMER OF WARRANTY: Company warrants that for a period of 60 days from the date you purchase this SOFTWARE (or purchase or adopt the accompanying textbook), the Software, when properly installed and used in accordance with the Documentation, will operate in substantial conformity with the description of the Software set forth in the Documentation, and that for a period of 30 days the disk(s) on which the Software is delivered shall be free from defects in materials and workmanship under normal use. The Company does not warrant that the Software will meet your requirements or that the operation of the Software will be uninterrupted or error-free. Your only remedy and the Company's only obligation under these limited warranties is, at the Company's option, return of the disk for a refund of any amounts paid for it by you or replacement of the disk. THIS LIMITED WARRANTY IS THE ONLY WARRANTY PROVIDED BY THE COMPANY AND ITS LICENSORS, AND THE COMPANY AND ITS LICENSORS DISCLAIM ALL OTHER WARRANTIES, EXPRESS OR IMPLIED, INCLUDING WITHOUT LIMITATION, THE IMPLIED WARRANTIES OF MERCHANTABILITY AND FITNESS FOR A PARTICULAR PURPOSE. THE COMPANY DOES NOT WARRANT, GUARANTEE OR MAKE ANY REPRESENTATION REGARDING THE ACCURACY, RELIABILITY, CURRENTNESS, USE, OR RESULTS OF USE, OF THE SOFTWARE.

5. LIMITATION OF REMEDIES AND DAMAGES: IN NO EVENT, SHALL THE COMPANY OR ITS EMPLOYEES, AGENTS, LICENSORS, OR CONTRACTORS BE LIABLE FOR ANY INCIDENTAL, INDIRECT, SPECIAL, OR CONSEQUENTIAL DAMAGES ARISING OUT OF OR IN CONNECTION WITH THIS LICENSE OR THE SOFTWARE, INCLUDING FOR LOSS OF USE, LOSS OF DATA, LOSS OF INCOME OR PROFIT, OR OTHER LOSSES, SUSTAINED AS A RESULT OF INJURY TO ANY PERSON, OR LOSS OF OR DAMAGE TO PROPERTY, OR CLAIMS OF THIRD PARTIES, EVEN IF THE COMPANY OR AN AUTHORIZED REPRESENTATIVE OF THE COMPANY HAS BEEN ADVISED OF THE POSSIBILITY OF SUCH DAMAGES. IN NO EVENT SHALL THE LIABILITY OF THE COMPANY FOR DAMAGES WITH RESPECT TO THE SOFTWARE EXCEED THE AMOUNTS ACTUALLY PAID BY YOU, IF ANY, FOR THE SOFTWARE OR THE ACCOMPANYING TEXTBOOK. BECAUSE SOME JURISDICTIONS DO NOT ALLOW THE LIMITATION OF LIABILITY IN CERTAIN CIRCUMSTANCES, THE ABOVE LIMITATIONS MAY NOT ALWAYS APPLY TO YOU.

6. GENERAL: THIS AGREEMENT SHALL BE CONSTRUED IN ACCORDANCE WITH THE LAWS OF THE UNITED STATES OF AMERICA AND THE STATE OF NEW YORK, APPLICABLE TO CONTRACTS MADE IN NEW YORK, AND SHALL BENEFIT THE COMPANY, ITS AFFILIATES AND ASSIGNEES. HIS AGREEMENT IS THE COMPLETE AND EXCLUSIVE STATEMENT OF THE AGREEMENT BETWEEN YOU AND THE COMPANY AND SUPERSEDES ALL PROPOSALS OR PRIOR AGREEMENTS, ORAL, OR WRITTEN, AND ANY OTHER COMMUNICATIONS BETWEEN YOU AND THE COMPANY OR ANY REPRESENTATIVE OF THE COMPANY RELATING TO THE SUBJECT MATTER OF THIS AGREEMENT. If you are a U.S. Government user, this Software is licensed with "restricted rights" as set forth in subparagraphs (a)-(d) of the Commercial Computer-Restricted Rights clause at FAR 52.227-19 or in subparagraphs (c)(1)(ii) of the Rights in Technical Data and Computer Software clause at DFARS 252.227-7013, and similar clauses, as applicable.

Should you have any questions concerning this agreement or if you wish to contact the Company for any reason, please contact in writing: Legal Department, Prentice Hall, One Lake Street, Upper Saddle River, NJ 07458. If you need assistance with technical difficulties, call: 1-800-677-6337.